MW00581588

DAVID O. MCKAY
AND THE RISE OF
MODERN MORMONISM

David O. McKay
and the
Rise of Modern Mormonism

BY

Gregory A. Prince

AND

Wm. Robert Wright

THE UNIVERSITY OF UTAH PRESS
Salt Lake City

09 08 07   5

 The Defiance House Man colophon is a registered trademark of
the University of Utah Press. It is based upon a four-foot-tall,
Ancient Puebloan pictograph (late PIII) near Glen Canyon, Utah.

LIBRARY OF CONGRESS CATALOGING-IN-PUBLICATION DATA

Prince, Gregory A., 1948–
  David O. McKay and the rise of modern Mormonism / by Gregory
A. Prince and Wm. Robert Wright.
     p. cm.
  Includes bibliographical references and index.
  ISBN-13: 978-0-87480-822-3 (cloth : alk. paper)
  ISBN-10: 0-87480-822-7
  1. McKay, David Oman, 1873–1970. 2. Church of Jesus Christ of
Latter-day Saints—History—20th century. I. Wright, Wm. Robert
(William Robert), 1935– II. Title.
  BX8695.M27P75 2005
  289.3'092—DC22

Frontispiece: Charcoal sketch of David O. McKay courtesy of Alan Moorehead.

In memory of Clare Middlemiss,
for creating the record.

It is always a difficult task to hold the scales of justice at even balance when weighing the deeds of men. It becomes doubly more so when dealing with men engaged in a movement that one believes had its origin with God, and that its leaders on occasion act under the inspiration of God. Under such conditions to so state events as to be historically exact, and yet, on the other hand, so treat the course of events as not to destroy faith in these men, nor in their work, becomes a task of supreme delicacy; and one that tries the soul and the skill of the historian. The only way such a task can be accomplished, in the judgment of the writer, is to frankly state events as they occurred, in full consideration of all related circumstances, allowing the line of condemnation or of justification to fall where it may; being confident that in the sum of things justice will follow truth; and God will be glorified in his work, no matter what may befall individuals or groups of individuals.

—B. H. Roberts, *A Comprehensive History of the Church of Jesus Christ of Latter-day Saints, Century I*

CONTENTS

Preface ix

Introduction xii

1 | Prophet and Man 1

2 | Revelation and Prophecy 30

3 | Free Agency and Tolerance 40

4 | Blacks, Civil Rights, and the Priesthood 60

5 | Ecumenical Outreach 106

6 | Radio and Television Broadcasting 124

7 | Correlation and Church Administration 139

8 | The Education System 159

9 | The Building Program 199

10 | The Missionary Program 227

11 | Temple Building 256

12 | Confrontation with Communism 279

13 | Politics and the Church 323

14 | An International Church 358

15 | Final Years 380

16 | Epilogue 395

Appendix 405

Notes 413

Bibliography 457

Index 473

PREFACE

Wm. Robert Wright

There has never been a prophet of the Church of Jesus Christ of Latter-day Saints about whom so much information is available, particularly about his private thoughts and struggles, as David O. McKay. The records that made this book possible came from over thirty-five years of painstaking work by President McKay's personal secretary and my aunt, Clare Middlemiss. As his secretary from 1935 until his death in 1970, she recognized the importance of President McKay's work and dedicated her evenings, weekends, and holidays collecting, documenting, and preserving the details of his life during the tenure of his presidency. Because of Clare, we can feel his emotions, understand his thoughts, see as he saw, and put his actions in the context of all it meant to be who he was. And through this active process of study and identification, we find ourselves enriched, if only partly, by his experience.

President McKay's day always began at a very early hour. Usually he would rise about 4:00 A.M. to study, to meditate, to seek inspiration, and to plan his day. When Clare arrived at her desk at 7:00 A.M. she would find Dictaphone cylinders with notes asking if the final form could be done that very morning. It was also her duty to make appointments, answer telephone calls, interview people who called at the office, and make President McKay's busy life run as smoothly as possible. After a full day at her office, she would return home where her work would continue. I often visited her in the evenings to find her laboring over numerous stacks of articles, pictures, and other information that she painstakingly organized into diaries, discourses, and scrapbooks. I talked to her of the events she documented, giving her counsel and advice whenever she asked. I promised her that, when her time came to leave her position because of ill health or death, I would take the greatest care of all her work and eventually publish books based on her records.

Through my relationship with Aunt Clare, I had the privilege and blessing of knowing President McKay personally. Clare never married and therefore doted on her nieces and nephews. Her fondness included invitations to her office from time to time. There I came to know him as a prophet and even as a friend. In September 1955, President McKay returned from a trip to Europe where he had dedicated the new Swiss Temple and visited the London Temple, which was under construction. Aunt Clare had been one of the entourage that accompanied him. My twin brother Richard and I went to the airport to greet Clare and take her home. The plane pulled up on the tarmac. We spotted Clare and were soon talking to her. We advised her that both of us had been interviewed by our bishop and that we had submitted our papers to go on a mission. It was doubly exciting, not just because there were two of us, but also because the draft board for the Korean War had just rescinded the rule that only one missionary could go from each ward every year. Clare was excited. At about that moment, Clare spotted President McKay, who was moving our way. She ran over to him and guided him to my brother and me, exclaiming, "The boys are going on a mission!" President McKay was delighted and asked where we were going. We replied that we had not yet received our calls. President McKay then got a twinkle in his eye that I shall never forget. He stood between the two of us, put his arm around Richard and said, "Richard will go to England," and then put his other arm around me and said, "and Robert will go to Switzerland." (He was right.) The warmth and personal attention shown to us in this instance was a hallmark of President McKay's life as a church leader, and one of the characteristics that made him so capable of leading a fast-growing organization through such interesting times.

The real McKay would be impossible to know and understand without Clare's extensive records. Still, we cannot claim to represent a past undistorted by the events of the years since McKay's death. All history is subjective and each generation rewrites it to suit its own ends. I believe, as any historical writer must, that the questions we have chosen to ask about David O. McKay's life and teachings are unique to our time and that their answers are therefore uniquely enlightening and useful to today's readers. It is my hope that future generations will look to the Prophet's thoughts and ask questions suited to their times. In order to make this possible, I have donated the materials preserved by Clare Middlemiss to the J. Willard Marriott Library at the University of Utah, where they will be available to scholars. I believe that McKay's timeless wisdom and spirituality offer lessons equally important and satisfying to all generations.

If it is possible to learn from history, biography should be fruitful ground. In this book we understand the past not through the generalized machinations of nations and peoples, but through the eyes of a single and great individual, David O. McKay. Theoretical considerations of history aside, we strove conscientiously for a true and accurate representation of the Prophet, and we would like to believe that our own attempt to understand McKay in his proper historical context will help readers of this book achieve the rewards that literature promises: to bring down walls between us and others, between our time and another time, and to make us more able to empathize, more human. We certainly attained such benefits in researching and writing this book. The more we learned about David O. McKay, the more he became a true and unique form, and not a Rorschach inkblot upon which we project our own biases and the biases of our time.

President McKay presided over the Mormon Church during a period that produced some of the most challenging issues the church has ever faced. He wrestled with the problem of blacks and the priesthood, moving toward the inclusion that would, under another president in 1978, reverse more than a century of church policy; he confronted Communism and the effects of the Cold War; he fought for free agency and tolerance; and he succeeded in the task of taking the church worldwide. The Middlemiss records reveal not only the personal experiences and thoughts of McKay, but also the spiritual and personal conflicts that these explosive issues caused among church leaders. Our ability to see the actions he took in the face of these events and the deliberations and struggles that led to those actions is something that is rare, not only for a Mormon prophet, but for any great historical figure. This book is the record of a remarkable man in a remarkable time, making decisions that led the Church of Jesus Christ of Latter-day Saints to grow and broaden. Because of his background, personality, interactions, and inspirations, he directed the church from relative obscurity to worldwide renown.

The detail, organization, and breadth of the records that Clare kept reflect her great admiration and devotion to McKay as well as her deep understanding of the historical significance of his work. Never before and perhaps never again will we have the same kind of insight and appreciation for a prophet's daily strifes, struggles, and strengths as we have here. To those who question the wisdom of scrutinizing the details of a prophet's life, I suggest that truth can only liberate, and that seeing the truth about a great man like David O. McKay will inspire the reader to greater attempts at personal greatness. For who could fail to be inspired by a man who impressed such greatness on all he met? In one of the many interviews we conducted, I asked a prominent non-Mormon citizen, "Why, in your opinion, was David O. McKay so revered and so greatly loved and admired?" He quickly answered, "He loved everyone." This incident illustrates what seems to be a universal memory among those who knew McKay.

During my tenure as president of the Washington D.C. Mission from 1989 to 1992, I met Greg Prince and immediately found that we had many interests in common. Greg's passion for LDS Church history led the two of us to plan the writing of this biography. So began our ten-year collaboration of work together on a project to which we have both been devoted.

We have dedicated this book to Clare Middlemiss in recognition of her extraordinary vision and her diligent work in preserving as much of the life of President McKay as possible, so that we, and later generations, have the remarkable opportunity to see what he saw and to learn from him. The publication of this book would have been a very great day for Clare, the realization of her hopes, and the justification of all her hard work.

Introduction

Gregory A. Prince

I was two years old when David O. McKay became president of the Church of Jesus Christ of Latter-day Saints in 1951. Nineteen years later, fresh off a proselytizing mission to southern Brazil and midway through my first year of dental school at UCLA, I heard the news on the radio that he had died at the age of ninety-six. Although I never met him, he had been a continual presence in my life through broadcast sessions of general conferences, articles and photographs in church publications, lessons about him, and prayers in his behalf at church meetings and at home. Distinguished yet seemingly approachable, he appealed to me not only as a church leader, but also as the ideal grandfather, an idea not too far-fetched, as one of his grandchildren lived in our congregation.

I had neither the interest nor the conventional tools to write a biography; indeed, English was my least favorite subject in school, with history only slightly behind. I came from a family of dentists and eagerly walked down that traditional road. Before I had taken more than a few steps, however, the road took a series of turns that I could never have imagined, that led me to write the biography and, in the process, taught me much about the "law of unintended consequences."

An exceptional pathology course in dental school in 1970, taught only that year in the entire four-decade history of the UCLA School of Dentistry, steered me into a Ph.D. program in pathology and a career in medical research, which in turn transplanted me from my native California to a two-year postdoctoral fellowship in Maryland, where my family and I still reside after thirty years.

A request by my father, then bishop of the Westwood (California) Ward, that I fill the slot of early-morning seminary teacher for high school students during my senior year of dental school, at a salary of $600 for the year, steered me into an interest in Mormon books. I spent not only the $600, but also countless sums in subsequent years to build a personal library that now numbers some 10,000 volumes and that ultimately made possible the writing of this biography two thousand miles away from the epicenter of Mormonism.

A three-day solo house-hunting trip to Maryland in 1975 steered me to the only affordable housing in the area, which happened to place me in the same congregation as Lester Bush, who, with his family, had moved there only one year previously. Lester had recently published a still-unsurpassed landmark article in *Dialogue: A Journal of Mormon Thought* on the history of the LDS Church's ban on ordination of blacks that had placed him at the cutting edge of Mormon history. He quickly became my closest friend, my tutor in Mormon history, and my role model as a person trained in one profession—medicine in his case—who became expert in another.

An unexpected call from my stake president, Don Ladd, to serve as elders' quorum president in 1977 steered me to what became an insatiable curiosity about Latter-day Saint priesthood. Dissatisfied with all of the material in my library— which included virtually everything that had ever been published on the subject— I audaciously and somewhat naively embarked on an eight-year project that resulted in the publication of *Power from On High: The Development of Mormon Priesthood* (Salt Lake City: Signature Books, 1995).

One final twist in the road steered me to the current biography. In 1989 Bob Wright was called to be president of the Washington D.C. Mission. We had never met. Shortly after his calling was announced but before he and his family moved to Maryland, I was in the LDS Church Archives in Salt Lake City and paid a call on my friend and former stake president, John Carmack, a member of the First Quorum of the Seventy and managing director of the Historical Department. He told me that the new mission president in our area had a large family (eight children), too large for the existing mission home to accommodate, so the church was contemplating the purchase of a new mission home in Darnestown, Maryland. He asked if I knew the area and if I thought the home would be a wise investment for the church. I replied that it was only a couple of miles from our home and that it was an excellent neighborhood. The purchase of that home brought the Wrights into our ward congregation and into our lives.

Shortly after Bob and Janet got settled in the area, we became friends and invited them over for dinner. I was writing *Power from On High* at the time; and since they expressed an interest in it, I gave them a few draft chapters. The next time we had them over for dinner, Bob made an offer I couldn't refuse. He said his aunt, Clare Middlemiss, had been David O. McKay's private secretary for thirty-five years; and during that entire time, she had steadily worked on compiling, almost entirely on her own time and without compensation from the church, an extensive record of McKay's life and ministry with the intent of writing his biography. While he was alive, there was barely time to compile the record (see the more detailed record in the Appendix), and no time to write the biography. After his death, Clare's health began to fail, and she never realized her dream. Having read my chapters, Bob asked that I work with him to write the biography, using as a foundation the voluminous papers that Clare had left to him. It is not possible to overstate my indebtedness to Clare, whom I never met, and to Bob, who became and remains one of my closest friends.

With no training in either historiography or biography, I chose to follow my instincts and use the only tools at my disposal, those of scientific methodology. I believe that this is a valid approach for nonfiction writing, be it science or biography, depending on the author's ability to gather and analyze data.

I was astounded at the detail of the record that Clare Middlemiss had compiled, particularly the diaries. Yet I could also see that the title "diaries," which is what both Middlemiss and McKay called them, was something of a misnomer. While there are abundant first-person dictations in the diaries (it is all typescript), they are only a small minority of the total record. The remainder consists of extracts from the minutes of various meetings, memoranda, letters, newspaper clippings, from 1967 on photocopies of Alvin R. Dyer's daily record, and other materials. As a result, the diaries are rarely introspective. Once I began to work my way through them, I could see that, rich in information though they are, they are but part of a larger picture, and I identified three other "databases" needed to complete the picture.

One was the published record, which included books, magazines, scholarly journals, newspapers, pamphlets, master's theses, and doctoral dissertations. Most of these were already in my personal library, and I worked for several years to enter thousands of pages of verbatim material into the computer—material that dealt with David O. McKay personally or with the period of his church presidency. The number of published sources reflected in the text and bibliography is far smaller than the total number in the database. In no instance did I ignore the work of others; however, wherever primary sources were superior, I gave priority to them and did not reference secondary sources.

A second database consisted of unpublished materials in several archives. By far the most important of these was the Historical Department Archives of the Church of Jesus Christ of Latter-day Saints, repository of the 215 volumes of scrapbooks kept by Clare Middlemiss and her assistants, scores of transcribed oral histories, and an assortment of other manuscript materials. I am particularly indebted to Steven Sorensen and Ronald O. Barney for personal assistance with manuscript materials, and to William W. Slaughter for providing many of the photographic images that enliven the text of this biography. The church collections of official minutes of meetings of the First Presidency, Quorum of the Twelve Apostles, and other general councils and general boards; diaries of other General Authorities; official correspondence; and some oral histories are, by church policy, not made available to researchers. This biography thus cannot make a claim to have drawn on all existing sources, but rather on those currently accessible.

Second in importance was the Manuscript Division of Special Collections housed in the Marriott Library of the University of Utah. It is the repository of the

David Oman McKay papers, a massive collection consisting of the papers of David O., his wife, Emma Ray Riggs McKay, and their children, Lou Jean McKay Blood and David Lawrence McKay (donated by grandchildren Joyce McKay Bennett and Douglas McKay), and the David O. McKay diaries, discourses, and other records (donated by Wm. Robert Wright). The Manuscript Division also houses dozens of transcribed oral histories that contributed for this biography. I am doubly indebted to Gregory C. Thompson, director of Special Collections, who assisted me in accessing those collections, then later steered me to the University of Utah Press as my publisher.

The third database did not exist at the time we began this project. It now consists of the transcripts of over two hundred interviews that Bob and I conducted beginning in 1994. To our continuing surprise, almost none of the interviewees previously had been interviewed on the record on the subject of David O. McKay. Their cooperation was extraordinary, extending all the way to the only three surviving apostles called by President McKay to be General Authorities: Gordon B. Hinckley, the current church president; Thomas S. Monson, his first counselor; and Boyd K. Packer, acting president of the Quorum of the Twelve. Only later did we come to realize that much of the information contained in these interviews, the transcripts of which number over 5,000 pages, had never been recorded. Since we began conducting the interviews, some three dozen of the interviewees have passed away, leaving the transcripts as an irreplaceable treasure trove of information on the McKay years. These transcripts, currently in my personal papers, will doubtless provide a wealth of information for future scholars of the McKay years. Indeed, we quoted fewer than half the interviews in this biography, thus leaving much grist for other mills.

We worked for eight years to compile and sort our master database, which amounts to 15,000 single-spaced pages in electronic format. Once the compilation was complete—which meant that we had made a good-faith effort to examine all available published and unpublished materials relating to the McKay years, as well as interviewing anyone we could identify who had something important to say about them—I went through every page, line by line, and did an electronic cut-and-paste job to sort all of the data into subject files. Over one hundred subject files emerged from this process. I did not begin to outline the biography until the sorting was completed. At that point, I was able to step back and look at the files, whereupon it became apparent immediately what the important topics were. There were some surprises at this point, for some topics that I would have assumed to be important turned out to be less so, while others that I would have overlooked in my research had I determined the chapter headings in advance turned out to be of crucial importance. I include the chapters on broadcasting, correlation, and ecumenism in this list.

It also became apparent that a strictly chronological approach would be chaotic. As a result, the organization of this book is topical, with each subject being treated chronologically within its own chapter. The first chapter gives an overview of David O. McKay as both man and prophet, while the second and third chapters describe the spiritual foundation of his faith—essential for understanding his presidency. Chapters 4 through 11 deal with topics to which McKay assigned significance and those that acquired significance from the turbulent postwar times. Chapters 12 through 14 focus on the church and the new relationship it negotiated with a changing world. Chapters 15 and 16 conclude the McKay years and reflect on his legacy.

Writing the biography occupied two years. The division of labor was that I did the actual writing, while Bob did the critiquing. It turned out to be a very productive and collegial arrangement.

Given the wealth of data, we were able to stand behind the biography, not in front of it. While we have attempted to write an analytical biography rather than merely a descriptive one, the analysis consists largely in ordering massive amounts of data into a coherent narrative that allows the subjects to speak in their own voices, then connecting a few dots along the way while allowing the reader the challenge and joy of connecting others. In order not to get in the way of the data, we have avoided making sweeping conclusions that would have presumed we could climb within the consciousness of these people. Where the data are silent, we have tried to follow suit.

Our goal was simple: to write truthfully of a man who was one of the most important—if not *the* most important—figures in twentieth-century Mormonism. Our title has the feeling of inevitability for us. McKay stood at the crossroads where modern Mormonism took its shape and direction. In creating this biography, we were guided by the definition of truth in a revelation articulated by Joseph Smith, which continues to be the best I have ever encountered: "And truth is knowledge of things as they are, and as they were, and as they are to come."[1] It does not consist of things as we wish they had been. There is a risk in approaching a subject in this manner, of course, but with this subject we felt the risk was small. Nonetheless, we were determined to go wherever the data took us. For both Bob and me, the journey led to the conclusion that David O. McKay was not only a great man, but a greater one than we had heretofore appreciated.

Along the way there were surprises, mostly because the richness of our data allowed us to explore the recesses of LDS Church governance at its highest level.

People have often asked me, "Has this project been faith promoting or faith erod-
ing for you?" My consistent response—and I speak for Bob as well—has been that
it has been enormously faith promoting. This came as no surprise to me, for I
believe strongly that the only thing that can truly promote faith (rather than shield-
ing people from reality) is the truth. Juanita Brooks, a role model and former
neighbor in St. George, Utah, said that the church embraces all truth—not just
truth that happens to be useful for pursuing an agenda—and that those church
members who cannot deal with the whole truth might be in the wrong place.[2] I
believe that completely and wish I had said it first.

The picture of David O. McKay that I gained was of a great, complex, three-
dimensional man whose imprint on Mormonism was indelible and will likely forever
influence its destiny. To be sure, he had some weaknesses, and we have attempted
to be honest about them, while placing them in an understandable context. His
strengths and weaknesses are discussed in detail in the first chapter but are also recur-
rent themes throughout the book. It is our hope that the reader will be willing to
go along for the whole ride. We feel confident that such a reader will not only gain
a better appreciation for what it means to be great but also understand that kernels
of greatness are inherent in all of us, despite our imperfections. Making great people
accessible through honest biographies lifts us without degrading them.

We realize that truth can be jolting, particularly to those whose lives have been
shielded from it. There will doubtless be some who after sampling a few pages will
choose not to go along for the whole ride. We wish them no ill and trust that they
will continue to pursue their own faith journeys by their own rules. However, we
have taken pains to tell the story of David O. McKay with sufficient care and context to take what we hope will be a broad spectrum of readers to a position of comfort with "things as they were," hoping to convey not only an accurate understanding of how we came to be what we are as a church, but also of how and where
we—as a church and as individuals, whether LDS or not—are likely to go from here.
Regardless of an "outsider's" feelings about the church over which David O.
McKay presided, people of all stripes can learn much from this man. Along these
lines, the LDS reader will doubtless note that we have attempted to minimize, or
at least to explain, specialized LDS terms, in the hope of providing complete access
to the narrative for the non-LDS reader as well.

If we have succeeded in our goal, our satisfaction will not come from any
notion that we have written something "definitive," but rather from knowing that
we have helped people to understand a great man and the enormously important
yet complex era of Mormon history over which he presided. Perhaps our work will
eventually allow someone else to lay claim to writing something "definitive." That
would be pleasing to us.

Acknowledgments

In addition to those individuals already mentioned above, it is both a duty and my great pleasure to acknowledge those who played special roles in the researching and writing of this book, while necessarily overlooking many of the hundreds of others who also played influential and encouraging roles.

First and foremost I thank my wife, JaLynn, and my children, Chad, Lauren, and Madison, who bore the brunt of ten years of hard work that consumed so much of the time on which they had the best claim. They understood from the outset the importance of this project and gave unwavering support. They are also eager to get me back.

Once the decision was made to transfer the Middlemiss papers, which were in Salt Lake City, to my stewardship, the daunting task of shipping the priceless record to Maryland was undertaken by Sam Weller, owner of Zion Bookstore, Inc., and his assistant, Joan Nay, who gave it her personal attention and has watched over the project ever since. In addition, Sam and Joan have been trusted friends who have assisted me, for over three decades, in building a private library, which they half-jokingly refer to as "Sam Weller East," that allowed me to do much of my research at home. Midway through the project, Sam turned over the management of the store to his son Tony, and I am indebted to Tony for perpetuating the same level of support and friendship.

Transferring the essential material from the McKay diaries into electronic format was a crucial process that took over two years, as little could be scanned. Most of that work was done by my assistant, Sonja Schmieder. Though not a Latter-day Saint, either then or now, Sonja took the project on with a fervor equal to my own and, upon concluding it, told me, "David O. McKay is my hero."

Gary Topping, archivist of the Catholic Diocese of Salt Lake City, co-researched with me the fascinating interaction of David O. McKay and Duane G. Hunt, the Roman Catholic bishop of Salt Lake City, which became the core of the chapter on ecumenism. Each of us had looked at our "own" man independently yet simultaneously and, by a remarkable coincidence, came to learn of the other's research. Combining resources allowed us to portray a whole that was more than the sum of its parts.

I have relied upon many people to read drafts of some of the chapters, but I would like to single out four who read all of the chapters and responded with critical and helpful suggestions: L. Ralph Mecham, director of the Administrative Office of the United States Courts; J. Alan Blodgett, former Chief Financial Officer of the Church of Jesus Christ of Latter-day Saints; Floyd A. O'Neil, professor emeritus of history of the University of Utah; and Dr. Chase N. Peterson, president emeritus of the University of Utah.

The publication of this book by the University of Utah Press is most appropriate, as David O. McKay remains one of the university's most distinguished alumni. I am grateful for the cooperation of the press's editor-in-chief, Jeffrey Grathwohl, and acquisitions editor, Peter DeLafosse. Peter has been my chief contact at the press, and he made it a personal priority to ensure that the finished product met the highest standards of a superb university press. I also thank Lavina Fielding Anderson, of Editing, Inc., for her assistance during the editing process.

It has been a sobering yet strengthening responsibility to document and interpret the life of this extraordinary man. For the record thus produced, including any deficiencies, I accept full responsibility.

DAVID O. MCKAY
AND THE RISE OF
MODERN MORMONISM

1

PROPHET AND MAN

Two men walked directly in front of the hearse bearing the body of George Albert Smith, eighth President of the Church of Jesus Christ of Latter-day Saints, as it traveled west along South Temple Street toward the Tabernacle. One, the shorter and stockier of the two, was an internationally renowned attorney, statesman, and diplomat, J. Reuben Clark Jr. The other, tall, athletically trim, and crowned with a mane of flowing white hair, was well known within the church and the state of Utah, but virtually unknown elsewhere. Within a short time, however, David O. McKay would become the internationally recognized symbol of Mormonism, the man who transformed a parochial Great Basin organization into a respected worldwide religion.

AN UNCONVENTIONAL LEADER

Six years earlier, upon the death of Heber J. Grant, George Albert Smith, who had been serving as president of the Quorum of the Twelve Apostles since 1943, assumed the church presidency, retaining Grant's first and second counselors, Clark and McKay. Smith's health had been marginal for much of his life, particularly for the latter half of his presidency. In mid-March 1951, Clark and McKay received word from Dr. LeRoy Kimball that Smith had suffered a stroke in the middle of the night, leaving his right side paralyzed.[1] From that point, his condition gradually deteriorated until April 2, when it plummeted. McKay noted: "At 10 o'clock I received word from the doctor that President Smith was in a very serious condition. I went immediately to the house and was shocked at his appearance. He did not seem to recognize me—the first time during his sickness. I realized that possibly the end was not far off. It came as quite a shock to my nervous system, for I fully sensed then what his passing means."[2]

For over a half-century, the passing of the church president meant that the man with the longest tenure among the Quorum of the Twelve became the new church president, and McKay had been that man for a year, since the death of George F. Richards.[3] Despite the emotional preparation of this lengthy terminal illness, the inescapable fact of this final event confronted him with shocking finality. On

1

April 4 the Smith family asked McKay to give the ailing President a blessing of comfort. "In doing so," he wrote, "I broke down with emotion." Later in the evening McKay was summoned again to the Smith home, arriving "just a few moments prior to his passing."[4]

At the death of a church president, the First Presidency is automatically dissolved, with temporary stewardship of the church transferring to the collective Quorum of the Twelve. As senior member of that group, McKay thus automatically headed the interim government. Fully aware of the role reversal that Smith's death had just caused, Clark, who was first counselor, placed his arm through McKay's as the two men left the bedroom and said, "I want you to know that I accept you as my file leader, and that I will do anything you wish me to do."[5] Clark assumed, with ample historical precedent to back him up, that he would retain his position in the soon-to-be reorganized First Presidency.

Smith's death came just two days prior to the beginning of the annual general conference in April. (A semi-annual general conference is held each October.) Following the afternoon session on Sunday, April 8, McKay presided over a meeting of the fourteen surviving apostles in the Salt Lake Temple. They voted unanimously to sustain him as the ninth president of the church, whereupon he presented for their approval the names of his counselors: Stephen L Richards[6] as first counselor and J. Reuben Clark Jr. as second counselor. Both men were apostles; and for McKay to call Richards as his first counselor was a natural move, for Richards was his closest friend among all the General Authorities. But for Clark it was a devastating blow, not only because it signaled something of a demotion to him,[7] but also because it was unprecedented in the history of the church for a retained counselor in the First Presidency to be shifted from first to second.

McKay was not a conventional leader, and this was but the first of many unconventional moves he made after becoming president. The next came a short time later, when he informed his colleagues that D. Arthur Haycock, who had served as private secretary to the two previous church presidents, would be reassigned as an assistant to Joseph Anderson, secretary to the First Presidency.[8] In Haycock's place, McKay retained his personal secretary of sixteen years, Clare Middlemiss. Never before (or since) had the private secretary to a church president been a woman. During the subsequent nineteen years, Middlemiss would become arguably the most powerful woman in the history of the church, and would chronicle McKay's activities in unprecedented detail.[9]

The day after meeting with the Quorum of the Twelve, McKay presided over a Solemn Assembly in the Tabernacle and presented the new First Presidency for the sustaining vote of the congregation. Already, the mantle of his new job had settled over him. Middlemiss later recalled:

Well do I remember President McKay's sadness, and how ashen his face as he felt the full impact of the responsibility that had fallen upon him. Now he faced presiding at a funeral of a President of the Church, and also of presiding at a General Conference. It was a humbling realization for President McKay. He assumed his new and weighty responsibilities with the spirit of humility.

Just before the Solemn Assembly, I remarked to President McKay how much better he looked, and he said, "I know my course!"[10]

David O. McKay was perhaps the most charismatic man to preside over the church since its founder, Joseph Smith. On many occasions, even as a counselor in the First Presidency, his mere presence had an electrifying effect. One man recalled:

I was a young boy many years ago when President McKay, a counselor in the First Presidency at the time, came to eastern Utah to dedicate some new chapels in our valley. When I saw President McKay I had the same impression some other people have had as I witnessed a spiritual glow which radiated from him, but this sort of thing was a new experience for me. After the meeting, even though I was somewhat intimidated, my mother placed me in line with some other children to shake his hand. This was almost 60 years ago but I still remember vividly the indescribable feeling which came into my being when he shook my hand and said a few cheerful words to me.[11]

The effect was not confined to church members. Keith Wilcox, who many years later became a General Authority, was an eyewitness to an extraordinary event at the passenger depot in Ogden, Utah, during the early 1940s:

I was able to get a job with Western Union, part of which was to take messages down to the main train depot in Ogden.... I'll always remember one night when I had taken my telegrams down. I'd stand and just quite loudly give the name, "Telegram for so-and-so. Telegram!," so that everybody could hear it. I had gotten so I could get to everybody coming back. It was a huge group of people, bustling back and forth, very loud, very noisy. Really, the world was going by there. But one night I was down there, and I had an experience I will never forget. Here I was, busy trying to get my telegrams, and suddenly there was a quieting effect. The sound began to diminish in this huge tunnel. It got quite quiet! I looked up from what I was doing, and a lot of people had stopped, and were staring. I had never seen this happen. Ever! I couldn't imagine what had happened. I looked around, and here came David O. McKay.... He had come up on the train and gotten off in Ogden. He just walked down the steps and turned and started to walk up, and people literally froze. They just said, "Who is that man?" I could hear them. "Who is that? Who is that?" They were just spellbound. And all he was doing was walking up, like anyone else. But as I looked up, there was just—almost like a radiance around his head. He was so different than anyone else that you'd ever seen in that depot. He just emanated, and there was just kind of a spirituality about him, a friendly, wonderful radiant man. I'll never forget that, and how the people stopped and turned around. I could see them. "Who's this? Who was that?"... I've never seen any individual affect a crowd like he did. And he wasn't trying. He was just being himself.[12]

The effect was no less striking after McKay became church president. A recent British convert drove to London's Royal Albert Hall in 1955 to attend a concert by the Mormon Tabernacle Choir, which was on its way to Switzerland for the dedication of the new temple. Arriving several hours early, he decided to sit alone in the balcony and read the newspaper while the choir rehearsed:

After they had been practicing for about an hour, in the middle of a song they stopped, and they all stood up. I thought, "What's going on?" I looked around, and this white-haired gentleman came walking down the aisle. He said, "Sit down," [to the choir] and then he sat down in the stalls. I looked at this, and I didn't know who he was. The missionaries never even mentioned the Prophet, David O. McKay. As I looked, the atmosphere that came from him radiated, and made me vibrate right through. I was overwhelmed with the Spirit that came from him. Volumes of tears started to roll down my face. I was absolutely sobbing with the Spirit, it was so powerful. I thought, "What's the matter with me? Am I having a nervous breakdown? What's this?" I couldn't understand it at all. This was a unique experience that I had never before experienced in my whole life. I just looked at him sitting there and thought, "That must be the Prophet." I didn't even know his name.[13]

And again, the effect was not restricted to church members. Robert Simpson, who later became a General Authority, was eyewitness to one such occasion:

I was attending a large conference of educators. I guess it was all of the educators in Southern California. I was there for the telephone company because we were in a public relations program involved with schools. I wasn't aware of it, but President McKay was an invited guest. As he came into the room, literally, that room stopped, and everybody said, "Who is that?" It was not just the appearance, but there was a feeling there that dominated that group of educators. He absolutely captivated that room, just by his appearance and the spirit that he emanated.[14]

MISSIONARY, TEACHER, AND APOSTLE

David O. McKay was born in 1873 in the small, rural Utah town of Huntsville, Weber County, to David McKay and Jennette Evans McKay. According to a cousin, he was a discipline problem as a boy:

> In our family they tell the story about D.O. and the thrashers. Every fall the thrashing crew would come through the community. The thrashing machine would come in and set up, and all the farmers would gather around to get the thrashing for each farmer done. This was a big day on any farm, and the catch was that when they came, you always had to feed them. The family tells of the time when Aunt Jennette was planning to feed all these thrashers. Her sister was there, and they were planning to do the feeding. His aunt turned to his mother and said, "Look, if you'll take care of that boy, I'll feed the thrashers." He was that rowdy as a boy, and I believe it's true. He was an intense athlete. He grew up at a time when, with handling animals, it was a very rough time. When you broke a horse, you *broke* that horse.... President McKay just had an absolute tenacity, that "nobody's going to get the best of me."...So he evolved, and I guess we all do, to a kinder, gentler phase as we get older.[15]

At age thirteen, David O. and his brother Thomas, age eleven, received patriarchal blessings from Presiding Patriarch John Smith. Edward McKay, David O.'s son, saw both blessings shortly after Thomas's death:

> The remarkable thing about Uncle Tommy's blessing was that it stated that if he lived the laws of health he would live until his 73rd year. He died at age 72, his 73rd year. President McKay's blessing stated, among other things, if he lived to be worthy of it that he would sit in the leading councils of the Church. Very impressed by these blessings, I discussed them with Father, and asked him if he remembered the incident of the patriarch coming to Huntsville and giving them those blessings when they were children. He thought a minute and said, "No, I can't remember Patriarch Smith, but I remember his horse!"[16]

As a boy David O. obtained a job carrying mail from Huntsville over the mountain by horseback to the mining camp of La Plata. The journey took nearly a full day, and the literature and poetry that he read and memorized along the way became his lifelong love. He taught school in Huntsville briefly, but an inheritance to his mother upon his grandmother's death changed his career plans. According to David O's son Edward, "She left $5000.00...[and] insisted that every cent of that be used for the education of the children. So David and Thomas left Huntsville for Salt Lake with a horse and buggy and the cow trailing along behind them to give them milk while they were down there."[17] While a student at the University of Utah, McKay played on the football team, met Emma Ray Riggs, his future wife, and graduated as class president and valedictorian in 1897.[18]

His career plans were put on hold by a two-year mission call to Scotland, the land of his ancestry and his father's earlier missionary service. To his mind, the timing was not good. His eldest son, David Lawrence, recounted: "When he received his call to go on a mission it came at a most inopportune time. He had just graduated from college and had been offered a fine position teaching at Weber Academy. He discussed this with his father, and said, 'I'd like to go on a mission some day, but this just isn't the time.' His wise father said, 'It is your decision to make, David, but this is a call from the Lord.' So David reluctantly accepted."[19]

Nonetheless, he had misgivings that stemmed from unresolved doubts about the work he was being called to perform. Solid advice from an unexpected source allowed him to plunge ahead in spite of the doubts. He wrote much later to a wavering missionary:

> Over fifty years ago, when I was about to leave for my first mission, an agnostic friend said to me, among other things: "David, teach only that which you feel to be true—things about which you are in doubt, keep to yourself until your doubt is removed." Following that injunction, I went from what was known to what was unknown with respect to doctrine and Church policies, and today, believe me, doubts that shook me as a young man, as doubts are now shaking you, became as clear as Thomas' assurance of the resurrection of the Savior when he said, "My Lord and my God."[20]

McKay distinguished himself in missionary service—his mission president called him "one of the best men in the mission"[21]—but he never forgot his journey from skepticism to faith and occasionally used it as an object lesson to help others who doubted. In 1927 he spoke to a group of departing missionaries that included future BYU professor Hugh Nibley:

His whole talk was about how skeptical he had always been about the gospel. He said he had never believed it for most of his life and was very skeptical. And of course, he was made an apostle, and he was an apostle at that time. He did believe it, we assumed. He showed a side of skepticism, at least different from all the others. I don't think the others had ever been as skeptical as he was.... When he was made an Apostle, a lot of people were shocked. "David McKay, an Apostle?" Because he had been quite open and honest in expressing his doubts about things. So God moves in a mysterious way.[22]

Two experiences in Scotland softened McKay's skepticism and helped to shape the rest of his life. The first occurred early in his mission, at a time when home-sickness and doubt plagued him. Many years later he recounted the experience to Jack Dempsey, former world heavyweight boxing champion and lapsed Mormon:

I had become discouraged and homesick one day. Among other things, a Scotch woman had said to me as I handed her a tract: "Ye better gae hame; ye canna have any o' oor lassies!" Well I did not want any of their lassies; I had left a sweet one at home, but it made me discouraged to think of the ill-will which these people had toward the Mormons.... We had been assigned to Stirling, that historic town of which we read in the "Lady of the Lake" where James Fitz James won the championship, and James of Scotland had his dogs and his orchards to keep. Well, I was very interested in these things. We had just been on a tour of old Stirling Castle, and it was afternoon when we left that historic site and started out east of town.... As we were coming back into town, I saw on my right an unfinished dwelling, over the front door of which was a stone on which there was some carving. That was most unusual, so I said to Elder [Peter G.] Johnston: "I'm going to see what that is." I was half way up the graveled walk when there came to my eyesight a striking motto carved in stone—it read "WHATE'ER THOU ART, ACT WELL THY PART." I repeated it to Elder Johnston as we walked in to town to find a place for our lodging before we began our work. As we walked toward our destination, I thought about this motto, "Whate'er Thou Art, Act Well Thy Part," and took it as a direct message to me, and I said to myself, or the Spirit said to me, "You are a member of the Church of Jesus Christ of Latter-day Saints; more than that— you are here in the Mission Field as a representative of the Church, and you are to act well your part as a missionary, and you should get into the work with all your heart." I then said to Jack Dempsey: "I congratulate you as a man who has acted well your part—one who has brought honor to your profession."[23]

The second formative experience occurred in the latter half of his mission, during a missionary meeting in Glasgow. Several of the participants wrote detailed accounts of the meeting at the time it occurred, but McKay never spoke of it publicly until he was sustained as a member of the First Presidency in 1934:

> During the progress of the meeting, one Elder arose and said: "Brethren, there are angels in this room!" Strange as it may seem the answer did not startle us. It seemed wholly proper; it had not occurred to me that there were divine beings present: I only knew that I was overflowing with gratitude for the presence of the Holy Spirit. I was profoundly impressed, however, when President James McMurrin arose and confirmed that statement by pointing to one brother sitting just in front of me and saying: "Yes, brethren, there are angels in this room, and one of them is the guardian angel of that young man sitting there." Tears were rolling down his cheeks, not in sorrow or grief, but as an expression of the overflowing spirit.
>
> Brother James McMurrin then pointed and said: "One is the guardian angel of that young man there," and he pointed to one whom I had known from childhood, a son of the late David Eccles. Young David C. was also crying. We were all crying. I have named those preliminaries that you might in a measure have a picture of the setting in which President James McMurrin—no truer man ever lived—turned to me and said, paraphrasing the words of the Savior to Peter: "I say, Brother David, Satan hath desired thee that he may sift thee as wheat, but I have prayed the Father for thee." And then he added: "If you will keep the faith you will yet sit in the leading councils of the Church."[24]

Upon returning from Scotland in 1899, McKay joined the faculty of Weber Stake Academy (now Weber State University). On January 2, 1901, he and Emma Ray Riggs were married in the Salt Lake Temple. They had been married for sixty-nine years when McKay died. They raised six children to adulthood, a seventh having died as a young child.

McKay became the fourth principal of the Weber Academy in 1902. One of his students was Joseph Anderson, who later became secretary to the First Presidency. He wrote, "I've never had a teacher anywhere near the equal of President McKay."[25]

In late 1905 a crisis occurred within the Quorum of the Twelve Apostles that soon impacted the remainder of McKay's life. Two members of the quorum, Matthias F. Cowley and John W. Taylor, were obliged to resign because of their refusal to disavow the further practice of plural marriage. By the time of the April general conference of 1906, Apostle Marriner W. Merrill had died, resulting in three vacancies within the quorum. James E. Talmage, who later was sustained to the same quorum, wrote, "These were filled on nomination and vote by the following: Orson F. Whitney, George F. Richards (a son of the late Apostle Franklin D. Richards) and David O. McKay (a former student of mine). They are good men, and I verily believe selected by inspiration."[26]

McKay was different from the other two, both of whom were descendants of prominent early LDS leaders and polygamous families. This difference had not been inconsequential to Joseph F. Smith, the church president who called McKay to the Twelve. A friend later wrote, "Although a boy of only sixteen years, I recall the words of President Joseph F. Smith when you were chosen as an Apostle. He said there was nothing about your name that suggested importance in the Church, but the Lord wanted you in that position."[27] Nor did it go unnoticed by the non-Mormon *Salt Lake Tribune,* which exempted McKay from its ongoing diatribe against LDS leaders. The following year, the *Tribune* singled out a newly called apostle, Anthony W. Ivins, linking him with McKay, for special recognition: "As there had to be a filling of the vacancy, we certainly approve of A. W. Ivins. We could not have made a better choice ourselves, and this is about the first occasion (unless we except McKay) that we could have said the same."[28] For the remainder of his life, McKay would be a bridge uniting the LDS and non-LDS communities.

During McKay's tenure as a member of the Quorum of the Twelve, he suffered an accident that nearly took his life and that gave him strong confirmation about the necessity of following impressions of the Spirit. It happened on March 23, 1916, when he was driving his brother Thomas in their Model T Ford. Lawrence McKay recounted the incident as it was told to him by his father: "He had a feeling that he shouldn't go on, but he disregarded it and went on. Uncle Tommy said, 'There's a rope!' He ducked. The rope hit the radiator, bounced, and hit the windshield, knocking it back on its hinges. It then hit Father across the mouth, broke his jaw, and took out a lot of teeth. If it had been higher it would have blinded him, or if it had been lower, it would have killed him."[29]

The damage was so severe that Peter Johnston—the former missionary companion who had been with him in Stirling—did not recognize him in the hospital. McKay wryly reported the visit to his colleagues, "As he passed the room, he did not recognize the man lying there on the bed, but he came back, and the nurse said, 'Yes, that is he.' He stood at the bed and looked. 'Well,' he said, smiling as best he could, 'the eyes are the same anyhow.'"[30] The following day, Apostles Orson F. Whitney and Heber J. Grant visited him and gave him an extraordinary blessing, which McKay related in a letter to his fellow apostles eleven days after the accident:

> Both Brother Whitney and Brother Grant blessed me that I should be free from pain, should not be permanently disabled, not disfigured, and Brother Grant, that I should not be scarred. I believe I shall realize these blessings, for they were given in faith, and in the spirit of the true brotherhood of Christ. Already part of them have been fulfilled. Notwithstanding the fact, that the left cords in my neck were wrenched, my lips lacerated, all my teeth excepting five (four below and one above)—knocked out or loosened with fractured bone, and my upper jaw fractured, I have been practically free from pain. I acknowledge this as a direct blessing from the Lord. My face is almost entirely healed, and it looks as though I shall be practically free from scars.[31]

The blessing was fulfilled literally, to the amazement even of Grant, who years later confided to McKay, "David, I do not see any scars, but when I took my hands off your head, I wondered about what I had said, whether I had made a mistake."[32] The experience had a lifelong effect on McKay, an object lesson not only of the power of prayer, but also of the consequences of ignoring promptings of the Spirit.

THE CALL TO THE FIRST PRESIDENCY

McKay had long since caught the attention of Heber J. Grant, who became church president in 1918 when Joseph F. Smith died of influenza during the Spanish flu pandemic. Grant had first taken special notice when McKay was a young man attending a party in the Grant home. Grant's daughter Lucy reminisced about the event in a letter to McKay when he was church president:

> One night at our home on 2 East St. when you were attending the "U" at this same time our sister Ray [Rachel Grant Taylor] was there, Ray had a party at our house and you were one of the guests. Father and Uncle Tone [Anthony W.] Ivins were in the dining room and Father said to Uncle Tone "Let's go into the parlor and look over that group of young people." After a little visit they came back into the dining room and discussed the group. I remember so well that they both thought David O. McKay was an outstanding young man and Father had his eye on you from that very moment.[33]

In September 1934, this same Anthony W. Ivins, a counselor in the First Presidency, died. Upon returning to his home following the funeral service, McKay received a phone call from President Grant, asking the younger man to come to Grant's home. "On this occasion, he informed that he had chosen me to succeed Pres. Ivins in the First Presidency. The call coming so suddenly, I was entirely overcome. After an extended interview, when I arose to leave, he put his arms around me and kissed me."[34]

Since 1906 David O. McKay had sat in the "leading councils" of the church, and now he sat in its highest council. But there was one more step ahead of him, one that was first predicted in Jerusalem by his traveling companion, Hugh J. Cannon, during their 1921 global tour of foreign missions. In 1951, Cannon's daughter had written him a note alluding to that prediction; and in responding, McKay filled in the details:

> He [Cannon] was the first one who ever mentioned the matter to me. If I remember rightly it was on the evening of November 3, 1921, when your father and I returned from the Mt. of Olives to the Hotel Allenby just outside the walls of Jerusalem. We had spent the afternoon in meditation and prayer on the site where we thought Jesus had stood when He looked over the city and said: "O Jerusalem, Jerusalem, thou that killest the prophets, and stonest them which are sent unto thee, how often would I have gathered thy children together, even as a hen gathereth her chickens under her wings, and ye would not!" It was one of our most impressive and sacred associations on our world-wide tour. As we returned to our hotel room to rest, there was a moment or two of silence, and then your father said: "Brother, [I have] a distinct impression that one day you will be President of the Church." I answered: "Oh, that day will probably never come," or something to that effect, and nothing more was said about it.[35]

That day came on April 9, 1951.

DEVELOPING A NOBLE CHARACTER

In answer to the question, "What do you consider is the most important purpose of life?" McKay wrote, "To develop a noble character."[36] He developed the character traits that served him well as church president through intense self-discipline. One cousin recalled: "I knew what time he got up in the morning, and he was up at 4:30 every morning. My bedroom was on the south side of this house, and that old squeaky pump was on the north side of that house. I knew what time he got up in the morning, because that old squeaky pump would go, so I could hear. What time he went to bed, I don't know. But he disciplined himself, and he had a set of goals, and I think he probably had to the tune of about 13 of them that he set out very young."[37]

Another cousin commented on McKay's success at character development: "The fact that I never heard negative things about President McKay in Huntsville should produce some insight into his character, because a little town like that has so many cross-threads of jealousy, pettiness, and genuine complaints, as well as false ones."[38]

One of McKay's early challenges was to control his tongue:

> I picture now, in memory, a fork raised in Father's hand when one of us boys began to find fault with our day school teacher, stopping us. He did not want to hear about the faults of that teacher around the table. I recall, too, a rebuke written by Father when I was in the mission field. I had seen the acts of an elder whom I condemned because I thought he was ungentlemanly in his treatment of some members of the Glasgow Branch who were returning from a street meeting. And I wrote home to Father regarding it. This happened during my first month in Glasgow. He wrote a letter in which he quoted, "first cast out the beam out of thine own eye; and then shalt thou see clearly to cast out the mote out of thy brother's eye." (Matthew 7:5.) He thought that would be pretty hard, I suppose, and he softened it by saying, "Your mother is looking over my shoulder as I write and she says, 'Don't write that to the boy,' but I tell her that you are His servant and you know the spirit in which it is given." I did not write any more criticism of any of my associate missionaries.[39]

Nor did he speak criticism of his associates upon becoming a General Authority. Joseph Anderson, who for decades took the minutes in First Presidency meetings, noted that there were numerous occasions that could have elicited angry outbursts: "I have seen him under extreme pressures when under such conditions he could easily have lost his temper, but I never knew him to say an angry word. He may have felt annoyance, and rightly did on certain occasions, but he had great control over his speech, his language, and his attitude."[40] When his secretary asked how he managed, he told her his secret: "I learned many years ago, when I felt this surge of anger or retort coming over me, to put my tongue way back in my mouth and clamp my teeth down on it, and not to say the unkind and hurtful thing. Every time that I did that, I found that it was easier the next time to control my feelings."[41]

Controlling anger was one thing but controlling stubbornness was another, and McKay was much more accomplished at the former than the latter. A cousin attributed this to his Scottish heritage: "Some of the traits of the McKays, and I visited with some of our relatives in Scotland and it carries right through, are that they have strong feelings about right and wrong, and they know when they are right. When others aren't in agreement with them, *they* are wrong!... My Dad was this way. When he knew he was right, nothing stood in his way. He didn't care about public opinion or anything. Uncle Dade [David O.] was this way."[42]

Sometimes the stubbornness was an impediment, while at other times it served McKay well. For example, even as he aged, he insisted on putting in hours of hard physical labor at his Huntsville farm, despite the risk to his health. A cousin recounted an episode shortly after McKay had had eye surgery:

> I went over here one day when he'd had a cataract operation, and it hadn't been too long. He'd come up here and cut the lawn with a team of horses and an old hay mower. He'd do that. It was just kind of a therapeutic thing. He had a team of horses that nobody else used—fence breakers—but he loved them, and that's all that mattered. But they'd pull as much from the reins as they would with the tugs. Well, having had a cataract operation, you do a lot of straining, and that's not very good. So I said to him, "President, I don't think you ought to be doing that. You just had an eye operation." "Well," he says, "Lawrence can't do it. He just had a cataract operation." I said, "But so did you." And he just said, "Well, that's different."[43]

On another similar occasion things got out of hand and McKay wound up going to the emergency room of the hospital. One of his grandsons told the story:

> He was up in Huntsville, the two of them, my dad [Llewelyn], and he. They were moving some logs. They would have some horses there that would help them, and they were moving a whole bunch of logs. They were really heavy. They had an accident, and one of the logs fell right across his legs and stayed there. He was unable to move. My father was going to run and get help from the police or hospital or somebody. "Oh no, Llewelyn, get a chain, put it across the log and pull on it, like a horse," which he did. He got the log off his leg. He said, "Okay, we'll take you right to the hospital. You have broken some blood vessels." His leg was bleeding. He wouldn't go until he got the logs taken care of, another half-hour, anyway. Finally, he realized that he was very silly to do that. But he wanted to get things done. They took him to the Dee Hospital in Ogden. They patched him up, and my dad drove him home. When they got home on East

South Temple, he hobbled in. My grandmother just lit into him: "You have got to stop this, Dade! You are just getting too old for this type of thing." In all seriousness, he said, "No, when you stop, you die."[44]

THE IMPORTANCE OF A STRONG FAMILY

David O. McKay cherished his own family and spoke frequently and passionately about the supreme importance of strong families. He borrowed a phrase from sociologist J. E. McCulloch, and made it a mantra for the entire church: "No success in life can compensate for failure in the home."[45] He and his wife, Emma Ray Riggs McKay, whom he always called Ray, led by example. On their thirty-first wedding anniversary he wrote, "During that time I cannot recall that she has spoken a cross word to me. She has been an ideal sweetheart, a charming companion, and a loving wife."[46] And Sister McKay came close to this idealistic portrait. Speaking to BYU students, she related an apparently hypothetical example, but one that had actually occurred:

> There are many qualifications that a woman should have to be a good wife and mother, but the most important is patience—patience with children's and husband's tempers, patience with their misunderstandings, with their desires, with their actions.
>
> Suppose you ask your husband to carry a mattress downstairs, and instead of carrying it carefully so that not a speck of dirt touches its clean coverage, he throws it through the window upon the lawn below. He probably did not think of the grimy dirt from the window frame soiling the cover nor of the possible dirt that might be on the lawn. All he wanted was to save time and energy and get the thing over with in a hurry. Will you rave and rant at him, call him a stupid creature who never does things right, or will you think, "Oh, what's the use! The thing is done. Better make the best of it"? Always the latter if you can make yourself be calm.[47]

McKay was loving with his children, but he was also a strict disciplinarian. A granddaughter recalled, "You didn't ever question what he said. It was the way he said it. You knew you had to do what he told you to do."[48] Lawrence learned that lesson at an early age:

> We were riding to Huntsville in the surrey. Father was driving with Mother beside him on the front seat, and Llewelyn and I were sitting on the rear seat. I was not very old, and I was scuffling with Llewelyn. This was dangerous, of course, because one of us could fall in

front of the wheel. Father quietly told me to stop. I persisted. Then Father let me out of the carriage.

I can still remember walking up the hill, seeing the team and surrey going along, getting farther away by the minute. I was old enough to have walked the rest of the way and was certainly in no danger on the country roads of those times; but Father let me walk just far enough to contemplate the lesson in sufficient leisure, then stopped and waited for me. I was a much-chastened boy when I climbed back into the surrey. There was no more teasing or quarreling.[49]

McKay performed hundreds of marriages over the decades, and always dispensed advice to the newlyweds about how to build a successful marriage. One husband, for whom McKay had performed the ceremony six decades earlier, recalled the advice: "He said, 'I would like to say a few words which are not in the marriage ceremony. At this point, Brother Hodson, you will place a ring on her finger signifying a never-ending circle of love and continuing faithfulness for both of you.' He paused and smiled, his bright eyes seeming to penetrate our very souls. He went on: 'Brother Hodson, continue to court her, be kind to her and trust her.' He paused again and then said: 'And always admire her new hat.'"[50]

Nothing touched McKay more than the sight of a loving family, and rarely was there a more open expression of family love than the departure of a child for the mission field. Often the love came in the form of tears, particularly between mother and son, which some thought to be unseemly: "One of the bystanders said, 'I'm going to talk to President McKay about all this crying. I don't like this. This is all unnecessary.' So he went to talk to President McKay and President McKay looked at him and said, 'You say tears, do you? Those tears are all right. I'll take a chance on those tears. You let those mothers and those boys cry as much as you want. That's real affection.'"[51]

Failure in the home distressed David O. McKay as much as success in the home pleased him. When he was church president, it fell to him alone to make the final decision when a couple applied for cancellation of their temple marriage—the ecclesiastical equivalent of a divorce—and he referred to it as "the most depressing duty there is!"[52] He reserved special wrath for husbands who abused their wives. One bishop recalled a rare occasion when McKay lashed out publicly at such behavior:

There was a special priesthood meeting to be held at the Assembly Hall. We were all gathered in there, bishops and counselors, and President McKay was late. We kind of just buzzed around wondering what had happened, if anything. Finally, he came in, and he apologized, but he was very stern, very stern. It was very surprising in a way, because he talked about the reason why he was late, and he said that this sister had come to him and told him about her woes with her husband, and how she had been maltreated and so forth. He raised his voice and he said, "After listening to her, I was determined that that man should no longer have the Priesthood!" It fell like a big stone on us in the audience, you know, because he was very adamant about it and very stern. It was one of the more tense moments that I can remember during his administration as head of the Church.[53]

Consistent with McKay's feelings about the sanctity of the family were his actions toward women and children. All women received his respect. He would not enter a doorway ahead of a woman, and he insisted on helping whenever possible. Following a meeting with McKay during the wintertime, Primary General President LaVern Watts Parmley went into the outer office and reached for her overshoes, only to be overtaken by the president. "He got down and put on my galoshes. I said, 'Oh President McKay, you can't do that!' But he was so courteous that he couldn't think of letting me put on my galoshes so he put them on."[54] Indeed, family members learned that the only way to deal with the system was to beat it. One granddaughter recalled, "Mother took off her boots in the wintertime, before we rang the doorbell, because she said if she didn't take them off, he would be down on his knees, helping her with the boots."[55]

McKay always rose to his feet when a woman entered the room, and one of the most touching vignettes from his life resulted from this courtesy. A granddaughter-in-law recalled this incident, which occurred just six weeks prior to his death:

> We got a phone call from one of the nurses. She said, "Dick, your grandfather would like you to come to dinner."... So, we went down, and he was already seated in the dining room with Mama Ray, his wife. We came in through the kitchen, I think, and went right into the dining room. As I came in, we greeted them, and all the time he was struggling to get to his feet. I said, "Oh, Papa Dade, please don't do that." He continued, and it was probably not just seconds, it was minutes before he could get to his feet. He finally rose to his full stature, and he looked at me when I was protesting that this was too much to ask, and he said, "You wouldn't take that honor away from me would you?" And I had nothing to say.[56]

He had a special fondness for children that lasted throughout his life, and he was able to act and speak at their level. A letter written from a missionary to McKay in 1934 reminded him of an earlier time as a junior apostle: "It doesn't seem so long ago since you used to play marbles with my brother and me at conference time in

Montpelier."[57] Another written in 1960 noted, "[My father] tells me that you used to get down on your hands and knees and let me ride on your back when I was very young and you visited in our home at Stake Conference time."[58] Elaine Cannon, long associated with the church's youth programs, recalled "one time when a Lamanite [Native American] child came, and Clare tried to push him onto somebody else. President McKay heard of it, and oh, boy, he was angry. He said, 'I'm not that unapproachable.'"[59]

He not only played with children—he taught them, and with special effect. Following a chapel dedication in California, a young mother wrote him a note of special appreciation:

> As a Mother of two little children who were held spellbound by your words when you addressed yourself to the youngsters at the morning meeting, I can't thank you enough for the impression you made upon their little minds. My five-year-old son came home that morning and repeated almost word for word your illustration of the water and the glass, the inky water, and the further words concerning this illustration. My eight-year-old daughter is still talking about you, and about having shaken your hand.... I asked her what impressed her most about the meeting and she answered, "President McKay spoke to us children, and we could understand what he meant."[60]

As age limited McKay's mobility, his time with children diminished, much to his dismay; and holiday gatherings with grandchildren took on special significance. His granddaughter-in-law recalled a Halloween tradition:

> We used to take the children trick-or-treating down at the Hotel Utah.... We would just trip the kids in their little costumes through the [lobby].... He just was so thrilled. He said, "You know, that is one of the things in my life that I have missed. I have been traveling, and all of these other things take my attention, but to have children crawling on my lap and running their fingers through my hair"—and doing things on the couch as they would crawl all over him—he said, "you just can't imagine how important that is to me." He would always come to the door and wave good-bye to us and say, "Please come again soon."[61]

One of McKay's last trips away from his apartment in the Hotel Utah was to Ogden, for the dedication of the new McKay-Dee Hospital. Though confined to a wheelchair, he insisted on a complete tour of the facility that had been named in his honor. Architect Keith Wilcox, who escorted him on the tour, recalled his reaction when they reached one section of the hospital: "He got up to the pediatrics area where the children would be, and he shed tears. 'You mean children have to be in this hospital?' You know, he was just trying to imagine children having to be brought to a hospital. It just got to him."[62]

IMAGE AND DEMEANOR

Image is crucial to any leader; and David O. McKay, perhaps more than any of his predecessors since Joseph Smith, intuitively understood the importance of image and the means by which to cultivate it. Throughout his life, but particularly during his presidential years, he tried to strike a balance between pride in his image and humility in his demeanor. Generally, he was most successful.

Image building is made easier when the starting material is good, and McKay had an impressive physical presence. Genetics gave him his height, but years of farm work and athletics clothed the frame with a muscular build. Early in his presidency the *Salt Lake Tribune* called him "six feet two and 199 pounds of the kindliest, fairest and most understanding man one has the pleasure of meeting."[63]

Equally impressive as his build was his manner of dress, which was influenced by his two years of missionary service in Scotland. "There was a generation of Mormons who went to Europe on missions before World War I, and David O. McKay was in this group. They came home and brought with them some European demeanors," recalled Douglas Alder, who also served a mission in Europe. "They went over, and they came back with an attitude of refinement and elegance."[64] Where most of his fellow General Authorities dressed in dark suits, McKay often wore white doublebreasted suits during the summer, and the effect was stunning, according to Alder's wife, Elaine: "In this white suit, clear down to the white shoes, he'd walk through that door, and it really took your breath away, as many times as you saw him."[65]

Topping it off was a magnificent mane of flowing white hair that he intentionally left longer than men conventionally wore their hair in the 1950s and 1960s. His barber told the story:

> I was a barber with his son, Bob McKay, the jeweler. He wore his hair full, not shaggy, but full, and Mrs. McKay liked his. David O. went to the Deseret Gym which was right next door to his office, and they used to just kind of clean him up like a missionary haircut, all the way around. He had this beautiful white hair, and so she sent him up to me with restrictions of what I should do, but [basically she wanted it to be] like her son Bob. After she would call me on the phone and say, "Oh, I'm so happy with this. You are doing so great with him. Just keep it up." So I did.[66]

Some thought McKay took it too far, that he crossed over the line from image into vanity, but most understood the importance of what he was doing. One of his cousins noted: "On the broad scale of things, aura, image become overwhelmingly powerful. This was President McKay's long suit. His son Llewelyn once said, 'If father had any faults, they would be two. One, he drives too fast. And two, his vanity.' Appearances were very important to President McKay. And as a leader, this made sense."[67]

Taken together, all of the attention to detail resulted not just in an immaculate image of a Prophet—indeed, it is no accident that he is the one church president of whom countless people still say, "He *looked* like a Prophet"—but also an uplifted image for an entire church. And it happened when it was most needed. "What a happy period, what a Camelot it was, to have a Prophet, just when we needed him," commented Elaine Cannon. "The Depression is over, the War has cut everybody to the quick, and here he comes, and everything is going to be all right."[68]

Despite this striking and glamorous image, behind it was a man of humility. Part of his humility came from remembering past failures. Some seven decades after the fact, he still spoke publicly about failing the first time he blessed the sacrament:

> We did not have the prayer on a printed card before us then as is frequently the case now. We were supposed, as priests, to memorize it. The Sacrament table was just under the pulpit, and father, the bishop, always stood right over the one who asked the blessing upon the bread and water. I thought I knew the prayer. But I had memorized it privately, and when I knelt and saw the audience before me I became flustered. I remember when I got to "that they are willing to take upon them the Name of thy Son," things went blank and I said, "Amen." Father said, "And always remember him . . ." I was half rising from my knees, but I knelt down again and said, "And always remember him. Amen." Father said, ". . . and keep his commandments which he has given them." I knelt down again, ". . . and keep the commandments which he has given them. Amen." "And always remember him that they may have his spirit to be with them. Amen." I suffered all the pangs of failure, but I am glad that we did not give up.[69]

But more of it came from an understanding of humankind's subordinate status to Deity. When artist Arnold Friberg was commissioned to paint a series of scenes from the Book of Mormon, McKay told him, "Now whatever you do, don't paint Christ into the Book of Mormon." Friberg replied, "That's the high point of the book. Why not?" "Oh," he said, "the finite cannot conceive of the infinite."[70]

McKay's humility was expressed both in actions and in words. A prominent physician recalled an episode that had occurred decades earlier:

> The Prophet David O. McKay visited our Sacrament meeting and I was a Deacon passing the Sacrament. One of the Deacons bumped the Sacrament bread tray against the railing going up the stairs to serve President McKay. A few pieces of Sacrament bread tumbled off the tray onto the floor. Embarrassed, and hoping no one would notice, the Deacon looked away, and continued serving, President McKay first and next the Bishopric and others on the stand.
>
> A few moments later, in a manner so as to attract the very least amount of attention, the Prophet quietly bent forward, picked up the errant bread pieces, and slipped them into his coat pocket. He had captured our complete attention. We waited to see what came next. At the end of the meeting, he made his characteristic quiet exit from the side door, where he removed the Sacrament bread pieces from his pocket and gently placed them atop the shrubs where the little birds might find them. He spoke not a word about the incident (to the great relief of all of us) but by his quiet actions he taught us a most profound lesson about reverence for the Sacrament.[71]

On one occasion Paul H. Dunn, a newly appointed General Authority, approached McKay with a request:

> I said to him, "President McKay, some day I would like to just have a little while with you to ask some questions that kids have been asking me for thirteen years." That quick, he said, "Well, I don't have anything scheduled for the next hour or so, let's do it now." And so I sat there and asked him every question I could think of that those college youth were asking me. I guess a full 40–50% of his responses were, "I don't know. I don't know. The Lord hasn't told us yet."[72]

The combination of powerful image on the one hand and selfless humility on the other was a difficult balance to strike, but his ability to do so affected the entire church over the course of his presidency. His personal physician commented on the balance: "He was always very neatly attired. I think his personality bridged the gap between what could have been a formidable sort of man, bridged the gap to Church members and the public. He came over as a very kindly, human man, very loving and thoughtful. And he was what he was, whatever the day or time or circumstances."[73]

A DISTASTE FOR BUREAUCRACY

For all of his strengths in other areas, David O. McKay's skills as an administrator were limited. In large part, this was due to his distaste for bureaucracy. He told his secretary, "Men must learn that in presiding over the Church we are dealing with human hearts, that individual rights are sacred, and the human soul is tender. We cannot run the Church as we would a business."[74] Much more interested in people than in flow charts and policies, he often frustrated subordinates who were used to firm decisions that subordinated humane factors. Ernest L. Wilkinson, the president of Brigham Young University, wrote in his diary, "President McKay is a great spiritual leader, but he is not an executive, or he would not permit all of these reconsiderations, which take not only my time, but his."[75]

In dealing with subordinates, he preferred to give them the general outlines of what he wanted accomplished, then leave it to them to fill in the details. Sometimes this approach backfired, as in the case of the building program, where more attention to detail on his part would doubtless have reversed the financial drain before it reached crisis proportions. But generally it was a benevolent policy that empowered people to use their creativity to "magnify their callings," knowing that they had support from the top. To one mission president who was departing to Denmark, he said, "The less we hear from you, the more we'll love you. You will be a long way away from home. Now just go over and do a job."[76]

Another mission president was called to open a new mission in Scotland:

> I asked President McKay, "Where do you want the mission home?" He said, "I thought I told you the Lord called *you* to be the mission president over there." I said, "Thank you." I got the message. . . .
>
> I was given a bundle of checks an inch thick when I left to open the mission. I said, "President, we are just coming out of a depression." President McKay was as great a miracle prophet as ever lived on this Earth. I said, "What are these for?" He said, "The Lord will tell you." I bought over twenty-eight chapel sites. We have a chapel on every one of them.[77]

To those accustomed to a bureaucratic management style, McKay's approach was a source of continual frustration, particularly to administrators like Harold B. Lee who were struggling, at McKay's request, with the task of correlating the church's sprawling structure. Although there clearly were weaknesses in McKay's approach to management, the overall effect was quite striking. Quinn McKay, a cousin who spent his academic career researching and teaching management, summarized the factors that made McKay's leadership style work:

> I think President McKay and President Harold B. Lee are two fascinating contrasts in leadership. President Lee led by being an

administrator. He watched for the critical policies, and he had a
say.... He knew, administratively, how to make decisions that caused
things to happen....

President McKay took off, he'd go off traveling and make appearances, and stacks of decisions sat on his desk, time after time. But he
was an effective leader, in this sense. When you're leading in small
groups, policy decisions that you make and face-to-face influences,
you can lead and be effective in doing it.... President McKay, I think,
did not understand organization. He didn't understand administration. If it weren't for this personal aura that he had, he would have
had a tough administration. But that personal aura was so great that
he ruled by the grassroots, and not by the structure.[78]

A granddaughter said, "Mamma Ray told me once, 'I think if Dade had his way
he would spend his entire time marrying people and preaching funerals, because
he just feels that's a real way to be with them and help them.' He was just happy
with people."[79]

Indeed, style rather than structure enlivened the church during the McKay
years. He brought an infectious optimism to the job, and it spread widely. He had
it before he became church president, and he did not lose it afterwards. A 1939 publication captured what he always was:

The religion which David O. McKay preaches and practices is a cheerful one, encouraging everything that makes life rich and full and effective, cultivating in every way the romance and gladness that comes
from abundant living. It is not a straight [*sic*] jacket, it is not a killjoy,
there is nothing forbidding in its aspects, nothing inhibited by it that
would contribute to one's permanent peace and happiness. It dis-
courages only those things which would abridge one's usefulness or
curtail his righteous possibilities. From the blazing altar of his own
heart, David O. McKay kindles the love for truth in the hearts of his
associates.[80]

Arch Madsen, whom McKay recruited to head church-owned KSL television
and radio, said of him, "He was the youngest man I ever worked with, and he was
ninety years old then."[81] McKay told a colleague, "My, Brother Murdock, what
wouldn't I give to live another fifty years, when you see some of the most wonderful
things taking place."[82]

Because of his optimism he was able to see past things that were stumbling
blocks to other church members and even to chuckle as he accepted human foibles.
He told his fellow General Authorities, "Now, Brethren, don't you worry too
much. It's good for every dog to have a few fleas."[83] Besides, he said, "Perfect

people would be awfully tiresome to live with; their stained-glass view of things would seem a constant sermon without intermission, a continuous moral snub of superiority to our self-respect."[84]

And so, he gently chided Apostle John A. Widtsoe, whose wife advocated such a rigid interpretation of the Word of Wisdom as to proscribe chocolate because of the stimulants it contained, saying, "John, do you want to take all the joy out of life?"[85] But he didn't stop there. At a reception McKay attended, the hostess served rum cake. "All the guests hesitated, watching to see what McKay would do. He smacked his lips and began to eat." When one guest expostulated, "'But President McKay, don't you know that is rum cake?' McKay smiled and reminded the guest that the Word of Wisdom forbade drinking alcohol, not eating it."[86]

During intermission at a theatrical presentation, his host offered to get refreshments: "His hearing wasn't very good, and I got right down in front of him and I said, 'President McKay, what would you like to drink? All of our cups say Coca Cola on them because of our arrangement with Coca Cola Bottling, but we have root beer and we have orange and we have Seven-Up. What would you like to drink?' And he said, 'I don't care what it says *on* the cup, as long as there is a Coke *in* the cup.'"[87] McKay's point was simple and refreshing: Don't get hung up on the letter of the law to the point where you squeeze all of the spirit out of life.

The humor with which he dealt with such incidents served him well in other venues of life. He loved hearing and telling stories about the Scots. On the golden anniversary of Weber College he said: "A man's wife having died, his neighbor came in and expressed his condolence at Sandy's loss, and then praised the virtues of that good wife. She was loving, devoted and always true to her husband. Sandy listened and finally said, 'Aye, Thomas, what ye say is true, she was a' that and more: She was a good wife tae me, and I cam' near tellin' her sae, aine or twice.'"[88]

On occasion he was the target of the story and proved he could take as well as give. In a meeting in Los Angeles he said:

> When our sister asked if any Scotchmen were present, and President Russon said, "Oh, here's a Scotchman, but he can take it,"—whenever we hear jokes on the Scotchmen I like to retaliate with a story of the Scotch business man who went down from Glasgow to London to attend a business meeting. When he came back and reported to his Board of Directors, and they had accepted his report, one of them said, "Well, Thomas, now you've given us your report, tell us what you think of the Englishmen." Thomas replied, "I didna meet any Englishmen. My business took me only to the heads of departments."[89]

He could lapse into an authentic Scottish accent with ease and played tit-for-tat with another president who was good at turning an accent on and off. One of the secretaries in his office related:

> [Lyndon] Johnson could turn that southern accent on like you wouldn't believe. "Why I said to my good friend . . ." you know, with this big Southern accent. Then he'd turn around and say something to his friends, without an accent. I thought, "Oh, wait a minute!" President McKay picked up on it and started speaking with a Scottish accent. It was so cute! He was telling him this joke and he did it with a Scottish accent, and Johnson was having the hardest time understanding. It was so cute, and he laughed his head off after he got through. He could tell jokes better than anybody I ever knew.[90]

Humor was therapeutic for McKay, and he urged others to take the same medicine. Speaking to a group of former missionaries he said, "I believe in having good times, in laughing, relaxing, and seeing the sunny side of life. We are far too sober, have too much worry."[91] And he pitied those who couldn't laugh, saying, "I feel a little sorry for those that have such long faces that they have to sleep on their pillow lengthwise."[92]

As the ravages of age took a mounting toll, McKay was able to buffer the effect with humor. His housekeeper related one incident just after President McKay had turned ninety-five:

> He told us about it at the dinner table. After a session of General Conference, President McKay was riding in the elevator in Hotel Utah up to their apartment. On the elevator was a young boy who had followed President McKay into the elevator. On the way up, the boy said, "President McKay, I would like to shake your hand once more because you may die pretty soon." President McKay said that he thanked the boy and said to him, "Young man, you never heard of a man dying at 95." The amazement of the boy amused him so much that he told us about it.[93]

Humor even allowed him to handle with grace an otherwise embarrassing situation. His nurse recalled such a situation, which occurred as she helped him from his wheelchair into his desk chair:

> As he stood up, I had him on each side of the midriff, holding on the sides, and he had his hands on the desk. I just kicked the wheelchair back a ways so that when he would pivot around he wouldn't hit his ankles on the footrest of the wheelchair. Just as I did that, his knees

buckled. I was in a panic, and I thought, "Oh, my gosh! If he were to fall, I'd never get him up." I didn't realize until I had been taking care of him how big a man he really was. Anyway, as I did that and his knees buckled, the only thing I could think to do was sit under him. So he was really sitting in my lap, with his hands resting on the desk, and I could see his hands were shaking. I was trying to pivot him into this chair; and when I saw his hands quivering, I thought, "This is great, I've scared this poor man to death!" So as I went to pivot him around, to try to reassure him I said, "President McKay, don't worry about it, I've got you." Then he just kind of chuckled and said, "Well I know, honey, but it's just that you've got too much of me!"[94]

A Spiritual Leader

But of all the character traits that David O. McKay possessed, the most important was his deep, authentic spirituality. In his first address as church president he affirmed: "No one can preside over this Church without first being in tune with the head of the Church, our Lord and Savior, Jesus Christ. He is our head. This is his Church. Without his divine guidance and constant inspiration, we cannot succeed. With his guidance, with his inspiration, we cannot fail."[95]

The extent to which he sought and received divine guidance was apparent to those close to him. Joseph Anderson, secretary to the First Presidency, recalled: "I've been with President McKay in his later years when I've marveled at the way he has handled a situation. He was directed by the Lord. I could tell it. I didn't hear him say, 'Thus saith the Lord' or anything of that kind, but the spirit of the Lord was working on him."[96] Apostle Marion G. Romney went one step further: "I testify to you that that Spirit is active daily in the President of the Church.... I have heard him say frequently, 'The Lord has spoken.'"[97] When Henry D. Moyle died in 1963, creating a vacancy in the First Presidency, McKay sought divine guidance in selecting a replacement. As the son of Hugh B. Brown, his other counselor, tells the story:

> President McKay came to Dad—and this was all from Dad telling me—and said, "I'm being urged on this side and that side to appoint this man or that man. I'm going across to the temple to find out whom the Lord wants." When he came back, he went in to see Dad, and said, "The Lord wants N. Eldon Tanner. Can you work with him?" Dad said, "Well, President McKay, you may have forgotten, but this is my nephew. I've known him all my life. He's like a son to me. Of course I can work with him." "Oh, he's your nephew? Well, he's the man the Lord wants."[98]

The idea of talking directly to God and receiving a direct response is foreign
to most people in today's largely secular world, yet belief in "direct revelation" is
the foundation of the Latter-day Saint religion. On one occasion a boy who flip-
pantly questioned McKay on the subject received an unexpected answer:

> My younger brothers both worked at Nielsen Brothers Service Station
> on 1st South and 9th East. President McKay used to leave his car there
> for servicing very often, and then they'd drive it down to him. There
> was this third kid who worked there, who was inactive in the Church,
> sort of a hard-looking kind of a guy. One night it was his job to take
> the car down, pick up President McKay, and drive him home on
> South Temple. He had the temerity to say, "When was the last time
> you talked to God, President McKay?" No properly brought-up LDS
> kid would ever do that. You might wonder, you might think about
> that, but who would say that? This kid came back to the service sta-
> tion really quite shaken and shared this story with the other kids. It
> was my brother, Bill, who told me this. President McKay said, "It was
> last week." Now, he left everybody wondering what he really meant
> by that, whether he was praying, talking to God, or whether it was
> another kind of experience. But the way it was said, it really left this
> kid shaken up, and Bill said it really turned him around.[99]

Finding the right venue in which to seek inspiration was not easy, given that
McKay and all other modern church presidents have had to fill the dual roles of spiritual leader and head of church government. McKay's diaries show that, day in and
day out, there were few gaps in his daily schedule of meetings, interviews, and telephone calls. And so he worked around his schedule, carving out time in the early
morning hours for things he could not do during business hours. Coauthor Bob
Wright, then a missionary in Switzerland, received a letter from his Aunt Clare
Middlemiss in the summer of 1956. Included was a description of

> how [President McKay] would seek the will of the Lord. He had told
> her that he would come over to the office very early in the morning,
> never much after 6:00 o'clock, and sometimes earlier than that. Five
> o'clock regularly. He would sit in his office and meditate. I think that
> is the word that she used, "meditate." I remember that, because I
> really hadn't heard up to then—and still haven't heard in the Church,
> in Sunday School or anything else, very often—the word "meditate."
> I don't think we think about it that much. We talk about, maybe,
> pondering. That's something I hadn't heard. But it really went to my
> soul. She said he thought it was best in the morning when he was not
> tired, but invigorated and quiet, and no phone ringing and no inter-

ruptions. And he would contemplate and meditate the issues of the day.[100]

At other times, he would retreat to his beloved Huntsville. His housekeeper recalled, "He needed to go to Huntsville to be away from all the people who would give him advice. He wanted the Lord's answer. When the problems came into the Church, he had to be by himself, not to listen to every person giving him advice. So that's why he loved to go to Huntsville."[101] An assistant also spoke of the Huntsville retreat: "I'd take him to the Huntsville house,...make a fire and he'd just sit in front of it when he was particularly weighted down with problems."[102]

With his spirituality came a profound appreciation of the role of earthly life as but one step in an ongoing process. Death is not to be feared, for it is the transition from one step to the next. One General Authority stated, "I talked to President McKay one time, in one of my question sessions, and I asked him, 'What is it like to die?' He said, 'Oh, that's easy. It's like going from this room to that room.'"[103] He used different yet equally simple symbolism to explain resurrection to one of his sons: "At times when they would be riding in the mountains, Llewelyn would say, 'I don't understand this resurrection business.' So, his father would plan to go to the mountains so he could explain it to him. He would go in the early spring, when the flowers were just coming up, and he would say, 'We were here in the fall, and those flowers were all dead. It's springtime, and they are all back.' That is how he would explain the resurrection to his little children and his grandchildren."[104]

Huntsville was the setting for one of the more sublime vignettes of his life, related by his daughter-in-law:

> It was the time when he turned 90, and the *Life Magazine* people were there to take pictures. He was tired, so he and Mama Ray were going to walk back across the street to his home and lie down for a little while. So, I walked back over with them. I guess the front door was open, and he went to close it. He said, "Vivian, come here. I want to show you something." It was fall, September, and the colors were all changing. He said, "I want you to look out there. That is what the Celestial Kingdom looks like." I said, "Papa Dade, is that a prophetic statement, or is that a man who loves his home?" He thought for a minute and he said, "Maybe a little of both."[105]

TRIBUTES FROM AROUND THE WORLD

Men who successfully lead large organizations for many years are always the subject of perfunctory tributes, and David O. McKay garnered thousands along the way, as well as in memoriam. Several, however, were extraordinary by any standard and serve to conclude this portrait.

In 1955 McKay received several officials of the General Motors Corporation in his office, along with Gus Backman, executive secretary of the Salt Lake City Chamber of Commerce. After the meeting, Backman told Clare Middlemiss: "I thought you would be interested in a remark made by Mr. N. C. Dezendorf [Vice-President of General Motors] regarding President McKay as we were going down the steps of the Church Office Building following our interview with President McKay. He said, 'There is the most god-like man I have ever met. If you wanted to make a man in the image of God, there is the pattern!'"[106]

In 1956, Sterling McMurrin, then professor of philosophy at the University of Utah, met Walter Reuther at the high-powered Aspen Institute for the Humanities where, by invitation, McMurrin lectured from 1954 to 1960. Reuther, who was then the president of the United Auto Workers and vice-president of the AFL-CIO, indicated that he would like to visit Salt Lake City following the summer session at Aspen. McMurrin recalled the visit:

> It was Reuther who had the great battles to drive Communism out of the unions. In my opinion, he was a really great statesman, a remarkable human being. I've never known anyone who impressed me more favorably than Walter Reuther.... I arranged with him to meet with President McKay. We met in President McKay's conference room. We had a wonderful session.... As we went out of President McKay's conference room, Reuther said to me, "I have met with many of the leading people of the world"—and that was very, very true—"with presidents, prime ministers and some kings. I have never in my life met a person who left such a great impression on me as this man has."[107]

Reuther later commented to Marion D. Hanks of the First Council of Seventy, who was present at the meeting: "I doubt that another generation will produce a character like that."[108]

In September 1962 Lady Redding, the first woman ever to serve in the House of Lords in England, was escorted to McKay's office by Belle Spafford, general president of the Relief Society:

> When that interview was over, President McKay walked to the door with us. He took hold of my arm and pulled me back. He said, "Sister Spafford, today we have been in the presence of true greatness. That is a great woman." I stepped through the door, and she hooked arms with me, and she said, "Mrs. Spafford, I know you revere Doctor McKay as a great religious leader. He's far more than that. He's a

great man judged by any standard. I've met many great men in my life. I have never met a greater man than I have just met this morning."[109]

No less impressive was a simple statement, made in a private setting by a man who later became church president: "I was riding with President Harold B. Lee from Manti once, and I said—kind of a stupid thing—'I always wondered why you weren't the counselor to President McKay.' And he grinned, and he thought for a minute, and then said, 'The world produces few David McKays, and it's those few who change the world.'"[110]

2

REVELATION
AND PROPHECY

David O. McKay was a holy man. He was at his best when filling the prophetic role—not foretelling the future, as many people erroneously understand the word, but in calling people to God's service and a godly life. Unfortunately, as the church grew in size and complexity, greater and greater amounts of his time had to be devoted to administrative functions, a dilemma that was not resolved until years after his death, when most administrative functions were handed off to the Quorum of the Twelve. Nonetheless, he is best remembered for having filled the prophetic role unlike any other church president in modern times.

At the bedrock of his spiritual convictions was the absolute assurance that God continues to communicate not only with the prophet of the church, but also with lay members. On several occasions, when asked to enumerate the differences between the LDS Church and others he responded, "The first difference is that the Church claims divine authority by direct revelation."[1] In the second editorial he wrote upon becoming church president, he elaborated on what "direct revelation" meant to him: "God does reveal today to the human soul the reality of the resurrection of the Lord, the divinity of this great work, the truth, the divine and eternal truth, that God lives not only as a power, an essence, a force—as electricity—but as our Father in heaven."[2]

The recipient of such revelation, which he hoped would be every church member, would thereupon be the possessor not just of some sort of mystic knowledge, but of an iron conviction that would have practical benefit throughout life:

> You can pass through the dark valley of slander, misrepresentation, and abuse, undaunted as though you wore a magic suit of mail that no bullet could enter, no arrow could pierce. You can hold your head high, toss it fearlessly and defiantly, look every man calmly and unflinchingly in the eye as though you were a victorious king, returning at the head

of legions, with banners waving and lances glistening and bugles filling the air with music. You can feel the great expansive world of more
health surging through you as the quickened blood courses through
the body of him who is gladly, gloriously proud of physical health. You
will know that all will come out right in the end; that it must come;
that all must flee before the great white light of Truth, as the darkness slinks away into nothingness in the presence of the sunburst.[3]

McKay was reserved in speaking directly of revelations to himself and left none
in written form, but his closest associates were well aware of the process. Alvin R.
Dyer, a counselor in the First Presidency at the time of McKay's death, was interviewed for McKay's obituary in the *New York Times:* "Mr. Dyer expressed the view
that revelations through Mr. McKay, although not reduced to writing, were perfectly valid. Divine inspiration, he remarked, could take many forms. He recalled
several temple meetings on church matters in which Mr. McKay had buttressed his
presentations by adding, 'Thus saith the Lord.'"[4]

A CHURCH OF MIRACLES

The church into which David O. McKay was born was a church of miracles. Members not only expected and received revelation—direct manifestations of a spiritual
nature—but also shared them freely with others, in private conversations, in
monthly testimony meetings, and in print. Indeed, while McKay was still a
teenager, the church, in an effort to encourage children to share such manifestations, initiated a special column, "For Our Little Folks," in the *Juvenile Instructor,*
then a magazine for children. The column ran for fifteen years and included hundreds of accounts of spiritual manifestations, all written by the children who witnessed or experienced them.

McKay's own experiences with personal revelation began while he was a young
child, with an answer to a prayer that not only resolved the crisis of the moment,
but also enabled him to accept at face value current and historical accounts of revelation to others in the church:

> When a very young child in the home of my youth, I was fearful at
> night. I traced it back to a vivid dream in which two Indians came into
> the yard. I ran to the house for protection, and one of them shot an
> arrow and hit me in the back. Only a dream, but I felt the blow, and
> I was very much frightened, for in the dream they entered the house,
> a tall one, and a smaller one, and sneered and frightened Mother.
>
> I never got over it. Added to that were the fears of my mother,
> for when Father was away with the herd, or on some mission, Mother

would never retire without looking under the bed, so burglars or men who might enter the house and try to take advantage of Mother and the young children were real to me.

Whatever the conditions, I was very much frightened. One night I could not sleep and I fancied I heard horses around the house. Mother was in another room. Thomas F. by my side was sleeping soundly. I became terribly wrought in my feelings, and I decided to pray as my parents had taught me.

I thought I could pray only by getting out of bed and kneeling, and that was a terrible test. But I did finally get out of bed and kneel and pray to God to protect Mother and the family. And a voice, speaking as clearly to me as mine is to you, said, "Don't be afraid: nothing will hurt you."

Where it came from, what it was I am not saying. You may judge. To me it was a direct answer.

I say it has been easy for me to understand and believe the reality of the visions of the Prophet Joseph. It was easy for me in youth to accept his vision, the appearance of God the Father and His Son, Jesus Christ, to the boy praying. I thought of nothing else.[5]

Later in his childhood, McKay approached God in prayer with another request, assuming incorrectly that the response would be equally direct and dramatic:

I realized in youth that the most precious thing that a man could obtain in this life was a testimony of the divinity of this work.... But somehow I got an idea in youth that we could not get a testimony unless we had some manifestation.... I remember riding over the hills one afternoon, thinking of these things, and concluded there in the silence of the hills was the best place to get that testimony. I stopped my horse, threw the reins over his head, and withdrew just a few steps and knelt by the side of a tree.... I knelt down and with all the fervor of my heart poured out my soul to God, and asked him for a testimony of this gospel. I had in mind that there would be some manifestation, that I would receive some transformation that would leave me absolutely without doubt. I got up, mounted my horse, and as he started over the trail I remember rather introspectively searching myself, and involuntarily shaking my head, said to myself, "No, sir, there is no change; I am just the same boy I was before I knelt down." The anticipated manifestation had not come. Nor was that the only occasion. However, it did come, but not in the way I had anticipated. Even the manifestation of God's power and the presence of his angels came, but when it did come it was simply a confirmation; it was not the testimony.[6]

Several years passed with no answer to his petition. He went to the University of Utah with the expectation of obtaining a teaching position immediately after graduation, but his plans were altered by a mission call to the British Isles. He left Utah for the mission field in August 1897, still with no answer. "I still had not heard a voice…. I still had that same desire that made me kneel on the hillside."[7]

The answer came months later, while McKay was working in Glasgow. A dispute between two men in the branch led to one of them taking offense and declaring, "I'll never come back here as long as that man is in the presidency of the branch." As McKay grappled with the problem, the voice he had so long sought finally came, giving him the answer to resolving the dispute:

> I heard the voice that I had prayed for on the hillside. It was not so loud as I had anticipated. The inspiration came what to do to settle those [disputes], . . to bring about those men, to bring about unity in the branch, and further the work of the Lord without such antagonism…. I heard the voice, got in touch with the Spirit, as never before, the prayer on the hillside was answered, not the way I had anticipated, but the way the Lord intended it to be answered. That was the beginning of the revelation of the Spirit to my soul.[8]

PERSONAL REVELATION

In his earlier account of the incident, McKay alluded to another experience on his mission, when "even the manifestation of God's power and the presence of his angels came."[9] It was the most remarkable revelatory experience that McKay ever recorded; and despite his general reticence about spiritual experiences, he occasionally referred to it publicly after being called to the First Presidency in 1934.

The incident occurred in a missionary priesthood meeting in Glasgow on May 29, 1899, three months before McKay completed his mission. In addition to the later accounts of the meeting, contemporary accounts include the minutes of the British Mission and the diaries of eight men, including McKay, who were present.[10] McKay's diary account is modest, downplaying his own role while affirming the miraculous nature of the meeting:

> As the elders began to give their reports, it became evident that an excellent spirit of love and unity was amongst us. A peaceful heavenly influence pervaded the room. Some of the elders were so affected by it that they had to express their feelings in tears.

Just as Brother Young [a missionary] sat down after giving his report, Elder Woolfenden [another missionary] said: "Brethren, there are angels in this room! I see two there by Brother Young. One is his guardian angel. The other is a guardian angel, too; but I don't know whose it is." Everyone present, impressed with the spirit of the occasion and sensing the divine influence, could testify to the truth of his remarks. Although he was the only one who saw them, yet we each felt their presence. Elders wept for joy and could not contain themselves. Sobs came from different parts of the room and they seemed fitting, too, for "it seemed manly to weep there." At the conclusion of the reports, all joined with me in a prayer of thanksgiving to the Lord for his blessings and manifestation.

President James McMurrin then addressed the meeting, saying among other things that the "Lord has accepted our labors and at this time we stand pure before him." . . . It was the best meeting I have ever attended.[11]

What McKay described simply as "among other things" was a remarkable prophecy by McMurrin about McKay, which McMurrin wrote in his own diary account of the meeting: "We were nearly all melted to tears, my own flowed freely, and I was impressed to say, 'Yes, there are angels in this room, and let me say to you, Brother David, Satan has desired you that he may sift you as wheat, but God is mindful of you. If you keep the faith you will yet sit in the leading councils of the Church.'"[12]

Seven years after McMurrin's prophecy, McKay was called to the Quorum of the Twelve, one of the "leading councils of the Church." In 1919, twenty years after the prophecy, he first mentioned it publicly in an address at the October general conference. However, as in his own diary account, he downplayed his own role in the manifestations, noting merely that McMurrin "turned to me and in prophetic word pronounced my future." He also downplayed the role of the manifestations in nurturing his own testimony by adding, "The testimony that this work is divine had come, not through manifestation, great and glorious as it was, but through obedience to God's will, in harmony with Christ's promise, 'If ye will do the will of my Father which is in heaven, ye shall know whether the doctrine is of God or whether I speak of myself.'"[13]

It was not until McKay was called into the "leading council"—as second counselor in the First Presidency in 1934—that he shared publicly what James McMurrin and the other missionaries had recorded in their own diaries thirty-five years earlier. After recounting the story of the guardian angels, he turned autobiographical:

I have named those preliminaries that you might in a measure have a picture of the setting in which President James McMurrin—and no truer man ever lived—turned to me and said, paraphrasing the words of the Savior to Peter: "I say, Brother David, Satan hath desired thee that he may sift thee as wheat, but I have prayed the Father for thee." And then he added: "If you will keep the faith you will yet sit in the leading councils of the Church."

I think I have told that but once or twice. I told it last Thursday to my fellow workers of the Twelve.

Since President Grant called me to this position that scene has come back as vividly as though it were only last week. Brother McMurrin has gone to the other side and is associated there with his brother Joseph—two of the noblest defenders of truth that this Church has seen. I knew he was inspired. It has been an anchor and an encouragement to keep the faith, not that I have had any desire— I never have had a desire to be promoted in the Church, I mean for the honor that comes; my heart has been free of that, but it has been full of desire to serve.[14]

McKay's reluctance to divulge all of the details of the 1899 manifestation was consistent with his feelings about revelation throughout his life. While dramatic forms of revelation do exist, they are generally for private and not public consumption. He commented in a 1919 address: "I seldom speak of manifestations that have come to me. I do not know whether it is the Scotch reticence or what, but I do not like to speak of some things which are most sacred to me. I am glad to say that I have had many, which I treasure as most sacred."[15]

Along these same lines, he gently rebuffed an intrusive correspondent: "Your letter of February 4, 1949, ask[ed] me to write a letter setting forth one or more of 'my circumstances in which I received, as an ordained apostle my special eye and ear witness of the gospel, and that Jesus Christ is the Son of the true and living God, our Eternal Father.' There are some divine communications given to individuals, particularly to leaders of the Church, which are not for the public."[16]

In a similar vein, he admonished two church members who had written him letters about their remarkable experiences at the dedication of the Los Angeles Temple not to publicize them, while at the same time he acknowledged the validity of what they had experienced. To one he wrote: "We rejoice in the spiritual gifts which are enjoyed by the faithful Latter-day Saints. We are happy that the dedication of the Los Angeles Temple has blessed so many thousands, and that they so fervently acknowledge the increased support of their testimonies. It is well to regard these experiences as sacred, and that they be preserved for the benefit of the individual who has them, and therefore, that they be not given to the public."[17]

To the other he wrote: "With great appreciation I have read your letter of March 16, 1956. It is true, as you say in that letter, that such experiences are very sacred and are best to be regarded as being for the personal benefit of the individual who has them. I suggest that you cherish your memory of the experience as a part of your testimony, but that you do not publicize it."[18]

REVELATION FOR THE CHURCH

McKay's position as church president placed him in the unique position of seeking revelation for the benefit of the entire church. He was discreet about disclosing details of such revelatory experiences; consequently, such accounts tend to come from his colleagues.

In 1958 the London Temple was dedicated and Selvoy J. Boyer was called to be its first president. McKay asked Boyer to compile a list of a dozen couples who might be considered as temple workers, which list McKay would examine upon arriving in London for the dedicatory ceremonies. Boyer later recounted the unusual occurrence:

> The next Saturday he came. When he got through instructing us he said, "Have you got your list?" And I had it. He went over that list. That's one of my faith-promoting experiences. He'd never met the men nor their wives. He said, "Go ahead and read their names." And I read them. "Brother and Sister So-and-so." He said, "Yes. Set them apart as ordinance workers." This was my engineer. "Brother and Sister So-and-so." This was my gardener. He was a deacon. "Set them apart." "Brother and Sister So-and-so." He had their genealogy. He said, "Don't set them apart." "Brother and Sister So-and-so." "No." When I got done with all twelve names, I got six couples. That's all I needed. And he was right on the beam. Those people he turned down didn't stay with the Church nor the program.[19]

A similar incident occurred when McKay traveled to Glasgow, Scotland, to organize the first stake in that country:

> At one point the Prophet turned around to Elder [Bernard P.] Brockbank, who was sitting next to me, and he said, "Who is that man down there?" And President Brockbank mentioned a name. President McKay said, "That man is evil." And Brockbank was shocked, because the man was one of our branch presidents. But President McKay said, "That man is evil." So Brockbank took him aside afterwards and gave

him a searching interview and found out that he'd been having an adulterous relationship with several people over the years. And of course he was excommunicated. But just sitting there the Prophet pointed to this man and said, "That man is evil." It was a great testimony to me, and to many others, when they heard about it.[20]

When the New Zealand Temple was dedicated in 1959, a group of former missionaries who had served in that country chartered a plane to attend the dedication. One of the missionaries was Robert L. Simpson, who described a brief, seemingly inconsequential visit with McKay in the temple:

> I'd never met President McKay to that point; and on that first day of the dedication, I was walking down the corridor of the temple.... A friend of mine caught me by the arm, and said, "Brother Simpson, step into this sealing room. I want you to meet someone." As I stepped into the room, there were just two people there, President and Sister McKay. It just took my breath away to think that I was going to be able to meet the Prophet in this very sacred building, in New Zealand, of all places, which I love very much. I'll never forget President McKay, with that kindly look in his eyes and that slight smile on his lips. He reached out his big right hand and he pulled me in really close. He put his left hand on my shoulder, and he proceeded to look into my eyes. He looked and he looked. It must have been the better part of a minute, maybe 45 or 50 seconds. Then, he made his first gesture. He gave my hand a shake, my shoulder a squeeze, and said, "Brother Simpson, I'm pleased to know you." ...
>
> Well, it was about six or seven weeks later. I'm in my office at the Telephone Company in Southern California. The telephone rang at about 9:30 in the morning. "Brother Simpson, this is President David O. McKay calling.... Based on our personal interview in the New Zealand Temple, I feel inspired to call you to preside over the New Zealand Mission. How soon can you leave? We need you down there within the month."
>
> The "interview" hadn't consisted of a single question. "Brother Simpson, I'm pleased to know you." That was the extent of it. We sometimes think of the term, "Prophet, Seer and Revelator," but the term "Seer" took new significance on that day, because I thought he was actually able to look into my heart and soul, and know what was there.[21]

On rare occasions, McKay did speak privately of his revelatory experiences as church president. In the spring of 1956, an employee in the church film department

noticed that McKay was working late and, having a few extra feet of film in his cam-
era, asked if he would consent to bear his testimony for a film record. McKay
agreed and, in the course of his brief statement, made a remarkable observation:
"My testimony of the Risen Lord is just as real as Thomas's on that occasion [John
20:27–29]. I know that He lives. I know that He will confer with His servants who
seek Him in humility and in righteousness. I know because I have heard His voice,
and I have received His guidance in matters pertaining to His kingdom here on
earth."[22]

McKay made a similar statement five years later during an interview by John
Cook, a reporter for the *Sacramento Union*. Ted L. Cannon, the church's press representative, was present at the interview and wrote an account:

> Mr. Cook then said he was hesitant about asking his next question, and
> that he hoped President McKay would understand the spirit in which
> he was asking—not for a part of his story, but strictly from a personal
> inquiry standpoint, and that he hoped the President would not
> answer if he did not feel it was a proper question. He then asked Pres-
> ident McKay if he had ever seen the Savior.
>
> President McKay answered that he had not, but that he had heard
> His voice—many times—and that he had felt His presence and His
> influence. He then told about Peter (saying that he was his favorite
> among the apostles, even more so than Paul with all his education
> and learning—that Peter was a rough, simple man, but sincere) and
> he told how Peter had spoken of being partakers of the divine spirit—
> of the divine nature, and explained what he felt that to mean.
>
> Then he told how some evidences were stronger even than that
> of sight, and recalled the occasion when the Savior appeared to His
> disciples and told Thomas, who had doubted, "Reach hither thy fin-
> ger, and behold my hands; and reach hither thy hand and thrust it into
> my side, and be not faithless, but believing." And he said he liked to
> believe that Thomas did not actually look up, but knelt at the Savior's
> feet and gave his answer, "My Lord and my God." And then the Pres-
> ident repeated the words of the Master, "Because thou hast seen me,
> thou has believed; blessed are they that have not seen, and yet have
> believed."
>
> President McKay then smiled, and said, "That is quite a testi-
> mony I have given you.... I don't know when I have given this
> before."[23]

Prayer and Meditation

While McKay did, on occasion, experience the more dramatic forms of revelation and readily acknowledged the experiences of others, his mainstay was the more subtle impressions derived from prayer and meditation. Particularly in the earlier years of his presidency, when his health allowed more independent movement, he would often spend part of Sunday alone in the Salt Lake Temple, meditating and praying. Typical diary entries during that period were: "Spent several hours in the Temple this morning in meditation, study, and planning for the Church." "Spent most of the day in the Salt Lake Temple—studied and meditated on Church problems." "Spent about two hours at the Salt Lake Temple, studying the Temple ordinances, and meditating on Church problems." "Spent the morning alone in the Salt Lake Temple in study and contemplation."[24]

At a meeting in the Salt Lake Temple in 1956, McKay summarized to his fellow General Authorities the process by which he received the "whispering of the Spirit" that allowed him to lead the church:

> President McKay said it is a great thing to be responsive to the whispering of the Spirit, and we know that when these whisperings come, it is a gift and our privilege to have them. They come when we are relaxed and not under pressure of appointments.... The President said that the point he had in mind was that when we are relaxed in a private room, we are more susceptible to those things; that so far as he was concerned his best thoughts come after he gets up in the morning, and is relaxed and thinking about the duties of the day; that impressions come as clearly as if he were to hear a voice, and those impressions are right; that if we are worried about something, and upset in our feelings, the inspiration does not come. If we so live that our minds are free from worry, our consciences are clear, and our feelings are right towards one another, the operation of the Spirit of the Lord upon our spirit is as real as when we pick up the telephone; but when they come we must be brave enough to take the suggested action. The Lord will approve it and the Brethren will approve it, and we know it is right. The President said it is a great consolation in this upset world today to know that our Savior is directing His work. He then said: "I value that testimony!"[25]

3

FREE AGENCY
AND TOLERANCE

David O. McKay was an intellectual. He cherished the things of the mind, cultivated his own intellect throughout his life, encouraged his fellow Latter-day Saints
to do likewise, and vigorously defended the consequences of intellectualism. He did
so, not as a matter of personal preference, but because he saw it as one of the key
Christ-like virtues. Commenting on a classical painting depicting Jesus in the Temple he noted, "In that picture the artist has combined physical strength, intellectual fire, moral beauty, and spiritual fervor," and he held these traits up as the ideal
for all.[1] "The Church of Jesus Christ of Latter-day Saints," he said, "makes an
appeal to all men to seek the higher life, intellectual and spiritual, and to incite
them to greater intelligence in striving for the abundant life."[2] Such a lofty appeal
was consistent with one of the most sublime revelations received by Mormonism's
founder, Joseph Smith, who proclaimed, "The glory of God is intelligence."[3]

TWO SIDES OF THE SAME COIN

In encouraging intellectual inquiry, McKay drew no boundary lines. While on the
one hand he vigorously proclaimed that the church he headed was Christ's true
church, he openly acknowledged that truth was to be found everywhere and that
no institution, not even the true church, held a monopoly on it. By training and
by profession, he was an educator; and his extensive reading in the world's great
literature furnished his mind with beautiful and powerful passages that he greatly
prized. Indeed, great literature was scripture to him, and he quoted it more frequently in his public addresses than he did the scriptural canon of his own church.

Unbounded intellectual inquiry carries risks, for it inherently challenges the
core beliefs and values of the seeker at each turn of the road. Yet McKay never
wavered from encouraging his fellow Latter-day Saints to undertake the journey,
for he understood the consequences of the alternative pathway and quoted the
words of a poet, set to music in a Mormon hymn, to underscore the point:

Freedom and reason made us men;

Take these away, what are we then?

Mere animals, and just as well

The beasts may think of heaven or hell.[4]

Reason without freedom is insufficient. Thus, McKay held that, once life began, the most important principle driving that life is free agency. He made the point often, though never more pointedly than when he offered the blessing on a White House dinner at the invitation of President Dwight D. Eisenhower. When the meal itself began, he recalled: "After that it was just a pleasant social chat, a regular social dinner, excellent dinner. The man on my right started a conversation. He said 'You mentioned in your grace the freedom of the individual. Is that fundamental?' I said, 'Next to life itself.' He was a Presbyterian by training. He said, 'They crowded me so much I have finally left churches,' but he said, 'I believe in that freedom of the individual and developing oneself.' I said, 'That is fundamental in the Mormon Church.'"[5]

Free agency is of paramount importance, not merely as an abstract dogma, but because it is the only way in which humankind can progress toward internalizing godlike qualities:

> As real to us as the consciousness of life itself is the awareness of the ability to make a choice. There exists an eternal law that each human soul shall shape its own destiny. "No one individual can make happiness or salvation for another." "Even God could not make men like himself without making them free." Dr. Iverach of Scotland is quoted as saying, "that it is a greater manifestation of divine power to make beings that can make themselves than to make beings that cannot, for the former are men and the latter are puppets, and puppets after all are only things." [It is] another way of saying that free men must live in a world of moral order, in which men are made by education and experience.[6]

Communism's deprivation of its adherents' free agency was the basis for McKay's adamant opposition to Communism.[7] Communism, however, was not the only political threat; and in the midst of World War II, when Nazism was a more urgent danger to free agency, McKay framed the subject in the context of the premortal "war in heaven," a foundational Mormon belief:

> Think of it now—the value of freedom of choice! That was the great principle involved when war arose in Heaven when Lucifer would have deprived God's children of the right to choose. Lucifer said to

> the Lord: I'll go down and bring all your children back, but you give
> me the glory. Jesus, however, said: Send me and the glory be Thine.
> Satan's attempt to deprive the children of men of their free agency
> brought contention in Heaven—the only time about which we have
> any record that God would permit war in Heaven. And yet, the Lord
> would not deprive even the Adversary of the right to choose; and so
> Satan "turned away." But Christ came and died that you and I might
> have freedom of choice.... Your sons and mine are out fighting for
> that principle. In the last analysis that is the great question in this war
> so far as the Allies are concerned—whether we shall have the right to
> worship as we please, whether we shall have the right to think as we
> please.[8]

But it was not only governments that he saw as instruments of such adverse
action. All organizations, even churches, ran the risk of depriving their members of
free agency, and McKay's comments to this effect still stand as a timely warning to
his own church:

> Among the immediate obligations and duties resting upon members
> of the Church today, and one of the most urgent and pressing for
> attention and action of all liberty-loving people, is the preservation of
> individual liberty. Freedom of choice is more to be treasured than any
> possession earth can give. It is inherent in the spirit of man. It is a
> divine gift to every normal being. Whether born in abject poverty or
> shackled at birth by inherited riches, everyone has this most precious
> of all life's endowments—the gift of free agency; man's inherited and
> inalienable right.... This principle of free agency and the right of each
> individual to be free not only to think but also to act within bounds
> that grant to every one else the same privilege, are sometimes violated
> even by churches that claim to teach the doctrine of Jesus Christ. The
> attitude of any organization toward this principle of freedom is a
> pretty good index to its nearness to the teachings of Christ or to those
> of the Evil One.[9]

McKay made no secret of his passion for free agency, speaking frequently on
the subject in public settings. As a result, in the early 1960s his feelings attracted
national attention. At issue was an ongoing debate over a tendency toward news
suppression within Utah. A professor at the University of Utah, Waldemar P. Read,
was particularly critical of what he termed a "stifling sameness of belief." McKay's
response to the debate, chronicled by nationally syndicated columnist Drew Pearson, was straightforward: "President McKay, while not commenting directly on
Professor Read, made it clear that he is against the stifling of news and ideas. He

remembers all too well the persecution suffered by the Mormons in their early days, and believes his churchmen must vigilantly champion free discussion, a free press, and the free forum of ideas. He is not fearful that the American system or the Mormon Church will suffer from listening to or reading news with which they may not agree. Quite the contrary."[10]

Even in death, McKay's passion for free agency continued to echo. An obituary in a Washington, D.C., newspaper noted, "Mr. McKay brought to the presidency a strong sense of individual freedom, which he retained through the years. 'I believe in freedom of choice for the individual,' he declared in an interview on his ninetieth birthday."[11]

Given free agency, some will inevitably make incorrect choices that affect not only themselves but also their churches adversely. As a church leader McKay understood this, but he understood also that tolerating such people and the consequences of their choices was a small price to pay for the benefits of such a policy. Well aware that free agency and tolerance are two sides of the same coin, from the outset of his tenure as church president he set a tone of tolerance that has not since been equaled. The year after becoming president he wrote in one of the church magazines about the Parable of the Tares:

> A man went out and sowed his seed and expected a good harvest, but at night an enemy came and sowed weeds or tares right in the midst of the corn, so that when the crops grew, there were the tares and weeds right with the corn. The application here is wonderful; I should like to give it to the whole Church. There are tares in the Church—indifferent, not sinful people, who deal unjustly and unrighteously, with their neighbors.... It is folly to say to the president of the Church or to say to the presidency or superintendency of any of the auxiliary organizations, "You remove that man, or you remove that woman, or else I will stop coming to Church." The Savior said, "No, do not pull up the tares or you will destroy the wheat; let them grow together, and in the time of harvest bind your tares to be burned and harvest your good crop." Oh, what a beautiful message![12]

He lived what he preached and, time after time, instilled in his fellow General Authorities an appreciation for the importance of tolerating the tares. Three anecdotes illustrate this value well. Hugh B. Brown, his counselor in the First Presidency, once told McKay of an incident that occurred when he was a young counselor in a bishopric, and a young woman in the congregation confessed to an indiscretion:

> The Bishop asked her to go in the other room while we talked it over, and when she left he said: "Brethren, what do you think we ought to

do?" The first counselor said, "I move we cut her off the Church." I said, "I second the motion." The kind old Bishop said, "Brethren, there is one thing for which I am profoundly grateful and that is God is an old man. I am not going to cut her off the church.".... That young woman became the Stake President of the Relief Society up in Canada later on, to our chagrin, for if we had had our way, she would have been cast out of the Church. When I told that to President McKay, he said, "Brother Brown, let that lesson guide your judgment day by day. Remember that God our Father does not judge us until the end, and He gives us a chance to repent and come back."[13]

Richard L. Evans of the Quorum of the Twelve Apostles told of a similar incident: "One morning in President McKay's office some of us were assembled by appointment to discuss a somewhat serious personnel problem, the easiest solution to which (but not necessarily the most just) seemed to be to relieve one particular person of duties that he had long and faithfully (but somewhat troublesomely) performed. The President paused and earnestly looked at us as he said: 'Human hearts are very tender, and human lives are very precious. Let's solve this problem without hurting a very tender heart.'"[14]

And Paul H. Dunn, of the First Council of Seventy, spoke of McKay's attitude toward those who were outside the mainstream—not in action, but in thought. After spending a decade as a teacher in the Institutes of Religion, Dunn was called by McKay to be a General Authority at the unusually young age of thirty-nine:

> Here I am a young buck coming into the system, and the circulation is, "Let's excommunicate the Sterling McMurrins of the Church, and weed out the liberals." That got thrown around a lot. Even poor Lowell Bennion got thrown into some of that. If it hadn't been for President McKay, we'd have had a fiasco on Lowell Bennion. There's one of the sweetest, great Christians of the world. I would be totally surprised if all of heaven isn't a Lowell Bennion philosophy. There isn't a kinder, more gentle Christian in the world. And yet there were those in the system who tried to weed him out, because he kept the President McKay kind of vision open. . . .
>
> The George Boyds and the Lowell Bennions kept people in the Church whom nobody else could have. Philosophically, they could go with you on the trip through your frustration in thinking, and bring you back. Not many people could do that. I worked with George for many years down at the University of Southern California. I watched him save kids that nobody else could. And yet there was that element in the Church that tried to get him bumped, because he

didn't teach what they taught. I've found in the Church, and this is what gave me great comfort with President McKay, that there is room for all of them, not just a few, not just those here or there, but the whole spectrum. President McKay would say, and two or three times I heard him say privately, and once or twice publicly in meetings where I sat, that "if you would have to take action on that kind of a person thinking that way, you'd better take action on me, too."[15]

Although McKay preferred to "live and let live," there were several notable occasions on which he turned activist. Five vignettes are particularly noteworthy. The first two involve General Authorities. Speaking to BYU President Ernest Wilkinson on a different matter, McKay defined special boundaries within which he expected teachers at BYU, as well as General Authorities, to operate. As Wilkinson recorded McKay's instructions, McKay stated that "there was all the difference in the world between whether a man should be excommunicated because he may not accept all the views of the Church, and whether he should still be employed on the faculty of BYU. He told me that I would have his complete support in refusing to renew the contracts of any teachers who did not teach the doctrines as they were interpreted by the leaders of the Church."[16]

Defining the doctrines was the domain of the church president, and on two notable occasions McKay had to deal with General Authorities who thought otherwise. Trying to strike a balance between tolerating their divergent personal beliefs on the one hand and limiting their ability to advance those beliefs as normative for the church on the other, he met with only limited success. The first involved the anti-scientific stance of Joseph Fielding Smith, and the second was Bruce R. McConkie's publication of the unauthorized *Mormon Doctrine*.

THE EVOLUTION DEBATE

In the first half of the twentieth century, the debate surrounding biological evolution was as heated within Mormonism as in other American Christian churches. It extended into the Quorum of the Twelve Apostles, with three scientists—James E. Talmage, John A. Widtsoe, and Joseph F. Merrill—supporting evolution, and Joseph Fielding Smith vehemently opposing it. A moratorium that was initially imposed by Church President Heber J. Grant[17] prevailed until the last of the three apostle-scientists died in 1952. At that point, Smith acted on his own volition to publish *Man, His Origin and Destiny* (1954), whose central theme was a condemnation of evolution.

Among all General Authorities, David O. McKay had a unique perspective on the subject of evolution. When he attended a showing of the movie *Inherit the*

Wind, a dramatized version of the Scopes Trial, he noted in his diary, "I was especially interested because I had personally met William Jennings Bryan on three occasions, and had followed the real court trial. When I was Principal of Weber College, William Jennings Bryan, at my invitation, came to Ogden and addressed the students of the College."[18]

Although McKay never made a public statement affirming his acceptance of biological evolution, he was sympathetic to that viewpoint. The closest he came to a public affirmation was his address in 1946 at the funeral of May Anderson, general president of the Primary Association for children (1925–39). Using evolution as an argument in favor of resurrection in the same manner that St. Paul had used baptism for the dead (1 Cor. 15:29), McKay went so far as to borrow from Charles Darwin to make his point:

> Among the generalizations of science, evolution holds foremost place. It claims: "Man is a creature of development; that he has come up through uncounted ages from an origin that is lowly." Why this vast expenditure of time and pain and blood? Why should he come so far if he is destined to go no farther? A creature which has traveled such distances, and fought such battles and won such victories deserves, one is compelled to say, to conquer death and rob the grave of its victory. Darwin said... "Believing as I do that man in the distant future will be a far more perfect creature than he now is, it is an intolerable thought that he and all other sentient beings are doomed to complete annihilation after such long-continued, slow progress. To those who fully admit the immortality of the human soul, the destruction of our world will not appear so dreadful."[19]

In private, McKay was even more direct. In meeting with Sterling McMurrin at a time when McMurrin's church membership was in peril, McKay brought up the subject of evolution. "I would like to know just what it is that a man must be required to believe to be a member of this Church. Or, what it is that he is not permitted to believe, and remain a member of this Church. I would like to know just what that is. Is it evolution? I hope not, because I believe in evolution."[20] He kept his views private, however, for a simple reason that he raised in another private conversation: "The thing you need to remember about evolution is that the Lord has never revealed anything about the matter. People have their opinions but the Lord has not revealed the details of how He created the earth."[21] As church president, McKay knew that anything he said publicly, even if nuanced as personal belief only, would be interpreted by many church members as church doctrine. In the absence of definitive revelatory knowledge on the subject, he therefore refrained from public comment. He clearly wished that other General Authorities would do likewise and saw Joseph Fielding Smith's failure to do so as problematic.

Shortly after publishing his book, Smith compounded the problem by putting pressure on the church's seminaries and Institutes of Religion to make it an official course of study. Joy Dunyon, of the Church Department of Education, was so upset at the proposal that he asked for an appointment with McKay to discuss the matter. McKay, though aware of the book's publication, had not heard about Smith's action to make it a course of study. He asked Dunyon to ascertain if the book had been approved for such use by the Reading Committee of the Quorum of the Twelve. "If the book has not been approved," he told Dunyon, "then it should not be used as a text book, or considered in the class, more than any other private book."[22] One week later, Dunyon returned to McKay and reported that the book had not been approved by the committee.[23] McKay's papers do not include any response to Dunyon.

However, about a month after meeting with Dunyon, McKay brought the matter before the First Presidency:

> Among items considered were the number of letters that I had received from seminary and institute teachers regarding President Joseph Fielding Smith's book, *Man, His Origin and Destiny*. The Brethren were agreed that inasmuch as this book has not been passed upon by the Church that it should not be used as a study course in the seminaries and institutes. They felt that the matter therein discussed is really not essential to the advancement of the cardinal principles of the Church.[24]

The First Presidency decision notwithstanding, the following week Smith promoted his anti-evolution views at a summer seminar for Institute of Religion instructors at BYU.[25] Several instructors who attended the seminar, whose views on the subject clashed with Smith's, subsequently appealed directly to McKay for guidance on how to treat the topic in their classrooms. One month after the BYU seminar he met with four of them in his office: Joy Dunyon, Lowell L. Bennion, T. Edgar Lyon, and George Boyd. The latter three were all on the staff of the Institute of Religion serving students at the University of Utah, and Bennion was then its director. Although the meeting lasted for two hours, McKay's diary entry was brief and to the point: "I told them that that book should be treated as merely the views of one man.... It is true that [this] one man is President of the Twelve, and [that] makes it more or less authoritative, but it is no more to be taken as the word of the Church than any other unauthorized book."[26] Boyd's account of the meeting captured more emotion: "When we left he said, 'You go ahead and teach the way you've been teaching (we had outlined for him our way of handling the subject of science and religion), and if you have any trouble you come to me.' We learned during the interview that President McKay was very much disturbed himself over the publication of the book. I recall a statement that he made. He said, 'We have known what Joseph Fielding Smith has thought on this subject for years. The sad part is, now it's in print.'"[27]

For McKay, the fact that Smith personally held anti-evolution viewpoints was neither a surprise nor a problem. The problem came when he published those views, for simply by virtue of his standing as president of the Quorum of the Twelve Apostles, Smith's published views on *any* religious subjects carried inordinate weight for many Latter-day Saints. Furthermore, McKay's refusal to discuss the topic in public, on the grounds that the Lord had not yet spoken on the matter, meant that Smith's views went unanswered—in effect, giving them quasi-official standing.

During this same time frame, one of McKay's sons spoke to a study group on the subject and affirmed his father's tolerance for privately held views. According to Sterling McMurrin, a member of the group: "Llewelyn McKay stood up and said, 'I've talked to my father about this book, and he doesn't like it. He doesn't agree with it. He would like it to be known that this book doesn't represent the church's position and that it must not be used for teaching any religion classes.' Then he added that President McKay said Joseph Fielding Smith was free to say or write what he wanted to, so long as he didn't claim it was church doctrine."[28]

Publication of Smith's book was, of itself, problematic, but the one problem also created another. In occasional private conversations or, more often, in response to written inquiries, McKay responded simply that the book did not represent the church's position on the subject of evolution. His papers contain no record of a meeting with Smith to discuss the matter. Though McKay was not overtly critical of Smith, stories began to circulate that there was a rift between the two men, a rumor that was groundless but that was nonetheless very troubling to McKay. In June 1955, McKay summoned Ernest Wilkinson and William E. Berrett, who had supervision of the seminaries and Institutes of Religion, to his office for an uncharacteristically terse meeting, which Wilkinson reported in his diary:

> President McKay began the conference by stating that when he received complaints or had something against an individual, he thought the best way was to take it up with them direct, and that his complaint in this case was one against Brother Berrett, and that he had asked me to be present so that I could sit in on it. He said he had been advised that Brother Berrett had said there had been a rift between President McKay and President Joseph Fielding Smith, which could not be healed until President McKay died. President Berrett replied

that the assertion with respect to the rift had come from our Seminary teachers, several of them reporting to him that they had talked separately to President McKay and President Smith over President Smith's latest book.[29]

McKay was essentially boxed in by his own standards of conduct. At no time during his tenure as church president did he ever speak publicly in criticism of any other General Authority, and he would not depart from that standard with Smith. Neither, however, would he allow himself to speak out to quell the rumor of a rift between the two men. Instead, he took an indirect approach that stayed within the bounds of his own standards. Unfortunately, it had little effect.

His first move can be deduced from a speech given shortly thereafter by his counselor, J. Reuben Clark Jr., at BYU. "When Are the Writings and Sermons of Church Leaders Entitled to the Claim of Being Scripture?" This addresss reaffirmed the unique position of the church president in defining doctrine.[30] He later also sent his other counselor, Hugh B. Brown, to BYU to speak on the same subject, reportedly instructing him, "You go down there and drive a wedge into the kind of theology that President Smith is advancing."[31] In 1965 McKay authorized a BYU scientist to write a pro-evolution article that was published in the church magazine for teachers, *The Instructor*.[32] And finally, in the late 1960s, he authorized William Lee Stokes, a geologist on the faculty of the University of Utah, to publish a letter that he had written to Stokes in 1955 that stated, "The book, 'Man, His Origin and Destiny' was not published by the Church, and is not approved by the Church."[33]

However, all of the countermeasures were indirect and all came through persons either outside the hierarchy or junior to Smith within the hierarchy. As a result of McKay's tolerance and his unwillingness to contradict a fellow General Authority in public, Smith's views, which remain in print to this day, came to be embraced by a substantial proportion of the church membership as the official position.

THE CONTROVERSY OVER MORMON DOCTRINE

A similar situation occurred when Joseph Fielding Smith's son-in-law, Bruce R. McConkie, then a member of the First Council of the Seventy (1946–72) quietly wrote and published an encyclopedic book with the presumptuous title of *Mormon Doctrine* (Salt Lake City: Bookcraft, 1958). He did not submit it to the Reading Committee prior to publishing it, and his father-in-law, whom McConkie quoted voluminously in its pages, later said that he "did not know anything about it until it was published."[34]

Mormon Doctrine was an immediate success on the bookstands, largely because it gave succinct answers to a plethora of doctrinal questions and did so in an authoritative tone in spite of the author's disclaimer that he bore "sole and full responsibility" for the contents. McKay's initial reaction to the book was not favorable. In a First Presidency meeting, he said that "the General Authorities of the Church should be informed that the First Presidency expect no book to be published unless it be first submitted." The dilemma for him was the same that he had faced four years earlier with Smith's book: "In the minds of the people the General Authorities in their individual capacities cannot be separated from them in their official capacities."[35] McKay was tolerant of McConkie's individual views but objected, as he had with Smith, to McConkie's implication that those views represented official church doctrine.

McKay's first step was to obtain a copy of the book and study it. One of his secretaries noted, "He went through the whole thing. He had paper clips [on the pages where he had a question], and there were hundreds of them there."[36] Then he summoned two senior apostles, Mark E. Petersen and Marion G. Romney. "I asked them if they would together go over Elder Bruce R. McConkie's book, *Mormon Doctrine* and make a list of the corrections that should be made preparatory to his sending out an addendum to all members of the Church who have purchased his book."[37] Having a General Authority send such an addendum would have been unprecedented, an indication of the seriousness with which McKay took McConkie's breach of propriety.

Petersen and Romney took ten months to critique the book and make their report to the First Presidency. Romney submitted a lengthy letter on January 7, 1960, detailing what he felt were the most egregious errors in the book and noting: "Its nature and scope and the authoritative tone of the style in which it is written pose the question as to the propriety of the author's attempting such a project without assignment and supervision from him whose right and responsibility it is to speak for the Church on 'Mormon Doctrine.'" On the same day, Petersen gave McKay an oral report in which he recommended 1,067 corrections that "affected most of the 776 pages of the book." Their reports placed McKay on the horns of a dilemma: How could he regain control of doctrinal exposition without destroying McConkie's credibility and career? McKay summarized the problem in the same diary entry: "It was agreed that the necessary corrections are so numerous that to republish a corrected edition of the book would be such an extensive repudiation of the original as to destroy the credit of the author; that the republication of the book should be forbidden and that the book should be repudiated in such a way as to save the career of the author as one of the General Authorities of the Church."[38]

The following day, McKay and his counselors made their decision. The book "must not be republished, as it is full of errors and misstatements.... We do not want him to publish another edition. We decided, also, to have no more books published by General Authorities without their first having the consent of the First Presidency."[39]

Three weeks later, prior to meeting directly with McConkie or the Quorum of the Twelve, McKay met with Smith. After informing him of the First Presidency's unanimous disapproval of his son-in-law's book, he walked through the proposed remedy:

> I then said: "Now, Brother Smith, he is a General Authority, and we do not want to give him a public rebuke that would be embarrassing to him and lessen his influence with the members of the Church, so we shall speak to the Twelve at our meeting in the Temple tomorrow, and tell them that Brother McConkie's book is not approved as an authoritative book, and that it should not be republished, even if the errors (some 1,067 of them) are corrected."
>
> Brother Smith agreed with this suggestion to report to the Twelve, and said, "That is the best thing to do."
>
> I then said that Brother McConkie is advocating by letter some of the principles as printed in his book in answer to letters he receives. Brother Smith said, "I will speak to him about that." I then mentioned that he is also speaking on these subjects, and Brother Smith said, "I will speak to him about that also."[40]

The next day, McKay met first with McConkie and informed him of their course of action, to which McConkie replied, "I am amenable to whatever you Brethren want." McKay then met with the Quorum of the Twelve, using what was, for him, extremely strong language:

> At Council meeting I reported to the Brethren our decision regarding Elder Bruce R. McConkie's book *Mormon Doctrine,* stating that it had caused considerable comment throughout the Church, and that it has been a source of concern to the Brethren ever since it was published. I said that this book had not been presented to anyone for consideration or approval until after its publication. I further said that the First Presidency have given it very careful consideration, as undoubtedly have some of the Brethren of the Twelve also, and that the First Presidency now recommend that the book be not republished; that it be not republished even in a corrected form, even though Brother McConkie mentions in the book that he takes all

responsibility for it; and that it be not recognized as an authoritative book.

I said further that the question has arisen as to whether a public correction should be made and an addendum given emphasizing the parts which are unwisely presented or misquoted or incorrect; but it is felt that that would not be wise because Brother McConkie is one of the General Authorities, and it might lessen his influence. The First Presidency recommend that the situation be left as it is, and whenever a question about it arises, we can answer that it is unauthoritative; that it was issued by Brother McConkie on his own responsibility, and he must answer for it. . . .

I then said that the First Presidency further recommend that when any member of the General Authorities desires to write a book, that the Brethren of the Twelve or the First Presidency be consulted regarding it. . . . I said it may seem all right for the writer of the book to say, "I only am responsible for it," but I said "you cannot separate your position from your individuality."[41]

The president of the church, since the days of Joseph Smith, was the single individual who could put forth the official doctrine of the church. This position itself had been canonized in Doctrine and Covenants 28:1; yet by the title of his book and the tone of the content, McConkie had violated that policy. Short of a public repudiation—a step McKay never took where any fellow General Authority was concerned—it was his strongest form of reprimand, a balancing act between tolerance for the divergent individual views of a General Authority and institutional discipline.

McKay's message seems to have been unambiguous. Nonetheless, McConkie audaciously approached McKay six years later and pushed for publication of the book in a revised form, albeit with the same title and general tone. At that point, McKay, age ninety-two and in failing health, did not take the matter up with his counselors or the Quorum of the Twelve. Rather, he said that "should the book be re-published at this time," McConkie would be responsible for it and "that it will not be a Church publication."[42]

Three days after meeting with McKay, McConkie wrote in a memo to Clare Middlemiss, McKay's secretary, "President McKay indicated that the book should be republished at this time."[43] McConkie, who practiced law prior to becoming a General Authority, was well versed in the legal meaning of words; and so one is hard pressed to conclude that he misunderstood McKay's cautionary statement, "should the book be re-published," as a mandate to republish. Instead, he moved with the same boldness of eight years earlier, and published a second edition of *Mormon*

Doctrine. The book became one of the all-time best sellers in Mormondom, achieving the near-canonical status that McKay had fought unsuccessfully to avoid, and setting a tone of doctrinal fundamentalism, antithetical to McKay's personal philosophy, that remains a legacy of the church to this day.[44]

Three additional vignettes involve lay church members whose beliefs or writings raised the ire of church officials. In two instances McKay intervened to block efforts by fellow General Authorities to initiate excommunication proceedings, while in the third he showed extraordinary tolerance and compassion toward a niece whose excommunication predated his becoming church president. Each of the three cases sent a strong message that is no less appropriate to today's church: Mormonism is a broad tent with room beneath it for a wide spectrum of beliefs. Or, in the words of a British stake president, "We're here to heal people, not to kill them."[45]

JUANITA BROOKS AND THE MOUNTAIN MEADOWS MASSACRE

Juanita Brooks was a young schoolteacher in southern Nevada when the family of an elderly man summoned her to his deathbed. He had taken a liking to her and had hinted that there were things he had seen but never spoken of that he wished to relate to her. Brooks had never followed up on that invitation, although she meant to; now as he lay dying, he could only cry out in anguish, "Blood, blood, blood!" Then he died. When Brooks asked the family for an explanation they replied, "Didn't you know? He was at Mountain Meadows." Though she had grown up within a few miles of the site of the 1857 Mountain Meadows Massacre, one of the darkest episodes of Mormon history, this mention was the first she had ever heard of it.[46]

Driven by the old man's words, Brooks spent over two decades carefully researching a topic that many in the church preferred to leave buried along with the victims of the massacre. In 1950, despite efforts to block its publication, Stanford University Press published *The Mountain Meadows Massacre*. Although the book was greeted by critical acclaim, remains a classic of Western American history, is still in print today after over a half-century, and is widely considered to be one of the foundational works of the New Mormon History, it resulted in ostracism both locally and at church headquarters for the author. One friend, recalling that Juanita had previously been president of the stake Relief Society, mused: "I did not know of any prominent Church position she held after that. Not a single one. Not at a ward or a stake level."[47] The ostracism also extended to her family, including her husband, the sheriff.

Brooks continued her research, focusing on the chief figure in the massacre, John D. Lee. Lee, who was excommunicated by the church and then executed by a firing squad at the site of the massacre, was the only person disciplined for the episode, despite Brooks's finding that many others shared the blame. Her careful research, combined with consistent pleas to church leaders by the Lee family, eventually resulted in McKay's decision to have a committee investigate the matter. The committee, chaired by Apostle Delbert L. Stapley, recommended to McKay that Lee's church membership be restored. He agreed; and in 1961, one of Lee's grandsons was baptized by proxy for his grandfather.

Church leaders, understanding that Lee's reinstatement was a tacit admission that Lee had unjustly been made a scapegoat by an earlier generation of leaders, attempted to suppress the news. Brooks, however, felt strongly that the information should go into the Lee biography, which was about to go to press. Her biographer noted, "It was more than a restitution for the disgraced pioneer; it was a personal vindication for Juanita, who had for years suffered a shadowy disgrace among her conservative friends and relatives for having espoused his cause."[48] Accordingly, she determined to add a paragraph to the biography announcing the reinstatement.

Upon hearing of Brooks's publication plans, Stapley requested a meeting with her, during which he threatened adverse action if she published the paragraph. According to R. J. Snow, who heard the story from Brooks:

> [She] was warned by one of the Council of the Twelve that if she did that, the action on John D. Lee which restored his priesthood and restored him to full fellowship in the Church might be rescinded. She defiantly said she had always believed that priesthood authority could bind and loosen on earth things which would be recorded in heaven. She did not worry that the simple fact of publication of something that had actually occurred under that authority would be reason to rescind the priesthood action. And she said, "As far as I'm concerned it is a fact and it will be published." And it was, and there was no rescission of the action.[49]

Although no adverse action was taken to reverse Lee's reinstatement, Stapley felt that she had been insubordinate and strongly recommended to McKay that she be excommunicated. Commenting later to William Delves, an Australian stake president, Stapley related McKay's response: "President McKay is a more compassionate man than I am, and he said, 'Leave her alone.'" Delves subsequently became part of the story:

Eighteen months later, in October 1965, I again traveled to General Conference.... I returned from a General Conference session one afternoon to the [Jack] Prince home to find that they had a visitor, an affine to whom the Prince family was connected by some complex inter-marriage relationship, but who was affectionately introduced as "Aunt Juanita." I came into the living room and was brought face-to-face with Juanita Brooks. . . .

During the conversation, I told "Aunt Juanita" of my relationship with Delbert L. Stapley, and the story I have just related. I can do no better now than quote what I recorded at the time: "In this life I was not permitted to see the plates of the Nephites, but I did see the tears in Juanita Brooks' eyes when I told her of President McKay's instruction to 'leave her alone.'"... Brooks thrust out both of her hands and I took them firmly in mine. No words were exchanged, none were necessary.[50]

STERLING MCMURRIN AND CHURCH ORTHODOXY

Sterling M. McMurrin was one of Utah's most distinguished educators. His lengthy career as a member of the philosophy and later history faculty at the University of Utah was highlighted by service as vice president of that institution and, at the request of U.S. President John F. Kennedy, the nation's Commissioner of Education. In the early 1950s, however, his unorthodox religious beliefs raised the ire of two senior apostles—Joseph Fielding Smith and Harold B. Lee—who moved to have him excommunicated. When David O. McKay got wind of their intentions, he telephoned McMurrin directly and asked for a private meeting. That meeting took place at the University of Utah on a Sunday morning, March 14, 1954.[51] McMurrin's account of the meeting portrays McKay at his finest:

The discussion with President McKay lasted for some time, I think perhaps about an hour and a half, and in every way he was not only friendly, but affectionate in his whole attitude toward me—not a word of criticism or reproof, or in any way disapproval.... Then he just hit me on the knee, and took hold of my knee and said, "They cannot do this to you!" I didn't say anything. He said, "They cannot do this to you! They cannot put you on trial!"... I said, "Well, President McKay, you know better than I what they can do, but it appears to me that they are going to put me on trial." He said, "They cannot do it!" And then, there was a rather long pause, and he said, "Well, all I can say is, that if they put you on trial for excommunication, I will be there as the first witness in your behalf." Well, I was rather visibly moved by this expression of his, and said, "Well, I don't think that I could find a much better witness." I kind of laughed, and he laughed, and it sort of broke the tension of the situation. . . .

I should have been censured for being such a heretic, and here President McKay wasn't even interested in raising a single question about my beliefs, but simply insisted that a man in this Church had a right to believe as he pleased. And he stressed that in several ways. . . . It was really a quite remarkable experience, to have the President of the Church talking in such genuinely liberal terms. Always after that, President McKay was most friendly to me. I would encounter him on some occasions, and had some correspondence with him. He would write to me in not only a friendly manner, but even in a kind of affectionate manner.[52]

Several days after the interview an appreciative McMurrin wrote gratefully to McKay: "You have always been a symbol to me, as to countless others, of the religion that reaches out to include rather than exclude, that unites rather than divides, that is concerned with large moral and spiritual issues."[53]

McKay did not get his chance to testify in McMurrin's behalf, for when word of his offer reached the two apostles, the ecclesiastical action died a quick death.

As news of McKay's intervention spread, others expressed their gratitude. Particularly noteworthy was a letter from M. Lynn Bennion, the superintendent of Salt Lake City Schools and brother of the beleaguered Lowell Bennion: "I believe that Sterling will make a great and lasting contribution. I am most anxious that he be permitted to make that contribution in our community and within the Church to which we belong. There is a fundamental issue at stake in the case being formulated against him. You expressed it directly when you spoke of man's right of freedom to think and to worship within the Church. God bless you for taking this stand. It is our most precious possession and worth every sacrifice to maintain."[54]

Although McKay maintained a cordial relationship with McMurrin and made no attempt to alter his private beliefs, he was occasionally displeased when McMurrin made public statements that put the church in a bad light. In 1960, when McMurrin spoke at the Salt Lake Branch of the National Association for the Advancement of Colored People (NAACP) and criticized the church's exclusion of blacks from its priesthood, McKay recorded in his diary without further comment: "This talk was under consideration at the First Presidency's meeting this morning."[55] That did not damage their relationship, however; and several months later McKay telephoned McMurrin to offer his personal congratulations on McMurrin's appointment as vice president of the University of Utah. The subsequent exchange of letters between the two men speaks to the genuineness of their friendship:

> Dear President McKay,
>
> It was most gracious of you to call me as you did a few days ago relative to my appointment as Vice President of the University. Nothing could mean as much to me on such an occasion as an expression of your friendship. . . .
>
> It would be quite impossible for me to adequately express my personal affection for you or my deep appreciation for the meaning of the Church and the world of your life and work. Your unfailing humaneness and the sincere compassion of your soul have over the years been so indelibly written into the character of your office that they are now a part of the capital of virtue that the Church will transmit to future generations. To know your personal friendship is for me a most precious thing, as it is for so many others.[56]

McKay responded with equal appreciation:

> My Dear Dr. McMurrin,
>
> You have heard of course of the old saying that a certain "hot place" is paved with good intentions. Since receiving your most gracious letter of September 13, 1960, I have contributed my share to that proverbial "pavement."
>
> The reason I did not write you, as I am doing now, to tell you how much I appreciate your letter, is because I intended to call on you and have a heart-to-heart talk with you. It is really surprising how one can permit things of minor importance to consume time and contribute to procrastination.
>
> This morning, I am just going to tell you that your letter is now preserved among my most treasured possessions, that I cherish your friendship, and give you my confidence and prayerful wishes for your continued success in the Presidency [*sic*] of the University of Utah.[57]

In 1968 McMurrin again came to McKay's attention over critical remarks concerning the church's policy excluding blacks from the priesthood. The remarks, again delivered at a local meeting of the NAACP, were published in the *Salt Lake Tribune*. McKay dictated in his diary: "Some of the Brethren are very upset over Dr. McMurrin's attitude toward the Church, and feel that he should be tried for his membership. . . . Although I was disturbed over Dr. McMurrin's statements and attitude, I made no commitment concerning this matter."[58]

Three weeks later, McMurrin's speech again was discussed in a First Presidency meeting. Joseph Fielding Smith, who had been named an additional counselor to McKay since October 1965, recommended "that this man should be excommunicated from the Church."[59] McKay again declined to take such action, and the matter was never raised again. McMurrin survived McKay by a quarter-century and remained a church member throughout his life.

THE EXCOMMUNICATION OF FAWN MCKAY BRODIE

The final vignette deals with an episode that struck close to home, the excommunication of Fawn McKay Brodie, the daughter of David O. McKay's brother Thomas. In 1945 Brodie published a scholarly biography of Joseph Smith, *No Man Knows My History: The Life of Joseph Smith the Mormon Prophet* (New York: Alfred A. Knopf). Outside church circles the book received critical acclaim, establishing Brodie's reputation as a formidable biographer whose later subjects included Thomas Jefferson and Richard M. Nixon. Within the church hierarchy, however, the book attracted intense fire. McKay, whose words in public were always measured, privately lamented "the viciousness and inaccuracy of the writer."[60]

A year following the book's publication Brodie, who resided in the East at the time, was excommunicated by local church leaders. There is no evidence that McKay had any role in his niece's excommunication, yet Brodie was suspicious. She told a friend, "I suppose I shall never know exactly what brought the action about, but if my uncle did push the thing through, such an action wouldn't surprise me."[61] Her ill feelings toward her uncle were reciprocated. McKay's oldest son recalled, "I remember one comment he made, 'A bird fouling her own nest.' Thomas E. [Brodie's father] broke into sobs about the girl and her book. Father was just stern."[62]

Five years after Brodie's excommunication, McKay became church president; and three months thereafter, he encountered her at a family gathering in Huntsville on the Fourth of July. His diary entry is unique among all of his papers in reflecting distaste and intolerance toward another person: "After the meeting [a ward Fourth of July service] we went directly to the old home. I had a great disappointment upon my arrival there—the first persons I met were the Brodies who are visiting here from New York. Their presence put a damper on the entire day for me. I shook hands with Mr. Brodie, but refused to recognize Fawn—I just cannot bring myself to accept her."[63]

With the passage of time, however, McKay went through a remarkable transformation. While never reconciling himself to Brodie's book, he eventually did what he was not able to do in 1951 and brought himself not only to accept her, but to love her. Russell Mortensen, one of Brodie's close friends, described the transformed relationship:

> She was treated so gracefully by her uncle, who was the President of the Church, David O. McKay, in spite of her excommunication that he felt pretty good about her.... Because of David O. McKay's attitude toward her, she continued to have a close family relationship with him. Whenever there was a McKay family reunion, she was always there. And she said to me that David O. McKay, every time he saw her until the day he died, put his arm around her and said he loved her. You can't ask for any better blessing than that.[64]

For her part, Brodie reconciled her feelings toward her uncle. Ann Hinckley, another close friend of Brodie, recalled: "I think she thought he was quite a remarkable man, from everything that she ever said to me about him.... That was the impression that I got. I don't recall that the mention of his name or an article that appeared in the newspaper ever triggered any kind of a response from her that would be less than generous or respectable."[65]

The story of their relationship ended when Brodie coincidentally was in Salt Lake City after McKay died, and his body lay in state while the public paid its respects. Russell Mortensen was with her, and described the scene:

> We were at the Alta Club having a Westerners' meeting [a local historians' group] in the evening, catty-corner across the street from the Beehive House and the Lion House.... David O. McKay had died and there was a long line this evening, seven or eight o'clock, coming down State Street around the corner to the Church Office Building. She and I stood in the main room on the second floor of the Alta Club watching this business going on, and she told me about her uncle and his attitude toward her when she was excommunicated in New Haven, Connecticut, for writing *No Man Knows My History,* a biography of Joseph Smith. His attitude toward her was—when she came to a family reunion, he said nothing to her about this book but put his arms around her and kissed her and hugged her and said, "Fawn, you're one of my favorite nieces."[66]

4

BLACKS, CIVIL RIGHTS, AND THE PRIESTHOOD

Even those whose own memories extend to the 1950s and earlier are shocked as they revisit, in detail, the manner in which African Americans were treated in the United States. Until 1954, with the U.S. Supreme Court's decision in *Brown v. Board of Education,* segregation and discrimination were the law of the land; and states and cultures differed only in the degree of their racism. The Latter-day Saints, whose very presence in the Great Basin was the result of being a persecuted minority driven at gunpoint from Missouri and Illinois, were nonetheless intolerant of blacks. This attitude was, in part, due to their being products of their time, and in part to a tenet of their religion, carried over from the pre-Civil War era, that excluded blacks from the church's lay priesthood, and thus gave ready justification to those whose inclinations were already racist.

During David O. McKay's administration, two separate strands—each with a separate agenda and outcome—were closely intertwined. The first was civil rights; and on that issue, David O. McKay was clearly a product of his time and locale: resistant to change and unprogressive. The second strand was priesthood; and on this issue, in a story that has never been told, he struggled against the policy developed beginning with Brigham Young that forbade the ordination of worthy black men, repeatedly seeking divine guidance.

In sum, as a result of his simultaneous resistance and progressiveness on these two issues, he set the stage for change in small ways and moved to offer comfort and great-hearted inclusiveness wherever he felt he could, even while the church, under his leadership, grimly clung to a hard-line status quo. For three decades, even though he held his feelings close and, unlike some of his fellow General Authorities, never fanned the flames of racism in public statements, he was strongly opposed to racial integration and mistrustful of the civil rights movement and its leaders throughout his life. In this regard, he was of like mind with most of his closest associates in the church hierarchy—Hugh B. Brown being the most notable exception. Yet unlike them, he simultaneously moved toward extending priesthood blessings to black men within the church. His civil rights record is one of missed opportunities; but he deserves more credit than he has ever received for preliminary work on reversing the ban on priesthood ordination for black men that had persisted for more than a century.

THE STATUS QUO

McKay grew up in the small Utah town of Huntsville, in which no blacks resided. He traveled to nearby Ogden, a railroad town whose small population of blacks was nonetheless the largest in Utah, for his secondary schooling. Still, he had little direct association with blacks throughout his life.[1] He first traveled outside of Utah in 1897 to serve a two-year proselytizing mission to Scotland and, while crossing the Atlantic Ocean, was greatly disturbed at the racist remarks one of his fellow missionaries directed toward the Fiske Jubilee Singers, an internationally renowned black group from the South that was making its fifteenth transatlantic concert tour. "As the missionaries lined up to register, one of the University boys said, 'I'll not sit at the table with any negroes,' and some of them heard him." McKay noted that throughout the voyage the missionaries were not obliged to sit with the singers, but neither were they honored at any time with an invitation to sit at the captain's table, where the singers frequently dined. Near the end of the trip, one of the sopranos favored the passengers with a solo, whose chorus "impressed me very much because of the remarks made at the time of the assignments to the seats in the dining room." He recorded the words and frequently referred to them throughout his life:

> If you want to know a Christian,
>
> Just watch his acts and walks.
>
> If you want to know a Christian,
>
> Just listen how he talks.[2]

The following year he attended a concert in Glasgow given by the same group. "The audience was small, but the singing was nonetheless excellent. At the close I stepped to the front and shook hands with them. They seemed pleased to see me, and I am sure I was glad to see them." But then, in the same diary entry, he revealed his prejudice: "Although, I do not care much for a negro, still I have a warm spot in my heart for these beautiful singers."[3] Over a quarter-century later, when serving as president of the European Mission, McKay referred again to the Jubilee Singers in an article entitled "Persons and Principles" that he wrote for the church magazine. "Of what value are the lofty principles of Christianity if they are not introduced into our daily lives? . . . It is not easy I know, but the true Christian is he who exemplifies in his 'acts' his 'walks' and his 'talks' that which his tongue says he believes."[4] Indeed, it was not easy.

As McKay rose within the church hierarchy, civil rights were far from the public consciousness. Though Latter-day Saints were not exemplary in their treatment of blacks, they were no different from the rest of the country, and they were rarely singled out for special mention. For example, in a widely read and highly respected study of Mormonism published in 1957, six years after McKay became church president, Catholic sociologist Thomas F. O'Dea devoted an entire chapter to "Sources of Strain and Conflict," yet made no mention of the subject of race.[5]

As second counselor in the First Presidency (and thus as third-ranking member of the church hierarchy) from 1934 until 1951, McKay occasionally indicated his feelings toward civil rights, albeit never in a public setting. During World War II, under pressure from local businessmen, he declined to extend to black servicemen the use of a church facility. M. Lynn Bennion later told a study group to which he belonged:

> As a member of the USO Council I asked President McKay if the Church-owned Deseret Gymnasium could be opened to the soldiers just as the YMCAs all over the country had opened their doors. President McKay's quick response was: "Yes, their uniform will be their entrance ticket." At the next Council meeting I was informed that some of our soldiers had been turned away by the gymnasium authorities. President McKay inquired and was told that they were negro soldiers and that business men in town, who used the gym would not tolerate swimming with negroes. He asked me to try to "smooth the matter over," a painful task for me. At the time black soldiers had their own USO location in Salt Lake City. I was disappointed in President McKay's not taking a stronger stand.[6]

A few years later, McKay discussed with a local church leader in Arizona pending civil rights legislation within that state. Noting that similar legislation had been discussed (and defeated) in Utah, McKay voiced his strong opposition to any law that would "punish any Hotel Manager who would discriminate against colored people." He advised the leader not to bring the church into the public debate in opposition to the legislation, but to "let us use our influence quietly." He favored the status quo. "The fact is that no matter what the law says, there is going to be discrimination against the colored people, and I advised Pres. [Lucian M.] Mecham to simply take the stand to let conditions remain as they are for the present without involving the Church in any way."[7]

McKay's Inner Circle

At the time McKay became church president in 1951, General Authorities had life-long tenure. This meant that all of the men in the hierarchy who made up his for-mal (First Presidency) and informal inner circles had been selected by his prede-cessors. A decade would pass before one of his own selections, Hugh B. Brown, would move into one of those positions. In the meantime, nearly all of the voices he heard on a regular basis were opposed to expanded civil rights for blacks.

Stephen L Richards, first counselor in the First Presidency and McKay's clos-est friend, was ambivalent on the issue and left no record of public or private pro-nouncements. His death in 1959 came before the civil rights movement achieved much prominence.

McKay's second counselor, J. Reuben Clark Jr., had a highly successful legal and government career prior to entering church service in 1933, when he completed a tour as U.S. ambassador to Mexico. Though his selection as a General Author-ity occurred twenty-seven years after McKay's, he entered the First Presidency one year prior to McKay and was his ecclesiastical superior for seventeen years until McKay became president. Brilliant and autocratic, Clark was often the dominant voice in the First Presidency during those years, particularly during the extended periods when the two presidents he served, Heber J. Grant and George Albert Smith, suffered poor health and ceded day-to-day management of church affairs to him. His voice consistently discouraged the expansion of civil rights. While serv-ing under Grant, Clark authorized local church leaders in Salt Lake City to join "a civic organization whose purpose is to restrict and control negro settlement."[8] The following year he discussed with Smith, who succeeded to the presidency follow-ing Grant's death in 1945, the use of LDS chapels "for meetings to prevent Negroes from becoming neighbors."[9] And in 1957, now serving a subordinate role to McKay, he instructed Belle Spafford, general president of the Relief Society (the church's organization for women), "that she should do what she could to keep the National Council [of Women] from going on record in favor of what in the last analysis would be regarded as negro equality."[10]

Henry D. Moyle, who moved into the First Presidency upon the death of Stephen L Richards in 1959, encouraged an initiative to persuade the U.S. Depart-ment of Defense not to deploy troops as planned to an army base in Tooele, Utah, because "there will be two to three hundred Negro families in this contingent." Instead, he hoped the army could be persuaded to send them to California bases.[11] Two years later, in a First Presidency meeting, he spoke out strongly against John F. Kennedy's proposed civil rights legislation. A successful attorney and law school professor prior to entering full-time church service, Moyle "expressed the opinion that it is unconstitutional because it takes away a man's right to contract, and to do business. He said there is no such power given to the Federal Government by the Constitution."[12]

Joseph Fielding Smith, the guardian of orthodoxy and the man to whom McKay referred doctrinal questions, was president of the Quorum of the Twelve Apostles during McKay's entire tenure as church president; he was also McKay's successor. While generally not a participant in the public debate on civil rights, Smith's lack of sensitivity to the issue was revealed by his 1963 statement published in a national magazine and widely quoted thereafter: "'Darkies' are wonderful people, and they have their place in our Church."[13]

Harold B. Lee was the second senior apostle during McKay's presidency and succeeded Joseph Fielding Smith as church president in 1972. He was one of the most outspoken opponents of civil rights among McKay's advisors. As a member of the Board of Trustees of Brigham Young University he was in favor of barring blacks entirely from the university. In 1960 he scolded BYU President Ernest L. Wilkinson for the presence of black students on the campus, saying, "If a granddaughter of mine should ever go to the BYU and become engaged to a colored boy there, I would hold you responsible."[14] His daughter confided to a friend, "My daddy said that as long as he's alive, they'll never have the priesthood,"[15] a prediction that proved to be correct.

Apostle Ezra Taft Benson had an exceptionally high national profile by virtue of his simultaneous service as an apostle and as Secretary of Agriculture in Dwight D. Eisenhower's cabinet (1953–61). Restrained in his public comments while serving in this position, he afterwards became an outspoken critic of the civil rights movement. A friend and confidant of Robert Welch, founder of the John Birch Society, Benson tried unsuccessfully to obtain McKay's permission to serve on its board of directors. Undaunted by McKay's consistent refusals, he repeatedly endorsed in public settings the racist agenda of Welch. (See chap. 12.) Speaking publicly against proposed federal civil rights legislation in 1963, Benson "charged. . .that the civil right's movement in the South had been 'fomented almost entirely by the communists,'" and went on to say that "the whole civil rights movement was 'phony.'"[16] In a private meeting with McKay in September 1967, Benson "briefly talked about the plight of the Negroes in this Civil Rights Issue, and how the Communists are using the Negroes to further their own schemes to foment trouble in the United States."[17] He obtained McKay's consent to address the subject publicly in the church's general conference a week later.

Mark E. Petersen spent his entire career in journalism, rising through the positions of editor and general manager of the church-owned *Deseret News* to become president of the Deseret News Publishing Company while serving as an apostle. In a 1954 talk to Church Education System employees a decade after becoming an apostle, he invoked God's will as the rationale for maintaining a segregated society: "I think the Lord segregated the Negro and who is man to change that segregation? It reminds me of the scripture on marriage, 'what God hath joined together, let not man put asunder.' Only here we have the reverse of the thing—what God hath separated, let not man bring together again."[18]

The only member of McKay's inner circles who was not a General Authority was Ernest L. Wilkinson. Nonetheless, by virtue of his two-decade tenure as president of Brigham Young University, which coincided almost exactly with McKay's term as church president, he wielded enormous influence on McKay. In a 1960 diary entry he expressed sentiments similar to Petersen's six years earlier as justification for reversing a subordinate's decision to hire a black professor to teach a summer course at BYU: "I wish we could take him on our faculty, but the danger in doing so is that students and others take license from this, and assume that there is nothing improper about mingling with the other races. Since the Lord, himself, created the different races and urged in the Old Testament and other places that they be kept distinct and to themselves, we have to follow that admonition."[19]

McKay eventually added two men to the body of General Authorities who exercised considerable influence with him and had a significant impact on the church's attitudes toward civil rights. In 1958 he called Alvin R. Dyer, then a heating and air conditioning contractor, to the position of Assistant to the Twelve Apostles, then in 1968 brought him into the First Presidency as an additional counselor. Dyer made known his feelings about blacks when he told a group of missionaries in 1961:

> I suppose you have heard someone say, or you have heard missionaries say or ask the question, "Why is a Negro a Negro?" And you have heard this answer, "Well they must have been neutral in the pre-existence or they must have straddled the fence." This is the most common saying—"They were neither hot nor cold, so the Lord made them Negroes." This of course is not true. The reason that spirits are born into Negro bodies is because those spirits rejected the Priesthood of God in the Pre-existence. This is the reason we have Negroes on the earth, as a result of a curse placed upon them.[20]

Although most of the internal discussions about civil rights had occurred by the time Dyer joined the First Presidency, he became a prominent and negative voice in the debate over whether blacks should be ordained to the priesthood.

The sole voice of moderation on the subject of civil rights within McKay's inner circle was Hugh B. Brown. McKay called Brown to the office of Assistant to the Twelve in 1953, then elevated him to the Quorum of the Twelve Apostles in

1958 and to the First Presidency in 1961. Brown pushed hard for the church to speak out in favor of increased civil rights, often as a lone voice among the General Authorities. He achieved some notable successes, but other General Authorities disliked his activism. Members of his family felt that this issue was the reason he was released from the First Presidency upon McKay's death, something that had not occurred to a sitting counselor since the death of Brigham Young nearly a century earlier.[21]

THE CIVIL RIGHTS ACT

McKay's first civil rights challenge as church president came only days after he was sustained to that position in 1951. Nobel Laureate Ralph J. Bunche visited Salt Lake City to speak at the University of Utah and was booked at the church-owned Hotel Utah, then the grandest hotel in town. Upon arriving, however, he was refused accommodation by the hotel, whose policy was to exclude blacks. Only after obtaining McKay's consent did the hotel management make a one-time exception to its policy and allow Bunche to stay—on condition that he take all his meals in his room.[22]

The Supreme Court's *Brown v. Board of Education* decision in May 1954 signaled the beginning of a lengthy process by which the legal framework that sanctioned racial segregation was dismantled. Within Utah at that time, discrimination was rampant. In November of the same year, W. Miller Barbour, a field director for the National Urban League, published a report in *Frontier* magazine: "In large areas of Utah, Nevada, and southern Arizona, and in most of the smaller towns, the discrimination is almost as severe as in the south." Regarding trailer parks, "We encountered complete rejection in Utah."[23] The same month, in a "Symposium on the Negro in Utah" held at Weber College in Ogden, Harmon O. Cole, who described himself as "a person of Negroid ancestry," confirmed Barbour's report: "We are not free to eat or to sleep where we want, nor, in a theater, can we sit where we choose; we are even, in some instances, refused the common courtesy of going openly to a hotel to see a Caucasian friend.... A few months ago, my wife was asked to come to a hotel in Salt Lake City to call on a Caucasian friend. She was asked at the desk to take the service elevator to her friend's room, since Negroes were not allowed to use the passenger elevator."[24]

At the same meeting, Wallace R. Bennett (not to be confused with U.S. Senator Wallace F. Bennett) described the state legislature's repeated failure to outlaw racial discrimination: "In 1945, an equal rights act was introduced in the [Utah] Senate which would have expressly prohibited 'discrimination on account of race in admission to any place of public accommodation.' The bill died in committee, however, as it did again in 1947, 1949, and 1951. No effort was made in 1953."[25]

Two years later, as the national civil rights movement gained momentum, the church-owned *Deseret News* published an editorial conceding that "even in the South, thinking people are admitting that racial desegregation is inevitable." While advocating "moderation and gradualism," it nonetheless called for "working toward the full civil and personal rights that justice and human dignity demand." The editorial concluded, "This is a time for acceptance of inevitabilities, and acceptance of the concept of working toward them calmly, gradually and open-mindedly."[26] Absent from the published version, however, was language that advocated desegregation of schools—language that had been deleted at McKay's direction. In his diary, McKay explains that he had instructed O. Preston Robinson, the paper's general manager:

> I had no objection to the editorial's being printed as it now stands with the exception of the reference to segregation in the school room. I said that there is a different problem attached to this subject; for instance there may be a district where the negro is in the majority; that there might be three or four white children. Inasmuch as the negro child is two or three grades below the white child of the same age, it would not be fair to force the few white children to attend—furthermore, the negro really prefers to attend a school for the colored people. I therefore instructed Dr. Robinson to leave the reference to the school room out of the editorial.[27]

Two years later, Henry A. Smith, president of the Central Atlantic States Mission, in Virginia was approached by the Charlottesville Educational Foundation, which sought "to provide educational opportunities for all children in the event of school closings," with a request to use an LDS chapel in such a contingency. The local leader relayed the request to McKay, who declined to make the building available, stating that "the Church had better not take sides, especially on the question of segregation."[28]

The 1960s began with the election of John F. Kennedy as president of the United States, and one of the important items of Kennedy's legislative agenda was civil rights. McKay was opposed to such legislation but generally held his views closely, never making a public statement against it. Privately, he objected to what he viewed as federal intrusion upon states' rights. He told Keith A. Jensen, first counselor in the South Carolina Stake presidency, "We should like to leave the solution for the Southern States people to handle. If the Government judiciary had kept out of this the Southern States would have handled it properly." But, he added, "We shall never be condemned for what we do not say."[29]

Midway through 1961, McKay made a move that had major repercussions on Mormonism's response to civil rights. In response to the failing health of his eighty-nine-year-old first counselor, J. Reuben Clark Jr., McKay brought Hugh B. Brown into the First Presidency as an additional counselor, something that had not been done since the presidency of Brigham Young. Brown, a politically active Democrat, brought into McKay's inner circle for the first time a liberal social philosophy that included strong pro-civil rights sentiments.

Only a few weeks later Brown's feelings were stoked by a letter from Stewart L. Udall, a Mormon from Arizona who served as Secretary of the Interior in the Kennedy administration. Udall wrote to Moyle and Brown: "I am deeply concerned over the growing criticism of our church with regard to the issues of racial equality and the rights of minority groups.... It is my judgement that unless something is done to clarify the official position of the church these sentiments will become the subject of widespread public comment and controversy."[30]

In June 1963, as President Kennedy sought to widen support for his proposed civil rights legislation, he invited McKay to attend a White House meeting of religious leaders to discuss the subject. Only an hour after reading Kennedy's telegram, McKay received a visit from J. Willard Marriott Sr., the Mormon hotelier from Washington, D.C., who was visiting in Salt Lake City: "We talked about the Civil Rights and the negro problem and disturbing conditions as they exist in the government today. I took the liberty of letting him read President Kennedy's telegram. He agreed with me that it would not be wise for me to go."[31]

McKay declined the invitation but, several days later, met with James E. Faust, president of the Cottonwood (Salt Lake City) Stake, a Democrat, and president of the Utah State Bar. In the latter capacity, he had received an invitation to a related meeting and was asking whether he should accept. McKay again shared his concerns over Kennedy's proposed legislation:

> I told Brother Faust that he should go and find out what President Kennedy is trying to do. I said that I did not like to see a law passed which will make the Hotel men violators of the law if they refuse to provide accommodations for a negro when their hotels are filled with white people, or restaurant men made violators when they decline to serve colored people. I said that businessmen ought to be free to run their own businesses, and not become law breakers if they choose to employ certain people; that if we have such a law as that, then it is unfair to the majority of the citizens of this country.[32]

Faust attended the meeting, reported to the First Presidency, and received McKay's clearance to be part of local committees that, at Kennedy's invitation, would offer informal feedback on civil rights.[33]

A month after McKay's meeting with Faust, Stewart Udall again wrote to Hugh B. Brown, voicing continuing concerns over the church's failure to support the civil rights movement. Brown, now a seasoned member of the First Presidency, responded optimistically to Udall, citing the recent announcement of a mission to Nigeria, the church's first ever to black Africa, and an internal reevaluation of the church's long-standing policy barring blacks from the priesthood. The subject, wrote Brown, is "of very great and, I think, urgent importance to all of us."[34]

Two months later, the civil rights issue in Utah came to a head. Concerned that Utah was the only western state that had not passed laws guaranteeing basic civil rights for minority groups, local NAACP officers tried without success to meet with the First Presidency and enlist their support of such legislation. As a result of the rebuff, they decided to picket Temple Square during the church's upcoming October general conference. Alerted to their plans, Sterling M. McMurrin, who had served as Kennedy's U.S. Commissioner of Education until autumn of 1962, attempted to mediate a settlement. He met with Hugh B. Brown and suggested a face-to-face meeting with the NAACP officers. The night prior to the first session of the general conference, Brown met with the officers and worked out a deal: He would read a statement of the church's support of civil rights during one of the conference sessions, in return for which the planned demonstration would be cancelled.[35]

Unbeknownst to McKay, Brown asked McMurrin to draft the statement.[36] Working on a tight deadline, McMurrin wrote a document that McKay approved with only one minor change. Brown was pleased with McKay's approval but disappointed when he told Brown merely to include it in his prepared address, rather than presenting it as an official First Presidency statement.[37] Brown read the statement on Sunday morning—the session with the widest television and radio coverage:

> During recent months both in Salt Lake City and across the nation considerable interest has been expressed in the position of the Church of Jesus Christ of Latter-day Saints in the matter of civil rights. We would like it to be known that there is in this Church no doctrine, belief, or practice that is intended to deny the enjoyment of full civil rights by any person regardless of race, color, or creed.
>
> We again say, as we have said many times before, that we believe that all men are the children of the same God and that it is a moral evil for any person or group of persons to deny to any human being the right to gainful employment, to full educational opportunity, and to every privilege of citizenship, just as it is a moral evil to deny him the right to worship according to the dictates of his own conscience.

> We have consistently and persistently upheld the Constitution of
> the United States, and as far as we are concerned that means uphold-
> ing the constitutional rights of every citizen of the United States.
>
> We call upon all men everywhere, both within and outside the
> Church, to commit themselves to the establishment of full civil equal-
> ity for all of God's children. Anything less than this defeats our high
> ideal of the brotherhood of man.[38]

McMurrin paid close attention and thought it was successful. Wishing to max-
imize the impact of the statement while complying with McKay's request, Brown
"read it at the beginning of his sermon very much as if he were reading a separate
official statement from the First Presidency. Then he set it aside and proceeded
with his own address. It was most effective"[39]—so effective, in fact, that two years
later the *Deseret News* reprinted it as a "statement given officially" at the 1963 conference.[40] Albert B. Fritz, president of the Salt Lake City NAACP chapter, praised
the statement, adding, "Through this statement we are asking all NAACP branches
throughout the nation not to demonstrate or picket any LDS missions or
churches."[41]

However, in spite of the statement and intense lobbying by the NAACP, the
Utah State Legislature enacted only one minor piece of civil rights legislation in the
1963 session, a repeal of the state's onerous anti-miscegenation (racially mixed marriage) law. A month after Brown's general conference address, Charles Nabors, a
member of the executive board of the Salt Lake City NAACP chapter, offered his
opinion that Utah "has potentially the worst race problem in the United States."[42]
Nabors's statement, though harsh, was given credibility one month later when
Apostle Ezra Taft Benson, speaking at a public meeting in Logan, denounced the
civil rights movement as having been "fomented almost entirely by the communists." According to a report in the church-owned *Deseret News*:

> "The whole slogan of 'civil right' as used to make trouble in the South
> today, is an exact parallel to the slogan of 'agrarian reform' which they
> used in China," he added.
>
> "The pending 'civil rights' legislation is, I am convinced, about
> 10 per cent civil rights and 90 per cent a further extension of social-
> istic federal controls." Elder Benson said, "It is part of the pattern for
> the communist take-over of America."[43]

Following the assassination of John F. Kennedy in November 1963, David O.
McKay became the first religious leader whom Lyndon B. Johnson invited to the
White House. Although the two had met previously, a special and unexpected
chemistry now developed between the conservative Republican Mormon church-

man and the liberal Democratic president, which persisted for the remainder of McKay's lifetime. In July 1964, when Johnson's Civil Rights Bill became law, he invited McKay to serve on a national committee. In spite of having declined a similar request one year earlier from President Kennedy, McKay accepted Johnson's invitation, indicating in his telegram the personal reason for his decision, while still expressing reservations about the new law: "While walking by your side in the White House on January 31, I decided when national difficulties crossed your path that I would attempt to lighten your load whenever possible. The Civil Rights Bill is the beginning of troubles that will require the truest and best statesmanship of the President of the United States."[44] To his diary, McKay confided, "The Civil Rights Bill is now passed and it is the law of the land. Some of it is wrong—the Negro will now have to prove himself."[45]

Several months later, in the spring of 1965, the local NAACP chapter pressed the church "to take a public position in regards to the moral question of discrimination in housing and employment in Utah."[46] Upon being informed that the First Presidency would remain silent on the issue, the NAACP leaders immediately organized a series of marches in front of the Church Administration Building. In an effort to placate the marchers, N. Eldon Tanner suggested that McKay authorize the *Deseret News* to republish Brown's 1963 civil rights statement. McKay resisted the suggestion: "I said that we have said all we are going to say and all that we should; that I do not favor our repeating what had previously been said on the subject."[47] Nonetheless, after further discussion he relented; and the following day the *Deseret News* reprinted the 1963 statement, now elevated to "official" status. Two days later the marchers disbanded.

The memory of that crisis had barely subsided when Ezra Taft Benson again stoked the flames of controversy. Recently returned from a prolonged church assignment in Europe, he lashed out at the civil rights movement in his April 1965 general conference address: "What are we doing to fight it? Before I left for Europe I warned how the Communists were using the civil rights movement to promote revolution and eventual takeover of this country. When are we going to wake up? What do you know about the dangerous civil rights agitation in Mississippi? Do you fear the destruction of all vestiges of state government?"[48]

The following year, in May 1966, the ongoing dispute with the NAACP flared up again. The Salt Lake City chapter issued a stinging resolution charging that the church "has maintained a rigid and continuous segregation stand" and has made "no effort to counteract the widespread discriminatory practices in education, in housing, in employment, and other areas of life."[49]

In 1967, as race riots broke out in Detroit and other cities across the country, the relationship between the church and the civil rights movement plummeted to a new low. At 4:00 A.M. on a Sunday morning, Hugh B. Brown was awakened by a disturbing telephone call. "The Salt Lake City Police advis[ed] me that four car-loads of Negroes armed with machine guns and bombs were reported coming to Salt Lake City for the purpose of inciting a riot," he recorded in his diary, "and par-ticularly to destroy property on the Temple Block."[50] When Brown relayed the word to McKay three hours later, McKay was horrified, telling Brown that "every-thing possible must be done to guard that sacred spot." The rumor was unfounded, but this fact was not determined until, as a precautionary move, more than 3,000 visitors were denied access to the weekly broadcast of the Mormon Tabernacle Choir.[51] In the aftermath of the scare, church leaders took unprecedented steps to protect themselves and their families, including switching to unlisted home tele-phone numbers for all General Authorities and no longer publishing General Authority stake conference assignments, as "people with improper motives could take advantage of this information by burglarizing the homes or otherwise making trouble for the families of the brethren."[52]

In this atmosphere of near-hysteria, Ezra Taft Benson once again entered the picture. Having taken criticism from some of his colleagues for prior public state-ments linking the civil rights movement and Communism, Benson asked McKay's permission to address the subject once more in the upcoming October 1967 gen-eral conference. McKay summarized their meeting in his diary: "He briefly talked about the plight of the Negroes in this Civil Rights Issue, and how the Commu-nists are using the Negroes to further their own schemes to foment trouble in the United States. He said that he would talk on this subject from the viewpoint of bringing peace in our country instead of uprisings of the Negroes in riots, etc. I told Brother Benson that under these circumstances, he may go ahead with his subject."[53]

Given McKay's blessing, Benson hit hard:

> There is no doubt that the so-called civil rights movement as it exists today is used as a Communist program for revolution in America, just as agrarian reform was used by the Communists to take over China and Cuba.... We must not place the blame upon Negroes. They are merely the unfortunate group that has been selected by professional Communist agitators to be used as the primary source of cannon fod-der. Not one in a thousand Americans—black or white—really under-stands the full implications of today's civil rights agitation. The plan-ning, direction, and leadership come from the Communists, and most of those are white men who fully intend to destroy America by spilling Negro blood, rather than their own.[54]

When Martin Luther King Jr. was assassinated just days before the April 1968 general conference, McKay, in failing health at age ninety-four and thoroughly disenchanted with the civil rights movement, saw no reason to mention it at conference. However, unwilling to let King's death go unnoticed, Hugh B. Brown, in conducting one of the sessions of the conference, eulogized King: "At this time we express deep sorrow and shock at the news of the passing of a man (Dr. Martin Luther King) who had dedicated his life to what he believed to be the welfare of his people. It is a shocking thing that in this age such a thing could happen. We pray God's blessings upon his family, his friends, and those associated with him."[55] McKay noted in his diary that Brown had made the statement "of his own accord."[56]

ORIGIN OF THE PRIESTHOOD BAN

When viewed in virtually any other context, David O. McKay was a humane, kind man of exemplary tolerance of those different from himself. It is precisely for this reason that his harsh attitude toward civil rights, which he maintained until his death, is so jolting. Some of the elements that made up that attitude are clear. His animosity toward blacks dated to an early time in his life and was evident in his diary entry as a young missionary in Scotland in 1898. For all but five of his ninety-six years of life, he lived in Utah, a state with a chronic record of discrimination and lack of civil rights legal protection. At the time he became church president, not one member of his formal (First Presidency) or informal inner circles was a voice of support for civil rights; indeed, many of his closest advisors were vehemently opposed. And certainly Ezra Taft Benson's persuasive (to McKay) linkage of Communism (one of McKay's greatest fears) and civil rights did much to distance him from offering any support to the movement.

But perhaps the greatest negative influence on McKay was theological. From the days of Brigham Young on, blacks were denied ordination to a priesthood that was available to all other worthy males. Though never a doctrine supported by revelation, the exclusionary policy came to be assumed as divine in origin, and gradually a thick web of leadership discourse emerged to rationalize it. In one common iteration, as noted earlier in this chapter, sub-par conduct in a pre-mortal existence was invoked as the reason for the "curse." It is not a stretch to see how such a belief could easily dovetail with anti-civil rights feelings. Although McKay left little record explaining the genesis of his attitudes, it is likely that this issue played a significant role. Yet herein lies an enormous irony. Even though McKay was consistently non-supportive of civil rights, he differed dramatically from his conservative advisors in dealing with the subject of blacks and priesthood ordination, first distancing himself from the folkloric explanations of the policy, then taking unprecedented steps

to open a proselytizing mission in black Africa, and finally circumscribing for pragmatic and compassionate reasons the policy itself in a manner that not even his
closest associates appreciated while he was alive. And in so doing, McKay laid the
foundation for the 1978 revelation to a successor, Spencer W. Kimball, that abol-
ished forever the discriminatory policy.

The origins of the policy are obscure, but postdate Joseph Smith, Mormonism's founding prophet.[57] When the main body of Mormons moved to Utah
in 1847, the LDS Church entered a prolonged period of isolation that kept race relations on the back burner. By the turn of the twentieth century, when David O.
McKay became an apostle, few Mormons were even aware of the policy. Indeed,
McKay himself did not confront it for another fifteen years. In 1957, he recalled:

> I first met this problem in Hawaii in 1921. A worthy [black] man had
> married a Polynesian woman. She was faithful in the Church. They had
> a large family everyone [*sic*] of whom was active and worthy. My sym-
> pathies were so aroused that I wrote home to President Grant asking
> if he would please make an exception so we could ordain that man to
> the Priesthood. He wrote back saying "David, I am as sympathetic as
> you are, but until the Lord gives us a revelation regarding that mat-
> ter, we shall have to maintain the policy of the Church."[58]

The policy remained an obscure issue for another two decades, until in 1947
the First Presidency instructed Heber Meeks, president of the Southern States Mission, to investigate the possibility of proselytizing in Cuba. Meeks wrote to his
friend Lowry Nelson, a sociologist at Utah State Agricultural College (now Utah
State University) who had spent a year studying rural life in Cuba: "I would appreciate your opinion as to the advisability of doing missionary work particularly in the
rural sections of Cuba, knowing, of course, our concept of the Negro and his position as [to] the Priesthood."[59] Nelson was stunned by the letter and wrote in
response: "Your letter is the first intimation I have had that there was a fixed doctrine on this point. I had always known that certain statements had been made by
authorities regarding the status of the Negro but I had never assumed that they constituted an irrevocable doctrine."[60]

Nelson wrote the same day to George Albert Smith, then church president, asking for clarification of the policy and adding: "The many good friends of mixed
blood—through no fault of theirs incidentally—which I have in the Caribbean and
who know me to be a Mormon would be shocked indeed if I were to tell them my
Church relegated them to an inferior status."[61]

Nelson's letter evoked a written response from the entire First Presidency,
including Second Counselor David O. McKay, that vaguely rationalized the policy

as part of "the doctrines that our birth into this life and the advantages under which we may be born have a relationship in the life heretofore." The letter, in a historical inaccuracy that was not corrected for another twenty-five years, stated that the policy had originated with Joseph Smith, and labeled it a "doctrine of the Church, never questioned by any of the Church Leaders."[62] Lowry later noted, "As much as I was 'stunned' at Heber Meeks' question...this letter from the First Presidency was shocking.... There is no doubt in my mind that [J. Reuben Clark] drafted this letter to me."[63]

Although just a signatory to the First Presidency letter to Nelson, McKay penned his own thoughts on the subject several months later in response to a correspondent. He cited one scriptural precedent for the policy, a single passage from the Book of Abraham in the LDS canon of scripture.[64] For him, this passage appeared to answer the "who" if not the "why" of the policy and he added, "However, I believe, the real reason dates back to our pre-existent life." Unlike his more conservative General Authority colleagues, however, he did not pretend to know the details, and he declined to invoke either a "less valiant" or a "curse of Cain" explanation. In further departures from these colleagues, he allowed for the eventual reversal of the practice without restricting it to a postmortal period; and most significantly, he declined to call it a "doctrine." To him there was a distinct difference between a "policy" in the church, which he saw as conditional and thus changeable, and a "doctrine," which was immutable. The distinction was lost on his colleagues but was crucial in the final months of McKay's life.[65]

Several months later, McKay met with a group of former missionaries in his home, and "among other things discussed the Negro question which seems to be coming up frequently these days."[66] He did not, however, record the details of the discussion in his diary. Later in 1948 the question came up even more frequently with the appointment of a new president to the South African Mission. One of the earliest in the church, established in 1853, it was the only LDS mission on the African continent until 1980.

Prior to his departure, Evan P. Wright, the new mission president, met with the First Presidency and received detailed instructions about the problem of race in South Africa, a problem greatly exacerbated by the South African government's policy of apartheid. McKay recorded in his diary: "The color bar in South Africa was tightly drawn and any relaxing on the part of the church would breed discontent on the part of European members and friends." The First Presidency informed Wright that some earlier mission presidents had not strictly observed the ban on ordination of blacks, which included men with *any* proportion of black ancestry. "As a result, some difficulties arose although relatively few people with mixed blood were ordained or even baptized." Wright's mandate was clear: "No man was to be ordained to or advanced in the priesthood until he had traced his genealogy out of Africa."[67]

Upon arriving in South Africa, Wright found that stating the policy was quite different from implementing it. Tracing all of one's ancestral lines out of Africa was an onerous burden, so Wright reassigned six of his missionaries from proselytizing to genealogical research. A year after arriving, he reported his action to the First Presidency: "In the South African Mission we are doing a lot of genealogical research, at the present time so that more men may be ordained to the Priesthood and they in turn will be able to take places of leadership in our various branches. I have six missionaries spending much of their time doing genealogical work both instructing the members in connection with this work and assisting in family research."[68]

In spite of the elders' doubled efforts, they met with little success. Mormonism's reliance on priesthood ordinations bestowed upon the male laity thus created a crisis in local leadership. In April 1952, a year after McKay became church president, Wright described the situation to him: "A very serious problem relating to the South African Mission concerns the problem of the Priesthood. We are doing a lot of genealogical research but many of our people haven't been able to trace their lines out of Africa and therefore are not eligible for ordination to the Priesthood. Other individuals have run into slave lines from three to six or seven generations ago and as a result of this many questions have been raised which will seriously effect [sic] future missionary work in South Africa."[69]

Two months later, Wright again wrote to the First Presidency, this time with a greater sense of urgency:

> In the South African Mission we are badly in need of leadership through the priesthood, and I am most anxious to ordain men as fast as we possibly can. If we could have another fifty or hundred priesthood bearers in the mission our work would move forward more rapidly and successfully.... Apparently this is the only mission in the Church where it is necessary for a man to trace his genealogy to establish his eligibility for the priesthood. As a result, the members of the Church in this country feel that they are penalized.[70]

Wright also described a situation nearly identical to one that, less than a decade later, would launch Mormonism's first foray into black Africa: "In my time I have had native chiefs and officials ask me to come and baptize two or three thousand of their people. I always try to explain that the priesthood isn't conferred upon [black] Africans and at the present time we aren't laboring among them."[71]

MISSION TO SOUTH AFRICA

Several times during his five-year tenure as mission president, Wright urged the First Presidency either to visit South Africa themselves or to send another General Authority, pointing out that it was the only mission in the world that had never been visited by a general officer of the church.[72] McKay, in fact, had planned to visit South Africa during his around-the-world tour of LDS missions in 1921, "but much to our disappointment lack of time and difficulties of transportation deprived us of this joy."[73]

In 1953 Monroe McKay, a cousin, returned from a mission to South Africa and made a personal plea for McKay to visit that mission. Monroe drove to Huntsville, where President McKay was enjoying a respite from ecclesiastical duties by mowing on the family farm:

> As I walked across the lawn, he stopped the horses. The iron seat on those old mowers had three bolts, and two were missing, as was typical of the old machinery in those days. And he turned that seat around to face me as we started to talk. I gave him this account. He had big hands, and he wrapped them around his knee, and threw back his head and laughed with a nice, pleasant laugh. He said, "I'm going to tell you something, Monroe, that I haven't even told my counselors. I've already decided to go!" So I knew it before anybody else, except him.[74]

In January 1954, McKay embarked on a tour of three continents: Europe, Africa, and South America. There was no ambiguity in his mind as to the purpose for the second leg of his tour. On the long flight from England to South Africa, he discussed the matter with A. Hamer Reiser, who acted as his traveling secretary. According to Reiser, McKay "said he had that problem to consider, what to do about the present practice in South Africa of not conferring the priesthood."[75]

Shortly after arriving, McKay addressed a special meeting that included the new mission president (Wright had completed his assignment the previous year) and the missionaries. He began his remarks by saying, "To observe conditions as they are was one of the reasons that I wished to take this trip," and immediately addressed the issue of priesthood. "For several years the Coloured question in South Africa has been called to the attention of the First Presidency. We have manuscripts, page after page, written on it." He then spoke of the genesis of the church policy but in more tentative terms than his predecessors. "Now I think there is an explanation for this racial discrimination, dating back to the pre-existent state." He also spoke tentatively about the permanence of the policy, saying that it would be followed "until the Lord gives us another revelation changing this practice."

With a significance none of his audience could have appreciated, three times during his address he used the word "policy," but never the word "doctrine."[76]

What he did not do was to change the policy banning ordination of blacks. In
fact, he reiterated it by saying, "until a new revelation comes, the Church will
observe the policy of withholding the Priesthood from men of Negro ancestry."
Nonetheless, what he did next was highly significant.

> Now I am impressed that there are worthy men in the South African
> Mission who are being deprived of the Priesthood simply because they
> are unable to trace their genealogy out of this country. I am impressed
> that an injustice is being done to them. Why should every man be
> required to prove that his lineage is free from Negro strain especially
> when there is no evidence of his having Negro blood in his veins? I
> should rather, much rather, make a mistake in one case and if it be
> found out afterwards suspend his activity in the Priesthood than to
> deprive 10 worthy men of the Priesthood. . . . And so, if a man is wor-
> thy, is faithful in the Church and lives up to the principles of the
> Gospel, who has no outward evidence of a Negro strain, even though
> he might not be able to trace his genealogy out of the country, the
> President of the Mission is hereby authorised to confer upon him the
> Priesthood.[77]

McKay had not decided on this policy change before beginning the trip. Only
two days later, he wrote to his two counselors, informing them of the change for
the first time. Neither, however, was the decision impromptu, for in the letter he
explained: "After careful observation and sincere prayer, I felt impressed to modify the present policy."[78] The effect on the mission was immediate. Shortly after returning to Salt Lake City, McKay received a report from the new mission president:

> I wish you could have been with me in Johannesburg and Durban
> when I met with some of the Brethren and explained that it was possi-
> ble for them to receive the priesthood. Tears ran down their cheeks and
> they were so overcome they could hardly speak. The Brethren were
> very humble and they expressed their willingness to serve the Lord and
> magnify the priesthood. I know that your short visit here was the
> greatest blessing that had come to the South African Mission.[79]

The effect of the policy change extended beyond South Africa. By assuming the
absence of black lineage unless there was proof to the contrary, McKay established
a precedent that he repeated many times throughout the remainder of his life, thus

opening doors that previously had been shut. In 1957, for example, a wedding in one of the LDS temples was in doubt because of an unproven rumor that the bride had had a black grandmother. After some investigation of his own to confirm that there was no evidence to substantiate the rumor, McKay spoke to an associate who was advocating that the temple marriage proceed, and who later reported the conversation: "[President McKay] said, 'When problems like this come to me I say to myself, Sometime I shall meet my Father-in-Heaven and what will he say?' And I said to him modestly, 'He'll forgive you if you err on the side of mercy.' He smiled at that and said, 'But don't you think it's too late to do something about it?' I said, 'No sir.' He said, 'Leave it to me.'"[80] McKay then called the local ecclesiastical leader and said, "Since there is no absolute proof of Negro blood, I am going to give Miss Marshall the benefit of doubt."[81]

Two years later, in a virtually identical case, McKay phoned the local church leader and, after confirming that the case was founded wholly on rumor, instructed the leader to proceed with the planned temple wedding. Then McKay said, "Whenever we can face our Heavenly Father and say we did this and can justify ourselves, why I feel I can sleep, and I hope you can."[82] Time after time similar cases were brought to his attention. A fellow General Authority, who frequently sat in on meetings where such matters were decided, later recounted, "President McKay would always say, 'Well, if we don't know, give him the benefit of the doubt and go ahead and ordain him.'"[83]

CONFRONTING THE PRIESTHOOD BAN

As welcome as these cases were, however, they did not address the basic question of the ban on ordination. It appears, however, that McKay's South African trip caused him, for the first time, to explore the possibility of abolishing the ban. Upon his return he took two apparently unprecedented initiatives. The first occurred in March 1954, only three weeks after his return, during his private meeting with Sterling M. McMurrin, who was then under fire from Harold B. Lee and Joseph Fielding Smith, who were pressing for his excommunication because of his heretical beliefs. (See chap. 3.) McMurrin would, in 1963, write the statement on civil rights that Hugh B. Brown read at general conference. McMurrin candidly discussed his beliefs with McKay, including his rejection of "the common Mormon doctrine that the Negroes are under a divine curse." McKay's response caught him off guard: "He said, 'There is not now, and there never has been a doctrine in this Church that the Negroes are under a divine curse.' He insisted that there is no doctrine in the Church of any kind pertaining to the Negro. 'We believe,' he said, 'that we have scriptural precedent for withholding the priesthood from the Negro. *It is a practice, not a doctrine, and the practice will some day be changed.* And that's all there is to it.'"[84]

McMurrin elected not to publicize McKay's response, and McKay did not share his feelings with even his closest associates in the First Presidency and Quorum of the Twelve Apostles, a fact that created a crisis in the closing months of McKay's life. Nonetheless, his statement to McMurrin indicated that he was approaching the subject of the priesthood ban in a manner different than any of his predecessors since Brigham Young.

The second initiative, apparently at the same time as the McMurrin episode, involved a direct frontal challenge to the policy. Leonard J. Arrington, who later became Church Historian, described it:

> A special committee of the Twelve appointed by President McKay in 1954 to study the issue concluded that there was no sound scriptural basis for the policy but that the church membership was not prepared for its reversal.... Personally, I knew something about the apostolic study because I heard Adam S. Bennion, who was a member of the committee, refer to the work in an informal talk he made to the Mormon Seminar in Salt Lake City on May 13, 1954. McKay, Bennion said, had pled with the Lord without result and finally concluded the time was not yet ripe.[85]

Three things are significant about Arrington's account. First, as he had told McMurrin, McKay saw the issue as changeable policy rather than immutable doctrine. Second, as he had stated in South Africa, even though it was a policy that was changeable, it would require a revelation from the Lord to change it. He did not make it clear why he felt a revelation was necessary—that is, whether it was because the policy had been instituted by the Lord in the first place, or whether this man-made policy had become so firmly entrenched that changing it would require the force of revelation to convince church members that it needed to be changed. And finally, apparently for the first time, he took the matter directly to a divine source. It was not the last time that he did so, and not always did he achieve the same result.

In 1955, McKay visited the South Pacific, retracing some of the steps of his 1921 world tour. He met with a small group of church members in Fiji, where the church had never done any missionary work because of the Negroid appearance of the Fijians. Noting that the "race problem would be no worse than in South Africa or Brazil," he instructed the president of the adjacent Samoan Mission to explore the possibility of beginning proselytizing efforts in Fiji.[86] He later instructed Wendell Mendenhall, chairman of the Church Building Committee, and Edward L. Clissold, president of Oahu Stake, to investigate the relationship of the Fijians to other Polynesian groups (none of whom were under priesthood restrictions), with the clear intent of determining if the ban on priesthood would extend to Fijian men.[87] Following a trip to New Zealand four years later, he reported to his counselors that "there is evidence that [Fijians] are not of the Negroid races"[88] and authorized their ordination to the priesthood, thus narrowing the ban to blacks of African origin.[89]

As McKay continued to wrestle with the issue, his explanation of its justification underwent a significant change. On two occasions three years apart—both of them, ironically, at press conferences in London where McKay traveled to dedicate new church buildings—he responded to reporters' questions, but with different answers. In 1958 he ascribed the policy to unspecified events in pre-mortal life— the traditional explanation—but was careful not to go any further and add the also-traditional link either to a curse or to Cain: "We also believe in pre-existence that what we were in the world before we came here determines our position in this life and what we do in this life will determine our position in the next and so on. The Negro is very happy to receive the privilege of coming into this dispensation (this mortal existence) and receive the blessings which are his."[90]

Three years later, however, he abandoned the preexistence rationale, invoking instead the single verse in the Mormon canon that deals, albeit only indirectly, with the subject: "We have the Pearl of Great Price, a translation by Joseph Smith of an early account of the creation of the world. In that is a passage which refers to a son of Egyptus, who claimed the right of Priesthood by descent. But descendants could not have it because they were descendants of colored people. That Pharaoh was a righteous man but was not given the priesthood because of his descent from Egyptus, who had colored blood in her veins. That is the only reason. It is founded upon that."[91]

MISSION TO NIGERIA

McKay's first initiative relating to the priesthood ban had involved an African country but had addressed only white church members. His attention now shifted to another African country, Nigeria, and focused on its population of blacks, the largest in the world. Because of the ban on ordaining black men to the priesthood, LDS proselytizing initiatives to Africa, spanning a full century, had been limited to white populations in South Africa and, later, Rhodesia. In 1946, however, church officials in Salt Lake City received a letter from O. J. Umordak, a Nigerian, requesting church literature and missionaries. In spite of the inevitable difficulties posed by the priesthood ban, the Quorum of the Twelve Apostles considered the request seriously because of "our responsibility in proclaiming the Gospel to the world."[92] A year later, the Twelve gave further consideration to Umordak's request but decided to postpone further action "until the material regarding the negro question has been assembled and the Brethren have had an opportunity to look it over and digest it."[93]

No follow-up occurred for more than a decade. In the late 1950s, another Nigerian, Honesty John Ekong, wrote with a similar request for literature and missionaries. The request was given to LaMar S. Williams, an employee in the Missionary Department, who began to send pamphlets and overruns of the church magazines each month, sometimes several hundred pounds per shipment.[94]

A short time later, in 1960, church leaders requested that Glen G. Fisher, who had just been released as president of the South African Mission, visit Nigeria on his way home to assess the situation. Fisher reported that the local people had, using church literature, essentially converted themselves to Mormonism and, in the absence of personal contact with the church, had organized several congregations.[95]

The following year, McKay decided to take action on the matter, telling his two counselors, Henry D. Moyle and Hugh B. Brown, in June 1961: "I said that we cannot escape the obligation of permitting these people to be baptized and confirmed members of the Church if they are converted and worthy, but they should be given to understand that they cannot perform these ordinances nor can they hold the priesthood."[96]

It was clear that such an initiative would involve special logistical challenges unlike those of other missions, for without local clergy the Nigerian congregations would be dependent on white, usually foreign, missionaries for most official functions, performing ordinances, conducting meetings, and assuming most administrative functions—unless, of course, the policy was reversed. McKay had no illusions about the implications as he continued the discussion a couple of weeks later with his counselors: "I said that in this matter we are facing a problem greater than the Twelve of old faced when the church was shaken by the question of whether or not the Gentiles should have the gospel. I said that the Lord would have to let us know, and when he is ready to open the door he will tell us. But until he does, we shall have to tell these people in Nigeria that they can go so far and no farther."[97]

The next day in his weekly meeting with the Quorum of the Twelve, McKay began his discussion of the issue by describing in detail the decision in ancient times to carry Christianity beyond the Jews. He then summarized recent events regarding Nigeria and said "that in the past two attempts have been made to have the President of the South African Mission visit these people in Nigeria, but because of political conditions they have not had a good visit with them."[98] In mid-October McKay dispatched LaMar Williams to Nigeria on a fact-finding assignment. In particular, he wished Williams to determine how it might be possible to administer a Nigerian church in the absence of native lay priesthood.[99]

Williams, upon arriving in Nigeria, immediately confronted the core issue:

> I explained that they could not hold the priesthood. This was one
> thing that I was asked by President McKay to tell them, that they
> couldn't hold the priesthood, that it wouldn't be given to them. They
> could have the gospel and all the blessings of the gospel, but we
> would have to have missionaries to preside over them and to perform
> the ordinances. Reverend Udo-Ete stood up folding both arms out,
> and then putting his right hand underneath the left arm, he said, "I
> only want to walk under the priesthood," demonstrating that they
> were willing to let the priesthood be there and not to hold the priest-
> hood, just as long as they could have membership in the true Church
> of Jesus Christ.[100]

Williams reported to McKay that the people were sincere in their desire to affiliate
with Mormonism and counted nearly one hundred congregations, totaling some
5,000 people, who wished to be admitted to the church.[101]

On January 9, 1962, McKay once again brought up the matter with his counselors. In this significant meeting, the discussion took a dramatic, new turn. McKay,
noting that several hundred Nigerians had already taken upon themselves the name
of the church, asked for their opinion on an appropriate response to the Nigerians'
request for missionaries. He cautioned, "It is as great in the Church today as the
question that nearly split the primitive Church when they preached only to the
Jews." Moyle responded, "Sooner or later it will have to receive the same answer."
After reviewing briefly the story of the revelation to Peter that opened the door to
the gentiles, McKay, while acknowledging Peter's role, emphasized that "it took
the Lord to do it."

After they discussed the difficulty in running even the auxiliary programs of the
church in the absence of local priesthood, Brown made a proposal that had not been
previously considered: "I wonder if the time is coming when we will give the Lesser
Priesthood to them."[102] Such a move would have allowed much of the week-to-
week activity of the church to be implemented, as the "sacrament" (communion,
or the Lord's supper), the only ordinance regularly connected with worship services, is a function of the lesser priesthood. McKay, however, responded, "You do
that and you give them the priesthood." Brown replied, "That's the opening of the
door. I don't think the time has come, but it may come when the Lord directs it."

After some discussion, including a decision to present the matter to the Quorum of the Twelve the following week, the meeting concluded with an exchange
between McKay and Brown. McKay said, "They are entitled to the gospel, but
the priesthood is another thing." Brown replied, "You don't intend to decide any

change on that at this time,"—a half-question, half-statement—and McKay concluded, "You can't deal with this in a proper way unless you do. God bless you, brethren."[103] Although it appeared that McKay was on the verge of reversing the policy, he did not make the expected proposal to the Quorum of the Twelve. For undisclosed reasons, he instead placed the matter on the back burner.

The related question of a mission to Nigeria, however, continued to occupy his attention. Two months later, with the support of his counselors, McKay proposed to the Twelve that a Nigerian Mission be organized and that it be placed, for administrative purposes, under the West European Mission (headquartered in England) rather than the South African Mission, to minimize the possibility of antagonizing the South African government, which was opposed to proselytizing among blacks. The primary purpose of the mission would be to baptize the thousands of Nigerians who had already converted themselves to Mormonism. If this phase of the mission's work were successful, the church would assist local members in constructing meetinghouses. The Twelve unanimously approved the proposal, although Harold B. Lee expressed concern for the safety of the white missionaries. McKay concluded the meeting by stating that "this is just as important in our history as when James presided over the Council that gave consideration to the matter of carrying the gospel to the Gentiles."[104]

Two days later, on March 3, 1962, McKay instructed LaMar Williams to prepare to leave for Nigeria,[105] but a short time later McKay told him he would have to delay his departure for at least several months, "because of political problems the Church was having over its racial policies in anticipation of the forthcoming election [1962]."[106] Paramount among those problems was George Romney's decision to run for governor in Michigan, a state whose African American population would be a significant factor in the election. McKay wrote to N. Eldon Tanner, who as president of the West European Mission would supervise the Nigerian Mission: "Nothing will be done about it until after the November election."[107] After discussing the matter further in a subsequent First Presidency meeting, he wrote: "We felt that it was best that nothing be done about the matter until after the November election for the reason that if we were to baptize a considerable number of negro people at this time, certain politicians might take the view that it was done to influence the negro vote in favor of George Romney in his candidacy for Governor of Michigan."[108]

About three weeks before the November election, McKay again discussed with his counselors the logistical problems of trying to administer the church in Nigeria without local priesthood leaders. Moyle pointed out the obvious: "It is almost inconceivable to carry on the work of a stake without the priesthood." Acknowledging the problems, McKay nonetheless was resolute in moving forward with the

Nigerian Mission and looking beyond merely baptizing new members: "We have got to look forward and bring the mission organization to thousands of negroes.... We shall help them build their meetinghouses and these meetinghouses will soon be used as school houses in helping the children to read. When the children join the Church, the next thing will be to have them learn to read."[109]

In that important January 1962 First Presidency meeting, Hugh Brown had raised the question of ordination to the Aaronic Priesthood, but now McKay did, musing: "If we could just give them the Aaronic Priesthood. I suppose there is no way to differentiate. The Lord will have to do it." Brown responded, "I secretly hoped that the time would come when we could give them the Aaronic Priesthood." Once again, however, McKay made it clear that the final decision was not in his hands. "Only the Lord can change it, but that is what we are facing, Brethren, and we have gone so far now that we shall have to go down to Nigeria and baptize these people."[110]

LaMar Williams was formally set apart and received his formal commission on November 21, 1962, after Romney's successful election. He recalled McKay's personal charge in the blessing: "This is a new appointment, a new assignment, not only to you individually but to the entire Church, going to a people not entitled to hold the priesthood but entitled to other blessings of the Church, including eternal life in the Celestial Kingdom. We bless you that you may have sympathy for the people in this work and recognize their citizenship in the kingdom of God."[111]

Williams had planned to leave immediately for Nigeria, but his departure was delayed because the Nigerian government had not yet issued his visa. N. Eldon Tanner, a Canadian citizen, had no problem obtaining a visa and spent two weeks in December 1962 visiting Nigeria and meeting with government leaders. Tanner had been involved in oil and gas development as a government official in Alberta and, in that capacity, had previously met some of these officials as they consulted with Canadian officials about developing Nigeria's petroleum reserves. As a result, he was well received and was assured that the government would approve the sending of missionaries, including issuing visas, in only three weeks. Encouraged by this news, Tanner offered a prayer dedicating Nigeria "for missionary work to be conducted as directed by the Lord through his Prophet."[112]

Tanner returned to Salt Lake City in January and made his report to McKay, who dictated in his diary: "After listening to Elder Tanner's report, I was deeply impressed that it was most fortunate that I had appointed Elder Tanner to go to Nigeria to look into the opening of the work there. I do not know of another man who could have met the conditions so favorably and intelligently as Brother Tanner did."[113] Buoyed by the news, McKay expanded Tanner's mandate by instructing him to make application for twenty missionaries as soon as the permit was

issued. The following day, the church issued a press release announcing the opening of the Nigerian Mission. It said nothing about the problem of priesthood ordination.[114]

In spite of the government's assurance that the permit would be issued by the
end of January, church leaders received no news throughout January and February. Then, early in March, a Nigerian college student wrote an article that effectively
put the entire initiative on hold. Ambrose Chukwuo was enrolled at California
State Polytechnic College in San Luis Obispo. In the first weeks of 1963, he
accepted an invitation to attend an LDS worship service and, in a conversation
afterwards, first learned of the policy banning ordination of blacks. Already disqui-
eted by the conversation, he was outraged when he read John J. Stewart's recently
published *Mormonism and the Negro,* 2d ed. (Orem, UT: Bookmark Division of
Community Press Publishing, 1960). Although Stewart was not a church official and
the book was not endorsed by the church, it did convey the sentiments of many
ranking church officials. Chukwuo wrote an angry letter to the *Nigerian Outlook,*
published in Enugo, Nigeria, that included extensive quotations from the book. The
letter, which appeared on March 5, 1963, read in part: "I do not think that many
people know about this religion in Nigeria; but if you read one of their books *Mormonism and the Negro,* you will realize that such a collection of madmen have no
right to go under the name Christians. The Mormons believe that the Negro is a
race of outcasts who are undergoing some punishment in this world for what they
did in a previous existence. They are 'fallen angels.'"[115]

The editor of the paper fanned the flames further with his introduction to the
letter: "Evil Saints": "Our correspondent has gone into great pains to expose this
organisation because he fears it may come to Nigeria thoroughly disguised....
These so-called Latter Day Saints must be recognized for what they are—godless
Herrenvolkism—and must not be allowed into the country."[116]

Other Nigerian students wrote similar letters to government officials in their
homeland, with an immediate negative response. At first, the government questioned the church's financial reliability and demanded a substantial cash deposit "as
a guarantee that the missionaries will return." McKay bristled at the move and said
that no deposit would be made in Nigeria. Henry Moyle, trying to resolve the crisis, suggested a compromise: depositing the sum at Barclay's Bank in London,
which had offices in Nigeria. Not yet aware of Chukwuo's letter, McKay "expressed
the belief that one of the Nigerian churches, knowing of the interest of 4,000 people
to become Latter-day Saints, are [*sic*] opposing the missionaries coming in."[117]

Working through contacts at First National City Bank and the Kennecott
Company, Moyle soon assured McKay that the financial transaction would be taken
care of.[118] A week later, however, Tanner received a letter from Nigerian authori-

ties that imposed additional conditions: "1) The body must be one that practices cooperation with other Christian bodies; 2) It must be one that is recommended by the Christian Council of Nigeria or by overseas bodies already recognized in Nigeria; 3) It must be one whose work will be welcomed by the regional authorities."[119]

McKay, expressing confidence that Tanner "is the only man in the Church who can do it," instructed him to return to Nigeria and attempt to resolve the impasse after April general conference, only two weeks away. By that time, Tanner and other church leaders had learned about the Chukwuo letter and those of his fellow students. In May, Tanner gave McKay a blunt report: "A group of Nigerian students in San Luis Obispo, California are leading the attack and flooding Nigeria with literature and propaganda against the Church. Brother LaMar Williams went to talk to these students, and reported that these students base their whole objection to our Church on the fact that we discriminate against them in that we do not give them equal opportunity with white people in the Church."[120]

McKay, commenting on Tanner's report in his diary, added that, in addition to its earlier demands, the Nigerian government now required that the church "explain our position as far as the attacks which were made against us were concerned." Tanner postponed indefinitely his plans to return to Nigeria.

In late May 1963, McKay again met with Tanner and Williams. Estimates of the number of Nigerians seeking baptism had now risen from 4,000 to 7,000, and the three men agreed that the initiative to open the mission should be continued. However, in the face of government opposition McKay decided not to push the matter any more from Salt Lake City. Rather, "Elder Tanner was directed to write to leaders of Church groups in Nigeria who have been corresponding with the Church for some time, acknowledging them as leaders of their groups. These leaders were to be advised that, as and when they were able to obtain government permission for the Church to do so, it would send in representatives to assist them with their Church program."[121]

Only days after putting the Nigerian matter on hold, McKay was blindsided by his second counselor, Hugh B. Brown, who went public in his attempt to reverse the ban on priesthood ordination. Wallace Turner published an interview with Brown in the *New York Times* on June 7:

> The top leadership of the Mormon church is seriously considering the abandonment of its historic policy of discrimination against Negroes.... One of the highest officers of the church said today that the possibility of removing this religious disability against Negroes has been under serious consideration. "We are in the midst of a survey looking toward the possibility of admitting Negroes," said Hugh

B. Brown, one of the two counselors serving President David O.
McKay in the First Presidency of the Mormon church. "Believing as
we do in divine revelation through the President of the church, we all
await his decision," Mr. Brown said.[122]

McKay was not a man to be pushed and, indeed, only two days earlier, had
reacted strongly to pressure from the outside by saying, "We shall make no con-
cession to the NAACP. They are trying to take advantage of this situation to make
the Church yield equality in the Church."[123] He was no less resistant to pressure
from the inside, even from his third-in-command. Brown's initial defense, when
McKay called him on the carpet, was to claim that he had been misquoted. However, the church press officer, Theodore Cannon, who had been present at Turner's
interview with Brown, confirmed to McKay that Turner had quoted Brown accurately. Indeed, "Brother Cannon said that he was able to persuade the reporter to
leave out a lot of material which was not too favorable to the Church." Cannon
also passed on the word that a reporter for the *National Observer*, a weekly edited
by Robert Dirks, had asked for an interview with McKay in light of the *Times* article. McKay, with obvious disgust, told Cannon that the reporter "should see President Brown and let him straighten the matter out."[124]

The latter half of 1963 did not hold much good news for McKay. The Nigerian initiative had floundered to a halt; and the one seemingly positive development
on this front, a letter to McKay from U.S. Senator Wallace F. Bennett (R-Utah)
announcing that visas had been issued and would shortly arrive, proved premature.[125] Brown's statement had caused McKay and the church great embarrassment
and likely fed the resolve of the NAACP to press the church for change, resulting
in the threats of picketing that led to McMurrin's drafting of the civil rights statement that Brown read at October general conference.

Furthermore, a nationally syndicated article by writer Clare Boothe Luce, a
former Congresswoman and ambassador, discussed the possibility that George
Romney, who was making an impressive showing as Michigan's governor, might
become the Republican presidential nominee the following year. Without attribution, it basically took up where Brown left off: "In recent years many Mormons have
vigorously protested the Negro doctrine of their church. It is not at all unlikely that
in the months to come President McKay may have a Divine Revelation on the subject which will assure the Negroes equality of soul with that of men of other races.
And those who know Romney personally believe that he is devoutly praying that
such will be the case."[126]

Moyle, the first counselor, drafted a letter to Luce attempting to relieve the
pressure of the national publicity. After suggesting minor revisions, McKay
approved the letter, which reaffirmed what he had maintained throughout his pres-

idency: that the policy could not be changed simply by executive order. "There would be no hesitancy upon the part of the priesthood of the Church today to confer the priesthood upon the negro were we so authorized. There is not the slightest possibility of our announcing any revelation upon this subject or changing the direction which the Lord has already given, until the Lord actually so directs. Until a revelation upon this subject is actually received no change can be made. When or if such a revelation is to be received, obviously we do not know."[127]

Five days after sending the letter, Moyle, who had a long history of heart disease, died in his sleep. With Moyle's death, Brown became the first counselor, and McKay called N. Eldon Tanner, whose steady hand in the Nigerian initiative had so impressed him, to join the First Presidency as second counselor.

The next month, after October general conference, J. D. Williams, a University of Utah political science professor and former LDS bishop, took Brown's statement one step further and, boldly (and correctly) predicted to a *Time* magazine reporter that "the change will come, and within my lifetime."[128]

The year ended with more controversy. In a December meeting of the American Folklore Society in Detroit, BYU English professor Thomas E. Cheney gave a paper in which he predicted that the time would soon come when the church policy on ordination of blacks would be reversed. A reporter from the *Detroit Free Press* attended the meeting and asked Cheney for a copy of his paper to write a story for his newspaper. "I was not unhappy to have people know what I had said," Cheney reminisced, "because I knew that I had spoken the truth. But I wanted it to be reported accurately, so I gave the reporter my paper and told him to report only what I had said."[129]

Cheney was still in Detroit the following morning when the article was published with a headline, "End to Mormon Bias Against Negro, Seen by College Professor." "The thing that upset me was the statement, 'Mormon Bias Against Negro,' since I did not consider that the Mormons necessarily had a bias against Negroes," Cheney reflected. The United Press picked up the story and it ran in papers throughout the country.

By the time Cheney returned to Provo, "my name was being repeated on the radio all over the country." Upset with the story, McKay called Earl Crockett, acting president of BYU. Crockett, while sympathetic with Cheney, suggested that Cheney withdraw his pending application for promotion to full professor and postpone it for a year, as it was unlikely to be approved in the current climate. Meanwhile, Cheney sent a copy of his paper to Hugh B. Brown, who, undoubtedly still smarting from his *New York Times* episode earlier in the year, "told me that he was aware of the way the press had of misdirecting the things that were said." Brown read the paper and told Cheney that he approved of it.[130]

The year 1964 opened on a more positive note. Early in January, LaMar Williams finally received a temporary visa to Nigeria. McKay, pleased with the news, instructed Williams to meet with government officials in Nigeria and "be prepared to organize the Church there if the government officials will give permission for our missionaries to enter." Tanner added his endorsement, saying that "those people in Nigeria are very sincere, they have read our literature, they are well informed, are thoroughly converted, and are prepared to accept and live the Gospel without holding the Priesthood."[131]

Williams left for Nigeria on February 4 and spent nine days in the country. Although he was successful in visiting many prospective church members, he was frustrated in his attempts to meet with the premier of the eastern portion of the country. Without that individual's permission, the Minister of Internal Affairs of the federal government in Lagos refused authorization to establish a mission, and Williams returned to Salt Lake City empty-handed.[132]

Little changed for more than a year because of the Nigerian government's opposition. Williams's tourist visa would not allow proselytizing nor a long-term stay. Undaunted, he continued to press the government to issue him a permanent visa and pressed church leaders to continue the Nigerian initiative. His efforts produced a partial backfire. Even though the First Presidency had not met with Williams for some time, "the thought was expressed" in a meeting in April 1965 "that Brother Williams is a little over-enthusiastic about this matter, and that perhaps if and when he goes to Nigeria he may not use the best judgment." Nonetheless, by the end of the meeting, McKay agreed that, if Williams could obtain a visa, then he "should go to Nigeria…and arrange for the baptism of worthy converted Nigerians and effect a proper organization among them."[133]

Early in June, Williams's request for a visa was refused. McKay decided that "the matter should not be pushed."[134] Nigeria, however, lingered on McKay's mind. Two weeks later, James Larkin, a Mormon living in New York City, telephoned Tanner in Salt Lake City. Larkin's call was prompted by an article in *Time* entitled "Nigerian Mormons," which reported that 7,000 people had associated themselves with Mormonism, in spite of the absence of an official Church presence.[135] He claimed a "close relationship" of two years "to the government in northern Nigeria" and proposed that he might run interference for the church there. As the First Presidency discussed his suggestion, McKay said that, in spite of their recurring frustrations, "I am convinced, after studious thought and prayer, that we should go into Nigeria and give them what we can give them in accordance with the revelations of the Lord. As of now, the Lord has not yet revealed to us that we should give the Negro the Priesthood, but we can baptize them, give them membership in the Church, and give them the benefit of the Auxiliary organizations."[136]

A week later when McKay met directly with Larkin, the discussion took on a new and ominous tone, the full implications of which would not become apparent for several months. McKay recorded in his diary: "Brother Larkin said that strangely enough the local Nigerians who call themselves Latter-day Saints are members of a political party, which is currently playing the least role in the federal government; therefore, their opinions, unfortunately, because it is a democracy, would not carry as much weight as if they might have come from the northern regions, whose leaders control the federal government."[137] That political party was composed primarily of Biafrans, who would become victims in a bloody civil war when it erupted in July 1967. McKay, perhaps sensing trouble, said, "I think the time has not yet come to go into Nigeria."

In August, LaMar Williams finally received a visitor's visa, along with an assurance that it would likely be converted into a permanent visa. After such a protracted and frustrating effort to obtain the visa, the news injected an immediate spirit of optimism. Tanner, who gave McKay the news, asked if Williams should go to Nigeria. McKay answered in the affirmative. He directed that a letter signed by the First Presidency and addressed "To Whom It May Concern" be given to Williams, indicating that he was visiting Nigeria in an official Church capacity.[138]

By now it was late August 1965. Williams met with the First Presidency and received his instructions. In Nigeria he should as quickly as possible try to obtain a permanent visa so that he could remain and establish a permanent mission. In the meantime, he was to baptize those who he felt were adequately prepared and set up the auxiliary organizations of the church, which could function even without local priesthood. In a gesture indicating McKay's intense interest in Nigeria, he told Williams to report directly to the First Presidency, rather than through the West European Mission, as previously instructed.[139]

Williams immediately began preparations for his journey and was ready to go by mid-October. Shortly before his departure, however, McKay had Clare Middlemiss tell Williams that "he is not to be set apart as a Mission President, nor is he to do any baptizing in Nigeria at this time."[140] McKay's new hesitancy was due to his concern over the visa problem. If Williams were to be denied a permanent visa and thus return home prematurely, any fledgling church organization would likely die. Therefore, McKay told him to make a permanent visa his first priority. If he succeeded, then performing the baptisms would be the next step. Tanner concurred with McKay's thinking, adding optimistically that he felt it would be only a matter of days before the permanent visa would be secured.

In mid-October, a year and a half after launching his efforts to obtain a visa, Williams set out for his third trip to Nigeria. For three weeks he worked with government officials, obtained an extension of his tourist visa, and made arrangements for a long-term stay.

Meanwhile, half a world away, Williams's fate was being debated in a crucial meeting of the First Presidency and Quorum of the Twelve in the Salt Lake Temple. Harold B. Lee, a senior apostle and second in line for the church presidency, was the most vocal of all General Authorities in opposing any reversal of the ban on priesthood ordination. He voiced strong reservations to Williams's mission:

> Elder Lee said that Evan Wright, the former President of the South African Mission and one who had lived in South Africa for some years, had told him (Brother Lee) that he was shocked on one occasion to hear Brother Williams say that in his (Brother Williams') judgment the Negroes should receive at least the Aaronic Priesthood. Brother Wright said that if that statement were made in South Africa, or if they learned about it down there, it might close up our missionary effort in South Africa because there is a very strict policy of segregation.... Elder Lee said he wondered if this long delay in getting a permanent visa may not be evidence that the Lord is not ready to have this work done.[141]

Tanner pointed out that Williams was in Nigeria with the permission and blessing of the First Presidency, but Lee pressed his case. He referred to a discussion by the Twelve several years earlier in which a proposal to organize a small branch for black Mormons in Salt Lake City had been greeted initially with enthusiasm. However, as word of the proposal spread and reached the NAACP, Lee said, "they were demanding that the church bring them in as full-fledged members with the Priesthood and all." At that, Lee said, the matter had been dropped. The implication of Lee's remarks was clear: He believed that a mission to Nigeria would open a door that they would not be able to close.

Lee was followed by Mark E. Petersen, whose segregationist statement at BYU years earlier had disqualified him from visiting Nigeria when he replaced Tanner as president of the European Mission.[142] "Elder Petersen said that personally he would like to see Brother Williams called home and kept home, and that we proceed no further with this program. He thought it would do us great damage."[143]

The next man to speak was Ezra Taft Benson, who had long voiced both in public and private his distaste for civil rights, which he linked directly to a Communist conspiracy:

> Elder Benson said he shared the feeling of the Brethren who had expressed themselves on this question, that he was confident in his own mind from a study he had made of the Negro question that we

are only seeing something being carried out today that was planned by the highest councils of the communist party twenty years ago, and that Martin Luther King is an agent, if not a power in the Communist party. He said that this whole thing is being directed and supported and promoted by agents of the Communist party, that the Negroes are being used in this whole question of Civil Rights, integration, etc., and that the NAACP are largely made up of men who are affiliated with from one to a dozen communist-front organizations, and he thought they would do anything in their power to embarrass the Church. Elder Benson thought we ought to be very careful what we do in the Negro field, whether it be in Nigeria, here, or any other place in the world, and he felt that so far as Brother Williams is concerned, his work in Nigeria should be terminated and he be brought home to report.[144]

Gordon B. Hinckley mentioned his recent conversation with the returning president of the South African Mission, who had similarly "expressed the fear that if we took an interest in the Negroes it would jeopardize our position in South Africa." At this point Petersen moved that Williams be brought home at once, a motion that was seconded and unanimously approved. McKay, though present at the meeting, declined to exercise his prerogative as church president and veto the proposal, perhaps yielding to his own periodic reservations about the Nigerian initiative. Among those apostles who did not express an opinion in the debate was Spencer W. Kimball. As church president thirteen years later, he received the revelation that reversed the policy and initiated a permanent church presence in Nigeria.

Two days later, Williams received a telegram advising him to return immediately to Salt Lake City. He left Lagos the same day and immediately reported to the First Presidency, an event that marked the first time that McKay's two new additional counselors, Joseph Fielding Smith and Thorpe B. Isaacson, had attended an official First Presidency meeting. Williams reminisced,

> During the conversation and interview I was not really informed as to why I had been called back home or why they were discontinuing negotiating with the government. I wasn't quite able to discover it. The spokesman for the group was Thorpe B. Isaacson, who had been selected as one of the counselors to the First Presidency. He seemed to be carrying on most of the conversation. President McKay remained almost silent, as did the other counselors, who only asked a few questions. Finally Brother Isaacson stated that we were just asking for a lot of problems. I replied, "Since when did the Church start

running away from problems?" He said, "There's no use asking for them."[145]

Williams was naturally disappointed. He said that he had ascertained that as many as 20,000 Nigerians desired baptism. He had already received a ninety-day extension of his visa and felt that he was making good progress when he received the telegram.[146] He pleaded for one or more of the General Authorities to visit Nigeria and assess the situation firsthand prior to a final decision to abandon the mission, but to no avail. After discussing the matter thoroughly among themselves and listening to the minutes of the joint First Presidency/Twelve meeting the previous week, the five members of the First Presidency decided unanimously "that for the present we should postpone any attempt to carry out a program in Nigeria, that we should leave the situation as it is."[147]

In July 1967, the Biafran War broke out. Interviewed some sixteen years after returning from Nigeria, Williams mused:

> The war was in the very area that I had been doing missionary work or trying to establish the Church. I would have been right in the center of that conflict had I remained. It wasn't until then that I felt that the Lord had something to do with getting me out of Nigeria. It wasn't the time for the Church to be established. I was on a plane traveling with President [Harold B.] Lee from Los Angeles when he made this statement, "LaMar, it's just a matter of timing in establishing the Church." And he was right. The time was not right.[148]

EFFORTS TO LIFT THE PRIESTHOOD BAN

For several years the dialogue regarding the priesthood ban had been dominated by Nigeria, yet there were significant developments outside the Nigerian initiative. In 1954, McKay had opened the question of whether Fijians, whose features are clearly Negroid in appearance, were also included in the priesthood ban. After four years of investigation, he ruled that they were not. A related question surfaced in 1964, when the president of the Australian Mission requested a ruling from the First Presidency on whether Australian aborigines could be ordained to the priesthood. In March, the First Presidency replied, "We are pleased to give our consent to the conferring of the priesthood upon such of these brethren as may be otherwise worthy, in the event that there is no definite evidence that they have negroid blood."[149]

A similar question arose two years later, this time involving Africa. In response to an inquiry about whether the ban on priesthood included Egyptians, McKay ruled that it did not, despite his use four years earlier of the Book of Abraham's linking of Egypt and the curse of Cain to justify the ban: "I referred to the decision made by me while in South Africa some years ago to the effect that unless there is good evidence that the individual has Negro blood, he should be considered as entitled to receive the Priesthood and Temple blessings if otherwise worthy."[150]

The next three years saw no dramatic change on the issue. Rather, a series of decisions further defined the policy. Since these were decided on a case-by-case basis, some leaned toward greater inclusion while others sharpened the division. Could black men serve in leadership roles in the Church's auxiliary organizations? Yes.[151] Could temple ordinances, not available to blacks because priesthood ordination for men was a prerequisite, be performed by proxy in behalf of deceased blacks? No.[152] Could black children who are legally adopted by white church members be "sealed" to them? Yes.[153] Could black children enter the temple in order to participate in proxy baptisms in behalf of the deceased? Yes.[154]

In May 1967, Interior Secretary Stewart Udall, who earlier had written to the First Presidency urging greater LDS participation in the civil rights movement, published a letter to the editor in *Dialogue: A Journal of Mormon Thought*, a Mormon scholarly quarterly, that criticized the continuation of the priesthood ban:

> This issue must be resolved . . . by clear and explicit pronouncements
> and decisions that come to grips with the imperious truths of the con-
> temporary world. . . . It must be resolved because we are wrong and
> it is past the time when we should have seen the right. A failure to act
> here is sure to demean our faith, damage the minds and morals of our
> youth, and undermine the integrity of our Christian ethic. . . . Every
> Mormon knows that his Church teaches that the day will come when
> the Negro will be given full fellowship. Surely that day has come.[155]

Before that spring 1967 issue appeared, Udall sent a copy of the letter to McKay, along with a cover letter that stated, "I want you to personally know that I have expressed myself with humility and utter honesty—and always with the prayerful thought that my action will, in the long run, help, not harm, the church."[156]

Shortly after that issue of *Dialogue* was published, several prominent Mormon intellectuals approached Hugh B. Brown, asking that he request of McKay an official declaration of church policy toward blacks. Such a declaration would have clarified the matter for all parties, for most of the decisions that had been made over the past several years, including those relating to Nigeria, had never been publicized; and few church members outside the First Presidency had an accurate understanding of the church policy. After discussing the matter with his counselors, however, McKay "did not feel that anything was to be gained by making an official declaration on the subject," and ruled against publishing one.[157]

A year later, in June 1968, Sterling McMurrin, in an address before the Salt Lake Branch of the NAACP, criticized the continuation of the priesthood ban: "For any church to deny full religious fellowship to an individual on grounds related essentially to his race or color is an almost unbelievable moral deficiency that deserves the most rigorous condemnation."[158] Several days later, McKay met privately with Alvin R. Dyer, recently installed as an unprecedented fifth counselor in the First Presidency, and discussed McMurrin's speech. Dyer reported that "some of the Brethren [General Authorities] are very upset over Dr. McMurrin's attitude toward the Church, and feel that he should be tried for his membership." Dyer, while vehemently opposed to reversing the priesthood ban, nonetheless suggested moderation in handling the McMurrin case. "The Church is under such criticism regarding its stand on the Negroes holding the Priesthood, it would be unwise at this time for the Church to take steps to excommunicate Dr. McMurrin." McKay responded, "Although I was disturbed over Dr. McMurrin's statements and attitude, I made no commitment concerning this matter."[159]

Three weeks later, in June 1968, the McMurrin speech was the focus of a full First Presidency meeting. Joseph Fielding Smith, third counselor, had urged in 1954 that McMurrin be excommunicated for heresy, an initiative that, ironically, had resulted in McKay's private meeting with McMurrin, not only squelching the excommunication effort but also being the setting in which McKay stated his belief that the priesthood ban was a matter of policy and not doctrine. Smith now urged, once again, that McMurrin be excommunicated. Dyer, no less incensed with McMurrin than Smith, continued to urge moderation.

According to the meeting minutes in McKay's diary, "President Dyer ventured the thought that if this were done it could do the Church more harm than good, and perhaps in the eyes of the Lord[,] Sterling McMurrin has already been excommunicated from the Church on the records which are without question of greater potency than those which we keep among men where our methods are less complete and effective." Dyer, however, urged his colleagues in the First Presidency to "state the truth as the Church believes it" and thereby discredit McMurrin's statements. McKay replied, "I think we should be careful as to how we handle this McMurrin case and the Negro question." As he had done a year earlier in response to Stewart Udall, he quashed the proposal to issue an official statement.[160]

A month later, in August 1968, Sterling McMurrin wrote a letter to Llewelyn McKay, a longtime friend and colleague at the University of Utah, and also sent copies to the three other McKay sons.[161] The letter would become the vortex of a whirlwind in the final months of McKay's life: "I am writing this letter, with copies to your brothers Lawrence, Edward, and Robert, to tell you of a conversation with your father in the Spring of 1954.... I recall telling you of this conversation not long after it took place, but I'm interested now in detailing a small part of it in writing, as I believe it is of such importance that it should be a part of your family record."

McMurrin then described that part of his March 1954 conversation with McKay in which the church leader had stated his own belief that the priesthood ban was policy, not doctrine, and therefore susceptible to change. McMurrin added: "I am able to report your father's words with near accuracy because they were strongly impressed upon my memory and because within a few hours after our meeting I made a detailed recording of the entire discussion."[162]

In about 1980, McMurrin dictated a reminiscent analysis of his underlying reason for writing the letter: "I was a little afraid that President McKay might die without coming out with a statement such as he had given me, that this divine curse business was not a doctrine of the Church, and that there is no doctrine whatsoever respecting the Negroes, as he put it, and that the practice of withholding the priesthood would be changed.... I was interested in making at least some kind of a written statement about this statement of President McKay's."[163]

Llewelyn, fascinated by the new information, read the letter to his father and then reported the visit to McMurrin, who made it part of his dictated reminiscence:

> [Llewelyn] said, "Father was very lucid, very interested and very much aware. He was in good shape." Apparently, from what Llewelyn has said, President McKay [ninety-five years old] was somewhat disoriented on some days, but on other days and at other times, he was in very good mental shape, and he assured me that that was the case on this occasion. He said, "I read the letter to him, and when I got through, he said, 'That is exactly what happened, and that is exactly what I said.'"[164]

Llewelyn's brother, Edward, echoed his statement when he wrote a letter responding to McMurrin's letter: "In my discussions with father, I have gathered the same impression as you. He is much more liberal on this subject than many of the brethren."[165]

McMurrin had not intended that his letter be publicized. Sometime later, however, one of his former students, Stephen Taggart, got wind of it. Taggart was then a graduate student at Cornell University, working on a Ph.D. in sociology. He was writing a paper on what he believed to be the Missouri origins of the church position on blacks, which he had decided to research when he heard McMurrin's 1968 speech to the NAACP chapter. He came to McMurrin with a draft manuscript and asked about McMurrin's 1954 meeting with McKay. McMurrin told him of his recent letter to Llewelyn McKay: "He wanted to put it in his book. I told him that

I thought it was, as far as I was concerned, OK, but I would prefer that he check it all out with Llewelyn McKay. And he did check it out with Llewelyn, and Llewelyn confirmed the matter just as I have described it here, and Taggart put it in the book, with footnotes to the effect that he had checked it out with Llewelyn McKay, and Llewelyn had confirmed it."[166]

By late 1969, a copy of Taggart's manuscript, which now included McMurrin's letter to Llewelyn McKay, came into the possession of Hugh B. Brown, first counselor in the First Presidency.[167] Remarkably, Brown had been completely unaware of McKay's earlier statement to McMurrin, in spite of having been a member of the First Presidency for eight years. Astounded by the news, Brown, who had long advocated reversing the priesthood ban, gave a copy of Taggart's manuscript to Lawrence McKay, the eldest of McKay's four sons, and suggested that he take up the matter with his father. Lawrence complied with Brown's request, in the process initiating an unprecedented storm of controversy that pitted some of the church's top leaders against each other for the remaining months of McKay's life, yet which remained largely unknown to anyone else.

On September 10, 1969, Lawrence and Llewelyn McKay visited their father to discuss Taggart's manuscript and its possible implications. Fatefully, as they entered their father's apartment they encountered Alvin R. Dyer, who had escorted a visitor there. They asked that Dyer stay. He readily agreed and described the meeting in his diary:

> We sat in the President's office, the President seeming quite alert and roused for the discussion to follow. Lawrence explained that on the basis of his father's statement to Sterling McMurrin some time ago, that the withholding of the Priesthood from the Negro by the Church was a practice and not a doctrine. An article had been written for "Dialogue Magazine" by a Brother Taggart, who is the son of the President of Utah State University, which had received more or less an endorsement by Llewelyn based upon the reported interview which President McKay had had with Sterling McMurrin. This article seemed, in Lawrence McKay's mind, to bring the whole Negro question regarding the right to hold the Priesthood into focus, and that if this truly was a practice and not a doctrine, as Sterling McMurrin had inferred from President McKay's statement to him, then why was this not the time to drop the practice. He asked his father if this was not perhaps the time to announce that the Negro could be given the Priesthood, which he alone could announce, and to do so now voluntarily rather than to be pressured into it later.[168]

Dyer, who had not yet seen Taggart's manuscript and who was adamantly opposed to a reversal of the priesthood ban, forcefully entered the conversation at this point, feeling that it was "my responsibility to make some comments concerning this vital matter." He thereupon reiterated prior explanations of the ban, including the "curse of Cain" that McKay seemingly had abandoned years earlier. After completing his remarks, Dyer asked Lawrence for a copy of Taggart's manuscript, saying, "I would be pleased to study it and make a report to the President. President McKay asked that I do this. Lawrence then stood up and said, 'Perhaps, father, we had better leave this with you and you can think about it.'"[169]

A week later, Dyer met with three other counselors in the First Presidency: Brown, Tanner, and Smith. McKay, who had turned ninety-six earlier that month, was unable to attend because of failing health. In briefing the other counselors concerning the prior week's meeting with McKay's sons, Dyer denounced Taggart's article, saying that he "considered it one of the most vicious, untrue articles that has ever been written about the Church." Dyer said that he intended to continue to study the article, and would show "what the true facts are and give the references."[170]

The following week, McKay's counselors met with him and further discussed the Taggart paper. Their central concern was Taggart's inclusion of McMurrin's description of McKay's beliefs. Two of the counselors, Dyer and Joseph Fielding Smith, questioned McMurrin's veracity. Tanner, however, countered that he had received a letter from a man whose credibility he accepted, which "mentions that in conversing with President George Albert Smith's son recently he stated that President Smith had said that categorically the Church's position on the negro question was one of custom and not of revelation."[171] Joseph Fielding Smith countered, "He is wrong on that," without offering supporting evidence. McKay had said nothing up to that point; but although he was weak, he was "very lucid" that morning. "The brethren asked me if I wanted to make any ruling on the matter and I answered that I did not want to make any statement on the question this morning."[172] It was the last time McKay discussed the subject in a First Presidency meeting.

The debate now shifted from McKay back to the members of his inner circle. Two weeks after the First Presidency meeting, on October 8, 1969, Dyer met privately with Brown to discuss Taggart's article and its implications. According to Dyer's diary, both men had studied Taggart's article and had come to opposite conclusions. Brown maintained, "We should give the Negro the Priesthood, that we had only one scripture in Abraham that suggested otherwise." Dyer countered that the priesthood ban was doctrinal, and thus immutable, and invoked other writings

of Joseph Smith to give scriptural support to his position, apparently unaware that
blacks had been ordained under Smith and that the ban had begun with Smith's
successor, Brigham Young.

Brown then referred to the purported statement of George Albert Smith,
McKay's predecessor, that withholding the priesthood from blacks was a practice.
"Yes," Dyer replied, "but a practice based upon principles that have been revealed
from the Lord." Brown, to whom Dyer was subordinate in the First Presidency hierarchy, saw the futility of further verbal sparring and ended the discussion by saying, "We will wait and see what the next President of the Church will do." As an
aside in his diary, Dyer wrote that Brown "had tried twice of late to get President
McKay to withdraw the withholding of the Priesthood from the Negro, but President McKay had refused to move on it."[173]

Brown remained convinced that the priesthood ban could be reversed administratively, in spite of McKay's unwavering insistence that such change could occur
only by revelation and his consistent application of the ban in cases of known black
ancestry. Nonetheless, he made no further attempt to persuade McKay. For his
part, Dyer, in spite of his protestations, was now aware of the fact that there was
strong evidence that McMurrin's account was accurate. He did not understand
McKay's position and thus feared that the policy could, indeed, be changed by simple administrative action. Subordinate to Brown, Dyer moved to enlist a powerful
ally, Harold B. Lee, in an attempt to block such action.

Harold B. Lee was, at this time, acting president of the Quorum of the Twelve,
due to the fact that the president of the Quorum, Joseph Fielding Smith, had
joined the First Presidency in October 1965. By precedent established a century earlier, Smith would become president at McKay's death, and Lee would in turn succeed Smith. Smith was ninety-three years old and in fragile health by the time
McKay died in 1970, so it was already apparent in the final months of McKay's life
that Smith would cede much of the day-to-day supervision of the church to Lee, a
fact not lost on senior church officers. Furthermore, while Smith and Lee were currently subordinate to Brown in the church hierarchy, the situation would immediately be reversed at McKay's death: The entire First Presidency would temporarily
be dissolved, Brown would revert to a junior position of seniority within the Quorum of the Twelve, and Smith and Lee would hold the highest positions within the
hierarchy. Thus, Lee had enormous influence within the hierarchy in the final
months of McKay's life, and his own strong feelings that the priesthood ban should
not be reversed made him a logical ally for Dyer. Indeed, only two weeks after
the Brown-Dyer meeting, Lee told BYU President Ernest L. Wilkinson in late
October that he "would not consent to any change of policy as respects the Negro
problem."[174]

Lee took the unprecedented and, in some respects, presumptuous, action of beginning to draft a First Presidency statement that would block any attempts to modify the policy.[175] The statement went through several drafts,[176] finally including language insisted on by Brown that strongly endorsed civil rights at the same time that it closed the door on a reversal of the priesthood ban.[177] By the time the statement was finalized, McKay's condition had deteriorated to the point where he was unable to sign it. It carried the signatures only of Brown and Tanner, the highest ranking of the five First Presidency counselors.

The eighty-six-year-old Brown, however, signed only under great pressure, as related by his grandson: "[Grandfather] suffered from advanced age and the late stages of Parkinson's disease and was ill with the Asian flu. With Grandfather in this condition, Elder Lee brought tremendous pressure to bear upon him, arguing that with President McKay incapacitated Grandfather was obliged to join the consensus within the Quorum of the Twelve. Grandfather, deeply ill, wept as he related this story to me just before he signed the statement that bore his and President Tanner's names."[178]

The First Presidency statement was sent to all local church leaders, many of whom read it to their congregations. It began by acknowledging the diversity of opinions that had been circulating throughout the church, reaffirmed in strong language the pro-civil rights statement of 1963, and finally stated unequivocally that the priesthood ban would not, and could not be changed except by revelation to the church president, alone:

> In view of confusion that has arisen, it was decided at a meeting of the First Presidency and the Quorum of the Twelve to restate the position of the Church with regard to the Negro both in society and in the Church.... We believe the Negro, as well as those of other races, should have his full Constitutional privileges as a member of society, and we hope that members of the Church everywhere will do their part as citizens to see that these rights are held inviolate. Each citizen must have equal opportunities and protection under the law with reference to civil rights.... From the beginning of this dispensation, Joseph Smith and all succeeding presidents of the Church have taught that Negroes, while spirit children of a common Father, and the progeny of our earthly parents Adam and Eve, were not yet to receive the priesthood, for reasons which we believe are known to God, but which He has not made fully known to man.... Until God reveals His will in this matter, to him whom we sustain as a prophet, we are bound by that same will. Priesthood, when it is conferred on any man comes as a blessing from God, not of men.[179]

Even though the statement closed the door on an imminent change of the policy, it differed from earlier statements in making no mention of a "divine curse" and in avoiding the use of the term "doctrine." Although the statement was dated December 15, 1969, its release to church leaders was delayed for over a week and then was jarred loose only by external forces. Almost simultaneously, on Christmas Day, an article in the *San Francisco Chronicle* brought the Mormon ban back into the center of the limelight. *Chronicle* reporter Lester Kinsolving quoted Brown as saying that the church's priesthood ban "will change in the not too distant future" and that it would occur "in the ordinary evolution of things as we go along, since human rights are basic to the church."[180] The details of how Brown made this statement—whether Kinsolving approached him or whether Brown invited such an opportunity through an intermediary—are not known; but he was apparently acting out of frustration and grief over the First Presidency statement. On the same day the article appeared, he telephoned Sterling McMurrin "and told me that he wanted me to know that he signed this document under great pressure."[181]

The day after Christmas, Dyer met with McKay and informed him of the *Chronicle* article. Dyer had spoken over the phone with Tanner, who was vacationing, and the two were in agreement that the First Presidency statement, which had been intended only for internal dissemination, should be published in order to "counteract the confusion and misunderstanding that had developed" because of Brown's statements.[182] During the meeting on December 26, McKay initially had approved its publication in principle, stating that "the whole article was a fine statement and should be given to the press," without indicating when. Lee, however, was still hesitant to make it public. After the meeting with McKay, Petersen called Dyer and relayed Lee's suggestion that Dyer delay its publication yet again. Dyer recorded Lee's motives—keenly attuned to the public relations effect—in his diary: "Brother Lee was fully aware of what had developed and said that it was not so much a matter of publishing it.... It was a matter of timing. He wondered if, by withholding it at the present time, it would lessen the possibility of further breach in the impression that President Brown had given to the members of the Church by his reported statements. He also felt that inasmuch as the Quorum of the Twelve had thought that the article should not go to the press in general, that perhaps it should be withheld until it could be discussed further."[183] Dyer agreed.

This consensus was compromised by word that *New York Times* reporter Wallace Turner had obtained a copy and planned to print it. Church leaders quickly preempted Turner and published it in *Church News*, a weekly insert in the church-owned *Deseret News*, on January 10, 1970.

Eight days later, McKay died and the First Presidency automatically dissolved. Joseph Fielding Smith succeeded McKay as church president, with Harold B. Lee as his first counselor and N. Eldon Tanner as his second. Hugh B. Brown reverted to his position in the Quorum of the Twelve, the first time since the death of Brigham Young in 1877 that a counselor in the First Presidency had not been retained by a succeeding church president.

Neither Joseph Fielding Smith nor Harold B. Lee, who succeeded Smith as president, altered the priesthood ban. Lee died in December 1973, and was succeeded by Spencer W. Kimball, a seventy-eight-year-old apostle who had sat without speaking through the 1965 meeting of the First Presidency and Twelve. On June 8, 1978, President Kimball announced a revelation that extended the priesthood to all worthy males.[184]

In the years since 1978, many in the church have supposed that Kimball received the revelation because he asked the Lord, whereas his predecessors, including McKay, did not ask. This perception was reinforced by McKay's discretion in discussing the issue with only his closest associates. Indeed, as is apparent from the flurry of activity late in 1969, he declined to discuss parts of it even with fellow General Authorities, for reasons that he never made apparent either publicly or privately. Yet in the decades following his death, it has gradually become apparent that he wrestled with the subject for years and years, making it a matter of intense prayer on numerous occasions.

His earliest inquiry, as far as we have record, was referred to earlier in this chapter and occurred in 1954, shortly after his return from South Africa. Other inquiries followed, though generally the dates are not known. On one occasion his daughter-in-law, Mildred Calderwood McKay, who served on the general board of the Primary, the church auxiliary for children, expressed her anguish that black male children, who commingled with white children during their Primary years (through age twelve), were excluded from the Aaronic Priesthood when they turned twelve. "Can't they be ordained also?" she asked. He replied sadly, "No." "Then I think it is time for a new revelation." He answered, "So do I."[185]

Marion D. Hanks, a General Authority called by McKay in 1953, spoke with McKay in the late 1960s prior to traveling to Vietnam to visit LDS servicemen. Hanks related an incident from a prior trip to Vietnam, in which he had comforted a wounded black LDS soldier. As he told the story, McKay began to weep. Referring to the priesthood ban, McKay said, "I have prayed and prayed and prayed, but there has been no answer."[186]

Lola Gygi Timmins, a secretary in McKay's office from 1960 to 1968, recalled a day when he returned from a meeting with the First Presidency and Quorum of the Twelve in the Temple. The subject had come up in several such meetings; and obviously venting some private feelings, he told the secretaries in his reception room that he had inquired of the Lord several times on the matter, and that the answer was, "Not yet."[187]

But the most remarkable account came from Richard Jackson, an architect who served in the Church Building Department from 1968 through the time of McKay's death in 1970:

> I remember one day that President McKay came into the office. We could see that he was very much distressed. He said, "I've had it! I'm not going to do it again!" Somebody said, "What?" He said, "Well, I'm badgered constantly about giving the priesthood to the Negro. I've inquired of the Lord repeatedly. The last time I did it was late last night. I was told, with no discussion, not to bring the subject up with the Lord again; that the time will come, but it will not be my time, and to leave the subject alone." We were all, of course, a little dumb-struck. I don't think it has ever been written that that happened.... I've never told anybody about that. I can still see him coming in with a bit of a distraught appearance, which was unusual for President McKay. He always appeared as if he had everything under control.[188]

This uncharacteristic outburst in the presence of an astonished church architect highlights the contrast between two strands in McKay's thought that are, by today's standard, inseparably joined: civil rights for blacks and priesthood ordination for black men. The blurring, combined with McKay's own reticence, means that this difference has not been understood until now. By today's standards, David O. McKay's views on civil rights are jolting; yet in the context of his own time and place, his views were mainstream. He definitely was not "progressive" on the issue, even if measured by the low standards that would have earned such a label during his lifetime. On the one hand, he never advocated legislation or behavior that would worsen the status of blacks within the United States; indeed, his apparent desire was to preserve the legal status quo. Yet he also never advocated legal remedies to segregation and discrimination. He was, at best, a very conservative moderate.

He made a conscious decision not to enter the fray of the emerging civil rights movement that came of age during his presidency. On several occasions, most frequently at the behest of Hugh B. Brown, he had opportunities to reverse the church's long-standing legacy of racial discrimination. Yet each time he chose to turn away. Even the "official statement" on civil rights of 1963, which McKay did not intend to become official, was approved grudgingly and only in the face of the less favorable alternative of the NAACP's picketing general conference.

Given McKay's enormous moral stature, which particularly outside of Mormonism overshadowed that of his immediate predecessors, a move toward civil rights would have carried more than symbolic meaning. By sidestepping the issue, McKay missed an opportunity to send a strong signal to the entire church membership that change was in the wind—even to his conservative fellow General Authorities who, on other occasions and other issues, abandoned their opposition to McKay's initiatives once he made it clear that he spoke as the prophet.

In this context, his actions on the second strand—the ban on priesthood ordination—are all the more startling. He first softened the ban around the edges, intervening to extend priesthood blessings to individuals where he could, and repeatedly pleading with the Lord for a complete reversal. This record is nothing short of remarkable. Surrounded by voices that argued strongly in favor of maintaining the ban, save for the lone vision and voice of Hugh B. Brown, he nonetheless was willing to move in a different direction. On uncounted occasions, he sought unsuccessfully to call down the revelation that would have changed the ban, a revelation that came to one of his successors eight years after his death. This largely undocumented and almost wholly unknown struggle means that it is no stretch to assert that David O. McKay built the foundation upon which the revelation to Spencer W. Kimball rests.

5

ECUMENICAL
OUTREACH

Latter-day Saints have a long history of not getting along with others, and one explanation goes straight to the church's origin, Joseph Smith's "First Vision." Confused by the conflicting claims of various religions in western New York State where he resided, he asked the Lord in the vision which of them he should join. "I was answered that I must join none of them, for they were all wrong; and the Personage who addressed me said that all their creeds were an abomination in his sight; that those professors were all corrupt; that: 'they draw near to me with their lips, but their hearts are far from me, they teach for doctrines the commandments of men, having a form of godliness, but they deny the power thereof.'"[1]

Such a belief does not predispose to ecumenical feelings and, indeed, can easily sow the seeds of distrust and enmity among other faiths. Strained relationships between Latter-day Saints and others for more than a century after the founding of the church, which at one point triggered military action by the U.S. Army, attest to the difficulty of building friendships when one party considers the other to occupy an inferior position before God.

David O. McKay never soft-pedaled the claims of the church over which he presided. Writing in the *Improvement Era,* the church's official magazine, when he had been church president for five and a half years, he asked his readers,

> If at this moment each one of you were asked to state in one sentence or phrase the most distinguishing feature of the Church of Jesus Christ of Latter-day Saints, what would be your answer? Mine would be this:
>
> "Divine authority by direct revelation."
>
> There are those who claim authority through historical descent, others from the scriptures, but this Church stands out as making the distinctive claim that the authority of the priesthood has come directly from God the Father and the Son, by revelation to Joseph Smith.[2]

Yet in spite of reaffirming this message throughout his career and presiding over a far more successful proselytizing effort than any of his predecessors, McKay reached out to the non-Mormon world with unprecedented success, winning the admiration and friendship of religious and secular leaders throughout the world. Sterling McMurrin, a Mormon educator of national stature who served as U.S. Commissioner of Education in the administration of John F. Kennedy, paid private tribute to McKay on his ninetieth birthday:

> I am very sure that the most important thing that [the biographers and historians] will write about your large impact on your people is that it was during the period of your presidency and under the inspiration of your ideal and will that the Church overcame that measure of provincialism that was an inevitable quality of its early years and achieved sure grounds for the universality, inclusiveness, world mindedness, and ecumenical quality that must be its ultimate character. The difference that you have made in the life of the Church and the countless implications of that difference will quite surely be a major chapter in the histories of the future.[3]

Six years later, following McKay's death at the age of ninety-six, *Time* echoed McMurrin's sentiments in its eulogy:

> McKay was an affable new image of Mormonism to a world that had previously seen the Mormon leaders as dour, dark-suited figures. He was perhaps the first Mormon president to treat non-Mormons as generously as members of his own faith.... In his own generous, enthusiastic way, McKay had expanded his Church's horizons and involvement far beyond the abilities of any successor to contract them. If he had not completely destroyed Mormon exclusivism, he has certainly tempered it with his own remarkable vision of a much wider, friendlier world.[4]

Provincial thinking was the norm in nineteenth-century Utah. Having been driven from gathering places in Ohio, Missouri, and Illinois, the Latter-day Saints sought what they hoped would be lasting refuge within the Great Basin. Although their geographical isolation effectively lasted only a decade, the provincial mindset persisted for decades and, indeed, still persists among many Utahns today. McKay, reared in the small, agrarian Mormon village of Huntsville, had ample access to such thinking during his childhood. His schooling in the neighboring city of Ogden, however, began the process of transformation. Ogden was a railroad city, proximate to Promontory Summit where the Union Pacific and Central Pacific tracks were fused to complete the transcontinental railroad in 1869. With the railroad came a stream of diverse, non-Mormon émigrés whose demographics were unique within Utah.

Upon graduating from the Weber Academy in Ogden (later Weber State University) and the University of Utah, McKay embarked on the first of three prolonged international forays that gave him an exposure to the world unprecedented among church presidents. In 1897 he went to Scotland on a two-year proselytizing mission, rubbing shoulders along the way with the members of various Protestant churches. Two decades later he became the first General Authority to circle the globe as he toured the church's foreign missions. He visited many South Pacific, Asian, and Middle Eastern countries where Christianity was in the minority; and the extensive diary he kept documents his exposure to and appreciation of Eastern religions, Islam, and Judaism in their indigenous settings.

Two years after returning from this year-long global circumnavigation, he was appointed president of the European Mission, the highest-ranking LDS Church office in Europe. Although he was headquartered in England, where he also presided over the British Mission, his periodic trips to the Continent gave him first-hand experience with European countries, cultures, and religions far exceeding that of any previous church president. Reflecting on this experience many years later, he told a reporter from *Time*, "There is genuine affection between members of the Church and non-members. How did it come about? By getting to know and understand each other better. When you get to know a fellow, chances are you'll get to like him too."[5]

OUTREACH TO PROTESTANT DENOMINATIONS

An incident that occurred shortly after McKay became church president in 1951 illustrates the unprecedented inclusiveness of his worldview. On the afternoon of his seventy-eighth birthday, when he was recovering from gastritis, he received an unannounced visit from Episcopal Bishop Arthur W. Moulton.[6] Finding that he was taking a nap, Moulton, who was also seventy-eight, left a brief handwritten note on his business card wishing him a happy birthday. When McKay awoke and read the card he said to his wife, "I must dress and repay the Reverend's visit." He drove himself to Moulton's apartment building, climbed four flights of stairs, and knocked on the door. "When he came in and saw me standing there," McKay wrote in his diary, "his face lighted up, and he said: 'President McKay—why President McKay! This is the most wonderful thing that has ever happened to me—Why it's wonderful!! Come in, come in—sit down.'" McKay responded,

> Reverend Moulton the doctors were probably right when they told me
> that I should take a rest and see no more visitors for the day, and my

son was undoubtedly right when he explained to you when you called that I was under doctors [*sic*] orders to see no more visitors for the day, but it is *not* right for me to let your gracious, considerate call go unheeded, so I am here to pay my respects to you.

After visiting for a few minutes, McKay excused himself to return home. "As I picked up my hat to leave the Reverend came over to me, put his hands upon my shoulders, bowed his head, and gave me a blessing. I reciprocated by giving him a blessing." To appreciate the significance of this exchange, it is necessary to understand that the LDS Church does not recognize the sacraments of any other church. For an LDS church president to consent to be the recipient of such a blessing was extraordinary—perhaps unique in all of LDS history. McKay concluded his diary entry by writing, "I left the Reverend feeling satisfied that I had done the right thing by repaying his visit of this afternoon, and that much good would result from the contact we had with each other this day."[7]

McKay's relationships with other local Protestant churches were similarly affable. The minister of the First Methodist Church of Salt Lake City wrote to McKay in tribute: "Someone put it so well when they said, 'The man who writes upon the life of a community with a pen of service will never be forgotten.' This is so true of your splendid service to church and community, my good friend, that I want to share the thought with you. The honors which have come to you through the years speak well of this, and I trust the good Lord will spare you for many more years of service in His kingdom."[8]

In the same vein, the minister of Trinity Presbyterian Church of Ogden, responding to an LDS financial contribution that allowed the completion of a church remodeling project, wrote:

You are a mountain peak among men! How different perhaps would the history of the LDS Church be today and in the future if God had not raised you up and blessed the church through you as President. I search for new ways to express my deep, abiding and heartfelt gratitude for your letter, which touched my heartstrings as few letters have done in my twenty-two years in the ministry; and, I have received my full share of correspondence both great and small.... Your letter with the generous check enclosed came last Saturday. I announced it from my pulpit to the congregation. You could have cut with a knife the hushed awe. After the service of worship every person present had something to say each to the other and to me about the magnanimous gift and the spirit in which it was given.... This I shall never forget even if I live as long as some of the patriarchs of the Old Testament days![9]

McKay's benevolent influence among non-Mormons was not restricted to clergymen, extending at times even to children, as related by Reverend A. Cadman Garretson, a Presbyterian minister, during a tribute dinner to McKay:

> In a Presbyterian Church in Salt Lake City about a month ago, this incident really happened. I have been just busting to tell it to an audience or group of this kind. I give it to you as it was told to me. The Minister was visiting the children's Sunday School classes, and, having learned of the virtues of child participation, he asked the children to suggest things to thank God for in the prayer which he was about to lead. A small boy was first. "All right, Johnny," he said, "what do you think we should thank God for?" And Johnny said, "The sunshine." A girl held up her hand. "And what do you think we should thank God for, Mary?" "For the rain drops." And a third little youngster or girl held up her hand, and he said, "All right, and what do you think we should thank God for?" She said very clearly, "I think we should thank God for David O. McKay." Friends, in many ways the sentiment that that little girl expressed is just the reason for our being here today.[10]

OUTREACH TO THE JEWISH COMMUNITY

Latter-day Saints claim a special relationship to the Jews. This stems in large part from the narrative of the *Book of Mormon,* in which colonizers from the House of Israel migrated from Jerusalem to the New World and established the indigenous civilizations encountered by the Europeans. Indeed, modern Latter-day Saints consider themselves either natural or "adopted" members of the House of Israel.[11] McKay, because of his world tour in 1920–21, viewed that relationship on an even more personal level, as he recounted to his fellow General Authorities several decades later:

> I referred to a statement made by my father when I was a boy in my teens that the prophecy in the *Book of Mormon* that the Jews would return to the Holy Land would be fulfilled, and to a feeling that I had as a boy with regard to it. I remember saying (knowing in a general way of the conditions of the Holy Land, and the seeming impossibility of the fulfillment of that prophecy) to myself "if I live to see the fulfillment of that prophecy, I shall know that Joseph Smith is a prophet."
>
> I then called attention to the fact that on November 22, 1921, Elder Hugh J. Cannon and I stood in the city of Jerusalem, and witnessed the fulfillment of that prophecy, as on that day General

Allenby's proclamation that Jerusalem was to become a state for the
return of the Jews under the protection of the British government, was
issued.[12]

A short time later, in 1952, McKay acted on behalf of the church to purchase
$5,000 of Israel bonds. "This is done," he wrote, "merely to show our sympathy
with the effort being made to establish the Jews in their homeland."[13] Later, in connection with the 125th anniversary of the founding of the LDS Church, two prominent American Jewish leaders paid tribute to McKay and his benevolent relationship with the Jewish community. Dr. Israel Goldstein, president of the American
Jewish Congress, wrote: "I am happy to send you the April 25 issue of *Congress
Weekly*, a publication of the American Jewish Congress. The issue contains an editorial saluting the 125th anniversary of the Mormon Church and expresses the
heartfelt appreciation and admiration of the Jewish community for the Mormon
Church's high sense of dedication, and the aid and comfort which it has steadfastly
given the Jewish community."[14]

Rose L. Halprin, acting chairman for the Jewish Agency for Palestine, wrote
in a similar vein,

> We shall always remember that Orson Hyde, at the bidding of Joseph
> Smith, founder of the Mormon Church, undertook as early as 1840 a
> trip to the Holy Land, consulting, en route, leading figures of his day
> on the best means of bringing about the restoration of the Jewish
> people to Palestine. In Jerusalem he prayed to the Lord to "consti-
> tute her people as a distinct nation and government." Just a little over
> a century later, Zion was indeed restored. This early Mormon support
> of Jewish statehood helped make world public opinion more recep-
> tive to subsequent efforts by the Zionist movement. This, and the
> Mormons' universal dedication to the commonweal, to equity and
> justice generally, shall always be remembered by us with deep appre-
> ciation.[15]

Joseph Rosenblatt, a Jewish industrialist and Salt Lake City resident, gave elo-
quent tribute to McKay's inclusive spirit:

> We pay honor to David O. McKay—not that his theology is akin to
> ours, but really rather that it is not, for I think that we know him best
> as the ideal of what we look for in the great Americans. . . . In his very
> being and every deed we see in him the genius for freedom under law,
> the conviction that democracy is the highest expression of a dignified
> social order. We see every day his talent for harmonizing diversities and
> the inspired leadership which brings and secures enrichment from

varied cultural sources as he has brought them together from every
people, every land, every generation.[16]

RELATIONSHIP WITH ROMAN CATHOLICISM

The apex of McKay's relationship with the non-Mormon religious community
occurred in his ninetieth year, when Rosenblatt spearheaded a banquet in his
honor. *Time* reported the event:

> Last week in Salt Lake City, nearly 500 business and civic leaders, rep-
> resenting Judaism and a dozen Christian churches, gathered at a tes-
> timonial banquet honoring the ninth man in Mormon history to be
> in direct communication with God. . . . There could be no question-
> ing the sincerity of the praise for "David O." Joseph Rosenblatt, a
> Jew and president of the Eimco Corp., asked: "Does anyone know of
> any man who has lived with greater faith or purpose, and obedience
> to the exhortation of the Prophet Micah to do justly, to love mercy,
> to walk humbly with God?" A Catholic, President J. P. O'Keefe of Salt
> Lake City's Chamber of Commerce said: "All of us have been keenly
> aware of the advantages of living in Utah. And almost all these advan-
> tages can be attributed to the leadership of President McKay."[17]

Against a backdrop of such unqualified praise, McKay's uneven relationship
with Roman Catholicism stands in stark contrast. The roots of this relationship, as
with those of the more favorable Mormon-Judaic one, appear to extend to the
Book of Mormon, published in 1830. The book's first chronicler, prophet-leader
Nephi, saw in a vision of the future "a church which is most abominable above all
other churches," a church characterized by gold, silver, silks, scarlets, fine-twined
linen and precious clothing.[18] This church, "which is the mother of harlots," "sat
upon many waters; and she had dominion over all the earth, among all nations, kin-
dreds, tongues, and people."[19] The church was not named in the *Book of Mormon;*
but the concurrent anti-Catholic movement in western New York, where Joseph
Smith lived at the time the book was published, facilitated the linkage for those who
were inclined to make it. Indeed, one of the influential books chronicling that
movement employed the exact words of the *Book of Mormon,* "the Mother of Harlots," in describing the Roman Catholic Church.[20]

McKay never explicitly linked the Roman Catholic Church to these passages,
although one of his colleagues eventually did, much to McKay's distress. Nonetheless, he harbored deep personal distrust of Roman Catholicism. In 1830, Catholicism had been a minority movement in America, numbering only 318,000 (3 percent of the U.S. population). It mushroomed to over 20,000,000 (19 percent) by

the early 1920s.[21] While McKay's exposure to Roman Catholicism had been minimal in Utah, his appointment as president of the European Mission sent him into countries where it was the dominant church and where most Mormons were converts from Catholicism. In 1923 he visited Liège, Belgium, and wrote in his diary: "A Catholic Church celebration was held last night [Saturday]—People drinking and carousing until 6:30 this morning. O what a Godless farce that organization is!"[22]

As the presiding officer over all of the church's European missions, he also saw that the most successful proselytizing efforts spanning nearly a century had come from Protestant Great Britain, Scandinavia, Germany, and Switzerland, whose thousands of nineteenth-century converts, including his own grandparents, comprised the majority of territorial Utah's population. In contrast, proselytizing efforts to predominantly Roman Catholic countries had been limited—primarily to France, Belgium, and Italy—and had generally been unsuccessful. Missions to the British Isles (although not to Catholic Ireland), Scandinavia, Switzerland, and Germany operated continuously after their respective foundings between 1837 and 1854, while those to France, Belgium, and Italy, opened in 1850, were closed within fourteen years and not reopened until the twentieth century.[23]

Regardless of the attitudes McKay and his colleagues may have maintained in private, Mormon–Catholic relations within Utah had generally been cordial since the pioneer era, when Brigham Young intervened on behalf of Father Edward Kelly to resolve a disputed title to Catholic Church property in Salt Lake City.[24] Working from the unusual position of a minority church in heavily Mormon Utah, the Catholics assumed a live-and-let-live position that their Mormon neighbors reciprocated, at least as long as there was no apparent attempt by the Catholics to raid Mormon flocks.

In 1930, the centenary of the founding of Mormonism, the Catholics leased airtime on Sunday evenings on KSL, the Mormon Church-owned radio station, for a series of addresses by Catholic Bishop Duane Hunt in an attempt to shore up the faith of the Catholic minority. While not intended either as an assault on Mormonism or an attempt to lure Mormons to the Catholic fold, Hunt's addresses were not well received in some Mormon quarters. Nonetheless, the Catholics took the criticism in stride, the diocesan newspaper reporting that the Mormons "have done a good deal of anti-Catholic talking over the radio in recent months, but on the whole they are less intolerant than strongly Protestant communities."[25]

Equilibrium persisted over most of the next two decades, although Bishop Hunt privately expressed concerns over what he perceived as the weakening position of his church. Writing to a colleague in Kentucky in 1946, he enclosed a news clipping stating that 74 percent of Utah's population was LDS. Hunt complained:

"Concerning the growing Mormon domination in Utah, about which I tried to warn the Bishops last year, the enclosed is interesting. It is a copy of an item of news which appeared in the Salt Lake City *Tribune,* Tuesday morning, November 26. It shows that within this century the situation in Salt Lake City has completely changed, and in the wrong direction."[26]

The public equilibrium was upset one year later. In January 1948, J. Reuben Clark Jr., first counselor in the First Presidency and de facto president due to the failing health of Church President George Albert Smith, began a series of Sunday night radio addresses on KSL, in which he affirmed the core tenets of Mormon doctrine. At the same time, in a commendable gesture, the station made Sunday night airtime available to Bishop Hunt. Hunt did what Clark did: reaffirm the core beliefs of his own church. Clark, however, misinterpreted Hunt's addresses on the primacy of the Pope and the Holy See in Rome as an assault on Mormonism and wrote in his diary, "Bishop Hunt seemed to have declared war."[27] But it was Clark who waged the war. Speaking to his Catholic friend John Fitzpatrick, publisher of the *Salt Lake Tribune* and one of Utah's most prominent lay Catholics, he asked a rhetorical question: "What might be the situation if we went to Rome and applied for time over the Vatican station and they gave us the time for nothing...and then we proceeded to lambast the Catholic Church over their own station on the time which they had given us?"[28]

The printed texts of Hunt's radio addresses strongly belie Clark's charges. While he sometimes addressed doctrines over which Mormons and Catholics disagree, like the apostolic continuity of the Catholic Church, he did so as parts of a series of sermons on basic Catholic teachings, never as an isolated jab at Mormonism and never with any reference to Mormon teachings at all.[29] Thus, his astonishment was genuine when Fitzpatrick told him about Clark's indictment. "Oh, God forbid," Hunt exclaimed. "Do you mean that?"[30]

Clark was unimpressed by Hunt's response; and having concluded that Hunt had, indeed, declared theological war upon the Mormons, he responded in his own radio addresses with direct attacks on core Catholic beliefs. He also began to write an anti-Catholic polemic that he included as a 220-page appendix in a book containing the radio addresses, which was published the following year.[31] Furthermore, he made no secret of his antagonism toward the Catholic Church. Monsignor Jerome Stoffel, who occasionally substituted for Hunt in giving the radio addresses, was moved from the cramped studio normally used by Hunt to the spacious one used by Clark, while the station was doing some remodeling. After one address, he was walking out of the studio just as Clark was entering it to give his own address. Clark glowered at him, Stoffel recalled, as if to say, "What in the hell are you doing in my studio?"[32]

McKay was, at this time, second counselor in the First Presidency, and thus sub-ordinate to Clark. Although he was not yet directly involved in the Clark-Hunt dis-pute, he clearly sided with Clark. Following a meeting with a group of stake pres-idents in Ogden early in 1949, he wrote, "Another question that came up was the seeming determination of the Catholics to convert as many Mormons here in the West as they possibly can. There is no doubt but that there is an organized cam-paign on in this respect."[33]

Only two weeks later, he came into direct contact with Bishop Hunt over another matter, and its affable resolution was typical of McKay's mixed feelings of genuine benevolence and cooperation toward individual Roman Catholics, whether laity or clergy, but distrust and even animosity toward the church to which they belonged. At issue was an editorial in the *Salt Lake Tribune* pertaining to the high divorce rate in Utah. A Mormon friend of McKay was disturbed over the edi-torial, feeling that it was unfairly—albeit only indirectly—critical of the LDS Church. He voiced his concerns to Hunt who, feeling somehow implicated in the editorial, called McKay to clarify the situation. McKay assured him that he did not share his friend's feeling and affirmed that he felt the newspaper had the right to publish any facts and "to comment on anything that is News." Appreciative of the response, "Bishop Hunt then said he thought when anything like this comes up that it is better to get in touch directly; that he did not want any misunderstand-ing."[34]

In spite of the good personal feelings resulting from that exchange, McKay sin-gled out Hunt's institution several months later when, in a meeting with local LDS Church leaders in Idaho, he "admonished them to be on their guard against the attempted inroads of the Catholic Church."[35]

A month later, in August 1949, a pamphlet written for Utah Catholics and in-tended to raise money for underfunded Utah parishes, inadvertently caused a skir-mish that escalated nearly into theological warfare. The pamphlet, written by Rev. Leo J. Steck, Hunt's assistant, documented the impoverished condition of the Catholic Church in many areas of Utah. Only fifty-two priests were assigned to Utah, an area of nearly 85,000 square miles, six of the state's twenty-nine counties had only one priest, and sixteen counties were completely without the services of a priest. Steck requested donations to support the training of additional priests and the construction of more parochial schools (the state had only three) and churches. He also called for a Catholic center in Salt Lake City, as there was no adequate place for Catholic youth to gather socially. The pamphlet made no mention of the LDS Church or Mormon beliefs and carried no suggestion or implication of pros-elytizing among any non-Catholics within Utah. However, it was entitled "A Foreign Mission Close to Home!" and therein lay the problem.[36] In the Catholic vernacular, and certainly in the context of the pamphlet, *mission* meant a rudimentary, underfunded parish. In the LDS vernacular, however, *mission* meant only proselytizing. A Mormon who saw the pamphlet without reading its contents could thus easily have concluded that it was the first foray of a new initiative to lure Latter-day Saints away from their own faith into Roman Catholicism. One such Mormon was David O. McKay. Speaking to local church leaders in his hometown of Huntsville, "I presented to them the avowed activity of the CATHOLIC CHURCH here in Utah, and called their attention to a leaflet that designates Utah as 'a foreign Mission close at home.'"[37]

When Bishop Hunt found that the pamphlet had been widely misinterpreted by the Mormons, he was both hurt and enraged. On the same day that McKay spoke to the leaders in Huntsville, Hunt wrote to John Fitzpatrick, venting his frustration and anger:

> I cannot resist the temptation to get a few things off my chest. I refer to the pamphlet published by Bishop Steck this winter and which has apparently aroused some resentment among our neighbors.... There is absolutely no reason why anyone of any other church should pay the slightest bit of attention to this pamphlet. It contains not one iota of propaganda against any one else; it does not complain about any one else. It calls attention to a few priests in this Diocese who need financial assistance and of some of our poor missions. It was sent to Catholics only.... That anyone should be disturbed about this pamphlet of Bishop Steck's is wholly unreasonable. It makes me furious. Some day our Mormon neighbors will wake up to the fact that my regime represents the high point in the effort of the Catholic Church to be cordial.... To all of [our Utah priests] I give the same advice. "Never criticize any other church or its people; confine yourself exclusively to the Catholic religion." I have forbidden priests to reply to attacks made against us on the radio by prominent Mormons. I have forbidden them to reply to the contemptible attacks made in [LDS] ward meeting houses by ex-Catholics. I have forbidden comments about several books published about us during recent years. I have done everything possible to contribute to harmony.... Some day I will discuss the whole subject with you, but not at present. I am too angry. I must wait until I have cooled off.[38]

Things then went from bad to worse. Under direction from McKay and his colleagues in the First Presidency,[39] Apostle Mark E. Petersen, editor of the LDS Church-owned *Deseret News,* initiated a series of meetings with local church leaders throughout the Salt Lake Valley. Petersen asserted that "a powerful church is mustering all possible strength from all over America for an intensified and concentrated attack on us."[40] Leaving no doubt about the identity of that church, he painted a sinister historical picture: "About six years ago the authorities of the [LDS] church began to hear of Catholic movements in the east to raise funds for carrying on a campaign in Utah.... Bishop D. G. Hunt of the Salt Lake diocese had made trips to the east for the purpose of instigating anti-Mormon propaganda and at the same time to raise funds.... Loss of Mormons to the Catholics in Utah was mentioned. We recognize their right to proselyte, but they will not recognize our right to do so if they ever gain the upper hand."[41]

In the midst of Petersen's meetings, Hunt sent word to McKay through a mutual friend that he wished to speak with him personally in an effort to resolve the crisis. McKay responded, through the same intermediary, that he "should be glad to make a convenient time when he might see me."[42]

The meeting took place in Hunt's office at Holy Cross Hospital. Hunt explained that the sole purpose of the pamphlet had been to raise funds to continue the Catholic Church's ministry to its own members in Utah and that clearly both Catholics and Mormons were misinterpreting it. Hunt had already made a significant goodwill gesture to reduce tensions: "When we found out that our own people objected to it, and that your people especially had objected to it, we discontinued the distribution of the pamphlet." McKay dictated for his diary the conversation that followed. He replied,

> "We received a copy, it seems to me, only six weeks ago.... Naturally we were perturbed."
>
> "Well," said Bishop Hunt, "Catholics all over the United States are. I am very sorry; I hope you will believe me."

He went on to explain the different meaning of *mission* in the Catholic context.

> McKay responded dubiously, "I rather think, Bishop, that the people of the United States would not have that distinction in mind, because it says on the pamphlet, 'A Foreign Mission Close to Home.'"
>
> "I realize that it would be hard for me to make you believe otherwise," offered Hunt.
>
> "I believe it would be hard to make anybody believe otherwise," McKay rejoined stiffly.

Hunt persisted and finally succeeded in convincing McKay that the Catholics were not conducting a proselytizing campaign in Utah. McKay said he would carry that message to his associates in the First Presidency. Hunt then reassured McKay that he was a voice of moderation within the Catholic Church in Utah.

> I have been attacked recently by our Priests because the report has
> gone out that the Mormons are attacking the Catholics in Utah, and
> that I, as the Bishop, am doing nothing in retaliation, and I am not
> doing anything, and I do not propose to do anything. Whenever an
> article was about to appear, I have telephoned them to stop it, if I have
> known about it.... There is a feeling throughout the United States
> (this is from our side now) that the Latter-day Saints are persecuting
> the Catholics and are going to drive them out of the city, and they
> blame me for doing nothing about it.

Even though McKay had warmed to Hunt, he indicated that he had not been
totally convinced when he probed, "We understand that he [Steck, the pamphlet's
author] is especially skilled in missionary work, and that that is why he has been sent
to Utah." Hunt replied, "No, he isn't a missionary; that is not his work."[43]

Hunt followed up the meeting with a personal letter to McKay, in which he
sought to clarify the matter further:

> The attitude of the Catholic Church in Utah toward other Churches
> during this year has been and is precisely what it was last year and
> what it has always been. Our primary objective here as elsewhere is to
> safeguard the faith of our people and to administer the Sacraments to
> them. A secondary objective is to win converts. These come into the
> Church because they are attracted by some doctrine or devotion,
> never as the result of a direct approach by a priest, and never as the
> result of an attack upon the religion of their youth. We preach our doc-
> trines openly so that those who are interested may hear. We give out
> literature explanatory to [sic] our doctrines to those who ask for it.
> Such have been our methods in the past; such are our methods now.
> In other words and in summary, the disturbing pamphlet has not
> meant any change in our program or policies. In no way was it
> intended to affect our attitude toward Protestants and Mormons or
> our relations with them. It was intended merely as the means of rais-
> ing additional revenue for a few of our priests whose people cannot
> fully support them.[44]

McKay, professing himself satisfied with Hunt's explanation and apology, still
responded by insisting that the Mormon misinterpretation was inevitable:

> I am glad that I accepted your cordial invitation to have a personal
> conference with you on the question of the purpose of your having
> issued this objectionable pamphlet.... As I have already stated to you,
> when the leaders of the Church first read this appeal they understood

it to be the opening of a campaign in Utah to convert to Catholicism, members of the dominant church.... With this thought in mind, we took immediate steps to inform our people of what appeared to be an approaching campaign planned by the Catholics for the specific purpose named above. Your letter sets forth conclusively that there was no such intent, that there has been "no attack upon others," nor "any change in policies" of the Catholic Church here in Utah. Thank you for setting forth so clearly your attitude in this matter.[45]

In retrospect, it is clear that McKay and his colleagues badly and unfairly misinterpreted the pamphlet and subsequently took unwarranted and damaging action in retaliation. Hunt was justified in his irritation and showed commendable integrity and charity in initiating the healing process. McKay accepted Hunt's explanation, but only reluctantly. Furthermore, a double standard was in effect, although it never entered into the discussion. That is, McKay and his colleagues were vehemently opposed to any attempt by the Catholics to proselytize within Utah, yet made no apology about sending thousands of LDS missionaries to Catholic strongholds within the United States and foreign countries whose expressed intent was converting Catholics to Mormonism. Ultimately, McKay did exactly what he had accused Hunt of doing and took Mormonism to the gates of the Vatican when he reopened the Italian Mission after a hiatus of a full century.[46]

The patched-up Mormon-Catholic relationship then remained cordial for several years. Shortly after McKay became church president he visited Holy Cross Hospital to perform an administration of healing by the laying on of hands for a young LDS patient afflicted with polio. As he entered the building, he met Bishop Hunt, who greeted him cordially and introduced him to the Sister Superior.[47] A year later, Hunt wrote a letter and directed that it be read at Sunday Mass in every parish in the diocese. The letter touched delicately on Catholic-Mormon relationships and urged Catholics to be good neighbors under all circumstances:

You yourselves, precisely because you are Catholics, are often discriminated against. Accept such injustice uncomplainingly, I beg you, as the price to be paid for the true faith. It so happens that you are frequently approached by the zealous representatives of other churches who wish to win you over to their doctrines. For your guidance, I hereby give you a few directions. Never deny your faith. Never apologize for it. State frankly that you are Catholics. Be proud that you belong to the greatest institution in the world, the one Church that goes back to Christ, the one Church that is truly universal.... Do not condemn or attack other religions. What they teach is none of our business. Leave them alone.... Be good neighbors always. Be kind,

considerate, and unselfish. Obey the Ten Commandments and the
precepts of the Church. Love God and neighbor. Keep your minds and
hearts free from the bitterness of religious controversies.[48]

Several months later, McKay paid a high compliment to Hunt in speaking to
local LDS leaders in Ogden:

> I shall always respect Bishop Hunt and what he did the other day.
> Before I went to California, he asked for an appointment, came to the
> office, and said, "Frankly, we are contemplating building a high
> school up in Ogden.... I understand that if Weber College vacates the
> buildings on that block, some of them come back to you, but I think
> that this one is not included. I am here for the purpose of ascertain-
> ing whether or not you want that building. If you do, we will with-
> draw.".... Without hesitation, I said, "We want it." He said, "Then we
> will withdraw."[49]

The following year, McKay visited Brazil, with the largest Catholic population
in the Western Hemisphere. While in Rio de Janeiro, he walked up the hill of Cor-
covado, to the magnificent statue of Christ, "Cristo Redentor," that overlooks the
city. According to Asael Sorensen, the mission president who accompanied him,
"when he got up there and saw the statue with the arms outspread, he recited that
verse, 'Come unto me, all ye that labor and are heavy laden, and I will give you rest.'
Then he said, 'These people who have done this are spiritual.'"[50]

Nonetheless, occasional statements in private settings indicated that McKay
still drew a distinction between Roman Catholics, who in many cases were close
friends, and the church to which they belonged, which he continued to disdain. In
1953 he visited San Mateo, California, to dedicate a new church building. As he and
his host drove past a Catholic Church from which worshipers were emerging after
mass, he said, "There are two great anti-Christs in the world: Communism and that
church," pointing to the Catholic Church. "Then," recounted his host, "he put his
hand on my knee and said, 'Remember that.'"[51]

The following year, an advertisement appeared in the *Wall Street Journal* soliciting funds for the construction of a new abbey at the Catholic monastery in
Huntsville. The monastery had been founded in 1947 by the Trappist Order, which
had selected the property because its isolated rural setting would favor the monas-
tic lifestyle.[52] The fact that Huntsville was McKay's hometown was unrelated. The
monastery never engaged in proselytizing, yet McKay interpreted the campaign to
build a new abbey as part of "their campaign to convert Latter-day Saints." Speaking to a meeting of the First Presidency and Quorum of the Twelve Apostles, he
again linked Communism and Catholicism:

It is more apparent than ever, becoming more apparent each day, that two great organized forces, the purpose of which is to undermine the high principles of the Restored Gospel, are operating. One is Communism, which is moving aggressively over the face of the earth, fundamentally prompted by disbelief in the existence of God, a rejection of the life of Jesus Christ as the Savior of the world, and is against the Church. The other is the Catholic Church, which is showing more clearly than ever before that they are determined to counteract the influence of the Church in this western country.[53]

At the same time that he maintained a critical attitude toward Roman Catholicism, McKay continued to look favorably upon other churches. Less than a month after establishing a policy that discouraged LDS girls from wearing crosses because "this was a Catholic form of worship,"[54] he received, as a gift, a "Chrismah" charm, which combined the Byzantine Cross with the Star of David to symbolize "the essential unity of the world's great faiths." Much pleased, he noted in his diary: The same day, "I took the charm down to my son [Robert], owner and manager of the McKay Jewelry Shop and asked him to attach a pin to the charm so that I can wear it on my lapel when I so desire."[55]

Later the same year he spoke with Ezra Taft Benson, who was serving simultaneously as Secretary of Agriculture in Dwight D. Eisenhower's administration and an LDS apostle. Benson was about to embark on a world tour that would include a stop in Rome, and the American ambassador to Italy had suggested that a meeting with the Pope could be arranged. McKay, speaking for himself and his counselors, advised: "We are all united in the feeling that if you can in honor, and without embarrassment, avoid that conference it would be well for you to do it.... We have in mind particularly the effect upon our own people.... [The Catholics] have everything to gain and nothing to lose, and we have everything to lose and nothing to gain."[56] A week later, upon learning that the Trappists in Huntsville were seeking to buy additional land, he remarked to his fellow General Authorities, "The Catholic Church is against us, and wherever they can prevent our growth they are going to do it."[57]

In 1958 one of McKay's colleagues unwittingly initiated a series of events that ultimately led McKay to abandon his private hostility toward Roman Catholicism. Bruce R. McConkie, a member of the First Council of Seventy, the church's third-ranking presiding quorum, wrote an encyclopedic work that carried the authoritative title of *Mormon Doctrine,* but which was published without the consent or knowledge of his fellow General Authorities, including McKay and McConkie's father-in-law, Joseph Fielding Smith.[58]

McKay was infuriated when he found out about the book. Even before he saw it himself, he reacted to reports from his colleagues by instituting a policy (which remains in effect to this day) requiring advance approval from the First Presidency before any General Authority could publish any book.[59] In addition to studying the book himself, McKay quickly assigned two senior apostles to read the book and report their findings. Mark E. Petersen enumerated 1,067 errors that affected "most of the 776 pages of the book."[60] Among their criticisms and a focus of greatest concern was McConkie's treatment of Roman Catholicism. The entry under the heading "Catholicism" read "*See* Church of the Devil." Under that heading, he minced no words: "The *Roman Catholic Church* [is] specifically—singled out, set apart, described, and designated as being 'most abominable above all other churches.'" In support of his allegation, he cited "great and abominable" references from the *Book of Mormon,* even though the book does not make that connection itself.[61]

Bishop Duane Hunt, who had enjoyed several years of peace with his Mormon neighbors, was stunned. Immediately after the 1958 general election, he paid a courtesy call on newly elected Congressman David S. King to congratulate him on his victory. The experience was bittersweet for both men. Hunt carried a copy of McConkie's book; and with tears in his eyes he told King, a devout Mormon, "We are your friends. We don't deserve this kind of treatment!"[62] Hunt also took the matter directly to McKay. One General Authority reminisced, "I know the Catholic bishop at the time had a real affection for President McKay, no question about it. And President McKay had a feeling for him, and even went so far as to have Brother McConkie change a line or two in his *Mormon Doctrine* book that would have seemed a little hard on the Catholic Church at the time."[63] McKay's son Lawrence was even more direct in describing his father's reaction to Hunt. "[Bishop Hunt] called Father and said, 'Is this the attitude of the Church, that the Catholic Church is the 'Great and Abominable Church,' as expressed in this latest book of Bruce McConkie's?' That book was taken off the shelves" of Deseret Book.[64]

In the aftermath of the enormous embarrassment caused to the church and to himself by McConkie's book, McKay quietly abandoned his private criticism of Roman Catholicism for the remaining decade of his life. He had come to realize that Bishop Hunt was a true friend without a hidden agenda, and he valued that friendship greatly. In a note to Hunt following the funeral of McKay's closest associate, McKay wrote: "When, from the rostrum I saw you and my esteemed friend, John F. Fitzpatrick, sitting in the audience, paying tribute of respect to my departed friend and associate, Stephen L Richards, I wanted to shake your hands in personal appreciation. Thank you for your attendance at Stephen L's funeral rites."[65]

In addition to coming to terms with Hunt, McKay realized that the Catholic Church was not a threat to the LDS Church in Utah nor, for that matter, to the vitality of international Mormonism, whose emergence was the centerpiece of McKay's entire ministry as church president. Conversely, despite occasional skirmishes at a local level and successful LDS proselytizing among Roman Catholics, particularly in Latin America, Mormonism never posed a strategic threat to Catholicism. Indeed, in recent years the two churches have formally joined forces on occasion to pursue moral issues within the political arena.

Less than a year after the death of Stephen L Richards, as McKay and his fellow General Authorities were leaving the Salt Lake Temple following a meeting, they were shocked to hear the news of Hunt's sudden death. McKay prepared a statement for the local newspapers that conveyed genuine respect for Hunt, and grief at his passing: "We are deeply grieved at the sudden passing of this eminent and devoted leader of the many loyal and law-abiding members of the Catholic Church of the diocese of Salt Lake City. He gave to them the spiritual guidance that helped them to shape their lives in accordance with the teachings of his Church. They have lost a trusted and respected adviser."[66]

Beyond the words of written tribute, McKay paid unprecedented respect to Hunt by attending his funeral mass at the Cathedral of the Madeleine. It was the first high mass McKay had ever attended. "At the conclusion of the funeral services at 12 noon," he noted in his diary, "the new Bishop, The Most Rev. Joseph Lennox Federal, came out on the steps of the Cathedral to greet President [Henry D.] Moyle and me, and to thank us for coming to the services. I was very favorably impressed with him."[67] Federal, in turn, was very favorably impressed with McKay. A decade later he reciprocated the gesture by attending McKay's funeral. Then, as the cortege passed the Cathedral of the Madeleine on its slow, sad journey along South Temple Street to the Salt Lake City Cemetery, he ordered its bells tolled in a final demonstration of respect.[68]

6

RADIO AND TELEVISION BROADCASTING

The LDS Church's formal foray into broadcasting began in 1925 when it purchased majority ownership in radio station KZN and changed the call letters to KSL. It moved quickly to apply its new assets to religious purposes, broadcasting the October 1925 general conference. Four years later, KSL affiliated with the National Broadcasting Company (NBC) and immediately began weekly national broadcasts of the Mormon Tabernacle Choir, an ongoing series that continues to this day and is the longest running in American broadcasting history. On June 1, 1949, KSL television went on the air, the first commercial TV station in Utah. Four months later, for the first time, a general conference was broadcast over commercial television.[1]

Thus, when David O. McKay became president in 1951, he inherited a nascent broadcasting apparatus with largely unrealized potential. Gradually, he moved to unleash that potential. In October 1953, general conference was televised outside of Utah for the first time;[2] and six months later, out-of-state coverage expanded to ten stations in six Western states, an estimated potential audience of twelve million viewers.[3] Speaking at a special conference session at which a new proselytizing plan was unveiled, McKay spoke of electronic media's potential in carrying the message of Mormonism to the world: "Today it is a simple matter for us to teach all nations. The Lord has given us the means of whispering through space, of annihilating distance. We have the means in our hands of reaching the millions in the world."[4]

At the same time McKay was spreading his vision of the electronic church, however, KSL was entering a period of financial turmoil. Sensing the problem but unaware of its magnitude, McKay commissioned the church's financial advisor, William F. Edwards, to make a thorough evaluation of the station's business activities. Midway through 1958, Edwards made an interim report that, from a profit of $119,000 in 1954, the station's fortunes had declined to the point that it barely broke even in 1957, earning a profit of only $1,600. The situation was particularly sensitive because the president of KSL, Ivor Sharp, was the son-in-law of McKay's counselor J. Reuben Clark Jr. Edwards said that a full report would take another two or three months to complete and, "in the meantime, I ask that the First Presidency keep an open mind."[5]

Six months later, on January 22, 1959, Edwards again met with the First Presidency to discuss KSL's situation. He prefaced his remarks by stating that "there would appear to be no other company with more justification for the interest and attention of the First Presidency," then recommended that McKay become chairman of KSL, with his two counselors as vice-chairmen. Furthermore, he urged that Sharp be "retired" and a new president appointed. The First Presidency approved Edwards's recommendations. The discussion of whom to select as Sharp's successor centered on a current KSL employee, Jay Wright. Edwards, noting that Wright was an engineer, cautioned that "salesmanship and not engineering is the paramount challenge for success in this business. Therefore, there must be some reservation as to his ability to provide the necessary leadership to re-establish satisfactory operations." Nonetheless, he felt that it "would be much wiser to appoint him president and give him every assistance than to attempt to locate and employ someone with greater qualifications." The First Presidency concurred and selected Wright to be the new president.[6]

Wright was, in the estimation of his successor, "a genius of an engineer," but not equipped to manage the business operations "because he had no station experience."[7] By the following year it became apparent to the board of directors that KSL's decline was not reversing, and they initiated a search for a new president, this time looking outside the company.

THE GROWTH OF KSL

Arch L. Madsen was a Utah native whose relationship to broadcasting had been love at first sight. "I started at a very early age with an interest in radio, and all forms of communication, in fact," he reminisced. "I started a little tiny amateur radio station, out of old receiver parts." During high school he joined the Army Amateur Reserve System. Graduating from high school in the depths of the Depression, he enlisted in the U.S. Army, where he worked in radio communications. Upon returning to civilian life, he worked briefly for KSL as an engineer, started a successful commercial radio station in Provo, and eventually became a lobbyist in Washington, D.C., for the broadcasting industry.[8] He was working in Washington in 1960 when he was contacted by an old friend, BYU President Ernest L. Wilkinson, who was a member of the KSL board of directors.

In May 1960, Henry D. Moyle, by then McKay's second counselor, asked Wilkinson to research Madsen's qualifications, "because," Wilkinson noted in his diary, "they are considering the question of whether there should be a change of management at KSL."[9] Wilkinson did his homework quickly and, two weeks later, discussed Madsen with McKay:

> [President McKay] told me he had raised the question at the First Presidency meeting the day before as to the management of KSL, and that they had discussed Madsen. He wanted to know why Madsen had had so many jobs, and was kicked out of his last job in Chicago. I told him he was misinformed on that, that I had checked into the matter carefully and that Madsen quit the job in Chicago because he foresaw it was going to be under new ownership with new management, which actually happened, and that he had a very good job in Washington, D.C. President McKay said he was under the impression that Madsen was out of work. He thanked me profusely for having corrected him on these matters, and said that this new information would help him very much.[10]

Several months later, at the request of McKay and Moyle, Wilkinson invited Madsen to Salt Lake City to discuss the KSL situation.[11] On December 16, 1960, Madsen and Wilkinson met with McKay.

> We told President McKay that President Moyle had asked Brother Madsen to analyze the statement of KSL, which he did, and then, in response to questions from me, he told of his qualifications. We were with President McKay for forty minutes. Brother Madsen made a very fine presentation. President McKay later told me that he was very much impressed with Brother Madsen. From the presentation, I learned that KSL, although it is a 50,000-watt station, the largest in Utah, is now in third place in Salt Lake City, as far as reader [*sic*] interest is concerned.[12]

The following month, McKay and Moyle met with two members of the board of directors to discuss the future of KSL:

> I explained to them there are two things in the mind of the First Presidency regarding KSL. First, that we wondered if something can not be done to bring KSL to its proper place at the head of our broadcasting system, that it does not seem to be holding its own.... After discussing the matter, I said that the whole question is whether or not we are justified in considering a change of leadership, and that we are now asking their judgment.... I mentioned that I had had a conference with Brother Arch Madsen who is an analyst and who gave me quite a different viewpoint of reports than had been submitted to me heretofore by KSL.[13]

After the two board members left, McKay and Moyle decided to invite Madsen for a second visit and offer him the top post at KSL.

A week later, Madsen returned to Utah. He had an appointment with Moyle on a Monday and with McKay the following day, but he spent Sunday afternoon with Wilkinson. Wilkinson told him that he had recommended him for the position, then liberally dispensed advice concerning the terms on which he should insist, if he chose to accept the offer.[14] Madsen then met with Moyle and McKay, albeit reluctantly: "I had a list as long as your arm of the reasons I didn't want to come back. Although I seemed to be pulled in this direction, I'd given up all thoughts because I'd previously been employed here and the atmosphere was not right. KSL Radio was the fifth-rated radio here, and KSL Television, at a time when CBS really, really pressed it, was a poor third."[15]

Madsen freely expressed his reservations to McKay. Then it was McKay's turn:

> He gave me some instruction. I was only with him five minutes, and he turned me around completely. I had a wonderful job in Washington. I was working with all the top television stations and networks in the country. I got to know all of them, and out of that developed many employment opportunities. But he changed my mind in five minutes.... When we agreed that I would come, he said, "Now, I want you to promise me one thing. You are to report to me, or the man I delegate in the First Presidency, as long as I am the President of the Church. And if you're ever asked to report otherwise, I want you to make me a promise, that you'll have your letter of resignation on the desk of the official asking for it within five minutes. Because, if you don't, your life won't be worth living." That's the environment in which I came into KSL.... If it hadn't been for that man, they'd have had my head a dozen times. Now that's not a very pleasant thing to record, but it's the truth.[16]

While having direct access to McKay was crucial, it was McKay's vision of broadcasting in the church that persuaded Madsen to accept the job offer:

> He said, "We are not in the broadcasting business to make money. It is not an investment. But, you must make the stations profitable, because that is a sign that they are providing a healthy service to the community in which they are located. Broadcasting is not an ordinary business. It is not a dollar and cent affair. It has responsibilities far, far beyond the profit statement. We're in the business of broadcasting to learn *how* to use it to further the work of the Lord." That was my guiding star all the time, some twenty-three years that I was heading up Bonneville.[17]

In April 1961, Madsen began his new job, with the daunting challenge of reforming the operations of KSL:

> The stations here were in terrible shape. The operations were in shambles. I will let it rest at that, except to say that I was called in by the people at CBS and told that they had 200 affiliates, and KSL television was listed in the bottom ten, and the other nine had a reason to be there. I was also told by one of the top officials, "I've been around you Mormons quite a while, and you have a saying that the glory of God is intelligence." I said, "Yes, we do." "Well then, why the hell don't you practice it in broadcasting?" He just laid it on the line. The AM radio station was number five in the local market, and the FM station was a joke. That's what I inherited.[18]

Madsen presented to McKay his strategic plan for rebuilding the church's broadcasting operations: "First of all, we had to provide outstanding community service. Secondly, we had to have an excellent plan for personnel development. Thirdly, quality programming. And fourth, profitability. I went to the board with that after he had approved it, and I had a lot of opposition. They wanted profitability on top, and I said, 'Unless you take care of these three, you're not going to have it down here anyway. So that's where it belongs.' And President McKay supported me in that."[19]

A month after beginning the job, Madsen gave a progress report to the First Presidency. After the meeting, McKay remarked to Moyle, "We didn't make any mistake. That is the most informative report we have had on KSL."[20]

As he suggested to McKay, Madsen put a premium on human resources, particularly the improvement of skills among current KSL employees. One employee later described the process: "He created an understanding that we were in a very intensely competitive environment, and you're going to have to compete. He provided better compensation systems. He immediately brought forward a lot of encouragement to seek better education, more training. I am the recipient of dozens of very expensive, very important types of seminars that I've traveled to. I've done it for years. Arch brought those things there."[21]

To improve religious programming, Madsen looked beyond the Tabernacle Choir broadcasts to programs that emphasized religious values but kept Mormonism in the background. One early success involved Michael Grilikhes, a convert to the church who was a CBS executive in Los Angeles: "Every time CBS needed a thing having to do with the Tabernacle Choir, they discovered that I was a Mormon and said, 'You know those people; you go talk to them.' What had happened was that they were tired of the choir. They said, 'We've got to have something other than a choir concert. We're just tired of it. They get up and they're beautiful, but can't we do something else?'"[22]

The result was a televised special in 1962, *Let Freedom Ring,* which traced the history of the United States through song and the spoken word. Grilikhes enlisted the talents of his wife, actress Laraine Day, as well as non-LDS actors Richard Boone and Howard Keel. *Let Freedom Ring* won both a Peabody Award and a Freedom Foundation Award.[23] In the process, Madsen discovered the advantages of enlisting talent outside KSL, Utah, and even the church. He also became acutely aware of the dilapidated condition of KSL's equipment. Following the broadcast, he urged a mammoth upgrade. McKay noted in his diary in May 1962:

> Brother Madsen said that they have a problem with their equipment; that CBS, after the presentation of the "Let Freedom Ring" program, suggested that we do not try to feed the network again with our worn-out equipment. KSL has sent to the First Presidency a report of what is needed for complete installation, black and white, or color, submitting prices on each. He said that it is thought the finest equipment should be used for our projects. Brother Madsen said that if their request is approved, it is believed that they can make special arrangements to let CBS bring here at a nominal charge equipment installed in time for the April conference. I said that we would give whatever financial help is needed.[24]

It was a sweeping commitment; and with McKay's approval, Madsen pushed hard to convert KSL–TV to color broadcasting. A station executive later commented on the importance of that conversion: "Before that, no one in Salt Lake was doing any color. But Arch decided to do everything in color. He changed all of the equipment, went to all color cameras. All that bit. That was a hard thing to talk the ownership into. But he was of course very prophetic in that."[25]

After one year on the job, Madsen had turned KSL's fortunes around, and was building the foundation for a broadcasting empire. In May 1962 he reported to McKay:

- Worldwide, 330 stations carried the weekly Mormon Tabernacle Choir broadcasts.

- The April 1962 general conference was carried by fifty-two television stations, the first time the conference had been broadcast coast-to-coast.

- The president of CBS News had called Madsen four days earlier to inform him that the Tabernacle Choir would be part of the first satellite broadcast of a live television program to Europe, over the recently launched Telstar satellite.

- And finally, Madsen had made significant progress toward the realization of a decades-long dream of McKay's, to have a church-owned shortwave radio station.[26]

FORAY INTO SHORTWAVE BROADCASTING

The church's foray into shortwave broadcasting was a bold and risky venture whose lofty expectations ultimately slammed into technological and economic reality. The church had initiated efforts to obtain a shortwave license in the mid-1930s; but after lengthy consideration, the federal government had denied the application, and the matter remained dormant for a quarter-century.[27] But in April 1962, buoyed by the turnaround in KSL's fortunes, McKay gave Madsen "the responsibility of initiating negotiations for short-wave facilities."[28]

A month later, having consulted with experts in the field including Rosel Hyde, a church member who served on the Federal Communications Commission (and later chaired the FCC), Madsen proposed to McKay that the church build two shortwave stations. A transmitter in Puerto Rico "would permit us to reach Europe, South America and Mexico," while one in Guam would reach Australia, the Pacific islands, and much of Asia. (Because of the LDS ban on ordination of blacks of African origin, Africa was not a priority.) Hyde, however, had added a cautionary note—"that it is very likely that the right of private citizens to own and operate short-wave stations under the United States Government will probably be closed within a matter of days."[29]

Madsen estimated that the cost of building the two stations would be $2.5 million, with annual combined operating costs of $600,000. McKay responded enthusiastically: "I said that I do not hesitate for a minute; that it is one of the great things; that it is a dream of twenty years realized. I said that we should decide this morning to take it." He ended the meeting by voicing his vision of the potential of shortwave radio, calling it "the first great step to reach the world."[30]

James Conkling, former president of Columbia Records and vice president of CBS, was selected to be managing director of the shortwave stations, which would be part of a new church-owned entity, International Educational Broadcasting Corporation.

Two weeks after McKay gave the go-ahead for the shortwave stations, Conkling, Madsen, and McKay met. Madsen reported that potential sites had been located in Puerto Rico and Guam, and license applications had been filed. Conkling emphasized what Madsen already appreciated—that much of the success of the venture would be in the quality of the programming. According to McKay's record of the meeting, Conkling "explained that some time will be needed to bring everything into order and to translate or communicate the messages we have with proper

Portrait of President David O. McKay by Arnold Friberg. Copyright 2002 Arnold Friberg. Used by permission of Friberg Fine Art, Inc. (www.fribergfineart.com).

Portrait of First Counselor Stephen L Richards by Arnold Friberg. Copyright 2002 Arnold Friberg. Used by permission of Friberg Fine Art, Inc. (www.fribergfineart.com).

Portrait of Second Counselor J. Reuben Clark Jr. by Arnold Friberg. Copyright 2002 Arnold Friberg. Used by permission of Friberg Fine Art, Inc. (www.fribergfineart.com).

SOME NOTES AND MEMORIES OF HOW THESE PORTRAITS CAME TO BE

As recalled by the artist Arnold Friberg RSA

Back in 1955 I was heavily involved in working as chief artist and designer for Cecil B. DeMille, who was at that time producing his monumental motion picture "The Ten Commandments". DeMille told me he had known presidents Heber J. Grant and George Albert Smith, but had never met, but would like to meet, our present president. So I conveyed the nice invitation to Pres. David O McKay, who of course wished to meet DeMille.

In those days, to gain a bit of respite from the strains of his office duties, Pres. McKay and his wife often came to Los Angeles for a quiet complete rest. Even the local church members didn't know they were there. They didn't stay at the swankiest places, but at a nice quiet older hotel.

So next time he was down there, Paramount sent me in their limosine to pick up the McKays and bring them to the studio to meet DeMille. It was only natural that DeMille and McKay took to each other immediately, forming a strong and lasting friendship anchored in a deep mutual admiration and respect. I could recall many incidents between the two men, but I am here concerned only with the tale of these three portraits.

While down there, Pres. McKay decided he wanted me to paint his portrait. DeMille invited him to go into the studio prop department and select any chair in which he wanted to be painted. Out of several they offered him, he chose the one seen in all three of these portraits, perhaps taking a liking to the lions carved on the arm rests. And so I got started with a couple of sittings right there at Paramount studios.

Now, this was the time when crowds were taking the visitors' tour through the new Los Angeles temple prior to its dedication. Pres. McKay decided that in addition to his own portrait, that I should also paint one of each of his two counselors, all three portraits to be ready and completed in time to be placed in the temple at its dedication.

When I returned to Salt Lake City to complete the series of 15 large "Ten Commandments" paintings, DeMille gave me the chair so that I could continue the work on the work on the McKay portrait as well as painting the two of his counselors. All three men are painted sitting in that same chair, adding a note of unity to the po^rait trilogy. We still have this chair in our living room, and now known as "the DeMille chair."

All three men came individually to my Salt Lake City studio for sittings, and with intense concentration effort, I got as far as I could within their extremely limited time. In fact, the whole project had been initiated so close to the date of the temple dedication that there just wasn't time to develop the portraits to full completion. I could have finished them had they been able to grant me the time for sittings. Once the temple had been dedicated, they apparently lost interest, and never did come out for any more sittings.

And so the whole undertaking was forgotten. Of course I was not paid, and the portraits have languished ever since in the back storage room of my studio. I had the canvases removed from their stretcher bars and mounted onto Masonite to insure their safety from injury,

Now, seeing these portraits again after all these years, I feel good about them. For there is an immediacy and a directness of observation that can come only from painting direct from life, that can never result from painting from a photograph. In life, you feel the presence, the personal magnetism of the subject, and this stimulus is bound somehow to push its way up through the colors and to be felt in the painting.

I am surprised now, how far these portraits really were developed, when I recall how brief were the times of sittings. But I do dearly recall that at that time, under the powerful inspiration of DeMille, and of that monumental motion picture we were working on, that my talents simply poured out as in a torrent, and I was able to produce, under inhuman time pressure, what I could never accomplish today.

These portraits were painted for a certain time period. But as the years roll away, it is good to know that they will take their place as a historic record of our first presidency as it was at that time.

A. Friberg

Portrait of David O. McKay by John Hafen, 1907. Copyright by Intellectual Reserve, Inc.
Courtesy of the Museum of Church History and Art.

Artist's representation of Episcopal Bishop Arthur Moulton blessing David O. McKay on his seventy-eighth birthday, September 8, 1951. See chapter 5. Copyright 2004 by Rose Datoc Dall, *Blessing the Prophet*, oil on canvas, 30" x 40". Used by permission of the artist.

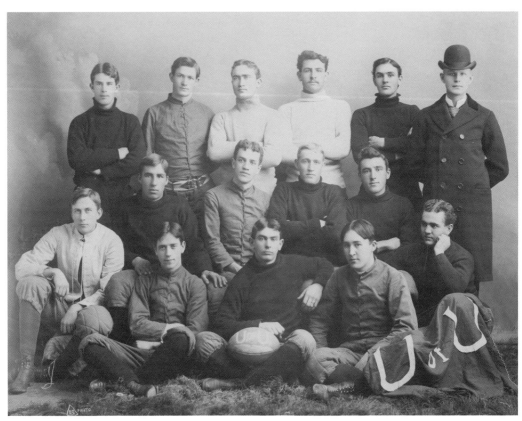

The 1894 University of Utah football
team. David O. McKay, top row,
second from left. Courtesy Special
Collections, J. Willard Marriott
Library, University of Utah.

"What e'er thou art act well
thy part." Inscription seen by
David O. McKay on his mission in Scotland. This motto
served as a guide for McKay
throughout his life. Courtesy
LDS Church Archives.

David O. McKay, center, visiting the German Mission while president of the European Mission, 1923. Gustav Weller, founder of Zion Book Store in Salt Lake City and father of bookseller Sam Weller, second row, right end. Courtesy Sam Weller.

Hugh Cannon and David O. McKay in Egypt on their 1921 worldwide tour to visit church missions. Courtesy LDS Church Archives.

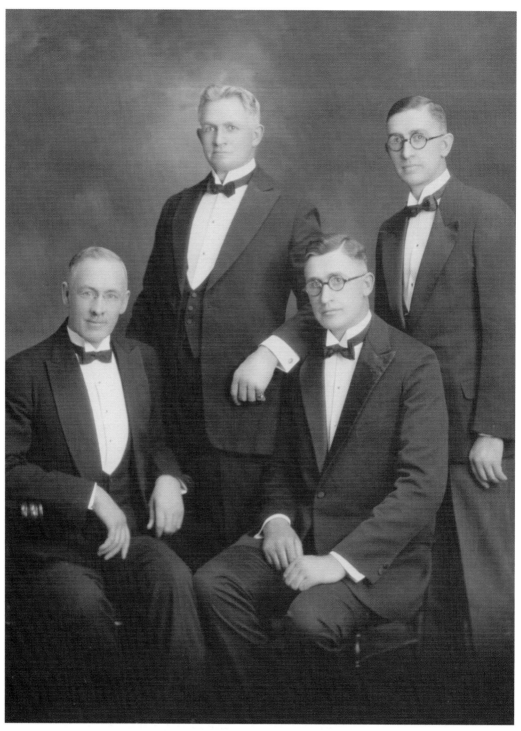

The McKay brothers, ca. 1920. Standing, from left, David O. and William. Seated, from left, Thomas and Morgan. Courtesy Rick Grunder Books.

Clare Middlemiss, Lottie (Mrs. Edward) McKay, Dr. Edward McKay, Emma Ray McKay, and David O. McKay boarding a plane on their 1955 European tour. Courtesy Wm. Robert Wright.

David O. McKay delivering an address at the dedication of "This Is The Place" Monument, July 24, 1947. Courtesy Wm. Robert Wright.

Clare Middlemiss, photographed about 1935 at the time she started working for David O. McKay. Courtesy Wm. Robert Wright.

Clare Middlemiss in David O. McKay's private office with the McKay diaries in the background, February 5, 1965. Courtesy Wm. Robert Wright.

David O. McKay and Bishop Joseph Milton Cottam at the dedication of the San Fernando California Stake Center, October 30, 1955. Courtesy Gregory A. Prince.

Joseph Fielding Smith, Clare Middlemiss, and Wm. Robert Wright at the October 1967 semi-annual general conference. Courtesy Wm. Robert Wright.

Emma Ray McKay, David O. McKay, and Clare Middlemiss in Scotland on their 1955 European tour. Courtesy Wm. Robert Wright.

taste and in appropriate ways to make them appealing to the people. He said there are dramatic ways of reaching the minds of people, and that these ways need not be dull, but must be according to good taste." McKay agreed, responding that "there will be large numbers, if we present the truth in a pleasant way, who will accept it, because most people are honest."[31]

McKay then addressed the financial issue, stating that while the church would finance the creation of the stations, they were to be self-sustaining through advertising. Conkling replied, "I am pleased that there is no aversion to making a profit, and that it be a self-supporting project." McKay concluded the meeting on a high note: "The Lord has helped us. It could not be better. It is a new step forward. It is not only a step, but it is really a bound into space in this space age. Now is the chance to teach the world. Watch your step carefully. We do not want to blunder."[32]

Only four months later, however, church leaders shifted course. Early in September 1962, the First Presidency and Quorum of the Twelve discussed an alternative approach. Richard L. Evans, the voice of the Tabernacle Choir broadcasts, argued for the purchase of WRUL in Boston, which had recently come on the market, instead of sinking "unnumbered millions into the creation, promotion and development of new stations." Mark E. Petersen agreed "that it would be much better to buy a going station than to pioneer a new one," a sentiment echoed by Delbert L. Stapley.[33] The First Presidency concurred. With this consensus, church officials moved quickly to negotiate the purchase of the station.

On October 10, 1962, church and broadcasting officials met with the First Presidency to complete the sale, for a price of $1,750,000. McKay asked John Kluge, representing the sellers, about the station's advertising potential. "Mr. Kluge said advertising goes out over the station to listeners overseas and that the potential overseas market is very large." Ralph Brent, an employee of WRUL, added that shortwave radio "is the biggest advertising medium in the world.... The *Reader's Digest* has nine million circulation outside the United States; there are 88 million listeners on short-wave receivers. This would mean that our potential is larger than the *Reader's Digest*." McKay, delighted with the information, commented jubilantly: "I said this is the realization of a dream come true. We have hoped for short-wave for 25 years. That was just in the imagination.... I remarked that some power has been working, that I am happy and thrilled with what they have explained and with the possibilities of this station.... This has been an historic occasion and more far-reaching than any of us can realize!"[34]

In December 1962, the FCC approved the sale of WRUL to the church.[35] Thus far the road had been smooth. In February 1963, McKay received good news and bad news about the shortwave program. The Voice of America had long broadcast from facilities on Long Island, but was relocating to Cape Hatteras,

North Carolina. James Conkling indicated that the transmitting equipment and real estate could probably be purchased from the government at a reasonable price. Such a purchase would have the dual benefits of reducing overhead and extending the coverage of the station. The bad news was that the station had lost $5,000 a week during 1962. Conkling minimized the problem and stated his expectation that "this year...it will be operating at a profit."[36] Two weeks later, the First Presidency approved an operating budget for the station of $750,000 for the calendar year, authorizing an additional $500,000 for purchasing the Voice of America transmitters.[37]

In November, the First Presidency met with Conkling to discuss the latest items of good and bad news. The good news was that advertising revenues for the year amounted to $300,000. Period. Offsetting that were grim figures about operating losses. Conkling, who earlier had estimated 1962 losses to be about $250,000, said that the actual amount had been $440,000. Losses for 1963 were going to be even worse—an estimated $575,000 after depreciation—and projected losses for 1964 at $400,000 before depreciation. The equipment was either old or obsolete, and Conkling estimated that it would cost $2,385,000 to bring the station up to current technological standards. He suggested that "by 1966 the operation can be nearer within income." An exasperated McKay, sensing that he had been sold a bill of goods with promises of an advertising market "larger than the *Reader's Digest,*" asked "if there is any possibility that WRUL will pay its way." Conkling replied, "I do not think it will be a money maker."[38]

In April 1964, McKay met with Madsen and asked bluntly, "What is our problem at WRUL?" In addition to mounting operating losses, the station's broadcasting signal was far poorer than expected, with mission presidents throughout the world complaining of poor reception. Madsen tried to be optimistic, saying that he hoped the mission presidents and church members "were not discouraged or disillusioned with the reception results from WRUL in many areas. With the installation of new equipment this could be vastly improved." McKay was not completely satisfied, wondering aloud if Conkling "really grasped the details and the concepts that were necessary for its successful operation." His parting comment to Madsen was an assignment to bring him "specific recommendations regarding an improvement in the WRUL situation as soon as possible."[39]

The financial hemorrhage increased. In July, Conkling requested a supplemental budget of $250,000 "to carry them through October 31."[40] By the end of the year, McKay's patience had run out; and in a meeting with Arch Madsen and Thorpe Isaacson, he announced his decision: "Since reports have come that conditions are not just right at WRUL, I asked Brother Madsen to serve as President of WRUL, and to make such investigations and changes as may be necessary so that this Station can be operated as was originally intended when it was purchased."[41]

A week later, having done some investigating into the situation, Isaacson urged McKay to delay replacing Conkling, arguing that Conkling "has great ability and wants to do a good job for the Church."[42] Indeed, Conkling was a talented executive who later served as the Voice of America director in the administration of Ronald Reagan. In retrospect, it appears that the problem was not Conkling, but the original decision to purchase the station in the face of bloated expectations and inflated promises. Conkling had had the misfortune of being commissioned captain of an already-sinking ship. By mid-1965, Conkling offered his resignation, which was accepted.[43]

At least one man had expressed reservations about the purchase of WRUL but to no avail. N. Eldon Tanner, who joined the First Presidency in 1963 after the station had been acquired, "said he opposed strenuously the purchase of WRUL... but was overruled."[44] In September 1966, with a request on the table for as much as $5 million to upgrade equipment, he applied the brakes. He told McKay that "he had recommended to the Board, which was approved, that a survey and study be made regarding short-wave reception in South America and Europe before any such expenditure is made."[45] Three months later, he reported that operating losses for 1966 would be nearly $600,000, "which is even greater than the loss last year"— this despite Conkling's earlier prediction that "by 1966 the operation can be nearer within income."[46]

The euphoria that had accompanied the purchase of WRUL only four years earlier was gone, and other cautionary voices began to join Tanner's. Early in 1967, McKay and his counselors listened to a sobering report by Gordon B. Hinckley, who had been assigned to make the survey Tanner had recommended:

> Elder Hinckley stated, and it has been substantiated by the engineers, that we can reach the areas [of South America] by an expenditure of probably five million dollars, but the question was raised as to what good we are doing if we give the signal and the people haven't the facilities or the interest, one or the other or both, to receive the messages. It was explained that we are competing whenever we go to one of these foreign countries like South America, South Africa, and Europe, with the governments of these countries who have their short-wave signals going out all over the world.... There is great doubt as to the wisdom of spending large sums of money to bring our station to a condition where it can compete with other stations if our message is not being received.[47]

Without question, Hinckley's message was received. The church gradually cut its losses and, in 1974, quietly sold its shortwave properties.[48] Alan Blodgett, who became the church's chief financial officer in 1969, later commented on the enterprise's demise:

> As for short-wave broadcasting, for a time it was felt by some that owning a facility would allow the Church to broadcast its message to both members and investigators on a broad scale. Any enthusiasm was short-lived, however, for it soon became evident that it is one thing to broadcast, and it is quite a different thing to get people to listen to your broadcasts. For Church leadership, the use of films, then satellite closed circuit connections proved to be much more effective and practical. To use broadcasting as a missionary tool, it was necessary to use a medium where there was a captive audience. Thus the development of high quality, high impact messages such as the "Homefront."[49]

The road to "Homefront," arguably the most successful broadcasting venture of the church to date, lay not in the failure of shortwave broadcasting, but in the success of the church's other commercial broadcasting interests.

KSL's return to profitability opened the way to acquiring other radio and television properties. According to Arch Madsen's recollections, Henry D. Moyle's business instincts led him to encourage McKay in that direction:

> I'll never forget his statement to President McKay. He said, "President McKay, this is an area in which the Church can have its cake and eat it too," which was absolutely right. We started looking around to expand.... We came to purchase KIRO in Seattle, which was by far the biggest part of our Bonneville organization. There was opposition to the concept, but he still maintained that you could have your cake and eat it too. We put $7.2 million in that operation; the current [1981] appraised value of the three stations [TV, AM and FM radio] is at least $150 million. And they provided us with the funds to build an organization and expand.[50]

The purchase of KIRO was completed in January 1964. The church's broadcasting interests now included three properties, KSL, KIRO, and WRUL, under different management. As he had done six years earlier, McKay turned to William Edwards for advice.

> I received a call from President McKay's secretary saying President McKay has a very major problem he has to resolve and he wants your advice before he makes the decision. I, of course, was immediately in

President McKay's office.... I sensed very quickly what the problem was. It had to do with the broadcasting interests of the Church. The Church owned KSL, which was profitable, the Church had acquired a group of stations in Seattle which were profitable, but the Church also had a short-wave broadcasting operation back in Massachusetts, which was losing over $500,000 a year. It would be quite obvious to any financial man to merge the profitable and unprofitable companies together so that you'd wipe out the deficit against the profits and you'd recover half of the deficit in tax savings. I was back to President McKay's office within a week or ten days with a tentative proposal. I could see his further thinking. I was back again within about a week with a plan for merging these companies and the creation of a holding company. Now for the first time he gave me permission to speak to an attorney. At the same time, Arch Madsen, President of KSL was working with President Brown and President Moyle on the creation of a holding company for the broadcast system, and I didn't know it. I didn't learn until about two years ago that they were working concurrently with my working. President McKay then approved the organization of the holding company and it was put into effect.[51]

BONNEVILLE INTERNATIONAL CORPORATION

The holding company, Bonneville International Corporation, was formed in March 1964, with Arch Madsen as its president. Having learned a lesson from its experience in shortwave radio, the church moved to acquire financially sound properties in television, and AM and FM radio. "Through profits and business borrowing," Blodgett confirmed, "Madsen was able to fund Bonneville expansions internally."[52] In 1966, Madsen spoke in general conference and reported that Bonneville's holdings now included twenty broadcasting facilities.[53] Bonneville International acquired additional radio stations in Kansas City[54] and Los Angeles[55] over the next three years.

To some it appeared that the goal of broadcasting to the entire world via church-owned facilities had not changed, merely that the tactics had shifted from shortwave to other media. Indeed, Spencer W. Kimball seemed to be suggesting as much when he addressed the newly appointed Regional Representatives of the Twelve in their inaugural meeting in September 1967:

> We now have ownership in 22 broadcasting facilities.... We are but in the beginning as we think of the future, as space becomes our ally, and as our message travels from the Rocky Mountain vastness in the 87 pound satellite Tele-Star [*sic*] 22,000 miles above the East coast of

Brazil, motionless in relation to the ground, from which 87 pound speck, the Gospel may bounce back to the earth to effectively cover one-third of the earth's surface. Another over the Pacific now brings another third of the world into our service area. And when a third brings in the balance of the world the scripture will be totally fulfilled which states, "For, verily, the sound must go forth from this place into all the world, and unto the uttermost part of the earth" (D&C 58:64). Now when every person has a TV or a transistor, all our programs can be broadcasted in all major tongues, then the poor and the rich, the educated and the illiterate may hear the truths in their own tongue, and iron curtains and bamboo curtains block us no more.[56]

But in fact, the church's communications ambitions were being reshaped. Madsen had taken as his motto McKay's instructions when interviewing him for the KSL job: "We are in it to learn how to use it, and that is your major assignment."[57] The learning curve had at times been steep and the shortwave experience a stinging one, but other factors also tempered the vision of global broadcasting. Alan Blodgett offered his analysis of the transition:

It is my view that Church leaders abandoned the dream of reaching the entire world through a broadcasting empire that they controlled for several reasons:

- The need developed for two very different broadcasting capabilities, one to send messages to members, and the other for proselytizing purposes.
- Television advanced over radio as the preferred medium because of its greater effectiveness, but the cost of television broadcasting facilities is vastly greater than radio.
- With the widely dispersed Church membership, having owned facilities to contact congregations throughout the world was not practical. It was much less costly to rent time, as needed, using the latest technology such as satellites or community access TV channels.
- While owned commercial facilities could be effective for broadcasting proselytizing messages, the content had to be controlled so as not to adversely affect publicity ratings or violate FCC regulations. Further, it is difficult to allocate prime time for church messages.
- Finally, federal regulations limit the broadcasting exposure that can be controlled by one owner, thus limiting the areas that could be served.[58]

Thus, the emphasis shifted toward programming. Madsen later reminisced: "The major reason we were in it was to get cash enough, and get exposure into enough market situations, with enough religions, to find an answer.... What we needed to focus our money on was the production of quality communications about the gospel. We have still just barely touched the surface. Barely."[59]

AN EMPHASIS ON PROGRAMMING

Any shift in programming would, of course, buck tradition and meet opposition within a conservative bureaucracy. Madsen broached this sensitive issue with McKay when McKay first indicated his desire to have Madsen manage Bonneville:

> We then discussed at length the problems of creating and producing Church television and radio programs.... I wholeheartedly recommended the establishment of a Church television and radio program department, which would report directly to the First Presidency. I explained that I felt this department should be manned by top people who would be well paid, and who would have the confidence of the First Presidency.... I informed the President that we could pay for these services from the profits of our radio-television operations. He told me he expected me to bring recommendations as to organization and personnel as quickly as possible, and to keep very close and in charge of this matter. I, in turn, told him that I would be delighted to do so, but that as far as the materials and subject matters covered by these programs, the individual in charge should report only to the First Presidency. I understood from our conversation that he agreed in this wholeheartedly.[60]

The challenge to Madsen was formidable: to make the message of Mormonism interesting to a non-Mormon audience. The staple of church programming since 1929, the Tabernacle Choir broadcasts, were, in Madsen's view, falling short of that goal for two reasons. First, the broadcasts had gone along unchanged for so long that they had become a familiar form with little content. "The Choir was fine, but when you analyze it, the Choir is known, but the people don't really know what it is."[61] And as a result, choir coverage had gradually declined: "The number of stations carrying the Tabernacle Choir on radio dropped, dropped, dropped. We could see, with the behavioral scientist's help, that a preacher—just a head—was the very weakest way to carry a program of religion."[62]

As he had done with *Let Freedom Ring*, Madsen looked beyond Utah for answers:

We started to write to the other churches, to find out what they were broadcasting, and offer free time on what we called "Prelude to the Sabbath." We, at one time, had a working relationship with over forty different religious groups who supplied programming material that we used.... In running this program, "Prelude to the Sabbath" (for which the Southern Baptists gave me an award), we hit on the idea that we were going to take the main problems people had in their lives and relate them to solutions found in the gospel. We called this the "Homefront," consisting of thirty- and sixty-second spots. We picked very smart writers and musicians. This series of programs is still running. It has won every award that they give in broadcasting in the United States. We even have awards from foreign countries, including a Bronze Lion from the Cannes Film Festival in France. The impact was tremendous. This is the way to go, because a station can fit it in, in various places. These announcements weren't released at 7:00 o'clock on Sunday morning. These announcements found their way into prime time programming, including the networks. CBS wiped out their policy of not accepting religious broadcasting to carry our spots, they were so good.... The last year I was there, I think the fellows brought me in an estimate that we had received free for the Church over $19 million worth of time on stations in the United States and Canada, in one year.[63]

McKay did not live to see "Homefront," which was launched the year following his death, but it remains the legacy of his vision of what broadcasting could do to promote the message of the church. Madsen, in a tribute to McKay's vision, described one of the more dramatic effects of "Homefront":

Our [non-Mormon] friends in the Dominican Republic wanted to broadcast the Homefront, so we sent a crew down. They broadcast there for seven years before we opened the mission. I had a memo from the first president of that mission, who told us what happened. He said, "The first year was very unsuccessful. But then I discovered that they were broadcasting our Homefront series. So I told the missionaries not to say that they were from the Church of Jesus Christ of Latter-day Saints, but when they went to the doors, to identify themselves as the Homefront missionaries. And the results were astonishing. In one year, those messages did more good than we could have done in ten years of knocking on doors." That's the thing that President McKay wanted us to open up, and that's what we tried to do.[64]

7

CORRELATION AND CHURCH ADMINISTRATION

During the presidency of David O. McKay, the church experienced unparalleled growth. It nearly tripled in total membership and became a significant and permanent presence throughout the world in countries that earlier had served primarily to feed convert-immigrants into the American body. However, such growth was a mixed blessing, and the response to these growth pains came to be known simply as "correlation."

The basic blueprint for church administration was contained in a series of revelations over the course of a decade to the founding prophet, Joseph Smith. While some in the church considered the word of God, as contained in these revelations, final and immutable, experience quickly demonstrated that, like the U.S. Constitution (which Latter-day Saints also consider a God-inspired document), the revelations were elastic. Thus, from the earliest days of its existence, the church's administrative structure consisted of a hybrid of revelation-mandated offices and organizations, and experience-mandated accommodations.[1]

For most of its nineteenth-century existence, the church's hierarchical structure was composed largely of men who accepted and practiced plural marriage. In 1890, as a precondition for Utah's statehood, church leaders publicly renounced the practice, yet privately continued it. By the turn of the twentieth century, it was apparent to most observers, and particularly to those in Washington, D.C., that the renunciation had been made with significant private reservations. Determined to end forever a practice that, along with slavery, had been one of the "twin relics of barbarism," the Congress chose as its battleground the seating in the U.S. Senate of Apostle Reed Smoot. Elected by the Utah State Legislature in January 1903, he was, ironically, one of the few monogamists among the church's General Authorities.[2]

139

The challenge to Smoot's seating in the Senate, which was in reality a challenge to the plural marriage-based culture of church life and administration, grew into a three-year-long public spectacle of Senate hearings that included the appearance under subpoena of Church President Joseph F. Smith. Stung by the harsh treatment he received from the senators and convinced that the church's continued existence was linked to its final renunciation of the practice of plural marriage, Smith issued a "Second Manifesto" in the 1904 general conference, in effect saying, "This time we mean it!"

It was a bitter pill for many Latter-day Saints whose entire lifestyle had been shaped by plural marriage. Two apostles, John W. Taylor and Matthias Cowley, were dropped from the Quorum of the Twelve Apostles the following year when they failed to follow Smith's leadership and renounce the practice. In the April 1906 general conference, Smith replaced one of them with a young schoolteacher whose family had never practiced plural marriage, David O. McKay. During the same conference, Smith made a prophetic statement to the conferees, which ultimately became the backbone of the modern correlation movement:

> We expect to see the day, if we live long enough (and if some of us do not live long enough to see it, there are others who will), when every council of the priesthood in The Church of Jesus Christ of Latter-day Saints will understand its duty; will assume its own responsibility, will magnify its calling, and fill its place in the Church, to the uttermost, according to the intelligence and ability possessed by it. When that day shall come there will not be so much necessity for work that is now being done by the auxiliary organizations, because it will be done by the regular quorums of the priesthood.[3]

Perhaps Smith looked backward and saw that the dismantling of plural marriage meant the end of "business as usual" throughout the church hierarchy and that restructuring would require a ground-up effort built upon the backs of the local priesthood quorums that had existed since the earliest days of the church, but that had never been fully utilized. Perhaps he looked forward and saw that the church's twentieth-century growth would be impossible with former administrative practices and that now was a convenient time to retool. He did not elaborate, and so we are left to guess the complete rationale behind his prophecy. However, there is no question as to its effect, both then and subsequently.

EARLY ATTEMPTS AT CORRELATION

By the turn of the twentieth century, the structure of the church resembled a patchwork quilt. The basic ecclesiastical backbone of General Authorities, stake (diocese) presidents, and bishops (local congregations) had been in place for a half-century. However, the lifeblood of the church, which gave it most of its identity, was a collection of auxiliary organizations that had all begun as grassroots initiatives addressing the needs of a growing and changing social and cultural body. The local success of these organizations subsequently catapulted them into church-wide adoption.[4] These organizations functioned nearly autonomously, for while the general president of each was selected by the church president, the selection of board members and the formulation of programs, financing, shaping of policy and handbooks, and the writing of lesson manuals was done within the organizations, with little or no input from the First Presidency or Quorum of the Twelve.

By 1908 the Young Men's Mutual Improvement Association, Young Ladies' Mutual Improvement Association, Sunday School, and one priesthood quorum (the Seventy), were publishing their own lesson manuals annually. In April of that year, Church President Joseph F. Smith organized the General Priesthood Committee on Outlines, assigned it to prepare lesson materials for the remaining five priesthood quorums (high priests, elders, priests, teachers, and deacons), and further charged it to correlate the instructional materials of all church organizations.[5] He asked David O. McKay, then a junior apostle, to chair the committee. Within the year it completed the first task; but it never accomplished the second, as the auxiliary organizations continued to chart their own courses.

Four years later, in 1912, Smith organized a Correlation Committee[6] with the specific charge to survey the curricula of all organizations, including priesthood quorums, and eliminate duplication. Once again Smith assigned McKay to head the committee.[7] Although the committee worked for several years, it failed to accomplish its primary assignment.

Joseph F. Smith died in the influenza pandemic of 1918. His successor, Heber J. Grant, was no less dissatisfied with the lack of coordination among church organizations, and in 1920 he selected Apostle Stephen L Richards (who in 1951 became David O. McKay's first counselor) to chair a new Correlation–Social Advisory Committee to accomplish the task.[8] After working for several months, the committee recommended that the Sunday School be given the primary responsibility for teaching, a move that would have curtailed much of the work of the other auxiliary organizations.[9] Grant and his counselors tabled the recommendation for over a year, then decided to reject it outright and maintain the status quo, thus acknowledging that each organization had a right to teach the gospel to its own members.[10] That decision continues to shape the church today, and subsequent correlation attempts generally have focused on coordinating the curricula of all organizations, rather than restricting curriculum development to one organization. Four months after rejecting its recommendation, Grant disbanded the committee.

Nonetheless, the need to coordinate an ever-burgeoning network of programs and organizations continued, and one committee followed another. One year after Grant's decision, McKay wrote to Richards from England, where he was presiding over the European Mission, encouraging him to continue the correlation effort: "It is indeed gratifying to learn that the Correlation Committee is still functioning, and that the excellent work of the social advisory committee is being carried on." He shrugged off the significance of the name change, quoting, "A rose by any other name will smell as sweet." He then made a suggestion that, over four decades later, redefined the entire organizational flow chart of the church by channeling all organizations through the Quorum of the Twelve: "I have one suggestion in regard to the Priesthood work, and that is this: The Presiding Bishopric should not act independently of the Twelve. The Aaronic Priesthood is an appendage to the Melchizedek, and the officers therein should ever work in harmony with and under the supervision of those in the Higher Priesthood."[11]

Correlation efforts continued sporadically through the 1920s, '30s, and '40s, with only minor successes. For example, in 1928, McKay, then serving a dual role as both apostle and general superintendent of the Sunday School, announced that the curricula of the priesthood quorums and the Sunday School, while remaining separate, would be reviewed and authorized by a common committee.[12] In another example, in 1929 the monthly magazines of the YMMIA and YWMIA, the *Improvement Era* and the *Young Woman's Journal,* were "wedded" into a single publication, with the YWMIA publication being subsumed into the YMMIA's. But the overall goal of consolidating and coordinating all church programs and organizations remained elusive, largely because of the autonomy exercised by the five major organizations: Relief Society, Sunday School, YMMIA, YWMIA, and Primary. In a 1938 memorandum to J. Reuben Clark Jr., Apostle John A. Widtsoe reiterated McKay's comment of fifteen years earlier: that policy decisions needed to be made by the Quorum of the Twelve rather than the auxiliary leadership.[13]

THE MODERN ERA OF CORRELATION

By the time McKay became church president in 1951, the auxiliary organizations gave the church a balkanized appearance. Organizational heads, while serving at the First Presidency's pleasure, had nearly complete autonomy and little First Presidency oversight. They also had complete responsibility for managing their own budgets and were responsible for raising operating funds in addition to those allotted from general church revenues. Joseph T. Bentley, general superintendent of the Young Men's Mutual Improvement Association, later characterized the strength and autonomy of his organization: "We paid our own expenses.... The Church didn't help the Mutual financially at all, nor *The Improvement Era* [its monthly maga-

zine]. But we were becoming stronger financially year by year.... *The Impr*
Era had developed into such a fine magazine and was so widely distributed that it
became a source, quite a large source, of revenue. Another thing we did, after I went
in, we localized and controlled our investments. We had a tremendous amount of
investments, both with Mutual and *The Improvement Era*."[14]

While not so flush with funds, largely because its monthly magazine, *The*
Instructor, did not take advertising, the Sunday School enjoyed similar independence. Lynn S. Richards, a member of its general board and later a counselor in its
general superintendency, described it: "The Quorum of the Twelve and the First
Presidency interfered very seldom with the actions of the General Board and the
Superintendency of the Deseret Sunday School Union.... We were pretty much
independent, of course, knowing what was expected of us. It was primarily to prepare the materials and try and ensure that they were more expertly presented and
better presented all over the world.... [We] decided who would write the manuals and who would do the traveling."[15]

Two General Authorities who sat on the other side of the table and saw the
strength and independence of the auxiliary organizations as an impediment, rec-
ollected the situation from their vantage point. A. Theodore Tuttle, a member of
the First Council of Seventy, noted:

> [We] could see the auxiliaries running the Church, as it were.... We
> had no Priesthood board but they had large and talented and power-
> ful Mutual boards and Sunday School boards and Relief Society
> boards and Primary boards. And they scattered throughout the
> Church teaching their message, and they were talented people and
> taught so well that the auxiliaries of the Church were far more effec-
> tive and powerful in the members' idea and view than were the Priest-
> hood quorums.... So I would say, to characterize the Church prior
> to Correlation, that the auxiliaries ran it and everything took second
> place to them.[16]

Loren C. Dunn, a member of the First Council of Seventy (1968–76), remembered "the very strong, high profile auxiliary organizations like the Young Men and
Young Women, which in some respects were almost a church of their own. They
had their own programs and their own lives."[17]

Even parts of the priesthood hierarchy existed semi-autonomously. John H.
Vandenberg, who served for many years as Presiding Bishop (1961–71), described
the loose manner in which his quorum, and through it the entire Aaronic Priesthood, related to the two quorums above it: "As to orientation, we had no orientation.... It seemed like our responsibility was mainly to do what the First Presidency asked us to do as messengers for them.... Our only relationship to the

Quorum of the Twelve was the relationship to the Correlation Committee through Brother [Harold B.] Lee."[18]

Other church organizations that did not have member constituencies had their own sets of challenges. At one point the Genealogical Society had forty-seven different divisions, "and they were not getting along with each other."[19] The business affairs of the church, which had been run almost in terms of a personal management style by prior church presidents, were fragmented, no longer manageable by such techniques. Wilford W. Kirton, the church's general counsel for decades, noted: "Because of the complexity of the temporal affairs of the Church—the housing of the membership, handling the funds of the Church, and so on—the size, and what is needed, we could be penny wise and pound foolish in terms of leadership in principal areas."[20]

And the overall curriculum, long the subject of unsuccessful attempts at consolidation and coordination, fell far short of what the General Authorities hoped and assumed it was teaching. Paul H. Dunn, who would in 1964 be called as one of the presidents of the First Council of the Seventy, did his doctoral project in 1960 when he was an Institute of Religion instructor in the Church Educational System, "for the Mormon Church, at the University of Southern California." His topic was a comparison of "what the Brethren thought ought to be taught, and what was being taught. They were miles apart.... I went through all of the curriculum of the college institute program to see if we were doing what the Brethren said we ought to do. That is where we found some real discrepancies. I made a recommendation of what we ought to be doing. When I became a General Authority, Brother [Harold B.] Lee said, 'You'll never know how that impressed me.'"[21]

Over the period of forty-five years between his calling as an apostle and as church president, David O. McKay had witnessed all attempts, both successful and unsuccessful, at correlating the church, and had participated directly in many of them. Upon becoming church president in 1951, he continued the effort to address the problems of a growing church and a formidable but fragmented church bureaucracy. Indicative of the kinds of problems he faced was a letter he received in the second year of his presidency from the general presidencies of the YMMIA and YWMIA, who unitedly bristled at the suggestion of several apostles that their organizations come under closer outside supervision:

> The Committee disapproved our selecting manuals whose immediate and direct objective was not the building of testimonies in the restored Gospel. As we interpret them, these letters recommend that the Mutuals select only theological or "gospel" subjects for class study, and recommend the rejection of purely cultural subjects, or subjects designed primarily to assist young people in applying Chris-

tian principles to the problems of life. To follow this suggestion would
constitute a complete reversal of that which we have conceived to be
approved policy.... Recently, other organizations within the Church
have entered into the recreation field, and have thereby created an
overlapping competitive area.... We might add, further, that the time
is propitious for receiving a new statement of objectives, since it has
been exactly 30 years since the First Presidency has taken occasion to
speak officially on this subject.[22]

McKay declined to answer their inquiry directly; but by allowing the status
quo to prevail, he reinforced the auxiliaries' autonomy and maintained the traditional separation between them and the Quorum of the Twelve.

On other occasions, particularly those that did not threaten the autonomy of
the auxiliary organizations, he implemented changes toward a more modern organizational structure. In 1952 the church centralized all disbursing and accounting,
which hitherto had been done within each organization and department.[23] Three
months later, in an effort to reduce the enormous workload of General Authorities, he announced that missionaries returning from their fields of labor would now
make their formal reports to local leaders rather than General Authorities.[24]

But the key area of the relationship of priesthood quorums (particularly of the
church's presiding quorums) to the auxiliary organizations remained problematic.
Although McKay had protected the autonomy of the auxiliaries, he acknowledged
that the status quo was retarding quorum development and function. In a First Presidency meeting in 1953, he noted the problem: "We have assigned very important
functions to other groups: teaching, recreation, and everything that might be incorporated in the quorum unit to strengthen its organization we have given to others."[25]

Three years later, Apostles Delbert L. Stapley and Adam S. Bennion met with
the First Presidency and recommended the appointment of a new general committee that would, once again, attempt "to correlate the courses of study given by
the Quorums and auxiliaries of the Church." McKay told them that their suggestion was "meritorious" and asked that they make it formal so that it might come
before the First Presidency and Quorum of the Twelve.[26] Four years thereafter, with
no explanation for the delay, McKay acted upon their recommendation and initiated the modern era of correlation.

On March 24, 1960, the First Presidency wrote a letter to the General Priesthood Committee, which was composed of members of the Quorum of the Twelve.
It began by referring to a meeting three weeks earlier of the First Presidency and
the Quorum, the minutes of which note:

Recommendation was made by the General Priesthood Committee and
the Council of the Twelve that the General Priesthood Committee be

permitted to make a study of the study courses of the Auxiliary
Organizations with a view of having a well-correlated plan of study.

Elder Harold B. Lee recommended that, in connection with the
matter of correlating the curriculum in the Church, it would seem to
be advisable to employ someone to make a curriculum study to assist
the Priesthood Committee in this project, the one to be employed to
do the detail work in connection therewith.

President McKay expressed the feeling that this is a step in the
right direction and said that the Committee might go forward with
this project along the lines suggested.[27]

In addition to the problem of overlapping curricula, McKay and his counselors
noted in their letter that for years the various organizations had prepared new
courses of study each year and implicitly questioned the need for such an ambitious
undertaking. They called for a thorough reevaluation of all curricula—priesthood
quorums and auxiliary organizations included. The letter concluded: "This is your
authority to employ such necessary technical help as you might need to bring this
about." Harold B. Lee, as chairman of the General Priesthood Committee, would
spearhead the effort. While the First Presidency letter clearly limited the scope of
his authority to matters of curriculum, it soon became apparent that Lee took the
letter as his mandate to enact sweeping changes that did not always meet with the
First Presidency's approval.

THE PRIESTHOOD AND THE AUXILIARY ORGANIZATIONS

From the time he was called to be an apostle in 1941, Harold B. Lee had a strong
desire to reorganize the church by placing the priesthood organization at the fore-
front. To do this, however, he would have to place limitations on the powerful
auxiliary organizations. As a junior apostle, his options were limited. "So, Brother
Lee fought a losing battle for a long time," recalled his son-in-law and biographer.
"He had his charts for correlation all prepared. But he rolled them up and put
them in his roll-top desk, and there they sat gathering dust for 15, 20 years."[28]

By 1960, Lee was not only the second most senior apostle, but also chairman
of the General Priesthood Committee within the Quorum of the Twelve Apostles.
Although the First Presidency letter of March 24 was directed to the entire committee, the minutes make it clear that Lee had been the driving force behind the
committee's recommendations. While his mandate was narrow, limited to curriculum reform, he did finally have a mandate, and he and his committee moved
quickly on two fronts.

First, it approached each organization directly. Writing to the Relief Society (and
similarly to the other auxiliary organizations), the committee asked for lists of

courses of study and copies of all manuals in order to address the issue of curriculum reform. However, it also included a request for "a statement of the Relief Society's assignment as you understand it to be from instructions received by the Relief Society from the First Presidency of the Church,"[29] thus signaling a broader intent.

On a second front, Lee called BYU President Ernest L. Wilkinson and asked to borrow one of his faculty members, Antone K. Romney, a professor of education then serving as dean of students, to chair a committee "to have charge of coordinating and revising all of the lesson plans of all Auxiliary Organizations of the Church."[30] Acting under Lee's direction, Romney outlined a plan that would examine church curriculum but go well beyond that goal to include "a study to determine the jurisdictions of the several auxiliaries and Church organizations."[31] He presented the proposal to the Education Committee of the General Priesthood Committee, which was chaired by his brother, Marion G. Romney, and included Harold B. Lee. The committee unanimously endorsed the plan on June 28, 1960, and approved Romney's suggestions for members of his committee.

Romney's task force worked for nine months, digging deep into the church archives to research not only curriculum matters, but also the history and mission of each auxiliary organization. In October, Romney went back to the Education Committee and asked a crucial question whose answer would shape his work and extend it well beyond curriculum reform: "'Is it your desire that this committee proceed in this line of thinking and attempt to bring suggestions forward which might point to a reorganization of the auxiliaries in such a way as to preserve their functions but to have activities administered through the Priesthood quorums of the Church?' An affirmative answer was given."[32]

On January 24, 1961, Romney met with his brother Marion, Harold B. Lee, and Mark E. Petersen to give a progress report on his committee's work. The three men "again suggested that all functions of all auxiliaries be placed under the operation of Priesthood Quorums."

On March 15, 1961, Antone Romney returned to the Education Committee and made a comprehensive proposal. His committee had looked closely at curriculum and, in the case of the Relief Society, "found that much material which has been covered in their theological lessons has been covered in Sunday School, MIA, and other auxiliaries." Noting similar problems among the other organizations, the committee "felt that it was impossible to limit the jurisdiction of these auxiliaries unless new assignments were made and clarified which would supersede the old." Noting in general the teaching of modern church leaders "that the Priesthood Quorums should become more active in the supervision and teaching of all things pertaining to the gospel," and quoting Joseph F. Smith's 1906 prophecy, they cautioned that the current auxiliary organizations and the priesthood quorums, which they termed a "double-wired organization" [redundant functioning], would continue to work at cross-purposes unless dramatic structural changes were made.

Feeling that "this problem should be recognized and that steps should be taken to correct the double-wired organization, and at the same time protect the functions which are carried on by the many auxiliaries which we now have," the committee recommended a solution that, although radical, was consistent with the feedback Romney had received from the Education Committee in his meetings in October and January. The essence of their recommendation was that all of the auxiliary organizations be dissolved as they were then functioning and that both the administrative structure and the curriculum be reorganized, not by organizational identity (e.g., Sunday School, Relief Society, etc.) but rather by age-group (children, youth, and adults) as priesthood-supervised organizations. In other words, the beloved and powerful auxiliary organizations would, for all practical purposes, cease to exist.

In spite of the Education Committee's earlier favorable reaction to the work of Antone Romney's group, such wholesale change was too much for even the progressive Lee to swallow. Romney's terse account of the meeting ended without editorial comment:

> After several hours of presentation to the Education Committee by the research committee, the Education Committee made numerous suggestions, and indicated that it would not be desirable for them to recommend such a complete reorganization of auxiliary work in the Church. It was thought that it would be wise for the research committee to make further study relating to correlation, maintaining the separate functions of the auxiliary organizations in their present form. The Research Committee returned to Provo and began anew on the coordination of the present basic Church organization.[33]

Perhaps Lee sensed that it would be impossible for him to get others, particularly the auxiliary leaders, to accept the demise of their organizations. And perhaps he himself, having been nurtured by these organizations throughout his life, simply could not bear to see them go. Regardless, his instructions to Romney's task force were clear: Do it again, and this time don't get rid of anything. That charge has essentially defined all correlation efforts up to the present time.

As Antone Romney and his task force returned to the drawing board, Lee proceeded to craft his own vision of correlation. One week after meeting with Romney, Lee wrote in his journal of a change that would be far-reaching: "I conducted a meeting of the Priesthood Committee where the principal item of business was to consider the final draft of a proposed overhauling of the ward teaching program of the past, under the new title of 'Priesthood Correlation Program,' with those participating as 'Priesthood Watchmen.' Twelve or 14 stakes will be selected for the experiment before launching as a Church-wide operation."[34]

"Priesthood Watchmen" had an ominous tone, as Lee later told a general conference while somewhat disingenuously distancing himself from his own terminology: "When this was discussed with President David O. McKay, some suggested we should call them watchmen—'priesthood watchmen'—but the President wisely counseled that we had better not let the membership of the Church think of the priesthood as detectives, that it would be better to call them the priesthood home teachers."[35]

While Lee moved forward with what became home teaching, Antone Romney's committee worked for four months to revise its recommendations. On July 10, 1961, Romney presented his new report to his brother: "The new purpose of the committee was to preserve the present organization as shown in the chart, but to suggest a system of correlation which would permit the reorganization of Church curriculum on age group levels, and which would coordinate the curriculum and activities and program of instruction offered to the several age groups."[36]

To accomplish this goal, the task force recommended that "a general all-church coordinating council should be formed," under whose direction three age-group committees (children, youth, and adults) would work to coordinate the activities of the existing priesthood and auxiliary organizations. The new recommendations were approved (date not specified) and implemented, and Lee became chairman of the powerful All-Church Coordinating Council.

In the October 1961 general conference, Lee unveiled his committee's work. In prefacing Lee's remarks, McKay, speaking for the First Presidency, made it clear that the mandate of the committee was curriculum reform: "We unite in saying God bless you all, and particularly we pray that the message given you this night by Elder Harold B. Lee and Elder Richard L. Evans regarding the correlating of our studies, Melchizedek, Aaronic, and auxiliary, may be understood and taken to heart. It is one of the greatest undertakings that have yet been presented to the Priesthood."[37]

Lee, for his part, emphasized the curriculum reform activities of his committee. He cited "an urgent need of correlation of studies among the auxiliaries of the Church, to avoid the necessity for new courses of study every year," and announced the establishment of "an all-Church co-ordinating council and three co-ordinating committees: one for the children, one for the youth, and one for adults" to work toward that goal. He made no mention of the radical reorganization that his own committee had first encouraged from Antone Romney's task force, then summarily discarded, but he foreshadowed his broader agenda when he spoke of "consolidation and simplification of…church publications, church buildings, church meetings."

Lee concluded his talk by referring to a recent and controversial decision by McKay to ordain the seven members of the First Council of Seventy to the office of high priest. Perhaps in an effort to pave the way for acceptance of his own subsequent reforms, Lee used the decision as an object lesson on the prerogatives of the sitting church president:

> Recently, Presidency McKay, acting under the inspiration of his calling, moved to enlarge the activities of the seventies, by ordaining some of the presidents of seventies to the office of high priests, with the explanation that it would make them more serviceable and more effective in their work. I was in one of the Arizona stakes, and I had one of the brethren ask, "Was it not true that the Prophet Joseph had said that it was contrary to the order of heaven that a high priest should be in that position?" I merely said to him, "Had you ever thought that what might have been contrary to the order of heaven in the early 1830's might not be contrary to the order of heaven in 1960?"[38]

There was irony in Lee's use of the story, for while he accepted McKay's decision, defended his authority to make it, and used it as a precedent of his own sweeping changes, he was not personally in favor of it. Upon becoming church president in 1972, "he quietly reversed that decision, calling and setting apart Rex D. Pinegar to the First Council without making him a high priest."[39]

McKay's initial reaction to Lee's correlation efforts was positive. According to Lee's biographer: "President McKay told Elder Lee that he had awakened one morning at 6:30 A.M. with a clear impression as to the proper theme for the general priesthood meeting of general conference in October 1961. He was impressed that the newly approved correlation program should be that theme and asked Elder Lee and Elder Richard L. Evans to speak on this subject."[40]

McKay's diary entry confirms this report. In describing the priesthood session of general conference, he recorded: "Elders Harold B. Lee and Richard L. Evans masterfully explained that three correlation committees will handle the activities and materials for three general age groups, and gave further details about the plans."[41] The following June, Lee and his new All-Church Coordinating Council gave "a progress report of their work on coordinating lesson materials for the Church," which McKay described in his diary as "an excellent work."[42]

However, it is apparent in hindsight that McKay and his counselors, while being apprised of progress in curriculum reform, were not being given all of the details of Lee's plans for correlation. McKay began to sense that there was more to it than he had been told, and in May 1962 he conveyed some of his concern to his secretary by saying, "We cannot run the Church as we would run a business."[43]

Several months later, in a meeting of the First Presidency, Henry D. Moyle, the first counselor, bluntly described what he saw as correlation's threat to the primacy of the First Presidency, initiating a remarkably candid discussion among McKay, Moyle, and Hugh B. Brown that highlighted the suspicion of all three about Lee and his plans. McKay dictated a lengthy description of the meeting for his diary:

> At the conclusion of the discussion, President Moyle said: "Do you think this correlation which has to do with primarily the class work in the various organizations, should transfer any of the responsibilities that are now placed in the Presidency to the Twelve, for genealogical work, as an example?"
>
> I said that the correlation work affects primarily the duplication of courses of study, and that it should not affect the organization of the Church.
>
> President Brown said that the Prophet [Joseph Smith] had a wonderful sense of propriety and of revelation when he said that it is the nature and disposition of almost all men when they get a little authority as they suppose to extend it, and to reach out for more and more.
>
> I quoted: "Hence, many are called and few are chosen. Why are they not chosen? Because they have not learned this one lesson, etc."
>
> President Moyle added, "That no power or influence can or ought to be maintained."
>
> And I quoted, "Only upon the principle of righteousness."
>
> I then said that these matters of correlation of our work are for all three of the First Presidency to decide; that when we are united, we can take the next steps and until we are united, we do not take any step.[44]

In their meeting the following morning, the three men continued the discussion. Their concern that Lee and his correlation agenda were extending beyond curriculum reform had not cooled overnight. McKay began:

> This correlation work is applicable to courses of study of priesthood and auxiliaries to avoid duplication. *That is the purpose of the correlation work.* That is the heart of it, and further than that as it affects the organization of the Church, we will have to decide and tell them so. That is where we stand on that.... It is easy to understand how the Apostasy took place in the early days.
>
> President Brown added, "Take the heads away, and you are done."

President Moyle said, "Leave this alone, and you get something contrary to the Church. That is the way the Roman branch of the Church took precedence. As big as we are now, the amount of assistance and instruction and supervision that we can give is essential to maintain the integrity of the Church and the efficiency of our work."

I said that we are holding that whole proposition up; that it is going farther than the correlating of studies. It is going to the point of suggesting a change in the organization of the Church. That is the vital point now.

President Moyle said, "This program was suggested in 1948; it is in the files." I said that I did not remember it.

President Moyle said that it was presented at great length to the Presidency and the Twelve; and I said, "Yes, but we didn't accept it." President Moyle replied, "No, we did not."

I said, "This latest suggestion is striking at the very heart of it. They wanted to see me, but I told them we shall have to take it under further consideration, and that is where it is standing."[45]

The next week McKay and his counselors met to discuss the presentations to be given the following evening in the priesthood session of October general conference by Lee and his committee members. Concerned that Lee would overstep his bounds, McKay said:

"It would be well to have these Brethren explain to the Priesthood specifically what we are going to do, and that we should consult with Brother Lee particularly in telling each one what to say.... This will enable the entire Priesthood to get the Correlation of the courses of study; *that there will be no change in Church Government, and that now is a good time to get that clearly defined.*" President Brown concurred in the plan and said that it would be a good time since the Stake Presidents and the Bishops will be present. President Moyle also agreed and said that the great coverage to the Priesthood will also make it advantageous.[46]

From his own standpoint, Lee was boldly advancing a new blueprint for correlation, despite uncertainty about whether McKay would undo what he had done. But opposition also came from other quarters, as both salaried bureaucrats and volunteer auxiliary staff moved to protect their own turf. Barbara Bradshaw Smith, who later served as Relief Society general president (1974–84), recalled, "President Lee said that was the hard part. Every time he would do anything, there was always somebody trying to change it."[47]

Correlation and Church Restructuring

In the October 1962 general conference, Harold B. Lee announced the home teaching program and described it as "the first tangible step forward that the Church will see on a church-wide basis" of the correlation process.[48] The new program, which would be implemented church-wide in January 1964, had McKay's endorsement even though it went beyond the mandate of curriculum reform. Home teaching differed from then-current ward teaching in two significant ways. First, home teachers (adult male priesthood holders) would have stewardship over the general welfare of the families to which they were assigned, rather than merely delivering a rote message each month that was published a year in advance. Second, while the bishops would administer the program at the local level, at the general level it would fall under the direction of the Quorum of the Twelve, not the Presiding Bishopric, who had supervised ward teaching.

This latter point became a bone of contention between Lee and Moyle. The two men had once been the closest of friends, but that friendship seemed to fade quickly when, in 1959, McKay bypassed several senior apostles, including Lee, and plucked the more junior Moyle from the Quorum of the Twelve to join the First Presidency upon the death of Stephen L Richards. Moyle's daughter later commented on the deterioration of their friendship:

> They were very close. I often heard my father say that if he could have chosen a brother, he would have chosen Harold B. Lee. He adored President Lee, and went out of his way to do things for Sister Lee, particularly when she became ill. But something happened to their relationship. When Daddy went up and told President Lee that he had become Second Counselor—Mother was with him and told me this—his [Lee's] face went completely red. He just could not seem to accept that Daddy had surpassed him in the hierarchy of the Church.[49]

Those feelings now came to the fore over the new home teaching program. Only three days before the April 1963 general conference session in which Lee was to present details of the program, Moyle voiced his objections in a First Presidency meeting that Lee attended. McKay's diary makes it clear that the mood of the meeting was tense, even combative:

> Brother Lee said this plan was presented to the Twelve and approved by them and commended. President Moyle said he had not approved of the plan but was very upset about it.... [Brother Lee] said the program has been developed step by step and has been brought to the First Presidency and the Twelve where it was approved and now is in

the process of being printed.... President Moyle said this takes it
entirely out of the hands of the Presiding Bishopric. Brother Lee said
I am telling you what has been developed by the First Presidency and
the Twelve.... President Moyle said he understood that the original
commission to the Correlation Committee was to correlate the ward
teaching messages to be delivered by the ward teachers and that the
committee would go no farther. Brother Lee said no step has been
taken that has not been explored and approved by the Presidency and
the Twelve. President Moyle expressed the opinion that the committee has gone beyond the letter of commission given it.[50]

At this point, McKay intervened and asked Lee to present the plan, for a second time, to the First Presidency and Quorum of the Twelve the following morning. Moyle then enumerated other areas where he felt Lee and his colleagues had
overstepped the boundaries of their assignment:

President Moyle commented upon the dismissal of Brother Hinckley
from the direction of missionary work without the knowledge of the
First Presidency and the giving of this function to the Priesthood Missionary Committee Representative. He said he understood that when
a change was made the Missionary Committee was to report to the
First Presidency directly. I expressed concurrence. President Moyle
commented also upon the taking over of the Genealogical work and
the selecting of a manager to take Brother Tanner's place.[51]

Lee sidestepped those issues, merely stating, "We shall have Brother Romney
make the presentation tomorrow." He then left the meeting, but Moyle continued
to press his case that Lee was moving beyond his authority and, in doing so, was
undermining the primacy of the First Presidency. "We have never agreed that the
Correlation Committee could dismiss Brother Tanner from the Genealogical
Department and Brother Hinckley from the Missionary Department. They have
been appointed by the Presidency."[52] In view of their recent discussions on the matter, McKay undoubtedly agreed with Moyle. Nonetheless, he declined to reverse
the decisions and, by his inaction, strengthened Lee's hand.

The following year, in September 1964, the growing power of correlation again
became the focus of a First Presidency meeting. This time, the discussion included
McKay, Hugh B. Brown, and N. Eldon Tanner, who had joined the First Presidency
in October 1963 after Moyle's death in September. McKay raised the issue:

I inquired if the counselors know what the Correlation Committee is
doing, and said that it is a matter that should be handled very carefully or it will get out of hand; that at present it is too indefinite for

the Church as a whole. President Tanner commented that he thinks
he knows what they are trying to do, but that he had some fear that
we are organizing this to a point where it would be somewhat in the
nature of regimentation, and that he thinks the program should be
very carefully checked before we go forward. I agreed implicitly, and
said that the Correlation Program must be carefully checked before
we go any further. We agreed that the Correlation people should submit to the First Presidency briefly, but fully the program of the Committee, and that the First Presidency would go over it to get it clearly
in their minds before it is given out to the Church.[53]

But Lee had the momentum and continued to pursue his ambitious agenda,
which included shifting the day-to-day control of the church from the First Presidency to the Quorum of the Twelve. In the process, he publicly invoked God's will
as legitimizing his efforts, reservations of the First Presidency notwithstanding.
Speaking to the general conference in October 1964, just one month after the First
Presidency's doubts about his efforts, he proclaimed: "My mind has been filled with
the realization that in 1964 and the year just preceding, we have been receiving as
pertinent and important divine direction as has ever been given to the Church in
any similar period in its history through the prophet and leader who now presides
as the President of this Church. You may recognize it in some of the developments
we know as the correlation program. You have seen it being unraveled bit by bit,
and you will see and hear more of it."[54]

To be sure, Lee and his colleagues did not lose sight of what had been their
primary charge—the coordination of curricula of the many church organizations.
But curriculum reform paled in significance next to Lee's other goals of reining in
the auxiliary organizations and placing day-to-day control of the church in the
hands of the Twelve. Predictably, the auxiliary organizations resisted the change.
Lee's son-in-law later described the process: "The changes were still painful to
make, when they actually came down to it, because the auxiliaries did not want to
relinquish their control. They had huge general boards. They had all the talent in
the Church marshaled at their command. Their conventions were showplaces.
They had the budget. BYU was making films for those Sunday School conventions,
and they were beautiful. It was a huge bureaucracy that was under attack. The
changes came slowly and painfully, but they were made."[55]

The auxiliary organizations were not the only groups to be threatened. Members of the First Presidency continued to express privately their concerns about the
growing power of the correlation movement, which was undermining their own
control. In May 1967, McKay, Brown, and Tanner again discussed the subject in a
First Presidency meeting:

President Brown stated that it seemed evident that the First Presidency is losing its grip on the activities that are going forward, and that more and more we are being regulated and ruled by committees.... He felt that the First Presidency is taking rather a second place to the committees in these matters. He explained that for example the handling of the Missionary Department, which heretofore has always been under one of the Presidency of the Church, is being carried on quite exclusively by the Missionary Executive Committee.... He said that he would like to pull back into the hands of the First Presidency some of the things that seem to be slipping from them.... I said that this should be taken under consideration immediately.[56]

Two days later, Brown expressed further reservations to McKay and Tanner about the amount of power that had already passed to the Quorum of the Twelve:

He said he considered the [correlation] program rather revolutionary and wondered if it should not have been given more consideration. He mentioned that there is [*sic*] a number of things about it that he felt we might not want if more thought were given; that it is something of a new system. President Tanner said he just wondered if I were happy about the whole thing. President Brown suggested the wisdom of dividing up the Auxiliary organization supervisory work among the counselors in the First Presidency. He said that at present the Twelve have great responsibility, and the First Presidency very little so far as the operation of the Church from day to day is concerned.... President Brown said that he would be glad to work in one or two of these organizations and carry the responsibility that is now being carried by the Twelve or their Assistants, if I felt it advisable.... President Brown then suggested the possible advisability of giving to the members of the First Presidency supervision of the missionary work, which he stated one of the counselors in the First Presidency supervised until the death of President Henry D. Moyle, when this was turned over to the Missionary Executive Committee. He thought it would be much better administered by the First Presidency with the assistance of the Twelve.[57]

McKay indicated that he would like to take the matter under advisement, but he subsequently declined to take the action that Brown had advocated. The basis of his inaction is not clear. Perhaps he saw that structural changes were necessary if the church was to be able to respond successfully to its phenomenal growth and that Lee's plan, regardless of its adverse effect on First Presidency prerogatives, was an appropriate solution. Or perhaps, as a ninety-three-year-old man in failing health, he simply would not or could not rein in the ambitions of a man twenty-six years his junior. Furthermore, the force of Lee's personality was undeniable. He was second in line for the office of church president, twenty-three years younger than the man in between (Joseph Fielding Smith), and had assembled an impressive array of supporters among the other General Authorities. Regardless of the reason, for the remaining three years of his life McKay took no overt action to counteract Lee's initiatives.

By the time of McKay's death in 1970, correlation had achieved mixed results. At a meeting of church leaders in 1971, Lee reported an impressive list of accomplishments:

> Even as I repeat them now it seems unbelievable that we have been able to do what we have done in this time: priesthood home teaching; family home evening; unified social services; the expansion and clarification of the missionary responsibilities of the seventies quorums; expansion of the home-study seminary course; bishops' training course; priesthood teacher development; libraries and how to use them; definition of a closer relationship between the Aaronic Priesthood and the MIA; improving and making more effective preparation, editing, translating, and distributing of teaching materials, and the distribution to meet the deadlines at seasonal beginnings; introduction of a Church-wide library program; the experimental study of the Church membership all over the world to achieve a feeling of closer relationship with the full Church program; the correlation and clarification of the LDS Student Association role to meet the unmet youth needs using the existing structure rather than a separate professional staff; and the correlation of military relations programs using existing Church structure instead of professionals. So we go on and on, and all of this under the direction of the Twelve.[58]

It was not, however, a clean sweep. The long-standing and deeply entrenched bureaucracies of the auxiliary organizations, particularly those headed by women, had managed to delay the implementation of some of the reforms that Lee had pushed. The Relief Society was arguably the most powerful of the auxiliaries, with a constituency that potentially included all women in the church. Since 1945 it had been headed by Belle Smith Spafford. And the Primary, the organization for the church's children, had been led since 1951 by LaVern Watts Parmley. Both women retained their positions and much of their organizational autonomy beyond Lee's death in 1973. Ultimately, however, the main elements of Lee's vision of correlation were accomplished: coordinating the functions of all church organizations, transferring their budgets to the General Church Operating Fund, and terminating their publications in favor of three age-grouped magazines that began publication in January 1971, one each for children, youth, and adults. They also, more significantly, came under the direct control of the Quorum of the Twelve. In the process, the power of that quorum was greatly enhanced, albeit at the expense of the First Presidency. Gordon B. Hinckley, an apostle at the time of these changes but currently church president, viewed the transfer of power benignly when he was interviewed in 1996: "My feeling has been to use the Twelve more.... The Church is growing so tremendously, just leaping forward in a tremendous way. Rather than think of more counselors in the Presidency, I've simply felt to use the Twelve. And that's been my philosophy of governing."[59]

As a final note, there was another, less benign aspect to correlation, probably not foreseen by McKay or Lee, that gradually took on a life of its own, and that continues to this day. It was aptly characterized by one General Authority whose tenure began in 1964, near the beginning of the correlation movement:

> I think what happened is what's happening in government today, as I see it now, thirty years later. For example, the Supreme Court is supposed to determine the constitutionality of a law, but very gradually, the Supreme Court starts to make the law. That's what is happening to correlation. Correlation creates nothing. That's the process. It has no authority to make a statement that creates a position or direction. That's totally out of harmony with what President McKay set up. Brother Lee understood that, and carried it out. Since the 1970s, I've seen that drift, where correlation now is telling me, if I write something to get through correlation, "You can't say that." And I write back and say, "Why?" And they say, "Well, because we think this is the interpretation." And I write back and say, "You're not the interpreter."... And that's where we get lost. Today, I see correlation, like the Supreme Court, becoming more and more the originator of the thought, rather than the coordinator of the thought.... So, while I think correlation is good, I think it's gone past its original commission.[60]

8

THE
EDUCATION SYSTEM

David O. McKay was a professional educator until his calling as an apostle in 1906, and education remained a paramount interest over the subsequent six decades of his life. His nineteen-year tenure as church president coincided almost exactly with that of Ernest L. Wilkinson as president of Brigham Young University, and the educational alliance of the two men transformed BYU from a bucolic college to the largest church-owned university in the United States. In the process of fostering church-sponsored higher education, McKay instilled into an entire generation of Latter-day Saints a love of the life of the mind coupled with a charge to go wherever truth led.

McKay's early role model was Mosiah Hall, in whose home he had been tutored in elocution as a child. Speaking at Hall's funeral over a half-century later, McKay reminisced, "Brother Hall started me out as a teacher—he had me assisting him in his school room the year I completed the 8th Grade."[1] After graduating from the University of Utah, McKay became the principal of the Weber Stake Academy (predecessor to Weber State University) in Ogden, the position he held at the time of his calling as an apostle.

His philosophy was that true education is liberal, painted by the broad brush strokes of all academic disciplines, unfettered by thin pencil lines of dogma. Speaking at the dedication of a church high school in New Zealand he said: "Members of the Church are admonished to acquire learning by study; also, by faith and prayer; and to seek after everything that is virtuous, lovely or of good report, or praiseworthy. In this seeking after truth, they are not confined to narrow limits of dogma, or creed, but are free to launch into the realm of the infinite for they know that 'truth is truth where'er it is found, whether on Christian or on heathen ground.'"[2]

Not only did he admonish church members to seek truth wherever it was to be found, but also to "learn uphill"—that is, to tackle progressively more difficult

159

intellectual challenges, as related by Hugh Nibley, a professor of ancient languages at BYU:

> I wrote the priesthood manual for 1957, you know, *An Approach to the Book of Mormon*. Well, there was a reading committee on it. Adam S. Bennion was the head of the committee.... The reading committee wiped out every lesson in that book. Now this is one thing in which I'm greatly obliged to President McKay. They kicked out every lesson in the book. They said it was over people's heads. And every time, President McKay overruled them. The book is exactly as I wrote it. They wanted to make hundreds of changes and get rid of the whole thing entirely, and President McKay said, "No. If it's beyond their reach, let them reach for it." Adam S. Bennion said, "It's over their heads." And President McKay said, "Let them reach for it." Now there's a great man. I liked that.[3]

Well aware that knowledge brought risk, McKay's response was to manage the risk, not proscribe the knowledge. Noting the "young man who, as his immature beliefs fall from him one by one, finds himself substituting science for religion, and the scientist for God," his response was to add religion as a refining influence on the young scientist, not caution him to retreat to safer ground. Similarly, he acknowledged the inherent risks of technology yet welcomed them, with one caveat. On the eve of the United States' entry into World War II, he sounded a cautionary note: "Twenty-five years ago an intoxicated man might tip the buggy over, but commonly the old horse will bring him home. Today a driver under the influence of liquor maims and kills.... As one result of the automobile has been to put hell on wheels, the airplane will put hell on wings unless righteousness too is speeded up. On the development of character depends whether the airplane shall bring prosperity or calamity."[4]

Indeed, the development of character stood ahead of career training as the primary goal of education:

> Character is the aim of true education; and science, history, and literature are but means used to accomplish this desired end. Character is not the result of chance, but of continuous right thinking and right acting. True education seeks to make men and women not only good mathematicians, proficient linguists, profound scientists, or brilliant literary lights, but also, honest men, with virtue, temperance, and brotherly love. It seeks to make men and women who prize truth, justice, wisdom, benevolence, and self-control as the choicest acquisitions of a successful life.

> It is regrettable that modern education so little emphasized
> these fundamental elements of true character. The principle [*sic*]
> aim of many of our schools and colleges seems to be to give the
> students purely intellectual attainment and means of gaining a
> livelihood, and to give but passing attention to the nobler and
> more necessary development along moral lines.[5]

The latter point overrode his Scots frugality and justified the huge expenditures on higher education that he consistently authorized. As a youthful apostle in 1926, he stated clearly his bias: "I am not in favor at all of spending money on higher education in Church Schools...but I hesitate about eliminating the schools now established, because of the growing tendency all over the world to sneer at religion." The goal was not to shield students from modern thought, but rather to have a place "where the principles of our religion may form part of the teaching of the schools."[6] "Let us seek to live intellectually," he urged, and church schools provided the ideal venue.[7] Although philosophical differences and economic exigencies often led to heated policy debates, education always held a favored position when the budgetary pie was sectioned.

THE GROWTH OF BRIGHAM YOUNG UNIVERSITY

Ernest L. Wilkinson's term as BYU president spanned the entire period that David O. McKay served as church president. Thus, to understand BYU during the McKay years, one must examine Wilkinson, both as a person and an administrator.

Wilkinson grew up in Ogden, graduated from BYU in 1921, then moved east to study law at George Washington University and Harvard. A successful law career in Washington, D.C., reached its zenith when he represented the Ute Indians in a lawsuit against the U.S. government and won a record $32 million award. His portion of the award made him wealthy and gave him the luxury of pursuing a second career.

In 1949 Howard MacDonald, the BYU president, resigned under pressure and opened the way for Wilkinson to throw his hat into the ring. After a lengthy search process, the list of candidates was shortened to seven, five of whom had solid academic credentials. McKay, who was on the search committee and the BYU Board of Trustees, personally favored Henry Aldous Dixon, president of Weber College in Ogden; but the search committee recommended to the First Presidency that Wilkinson, who had no academic experience, be given the job. The First Presidency, then consisting of George Albert Smith, J. Reuben Clark Jr., and McKay, unanimously agreed, and in July 1950 offered him an invitation to head BYU. Wilkinson accepted but did not begin the job until February 1951.[8]

Only two months after Wilkinson arrived on campus, George Albert Smith died, and Wilkinson suddenly had a new leader. Monroe McKay, a federal judge and cousin of David O., later commented on the dilemma Wilkinson faced. "Ernest Wilkinson clearly understood, I think, that President McKay was both the key and the problem. He must have known that President McKay had not been enthusiastic about his appointment, and what he set about to do was to lobby."[9]

The two men were of sharply contrasting personalities, yet Wilkinson succeeded in gaining McKay's consistent support. Wilkinson's daughter, Alice Wilkinson Anderson, later described the relationship: "I was impressed with what I viewed as an uncommon charismatic relationship between two men with seemingly opposite temperamental endowments. It was a relationship which was first seeded with respect but which then blossomed into friendship, visibly warm, and uncharacteristically comfortable, at least for my father."[10]

Wilkinson wasted no time in forging new ties. On April 9, 1951, the same day McKay was sustained as church president, Wilkinson phoned his office for an appointment.[11] The men met two days later; and Wilkinson presented a lengthy and ambitious agenda,[12] thus establishing the tradition of direct contact that was the foundation of his administrative strategy.

He took pains to maintain the contact, often employing unconventional means. For years, until McKay moved permanently into an apartment in the Hotel Utah in August 1960, Wilkinson would often arrive in the parking lot of the Church Administration Building before 6:00 A.M., wait until McKay arrived, and then intercept him on his way to his office. After McKay's move, "he would wait in the lobby of the Hotel Utah to catch the President as he was walking over to his office, because he didn't want to have him tied down immediately by a lot of other people that had problems that they wanted the President to solve. He wanted to get there first. And that determination, of course, made a real impression."[13]

Wilkinson also understood that Clare Middlemiss was the president's gatekeeper. "Wilkinson knew how to butter up the secretary, and he really worked very closely with Clare," commented John T. Bernhard, Wilkinson's administrative assistant. "I think she really went out of her way at times to tell him when it would be a good time to visit with the President.... He was very good at that. He talked more to her, actually, than to some of the Brethren about his chances of getting in to see President McKay."[14]

Occasionally, direct access required even more creativity. McKay's housekeeper recalled one such incident:

> Middlemiss wouldn't let him talk to President McKay. That was two
> or three months before he died. So he went to the hotel, and asked if
> he could talk to President McKay. They rang the telephone, and at the

time I was in the office with the medicine, because I was right there, and I picked up the phone. "It's Brother Wilkinson. He would like to see you. Will you receive him?" Well, he [McKay] hesitated, then he said, "Well, let him come." He didn't want to say no to him, so he [Wilkinson] came up. He was so grateful I let him see President McKay that he gave me ten dollars—he sent it through the mail. Of course, I kept it![15]

Access to McKay was crucial to Wilkinson's success, for he was not a consensus builder. If a direct approach did not win over BYU's Board of Education, he went around the board, time after time, and appealed directly to McKay, much to the chagrin of board members. Paul H. Dunn, a Seventy who began his service on the BYU Board of Trustees in 1966, recalled: "That caused a real frustration with the Twelve, and particularly Harold B. Lee. When they'd get through with a Board of Education meeting, it was not uncommon for Ernest Wilkinson to go over to the hotel with President McKay and follow up on some things that didn't go too well over at the meeting, where he got vetoed or turned down on something."[16] McKay's son, Edward, confirmed the observation. "I'm sure it ruffled some of the Brethren when Ernest would bypass them and come right to Father when he had a problem. The door was always open."[17]

At the same time that Wilkinson was working hard to maintain his own access, he consolidated his power by blocking similar access by other BYU employees. "He insisted to his Board of Trustees that all school matters must go through him—no more end-runs with faculty members taking complaints to their favorite apostles."[18]

While access to McKay was crucial, Wilkinson's forte was a combination of brilliance, prodigious energy, and meticulous attention to detail. James Fletcher, who was president of the University of Utah and had frequent interaction with Wilkinson, gave him the highest marks for intelligence. Fletcher's widow recalled, "Jim thought he was one of the smartest men he had ever worked with.... He thought things through. He could look at a problem and analyze it."[19]

Wilkinson's energy was boundless, in spite of a schedule that often reduced sleep to as little as four hours on some nights.[20] Joseph T. Bentley, BYU comptroller, recalled that he relentlessly drove himself and his associates: "He would spend nearly all his time at his office, even on Sunday, and he would expect that he could call his close associates any time, day or night, and expect them to respond.... I think that the present size and the quality programs at BYU are largely a result of the one-track, concentrated mind of President Wilkinson."[21]

Intelligence and hard work were coupled with thorough preparation. Clark, who had favored Wilkinson's appointment, said, "I've been on many Boards of

Directors, but I've never seen a Chief Executive Officer come to board meetings more thoroughly prepared than Ernest Wilkinson."[22] Dale T. Tingey, one of Wilkinson's assistants for the Institute of Religion program, described the process:

> He figured if you got enough material to overwhelm them, they couldn't answer it, and he was a master at that. We'd be working for weeks to make a presentation on why they ought to build a big building, or why they ought to reach out and do this. The Brethren would walk in there cold and smart and capable, but they didn't have anything to combat it with. He would be so prepared, and if he did get turned down he'd say, "They don't mean no, they just don't understand the situation." So we'd all go back to work again.[23]

Wilkinson paid so much attention to detail that he occasionally crossed over the line of propriety. Bernhard, his administrative assistant, recalled that Wilkinson covertly taped board meetings: "One of the things that Wilkinson told Clyde Sandgren to do was to bring this big briefcase, and then he'd have a tape recorder in the briefcase so that all of the comments that the Brethren made at the meeting would be recorded. I saw this thing in the briefcase, and I knew what was happening.... Wilkinson looked at it from the viewpoint of being able to pick up all of the side comments that were made during the meeting that he might have missed."[24]

Though Wilkinson's means were sometimes unsavory, they were effective in accomplishing his ends. Joseph Rosenblatt, a prominent Salt Lake City businessman and close friend of McKay, gave a particularly candid assessment:

> Wilkinson had a lot of bad habits, but he was a driver! He was imbued with the fact that BYU was going to be a great institution of higher learning. He screamed for money, and he got money.... That set the pattern for the growth of BYU, getting top people in there as professors and teachers and a willingness to spend money in order to achieve excellence. That was probably one of the greatest accomplishments.... With all his peculiarities of personality, he did do a great job and you have to give him credit for it. He was mean and he was vicious in the way he treated people, but the goal [of building BYU] was the same goal.[25]

Richard D. Poll, a BYU history professor from 1948 until he resigned in 1970 in the aftermath of the BYU spy scandal (discussed below), expressed a similar sentiment regarding Wilkinson's people skills: "The tragedy of President Wilkinson in my view—and I think it is a tragedy—is that he never discovered how to relate to the faculty. He thought of it as an ordinary employer-employee relationship, and a university can't operate on that basis."[26]

Nor, for that matter, did he discover how to relate to the General Authorities who constituted his Board of Trustees, particularly Harold B. Lee. Paul Dunn recalled: "There was no love lost between those two. It was strained every time the two sat, and they were always right across the table from each other. That always made it interesting. I'd come in, and I'd go clear down to the end, just so I could get a better view of the activity. It was like the gladiators!"[27] Harold B. Lee was a key player during and after the McKay years, and Wilkinson's strained relationship with Lee came back to haunt him after McKay's death.

David O. McKay made clear his dream for BYU before either he or Wilkinson became presidents. Speaking to the student body in 1948, he defined the reason for BYU's stature: "Its paramount purpose is character, ...to make great men, great scientists, great leaders. Any institution which is prompted by those incentives or aims is great. You will agree with me also that the Brigham Young University is destined to become greater than it is now. You may not agree with me when I say that I look upon the Brigham Young University as having resting upon it the greatest responsibility of any university in the world."[28]

Wilkinson agreed completely with McKay's vision but saw it in an even broader perspective, with BYU being the flagship of an entire system of church-sponsored higher education. Accomplishment of his own dream required broader powers, and he worked behind the scenes to acquire them. In March 1953, McKay created the framework that would give Wilkinson total control over church education by approving "the suggestion...that we place the Brigham Young University and Colleges, Institutes and Seminaries under one head." Meeting with Franklin B. West, the Church Commissioner of Education, the same day, McKay informed him of the plan. West agreed in concept but suggested that the commissioner be placed over all educational entities, including BYU, rather than having the BYU president over everything.[29] McKay disagreed, and three months later summarily informed West that his services "would soon be discontinued."[30] In July 1953, the church announced that Wilkinson would thereafter act as both the "Administrator" (later Chancellor) of the Church Unified School System and also as president of BYU.[31]

Wilkinson moved quickly to implement his master plan. One month after his appointment, he established a policy that would shape the educational plans of tens of thousands of LDS students over the following decade, until swollen enrollments dictated other options. "The policy will be that of encouraging Latter-day Saint boys and girls to attend our Church schools—that is, Brigham Young University and Ricks College, except where there are definite reasons for them attending other universities."[32]

The policy worked. Enrollment at BYU, in particular, began to climb rapidly, albeit requiring considerable sacrifice from some LDS families. Paul Dunn, who was an Institute of Religion director in Southern California during this period, described the dilemma: "We had parents who were going into financial debt to get their kid up to the 'Y' when they could go to a junior college in California, which in those days was darned near free."[33]

More students meant more classrooms and dormitories, and Wilkinson quickly began an unprecedented building program that has not since been equaled. Initially he had but one source of capital funding, and that was general church revenues. The magnitude of his plan exceeded those resources, however, and so he "told the [First Presidency] that the real challenge now at the BYU, in view of the enlarged educational system of the Church, was to obtain large contributions to our educational system from members of the Church who could afford to give, rather than to rely entirely on the tithing of the Church."[34] Two years later a full-time development office was approved, which since has raised over $1 billion.

In the meantime, Wilkinson had to rely on tithing dollars, and that meant courting the approval of his Board of Trustees, the Church Budget Committee, and, not least, David O. McKay. His overwhelming preparation for committee meetings was always reinforced by McKay's approval; and as a result, Wilkinson was successful even beyond his own immodest expectations. BYU's budget doubled from $3 million during his first five years; and in 1957 he confided to his diary: "When I became president and administrator, no one, least of all I, ever thought the budget would become so large in so short a time."[35]

The following year, however, the bloom began to fade from the rose. McKay's ambitious program of building chapels throughout the world was rapidly gaining momentum under the leadership of Wendell Mendenhall, chairman of the Building Department, and competition for budget dollars tightened. (See chap. 9 for an account of the budget problems created by the rapid building of chapels.) Late in 1958, McKay was given sobering budget projections for the following year. In 1951, Wilkinson's first full year at BYU, the education budget had been $3 million, or 13 percent of the total church budget. His request for 1959 (the church budget was on a calendar year) was $29 million, 37 percent of the total requests. Furthermore, the requested increase at BYU alone, $10 million, accounted for 57 percent of the total increase in requests. The understated minutes of the meeting note: "It was suggested that there was probably a need for a comprehensive, coordinated study of the church educational program including the development of a financial schedule." McKay directed that Wilkinson and Mendenhall, both of whom ran programs with insatiable appetites, work together to produce such a study.[36]

Ten months later, in October 1959, J. Reuben Clark Jr., who had recently been promoted back to his former position as first counselor in the First Presidency, passed along a friendly warning. Recorded Wilkinson in his diary: "He told me that there was criticism of the large spending at BYU."[37] In early December, Apostle Spencer W. Kimball, chair of the Budget Committee, dropped the axe by informing Wilkinson that "there would have to be a very, very drastic cut in our [BYU's] budget."[38] The following day Wilkinson got the details. In 1959 church expenses had exceeded income by $8 million, and budget requests for 1960 exceeded projected tithing revenues by $17 million. Although Wilkinson had requested only a 2.2 percent increase for 1960, far less than in earlier years, he was now asked to cut his proposed budget by $8 million—nearly 30 percent. He bristled at the request and pointed out that "in the past we had always lived within our own budget and had voluntarily cut down our own budget very substantially for the coming year"—a veiled shot at Wendell Mendenhall and his Building Department, which had notoriously overspent its budget.[39]

In February 1960, Wilkinson met informally with Clark but found no support there. Clark bluntly told him, "Ernest, I think you are money-mad at the 'Y'."[40] Undoubtedly stung by the rebuke from his mentor, Wilkinson nonetheless was buoyed by the fact that the one voice that counted the most, David O. McKay's, spoke no word of criticism. The silence of that voice allowed Wilkinson to fight vigorously and successfully to maintain BYU's budget at a level sufficient to sustain the continuing swell in enrollment.

In October 1966, Wilkinson made a summary report to McKay of BYU's progress during his tenure: Enrollment had quadrupled to over 20,000, in the process of which "BYU now has become a university of world-wide importance." Eighty "major, permanent buildings" had been constructed, yet they were filled to capacity. Demand for admission had not abated, but further expansion was problematic in view of the fact that three-fourths of the expense of educating each student was paid by tithing revenues. Wilkinson's recommendation was pragmatic. "The school can grow further only if we can build new buildings to accommodate the students, and these must be financed largely outside the school budget." McKay was delighted with the report. "I congratulated these brethren and told them that they had my prayers and heartfelt wishes for their success; that education has always been dear to my heart, and that this all pleases me very much."[41]

Given McKay's encouragement, Wilkinson continued to build. In 1969, six months prior to McKay's death, Wilkinson gave him a final, brief report: "I am devoting my full energies in preparation for the opening of school in September, when we will have 24,000 students. It is now the largest private University in the United States, and what is more important has the finest student body in the world."[42]

Richard Poll, even though he criticized Wilkinson's lack of people skills, was nonetheless highly complimentary of his success in building BYU:

I have felt that President Wilkinson made a great contribution to the university in two respects. One, he obtained from the General Authorities a commitment to the university such that its status could no longer hang in the balance as it did intermittently during the first fifty or sixty years of its history. Once President Wilkinson had begun to build the university, there was no longer any question that BYU was permanent; and since the Church is inclined to do everything it does first-class, it would be a quality institution within the parameters defined by its mission. The second thing is that he gave the university a first-class physical plant and the resources to reach out and develop what was potentially a fine university.[43]

ACADEMIC FREEDOM AT BRIGHAM YOUNG UNIVERSITY

While Ernest Wilkinson's legacy of buildings and infrastructure was authentic, benevolent, and lasting, his imprint on the intellectual life of BYU yielded mixed results. After a benign beginning he gradually became preoccupied, even obsessed, over issues of control over his faculty. He generally succeeded in gaining David O. McKay's expressed or implied approval of what he was doing; but on important occasions McKay gave his approval unwittingly, following explanations by Wilkinson that were either highly biased or overtly duplicitous. The effect on Wilkinson's targets was sometimes devastating, and ultimately he paid a high price.

McKay set the tone for intellectual life at BYU when he spoke at Wilkinson's inauguration ceremony in 1951 when he himself had been church president for only six months:

> This institution, unhampered by politics, uninhibited by fear of criticism from others, can teach in every class the existence of God, the divinity of Jesus Christ, the reality of the Restoration of the Gospel of Jesus Christ in its fullness, and can waken a desire in the lives of her students to spend their lives in the service of their fellowmen.
>
> God bless you teachers of this faculty, you students, that you may lift this school, if it has not yet attained it, to that height wherein it may be an example to all higher institutions in the world, that we may contribute to the new trend of thought of educational leaders that the great need of the world today is more spirituality, less atheism, more love of God, and for one's fellow men![44]

Such a lofty goal is easy to embrace but difficult in the extreme to achieve. Indeed, both Wilkinson and his eventual nemesis, Harold B. Lee, were in agreement with the goal; where they parted ways was over the "how," not the "what." Speaking to teachers in the Church Educational System in 1953, Wilkinson said, "In our Church Schools, the teaching of the Gospel is not confined merely to classes in religion, but is the proper subject to teach in all classes. This overall religious teaching in connection with biology and geology, for instance, is often more important than the teaching of formalized classes in religion."[45] Speaking to the same group the following day, Lee echoed Wilkinson: "The first purpose of our Church Schools I would name is: to teach truth, so effectively that students will be free from error, free from sin, free from darkness, free from tradition, vain philosophies and from the untried, unproven theories of science."[46]

The problem for Wilkinson was that the ideal repeatedly clashed with the reality of academic freedom. Once a line is drawn in the sand to define religious orthodoxy, to place it within each classroom and make it normative for all academic disciplines, some professors will cross the line. At that point, the battleground becomes academic freedom and personal free agency. The first major skirmish on the battleground was the payment of tithing.

BYU faculty were almost entirely LDS and as part of their employment arrangement agreed to abide by church standards, among which is the payment of tithing. Apparently on his own, Wilkinson decided that he should have access to the tithing records of his faculty to verify their compliance. He requested the information from Joseph Wirthlin, the Presiding Bishop, who forwarded the request to McKay. McKay refused to release the information to Wilkinson. Months later, Wilkinson returned to Wirthlin with an amended request. This time, rather than the dollar amount, he asked to know who among his faculty had paid full tithing and who had paid only partial or no tithing. This time McKay "told Bishop Wirthlin that President Wilkinson need not know amounts, but that he could be furnished information about whether or not they pay part or full tithing."[47]

The information he received startled him. "I was very much distressed to find the poor record of certain faculty members. I have not yet made a computation, but it looks to me that no more than one-half of the faculty are full tithe-payers." (He later revised that figure upward to five-sixths.) He examined the records in the context of annual salary reviews for his 600 faculty members and noted three options in his diary: "One is to pay little attention to it, as has been too much of our practice in the past." A second was to demand full tithe payment as a condition of continuing employment, which he also rejected, on the ground that "it ceases to be a voluntary offering." The third, which to him seemed non-coercive, was to say, "I am not going to require you to pay it, because it ceases to be voluntary. But since you have not voluntarily paid, it would seem you ought to look elsewhere for a position."[48]

He wrestled with the idea for several weeks, then adopted a modified position that "I should not increase the salaries or promote any of our faculty who do not pay an honest tithing." Pleased with his new position, he nonetheless acknowledged that "there will be an explosion at the BYU when it is known."[49] Three days later he modified his policy yet again. "The best solution I came up with during the day was that they probably should be treated the same way as they treated the Lord, a new application of the Golden Rule. Under this application, if they paid no tithing they would get no salary increase. If they paid half-tithing, they would get half the salary increase contemplated.... This still, however, did not seem to be the correct answer."[50]

Wilkinson then discussed the matter with two apostles, Marion G. Romney and Hugh B. Brown, who advised him against using coercion and recommended instead that General Authorities meet privately with errant faculty and urge them to improve their performance. They also suggested that he discuss the matter directly with McKay.[51] The meeting took place the following morning. Free agency was a bedrock principle with McKay, and Wilkinson's own account of the meeting suggests that he knew in advance what the outcome would be, and spoke disingenuously about the history of the matter. "I told him that it had been suggested to me by my executive committee that no salary increases should be given to those who were in that situation, but that I had my doubts that that was the proper way to handle it." McKay agreed, and said that "salaries should be predicated largely on professional ability."[52]

The next day Wilkinson worked through the salary increases, giving "almost exclusive consideration" to professional competence instead of tithe-paying status. Nonetheless, he was not in complete agreement with McKay, for he confided to his diary that "if, by the end of this calendar year, we still have members on the faculty who are either non- or token tithe payers, my present feeling is that we should take some action to have them replaced on the faculty."[53] Acting on that feeling, by the end of the spring semester of 1960, Wilkinson had effected the release of some thirty BYU employees over the issue of tithe paying, at which point the issue appears to have moved off his agenda.[54]

A much more vexing problem for Wilkinson was how to control (or eliminate) faculty whose liberal leanings ran contrary to his own conservatism, regardless of their adherence to religious guidelines. The problem first reared its head in 1954, following a private meeting between McKay and Sterling McMurrin, a philosopher at the University of Utah. Senior apostles Joseph F. Smith and Harold B. Lee were attempting to excommunicate McMurrin because of his liberal religious beliefs. Without necessarily agreeing with McMurrin's beliefs, McKay defended his right to hold them, and the excommunication plans were quickly dropped. Word of McKay's intercession spread to BYU, and its effect on the liberal-leaning faculty led Wilkinson to seek an audience with McKay.

The immediate issue at hand was a request for sabbatical leave from J. Golden Taylor, a professor in the English Department, whose views troubled Wilkinson.

> When I called Golden Taylor in to suggest to him that while we would approve of a sabbatical leave, we would not recommend his coming back unless his attitude toward the church leaders and general church doctrine were changed, he, Taylor, informed me that President McKay had had a conference with Sterling McMurrin, and had told McMurrin that there was plenty of room in this Church for diverse religious beliefs, and further said that if any excommunication proceedings were ever held, President McKay would appear as a witness in his favor.

The problem, Wilkinson explained, was that his dissident faculty were using the McMurrin incident to justify their own beliefs and actions. McKay, while confirming the report of his meeting with McMurrin, drew a crucial distinction that Wilkinson thereafter used as a mandate to control his faculty: "President McKay replied that there was all the difference in the world between whether a man should be excommunicated because he may not accept all the views of the Church, and whether he should still be employed on the faculty at BYU. He told me that I would have his complete support in refusing to renew the contracts of any teachers who did not teach the doctrines as they were interpreted by the leaders of the Church."[55] While McKay's principle dealt only with religious orthodoxy, Wilkinson later expanded it to include politics.

The issue of religious orthodoxy resurfaced early in 1959 when the History Department sponsored a symposium "at which," as Wilkinson put it in his diary, "they discussed the problem of whether or not the Mormon Church was going to be liberal." Word of the meeting reached J. Reuben Clark, who asked Wilkinson for a report. Wilkinson summarized his information-gathering effort in his journal: "This meeting apparently turned out to be the most vigorous criticism of Church tendencies and Church leaders that has been held on the campus since I have been here." As he interrogated those who attended, he pinpointed what he saw as his administrative dilemma: "If I strike out vigorously against those who were the ring leaders, it will make martyrs of them, and thereby accentuate, rather than minimize, what they have done. At the same time, it is apparent that we have some faculty members who do not accept wholeheartedly the divine nature of our Church, and I must find some way of getting rid of them."[56]

Three months later, in April 1959, the matter surfaced in a meeting of the Executive Committee of BYU's Board of Trustees where Wilkinson's testy relationship with Harold B. Lee complicated the discussion. Wilkinson reported that Kent Fielding, a faculty member in the History Department, was one of the "ringleaders" of the symposium and had since "admitted to Brother William E. Berrett that he did not have a testimony of the Gospel." When Berrett asked Fielding how he had been hired without a testimony, he replied that Harold B. Lee, who had interviewed him as part of the hiring process, never asked the question. Wilkinson had already told Lee that his omission had led to hiring a deficient faculty member; but "Brother Lee, whose main weakness as far as I can see is that he cannot accept criticism, had interpreted it as serious criticism on my part of him."[57]

With the Fielding case as a backdrop, Wilkinson and Lee engaged in a heated exchange over the symposium, which Wilkinson recorded in the following terms: Lee "said he had been disappointed that I had not gotten rid of about a third of the faculty who did not have a testimony of the gospel. I told him that I thought his estimate was altogether too high. His response was that he thought I must have been awfully naïve if I did not know the large number of our faculty who did not have a testimony. He was smarting very much under what I thought was my criticism of him for not having properly interrogated Brother Fielding."[58]

Despite Wilkinson's resentment, he took no action against Fielding for nearly a year, until J. Reuben Clark Jr. criticized his inaction. Commenting on Wilkinson's fund-raising efforts, Clark said, "You've got many more important problems down there than raising money. You've got some members of the faculty who are destroying the faith of our students. You ought to get rid of them."[59] Given this pointed reminder, Wilkinson interrogated Fielding six days later and concluded: "It was apparent he had no testimony of the gospel." He opted for an indirect approach to fulfilling Clark's instruction: "I informed him we would grant him a sabbatical leave for next year, but that he was not to return to the University unless he was approved by one of the members of the executive committee after having a conference with him. None of us, including Kent, thought he would be able to pass that conference."[60]

The Fielding case involved religious orthodoxy and thus fell clearly within the bounds of Wilkinson's earlier discussion with McKay. In 1962, however, Wilkinson successfully parlayed these instructions into political orthodoxy. Influenced by the right-wing extremist politics of Ezra Taft Benson, who had recently returned to Utah after eight years as Secretary of Agriculture in the Eisenhower administration, Wilkinson began to attack faculty members who, despite passing the litmus test for religious orthodoxy, were too far to the left of the political spectrum to suit him. Wilkinson, well aware of McKay's own fears of communism and socialism, played skillfully on those fears. Taking his cue from the John Birch Society, which he admired but did not join,[61] Wilkinson labeled the Democratic administration of John F. Kennedy as socialistic, accused an unnamed BYU political science professor of being too sympathetic with it, and used his own accusation as a guise to push for his dismissal. "I informed President McKay we had a member of our faculty who admittedly felt the government should engage in all of the new ventures that were being proposed for it, and which together have been characterized as the welfare state," he wrote in a memorandum that McKay included in his diary. "I told him this faculty member had forthrightly suggested that if he were out of step with our feelings at BYU he would be happy to locate elsewhere. President McKay emphatically told me to have him locate elsewhere."[62]

Wilkinson crossed a personal threshold late in 1963 when he decided to run for the U.S. Senate. In resigning his joint positions of president of BYU and chancellor of the Church Unified School System, he recommended that Earl Crockett serve as acting BYU president and Harvey Taylor as acting chancellor—"acting" because Wilkinson received from McKay a promise of his former positions if he lost the election.[63] Unwittingly, he thus set the stage for his eventual demotion.

He won the Republican nomination but lost by a wide margin (224,775 to 166,697) in the 1964 general election to the Democratic incumbent, Frank Moss. Ray Hillam, a BYU political science professor who later became Wilkinson's direct target, described the defeat as "a bitter rejection. [Wilkinson] felt betrayed by some of the faculty. He returned to BYU with vengeance and with a political agenda. His reactionary views had intensified and he set about to give an even stronger political tone to the university. He delivered right-wing speeches and he brought ultraconservative speakers and films on campus. He monitored the so-called 'liberal' faculty. Some of us who had not supported him in his quest for the U.S. Senate found ourselves targeted as well."[64]

In the eleven months of Wilkinson's absence, his power base had eroded. While McKay's support remained unwavering, other General Authorities who did not approve of Wilkinson's tactics began to move against him in subtle ways. One week after the general election, McKay informed his counselors of his earlier promise to Wilkinson to let him return to BYU—apparently this was the first they learned of it—and the three men agreed that "we are obligated to grant him this privilege if he desired to do so." Nonetheless, "it was also mentioned that many of the members of the Board feel that it would be better to have a change."[65]

According to his promise, McKay recommended to the Church Board of Education and the BYU Board of Trustees that they reappoint Wilkinson to both of his previous positions, president and chancellor. The motion passed.[66] One month later, however, in a move unprecedented in McKay's tenure as church president, the boards reversed their sentiment and recommended to McKay that Wilkinson be given only the BYU appointment and that Harvey Taylor be made permanent chancellor. McKay bristled: "I said that it would not do to make Brother Wilkinson President of the Brigham Young University and nothing else."[67] The board held firm, however, and one month later, on February 2, 1965, the First Presidency rewrote Wilkinson's letter of appointment. "A decision was reached that it should be modified and only that part which refers to the BYU sent to President Wilkinson and the balance of the letter sent to Harvey Taylor, who was appointed temporary Chancellor of the Unified Church School System."[68]

The following day, when the announcement of Wilkinson's de facto demotion was made public, he came to the regularly scheduled joint meeting of the BYU Board of Trustees and the Church Board of Education. He bristled at his demotion and confided to his diary his belief that Hugh B. Brown had engineered it, an allegation not substantiated by other sources. Although he tried to show a stiff upper lip by writing, "This might be a godsend to me," another part of his entry for the day suggests that he reacted by declaring war against aberrant professors: "There is no question that the Executive Committee [of the Board of Trustees], and in this I agree with them, has determined that we not have teachers at the BYU who will be advocating social and economic and political theories at variance with the fundamental beliefs of the Church Brethren. This may be a big step forward but the practicum enforcement of this is going to cause a number of real problems for me which, however, I am perfectly willing to face."[69]

While religious orthodoxy may have been possible to define, there was, in fact, no such thing as political orthodoxy within the church. Thus, it is highly unlikely that the executive committee meant what Wilkinson's diary entry suggests. In declaring open season on those "at variance with the fundamental beliefs of the Church Brethren," Wilkinson was giving himself *carte blanche* to go after any target of his choosing. Two days later Wilkinson spoke with Apostle Marion G. Romney, a member of the Board of Trustees, about "this whole problem of getting people who support the viewpoint of the *majority* of the Brethren on social and economic matters. He confided to me that if he had his own way he would go as far as to close down the BYU rather than permit teachers to teach anything other than the view of the General Authorities; but he did not think his viewpoint would be upheld by President McKay."[70]

Wilkinson did not share Romney's assessment of McKay, and two months later he tested the water. His target was Richard D. Poll, the political science professor whose "critical 'liberal' attitude" he found offensive. Wilkinson told McKay "that I was now attempting to put some voluntary restraints on Poll and others who had been quite liberal in their social and economic views; that I intended to let them know they could not stay at the 'Y' if they persisted in their critical attitude; that I merely wanted him to know and make sure that I would have his full support. The President told me to go ahead and that I would have his full support."[71]

The chapter that followed marked the low point in the intellectual life of BYU during Wilkinson's twenty-year tenure. On April 21, 1966, he preempted the weekly "Forum," to deliver a controversial address entitled "The Changing Nature of American Government from a Constitutional Republic to a Welfare State." In an effort to monitor the responses of suspect professors to the address, he recruited student "spies."[72] The plan was ill conceived and poorly implemented, and rumors of it soon began to swirl throughout the BYU campus. Wilkinson denied the rumors; but by early 1967, it was apparent that he had a scandal on his hands that was quickly mushrooming beyond his control.

On February 5, 1967, Wilkinson began a damage control initiative with McKay. On the theory that the best defense is a potent offense, he warned that "certain faculty members at the BYU" had a tendency to teach "Socialism and certain ingredients of the welfare state." He asked McKay to give him "a statement to the effect that we are not to advocate any facets of Socialism at BYU." McKay agreed to do so.[73]

Three weeks later, one of the student spies dropped a bombshell by confessing to the media what Wilkinson had been denying. The story was immediately picked up nationally. His operation exposed, Wilkinson raised the volume on his damage control. He met with McKay on March 6, 1967, one week after the student's confession. McKay made brief mention of the meeting in his diary and concluded by noting, "At my request, he [Wilkinson] sent me minutes of the views he discussed with me." Those minutes, included in the McKay diaries, were provided "in obedience to your continuing instructions that I keep you personally informed of any unusual developments at the Brigham Young University." Wilkinson downplayed the spy scandal by casting aspersions on the student. "It appeared that the student making the main accusations was very unreliable and apparently was guilty of a recent robbery in California for which he may be arrested," a serious charge that Wilkinson made no subsequent attempt to validate.[74]

Wilkinson then distanced himself from the scandal. "There is probably some truth to the charge that certain students had been organized to report on certain teachers, and that the administration may have advertently or inadvertently encouraged these students although not in the manner it took place."[75] In light of the subsequent internal investigation that showed Wilkinson to have engineered the spying from the outset,[76] it was a remarkably disingenuous statement, particularly to the church president. But it worked, and Wilkinson succeeded in brushing aside any further discussion of his espionage efforts to focus on the future.

His letter to McKay continues: "After a rather full discussion, you advised and instructed me as follows":

- "Teachers ought not to object to the Administration knowing what they teach, nor to students reporting on the same so long as the Administration is careful in properly evaluating the same."

- "Where students or teachers have complaints, they should take them up with the Administration, rather than resort to public declamation or newspapers and other media concerning the same."

- "It is my responsibility to see that Atheism, Communism and Socialism are not to be advocated by BYU teachers."

- The Board of Trustees should not investigate the scandal, a direct rejection of the recommendation of the American Association of University Professors.

- Wilkinson, alone, should investigate the whole matter and report back to McKay personally.

Wilkinson concluded: "Since I want to make sure that what I have said above is a correct statement of your instructions, and that I have authority to proceed, will you please approve this letter in the space provided below." McKay co-signed the letter; there is no record that he censured Wilkinson's espionage efforts, either in writing or in conversation.[77]

Wilkinson's maneuver, though duplicitous, was brilliant. In a single meeting, he managed to tarnish the character of the student who accused him, distance himself from the scandal, close the door on anyone else giving a different view to McKay, shut off any investigation by the Board of Trustees, appoint himself—the accused—as the sole investigator of the accusations, and restate and strengthen his own mandate to proceed as hitherto. And he succeeded in memorializing it all over McKay's signature. In earlier years, it seems far less likely that Wilkinson could have accomplished as much, but McKay was now ninety-three years old, and his contact with the world beyond his apartment was limited to those who entered it. With the cooperation of Clare Middlemiss, Wilkinson continued to have favored access to McKay, and the combination of frequent private meetings and McKay's explicit trust of Wilkinson virtually guaranteed that he would be able to place his own spin on anything that occurred—even a spy scandal—and achieve a favorable outcome with his patron.

Returning to the campus, Wilkinson continued his damage control initiative. In a memorandum to the faculty four days after meeting with McKay, he acknowledged the spying but obscured his direct involvement, stating: "Although there is misinformation in the charges, there was such a group, reports were made and the students were under the impression they were acting with the sanction of the administration."[78]

Four days after writing the faculty memorandum and only one week after his prior meeting with McKay, Wilkinson returned to McKay's apartment and made his final report on the "investigation." It was a briefer meeting, and once again involved neither a *mea culpa* from Wilkinson nor a rebuke from McKay. In fact, it involved no discussion at all of the scandal itself, consisting instead of two related issues. First, Hugh B. Brown, McKay's first counselor, had become aware of the spying and was attempting to carry out his own investigation. Brown had asked Wilkinson for documents relating to it, but Wilkinson had refused. McKay agreed with Wilkinson, saying, as Wilkinson reported in another memorandum that McKay included in his diary, that "under these circumstances I should stand my ground and not give the report to President Brown."[79] The unusual rebuff of a counselor may have had less to do with the merits of the case than the lingering effects of the 1965 rift within the First Presidency over the building program, which resulted in McKay's circumventing N. Eldon Tanner and Hugh B. Brown, his counselors, by adding two more counselors to the First Presidency. (See chap. 9.)

The second issue was Wilkinson's allegation that "we had now learned that last year we had a student who, in all probability, was a Communist on the campus" out of a total enrollment exceeding 20,000. Without producing any evidence to support his allegation or naming the accused student, Wilkinson said that "we had to be continually on alert against subversive students" and asked McKay's permission to hire "a man with Federal Bureau of Investigation detective experience to exercise surveillance on the campus." McKay approved the audacious request and once again co-signed Wilkinson's report of the meeting to indicate his explicit approval.[80] For McKay, the case of the BYU spying scandal was closed, and Wilkinson emerged not only unscathed, but even stronger.

While Wilkinson was successful in his damage control efforts with McKay, his experience on campus and with other General Authorities was altogether different and likely sowed some of the seeds that eventually sprouted to end his tenure at BYU. Shortly after the student spies began their work, Ray Hillam, a political science professor who was one of their primary targets, became the subject of hearings focused on the allegations of two of the students. Wilkinson appointed three of his vice presidents, Clyde D. Sandgren, Ben E. Lewis, and Earl C. Crockett, to conduct the hearings. Though structured to confirm the allegations against Hillam, the hearings backfired when a student spy broke ranks and testified that one of the vice presidents—Sandgren, the university's legal counsel—had, in fact, been part of the spy program.

Shortly after the hearings, Hillam and two colleagues violated Wilkinson's policy and met directly with N. Eldon Tanner, second counselor in the First Presidency, and Harold B. Lee, acting president of the Quorum of the Twelve. As the professors described layer upon layer of the scandal and its attempted cover-up, Lee responded, "One lie leads to another."[81] In 1967, after the public confession by one of the student spies, Wilkinson was called to task in a meeting of the Board of Trustees, which included Lee.

The matter did not die on campus; and in March 1968, the same committee that had intended to prove the allegations against Hillam concluded that he had been innocent of the allegations and that Wilkinson himself had initiated the spy ring and then, when word of its existence leaked out, denied his involvement. In an effort to make amends, the committee agreed to Hillam's request that Wilkinson make him a personal apology.

In March 1968 Wilkinson met with Hillam and attempted to explain the whole affair. The explanation included no apology but instead appeared to be an attempt to lay responsibility for it at McKay's doorstep. According to Hillam's own account of the meeting, Wilkinson told him that McKay had given him instructions that Communism and Socialism were not to be advocated at BYU. "He said," Hillam added, that "President McKay's instruction led him to seek feedback from faculty on his [Forum] address.... I was unhappy with his inclination to blame President McKay for his need to know."[82] Wilkinson's diary makes no mention of the meeting.

Had a similar scandal occurred at most universities in the United States, it likely would have resulted in the swift removal of the president. McKay's firm support of Wilkinson, however, temporarily shielded him from his detractors. Nonetheless, the bad taste of the scandal lingered, increasing the sense of alienation between Wilkinson and his faculty and strengthening opposition to him on the Church Board of Education and BYU Board of Trustees. As McKay's health deteriorated, rumors of Wilkinson's vulnerability circulated widely. Becoming increasingly anxious, Wilkinson met with McKay on July 25, 1969, less than six months before McKay's death, to seek reassurance. He summarized the meeting in a memorandum that, once again, he asked McKay to sign. According to Wilkinson's memo, McKay concluded the meeting by saying, "We have been very close over the years and I think we are now as close as we have ever been and I think you better continue as you are and not let rumors disturb you."[83]

When McKay died in January 1970, the comparatively vigorous seventy-year-old Harold B. Lee became first counselor in the First Presidency of the aged and ailing ninety-three-year-old Joseph Fielding Smith. Only five months later, facing the inevitable, Wilkinson tendered his resignation in the form of a handwritten, confidential letter to the First Presidency.[84]

Wilkinson's legacy provides material for a spirited debate on ends versus means. Even his detractors acknowledge that he was primarily responsible for the unprecedented growth of the university, in terms of both enrollment and physical plant. Indeed, on both counts there was more growth during the Wilkinson years than all other BYU administrations combined. One building today, the Student Union, carries Wilkinson's name, yet the entire campus bears his imprint.

But Wilkinson also left a darker legacy of coercion and distrust. Several key professors left the university as a result, as did his former administrative assistant, John T. Bernhard.[85] A more enduring effect was the curtailment of academic freedom. It is true that McKay gave Wilkinson the mandate of imbuing all classes in all subjects with the gospel of Jesus Christ. But the questionable means by which Wilkinson attempted to carry out that mandate left much sorrow in their wake. How effectively the goal could have been achieved through more benign means will remain a matter for debate.

CHURCH EDUCATION IN HAWAII

In 1921 Church President Heber J. Grant asked David O. McKay, then a junior apostle, to travel around the world and make an unprecedented tour of foreign Latter-day Saint missions. Upon reaching the Territory of Hawaii, he met with local church leaders and asked what they felt was most needed within the mission. According to the record made by Church College of Hawaii's first president, "All were united that a church school of higher learning was the greatest need.... Elder McKay said that he was very strongly impressed that such a church school was the big need of the mission, and that before many days he would write a letter to the First Presidency recommending that one be built."[86]

McKay returned to Hawaii in 1936, 1940, and 1941 as second counselor in the First Presidency, and each time he renewed the discussion with local leaders about a college. However, it was not until he became church president in 1951 that he was able to transform his dream into reality. After some discussion about the location, McKay settled on Laie, on the island of Oahu, where nearly a century earlier the church had purchased several thousand acres that had since become the home of the Hawaiian Temple.[87]

McKay dedicated the site in February 1955, then told local leaders, "I want the school to open in September. At Laie we have a chapel, a social hall, an old mission home, and the Saints have homes in which they could give up a room for a classroom. Let's get started."[88] Faced with a daunting task, local leaders improvised. Vaun Clissold, then president of the Honolulu Stake, recounted: "Fortunately at that time there was a great move on in Honolulu to get rid of the old war buildings. They were an eyesore and in the way of progress. So I went to the Army and bought building after building. We cut them in half and at one time we had sixteen sections of buildings moving to Laie. By September 1955 we had a library, a dormitory, a cafeteria, and several classrooms.... We opened up with 155 students, and it's been going strong since."[89]

The primary purpose of the Church College of Hawaii (later renamed BYU–Hawaii) was to provide higher education for LDS youth not only in Hawaii, but all of the South Pacific. The strategy worked, for in the first decade of its existence the percentage of Hawaiian LDS students attending any college soared from 3 percent to 40 percent.[90]

In 1951, the year McKay became church president, Apostle Matthew Cowley had his own vision of a church presence in Hawaii. Clissold recalled the genesis of what became the Polynesian Cultural Center:

> In 1951 Brother Cowley and I were in Laie and we were talking about the Saints who come up from the South Seas to go to the temple. He said that the Maori people had great difficulty in finding housing and it was expensive when they found it. He thought if somehow we could have a big Maori carved house at Laie that it would be an attraction to tourists and would be serviceable to the community, particularly to the Maoris when they came up, because they were accustomed to community living, you know, living in one big house. He said maybe they could put on an entertainment or two for tourists or somebody and in that way make a little money. I said, "Well, if that's true of the Maori people, it could also be true of the other people that come up. Each one of the Island groups could have a place where they could live and display their particular kind of craft or entertainment."
>
> That was about all that was said, but a couple of weeks later in the stake conference in Honolulu Brother Cowley said from the pulpit, "I can envision a time when there will be villages at Laie. They'll have a carved house out there for the Maoris, and there will be a Samoan village, a Tahitian village, and villages for other peoples of the South Seas." That was the kernel of that idea.[91]

Cowley died two years later, but Clissold and Wendell Mendenhall, who had been a close friend of Cowley, kept his vision alive. When David O. McKay dedicated the Church College of Hawaii, he caught the vision from Clissold and Mendenhall, seeing it as a means to preserve the various cultures of the South Pacific. McKay's vision was broad, recalled Michael Grilikhes, a CBS executive recruited to pull together the cultural and entertainment aspects of the center. "He didn't say, 'This is a gathering place for the [Church] members in the Pacific.' He said, 'This is a gathering place for the *peoples* of the Pacific.'" Church members and non-members alike joined to build and staff the center.[92]

As enthusiastic as McKay, Clissold, and Mendenhall were about the Polynesian Cultural Center, others viewed it as folly. McKay's grandson-in-law Howard B. Anderson, a member of the center's first board of directors and then president of the California Mission, noted that there was "opposition from many in the community and at church headquarters. Some thought it was a terrible idea, it wasn't anything the Church should be engaged in, and it would be a money loser."[93]

Despite such opposition, McKay nonetheless moved forward. At his direction, Mendenhall presented a detailed plan to the Quorum of the Twelve late in 1961. Michael Grilikhes recalled Mendenhall's account of the meeting. "Wendell went to the Council of the Twelve and said, 'This is what we are going to do, and this is what it is going to cost.' They said, 'No.' So he left."[94]

Some months later, Harold B. Lee, a senior member of the Twelve, stopped off at Laie for some business at the temple. Seeing the adjacent construction he asked, "What's that?" "Oh, that's the Polynesian Cultural Center." Upon returning to Salt Lake City he called Mendenhall into another meeting with the Twelve. "You were told no! No approval!" Mendenhall replied, "Brethren, I told President McKay you said no, and President McKay said, 'Build it!' Now if you brethren want to talk to President McKay about it, you go right ahead."[95] The construction proceeded without interruption because, noted Howard Anderson, "That's the way President McKay felt about the importance of the Polynesian Cultural Center."[96]

After "a normal business cycle, about three or four years," recalled Anderson, the Polynesian Cultural Center began to be profitable, and went on to become the largest tourist attraction in the Hawaiian Islands. "I remember one year we were getting an operating margin of 40 percent, with a 25 percent return on investment. You find me a business that can do that."[97]

As the center prospered, it began to serve a secondary function beyond the preservation of culture, one that had not originally been envisioned. Thousands of students at the adjacent Church College of Hawaii, most of whom had limited financial resources, eventually found paid employment there, and much of the center's profits reverted to the college. Thirteen years after the center opened, Clissold spoke of the benefits to the college: "According to our charter, the surplus of the Center, over and above the cost of operation, eventually goes to the school, in one way or another, either as a grant to the school or as scholarships to the students or as remuneration for services given by the students.... To date several million dollars have gone to the school through those channels."[98]

Criticism of the center, of course, muted as its success increased. At least two former opponents reversed field and openly acknowledged the error of their prior position. Anderson noted: "Nathan Eldon Tanner said to us, as a board, 'This thing will be a drag and a burden on the Church forever and ever. It will never succeed.' Well, when we proved him wrong, bless his heart, Nathan Eldon Tanner was the first one to stand up and say, 'I was wrong!' There is the greatness of the man."[99]

Perhaps even more impressive, albeit delayed, was the change of heart experienced by Harold B. Lee, whose outrage upon seeing the center under construction had resulted not only in Mendenhall's inquisition before the Twelve, but also in open criticism at a stake conference in Hawaii. Michael Grilikhes, one of the targets of the criticism, described the conference and, a decade later, Lee's reversal:

> When he went to the stake conference, in the Sunday afternoon session, he said something about Hollywood people coming to Hawaii, and they mustn't be allowed to create that kind of atmosphere, especially near the temple. The last thing we wanted to do was create any Hollywood thing. We wanted to do it so that it would do what President McKay wanted it to do. It is a cultural representative of the people, and everything was done perfectly in good taste. . . .
>
> Now, when Harold B. Lee became President of the Church, I got a call from Arthur Haycock [Lee's secretary]. Would I come over? I came over, and President Lee wanted to apologize to me. He said, "There are times when you don't know all of the matters, and sometimes even our judgment is flawed."
>
> We talked for a few minutes, and then I went back to Arthur's office. I said, "I don't understand this. He was so 'these Hollywood people,' and whatever." He said, "I've seen, over all the years that I've been the secretary for different Presidents of the Church, remarkable changes happen when somebody becomes the President of the Church. There are things you would normally think they would have forgotten long ago, or an attitude that they had, and they just become very different."[100]

The vision of McKay, Cowley, Clissold, Mendenhall, and others continues to bear fruits. BYU–Hawaii now enrolls over 2,400 students from more than seventy countries. The Polynesian Cultural Center remains one of the most popular tourist sites in the Pacific, attracting over a million visitors a year. Furthermore, the synergistic relationship between the two institutions continues to assist college students to fund their education.

THE JUNIOR COLLEGE SYSTEM

From 1888 to 1909 the church established thirty-three stake academies, roughly equivalent to modern high schools. Shortly after the turn of the twentieth century, most of these schools were discontinued as other educational options became available, while others were converted to two-year colleges. By the 1920s five such colleges remained under church ownership: Dixie (St. George, Utah), Gila (Thatcher, Arizona), Snow (Ephraim, Utah), Ricks (Rexburg, Idaho) and Weber (Ogden, Utah).[101]

In 1928, even before the Great Depression, church financial resources became severely strained, causing Joseph F. Merrill, the Church Commissioner of Education, to discuss with the Church Board of Education whether it would be possible to continue financing the colleges. Legislatures in Utah and Idaho were simultaneously considering whether to embark upon state-sponsored junior college programs, and Merrill suggested that the church explore the possibility of turning over its colleges to the states.[102] After investigating its options for a year the board decided, with one dissenting vote, to sustain a decision of the First Presidency to offer all of the colleges to the respective state governments and to rely upon church seminaries (religious classes for high school students) and Institutes of Religion (at the college level) to provide religious instruction. The dissenting vote came from Apostle David O. McKay:

> Brother McKay stated that he did not wish to be considered as not sustaining the First Presidency, but that he could not vote in favor of the elimination of junior colleges.... He favored the retaining of Junior colleges at this time because, by their elimination, the Church would lose its hold on the training of its teachers; and that in his opinion it would be better to curtail the establishment of seminaries for a time and hold the colleges, until the virtue of seminaries and institutes as substitutes for schools be more clearly demonstrated. He also expressed the thought that the local people involved in the junior colleges should be consulted and won over to any proposed eliminations before definite decisions are made.[103]

McKay's strong feelings, which led him to the highly unusual step of voting against a First Presidency recommendation, played a major role in later decades when the church attempted to reenter the junior college arena. His deference to the "local people" also factored into the divisive issue in the 1950s of whether to move Ricks College to another venue.

Notwithstanding McKay's opposition, in the early 1930s the church transferred Dixie, Snow, and Weber to the state of Utah, and Gila (later renamed Eastern Arizona Junior College) to the state of Arizona. It made the same offer of Ricks College to Idaho; however, on a narrow 23–20 vote, the Idaho State Senate defeated the transfer bill and thus it remained under church ownership.[104]

In 1948 J. Bracken Lee was elected governor of Utah. Lee was a fiscal conservative and, in an attempt to reduce state expenditures asked the state legislature early in 1951 to approve a bill that would discontinue support of the three formerly Mormon colleges, in effect, returning them to the church. The terms of the deeds twenty years earlier specified that they would automatically revert to the church if the state at any time ceased to operate them as educational institutions.[105] The First

Presidency, in which McKay was then second counselor, took an ambivalent position on the bill, and it failed to pass.[106]

Two years later, McKay as church president named Ernest Wilkinson as administrator of the Unified Church School System, whereupon the junior college matter assumed a higher priority. Wilkinson's grand vision, shared by McKay, was a system of church-owned junior colleges that would feed upper division students into Brigham Young University. An obvious first step was to regain ownership of Dixie, Snow, and Weber colleges; and two months after assuming his new role, Wilkinson obtained McKay's permission to approach Governor Lee on the subject.[107] Wilkinson subsequently reported to McKay: "Governor Lee had informed me that he was going to inform the legislature that one way they were going to get the money necessary for the public schools would be for the State of Utah to do away with its junior college program." Weber was the jewel of the three, even without its personal ties to McKay, for the other two were so small that it was not clear whether they should be continued under either ownership. McKay told Wilkinson that "while we were not asking that Weber be given back to us, that if it was, we would accept it and thank the Lord for its return."[108]

Wilkinson worked with Utah State Senator Orval Hafen, a St. George resident and strong proponent of Dixie College, to draft the legislation. It stipulated that the church was not asking for the return of the colleges but would accept them if they were returned. On December 9, 1953, after getting the governor's approval of the bill, a delegation from the legislature called on J. Reuben Clark Jr. of the First Presidency and informed him of its contents. He repeated McKay's sentiments: "if they [the colleges] were turned over to the Church, we should be pleased to operate them."[109]

When the bill was introduced the following day, vigorous and bitter opposition immediately broke out in Weber County. McKay attributed the opposition to the Catholic Church, which, according to an anonymous correspondent, was planning a Catholic college in Ogden. McKay related the story to Wilkinson, who noted in his diary: "After that letter, there was never any doubt in President McKay's mind that it was desirable to obtain Weber back."[110] In spite of Ogden residents' resistance, one week later the bill passed by comfortable margins in both houses of the legislature and was signed into law four days thereafter.[111]

Whatever the facts about the proposed Catholic school, opposition to the transfer was in fact broadly based, particularly in Ogden, with strong backing from Mormons and non-Mormons alike.[112] Having lost their battle in the legislature, the citizens began circulating petitions for a referendum on the issue. McKay was in the middle of a three-continent tour at the time, but his first counselor, Stephen L Richards, brushed off the possibility, writing to him: "It would seem that the proponents of the measure will have a rather difficult time getting the necessary ten per cent of the votes cast for Governor at the last election, or 33,000, in at least fifteen counties of the State, and that before February 19."[113] Richards's prediction was wrong, as supporters of a referendum had no trouble in obtaining the requisite signatures.

The referendum would not come up for vote until the November general election; but in May, Governor Lee wrote to the First Presidency asking where they stood on the referendum: "During the campaign to obtain signatures to the referendum petition...in some parts of the State it was represented that The First Presidency wanted these colleges returned to the Church, whereas in other parts of the State it was represented that The First Presidency did not want these colleges returned."[114] He asked that they respond to a series of questions, which were subsequently published with the First Presidency's answers. To the central question, "Will you please advise me as to whether you do or do not want Weber, Snow and Dixie Colleges returned to the Church?" the First Presidency responded ambivalently. "We shall be pleased to have Weber, Snow and Dixie Colleges returned to the Church, which is in a position to operate them in a first-class manner scholastically and otherwise."[115] The response left open an underlying issue of utmost importance to church members with decades of experience in looking to ecclesiastical leaders for guidance: Should they vote their conscience or vote the church position?

When pressed on the matter, McKay again gave mixed signals. Asked by the Utah Educational Association, most of whose members were LDS, what its members' attitude should be at the UEA's upcoming statewide convention, McKay said "they should use their own judgment; that the attitude of the Church is plainly stated in the First Presidency's public statement, which is that we are receptive if and when the State ceases to conduct these schools as state institutions."[116] Similarly, in a three-hour meeting with a delegation from Ogden that McKay summarized in his diary, McKay "told them that the Church is not making an aggressive campaign to have these schools turned back." A. L. Glasmann, owner of the *Ogden Standard-Examiner*, pressed the issue. "Do you want them back?" he asked. McKay declined to answer directly, stating that he did not wish to exert "undue influence." Glasmann continued, "Our people are saying that if members of the Church vote against turning these schools back to the Church, they are not good members of the Church and will be dealt with." McKay answered, "No member of the Church, General Authority or otherwise, will be dealt with if he votes his own convictions. That is what we want him to do."[117]

However, McKay, apparently by inference, had sent a different message to church leaders. In November, Wilkinson would say that he and others, including all of the stake presidents in Utah, "had been given the main responsibility with respect to the junior college issue."[118] They had taken what they interpreted as a mandate from McKay and were encouraging church members to support the transfer of the colleges to the church. However, late in September, Apostle Henry D. Moyle informed McKay of an upcoming meeting with local stake presidents "relative to the distribution of pamphlets concerning the Junior College situation." McKay's response suggests that he had never intended to advocate church sponsorship and was surprised at the level of advocacy that had nonetheless emerged. "I told him that the Stake Presidents are not to make a campaign that Gen'l. Authorities are in favor of the Church's taking over the Junior Colleges...also that they are not to quote the General Authorities."[119]

Now on the defensive, McKay went out of his way to communicate the church's neutrality. To Frank Browning, a friend in Ogden who questioned that neutrality, he wrote, "Every person entitled to vote should express at the polls his or her honest convictions regarding this important matter. A vote cast for the state to do so [continue support of the colleges] is not a vote against the Church."[120] One week later, upon being informed that "pamphlets in support of transfer (of colleges) have been mailed to residents under postal permit of some stakes and delivered by ward teachers," McKay replied adamantly that any such distribution "was done directly contrary to my instructions." In order to drive his point home, he authorized the publication of his communication to Browning.[121]

McKay's high-profile neutrality on the issue effectively silenced support of church leaders, thus conceding public debate to opponents of the transfer. The referendum to block transfer passed easily, by a 3–2 margin.[122] Wilkinson complained in his diary that he "had been 'undermined' by statements emanating from the President of the Church during the campaign, and I thought it was most unfair to those of us who had been given the responsibility."[123] Three years later, reacting to another disappointing situation, he went even further: "This matter disturbed me almost as much as the reversal of President McKay on the junior college situation, after he had instructed Brothers [Harold B.] Lee and [Henry D.] Moyle and me to do what we could to have the resolution carried by the state."[124]

For his part, J. Bracken Lee considered the defeat of the transfer a major disappointment of his eight-year administration. When he first learned of the referendum campaign, he called on the church to assess its level of support. As he explained later in an interview:

> "They [the transfer's opponents] will get it on the ballot and it will
> be defeated. That makes it necessary for me to get an absolute prom-
> ise out of the Church. I don't mean one or two. I mean the General
> Authorities from top to bottom."... So they met. Then they sent

Harold B. Lee up to my office as their representative. He said, "You have the absolute promise of the Church authorities that if you sign this bill and it goes on the ballot, the Church will support you and support that bill. It will let it be known amongst all of our people that we want them to vote to get those schools." I said, "With that promise, I'll sign the bill. I have your assurance that all the authorities are behind this?" "Yes." So I signed it. Then just about a week before the election, President McKay came out and made a public statement that they don't care about them. They could vote as they pleased. Now this is a disappointment to me because these are men that you would take their word. I had two or three of them with tears in their eyes come to me and tell me how ashamed they were and how sorry they were that this happened.[125]

Even with the benefit of hindsight, it is difficult to understand McKay's actions in this instance. Clearly, he was personally in favor of regaining the three colleges for the church, and clearly he telegraphed that preference to his close colleagues among the General Authorities when the issue first arose. It seems he did not anticipate that the issue would become as high profile and polarizing as it did, a conjecture supported by the opinion of Stephen L Richards that a referendum on the subject was not even a possibility. As the stakes rose, it is likely that he became acutely aware, perhaps for the first time, of the enormous influence he might exercise as church president, and elected to step back from the debate to allow church members unfettered exercise of free agency on an issue that bore no moral overtones. At the same time this issue was subjected to a referendum, another involving reapportionment of the Utah State Senate was also on the ballot (see chap. 13), toward which McKay took a similar approach. The two issues marked the first time since he became president that he had to decide whether to use the inherent power of his bully pulpit in a political forum, and he chose inaction. Unfortunately, in both instances, his withdrawal from the public debate left his colleagues dangling.

The Growth of Ricks College

With the defeat of the transfer legislation, two options remained for a network of junior colleges. One was to expand and strengthen Ricks College, which had never left church ownership, and the other was to build new colleges in areas of concentrated church membership throughout the West. Wilkinson chose to concentrate first on Ricks College, perhaps on the assumption that it would be the easier task. He was mistaken. The fight over Ricks's location turned out to be one of the most time-consuming matters of his entire presidency, a bitter disappointment, and the proximate cause for the demise of his entire junior college vision.

Within days of his appointment as administrator of the Unified Church School System, Wilkinson drove to Rexburg, Idaho, and visited the Ricks College campus. Founded in 1888 as the Bannock Stake Academy, Ricks had had a tenuous existence. It had nearly folded in the early 1930s after the state refused to accept it from the church. Church financial support during one year dwindled to a mere $10,000.[126] The campus that Wilkinson toured had an aged physical plant and a small student body, not the image to fit his master plan. Furthermore, Rexburg was an agrarian town with slow population growth. In contrast, Idaho Falls, only twenty-five miles to the south, had triple the population of Rexburg. It also promised to grow rapidly, thanks to U.S. Atomic Energy Commission offices that were being built to support a nearby nuclear reactor testing station. Wilkinson calculated that it would be less expensive to build a new campus in Idaho Falls than to rebuild one in Rexburg. On paper, at least, the move made good sense.

Wilkinson made no public announcement of his plans; but by early 1954, rumors of an impending move to Idaho Falls swirled about Rexburg, causing local priesthood leaders to send McKay a telegram on March 17: "We are very much disturbed over Ricks College being moved, it is our heritage, we were born and raised here and want to educate our children under its influence." McKay replied the same day, "Rest assured there will be no change in Ricks College."[127]

In the meantime, Wilkinson, who knew nothing of the telegrams, began lobbying General Authorities to support his cause. Reaction among members of the Executive Committee of the Church Board of Education was mixed. Joseph Fielding Smith, the senior apostle on the committee, would not consider any change, while Apostle Henry D. Moyle was a vocal proponent. Wilkinson noted, "It was a question with him of what was right and what would do the Church the most good. To the local sentiment, he said this was nothing but selfishness."[128] But even though both Moyle and Wilkinson dismissed "local sentiment" out-of-hand, it ultimately defeated his plan.

Despite Moyle's endorsement, Wilkinson was unable to muster sufficient support for a move and reluctantly carried out the will of the committee to recommend to the First Presidency the construction of a new building on the Rexburg campus. In his diary, he brooded, "This letter was sent with more reluctance than any letter I have yet sent, for I am completely convinced that it is a mistake to continue Ricks College at the Rexburg location."[129]

Three years later, in the spring of 1957, Wilkinson again pressed his case, this time directly with the First Presidency. And again he presented convincing arguments in favor of moving the college to Idaho Falls, first in a meeting that included the First Presidency and fifteen stake presidents from eastern Idaho, and a week later to the Church Board of Education. On April 18, 1957, the board unanimously approved the proposed move, "with the understanding, however, that the Stake Presidencies at Rexburg would be invited to meet with the executive committee, and that if they presented any new facts against this decision which should merit further consideration, the question would again be considered."[130]

The "new facts" came forward quickly. Only nine days after Wilkinson's apparent victory Steve Meikle, president of the Idaho Bank of Commerce in Rexburg, telephoned McKay and reminded him of the 1954 telegram. McKay initially was dismissive, writing in his diary, "This telegram, however, referred to the change from a four-year to a two-year college and had nothing to do with the move to Idaho Falls."[131] The following day his mood changed, for the telegram became the subject of a two-hour discussion within the Board of Education, including Wilkinson, who recorded the discussion with an air of disbelief:

> Brother [Henry D.] Moyle, who had been the one pressing hardest for the removal of the school to Idaho Falls among the board of education, took a flat and strong position against the move, in view of this alleged "commitment" from the First Presidency. President [Joseph Fielding] Smith then joined in the discussion, urging against it.... After two hours' discussion, it was finally resolved that President McKay and others should go to Rexburg to present the matter to the brethren there in an attempt to be released from any commitment that had been made, if any. I took the strong position that no commitment had been made, that President McKay, in wiring the Seventies Quorum, had merely informed them the decision of the First Presidency at that time (in 1954)... In a court of law they would have no standing. They would not even be heard to protest.[132]

One month later, McKay and Wilkinson drove to Rexburg for a site visit and spent nearly six hours inspecting all of the campus buildings in company with John L. Clarke, Ricks College president, the Rexburg Stake presidency, and Rexburg's mayor. McKay noted, "Much to my surprise, it would be less expensive to have the College in Idaho Falls than in Rexburg."[133] Wilkinson was not overstating the situation when he wrote that "every argument was in favor of transferring Ricks College to Idaho Falls,"[134] and thus he was both shocked and indignant when McKay issued a press release on July 11, 1957, announcing that the college would definitely stay in Rexburg: "that the school will grow where it is and that the support of the people of the area will be given and the honor of the General Authorities of the Church in their minds will be preserved."[135] Indeed, it was McKay's sense of honor, linked to his 1954 telegram, that swayed his decision. On July 11, 1957, he told the Board of Education that the college would stay in Rexburg. If the church moved the college, he explained, "justified or not, thousands of people, young and old, will be imbued with the thought that the assurance given by the First Presidency, by the President, and by the Church School Administration, that Ricks College will remain at Rexburg was not kept."[136]

As noted earlier in this chapter, "no" did not mean to Wilkinson what it means to most people: "They don't mean no, they just don't understand the situation"—even when the "they" was a prophet. In this instance he had an unlikely ally, Stephen L Richards, McKay's first counselor and perhaps closest friend. One year after the decision to leave the college in Rexburg was announced, Wilkinson confided to his diary, "In view of the fact that David O. McKay's decision to leave Ricks College at Rexburg had been based on fraudulent representations, I had not really known whether to put his decision [to construct a new building on the Rexburg campus] into operation. On seeing President Richards, he advised that I continue to do just as I had done, namely stall on the matter until we found some way of getting the full facts before the president of the board of education."[137] Several months later he gained another ally, in the form of a proposal for the state of Idaho to build a junior college in Idaho Falls, that emboldened him to lobby McKay for a reversal. "I am sure," he wrote in his diary, "that many would think I was foolhardy in raising this question with President McKay after he had decided in favor of leaving it at Rexburg, but even though he is a prophet of the Lord, I have been convinced in my own mind that a decision made by him based on misinformation could not stand the test of time."[138] Wilkinson's use of *misinformation* was problematic, for he viewed any factors other than quantitative data as irrelevant. Thus, he would have considered any recognition that McKay gave to a factor like local loyalty to a college sustained by love and sweat as leaving him "misinformed."

Wilkinson's new strategy, with an assist from Richards, worked. A state college in Idaho Falls, the reasoning went, would dwarf Ricks College and cause it to fade into insignificance. On October 31, 1958, Wilkinson again argued his case to the First Presidency, and McKay recorded his summary of the First Presidency's deliberations: "During our two-hour meeting we gave consideration to the letter signed by Presidents of the Stakes in the Idaho Falls area reviewing public interest and action being proposed by citizens of Idaho Falls for the circulation of a petition to the legislature for the establishment of a state college at Idaho Falls.... After consideration it was unanimously agreed to recommend to the Council of the Twelve and the Board of Education that steps be taken to establish Ricks College at Idaho Falls."[139]

Hearing the news of the reversal, Wilkinson was jubilant. His diary entry was unrestrained: "There is one moral to the Ricks transfer, namely that if one is right (as I was sure I was), one should not hesitate to question the decision of the President of the Church (President McKay had formally decided to leave Ricks at

Rexburg), as long as it is done properly. His first decision was wrong, and I am happy I had the courage to raise the question again. With the strong support of President Richards, who knows how to handle President McKay, we finally got this serious mistake rectified."[140]

Wilkinson's jubilation would doubtless have been tempered had he fully appreciated the "local sentiment" that he and Henry D. Moyle had earlier dismissed as insignificant. Within days of the announced move, Rexburg citizens, both LDS and non-LDS, began to protest vigorously. In the face of such protest, McKay initially held firm. "The decision," he said, "was precipitated by the possibility of a two-year state college being established in Idaho Falls." When McKay was asked, at a meeting of local church and civic leaders in Rexburg, if the question was open for further exploration, he answered, "No."[141] But when local voices appeared to question his own credibility and the credibility of the First Presidency, McKay's tone changed. In late November 1958, he voiced these new concerns to Wilkinson. Wilkinson tried to reassure McKay that verbal attacks on himself (Wilkinson) by Rexburg citizens were inconsequential. But while Wilkinson was used to shrugging off criticism, McKay was not and replied, according to Wilkinson's diary, "that they were attacking the First Presidency also, and particularly charging that he, the president, had broken his word.... He said he realized that there was no contract, but his word meant more than a contract."[142]

Further doubts entered McKay's mind in late December when he met with Delbert Taylor, president of the Rexburg Stake, and Taylor questioned Wilkinson's honesty. McKay said, "You seem to imply that Dr. Wilkinson has been scheming to get a reconsideration." Taylor replied, "I imply that indirectly." After further discussion, McKay reassured Taylor: "I get your point of view. The Church is dear to all of us. Whatever is the right thing to do, what the Lord wants us to do, we will do, and that will be right."[143]

Six weeks later, McKay met again with Taylor, this time in the company of Taylor's two counselors. McKay confided to the men, "I am concerned on this because my honor is at stake."[144] Three days later he wrote in his diary, "Very tired after a strenuous day of problems. The last six months have brought many hours of worry and concern over the Ricks College."[145]

In the meantime, the status of the college remained in limbo. While the decision to move it to Idaho Falls had been announced, no action had been taken to effect the move. It was a dynamic stalemate, with the citizens of Rexburg on one side and Ernest Wilkinson on the other attempting to make their case with McKay. The stalemate began to dissolve with the unexpected death of Stephen L Richards, Wilkinson's ally, on May 19, 1959.

A year later, with the college still functioning in Rexburg, McKay decided to pay a surprise visit to the campus. He invited Wilkinson to accompany him, but Wilkinson declined. Too late, he realized that his refusal had been a huge mistake.[146] The trip turned out to be pivotal, for McKay was able to experience, unfiltered, the remarkable spirit of the college that was the legacy of decades of local support and sacrifice. McKay's dictated report of the experience was enthusiastic: "I wanted to partake of the spirit of the School and see just what they are accomplishing under the adverse circumstances of this year, which was one of the most difficult years for Ricks College. I was very glad I made the trip—it was about 500 miles. It was one of the best trips I have made in many a year!"[147]

Within weeks of McKay's trip, Wilkinson began to see the handwriting on the wall. After meeting with McKay on the subject he wrote, "My impression is that President McKay really wants Ricks to stay at Rexburg."[148] The impression was strengthened two weeks later when McKay told Wilkinson, according to McKay's diary entry: "I had never really felt right about the decision" to move the college to Idaho Falls.[149]

In a lengthy and extraordinary meeting with his counselors (now J. Reuben Clark and Henry D. Moyle) and the Council of the Twelve on June 30, 1960, which McKay called "in very deed an Apostolic meeting," he laid out the history of the whole matter. The minutes of the meeting, included in his diary, quote him as saying: "All indications favor going to Idaho Falls," yet adding "he could not feel right about moving the school from Rexburg.... The President said that when he faced this problem he felt cloudy about the sale of the buildings, tearing them down, and the building of a new college at Idaho Falls.... He said his feeling is that whether they have a State junior college at Idaho Falls or not we should keep Ricks at Rexburg." He did not use the words *inspiration* or *revelation,* but his colleagues understood the importance of what he was saying and backed him solidly. Marion G. Romney's comment was typical: "He said he felt that the President's impression is more persuasive on what should be done than anything else." Similarly, Spencer W. Kimball, who later became church president, "said he was one hundred percent behind President McKay in what he felt to be the revelation of the Lord to him." The vote to sustain his recommendation was unanimous. McKay concluded the meeting on a somber note: "The President said that today as never before our charge as Apostles should be considered sacred, and one of those charges is that we keep this to ourselves."[150]

Nearly four months elapsed before McKay gave Wilkinson the news that Ricks College would remain in Rexburg. Wilkinson was deeply disappointed and, although outwardly bowing to McKay's decision, fumed privately to his diary: "Over the six-year period...I have spent more time on it than on any other single matter.... I still think I am right, as I know many of the General Authorities of the Church do, but when the President speaks, he overrules the rest of us." He then predicted: "This will mean that Ricks College at Rexburg will continue as a relatively small school, in contrast to the junior college they will have at Idaho Falls."[151]

McKay felt otherwise, and a year later, after attending a Devotional at Ricks College, contentedly told his counselors and the Quorum of the Twelve that "we had done the right thing in leaving Ricks at Rexburg."[152] History has proven his decision to be correct. The rumored state junior college in Idaho Falls never materialized; and despite a population reported in the 2000 federal census as 50,730, triple that of Rexburg, the only colleges in the city were Eastern Idaho Technical College (enrollment 595) and Vogue Beauty College. By contrast, over 11,000 students are currently (fall 2004) enrolled at BYU–Idaho (formerly Ricks College), a number equivalent to 65 percent of Rexburg's nonstudent population. Church President Gordon B. Hinckley not only authorized the school's expansion to offer a full four-year curriculum but also called David A. Bednar, the college president who managed the successful transition, to fill a vacancy in the Quorum of the Twelve in October 2004.

DEMISE OF THE JUNIOR COLLEGE SYSTEM

Were it not for the self-imposed distraction of Ricks College, Wilkinson likely would have succeeded in implementing at least part of his bold initiative to build new junior colleges even though, as matters turned out, such expansion would have certainly been curtailed in the early 1960s by a financial crisis precipitated by the church's ambitious building program. (See chap. 9.) He began to investigate potential junior college sites within months of becoming administrator of the Unified Church School System in 1953, but four years elapsed before the first site was purchased, and that was the proposed new campus for Ricks College in Idaho Falls. Eventually the church purchased additional sites in Utah, Arizona, California, and Oregon, but the Ricks College controversy put these plans on hold and jeopardized the entire program. On December 4, 1959, exactly one month after the Church Board of Education approved the purchase of properties in Phoenix, Portland, and the San Francisco Bay area,[153] Wilkinson received the shocking news that the church was in financial peril:

> We were informed that for the first time for a long number of years,
> the Church last year had spent $8 million in excess of its income, having called on its reserves for that amount, that this year, the requests
> for expenditures from the different departments of the Church were

$17 million in excess of the estimated income.... I told them I had committed myself to the governor of Arizona, to city officials and others at Fremont, and to the chairman of the planning board in Portland. Brother [Delbert L.] Stapley commented that he thought we would have to go through with those moral commitments.[154]

Wilkinson's persuasions prevailed and the land was purchased, but this action did not sit well with others whose budgets were severely trimmed. In January 1960 McKay and his counselors began to take a serious second look at the whole program. McKay wrote: "I stated that the whole question of Junior Colleges, institutes, and seminaries is before the First Presidency. The rapid expansion of the Brigham Young University and the matter of providing additional Junior Colleges in several places and giving training in basic courses in education rather than in the 'fringe' subjects were mentioned as warranting a full review of the general subject with President Wilkinson."[155]

Four days later, the executive committees of the Church Board of Education and BYU's Board of Trustees informed Wilkinson of McKay's decision. "This is a grave disappointment," he wrote, "after I've been working now for nearly three years under the assumption the decision was made to go ahead with them."[156] Three months later he presented to the executive committee of BYU's Board of Trustees a fifteen-year plan for developing junior colleges. "It was unanimously enthusiastically approved," he recorded. "This was a real step forward, and if approved by the board of trustees, will represent my greatest achievement as President or Administrator." Despite this grandiose pronouncement, however, he ended his diary entry on a seemingly prescient note: "Only time will tell."[157]

The Board of Education was scheduled to vote on the master plan on June 29, but a fluke occurrence caused it to be postponed. Six days before the meeting, a secretary to the First Presidency called Wilkinson and informed him that 421 missionaries needed to be set apart on that day, requiring all of the General Authorities on the board. Since summer vacations would occur shortly thereafter, the meeting would have to be postponed until the fall.[158] What Wilkinson did not know at the time was that, on June 30, one day after the scheduled meeting, McKay met with his counselors and the Council of the Twelve and dealt Wilkinson a severe setback by ruling against him in the Ricks College matter. The high-water mark of the junior college program had been reached, but it would take Wilkinson several years to realize it.

Wilkinson's rescheduled meeting with the combined Board of Education and Board of Trustees occurred on September 7, 1960. The main agenda item was the junior college master plan. McKay's two counselors, Clark and Moyle, came down hard on the plan. It looked for a while as if the junior college program might be killed outright, but Wilkinson gained a temporary respite by going toe-to-toe with Clark and Moyle. "Had I not been willing to stand up against the two counselors for an hour of running duel, this matter would have gone over for a year, and might have meant the end of the program."[159]

In October, McKay, after four months of delay, finally informed Wilkinson that Ricks College would remain in Rexburg. Deeply disappointed, he nonetheless waxed philosophical as the weeks passed. In late November he wrote, "I was, frankly, anxious to have the matter out of the way so that we could get going on a junior college program. This had been a roadblock to the entire program."[160] Rather than a roadblock removed, however, the Ricks College matter emboldened Wilkinson's opponents.

In May 1961 Wilkinson met with Moyle at Moyle's request. Sensing that Moyle was opposed to the junior colleges, "I thought I would beat him to the punch, and so I told him President McKay had been here the day before, and had asked me how large I thought BYU ought to grow. I told him it should not get any larger than 12,000, whereupon President McKay said he agreed that we must proceed immediately with our junior college program." Moyle's response was violent. He "thumped his hand on the desk" and adamantly stated that there would not be enough money to finance the junior college program "in your lifetime or mine."[161] Two weeks later Wilkinson played Moyle against McKay by reporting Moyle's announcement to McKay and asking "whether I should include any items in the budget next year for junior college construction. He instructed me to do so."[162]

Wilkinson was winning some battles but losing the war. In August 1962 after a meeting of the executive committee of the BYU Board of Trustees, he wrote, "It was apparent from the meeting that Brother [Harold B.] Lee is very much opposed to the junior college program."[163] Wilkinson continued to push his agenda with the supportive McKay, telling him in October 1962 that BYU would reach its enrollment limit in two years and that the junior colleges would be their only alternative for educating LDS students. McKay "instructed me to proceed with all haste; that we should first build the one at Anaheim.... I informed him we would need $5 million in the budget for junior college purposes for next year and he commented that if that is what we needed, we would have to spend it."[164] Five months later, however, the Executive Committee of the Church Board of Education thought otherwise and blindsided Wilkinson.

In January 1963, Wilkinson had announced to the stake presidents in southern California plans to break ground for the junior college at Anaheim. The board of education had not authorized either the announcement or the groundbreaking. This announcement perturbed the youngest member of the Church Board of

Education, thirty-eight-year-old Boyd K. Packer, a former regional supervisor of seminaries and Institutes of Religion, who had been called as an Assistant to the Twelve sixteen months before Wilkinson's announcement. Bypassing the other members of the executive committee, he wrote directly to the First Presidency on February 18. Wilkinson's announcement, he said, was one of "a series of events" that "has weighed so heavily upon my mind as to overcome my hesitancy to make expression of my feelings."[165] On March 1, 1963, the executive committee, of which Packer was a member, met in executive session without Wilkinson and held a long discussion of his letter.

One of Packer's colleagues who was not on the committee later described the letter: "[Packer] put a paper together that showed that the Institutes [of Religion] were the only way it [church education] could survive—the cost, the growing numbers, the expansion of the Church every place. You couldn't have enough colleges to reach them. It was a pretty impressive paper. I remember reading it, and I thought, 'Boy, he's been thinking about this.' He got that to President McKay, and that was the beginning of the end."[166]

Following a discussion of the letter, the executive committee voted unanimously "that the Church take steps to approve of the discontinuance of the actions establishing Junior Colleges throughout the Church." Four days later, again without Wilkinson, the executive committee met with the First Presidency to discuss the matter further. They reviewed Packer's letter. McKay asked the committee to verify that Wilkinson had acted without their knowledge. They did so.[167]

McKay then spoke of his own advocacy for church-owned colleges, relating how, more than three decades earlier, he had voted against a First Presidency recommendation to give the church's junior colleges to the states of Utah, Arizona, and Idaho. Yet while he still had a warm spot for church colleges, he acknowledged that their expense might be beyond the church's means. The question before them, he said, was "whether the junior college is worth the extra cost to introduce religion with all the secular subjects, or whether the institute [of Religion] will supply the religious training." Marion G. Romney, a member of the Executive Committee of the Church Board of Education, said that "he would favor the junior college where Latter-day Saint teachers could be used in every class, but he felt that the cost would be prohibitive to furnish college work to all the Church." After a lengthy discussion, McKay summarized the issue before them:

> [He] said he could not see that we could do anything else, that we
> have discussed the matter and have come to the conclusion that the
> seminaries and institutes can do the religious work.... [He] asked if
> as an executive committee they wanted to give official approval to the
> sentiment of this meeting. Elder [Harold B.] Lee said he thought it

should be a part of the minutes of this meeting that we take steps to approve the discontinuance of the actions establishing junior colleges throughout the Church. President [Henry D.] Moyle said he would like to make that motion, which he did, and which was seconded by Brother Packer. This motion was unanimously approved.[168]

Later the same day, Packer called Wilkinson and informed him of the executive committee decision. Wilkinson was devastated with the news, particularly since the proceedings had occurred "without my knowledge or without inviting me (although I am a member of the committee), with the First Presidency."[169] Never one to accept defeat, he maneuvered to reverse the decision. One week later, however, Marion G. Romney, usually Wilkinson's ally on the executive committee, cautioned him not to push the issue. "He thought the matter had already been decided. He urged me that if I did present it at all, that I be very careful in the manner I proceed, because there were some very deep feelings in the matter.... In the afternoon, I had a talk with Brother Packer on it. He went further than Brother Romney, and thought I ought not even present it."[170]

Undaunted, Wilkinson spent hours during the next two months preparing to appeal the committee's decision. On May 28 he made his presentation to the regular meeting of the full Church Board of Education. As Romney had warned, deep feelings came to the surface. Harold B. Lee, in particular, "launched into a tirade of the junior college program, saying that it had been decided, and now I apparently wanted to have it debated again. He further told Ben [E. Lewis, BYU's executive vice president] that Brother Romney had told me that if I brought it up again, I might be successful at present, because I was pretty persuasive, but that eventually I would lose."[171] Lee's words were prophetic.

Wilkinson continued to push his case hard over the next six months, at one point apparently turning the tide; but he was up against two inexorable opponents: antagonistic board members and economic exigencies. There simply was not enough money to build the junior college system that Wilkinson had envisioned; yet his earlier successes in obtaining huge capital budgets for BYU prevented him from accepting that reality.

There is no telling how long Wilkinson might have attempted to prolong the battle, but in December 1963 he effectively dropped the issue when he resigned to run for the U.S. Senate. He later noted that he "had spent more time on this junior college project than on any other single project."[172] Though he returned as BYU president after losing the 1964 election, both the BYU Board of Trustees and the Church Board of Education managed to persuade McKay not to also reappoint Wilkinson as chancellor of the Unified Church School System. His vision of a junior college system thus died a quiet death. The sites were either used for other purposes (in Portland, a temple was built on the site), or sold at substantial profits.[173]

McKay's Educational Legacy

The educational legacy of the McKay years has been rich. McKay himself instilled in an entire generation of Latter-day Saints an enhanced appreciation of the value of higher education that continues to this day. His desire to give LDS students secular education at church-owned colleges overcame his Scots frugality, and he approved unprecedented expenditures for the building of a new school (the Church College of Hawaii) and the expansion of two existing ones (BYU and Ricks College). Working hand-in-glove with Ernest L. Wilkinson, and occasionally in the face of opposition from some General Authorities, he took great satisfaction in seeing BYU grow from a small, insignificant college to the largest church-sponsored university in the United States. While Wilkinson sometimes overstepped the bounds of propriety in the way he pursued his agenda, there is no question that he deserves the credit, more than any other individual, for the impressive physical plant of BYU.

The major disappointment for McKay, as well as Wilkinson, was the demise of the ambitious junior college system that both had envisioned. One may speculate what might have happened had Wilkinson been less determined to move Ricks College to Idaho Falls. Had he left it alone, he might have been able to build other campuses before the 1959 budget crunch that effectively spelled an end to the dream. Yet one also wonders whether it was ever practical to think of providing secular education for all, or even most, LDS students. As church membership outside the United States mushroomed, beginning in the McKay years, it became clear that chapels, not colleges, were the greater need. Reluctantly, both McKay and Wilkinson turned to the seminaries and Institutes of Religion to provide religious education to those attending secular high schools and colleges. Today fewer than 10 percent of LDS college students can attend one of the three church-owned schools (now named BYU, BYU–Hawaii, and BYU–Idaho). That percentage will continue to drop as church membership increases in the face of capped enrollments. Yet the seminaries and institutes have effectively fulfilled their role, by 2002 serving over 740,000 students.[174]

9

THE
BUILDING PROGRAM

For the first quarter-century of his life, until a mission call took him to Scotland, David O. McKay's world was northern Utah. Glasgow, "a gloomy-looking place," was a far cry from bucolic Huntsville, and on his first morning in the city he recorded the first of many cultural shocks: "The people, many of them, are in a deplorable condition. Some of the women are bare-headed and bare-footed, ragged and dirty; and such women are raising children! It is a common sight to see women *reeling* along the street. It is enough to make a person sick. *Utah* is *dearer* than *ever.*"[1]

A second shock came more gradually, and its effect was lifelong. McKay had never known a place where the church met in any quarters other than its own chapels. When he was ten, the modest chapel in Huntsville was replaced by a large, ornate building that became the centerpiece of the town. In contrast, there was not a single church-owned chapel in the British Isles. The small, scattered congregations of Latter-day Saints, whose continuing existence was always a struggle because of a church policy that encouraged emigration to Utah, met in rented halls that were often deplorable and that worked against proselytizing efforts. McKay later recounted the dilemma: "People would ask, 'Where is your meeting place?'...We say, 'It is in Hall So-and-so,' giving the impression to an investigator that the Church was not permanently established."[2]

Following the turn of the twentieth century, the church quietly deemphasized the policy of "gathering," although it would be another half-century before it openly reversed the policy and encouraged people to stay where they were and build the church there. While the deemphasis may have marginally helped proselytizing activities, the continuing lack of appropriate meeting places remained a major impediment. During his 1921 world tour of the church's missions, McKay presaged what would become the cornerstone of his tenure as church president—the building of an international church—and linked it to such meeting places.

Addressing a group of Latter-day Saints in Adelaide, Australia, who had taken the initiative to build their own chapel, he said that he was "pleased to see members build good, strong, substantial buildings to show the world we intend to stay and stand forever."[3]

A year after his world tour, McKay was called to preside over the European Mission. In July 1923, he traveled to Denmark with Apostle (and U.S. Senator) Reed Smoot, who was attempting to leverage his political stature to improve relationships between the church and European countries. Smoot lamented the poor meeting conditions in Copenhagen:

> Headquarters back of a saloon and too large for the number of members of the church. I wish they had a better location and a modern church building.... It is in fair condition and kept clean but why do we also get in such poor locations and undesirable parts of the cities. I would like to sell the property and build a modern church building in a good location of the city and give people a chance to attend our services and our own members a place where they are not ashamed to ask friends not of our church. Some day this present policy will be exchanged and the sooner the better.[4]

Several weeks later, McKay echoed Smoot's sentiments in an impassioned letter to the First Presidency: "The Bradford branch, one of the largest in the British mission, is without a suitable place in which to meet. They hold services once a week in a schoolhouse, and they are storing their furniture, pews, organ, etc. in different places. The crying need of this mission is more respectable buildings in which to hold services."[5]

His plea went unheeded; and the following year as he handed over the mission presidency to Apostle James E. Talmage and returned to Utah, McKay urged him to continue to press the issue: "The need of suitable places of worship confronts the missionaries daily; several small churches should either be built or purchased. It will save you a great deal of worry if you will ascertain the Presidency's views in regard to this matter."[6]

Others later echoed McKay's frustrations. Edgar Brossard, former chairman of the U.S. Tariff Commission, spoke of his experiences as a mission president in France in the late 1950s:

> President Joseph F. Smith forty years ago or more said that a good chapel is worth twenty full-time missionaries as a proselyter. I think it's worth more than that, in my experience. And in France, we don't have them. We meet a lot of wonderful people and have an opportunity to convert them. But imagine how they feel, how shocked, when

they bring them to some of our little meeting places, where the best we can find to rent is one room, usually in some sort of mediocre club hall in a basement or upstairs, and in a not very desirable part of town. Sometimes we had to clean the place Sunday morning after their Saturday night parties—open the windows to air out tobacco smoke, pick up empty liquor bottles, clean out spittoons, sweep up litter, empty trash, arrange chairs and furniture, and other jobs.[7]

In the decades between McKay's return to Utah after serving as a missionary to Scotland and his calling as church president in 1951, three factors combined to forestall the kind of international building program that he envisioned. The first was the Great Depression, whose effects were no less devastating in Utah than elsewhere. Total churchwide expenditures on buildings, which included construction and maintenance, were only $890,000 in 1930, and by 1935 sank by nearly two-thirds to $320,000. (Twenty years later, the first year of Wendell Mendenhall's tenure as chairman of the Building Department, expenditures were nearly one hundredfold higher.)[8] The second factor was World War II. A secretary to the First Presidency explained: "The war had delayed [the] building of churches certainly. When the building business priorities were established...churches came way down the list of priorities."[9]

And the third factor was J. Reuben Clark Jr. Clark had been a powerful and autocratic first counselor to church presidents Heber J. Grant (1933–45) and George Albert Smith (1945–51). As both presidents suffered declining health for several years prior to their deaths, Clark became de facto church president, overshadowing McKay, the second counselor.[10] Fiscally conservative, Clark made no secret of his aversion to what he viewed as exuberant spending on buildings. Addressing the general conference in 1940, he said, "We have a tendency I think to make our buildings just a little too elaborate and too ornate."[11] In 1950 Clark acted unilaterally and abruptly to impose a moratorium on new chapel construction. McKay, clearly annoyed at being excluded from the decision, vented his frustration to a reporter: "Clarence Williams, reporter of the [Salt Lake] *Telegram* came in to discuss with me the story he had written and published in the *Telegram* regarding the church's decision to accept no applications for new chapels until 1951. I told Clarence that this is a matter that he will have to take up with [Presiding] Bishop [LeGrand] Richards and President Clark, that I have had nothing to do with the matter."[12]

While wartime exigencies and Clark's frugality frustrated McKay's vision of church buildings, they nonetheless laid the foundation for the building boom that accompanied McKay's ascension to the Presidency. Arch Madsen, who later headed Bonneville International, the church's broadcasting franchise, recounted, "President

[Henry D.] Moyle told me once that the church had built up quite a reserve during the war years, and they had a tendency to hold onto that. President McKay didn't believe in that, and neither did President Moyle."[13] A McKay grandson-in-law added, "As a result, there was money in banks all over the United States. The Church was hoarding cash, and President McKay said, 'Ah, we've got to get buildings built,' and that's when the policy was changed."[14]

AN INTERNATIONAL PRESENCE

David O. McKay became church president upon the death of George Albert Smith in early April 1951 and moved quickly to implement his vision. His first action, an unprecedented move that shocked many church members, was to demote Clark to second counselor, installing in his stead as first counselor McKay's lifelong close friend, Apostle Stephen L Richards. In doing so, McKay sent to Clark and to the entire church a strong signal that he, not Clark, would now set the agenda, and that the agenda would be a departure from past practices. Three weeks after becoming president, McKay, while visiting Los Angeles, "told reporters that the focus of the Mormon Church today is upon building."[15]

Although McKay's initial concern was chapels, he quickly broadened that vision. First, at the October 1951 general conference, McKay announced plans "for construction at some indefinite date of a 30,000-seat auditorium on the block north of Temple Square," more than thrice the capacity of the historic Tabernacle built nearly a century previously.[16]

On the same day he made this announcement, McKay spoke at the funeral of Robert Stayner Richards, a thirty-six-year-old father of two who died of polio. Stayner Richards, father of the deceased man and brother of McKay's first counselor, was president of the British Mission at the time his son died. Returning to Utah for the funeral, he met with the First Presidency and made a suggestion that catalyzed the development of the international church. Several months later, McKay described the meeting to the Quorum of the Twelve Apostles:

> For years it has been recommended that the branches in Great Britain
> and Europe be strengthened, but members of the Church in those
> lands when they get the spirit of the Gospel realize the importance of
> temple work, and notwithstanding some of them held good positions,
> they have given those positions up and have come here in order to go
> through the temple. While President Stayner Richards was in the City
> at the time of the death of his son last Fall, he consulted the Presidency
> and among other recommendations, asked if it would not be an
> opportune time to build a temple in Great Britain. The Brethren of
> the First Presidency considered it carefully and prayerfully and have

now come to the conclusion that if we build a temple in Great Britain we should at the same time build one in Switzerland; this latter temple would serve the people in Switzerland, Germany, Austria, and possibly Holland.[17]

The decision was unprecedented. For the first time in the history of the church, temples were to be constructed where there was not already a stake (diocese), yet McKay was confident that the temples would anchor the development of the church in Europe.

In April 1952, McKay made an administrative change that had an immediate effect upon the building program. He called LeGrand Richards, then serving as Presiding Bishop, to fill the vacancy in the Quorum of the Twelve caused by the death of Joseph F. Merrill and, at the same time, removed the building program from the portfolio of the Presiding Bishopric and placed it directly under the First Presidency.[18] This reorganization gave McKay immediate control of the program, and he frequently used his presidential prerogative in a manner that often frustrated his colleagues among the General Authorities but that often produced dramatic results.

For example, Belle S. Spafford, longtime general president of the women's Relief Society, had worked for years to raise funds for a Relief Society building; yet despite her efforts, the project had stalled in Clark's office. His attitude was: "We'll let you know when we're ready." In frustration she told her story to LeGrand Richards, who suggested a solution: "President Clark is not the President of the Church. You've got a new President of the Church, President McKay.... Go to him and tell him how embarrassed you are, that after having crowded the women to get their money in, that you can't go forward. The money is depreciating in value, building costs are increasing rapidly, and you're embarrassed as to what you can say to your women."[19] Spafford did as Richards suggested and, within ten days, had approval to begin construction.

When Clifton Kerr was called to preside over the British Mission, he was set apart by the First Presidency:

> President McKay seemed to be about through with his blessing when he hesitated a minute and then he went on and said, "You are to find a lot in the center of London where we can build the kind of a chapel to which we can take anybody, regardless of their situation in life." I got a vision of what he wanted from that blessing, so no sooner did we begin to travel around London than I began to look for suitable sites.... I called President McKay on the phone and I said, "I found the lot that I think you asked me to find." And I told him the problems. First, it was not zoned for religious purposes. It was zoned for

cultural or educational purposes. Then the price sounded like a lot of money for that much space, and there was also the question of not being able to get a deed to it. I described where it was, and he knew Albert Hall, which was right by it, and he said, "I have an idea where you are talking about. You go ahead and get the best price you can, get the longest lease you can, and I feel confident that the London County Council will give us permission to build on it.".... There wasn't a member living within seven miles of the place, so far as I knew. I remember one of the General Authorities came over and we talked about it and he said, "Who's going to meet there?" And I said, "I don't know. I have no idea. But President McKay said, 'Do this.'" The Building Committee wrote me and said, "We think maybe you ought to sell the property. Now is not the time to build a chapel." So I'm sure there were some misgivings. However, President McKay's instruction to me took precedence over the Building Committee's point of view. But going over then and going over later, as I did, I think it's fulfilled fully the dream that President McKay had for it.[20]

And finally, when McKay called Bernard P. Brockbank as president of the Scottish Mission, he gave the new mission president "a bundle of checks about one inch thick." Amazed, Brockbank expostulated: "'President, we are just coming out of a depression.' President McKay was as great a miracle prophet as ever lived on this earth. I said, 'What are these for?' He said, 'The Lord will tell you.' I bought over twenty-eight chapel sites. We have a chapel on every one of them."[21]

The major reason for new buildings was to establish the church as a permanent international fixture. During a trip to Europe in 1952 to inspect potential building sites, McKay told reporters that the purpose of the buildings was "to keep our adherents here instead of encouraging them to immigrate to Utah and other places in the United States."[22] Similarly, during a later trip to South Africa, McKay explained to reporters that the church's first priority in that country was "to establish church buildings so that we can hold our members in this country." He noted that the low number of Latter-day Saints in South Africa—1,800—was due to the constant flow of emigrants to the United States. "Hundreds have left the Union and settled in America and Canada, so that they could be near the great temples and thus enter into the fullest expression of the Mormon religion. This year alone, 25 have left South Africa. If we establish enough chapels here, this movement will be arrested."[23]

Results of the ambitious building program quickly became evident. At the October 1952 general conference, McKay joyfully announced that eighty-four new chapels had been completed and dedicated in the first nine months of the year, with another fifty-three scheduled for completion in the final quarter. Furthermore, 389 chapels were currently under construction, fifty of which were in the "missions," or outside existing stakes, many of them in foreign countries.[24] In the same announcement, he praised church members for opening their wallets to fuel the construction engine, stating that tithing receipts were up 217 percent from the previous year.

Shortly after the April 1955 general conference, Howard J. McKean died unexpectedly of a heart attack. McKean had been the effective though low-profile chairman of the Building Committee since 1946.[25] Two weeks later, McKay had lunch with several colleagues to discuss "the new building projects for the Church's great expansion program."[26] One of his guests, Wendell B. Mendenhall, would shortly take the church in directions few, if any, could have imagined.

RAPID EXPANSION OF THE BUILDING PROGRAM

Wendell Mendenhall was, at first glance, a strange choice to head the Building Committee, for he had little background in construction. "He'd been a rancher all his life, a stockman," described his friend and colleague, Vaun Clissold, a businessman in Honolulu. "But he was a very good businessman with a great sense of business, balance, and all that sort of thing."[27] He was also president of the San Joaquin California Stake and was well known among the General Authorities. In 1954, at McKay's request, he began to informally assist in the church's construction program in New Zealand,[28] largely because of his close friendship with George Biesinger, supervisor of the Church Building Committee of New Zealand.[29] A year later, McKay appointed him to supervise the construction of a temple in Hamilton, New Zealand, and an adjacent school.[30] Three months after McKean's death, McKay appointed Mendenhall as McKean's replacement.[31]

Mendenhall was a visionary and energetic man. "He was just a very powerful man," recalled Michael Grilikhes, who supplied entertainment expertise for the Polynesian Cultural Center, on whose board of directors Mendenhall served. "If he saw something that needed to be done, it got done.... Once he decided he was going to do it, it didn't make any difference what was in the way, he would do it."[32] But perhaps the most important factor in his success was that, like his predecessor since 1952, he reported directly to McKay and thus circumvented the church's bureaucracy.[33] Furthermore, he had McKay's personal confidence.[34] These same factors had fueled Ernest L. Wilkinson's long success in building Brigham Young University. (See chap. 8.) For nearly a decade, these factors also worked to Mendenhall's advantage.

J. Alan Blodgett, who later became the church's chief financial officer, stated that, under Mendenhall's leadership, the building program "took off like a shot...."

The church had built up large financial reserves during the war years,...and Mendenhall believed that these resources could be better deployed building the Kingdom."[35]

A major factor in Mendenhall's success was his creative expansion of a church program that called young men into service in the building trades, rather than the traditional proselytizing mission. Such "labor missions" had been commonplace in the early decades of the church but had largely disappeared in the first half of the twentieth century. Then, in 1950 a labor shortage in Tonga caused a crisis in the church's construction of a school. The resourceful mission president, Evon W. Huntsman, "then called young men to work and receive job training on the project. The church provided housing, local members gave food, and the building supervisor taught skills. Successful completion of the project led the program to be applied elsewhere in Tonga and then in New Zealand."[36]

Mendenhall greatly expanded the labor missionary program, first in the South Pacific, then in South America (1958) and Europe (1960),[37] all with McKay's enthusiastic endorsement.[38] While there were problems with the program, its overall effect was dramatic. Robert L. Simpson, who served for over three decades as a General Authority, described the effect:

> This building missionary program was instrumental in getting hundreds of chapels built, not only in the South Pacific, but over in Europe, chapels that might have waited another generation or two under the old thinking. Everything was accelerated. This idea of calling building missionaries: Down in New Zealand I could introduce you to hundreds and hundreds of young men who learned their building trade as building missionaries, building chapels in New Zealand under American supervision sent down under the direction of President McKay and supervised by Brother Mendenhall. It was a wonderful, wonderful thing.[39]

Already approaching a full head of steam, the building program received an unexpected boost when J. Reuben Clark died in 1959 and McKay called Henry D. Moyle to replace him as a counselor in the First Presidency. As a member of the Quorum of the Twelve Apostles, Moyle had shared with his colleagues irritation at Mendenhall's autonomy. One church employee admitted that the "Quorum of the Twelve often didn't know what maybe they should have known."[40] But changing seats also changed Moyle's outlook. Owen Cook, a member of the church's Pacific Board of Education and third president of BYU–Hawaii, worked closely with both men. As he described the situation: "President Moyle, when he went into the First Presidency, was thought by the brethren of the Council of the Twelve to be able to straighten out Brother Mendenhall. But instead of straightening out Brother Mendenhall, he joined forces with him."[41]

Moyle, trained as an attorney, had made a fortune in the oil business, and according to Robert Sears, a business partner, "had a great deal of wildcat background in his makeup. A wildcatter never knows if he's going to get an oil well or not. It's a gamble, and it's a big gamble. You just take that chance, and you're either broke when you get through, or you have a lot of money. That's the way all of these wildcatters were, and Henry had that same background and makeup."[42]

In addition to his willingness to take risks, Moyle quickly developed a grand vision for improving the church's image, especially abroad where it had been seen as a marginal sect for more than a century. Paul H. Dunn, who was, with Thomas S. Monson, coordinating ecclesiastical affairs in the South Pacific and who became a General Authority in 1964 when the full impact of the building program was apparent, described Moyle's vision:

> He had the idea of getting the Mormon image "out of the gutter."
> Mission homes, back before he took over, were kind of dumpy places
> around the world. And he went into the palatial concept.... When I
> was down coordinating the South Pacific, he bought a mission home
> in Christchurch, which is the showplace of all New Zealand. It had
> acres and acres of park, and this big palace in there. All of a sudden,
> people in New Zealand took notice of the Mormon Church, and said,
> "Who are these people?" Well, he did that in many, many parts of the
> world.... Having served [as supervisor in that area] I could see the
> value of it, because it enhanced what I was doing with people in town.
> I had entree to people you don't normally have entree to.[43]

Moyle, who as a young man had served as a missionary in Germany, was particularly concerned about improving the church's image in Europe. Within months of being called to the First Presidency, he traveled to Europe specifically to find chapel sites. William Erekson, then mission president in Switzerland, commented on Moyle's visit: "He was anxious to get a building program moving. I'm sure that there were others of the General Authorities who had the view of a worldwide Church, but I think none had a greater insight into the possibility than President Moyle.... He urged all the European Mission Presidents to press to get land and get it approved and purchased so that the Church could go ahead."[44]

Stanford Bird, an employee of the Building Department who was then working in England, recalled Moyle's abrupt mandate: "He gave me a checkbook and said, 'Start looking for properties.' That's when the building program started there.... It was constant and tremendous growth."[45]

Levi Berg Thorup, president of the Danish Mission, shared Moyle's vision:

> I'll never forget when I first arrived in Denmark.... As I looked at
> those building sites I can still remember how disappointed I felt,
> because they were so small.... The first trip that President Moyle
> made to Denmark, I took occasion then to invite [him] to go with me
> and look at these building lots. I said, "President Moyle, those lots are
> no good to us. We can't build a building that's representative of the
> Church on those kind of building sites." He said, "President Thorup,
> you're absolutely right. Let's sell all of them. Scrap them. That isn't
> the thing we've got to look forward to. What we've got to do is buy
> lots that are as big as an acre to five acres. We've got to build the
> Church up."[46]

Given Moyle's and Mendenhall's personal qualities coupled with McKay's
explicit and enthusiastic approval, they made a potent team. Mendenhall took pains
to ensure that McKay and his counselors were kept well informed. A. Hamer
Reiser, then an assistant secretary to the First Presidency, recalled: "What [Menden-
hall] was doing was very important, involving a great deal of money. Nobody
before had ever spent so much money for the Church and he quite properly needed
the ear of the Presidency and the informed participation of the Presidency in everything. And he helped them make decisions by presenting all the facts they needed
to decide upon a project.... Nothing got away without a decision, and an informed
decision, by the First Presidency. They knew what was going on."[47]

Only a year after Moyle joined the First Presidency, the *Church News*
announced "the largest building program in the history of the Church." By the end
of 1960, the article noted, 800 chapels worldwide would either be completed and
awaiting dedication, under construction, or have plans that had been completed and
approved.[48] A year later, Mendenhall and his committee reported to McKay that,
in Europe alone, 168 projects had been started in the prior nine months, including
purchases of real estate and buildings under construction.[49]

In August 1963, shortly before his ninetieth birthday, McKay traveled to Wales
to dedicate a new chapel in Merthyr-Tydfil, the birthplace of his mother. Speaking
to the congregation he expressed gratitude to members of the Building Department
not only for that building, but also for their progress throughout the British Isles:
"In the British Missions, you will be pleased to know, there are forty-six chapels
under construction now, and thirty-nine chapels going under construction before
the end of this year, a total of eighty-five buildings either completed or under way
for 1963."[50]

The following month, in a birthday tribute to McKay, Moyle summarized the
church's worldwide building accomplishments during McKay's tenure: "In the past

twelve years, under the direction of the First Presidency of the Church, we have built 56 percent of the 3,500 meetinghouses we now have in the world, 1,941 in number—more than were built in the preceding 120 years of church history. This was made possible by the organization of the church building missionary work program initiated in 1955 by President McKay under the inspiration of the Almighty. This program has made it possible to erect buildings in every mission of the Church, regardless of the financial condition of the people."[51]

The program's underlying purpose had been to build up the church, particularly in foreign countries where it had struggled for over a century. As the buildings were completed, the reports confirmed expectations. Moyle's son, who served in the early 1960s as a mission president in France, recalled: "The chapels that they built were really beautiful edifices.... All of a sudden the Church got out of the top of a bar and into a respectable, wonderful place to meet. And the people in the countries realized that. It makes a big difference how they accept you if they think you're of substance, rather than just some little cult. And I think that's what [my father] did. He differentiated us from being a cult to being a substantial religious organization, one that people would respect and listen to."[52]

In addition to strengthening existing church members, the building program catalyzed proselytizing efforts. William Bates, a British member who, in 1960, became a counselor in the first stake presidency in Europe (Manchester, England), recalled the striking effect: "It absolutely multiplied the number of baptisms, and it raised the status of the Church tremendously.... You know, can you imagine doctors and lawyers and architects going to a storefront building? They wouldn't go. You would feel, 'What's this? Kingdom Hall.' But it wasn't even a Kingdom Hall. It was like an insult to people to ask them to go there. 'Is this the best the Lord can do?'"[53]

Indeed, although other factors also contributed to proselytizing successes, 1961–65 saw the five highest annual numbers of convert baptisms in church history, triple those of the previous five years. Yet at the same time the successes were being tabulated, trouble was brewing just beneath the surface.

A FINANCIAL CRISIS

The primary problem was financial over-extension. Alan Blodgett, an employee in the Financial Department who became the church's chief financial officer in 1969, summarized the problem succinctly:

> Throughout World War II and up until 1958 the Church had accumulated sizable surpluses. The rapidly expanding building program and BYU expansion began taxing the church liquid resources by then,

however, and deficit spending began.... No longer could it be said that the church was living within its income. Deficit spending continued for about five years, and by 1962 a real liquidity crunch presented itself. Some writers claim the church was approaching bankruptcy, which is ridiculous. The church had vast holdings of real estate and other assets and virtually no debt. It had merely run out of cash. Out of necessity, the rate of expenditures was slowed in 1962, and further curtailed after President Moyle died and President Tanner took office [in 1963].[54]

The era of church deficit spending coincided with Moyle's service in the First Presidency. While Mendenhall had ratcheted up the level of construction since taking over in 1955, Moyle, appointed four years later, quickly pushed it to new heights. "He was furious that the Church was putting money in savings accounts all over the United States at 2 percent interest," described Howard Anderson, later a stake president in Los Angeles and McKay's grandson-in-law. "He is the one who said, 'Go out and buy real estate.'"[55] Rather than viewing the funding of new chapels as deficit spending, Moyle saw it as an excellent investment. New chapels, he reasoned, would result in new converts who, in turn, would provide new sources of tithing revenue that would service the debt.[56]

Moyle's more conservative colleagues among the Quorum of the Twelve, however, were not convinced by his argument and tried to hold his spending in check. Late in 1959, according to Ernest Wilkinson, himself no mean spender, the General Authorities voted that "they would not spend any more than their income.... This was a resolution that had never been passed by them before."[57] This resolution had the same effect as periodic attempts by the Congress to control deficits by passing balanced budget laws; and only six weeks later, the Church Budget Committee, chaired by Spencer W. Kimball, then an apostle and later church president, announced that "for the first time for a long number of years" the church's expenses exceeded its revenues, by $8 million. Even more troubling, the deficit for 1960 was projected at $17 million.[58]

While agreeing in principle to a balanced budget on the one hand, the First Presidency announced in October 1960 that it "had made some very heavy commitments for the construction of buildings in Europe, as well as a tremendous construction program in Salt Lake City." Wilkinson commented, "It was obvious that all members of the budget committee are very much concerned, and don't know how to act."[59] The heavy commitments included one hundred new chapels in Europe and a large, though unspecified number in South America.[60] Only a week later, McKay, in a move that undoubtedly sent mixed signals to Mendenhall, cautioned him "to move slowly on some of these important church buildings which is causing a vast expenditure of money; that these things had caused much concern in my mind."[61] A month later the budget committee found itself wrestling with a projected deficit for 1961 of $20–25 million. Despite belt tightening by the various departments, the deficit had been reduced only to $17 million by the end of December, resulting in an emergency meeting during the Christmas holiday of McKay, Delbert L. Stapley and Joseph L. Wirthlin (both members of the Budget Committee), and two representatives of the Finance Department: George Y. Jarvis, the church's chief financial officer, and an otherwise unidentified "Brother Olson." Wilkinson was not included. McKay recorded in his diary: "We then made further reductions in the budget bringing the amount over the estimated income down to $9 million."[62]

Good intentions notwithstanding, the Building Committee's expenditures during 1961 continued to spiral upward. In September, an incensed Ernest Wilkinson learned from the expenditures committee that $3.6 million had been shifted from the BYU budget to the Building Committee. "They had done this because, unlike ourselves, the Building Committee of the Church had not been operating within its budget, and was out of funds," he fumed. "I am going to make a very, very vigorous protest to President McKay."[63] Wilkinson's temper cooled, however; and the next time he met with McKay, four days later, he made no mention of the subject.[64] Hugh B. Brown, second counselor in the First Presidency, tried to exercise some restraint over the Building Committee by attempting to have Mendenhall meet with the entire First Presidency, rather than McKay alone, but without success.[65]

Six weeks after learning about the raid on BYU's budget, Wilkinson met with Apostle Delbert Stapley of the budget committee and learned that the fiscal situation had worsened yet further:

> He confided in me that they had requests for next year for $60 million in excess of the income of the Church. Further, that the reserves of the Church had been spent down to $10 million. I repeated to him what he already knew, that while it was none of my business, I had not approved of the manner in which President Moyle had been spending the reserves of the Church.... As one of the members of the budget committee, he has an almost insolvable problem. I pointed out to him that the reason he had such great demands was because of what I consider the reckless expenditures of the Church Building Committee. I am sure he agreed.[66]

The budget committee worked for the next month to pare down the deficit, giving instructions to all departments to cut their requests for 1962. McKay summarized their gloomy report: even though "they have all cut as much as they think they can cut," the projected deficit was still $20 million. On December 1, McKay met with Kimball, Stapley, and Vandenberg of the Budget Committee along with Jarvis and Wallace Hight, also of the finance department. They reached an agreement in the meeting to address both sides of the balance sheet. On the supply side they decided to initiate a campaign early in 1962, through stake conferences, to increase tithing revenue. McKay confidently noted, "We should hope to increase the tithing by $15 million in order to keep within our budget." On the expense side, they decided that "capital investments"—buildings other than chapels—simply would not be considered budget items.[67] Just how these projects would be funded was not yet explained.

Alan Blodgett, who joined the auditing department in April 1962, described the state of affairs that he first encountered:

> The church building program had expanded so rapidly over the previous two or three years that the finances were out of control. Budgets were being exceeded and the church's cash balances and liquid assets were rapidly being depleted. Another problem was an absence of an accounting for the moneys being spent.... Money was being sent out to the various areas in ever increasing sums as the tempo of the building program increased. The record keeping systems became bogged down, and tens of millions of dollars went unaccounted for. George Y. Jarvis, then Controller, referred to the advances for which there was no accounting as the "lump." At one time it reached $50 million, a very big sum for that period of time. The challenge was not only to get an accounting for moneys already spent, but to develop an accounting system that would provide immediate accountability for future expenditures.[68]

A month after Blodgett began his work, Moyle and Leland Flint, president of Zion's First National Bank, flew to New York City. Joined there by Harold B. Lee, who was in the city on other business, they met with officers of First National City Bank in an attempt to arrange financing for "capital investments," which could then be removed from the budget. Church leaders had initially favored issuing fifty-year bonds, but City Bank officials discouraged them from that strategy, instead offering the church a $20 million open line of credit.[69]

One week later McKay convened a meeting to discuss the New York proposal. Attending the meeting were McKay's two counselors, Henry D. Moyle and Hugh B. Brown; Apostles Joseph Fielding Smith, Harold B. Lee, and Marion G. Romney; Leland Flint; and Graham H. Doxey, manager of Zion's Securities Corporation, the church's holding company for its commercial assets. Of special significance was the presence of Smith and Lee, the next two men who would serve as church president. This was new ground for the church, a long-term borrowing plan that would impact its finances well into the future. McKay understood the implications and opened the meeting by asking "these Brethren to listen to this financial plan for the Church, so that they would be well acquainted with it pending any further changes in the leadership of the Church which may occur." He gave a strong endorsement to the proposal to initiate the line of credit (terms not specified in the meeting), saying, "The plan presented will enable us to obtain the finances we need without interfering with the regular income and expenditures of the Church."[70] The borrowing plan was approved in this meeting and endorsed by the Quorum of the Twelve the following week.

In spite of these measures, the deficits continued to mount. In July 1962, McKay announced to his counselors, "I feel that the time has come for a retrenchment, and for the rebuilding of the cash reserves of the Church; that non-producing properties must be sold so that the cash reserves of the Church can be built up."[71] He directed that a list be made of such properties.[72]

Among the properties considered for sale was the church's huge ranch in Orlando, Florida, which encompassed several hundred thousand acres adjacent to what is now Walt Disney World.[73] On this matter church leaders consulted with David M. Kennedy, a prominent Chicago banker and church member who later became U.S. Secretary of the Treasury in the Nixon administration. Over the course of many phone calls, he discussed with them the pros and cons of various options. "Finally I called them and said, 'This is being talked around. I hear the Church is in serious financial difficulties, from sources in New York and others. I think you're hurting your own image by trying to do this the way you are doing it.'"[74] As a result, the church pulled the property off the market but used it as collateral for substantial loans from First National City Bank.[75]

There was some good news amid the bad. The tithing campaign initiated early in 1962 achieved notable success, with receipts for 1962 being 10.8 percent higher than 1961.[76] Overall, however, the deficits continued to mount. Tithing was, by definition, 10 percent of income and thus could not be increased. However, additional revenue was generated by shifting more of the construction costs to individual congregations. During the building boom up to this point, congregations had been required to raise 30 percent of the total cost of new or remodeled buildings; McKay now authorized raising this ratio to 40 percent. McKay recorded in his diary the public relations reason: "The people need to have a higher participation in this so they will be more diligent in participating in maintaining the buildings."[77]

In late March 1963, Jarvis warned McKay of "a day of reckoning" if expenditures were not brought under control.[78] Under pressure from McKay, Mendenhall agreed, two months later, that the number of new chapels scheduled for 1964 "will be cut considerably. . .and then the Building Committee will be caught up on its schedule and can be put on a regular basis thereafter."[79] Mendenhall's optimism was illusory, however.

RESTORING FINANCIAL ORDER

Six months earlier than Mendenhall's blithe characterization of the Building Committee's "schedule," Moyle fell out of favor with McKay over irregularities in the missionary program, which Moyle supervised (see chap. 10), and was released as chair of the powerful Missionary Committee in January 1963.[80] Seeing Moyle's weakened position, others broke their silence and began to press their own complaints concerning the building program and BYU's budget, the two areas where, with McKay's sponsorship, individuals had too much autonomy for the comfort of the Twelve. Stanford Bird, one of Mendenhall's co-workers on the building committee, recalled the situation:

> It was right after [Moyle's demotion] that people began to complain about the costs of the building program. There were many, many, many accusations thrown up. . . . One time President Moyle said to me, "Stan, the Quorum of the Twelve and the General Authorities are so jealous of Wendell Mendenhall that they can't [*sic*] hardly stand it. He controls the finances of the Church more than anybody besides the First Presidency." He was the one who was really handling the money of the Church, in this building program. Of course, everybody was jealous. They wanted to go over there and tell him how to build his buildings and what properties to buy, because they used to do it. And all of a sudden, it was taken out of their hands.[81]

The complaints went beyond the amount of money that was being spent. In the aftermath of Moyle's demotion, criticisms focused on the line Moyle had crossed between putting church units in respectable buildings and spending lavishly. One of the first came from Apostle Mark E. Petersen, then serving as president of the West European Mission, who complained about the expensive furnishings in mission homes. As McKay recorded his report to the First Presidency shortly after April conference 1963, Petersen "could not" feel good about the expense: "He said he would not furnish his own home in such luxury, nor would the Mission Presidents furnish their own homes as such, because they could not afford it. He said some of the mission homes on the continent, and in England, have taken his breath away. He said that when the people look at these furnishings, they must think that their tithing supports such luxury. He said the people receive only $30 a week, and the women come to the Church with holes in their stockings, and the children are poorly clad."[82] Already chilly toward Moyle because of perceived mismanagement of the missionary program, McKay responded "What President Petersen says must be true; that they are extravagant."[83]

Moyle defended the expenditures, citing "the people received by the mission presidents in the mission homes; the public officials, prominent people, governors, and mayors of cities. He also mentioned the hard wear and tear upon mission property by missionaries, and many others who come into the home, and said the quality of the furnishings must be of good grade. He said that cheap furniture was purchased for the Paris mission home, but it did not hold up and had to be replaced." McKay was not swayed, however, and delegated to Petersen the responsibility for furnishing the Belgium–French mission home "as they think it should be furnished."[84]

In September 1963, Henry Moyle died of a heart attack while visiting the church ranch in Orlando, thus depriving Mendenhall of his most potent ally. Replacing Moyle in the First Presidency was N. Eldon Tanner, a soft-spoken man possessing keen business instincts, an intense desire to bring church finances back under control, and outstanding personal skills. Tanner's rise through the hierarchy was swift, a mark of McKay's confidence in him, as he moved from "private citizen" through the offices of Assistant to the Twelve and apostle, then into the First Presidency in only three years. A non-Mormon businessman in Utah who worked closely with him recalled, "Tanner had probably the greatest touch of anybody I've ever met, with respect to bringing people together and managing tough situations. He did it differently than anybody I've ever known."[85]

Shortly after Tanner joined the First Presidency, McKay entrusted to him oversight of the church's financial affairs: "After a discussion of these matters, President Tanner said that he is trying to get as clear a picture of the entire financial situation as he could, and that he would like to bring to me recommendations when he thought changes should be made. I indicated my approval of his doing this."[86]

One of Tanner's first suggestions, made early in March 1964, was to terminate the special relationship Mendenhall had with McKay by putting "policies of the Church relating to building" in the hands of a council on which would sit representatives from the First Presidency, Quorum of the Twelve, and Presiding Bishopric, but not representatives from the Building Department. McKay, while agreeing in principle, used the approach of general conference four weeks away as a reason for postponing "consideration and action" until the next month.[87] On March 20, Tanner again made the same suggestion in a First Presidency meeting, and McKay gave the same response.[88] While McKay did not acknowledge in any way that Mendenhall would no longer report to him under this new arrangement, he quietly exercised a "pocket veto," and Tanner did not make his proposal a third time, even after April conference.

If Tanner had had any doubts about the seriousness of the deficit problem prior to joining the First Presidency, those doubts were erased in a meeting with McKay and Mendenhall in July 1964. Mendenhall reported that, although the budget year was only half over, "the Building Committee had used all the money budgeted for their use in 1964." Yet there were an additional fifteen buildings scheduled to begin in the second half of the year for which local congregations had already raised their share. Discarding fiscal restraint, McKay "said that where the people had raised their money we should not hold up the building program" and commended Mendenhall "on the fine work that he is doing and on his accomplishments in the interest of the Church."[89] The mixed signals from McKay put Mendenhall in a terrible bind.

As Tanner began to dig into the details of the building program, he saw that the cost per building was significantly out of line with expectations and reported to McKay in September 1964: "The program is costing us $50,000 per month more than we anticipated."[90] Two weeks later, he discussed with McKay another report from Petersen documenting cost overruns on European chapels as high as $125,000 per building.[91] Part of the problem was failure to include inflationary costs when the first estimates were made, part was "the temptation to apply for funding on the low side to partially offset the constant complaint from the Committee on Expenditures members that buildings were costing too much," and part was, as Tanner pointed out to McKay, "that our accounting has been so far behind we have never known just what the costs were."[92] On the latter issue, Tanner told Jarvis that "we would hold him responsible to take care of this phase of the situation...as expeditiously as possible."[93] Six weeks later, in mid-December, Tanner conferred with Jarvis on his progress and brought McKay the disheartening news that, if McKay was serious that expenditures not exceed income, the building program's budget would have to be cut in half.[94]

While Tanner grasped the enormity of the problem at hand, he did not panic or overreact. He worked steadily with Jarvis and his group, implementing purchasing and accounting reforms to curb excess expenditures and delaying new projects to ease the cash-flow problems. As early as the end of 1964, "the money drain was coming under control."[95] Tanner felt that the problems could be dealt with from within and made no recommendation for changing personnel on the Building Committee. Had he been able to continue his work without interference, he likely could have restored order to the committee and returned the church to fiscal stability. He was blindsided, however, in one of the most unfortunate episodes of McKay's presidency.

Thorpe B. Isaacson, an Assistant to the Twelve, had McKay's confidence, for reasons that McKay did not note, either in his diary or to his colleagues. In Octo-

ber 1964, two months before Tanner made his "halve the building budget" report
to McKay, Isaacson met privately with McKay to discuss "building problems that
have arisen in the San Jose West Stake." McKay's office diary is not specific about
these problems, but he showed McKay several letters that he had received from
unidentified correspondents on the subject. McKay had already received a letter
about the problems from the stake president. "After considering this matter for
sometime [*sic*] and other problems associated with the Building Program of the
Church," noted McKay in his diary, "I asked Elder Isaacson to go to San Francisco
and look into this whole matter and then report back to me."[96] McKay's reference
to "other problems" and the flow of subsequent events make it clear that the situation in San Jose was merely the catalyst that unleashed pent-up frustrations.

Only minutes after Isaacson's departure, McKay met with his two counselors,
Tanner and Brown, and reported his discussion about Mendenhall and his department, not only on the part of Isaacson, but from other General Authorities as well.
Tanner was aware of Isaacson's intrusion into the San Jose matter and had already
spoken with Mendenhall about it. He responded to McKay's report with thinly
veiled irritation: "President Tanner said that it would seem to him that Brother
Mendenhall and Brother Isaacson should be asked to meet with the First Presidency
together before anything is done by Brother Isaacson or anyone else in the matter
of investigating the situation, so that the Presidency could hear both sides of the matter." McKay not only rebuffed Tanner's suggestion but "confirmed this request [to
have Isaacson travel to San Jose] by telephone interview with Brother Isaacson during the meeting."[97] He made no attempt to explain the extraordinary step of
bypassing his own counselor and reaching beyond, not only the First Presidency, but
also the Quorum of the Twelve to rely upon Isaacson, an Assistant to the Twelve.

On November 13, Isaacson gave McKay a brief report on the situation in San
Jose. McKay, who did not record any details, noted that Isaacson "will give a more
detailed report to me when I return from Oakland," for the dedication of the Oakland Temple.[98] No further meetings are recorded in the diaries prior to December
15, so it is likely that McKay's action on that day was based solely on the information that Isaacson provided to him in mid-November. On December 15, 1964,
without consulting his counselors, McKay appointed a committee consisting of
Isaacson and three apostles to reorganize the Church Building Committee and
"curtail" the building program's expenses. On the same day, he wrote a memorandum reporting this appointment to Brown and Tanner. Tanner, who was on
Christmas vacation, did not receive it until his return on December 30. The memo
read:

> After giving serious thought and study to reports that have come to
> me on the expenditures of the Church Building Committee, I have

decided to appoint a committee consisting of Elders Delbert L. Stapley as Chairman, and LeGrand Richards, Howard W. Hunter, and Thorpe B. Isaacson as members, with the special assignment of bringing about some adjustments and reorganization of the Church Building Committee. Since Elder Isaacson already has been looking into a serious condition of building matters in the San Jose Stake and elsewhere, I have asked him to work with the Brethren named above with a view of substantially curtailing the expenditures in the Church Building Department in light of conditions that have arisen in all parts of the world in regard to extravagance, waste, etc.[99]

Six days later, while Tanner was still out of town, Isaacson told McKay that his committee had already held "two or three meetings" but could not go any further until McKay "decided whether or not he wished the present Building Committee to be released." McKay "said that would be a rather difficult thing to bring about" but said he would "give it further consideration."[100]

When Tanner returned, the memo hit him like a thunderbolt. Fearing that a drastic decision regarding the Building Committee may already have been made, he told McKay on New Year's Eve that "he would like to sit down and talk with me alone about this matter before any action is taken."[101] The next meeting of the First Presidency was on January 5, 1965, attended by McKay, Brown, Tanner, and an unnamed secretary who took verbatim notes. At the meeting, Tanner "expressed himself quite freely about the administrative duties of the Church."[102]

The "administrative duties" included a single item, Isaacson's committee, and with uncharacteristic candor and no attempt to veil his irritation, Tanner unloaded his feelings. The transcript of the meeting filled nine pages of typescript, which are summarized in the following excerpts:

> [Tanner:] I came in here twice last year and recommended to you that we set up a committee to work with the Building Committee. Nothing was done about it. Isaacson comes in and recommends we set up a committee and you set it up immediately and the wrong kind of a committee in my opinion; they are men who are prejudiced against the Building Committee and their idea is to replace the leader without a study. I have nothing for Mendenhall, all I am interested in is straightforward administration of this Church, but when I made those recommendations last year no consideration was taken; Isaacson comes in here and says we should set up a committee and get rid of Mendenhall, without saying a word to us.... I want to tell you Isaacson is out to get Mendenhall, Mendenhall in whom you have had the finest confidence, whom you have given your support. The last time you and I

were together you congratulated him on the thing he had done, the progress he had made, the service he had given to the Church, and this man comes in and it looks like you are ready to kick him out.... You said this committee was set up to reorganize the Building Committee, and I said, "President McKay, I question the advisability of that; I would like to sit down and talk to you about it." I wanted to talk to you alone but it has come up this way and I want to express it here.... It is not the kind of committee that will do the job, it is only set up to get rid of Mendenhall and reorganize the Building Committee.[103]

McKay was caught off guard by Tanner's directness. Despite his own memo three weeks earlier about Isaacson's committee, he was evasive about the matter. While providing no details about the activities of Isaacson's committee, he did not hold back in expressing displeasure at what he viewed as audacity on Tanner's part. At one point he said, with obvious irony: "I am glad you unburdened yourself and pointed out my weakness." Brown, who said little throughout the meeting, eventually came to Tanner's defense: "I think it is a very good thing this matter has been brought out to the front.... I wish I had come out with it in the beginning and told you where I stood on it, but I thought I wouldn't do it." McKay replied, "What you are saying is that I have a third counselor in Brother Isaacson" (which indeed became the case a year and a half later). "I think you have," Brown responded.

The meeting did not resolve the issue but ended with Tanner's reaffirmation of both his loyalty to McKay and his own desire for clarity and consistency: "I would not do anything to offend you but I must tell you what I know and then I say it is entirely up to you what you decide, and I will serve as conscientiously and loyally as I can possibly do. You have a right to ask counsel from anybody, all I am saying is that as a counselor I cannot serve you nearly as well unless I know what is going on, and I think we should know before instead of after."[104]

Even though the ninety-two-year-old McKay had created this difficult situation, he reacted with personal pique to Tanner's candor. Tanner's biographer touched only tangentially on the incident but acknowledged that, "as a consequence, for a few hours [Tanner] felt he might possibly be released because of the strong position he had taken."[105] Two months later, McKay was still angry and fumed to Clare Middlemiss, "When I think that I had to sit and listen to a counselor rebuke a President of this Church because he valued the judgment of...Thorpe B. Isaacson whom I trust, I cannot get over it."[106] Seventy Paul H. Dunn, reflecting on the incident three decades later, attempted to provide some perspective: "There wasn't anybody, I think personally, more loyal or supportive of

David O. McKay than Eldon Tanner, from my exposure to him. If I were to try to define what happened, I think you have a man like Eldon Tanner, who was bold enough to share a concern or a feeling, and a President who wasn't tracking all that well, and misunderstood what his counselor was trying to do. Somewhere in there, I think you have the truth."[107]

The committee of the three apostles and Isaacson moved quickly. On January 21, 1965, less than five weeks after its organization and without consulting Tanner, its members recommended unanimously that Wendell Mendenhall be "released"—a euphemism for "fired," as his was a salaried career position and not an ecclesiastical appointment—and that "this release should be effective immediately." Their written report detailed a lengthy list of complaints against the Building Committee: "There has been great concern all over the Church regarding the extravagance, waste, high salaries, maintenance, costs for supervisors, travel, hotel, telephone, excessive building costs and other expenses, also domineering, in connection with the Church Building Committee until it has reached a point where many faithful members of the Church are deeply concerned, upset, and disillusioned; and ward, stake and mission leaders are questioning our laxity [in] handling so serious a problem."[108]

Although the committee called for Mendenhall's immediate release, McKay delayed action for several weeks, in large part because of his own poor health. He left Salt Lake City the morning after receiving the report, spent eighteen days resting in the church-owned beach house on Emerald Bay near Laguna Beach, California, returned to Salt Lake City, and only six days later was hospitalized for another twelve days.

At the end of March, McKay read Tanner and Brown a letter to Mendenhall "prepared for the signatures of the First Presidency" that extended to him "an honorable release" as chairman of the Building Committee. Brown was willing to go along with the action, but Tanner "expressed his personal opinion that Brother Mendenhall had done everything he had been asked to do conscientiously and [as] efficiently as anybody could have done." He also said that Mendenhall had agreed to explain Mark E. Petersen's criticisms about extravagance in Europe. McKay, while declining to acknowledge Tanner's points, agreed to bring the matter up in a joint meeting of the First Presidency and Twelve before taking final action.[109]

A week later, the First Presidency met as usual prior to joining the Quorum of the Twelve for their weekly joint meeting, at which time McKay noted, "A letter has been prepared which President Brown and I have signed, extending an honorable release to Brother Mendenhall." He did not state—but did not need to—that Tanner had not signed it. The three men then went into a four-and-a-half-hour meeting with the Twelve, during which "we discussed the serious problem of a reorganization of the Building Committee and the release of Wendell B. Mendenhall."[110] Apparently the matter was not resolved—McKay's diaries give no further details about the meeting—for the following week it was again a major agenda item in the joint meeting: "After a lengthy discussion, the Brethren unanimously voted that Brother Mendenhall should be released as of May 1, 1965."[111]

The following morning, April 16, the letter of release was sent to Mendenhall, then in Salt Lake City. This time it was signed by McKay and both counselors. Mendenhall was devastated. He met that evening with McKay, who noted in his diary that Mendenhall "was all broken up about it and cried and sobbed as he told what he had tried to do."[112] He asked for a one-year extension, which McKay initially granted, then rescinded after discussing it with the Twelve.[113] A week later, the church issued a press release that euphemistically "announced acceptance of the resignation" of Mendenhall.[114] In mid-May, McKay asked Mark B. Garff, a Salt Lake City contractor who had built a number of major buildings for the church and for Brigham Young University, to assume Mendenhall's chairmanship.[115]

Restructuring the Building Program

Less than a month after Garff accepted the position and before he had even assembled his new team, McKay made a brief diary entry that said much between the lines: "Went over a copy of the financial report of the Church as of May 28. I was pleased to know that our position is much improved over what it was a year ago."[116] In other words, Tanner's reform efforts had, in fact, already begun to bear fruit. Undoubtedly, this was why Tanner had been so passionate in defending Mendenhall and arguing against his release. Whether McKay realized that he had collaborated in scapegoating Mendenhall is not known, for he made no further comment in his diary.

For his part, Garff successfully pushed for an independent external audit of the building department, despite Tanner's objection that to do so would expose to non-Mormons "what he calls our 'dirty linen.'"[117] After several months of work, the auditors said that the records, particularly in foreign countries, were not complete enough to allow a comprehensive audit. While it was clear that there had been mismanagement within the department during the Mendenhall years, there was no evidence of financial impropriety, contrary to the hints. Michael Grilikhes, a close associate of Mendenhall, later commented:

> There were rumors going around...that he had been taking money and had big bank accounts. I said to a couple of people, "If anybody wanted to look, I'll bet that he's in the hole a couple of million dollars of his own money that he's spent on these things."... I can remember the three of us [including Mendenhall and Edward Lavaun Clissold] driving down to the Bank of Hawaii and signing personal

notes so that we could get the money to pay for things that we had to have. The others made sure that I got mine back, but I don't know what happened to them.[118]

In retrospect, it is clear that Mendenhall's group—as well as those church leaders from whom they took their orders, including McKay—made a series of errors that contributed greatly to the financial crisis. Alan Blodgett made a careful analysis of those errors:

- Rather than using standard plans, local architects were often used, buildings were very expensive, and often not as efficient for church needs as a standard plan building would have been.

- Buildings were often being built in anticipation of need rather than after the congregation grew sufficiently to warrant the building. The thought was that the buildings would draw new members, and help activate existing members. In some instances this plan succeeded, but some buildings were built that would take years to adequately utilize.

- In the rush to gear up the building program many mistakes were made. Too much was paid for some sites. Buildings were built in the wrong places, according to inadequate architectural plans or [were] too big. People were used with inadequate skills or training, resulting in inefficiencies and poor workmanship. Overseas, most projects were directed by building supervisors from the U.S., who often were ill equipped to handle the task in the area where they were assigned. Inadequate accounting no doubt contributed to funds being wasted, or even stolen.[119]

In light of those errors, it is tempting to debunk the efforts of Mendenhall, Moyle, and others who worked with them. But to do so would seriously underrate their considerable accomplishments. Blodgett appraised their achievement:

[The building program] did accomplish what Moyle sought after. It established the Church in the overseas areas, it facilitated missionary work, and it added to the strength of the Church in those areas. Not only this, many local members who were personally involved in the church building programs went on to become future Church leaders. Even though Moyle was badly criticized at the time for allowing expenditures to get out of control, and for excesses in both the missionary program and the building program, when viewed with the benefit of hindsight, he accomplished what no one with less determination could have accomplished. It is also true that the vast expansion of the missionary and building programs could not for long go

unchecked without doing damage to the Church. I believe that
Moyle and Mendenhall saw this and steps were already being taken
to curb excesses before they were relieved of their responsibilities.[120]

Once Tanner accepted the inevitability of Mendenhall's departure, he proposed in a First Presidency meeting on April 27 a major change in the way that the
Building Committee did its business: "President Tanner recommended that we
have the Building Committee separate from the actual operation, with one of the
Twelve as the head, in which event he would be in a position to confer with the
Twelve in regard to the various phases of the work, could listen to their criticism
and be able to report regarding the operations.... The member of the Twelve
would be the head as far as policy matters were concerned, and the man under him
would direct the actual construction work."[121]

Even though this structure diluted McKay's personal control over the Building Department, he responded favorably during the discussion; and a week later
on May 6, Tanner pressed the issue further, suggesting, "The Chairman of the
committee would sit with the Twelve and bring to them Building Committee
problems and listen to criticisms that might be raised." Tanner recommended that
the committee be chaired by Apostle Marion G. Romney, with Franklin D.
Richards and John H. Vandenberg as members. Since this move would shift
authority from McKay to the Twelve, McKay reacted more cautiously, agreeing only
to "take the matter under consideration."[122]

Two weeks later on May 19, when McKay called Garff to replace Mendenhall,
he discussed with Garff the new committee as well as the Isaacson committee,
which had not been disbanded. Garff bristled at the idea of having to work through
a committee, rather than directly with the First Presidency, perhaps because of how
the Twelve had dealt with Mendenhall. He bluntly said, "President McKay, you
cannot ask me to do this job and then dam the ditch with men with whom I cannot work." McKay, who had already expressed personal reservations in the May 6
First Presidency meeting about ceding power to the Twelve, agreed with Garff.[123]

The following morning, prior to meeting with the Twelve, McKay dictated a
memorandum for the meeting: "Yesterday morning (May 19) I met by appointment
in my apartment Brother Mark B. Garff, at which time I asked him to take over
the management of the Church Building Department. After talking over the whole
problem with him, I told Brother Garff that he is to report to no one but me and
to the First Presidency. I told him that both committees that have already been
appointed will be released. I am presenting this matter to you for your approval and
action."

Tanner was out of town, but Brown approved it. McKay then took it into the
meeting with the Twelve. Marion G. Romney, chair of the short-lived oversight

committee, moved that it be approved, and the council voted unanimously to do so.[124]

Garff then got to work. On June 1, 1965, he told McKay that he needed to have a "clean slate" of co-workers, to which McKay readily agreed, saying that he "should have a free hand in reorganization matters, and that I will sustain him in that." Although Garff's official duties would not begin for another month, he had already learned enough about the building program to be "astounded at the expenditures over in that department." That impression was reinforced only minutes later when, after Garff left, Middlemiss told McKay that one of Mendenhall's co-workers had told Isaacson's committee that "$250,000 per year could have been saved in overhead at headquarters of the Building Committee."[125]

One week later, Garff met with McKay and asked for approval of an entirely new Building Committee and for authority to "make the changes necessary to cut down the expense of the entire building department." These changes consisted of shifting to a contract basis of construction, stopping the labor missionary program, and imposing an immediate moratorium on new construction projects until the new committee could get "an understanding and agreement of how we should proceed." McKay gave blanket approval to all of Garff's requests.[126]

On July 1, 1965, Garff and his new committee officially began their work. Horace A. Christiansen, a banker and member of the new committee, interviewed thirty years later, recalled the abruptness of the transition: "It was a totally new committee, all of the previous committee had been released, and they left the office one night, and the next morning we walked in and took over, with almost no orientation. Admittedly, we were quite green, quite uninformed as to the procedures and program.... [We] had to learn through day-to-day experience."[127]

Within three months, Garff made a detailed and encouraging report to the First Presidency. He said he could cut central office expenses by at least $500,000 annually and would close several area offices for further savings. This action would not only reduce office expenses but also place controls on construction spending. "In the past, areas have spent money without supervision and without record[;]...there have been no checks or balances that can be found as to what they spent money for and how much they are using for themselves." Furthermore, he outlined major savings from cutting back on unneeded chapels and reducing the size of other chapels to fit better the needs of the local congregations.[128] McKay was so impressed by the presentation that he had Garff repeat it the following day at a special meeting of all the General Authorities. Garff and his assistant, Fred Baker, gave "practically the same [report] as they gave at the First Presidency's meeting yesterday." McKay asked for the repetition because "I wanted the General

Authorities to know about this new program, and to hear about their findings on the old program."[129]

After nine months in office, Garff gave another major report to McKay. The report contained both good and bad news. After reviewing South American projects, Garff concluded "that there are buildings there for which we have no need; that they were built by misrepresentation"—presumably about the size and strength of the congregations—to McKay.[130] Furthermore, in Europe, there were by his count five chapels, including stake centers, "with no congregations to fill them." On the brighter side, Garff had closed five area building offices and reduced the labor force by some two hundred people, at a savings of over $100,000 a month. He estimated that the total savings to the Church in 1966 would be $10 million. "I have tried with all my strength to do it," he said. "Things are now out in the open."[131]

Three factors combined to pull the church out of its cash crisis. Garff's cost cutting, of course, was a major help to the budget problem, although the speed of the actions no doubt caused personal hardship to some individuals. A second factor was the consistent increase in tithing revenue. Since the renewed emphasis on tithing in 1962, there had been double-digit percentage increases each year, which in 1966 amounted to 11 percent.[132] And the third was the temporary moratorium on new construction. "Since the term of meetinghouse construction is only about a year," explained Blodgett, reviewing this tumultuous period, "halting the start of new projects had a dramatic effect on cash flow within six months.... By the end of 1965 the financial crunch was over."[133]

In April 1967, Garff reported to McKay and several colleagues that the cumulative savings of the Building Department since he became chairman were $32 million,[134] and by 1969 the financial health of the church had improved sufficiently to allow the construction of three temples and a twenty-six-story Church Office Building, while still maintaining a positive cash flow.[135]

THE MENDENHALL-MOYLE YEARS IN RETROSPECT

If one focuses on the Garff years, it is easy to look with disfavor upon the excesses of the Mendenhall-Moyle years, yet to do so is an injustice. Both Moyle and Mendenhall had a vision of lifting the image of the church throughout the world, of instilling in members a pride in their church that they did not have when meetings occurred in rented facilities that included nightclubs and bars, and of using handsome buildings to assist missionary efforts. To a large extent, they succeeded in those goals, in spite of the fiscal mismanagement along the way that shadowed their final months in office. Furthermore, as Blodgett pointed out, "Mendenhall did some revolutionary things, such as start the Building Missionary Program, whereby members would be called to actually aid in the construction of buildings. There were problems with this program, with poor quality building sometimes resulting, but with adequate supervision from well-qualified supervising building missionaries, this was not serious. Many young men in overseas areas learned a lifetime trade skill though the program."[136]

Whether the mismanagement could have been corrected without Mendenhall's summary dismissal is an intriguing question. Certainly, Tanner's reforms had already begun to yield positive results prior to Mendenhall's release; and in that light, the drastic and unusually swift action recommended by Isaacson's committee appears to have been impulsive, as was McKay's wholesale acceptance of their recommendation. However, their rejection was likely fueled by Mendenhall's own actions over the prior years, which did not ingratiate him to many of the General Authorities. One later recalled:

> I had the whole South Pacific, I was the supervisor [of ecclesiastical programs] for four years, and I'd want to talk about a building, and I would call Wendell Mendenhall. He didn't have to answer to me as his supervisor. If he liked you, he'd listen. If he didn't, he'd say, "Don't call me, I'll call you." Here you are, you're in charge of that part of the world, ecclesiastically, from David O. McKay. But when you want to get something physical, to enhance the ecclesiastical, you've got a guy in the department who can block you. And that is not good administration.[137]

There is no question that, once the decision to release Mendenhall was implemented, Mark Garff was highly effective in restoring fiscal order, albeit at great personal sacrifice.[138] Yet something was lost when something was gained. Alan Blodgett commented on both:

> For me personally it was a good thing that the Church Building Committee was changed because of the excellent relationship I had with the new committee. [Still] I can't help but wonder, if more was lost than gained by making the change. The pace of the building program was set back by a couple years, and the local involvement was greatly diminished with the new contractor approach to building. I am a romantic, I was moved by all the faith promoting stories that came out of the Mendenhall way of building meetinghouses. Few faith-promoting stories were heard after Garff took over; he was all business.[139]

10

THE
MISSIONARY PROGRAM

In June 1829, nearly one year before the church's formal founding, a trio of revelations established proselytizing as a core concern. In separate revelations containing identical language John and Peter Whitmer were told: "The thing which will be of the most worth unto you will be to declare repentance unto this people, that you may bring souls unto me."[1] A third revelation addressed to Joseph Smith, Oliver Cowdery, and David Whitmer admonished them "to cry repentance unto this people. And if it so be that you should labor all your days in crying repentance unto this people, and bring, save it be one soul unto me, how great shall be your joy."[2] In the fall of 1830, two of these men, Oliver Cowdery and Peter Whitmer, joined two others to become the church's first itinerant missionaries.

David O. McKay's involvement in missionary work began with a two-year proselytizing mission to Scotland in 1897. It continued when, as a young apostle, he made a worldwide tour of foreign missions in 1920–21, then presided over the European Mission in 1923–24. Upon becoming church president, he made missionary work a central theme of his administration and achieved unprecedented success. While tens of thousands of missionaries shared in the task through the nineteen years of his presidency, three men stand out: Henry D. Moyle, Alvin R. Dyer, and T. Bowring Woodbury. All three men possessed strong personalities that enabled them to push into uncharted territory, yet with mixed results. Largely due to their enthusiasm and aggressiveness, the missionary program achieved unprecedented numerical success. But their insatiable appetite for ever-increasing numbers of converts took an increasing toll on missionaries, local members, and new converts that ultimately resulted in the reassignment of all three men and the general retrenchment of the program to which they had devoted their energy.

Henry D. Moyle was a wealthy attorney and oil entrepreneur in 1947 when the church president, George Albert Smith, called him to be an apostle. Moyle accepted the calling and promptly applied his abundant energy and wealth to church causes. Seven years later he was asked to serve on the Missionary Committee; and from that point on, the focal point of his life was missionary work. He later stated: "The greatest work I have ever been engaged in, bar none, is missionary work."[3] Upon joining the First Presidency in 1959 he was given charge of the entire missionary program. Despite a history of heart disease, which claimed his life in 1963, he threw himself at the assignment with apparently boundless energy and enthusiasm, taking the program to previously unimaginable heights. His daughter recalled a characteristic episode: "I met a man the other day who was a missionary in Germany in one of the smaller towns. He said that Daddy came in, and in two days he had contacted all of the newspaper reporters and they called meetings and they got these big write-ups in the paper and all the missionaries had to hustle to get information and get notices out. He said it was like a cyclone had hit them."[4]

Alvin R. Dyer had a successful heating and air conditioning business in Salt Lake City but set aside his business interests in the mid-1950s to accept a call to preside over the Central States Mission. Taking a radically different approach to the process of conversion, he focused on conviction, not information, or in other words, a "conversion experience," rather than intellectual persuasion achieved by a series of didactic lectures and pamphlets explicating scriptural arguments. He achieved unprecedented success in that mission, and his accomplishments were noted publicly in the April 1957 general conference:

> [Gordon B. Hinckley] cited one of the oldest missions in the Church, the Central States, established in 1831, which had 95 converts or an average of .8 per missionary in 1946 and in 1956 reached 746 converts for an average of 6.3 per missionary. President Alvin R. Dyer of the mission then presented slide films and charts to show how this has been accomplished in the mission.... President Dyer said "there is too much hedging in our approach. Drive to the point. Be positive in presentation, but at the same time do the job in a clear and simple way. Let's do it," he said.[5]

In 1958, shortly after Dyer's return to Salt Lake City, McKay called him as an Assistant to the Twelve, and a year later he was selected as the first president of the newly reconstituted European Mission, with responsibility for all European missions. He took with him the methodology he developed in the Central States Mission and left an indelible though controversial imprint on the church in Europe.

T. Bowring Woodbury left his native Salt Lake City during World War II and moved to Wichita, Kansas, to preside over Culver, a newly formed company that made trainer planes for the Navy. After the war he turned his energies to commercial manufacturing, with great success. The Central States Mission included Kansas;

and Dyer chose Woodbury, whom he had not previously known, to be one of his counselors in the mission presidency.[6]

In the summer of 1958, Woodbury received a phone call from David O. McKay. Opening the conversation lightly, McKay said: "Brother Woodbury, we have designs on you." He then issued a serious invitation: "I am calling this morning to ascertain if it is possible for you to get away from your business for two and one-half or three years.... We should like you to preside over the British Mission."[7] Woodbury accepted the calling, spent nearly three and a half years as president of the British Mission, and became the catalyst for a sea change in the missionary program.

Woodbury brought to the task not only the skills of a successful businessman but also a unique flair and personality. His son described his persona:

> My father was a very flamboyant man, in his dress and in the way he handled himself. I know that Elder [Stephen L] Richards told him that he'd have to be subdued because the British people were very conservative and they were poor at that point—we were only a decade after the war. He indicated that my mother should dress quite conservatively, and so on. My dad just smiled, and told me he totally disregarded that. He was going to do things the way he wanted to do them. And there was that air of independency that I think was enormously important.[8]

Even though the London Temple was being dedicated as Woodbury arrived in the country, the British church that he encountered was still struggling in the austerity years following World War II. Many thought that the glory days when Wilford Woodruff and Heber C. Kimball had baptized thousands were behind it. According to Moyle's son, the departing mission president, A. Hamer Reiser, had remarked to Henry D. Moyle, "I just don't think there's much of the House of Israel left in England. Maybe we should close the mission."[9] Such a thought never occurred to Woodbury, and he plunged into the job with an electrifying effect. One of his missionaries recalled:

> I entered a world dominated by one of the most charismatic and powerful personalities I had yet encountered in my life.... Missionaries, especially those who served under him for the first two years, worshipped Woodbury. British Saints were mesmerized by his eloquence and demeanor. There was an air of royalty about the Woodbury family and their lifestyle, mostly engendered by "By," as he was known to family and friends.... To the majority of these Saints, those were the golden years of the British Mission. Woodbury's powerful influence on

people should never be underestimated and can be scarcely under-
stated.... Woodbury wasn't just another mission president; he was
bigger than life and an absolute spellbinder. Awe-inspired loyalty to
the man and his ideas left little room for conjecture or debate. This is
especially true within the context of what was purported to be the
purest of all endeavors—bringing souls to Christ.[10]

RESTRUCTURING THE MISSIONARY PROGRAM

Although the fruits of the rejuvenated missionary program did not ripen until the
end of the decade, McKay planted the seeds shortly after becoming church president. In December 1951, McKay and his counselors in the First Presidency met with
the First Council of Seventy, whose portfolio included missionary work, and
"explained to them the First Presidency's decision, which had been approved by the
Council of the Twelve, to reorganize the missionary set-up in the Church."[11]
McKay not only gave his personal imprint to missionary work, but he also engaged
the senior echelons of the church hierarchy. In 1954 he reorganized the Missionary Committee, with senior apostle Joseph Fielding Smith as chairman and Henry
D. Moyle as a member.

Moyle's entry into the First Presidency in June 1959 shifted General Authority
involvement into a higher gear. Five months later, with substantial input from
Moyle, McKay announced the reopening of the European Mission, with Alvin R.
Dyer as president.[12] Two months later McKay appointed Moyle chairman of the
Missionary Committee,[13] and within weeks Moyle proposed that all missions
throughout the world be brought under direct General Authority supervision.[14]
The following year Moyle's recommendation was implemented: "The precedent-
setting decision will place the missions in nine regions and place one of the Gen-
eral Authorities in direct charge of each region. Appointed to preside over these
regions are three members of the Council of the Twelve, five Assistants to the
Council of the Twelve and one member of the First Council of the Seventy."[15]

Along with these supervisory changes, McKay appealed to the entire church
membership to become involved. A phrase he had first uttered in 1923 as president
of the European Mission became the motto of the church over which he now
presided: "Every member a missionary."[16] Speaking at a missionary farewell in
1953, he elaborated on the meaning of the phrase: "Brother [Cornelius] Zappey
[president of the Netherlands Mission], as all mission presidents, will have missionaries under him who are paying their own expenses and will give their time and
ability and wealth to spread the Gospel. We often think it is their responsibility. But
the responsibility to preach the Gospel and carry happiness to the world should rest
upon every member of the Church."[17]

Beneath these initiatives lay a sublime reality, the spirit of prophecy. On rare occasions McKay briefly mentioned such moments of prophetic insight. Henry Moyle related one such occasion to T. Bowring Woodbury, as the two met in the British Mission headquarters:

> I don't think I have ever been as touched by remarks of the most intimate nature in the entire time of my membership in the Church. President Moyle called to our memory the time that President McKay in the temple [in 1952] and speaking to the Twelve of the New Era that was to break forth in the Church, climaxed his words by saying, "These are the words of the Lord." President Moyle told us that he tingled and felt truly in his heart, long before the President had mentioned that "these were the words of the Lord," that they were prophetic, inspired and were revelation unto the Twelve.[18]

Four years later Moyle visited the missions in South America and, in speaking with Asael Sorensen, president of the Brazilian Mission, related a conversation with McKay just prior to his departure. Sorensen described that conversation:

> When President Henry D. Moyle was going to come down [1956], President McKay said, "Now when you get to South America you are going to have a revelation. The Lord will bless you with a revelation." So we met him [Moyle] at the plane and took him around to different places, and this was on his mind. He mentioned that to me a couple of times; he said that he had been told he was going to have a revelation. We took him out to Tijuca, in Rio, with the missionaries, and as he was speaking, he paused and then he said, "From this time on, the people in Brazil will have dreams and various experiences, and they will come in, in large numbers." Well, the missionaries after that started having all kinds of experiences with these people. These people had seen the missionaries in their dreams, they had seen the inside of our chapels in their dreams, they had seen copies of the Book of Mormon, they had seen missionaries with their white hats. (All the missionaries during my time wore those white hats.)... Some of them, when they would rap on the door and before they could even say a word, would have the people invite them right in, because they had seen them in their dreams, because of those white hats. They knew they were messengers with the truth.[19]

Two years later, as McKay dedicated the London Temple, he foretold a similar unfolding of missionary success in Europe. Edgar Brossard, a mission president attending the meeting, recounted the event: "At that time a tremendous event in

European Mission history took place. President McKay ushered in a 'New Era' of missionary work and conversion. He blessed the people of these European countries and prophesied that their minds and hearts, more than ever before, would be opened, and that this work would go forward in spite of everything. He blessed the missionaries with great spirit and discernment in searching out those most ready to accept the gospel."[20]

Thus, it was with divine assurance that a 1960 First Presidency circular letter, addressed to all missionaries, proclaimed, "Our potential knows no bounds. There is no limit to our conversions other than those we create for ourselves. We could readily show a hundred per cent increase over 1959, and we shall if you will but dedicate yourselves to perform the task."[21]

RESHAPING THE CHURCH'S IMAGE

There was no master blueprint for bringing together a missionary program that would transform the church. Rather, a series of events unfolded throughout the 1950s that came together by the end of the decade to set the stage for success.

The public perception of the church, particularly in Europe, had for decades been malign, fed by sensationalistic stories of polygamy. David O. McKay's frequent trips to Europe went far toward dispelling the negative image, as did the Mormon Tabernacle Choir's triumphant 1955 tour. Newspaper and magazine articles gradually changed from negative to positive.

Combining with the changing public perception was an intentional facelift on the church's physical facilities, led by Henry Moyle. Mission homes, particularly outside the United States, had been unimpressive buildings, sometimes rented, that presented an image of a tentative, poverty-stricken, and even furtive religious body. Moyle began to replace these buildings with impressive, sometimes even extravagant, quarters that projected an altogether different image. His namesake son, then president of the newly created French East Mission, recalled the effect:

> He wanted mission presidents to have an image with the people. It was on their level, on an equal level with them, rather than having them look down on them, and people in Europe tend to do that.... They felt important! He had this wonderful place in Munich, and President Gardner just beamed. You could just see it working. I went with Dad to many of these places, and we would meet with the mission president at their mission homes. Some of those that he bought, I guess, could be called too expensive or extravagant, but he just felt that it was so important to make the mission presidents feel important enough to go out and have the courage to really—with conviction and authority—talk about the Church, and do it as though the Church was on

the same level as any other church or any other people.... It was for
the image of the Church, and it helped those presidents think that
they were really something.[22]

The demographic profile of the mission presidents also changed to accompany
that of the upgraded mission homes. Moyle explained to one new mission president, a young professional who had put his promising career on hold for three
years: "I don't want these 70-year-old retired men, who are just looking to top their
Church careers by saying, 'I was a Mission President.' I want younger men out
there, vigorous, that know how to motivate people and get this missionary work
going. I want to see a hundred thousand converts a year."[23]

Along with younger mission presidents came fresh, often bold ideas. Henry D.
("Hank") Moyle Jr., who was in his early thirties when he was called to preside over
the newly formed French East Mission, saw an opportunity and jumped at it:

> I wrote the Church and I said, "I want to buy thirty thousand copies
> of the Book of Mormon. We have a new translation and we're run-
> ning out of the old one." And they said, "You can't do that. Thirty
> thousand? No!" So I called Dad and I said, "Dad, I really want to do
> this." And he said, "That's a lot of money." So I got hold of Presi-
> dent McKay and I said, "President McKay,"—Dad wouldn't agree to
> it either—"I really want to do this thirty thousand copies of the Book
> of Mormon. I've talked to Dad"—this was a little bit of a stretch—
> "and he said if we don't sell them within a year, he'll pay the differ-
> ence." President McKay said, "I'm behind you a hundred percent."
> So we went ahead.... I told the missionaries that we were kind of on
> the hook for those copies of the Book of Mormon, and that we had
> to sell them in three months or I was in trouble. I said, "We're just
> going to make this a program in our mission, and I don't want you
> to give them away, I want you to sell them. I think people value it
> more if they buy it. We've got to pay for them, so you've got to sell
> them. And I really don't want you to give any of them away, even if
> you can afford it." We got so excited about doing it. The missionar-
> ies never worked harder. We never put in more hours. We never bap-
> tized more people than while we were doing the Book of Mormon
> program. Just before Christmas the three months expired, and early
> in December they had sold all thirty thousand copies and I had to
> write a letter back to the Church and say, "We'd like to print another
> thirty thousand, please. We just sold all the first."[24]

In the British Mission, T. Bowring Woodbury turned music to his advantage
in major public relations initiatives. The Relief Society's official choir from Utah,

the "Singing Mothers," under the baton of Florence Jespersen Madsen, had a successful tour in 1961. One of his missionaries recalled:

> He made sure they were in every major hall and that there was free advertising, that there were tickets printed up even though it was a complimentary concert.... He knew how to promote things and make things happen.... He had anywhere from five to ten thousand people at each one of them. He filled the Royal Albert Hall. He filled the hall up in Birmingham. Each hall was filled and many people were standing outside because he knew how to put this on.... The people all over Britain went to these concerts and it literally opened, not one or two doors, but thousands of doors in each area.
>
> With the dedication and opening of Hyde Park Chapel [in February 1961], here again Woodbury goes to work and gets one of the finest organs on the continent there, you know, a new organ. He arranges to have Alexander Schreiner there.... We had famous organists represented from just about every church in the world come to London to watch Alexander Schreiner play this organ.... He did recitals for about a year.... Everything was a production. Everything was a promotion. Everything was tuned in to make things happen.[25]

Woodbury's innovations did not stop with cultural events. Only weeks after assuming his new duties, he scrapped the church's standard but cumbersome proselytizing plan and replaced it with a streamlined version that emphasized conversion rather than instruction, thus borrowing from his earlier experience as Alvin Dyer's counselor.[26]

Dyer called his plan the "manner of conversion," and he formulated it after extensive interviews with recent converts to Mormonism. A mission president who served under Dyer when he presided over the European Mission recalled:

> One of the questions he asked them was, "When did you first get the feeling that the gospel was true?" Seventy percent of those people interviewed said, "On the first contact of the missionary." Well, that told him something, that the Holy Ghost was inspiring people to get the feeling that the missionary was telling the truth. That's what he built his philosophy on: We're waiting too long. The Holy Ghost isn't going to work with people forever, and if He gives them a testimony and they keep putting it off and putting it off it disappears; and I found that to be true. If you don't strike while the iron is hot they can lose that testimony. But once they're baptized and have the Holy Ghost conferred upon them, then it stays with them.[27]

It was a radical departure from the prior plan, which called for months of missionary visits prior to baptism. Instead, the subject of a baptismal commitment was broached within weeks or even days, and a positive response led quickly to baptism. The change was not universally praised. Howard Anderson, who served as president of the California Mission in the early 1960s, explained: "They were putting people in the water in two and three weeks. Oh, the stake presidents were alarmed. How could anybody get a testimony and understand the workings of the gospel in that short time? It was a tough battle."[28] But it succeeded; and in 1960, with Woodbury working in England, Dyer orchestrating events in Europe, and Moyle out of Salt Lake City, the results began to emerge. As missionaries and mission presidents throughout the world became aware of the new movement, they were swept up in a wave of unprecedented enthusiasm and empowerment.

In France the catalyst was a dinner meeting with Moyle:

> The thing that broke it all open over there in the French Mission was a meeting they held at the top of the Eiffel Tower, in a restaurant, with all the missionaries. They got up there and challenged those missionaries to do something that they'd never dreamed of doing. They'd been getting maybe a hundred baptisms a year. All of a sudden they came in and said, "You can do more. You can do better. You can do a thousand." And the missionaries went out and they just decided, "Boy, we can do it!" It was the first time.[29]

In Germany a meeting with Apostle Spencer W. Kimball, later church president, set the tone. One missionary recalled that stirring gathering: "The Berlin missionaries had a sense, right or wrong, that we were called by the Lord basically to teach his gospel and keep the city free. Spencer Kimball came and in that very gravelly voice of his—he had just had his third or fourth operation on his larynx—he came to this chapel in Berlin. All the missionaries gathered for this conference, and in that gravelly voice of his he said, 'As long as you're in this city, this city will be free.' That kind of thing. It was very powerful."[30]

In Finland the enthusiasm was cumulative, rather than being jump-started by a single catalytic event. One of the missionaries recalled:

> We came to Finland and we could see that we were entering the mission field at a time that everyone felt the crest was just being formed and we were riding that heavy wave to the crest. It was an exciting thing. We felt we were part of destiny and that history was being made.... As we would look around the mission and see people working hard and dedication being correlated with success as measured by contacts and baptisms, I think there was something that was inspirational to young

elders. We felt this was the correct answer to the promise that if you do the work you will reap the rewards.[31]

And in Great Britain, where the movement had begun, the enthusiasm was palpable. Henry Moyle's daughter, Alice Moyle Yeats, described a meeting that she attended: "What Daddy and Woodbury did in England was controversial and caused a lot of comment later on, but they did get those boys working. There was another meeting they had in the mission home. I'll never forget it. You just felt like the ceiling was going to pop off the roof of the room because there was so much Spirit there. Oh, my goodness!"[32]

CONVERT BAPTISM QUOTAS

Total convert baptisms throughout the church actually dropped slightly in 1959, Woodbury's first full year as mission president. This dip was likely the aftermath of an apostate movement in the French Mission the year before that resulted in the excommunication of several missionaries and a general demoralization of hundreds of others.[33] Yet in spite of that downturn, there were signs within the British Mission that something new and special was happening. In May 1959, Woodbury and William Bates, an English convert who supervised the Mutual Improvement Associations within the mission, orchestrated a youth conference. Woodbury noted, "We had hoped for overall attendance of five to seven hundred and it was a such a joy to know that we had in attendance, one thousand five hundred twelve."[34] Bates saw it as the start of something: "We brought the people and got everybody involved in it. It was just wonderful, and things started to go like a dynamo. Some General Authorities came across and saw what we were doing, and were all enthused about the vivaciousness of the Church."[35]

Several weeks after the youth conference, Woodbury spoke at the groundbreaking exercises for a new chapel in Central London. Borrowing freely the term "New Era" that David O. McKay had used in dedicating the London Temple, he gave a progress report for the mission, which he recorded in his diary in the third person:

> President Woodbury then bore testimony to the fact that this was a New Era in the British mission, that there was a New Era in membership.... The baptisms for the first six months of this year had increased 77.6%. President Woodbury said there was a New Era in local leadership and that now ten out of fifteen districts were completely in local hands and that before the end of the year it appeared possible that all of the districts could be in local hands. He said that

there had been a New Era in reactivation of members. Although the series of conferences which will just be embarked upon are stressing integration and enlistment, the enlistment program has already begun by the auxiliaries of the Church and fifty-two members were reactivated in June. President Woodbury said that there was a New Era in service and referred particularly to the six hundred thirty-four district missionaries who were set apart and who were about seventy percent active going two nights a week to the doors of their friends to hold cottage meetings. This program has only been in effect a few short months and already there were one hundred four convert baptisms recorded by the district missionaries.[36]

The year 1960 was a banner year, not only in the British Mission but also throughout the church. Woodbury's emphasis on the development of local leadership bore fruit early in the year when Apostle Harold B. Lee traveled to Manchester, England, to organize the first stake in Europe. On March 27, 1960, the day the stake was organized, Lee commented to Woodbury, "This is the greatest event to happen in the history of the British Mission since its organization [in 1837]."[37]

Woodbury built on the conversion successes of the previous year by giving his missionaries a new goal: "It was decided that the British Mission would achieve five hundred baptisms in the months of July and August and that the North British mission would contribute a like number of baptisms and that these thousand baptisms would be a tribute to President David O. McKay and that we would cable him on his birthday, the eighth of September when he will be eighty-seven years old that we had reached our goal of one thousand baptisms as a tribute to him, our great prophet." This goal would be met, he felt, not through the time-worn method of "tracting," or going from house to house and making "cold calls," but through a system of referrals. "In the first six months of this year, we are having one convert baptism for every one thousand thirty-eight homes we call on in tracting. Whereas, with referrals, we are baptizing one of every 7.9 homes on which we call."[38]

Several days later Woodbury wrote to McKay, informing him of the pledge "to produce 1000 convert baptisms in July and August as a Birthday Tribute to you, our prophet."[39] McKay responded with unrestrained enthusiasm: "You and your associates in the British Mission have set standards and achievements never before equaled in the missionary cause—a goal of one thousand convert baptisms in July and August! What a blessing to those who accept the Truth and become adherents to the Restored Gospel of our Lord and Savior Jesus Christ! What an eternity of joy and happiness will be theirs, and what a great satisfaction to the missionaries who carry to a thousand souls during those two months the glad tidings of great joy!"[40]

The two missions exceeded their goal, baptizing 1,111 in two months. Several days before McKay's birthday, Bernard P. Brockbank, president of the North British Mission, wrote to inform him of the achievement and announced further that the goals for his mission were 2,000 baptisms during 1960 and "4,000 or more converts in 1961."[41] A jubilant McKay passed the information along to the *Church News*.[42]

Not to be outdone by Brockbank, Woodbury boosted the goal even higher for his mission. Projecting that the two missions "would baptize in excess of nine thousand in the year 1961 to break the highest former record in the British Mission which was in the year 1849," he set the mark of 350 baptisms a month, an annual total that was 200 higher than Brockbank's.[43]

At the end of 1960 the *Church News* gave glowing coverage to the missionary successes. Worldwide convert baptisms for the year increased by 70 percent over 1959, while the combined European missions showed an increase of 300 percent. The highest numbers came from the British Isles, with the two missions combining for 4,591 baptisms compared to 1,404 the prior year. Yet on a percentage basis, several other missions posted even higher gains: the French Mission, nearly 600%; the Netherlands Mission, 325%; the Swedish Mission, 315%; the Central American Mission, 315%; and the North German Mission, 235%.[44] The total number of full-time missionaries increased by 40 percent, due in part to a challenge by Moyle in April general conference and in part to a downward adjustment in the minimum age for male missionaries from twenty-one to nineteen and from twenty-three to twenty-one for women.[45]

In the summer of 1961, several missions mimicked the British Missions' prior birthday tribute to David O. McKay. Two additional missions had been organized in Great Britain, and they joined together to produce a "birthday present" of 1,274 baptisms in the month of August, more than double the rate of the previous year.[46] Similar tributes came from France, Central America, and other missions. McKay exulted in the results of these tributes, writing to each mission president, "My heart was filled to overflowing with gratitude and thanksgiving."[47]

The year 1961 ended with even more impressive gains than 1960: 35 percent increase in full-time missionaries and 83 percent increase in convert baptisms.[48] As Woodbury had predicted, total baptisms in the British Isles exceeded the record set in 1849—by an astounding 57 percent. Optimism was virtually unbounded, and Moyle predicted that worldwide convert baptisms during the following year, 1962, would double.[49]

The results for 1962 were impressive, but the increase over 1961 was 30 percent, far short of Moyle's prediction of 100 percent. The luster of the missionary program was beginning to fade. In 1963 baptisms dropped by 10 percent, then continued to drop each year through 1967 until they were down to 62,280, nearly half the peak of 115,834 reached in 1962. This happened in spite of consistent annual increases in the number of full-time missionaries and the injection of nearly 1 million referral cards from the Mormon Pavilion at the New York World's Fair in 1964–65.[50] The missionary program was in trouble.

MISSIONARY INCENTIVES

Signs of impending trouble had appeared several years before the numbers turned downward, yet they either went unnoticed or were intentionally ignored. Perhaps the first sign was, at the time, benign. It occurred in conjunction with the 1959 British Mission youth conference, in the form of an incentive proposal that T. Bowring Woodbury gave to his missionaries: "We had told every missionary that if he had fifty-six hours proselyting time for four weeks in advance of Butlin's Camp, that they could accompany the Saints here to this youth convention."[51] Initially the requirement had been for *each* missionary to work 56 hours per week, to compensate for the two days of "lost time" at the conference,[52] but Woodbury later relaxed the requirement and allowed for a mission-wide average of 56 hours.[53] The incentive worked well, the mission average exceeded the requirement, and the missionaries attended the conference.

Other incentive proposals soon followed, yet the terms became less benign. The requirement changed from hours of work, over which the missionaries had reasonable control, to baptisms. The process of religious conversion was thus transformed into a numbers game. Missionaries who met their quotas were rewarded: a trip to the London Temple,[54] a trip to church historic sites,[55] dinner with Henry D. Moyle,[56] or membership in the Extra Mile Club.[57] To his diary Woodbury justified the use of incentives in missionary work:

> The use of incentives in every aspect of life is become almost a universal law. We have the incentives of bonus wages for more production in industry; attractive commissions to spur piece-salesmen on to greater sales; and the incentive present in every field of greater position for harder work. In the Lord's plan, too, there are great incentives: we are promised a place in the Celestial Kingdom of glory, to dwell with our Father in Heaven himself, in return for a life of righteousness, serving him and complying with his commandments and, more specifically in the Lord's plan, there are incentives in His missionary program.[58]

In the instance of the youth conference in 1959, all of the missionaries in the mission were rewarded. As time progressed, however, and baptismal goals were pushed ever higher, not all missionaries met the goals. Those who failed to meet them were punished by exclusion, and the effect was emotionally devastating. One of Woodbury's missionaries noted: "I think he pushed some too hard. He pushed some that were incapable of being pushed. Others he didn't push hard enough. It was that the same pressure was applied to all. And here is where he was a little bit uneducated. You know, you can push some harder and some a little bit, and some you don't push at all."[59]

Franklin Murdock, a longtime employee of the Missionary Department, noted the poignancy of this kind of treatment:

> When we took the Singing Mothers over to the dedication of the Hyde Park Chapel, President Woodbury was there.... I had seen a lot of the missionaries standing outside of the chapel and there was Brother David Skousen from my old ward and I said, "David, let's go in and sit up to the front so we can hear better." I was a stake president then. He said, "I'm sorry, President Murdock, I'm not allowed to go in there." "You're not? Why?" He said, "I only got two baptisms this month. You have to have ten to be able to get a seat in this conference." And I could see David way back there outside and I said, "Oh, I don't like this."[60]

Hugh B. Brown of the First Presidency encountered the same situation at the dedication. According to Clifton Kerr, former British Mission president who returned for the event, "Brother Hugh B. Brown interviewed all the missionaries in the mission during the period of days we were there for the Hyde Park chapel dedication, and he said to me, "The morale of the one-third that have come somewhere near reaching their quota is good, but I have never interviewed missionaries as low in their morale as the other two-thirds who didn't meet their quota."[61]

Woodbury was not the only one to apply pressure for ever increasing numbers of baptisms. A missionary from the Finnish Mission recalled: "There were some aspects that I personally was not overly happy with at the time and that, after fifteen years of being back from the mission, I'm not overly pleased with now. They had a number of contests, and I think the time periods for these contests were fairly long—several months, maybe six months. For those who baptized the most people in this period of time, prizes were offered, which included, at least in one contest, a trip to the Lapland area."[62]

Levi B. Thorup, president of the Danish Mission, tried an incentive program only once: "We did have an 'incentive' at one time with the Copenhagen Districts and we took the district that had the most baptisms to Bornholm for a Sunday. It was a one day trip, and we decided it wasn't a good idea, and we never offered any other 'incentive' rewards after that."[63]

What might have been a benign idea at first had now taken on a malignant life of its own. It spun rapidly out of control. Competition within a mission soon became competition between missions. One General Authority later commented: "It doesn't matter how carefully you couch your instruction, there is that inter-mission competition which will exist. They may say, 'Well, we don't stress baptisms.' Nonsense. Every mission president is going to try to look good to his supervisor, who is a General Authority. Well, it's that environment where real trouble began. And then they were using David O. McKay as the motivation, and this was the kicker, I think. That's the last thing David O. McKay would want his image to be used for."[64]

Different missionaries handled the pressure in different ways. Some buckled. A missionary in Germany recalled the pressure that came from Alvin R. Dyer. "Dyer just kept the pot boiling, and the message that was coming across to various missionaries was, 'If you're not baptizing, there is something wrong with *you*.'" He quoted an LDS psychiatrist who estimated that "ten percent of the missionaries in Europe, because of the pressure, were suffering fairly serious psychological problems."[65]

Others responded by finding ways to meet the quotas. A missionary in Scotland, who arrived after the fact, spoke of a practice called "Chip and Dip," where missionaries took children out for French fries and then baptized them.[66] Apostle Mark E. Petersen, who was later sent to Europe to investigate the situation, reported to a friend, "I even found where they were giving silver dollars to kids if they'd be baptized."[67] It got worse: "The pressure got so great that the missionaries figured out how to deal with it. Missionaries aren't stupid. 'Hey, I know where we can get some names for baptisms!' So they went into the graveyards and started taking names off of gravestones, filling out baptismal certificates and submitting them as baptisms. Well, you know, it goes through the Church thing and comes back to a stake president, or to branch and district presidents saying, 'Where are these bodies that we've been baptizing?'…It got that ugly."[68]

THE "BASEBALL BAPTISMS" PROGRAM

Another form of adaptation, which still symbolizes what went wrong with the missionary program, came to be known as "baseball baptisms." The genesis of baseball baptisms was described by one of the missionaries who saw it happen:

> In the first summer of my mission, I witnessed the birth of the baseball program. There was no formal unveiling, fanfare, or hype. It was not credited by its creator as having been inspired: neither did it come from the active minds of Woodbury, President Moyle, or any other LDS leader. Its roots were in pragmatism and desperation.

Elder Gaylan Grover was the branch president in Swansea, Wales. One of his principal responsibilities was creating activities for the half-dozen young people who attended the weekly youth program that Mormons called MIA [Mutual Improvement Association]. It was summer; and since the MIA meetings were held in a rented school near a park, it seemed natural to take the kids outside into the late afternoon sun for any activity Grover could contrive. By his own admission, Grover knew nothing about English sports, and so, as he reported to us in our Welsh District supervising elders' meeting, he wrote home for a softball and bat.

At the next MIA meeting, after the equipment had arrived, there was an astounding response. Grover enthusiastically related the phenomenon: "Within ten minutes, we had thirty kids begging to learn the new game. They gathered around us from all over the park, joining in with our kids to play this new American sport." As the evening wore on, it struck the elders that they should get the names and addresses of these non-Mormon kids before they went home.

As Grover and his missionary companion subsequently visited the families, not only were they not rejected, they were welcomed into the homes as "young American friends from the park." Old barriers fell, psychological distance disappeared, and relationships were established. As if by magic, the elders were able to exploit these opportunities to teach. The baseball program had begun.[69]

On its surface, the program was a master stroke, a far more effective means of "opening the doors" than traditional (and highly inefficient) methods such as tracting and street meetings. "All we did was take out a softball and a bat, and start hitting the ball. And these kids just *migrated* right toward us!"[70] The original idea of using baseball as an entrée into the homes was sound. One Briton who served in the British Mission at the time noted, "We have never found a program that's been able to get into the families better than that program. Had it been used more correctly and not got such a bad reputation, maybe progress might have continued at that rate."[71]

Indeed, in its early phase the program was not abused and produced authentic results. One of Woodbury's missionaries described the initial success:

Tales of our success soon spread to London, Great Britain, America, and the world. I don't think it ever occurred to any of us, in those early days, that this was an "easy way" to meet the mission's ambitious new convert baptism goals.... It was simply a "super referral program." Instead of being dependent on members to provide names, missionaries could simply don sweatshirts, take their ball and bat to any park, and within ten minutes, have a crowd of English kids fighting to give their parents' names and addresses for the privilege of receiving a visit from the "young Yanks."[72]

Although the program began as a means of gaining introduction to parents, with the goal of converting entire families to Mormonism, it rapidly fell hostage to the increasing pressure for baptisms coming out of mission homes. Missionaries soon found that it was far easier to persuade impressionable children to convert than it was to persuade their parents, and so the profile of the program quickly changed:

> Children were easy to convert; adults were not. The temptation was: Why labor with the Jones adults when the Evans kids were also ready for conversion? The elements all came together to create the opportunity for abuse. Based on personal experience, my unequivocal conclusion is that abuse was not overtly planned, encouraged, nor condoned. It just happened. But once it happened, it was conveniently ignored, generally denied, and subsequently apologized for.... Unfortunately, in the beginning, when the abuses started and then increased, Woodbury was insulated from the truth by his missionary leaders. No one dared tell the emperor that his new clothes were an illusion and that he was indeed naked in the streets.[73]

Church policy from the earliest days forbids the baptisms of children under the age of eight, when they are considered to be able to make informed moral judgment. No evidence exists in McKay's papers that children under age eight were baptized; but the baptisms of minor children age eight and over with parental permission soon deteriorated into the baptisms of children without parental permission. Ultimately children were baptized without even knowing what was happening to them. A British member who was baptized prior to the baseball baptism era described an all-too-common scene:

> One Wednesday we went to MIA, we walked in, and there were about fifty or sixty boys and girls there. It was just a shock to us at that particular time. There were boys and girls everywhere.... Half of them didn't know that they were baptized. I know that is true, because we were asked to go home teaching to these boys and girls a year or two later, and I remember going to see one young lady.... I said, "Don't you ever remember being baptized? Don't you ever remember dressing in white and being put in the water?" "No." "Can't you remember anything?" She said, "Just a moment. Tea and coffee, Americans!" I said, "That's right. Do you remember now two young American

men who didn't drink tea and coffee?" She said, "I do." And that was
all she could remember of her baptism.[74]

As the baptismal numbers shot up, the effect on congregations was devastating, for local leaders, not missionaries, were held accountable for the new members once they were baptized. In one congregation, the baseball baptism program resulted in 104 new members, only two of whom remained active.[75] In another, the results were even worse. Wilfrid Clark, who was on the high council of the London Stake in the early 1960s, "went to one of the Bishops there. I said, 'Look, your home teaching is terrible.' He said, 'Come here, Wilf, and I'll show you something.' He opened his book and said, 'There are nearly ninety children there who were baptized, and I've never seen one. I've never seen one!'"[76]

While David O. McKay and many other church members still basked in the good news of missionary success stories, other General Authorities saw trouble brewing. Ernest Wilkinson, the president of Brigham Young University, recorded a conversation with Henry D. Moyle in September 1960, still the early months of the success stories: "He [Moyle] confessed also that he was having real opposition from some members of the Quorum of the Twelve on the accelerated missionary program that had been instituted. Many of the members thought that baptisms were being made so fast that the conversions would not be permanent. Among these were President Joseph Fielding Smith, Harold B. Lee, and possibly others."[77]

Indeed, Smith, who had chaired the Missionary Committee before Moyle had gone into the First Presidency, was pointedly critical in private. Early in 1961 he received an inquiry from Lowell Bennion, a teacher in the Institute of Religion at the University of Utah. Bennion described to Smith a conversation he had had with a returned sister missionary who was guilt-ridden because she and her companions, under "extreme pressure to meet baptismal quotas," bought candy bars and gave them to children as enticements to get baptized. Smith's reply was emphatic: "I am satisfied completely that the Spirit of the Lord is not in it.... I have learned from direct and accurate authority that in this great drive they have been baptizing [first] children who are not old enough to comprehend and frequently without the consent of their parents.... How long we will permit this thing to go on, I am not prepared to say, but the idea of baptizing and converting afterwards has never been successful and in my judgment never will."[78]

Two months later Smith conveyed a similar message to Ernest Wilkinson:

> I learned while I was in Salt Lake that some members of the Quorum
> of the Twelve (apparently, nearly all of them) are gravely concerned
> about the pressures being put on missionaries to baptize to fill a quota
> of baptisms. President Smith told me that he remembers when they
> released one Mission President because he insisted on quotas for his

missionaries. He then commented that now that seems to be the order of the Church, that he felt it was definitely wrong. This, of course, was a criticism of President Moyle and many of the Mission Presidents working under his direction. Brother Stapley also, who is very soft in his speech, was very critical of some of the Mission Presidents suggesting that if a boy converted so many people, he could shake hands with President McKay. He thought that promise was ridiculous, and I agree with him. All Mission Presidents from the world are being called to Salt Lake City for a conference the latter part of June, for ten days. These will be workshops. I am satisfied there will be some conflict of opinion there as to the methods of missionary work.[79]

Among the workshops at the mission presidents' conference in June 1961 was Woodbury's presentation of the baseball baptism program, which he showcased as one of his most effective means of conversion.[80] Well aware of McKay's general approval of the upswing in convert baptisms, other General Authorities remained silent, except for Hugh B. Brown of the First Presidency, who gave a nuanced warning to the mission presidents:

> Do not allow competition to become the chief incentive to work. Encourage them all, of course, to do their best, but let your competition from now on be with your own mission, your own past record, and not with any other mission. Teach your missionaries that their competition must be with themselves, and not with the other missionaries, but inspire them with ambition and enthusiasm.... When great movements get the impetus of a prairie fire there is danger. I hope I have not spoken out of place. I am just sounding this word of warning. In your enthusiasm to increase the flock, be careful you don't lose the shepherds. The Lord spoke about leaving the ninety and nine and going out to save the one; I am thinking in reverse order. You are asking the one to go out and get the ninety and nine, but be sure you don't lose the one.[81]

Brown's warning went generally unheeded, largely because David O. McKay was not yet convinced that there was a problem.

In February 1961, four months prior to the mission presidents' conference, McKay had traveled to Scotland. On the eve of his departure one of his assistants, A. Hamer Reiser, a former mission president who then served as assistant secretary in the First Presidency's office, had received a disturbing telephone call from a Scottish journalist in Glasgow:

He said, "It's being rumored around here that your missionaries are baptizing children without the consent of their parents." I said, "That can't be, because that's contrary to the regulations." I had known that. Then I told him, "I have been in Scotland and in Great Britain and was there for nearly four years as a mission president and I speak from my own knowledge that that's contrary to regulations. I can't say anything about what you know, because I don't know what you know. President McKay is interested in this very problem and we're coming to Great Britain in a few days, and among other things the President is going to look into that. We'll see you there then. Let's not try to handle this over long-distance telephone." And that was the end of that conversation.[82]

At the same time, two Scottish journalists contacted McKay's private secretary, Clare Middlemiss, and told her that there was a "lot of criticism in Scotland regarding the methods used by our Elders in getting new converts; that they are persuading teen-age boys and girls to join the Church and taking them out of the control of their parents." McKay instructed her to reply that "there was a misunderstanding, because one of the teachings of the church is that parents are to be held responsible for the training and teaching of their children."[83]

Upon arriving in Prestwick, Scotland, late in February, McKay was immediately confronted by the press: "One newspaperman asked if it is true that missionaries are baptizing young people into the Church without the consent of their parents. President McKay replied that he thought this was not true and that it is contrary to instructions given to missionaries to baptize children only with the consent of their parents.... One reporter asked if President McKay intends to correct the practice if it is found that the missionaries are baptizing minors without parental consent. President McKay answered in the affirmative."[84]

Later the same day, as McKay met with Bernard P. Brockbank, president of the Scotch-Irish Mission, and his missionaries in Glasgow, he was confronted by another reporter with the same question. According to the minutes of the meeting included in McKay's diary, "The matter of baptizing young people without the consent of parents was answered by President McKay in the same way he had met the problem in Prestwick." After the reporter left the meeting, McKay questioned Brockbank and the missionaries:

> He asked the missionaries if any had baptized young people without the consent of parents. Four indicated they had. President McKay asked each one to give the facts. The first said he had had to be content with the consent of the foster father. President McKay dismissed

this case as having been handled properly. The second said the young woman in question was twenty years of age, approaching 21. President McKay dismissed this as a rather close case, but advised the missionary, nevertheless, to seek the concurrence of parents. The other two cases were rather obscure, but President Brockbank assured President McKay that he knew the facts of each case, and that he considered that the missionaries had not gone contrary to instructions.[85]

McKay was satisfied with Brockbank's explanation, and complimented the mission president in an address to the missionaries later the same day, adding just a hint of a cautionary note:

> I was glad today to hear President Brockbank say, "Our youth program is used to bring parents into the church." The world is accusing you of using the children merely to add to your number of baptisms. I was surprised yesterday when somebody put into my hands a certificate or a blank and there was a place on that blank for parent's signatures—"This certifies that I give my permission for John Jones, whatever the name of the child may be, to be baptized." Well, I thought of this limitation—there's a chance for a virtue to become a vice in this Church. It's quite possible, I thought, that a parent would sign that letter without your having seen the parents, and you don't know whether the child or the young man or young woman had even spoken to the parents. That's just where there's danger, and the world's condemning you for it. I don't know, but I'm going to look it up. You see what I mean? We have to be very careful not to cross the limit [line]. Instead of baptizing that child without going first and seeing the parents personally, invite them, and bring the entire family in, or there might be some cause for condemnation.[86]

He told the press "he accepted the findings of Mr. Bernard Brockbank, President of the Scottish-Irish Mission of the Mormons, who had investigated all the cases mentioned at the Presbytery meeting, and had not discovered any foundation or truth in them."[87] The issue did not die, however; and as the criticism continued, McKay became combative. In response to charges from Scottish ministers that Mormon missionaries were baptizing young girls without parental consent, he lashed out: "The Church of Scotland may choose a representative to travel to our headquarters in Salt Lake City and investigate our faith—with all expenses paid by the Mormon Church. No minor can be baptized as a Mormon without the consent of her or his parents. These charges are ridiculous. It is an attempt to get something sensational against our Church."[88]

McKay's last stop on the trip was a meeting with T. Bowring Woodbury, and his parting message, according to Woodbury's diary, was a strong endorsement of business as usual:

> He asked me a little about the baptizing of youth and I told him that we had been able to go from twenty-four percent of youth baptized down to eight percent for January and February and that families baptized including adults had gone up to sixty-nine percent. He talked of criticism both written and spoken that is sometimes our lot. Then President McKay continued, "I want you to know that I am pleased with what I see, what has been done and what is being done and what's more, President Woodbury, I want you to know the Lord is pleased. Does anything else matter?"[89]

McKay returned to Salt Lake City seemingly convinced that the whole matter of youth baptisms was overblown. Yet troubling reports continued to filter in. Later in the year, he summoned Marion D. Hanks, a member of the First Council of Seventy, and asked what he knew of the reports. "Did they do this in my name?" he asked. Hanks answered in the affirmative. McKay then asked Hanks if he could assume the presidency of the British Mission. Hanks said that he would do whatever he was asked but that his recent agreement to serve on President John F. Kennedy's Council of Physical Fitness had committed him to a heavy traveling and speaking schedule. Upon hearing this, McKay told him to continue doing what he was doing. However, a couple of weeks later McKay again called him to his office and said that the situation could no longer wait and that Hanks would have to leave soon, which he did in January 1962.[90]

In October 1961, the First Presidency extended to T. Bowring Woodbury, who had already served nearly six months longer than his original calling had specified, an honorable release. "In thus extending your release," they wrote, "it affords us much pleasure indeed to say that you retire from your present position with our utmost confidence, good will and appreciation."[91] Woodbury and his wife gave an official report of their mission to the First Presidency almost a year later, and McKay's enthusiastic response suggests that he did not consider him to have been the problem: "Brother Woodbury reported his presidency of the British Mission from September 1958 to January 1962. They gave an excellent report!"[92] Nor did McKay know the details of the problem at the time he sent Hanks to England. According to a later memo from Hanks to Clare Middlemiss, "Pres. McKay and I also discussed at some length the condition of the British Missions when I was assigned to Britain. He told me he had not known what was going on and expressed appreciation that I had been able to stop the procedures which, he said, had cast a reflection that would take the Church years to correct."[93]

A First Presidency circular letter late in 1962 was the first official acknowledgment:

> While we appreciate the effort being expended to bring members into the Church, several instances have been brought to our attention where individuals may have been baptized without having exercised proper conversion to gospel principles. These unfortunate incidents prompt us to repeat the recommendation that mission presidents extend to missionaries a caution against baptizing individuals who have little knowledge or of appreciation for principles of the gospel.
>
> We are particularly concerned that children not be baptized as members of the Church without written permission of their parents. When contact with the family develops through a younger member of the family, it is expected that every effort will be made to interest the entire family, particularly the parents, in the principles of the gospel. If parents should consent to the baptism of their children, elders performing the baptism should make certain that the parents fully understand the significance of the baptismal ordinance and where possible that they attend the baptismal services. . . .
>
> We suggest that the attention of missionaries be directed to the number of conversions rather than the number of baptisms. It would be hoped that no missionary, motivated by his desire to increase his number of baptisms, would baptize individuals who had not experienced genuine conversion.[94]

Early in 1963 McKay made three personnel changes that signaled the end of the "baseball baptism" era. The first was to replace Alvin R. Dyer, president of the European Mission, with Theodore M. Burton. According to Levi Thorup, president of the Danish Mission, Burton immediately changed the atmosphere. "When President Dyer was released and President Burton came over, there had been so much talk about pressure that had been put on, particularly in England and those areas, that they decided nobody was going to have any pressure."[95] Dyer landed on his feet, eventually becoming an apostle and, later, an additional counselor in the First Presidency. Second, Apostle Mark E. Petersen was called to preside over the West European Mission (British Isles), with explicit instructions from McKay to discontinue the youth baptisms.[96]

And finally, on January 31, 1963, McKay replaced Henry D. Moyle as chair of the Missionary Committee with Joseph Fielding Smith, president of the Quorum of the Twelve and a strong opponent of Moyle-style missionary work. Although McKay invited Moyle "to keep his hand on the situation,"[97] the message was clear. Moyle never attended another meeting of the committee. Five months later, when

Moyle mentioned in a First Presidency meeting that he was receiving reports of decreasing baptisms from mission presidents, McKay told him curtly that "the Missionary Committee will be relied upon to react to the condition."[98] Paul Dunn, a Seventy, later commented on McKay's treatment of Moyle: "The interesting thing about David O. McKay, relating to this, was that the greatest strength of David O. McKay was also his weakness. That was his love of a person, and the trust he put in him. If he trusted you, you couldn't do any wrong, unless you went contrary to that trust. Then, that love turned to just the opposite. Henry Moyle found himself in that situation with David O. McKay."[99]

Moyle remained first counselor in the First Presidency; but without the missionary portfolio, which he had called his greatest work, he was an empty man. He confided to Marion D. Hanks, "I have been relieved of every responsibility except my title."[100] On September 18, 1963, Moyle died of a heart attack.

The tide of bogus baptisms abated, leaving in its wake thousands of de facto church members who had no idea of the fact, but who nonetheless fell within the responsibility of local church leaders. What to do with them became the subject of considerable debate.

In July 1963, six months after assuming his duties as president of the West European Mission, Mark E. Petersen wrote to the First Presidency with a proposal for beginning the clean-up. An audit within a single stake (Manchester, England) had identified one thousand youth with dubious credentials. One-third were classified as "knowing that they were being baptized when they became members and their parents are indifferent," another third as "not knowing that they were being baptized and having no interest in the Church now," and the remaining third as "children whose parents resent their having been baptized into the Church under the circumstances and in a manner in which they were." Both Petersen and the stake president recommended that the first third be assigned to the stake in the hope of bringing them into church activity but that the other two-thirds be assigned to the full-time missionaries, "to labor with them and to remove their names from the statistics and records." McKay was adamantly opposed to a wholesale purging of the records:

> The idea of saying: "Take them off the record" is not worthy of consideration. They are members and we must keep them and deal with them as members. Where parents refuse to let them be active, the responsibility must be upon the parents. Where we have permission to deal with these children we must do it in the best ways. It is a matter of saving souls rather than statistics. We must work with these young boys and girls. We shall follow the revelation of the Lord, and place the responsibility upon the parents and let the statistics be as they are.[101]

Statistics were one matter, but commitments to visit and fellowship thousands of indifferent "members" on a monthly basis were another. A month later Petersen pressed his case in person, in company with Marion D. Hanks, who was grappling with the same problem in London. McKay noted neutrally: "President Petersen has been having some difficulties pertaining to the large number of children who have been baptized into the Church without the consent or knowledge of their parents."[102] In October, Petersen again raised the issue, this time eliciting a response from McKay that, despite his earlier charge to Petersen, indicated lack of awareness of the full scope of the problem: "President Petersen said, 'This idea of indiscriminately going out and rounding up children, we do not want that[,] do we?' I said that I have never heard of such a thing, except in the Brighton area of England."[103]

However, the magnitude of the problem gradually became apparent to McKay; and early in 1964 he approved a First Presidency letter to mission presidents detailing the course of action to take with such members. "The letter recommends that the parents and children be worked with in an endeavor to convert them to the Gospel and to activity in the Church; that, however, if they insist upon having their names removed, action should be taken after a reasonable effort by regular ecclesiastical court procedure."[104]

The First Presidency letter, while formally establishing the procedure for dealing with the issue, failed to recognize the fact that individual mission presidents had already been dealing with it on their own initiative. In the North Scottish Mission, for instance, Phillip Jensen, the new mission president, made a quick assessment of the situation. One of his missionaries explained in a later interview:

> It didn't take him long to see what was going on. He called the whole mission together and said, "That's over with. It's stopped." . . . It wasn't too much longer that the next step occurred. Phil Jensen said, "We're going to take the Church records of these people, and you are going to go out and find all of these kids, and find their families, and talk to their parents." . . . That was the eye-opener. It was very earth-shaking, because you were meeting kids that would tell you—many of them, not all—they had no idea they had joined the Mormon Church. They thought they belonged to this person's—called the elder—team for soccer, the elder's team for baseball, the elder's youth group. We talked to their parents, and I was horrified to find out that many of these parents claimed that they had no idea that their child was on the records of the Church. . . . So we had to do this full survey, for all the records of these kids in the mission. From that point on we just proceeded at a very, very slow pace, with a very positive

philosophy and procedures. But the numbers were gone, absolutely gone.[105]

In the Central British Mission, James Cullimore, the new mission president, selected Elder James Foulger in 1963 to investigate the youth baptisms:

> I got called to go into the mission home, and I lived in the mission home, in the mission president's quarters, not with the other missionaries.... I had special assignments, but I didn't have a companion. The mission president was my companion.... It was a new job.... I think we had about 1,800 unattached, inactive youth. That's a lot. But I don't think it was anywhere near what they had in London.... You could not excommunicate anyone, or wipe them off the record without physically talking to them. That was part of the assignment, you had to talk to them.... Most all of them had their names removed from the records of the Church.[106]

In the British Mission, where it had all begun, Marion D. Hanks, the only General Authority serving as a mission president in the impacted area, took a harder line. Hyrum Smith, an elder who had been serving for "seven or eight months" was designated as "one of four missionaries to be sort of a S.W.A.T. team, to go out and find all these kids that had been baptized in the youth program, and make a determination on the spot whether their names stayed on the record or not. No courts, nothing like that. Just, 'You draw a line through the name, and their name gets taken off the record.'"[107]

One man recalled Hanks's charge to his father, a former bishop who, with his wife, was called to serve a mission under Hanks: "My parents were called on a mission to Great Britain shortly after the Woodbury problem was identified. My father, as an experienced stake mission president and bishop was commissioned by President Duff Hanks to visit 'swimming pool Saints' throughout the mission, interview them, and personally determine whether their names should be stricken from the rolls as unwittingly having been baptized—all this without the formality of a high council court. Dad later told me he had written off several hundred names."[108]

Despite such efforts, the problem defied complete resolution. Late in 1968, upon returning from a tour of missions in Great Britain, Apostle Spencer W. Kimball wrote to the First Presidency

> making suggestions regarding action that should be taken relative to the large number of children in Great Britain who were baptized in 1961–1963 without the proper consent of their parents, and sufficient understanding on the children's part.... President [Hugh B.] Brown suggested that we assign this project to Elder Kimball to follow

through on it and not involve the First Presidency in another directive letter.... President [Alvin R.] Dyer suggested that a note be given to Brother Kimball advising against the wholesale processing of these young people.[109]

This meeting occurred only a year prior to McKay's death, and the absence of further references to the matter over the remaining months suggests that the whole affair was simply shelved.

THE PROSELYTIZING CHALLENGE

With the benefit of four decades of hindsight, it is nonetheless still difficult to place the missionary program of the McKay years in a coherent context. Even objective data such as baptismal statistics do not tell an objective story. To be sure, there was an astounding increase in baptisms that coincided with the calling of T. Bowring Woodbury to the British Mission presidency, Alvin R. Dyer to the European Mission presidency and Henry D. Moyle to the First Presidency, all of which occurred between the summer of 1958 and the summer of 1959. Whereas in 1959 the total number of convert baptisms churchwide was 33,060, by 1962 it had nearly quadrupled, to 115,834.[110] Yet thousands of those baptisms—the total number is not known—turned out to be bogus, causing untold headaches and heartaches for local members, missionaries, and General Authorities alike, while tens of thousands were authentic.

The personalities of the era, particularly Woodbury, Dyer and Moyle, loom larger than life in comparison to today's highly bureaucratic and often anonymous church hierarchs. Despite the excesses that placed a dark mark on the era, all three men acted out of genuine concern for the church to which they belonged and to which they devoted their lives. Each retained his defenders. A. Theodore Tuttle, a fellow General Authority, said of Moyle: "He just took missionary work in those days and changed it.... [His] was the leadership and vision that caused that kind of thing to occur when he was chairman—not without opposition, but in spite of it."[111] Henry D. Moyle Jr. called Dyer "one of the greatest missionaries I ever ran across."[112] Of T. Bowring Woodbury, Alan Blodgett was unrestrained in his admiration: "He was intelligent, articulate, a fascinating conversationalist, very proper in dress and bearing. He was a delight to be around. No doubt the missionaries under him worshiped him and were eager to follow his direction. He was innovative and his new programs took Britain from virtually no baptisms to thousands."[113] Nonetheless, their best intentions and the numerical success that accompanied them stand juxtaposed to a darker legacy of disenchanted missionaries, unwitting converts, and overburdened local members. To this day, a discussion of the missionary program during those years will, in many quarters, guarantee sharp debate over ends and means.

Perhaps the best indicator of long-term success is the formation of new stakes, which require both an adequate population base and mature local leadership. By this measuring rod, the missionary efforts from 1959 through 1962 were highly successful. Ninety-one new stakes were formed during this four-year period, including the first ever in Europe (Manchester, England) and fifteen additional stakes outside of North America.[114] It was during this period that David O. McKay's goal of transforming the church into a truly international organization achieved credibility.

Yet the "how" remains as intriguing an issue as the "what." What is the best way of going about proselytizing? The answer continues to elude the church, in part because it is a multi-faceted question and in part because it deals with a moving target that changes over time. One thing that is clear is that the prevalent theory of conversion—that conversion would automatically follow baptisms—was wrong. It made baptisms the primary goal. Clifton Kerr, who had presided over the British Mission before the Woodbury era, commented on the theory:

> Brother Brockbank was there [as mission president] when I went back in 1961 [for the dedication of the London Temple] and he went on the train to Wales with us. We sat and discussed this.... At about this time there came into being among a few brethren the idea that missionaries bring them in and the branch fellowships them. This of course happened after I got home. They said, "Fellowshipping them is no concern of ours. That isn't our business. Our job is to bring them into the Church. If they don't stay, that's someone else's fault." Now, Brother [Hugh B.] Brown heard that too and he just couldn't accept it. But that was the thing they pursued: "You missionaries just get them in the water." Later Brother Brockbank said to me, "I guess we erred. We thought they'd stay in." But they didn't.... Now, it's a beautiful theory—get them baptized and turn them loose—but our branch presidents became disillusioned. The branch president of the North London Branch, who later became president of the temple, Brother Dougald McKeown, said, "I was being handed baptismal certificates of people and kids I had never seen and have never seen since." I heard that often.... Brother Moyle was a good friend of mine and I liked him. He's been in this home and we kept in touch after I got back. He was just very kind. But he said that once the Spirit of the Lord had borne witness that the Church is true and you've got them in the waters of baptism, they'll never leave again. I said,

"Brother Moyle, how can you say that? What's the motive that brought them in?"[115]

With respect to an allied issue, however, a spirited debate continues to this day: Is it better to baptize more people and retain a lower percentage, or baptize fewer people and retain a higher percentage? In 1967, Spencer W. Kimball, an apostle and future church president, weighed in on the problem at a seminar for the newly called Regional Representatives of the Twelve:

> Some years ago in what may have been a competitive enthusiasm there was a great increase in baptisms. We recognize that there were some abuses, for which we are sorry.... An unfortunate thing which came out of it was the reaction that set in. Missionaries began to talk about it, Saints began at home to talk about it, everybody was condemning the mass baptisms. Jokes were made about it. It spread, and missions afar off caught the spirit of it, the pendulum swung back, baptisms all over the world reduced. And it is our opinion, though there may have been errors in the big push, that perhaps far more people may have suffered by deprivation by the reactionary movement. Certainly we must learn to correct abuses without killing the program.... One group of missions, as indicated on the charts, their baptisms went from 4,692 up to 13,315, up to 20,504, and then when the pendulum began to swing back and a new consciousness and criticism evolved all over the world then it swung back to 12,717, 4,143, 3,565, and now slightly up to 3,672. We could have lost 80% of the 20,000 in 1962 and still saved more people to the Church, than if we saved 100% of the 3,500 which was our record a year ago. Now, I believe everyone will concede that on the 3,500 basis we are still losing members. If we lost 20% of the 3,500 and retained 2,800 we could have still lost 17,000 of our 20,000 converts of the 1962, and still be ahead in numbers. Of course, this is not what we want, we do not want abuses on either side.[116]

Kimball clearly thought that more was better; and during the first eight years of his presidency (1974–81), convert baptisms soared from 69,018 (nearly identical to the number in the final year of McKay's presidency) to 224,000.[117] And what of the McKay years? At least one insider gave them a thumbs-up: "On balance, it is my assessment that the net results of the Moyle/Woodbury missionary thrust was positive for the church. That was the turning point for the great growth of the church in Britain."[118]

11

TEMPLE BUILDING

One of the earliest themes in Latter-day Saint theology was that of "endowment," which derived from the admonition of the resurrected Christ to his disciples to remain in Jerusalem until they were endowed with "power from on high."[1] The theme was so dominant in Joseph Smith's fledgling church that it impelled a move from New York to Ohio just months after its organization.[2] By 1833 the concept of endowment became associated with a designated sacred space; and since that time, temples—buildings consecrated to special purposes that are different from the more public function of the numerous local meetinghouses—have been the focal point of Latter-day Saint religious life.

By the time David O. McKay became church president in 1951, the church had eight operating temples. Four of them had been constructed in the nineteenth century in Utah (St. George, Logan, Manti, and Salt Lake City), and four in the twentieth century in the Pacific and western North America outside of Utah (Laie, Hawaii; Cardston, Alberta, Canada; Idaho Falls, Idaho; and Mesa, Arizona).[3] By the time of McKay's death, an additional eight had been completed or were under construction. New temple construction was a high priority in the McKay administration for two reasons: to accommodate large and rapidly growing concentrations of church members in the United States, and to stem the tide of foreign immigration to Utah.

THE LOS ANGELES TEMPLE

Plans for two California temples began in 1934, coincident with McKay's being called to the First Presidency by Church President Heber J. Grant. Grant authorized a search committee composed of southern California church leaders to identify a temple site in the Los Angeles area. The committee found a twenty-four-acre parcel in Westwood that had been the residence of motion picture producer Harold Lloyd. In 1937 the church purchased the property.[4] Within months, church leaders initiated the architectural planning process, anticipating a modest-sized building with a capacity of two hundred.[5] The onset of World War II, however, delayed the plans for more than a decade.

Shortly after McKay became church president, he resuscitated and significantly but perhaps inadvertently enlarged the plans for the Los Angeles Temple, making it the largest temple ever built by the church. As the architectural work progressed, however, government limitations on the purchase of structural steel, imposed by the Korean War, threatened to delay construction indefinitely. McKay dispatched two representatives, Preston Richards and Edward O. Anderson, to Washington, D.C., to plead with the National Production Authority (NPA) for an exemption.

Upon arriving in Washington, the two men immediately called upon Utah Senator Arthur V. Watkins, who personally escorted them to the office of the NPA to argue their case. Although construction had not yet begun on the temple itself, Richards and Anderson argued that it was actually an integral part of a complex of buildings that included a Bureau of Information, the California Mission home, and the Westwood Ward chapel; and since construction was already in progress on the other buildings, the temple should be considered part of an ongoing construction program. Whether because of the merits of the case or Watkins's presence, the NPA official was sympathetic to their request: "We were given every kind consideration, and in the presence of Senator Watkins, Mr. [Rufe D.] Newman ruled that this project had been started in January 1951, before restrictions were placed on churches, therefore the project could continue with other buildings, such as the Temple, Bureau of Information, Boiler Room, Mission Home and other improvements on the project. He stated to Senator Watkins that he would give us a letter the following morning to carry back with us confirming this decision, which he did."[6]

Later in the day, Richards and Anderson told a local church member, who worked in the office of the supervising architect of the federal government, of their success. He replied "that he couldn't realize that we had received word so soon, as the Supervising Architect of the Government was required to wait many weeks for a decision on the Government buildings."[7] Eager to exploit their window of opportunity, McKay and his counselors traveled to Los Angeles the following week for groundbreaking ceremonies.[8]

The estimate of construction costs was $4 million, of which church members in the fourteen southern California stakes were asked to contribute $1 million. McKay attended the kick-off luncheon for the local fund-raising campaign early in February 1952 and was delighted to receive a phone call only two weeks later reporting that Los Angeles Stake (which included the affluent areas of Beverly Hills and Bel Air) had already contributed 238 percent of its quota, while South Los Angeles Stake, which started a week later, had also exceeded its.[9]

Local church members were eager to contribute labor in addition to money, but their intentions were frustrated both by the general contractor's ultimate decision to rely upon union labor (despite McKay's strong aversion)[10] and by a tragic accident involving donated labor on the Westwood Ward chapel only a block away. When a scaffold collapsed under two ward members, one escaped with minor injuries, but the other suffered a spinal cord injury that resulted in permanent quadriplegia and a lawsuit against the church.[11] As a result, the company insuring the temple construction gave "notice of cancellation of the rider for casualty insurance on the temple construction for the usual coverage for the workmen because they will not take the policy with the provision for contributed labor."[12]

On August 11, 1952, almost a year after the ceremonial groundbreaking, actual construction began.[13] As work progressed McKay was surprised at the emerging size of the building: "That was an enormous temple," recalled John M. Russon, president of the Los Angeles Stake, within whose boundaries the temple is located. "When President McKay came on the site and saw the foundations poured, he couldn't believe that he had approved a project as vast as that one. He said later that in looking at the blueprints it just didn't look like that big an operation."[14]

The rising infrastructure of the temple was an impressive sight atop a gentle slope that overlooked the Los Angeles Basin to its south. To this day it is an architectural landmark, not obscured by any nearby buildings. The focal point of the building is a gold-leafed statue of the Angel Moroni on the pinnacle. It was only the third statue to be placed on a temple (after the Nauvoo and Salt Lake temples), even though they are now standard and have even been retrofitted to some other temples. On viewing the scale model of the sculpted angel, McKay approved of everything except the face, which to him had "been depicted entirely too feminine" by sculptor Millard F. Malin. Four days later on a return visit to review the revised model, he noted that the eyes were now larger and farther apart, pronounced it "a good model for the statue that is to be made, and told the artist to go ahead with his plans."[15]

Construction proceeded smoothly throughout 1953, though more slowly than anticipated. Upon visiting the site in October, McKay was surprised to find that his plans for a cornerstone ceremony had to be altered slightly: "It had been suggested that the corner stone should be laid about January 20, 1954. However, while we were inspecting the corner stone, we found they have already chiseled in the stone 'Erected 1953,' so we shall have to hold these services in December."[16]

The twenty-five-foot statue of Moroni was placed on the 245-foot tower late in 1954, and a year later the construction was completed. By size and location, the temple was the most imposing built by the church to that date. Coupled with the fact that it was the first temple built outside a Latter-day Saint stronghold, it

The First Presidency, 1945: J. Reuben Clark Jr., Heber J. Grant, and David O. McKay. Courtesy Wm. Robert Wright.

The First Presidency, 1951: J. Reuben Clark Jr., George Albert Smith, and David O. McKay. Courtesy LDS Church Archives.

The First Presidency, 1951: Stephen L Richards, David O. McKay, and J. Reuben Clark Jr. Courtesy Wm. Robert Wright.

The First Presidency, May 26, 1962: Henry D. Moyle, David O. McKay, and Hugh B. Brown, with United Airlines chef Jack Staub, prior to departing for the Oakland Temple groundbreaking ceremony. Courtesy Wm. Robert Wright.

The First Presidency (including his two additional counselors) at the October 1966 general conference. Left: Joseph Fielding Smith, Hugh B. Brown, David O. McKay, N. Eldon Tanner, and Thorpe B. Isaacson. Courtesy LDS Church Archives.

Mark E. Petersen. Courtesy LDS Church
Archives.

Bruce R. McConkie. Courtesy LDS Church
Archives.

Alvin R. Dyer. Courtesy LDS Church Archives.

Douglas Stringfellow. Courtesy Special Collections, J. Willard Marriott Library, University of
Utah.

Robert Welch, founder of the John Birch Society, and Ezra Taft Benson at a John Birch Society rally in New England, 1966. Courtesy John Birch Society.

David O. McKay and George Biesinger,
supervisor of the Church Building Committee in New Zealand, with Maori
workers, ca. 1960. Courtesy LDS
Church Archives.

George Romney and David O.
McKay, ca. 1967. Courtesy LDS
Church Archives.

London Temple groundbreaking ceremony, August 27, 1955. Mission President A. Hamer Reiser (left), David O. McKay, and Sir Thomas Bennett, architect of the London Temple. Courtesy Wm. Robert Wright.

British Mission office staff, 1961. Mission President T. Bowring Woodbury is second from the right in the front row. Courtesy LDS Church Archives.

Emma Ray McKay, Cecil B. DeMille, Charlton Heston, and David O. McKay visiting Paramount Motion Picture Studios in Hollywood, California, 1955. Heston is costumed for his role as Moses in DeMille's film *The Ten Commandments*. Courtesy LDS Church Archives.

David O. McKay and "Sonny Boy" at the Huntsville farm, on McKay's eighty-eighth birthday, September 8, 1961. Courtesy Wm. Robert Wright.

Bishop Duane Hunt. Courtesy Catholic Diocese of Salt Lake City.

Sterling McMurrin. Courtesy Tanner Humanities Center, University of Utah.

Fawn McKay Brodie. Used by permission, Utah State Historical Society, all rights reserved.

Juanita Brooks. Used by permission, Utah State Historical Society, all rights reserved.

Wendell Mendenhall, chairman, Church Building Committee. Courtesy LDS Church Archives.

Church Building Committee, 1965. Chairman Mark Garff is seated. Courtesy LDS Church Archives.

David O. McKay and Emma Ray McKay on their fiftieth wedding anniversary,
January 2, 1951. Courtesy LDS Church Archives.

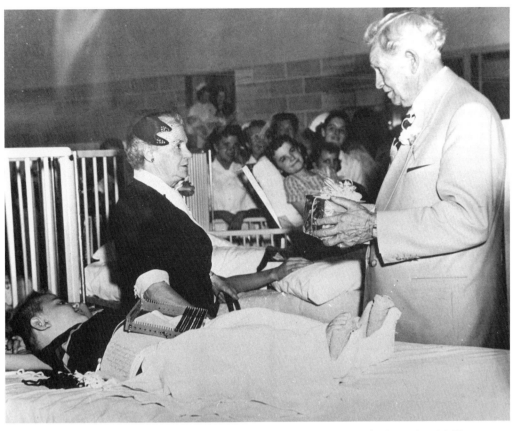

David O. McKay and Emma Ray McKay on a
Christmas hospital visit, ca. 1952. Courtesy
Wm. Robert Wright.

David O. McKay and Emma Ray
McKay at the Sacred Grove, 1951.
Courtesy LDS Church Archives.

President-elect Dwight D. Eisenhower and David O. McKay, 1952. Courtesy LDS Church Archives.

Ernest L. Wilkinson, President
Harry S. Truman, and David
O. McKay, 1952. Courtesy
LDS Church Archives.

Presidential candidate John F.
Kennedy, David O. McKay, and
Henry D. Moyle, September
1960. Courtesy LDS Church
Archives.

David O. McKay, Emma Ray McKay, and President Lyndon B. Johnson, September 1964. Courtesy LDS Church Archives.

attracted public attention all during construction. Thus, when church leaders announced that the temple would be open for public tours prior to its dedication, the response was enthusiastic.

One of the first people to see the inside of the completed temple was Cecil B. DeMille, then in the middle of directing the most famous of his movies, *The Ten Commandments.* Two years earlier, DeMille had hired Mormon artist Arnold Friberg of Salt Lake City to design costumes and sets for the movie and to paint promotional oil paintings. The temple was only a short distance from DeMille's studio, and he was curious about the building. A short time thereafter, Friberg met with McKay and conveyed a request from DeMille:

> During one of their conversations, on a certain subject, Mr. deMille said, "If I knew your President, I would telephone him upon this matter." Said he had met President Grant, and President Smith, but that he had never met President McKay. Brother Friberg told him that he was sure it would be perfectly all right to call me, but Mr. deMille was reticent about doing so. He said, however, that he would very much like to make my acquaintance. I told Brother Friberg that I would be in Los Angeles the first week in August, and at that time arrangements can be made for me to meet Mr. deMille.[17]

When the two men first met in August 1954, they instantly took to each other. Friberg described their first meeting: "DeMille said to McKay, 'Now this temple you're building up there, I'd like to go through that.' 'Oh,' McKay said, 'I'll take you through myself.' 'Now that's before it's dedicated, I may go through?' 'Yes.' 'Now after it's dedicated, I may not go through?' 'Oh,' McKay said, 'We'll take care of that. The first thing we'll do is baptize you!' And they both laughed."[18]

At the conclusion of the afternoon, DeMille presented McKay with a copy of the handbook for a previous movie, *Samson and Delilah,* which he inscribed: "To President McKay, with respect, admiration, and now affection." For his part, McKay responded with a note: "My dear Mr. deMille: Your graciousness to Mrs. McKay and me this afternoon we shall ever cherish as one of the most interesting and informative experiences of our lives.... In the generosity of your heart kindly remember our overwhelming interest."[19]

McKay was as good as his word and, two years later, took DeMille on the promised private tour. Unlike the visitations by public groups, which included a narrative by a trained guide, McKay allowed DeMille to set his own pace. "He just wandered around and looked, and absorbed the spirit of the place," recalled Friberg. McKay's only theological explanation to DeMille was: "The purpose of the temple is to take man from physical man to spiritual man."[20]

During the two months of public tours, nearly 700,000 people toured the temple.[21] In mid-March 1956, McKay dedicated it. A month later, he returned to take part in the first endowment ceremony to be performed in the new temple. The ceremony also marked another first: "The session was very well conducted," noted McKay, "and for the first time in the history of the church the old-style presentation of the endowment ceremony was given by tape-recording rather than by persons enacting the different parts. It proved conclusively to us that the ceremony can be done very impressively, and that this manner of presentation will probably be used in all the Temples."[22]

THE OAKLAND TEMPLE

In 1934, the same year Heber J. Grant authorized the search for a temple site in southern California, he appointed another committee to look for a site in the San Francisco Bay area. The committee considered several sites, but their preference was not for sale. When the Los Angeles property was purchased in 1937, "the conclusion of the Church authorities [was] that they should not undertake to build two temples at the same time in California." Nonetheless, the local committee members kept an eye on the site, which they privately called "Temple Hill." Two weeks after the bombing of Pearl Harbor in December 1941, the owner put the land on the market.[23] Over a year passed before the sale was completed; and during April conference 1943, Eugene Hilton, president of the Oakland Stake, presented the deed to the First Presidency. McKay noted with satisfaction that the "New Temple" would "be constructed as soon as the exigencies of war are over."[24]

The exigencies of both World War II and the Korean War passed without further action being taken, and the delay nearly cost the church the site. In 1957, church leaders had to work swiftly to check an attempt to condemn the land for the building of a public high school. Stephen L Richards, McKay's first counselor, asked Senator Watkins to intervene on the church's behalf with California's Senator William F. Knowland. Watkins agreed to approach Knowland, a personal acquaintance, "at the first opportunity...and see if Senator Knowland could legitimately approach his father, publisher of the *Oakland Tribune,* and see if he could quietly advise the school board and the citizens committee to forego this action."[25]

Only three weeks later in a First Presidency meeting, McKay reported that the strategy had succeeded: "President Richards reported that he has confirmation in writing that the temple property in Oakland will not be sought as a site for a high school; and that he has asked Senator Watkins to convey to Senator Knowland an expression of appreciation for the assistance he seems to have rendered."[26]

Three years later, on September 25, 1960, McKay dedicated a new tri-stake center in Oakland. "Impressed that the people were ready for the Temple," he told the

Church Committee on Expenditures in January 1961 that "the time has come to start building the Oakland Temple."[27] Meeting with local stake presidencies that same month, he reminded them of a prophecy made by Brigham Young in 1847, in which he stated that "in the process of time, the shores of the Pacific may yet be overlooked from the Temple of the Lord." McKay then said "that it was for the purpose of fulfilling that prophecy that we had met on this occasion."[28] The Oakland Temple was completed in 1964, and dedicated by McKay under remarkable circumstances. (See chap. 15.)

TEMPLES IN EUROPE AND NEW ZEALAND

While the Los Angeles and Oakland temples were on the drawing boards well before McKay's tenure as church president began, the construction of temples in Europe and New Zealand was his initiative from the start. The move was unprecedented on two levels: It was the first time temples were constructed outside North America (including Hawaii) and the first time they were constructed where stakes did not already exist. It was a calculated risk on McKay's part, but he was confident that such temples would anchor church members in their native countries, thus curtailing emigration to the United States and allowing the creation of overseas stakes.

Eight months after becoming church president, McKay acted on a recommendation by Stayner Richards, president of the British Mission, to purchase property for a temple near London. He discussed the matter with his two counselors, who "were unanimously in favor of erecting a temple in Europe and felt that Great Britain should have the first temple in Europe."[29]

A month later, McKay expanded the initiative by proposing a second temple on the European continent. Germany would have been a logical choice, for it had the largest LDS population. However, the Cold War was an overriding concern because a Soviet invasion of Western Europe, which many feared and some felt was inevitable, would likely have come through East Germany. As a result, McKay proposed Switzerland, which in spite of an LDS population of fewer than 3,000, was "probably the safest country in Europe, and more accessible than England to most of the other European countries."[30]

At the same time that the church's largest temple was under construction in Los Angeles, plans for the European temples moved in the opposite direction. With the low concentration of LDS members in Europe, temples smaller than any yet constructed would be sufficient. McKay described the new style of temple in a meeting with the Quorum of the Twelve early in 1952:

It is not contemplated that an expensive edifice would be erected but that temples be built that would accommodate the people under a new plan whereby temple ceremonies can be presented in one room without moving from one room to another, utilizing modern inventions therefore. It is thought that one room might be used and the scenery changed as needed and seats adjusted to accommodate the situation. It is felt that such a building could be erected and adequately equipped for about the cost of one of our present meeting houses, namely, two hundred to two hundred fifty thousand dollars.[31]

Upon returning from a trip to select sites in England and Switzerland, McKay announced the rationale for the new temples in an *Improvement Era* article:

One of the steps which will contribute to the stability and growth of the Church in Europe is the decision to build temples to provide ordinances and blessings which have never before been made available in Europe.... For some time it has been felt that many of the recent emigrants from Europe, especially among the older age groups, would have been happier had they had a temple in Europe whereby they could perform the sacred ordinances for themselves and for their kindred dead, rather than to have to come to America for this privilege. There has been some concern, too, to give these good people the endowment in their native tongue.[32]

Several potential sites in Switzerland fell through, leading McKay to write to Samuel Bringhurst, president of the Swiss-Austrian Mission: "Ever since we made the announcement that a Temple would be built in Switzerland, I have sensed the possibility of serious opposition, and have prayed most earnestly that the Lord would overrule conditions so that the Church will secure the proper site for the Temple."[33]

A month later, McKay received Bringhurst's welcome news that he had finally purchased a suitable site. McKay replied, "Surely the Lord has had a directing hand in this, for after five months' negotiations for the former site, all efforts failed, and when this property came on the market the deal was closed within one week!"[34] McKay was enormously pleased with the prospects of the new temples and, in a joint meeting of the Twelve and the First Presidency, shared both his enthusiasm and his vision. According to the minutes:

President McKay said that he felt that the right thing has been done, that when we voted here to undertake this, we voted for something which is entirely new in Church history, carrying temples to the people in Europe, with the understanding that they will build up

strong branches, making it unnecessary for them to sell out and go to
the expense of coming here, and depriving many who cannot come
here of the privileges of the House of the Lord, and they are worthy
people. The President said we have assurances of the guidance and
inspiration of the Lord in everything that has been done, and he testified that he was convinced we are doing the right thing. It is
believed that the temple in Switzerland can be completed by May,
1955, probably be ready for dedication before the Los Angeles Temple. He thought that nothing would be so helpful to the Church in
Europe as the dedication of that temple, and probably the dedication
in Great Britain.[35]

Though McKay's report made it clear that he was working under inspiration,
he later made the case even more explicitly in a letter to a stake president in Logan,
Utah, stating, "Recently the Lord revealed the fact that temples should be taken
to foreign countries, so people unable to come to the temple might have opportunity of doing the work in their own land."[36]

Early in 1953, McKay summarized the plans underway for the two European
temples in a memo to the Building Committee and, for the first time, mentioned
the possibility of a third temple, this one in New Zealand. He summarized in his
diary: "I said we contemplate building a temple there [Switzerland] that will cost
probably $300,000 or $400,000, that will take care of all the ordinances as we now
have them. Such plans will make it possible for us to build temples in Switzerland
and Great Britain and probably New Zealand, and give the people of those lands
an opportunity to do their temple work, who will probably never get a chance to
come here."[37]

Stephen L Richards visited New Zealand later the same year and, without making announcements, took the local pulse regarding the desirability of a temple.
Upon his return, he described in a First Presidency meeting "the desire of the
people that a Temple be built in New Zealand because of the practical impossibil-
ity of the Maoris coming to Hawaii," the nearest existing temple.[38] A year later, in
December 1953, McKay dispatched Wendell B. Mendenhall, who in July 1955
would become chairman of the Church Building Committee, to New Zealand to
identify potential sites.[39] In February 1955 the church publicly announced plans for
the temple.[40]

Although the temple in England had been the first envisioned, problems in
obtaining a clear title delayed its completion until 1958. As a result, the Swiss Temple was the first to be dedicated, in 1955. While all temple dedications are unusual
events, McKay's son, Edward, reported that the Swiss Temple's dedication was
marked by

one of the most spiritual experiences I've ever had. Prior to the prayer that was given, Father gave a talk. The Tabernacle Choir, of course, sang. The music was just heavenly. Father talked, and he said, "There are many here in the audience who have passed on, those who were instrumental in the preparation for the building of this Temple. The veil is very thin. They are here." That night we were talking about this at the hotel, and I said, "Father, when you mentioned that there were spiritual beings there who had passed on, no one doubted it." He said, "Yes, and my father was there, too."[41]

THE WASHINGTON D.C. TEMPLE

McKay initiated three other temples that he did not live long enough to see completed. After the Saints were driven out of Nauvoo in 1846, no LDS temple stood east of the Mississippi River, reflecting the fact that the center of church membership lay squarely in the Rocky Mountains. By the latter half of the twentieth century, however, a combination of eastward LDS migration and successful proselytizing efforts led to high concentrations of LDS members in the East, particularly in the suburban Washington, D.C., area.

There was no formal protocol for initiating a request for a temple, so stake and mission presidents of the Washington, D.C., area, with the assent of Franklin D. Richards, an Assistant to the Twelve, improvised and began on their own a process of identifying a site. Hugh B. Brown, second counselor in the First Presidency, learned of their initiative while touring the New England Mission and reported the information to McKay late in 1961. McKay, displeased, replied that "the stake presidents and mission presidents have no jurisdiction in a matter of this kind."[42]

Six months later the president of the Washington D.C. Stake, Milan D. Smith, sent a telegram to the First Presidency, "urging consideration of the purchase of a temple site in and near Washington, D.C., since suitable sites are decreasing and costs are increasing." The problem for McKay, however, was that he had recently received appeals for temples in Ogden, Utah; Nauvoo, Illinois; Palmyra, New York; Atlanta, Georgia; and Sweden.[43] The church's building program was burgeoning under Mendenhall (see chap. 9), already siphoning off the church's cash flow; authorizing all of the requested temples, especially since the Oakland Temple was still under construction, made it uncertain when any new temples might be possible.[44]

With no assurances from the First Presidency, the local leaders identified a fifty-seven-acre wooded parcel overlooking Rock Creek Park, only a few miles into Maryland from Washington, D.C., as a suitable site. Milan Smith phoned Hugh B. Brown with the details; and in September 1962, the First Presidency considered the proposal to purchase the property. The asking price of about $12,500 per acre seemed reasonable, with First Counselor Henry D. Moyle pointing out that the church had recently paid $10,000 per acre for a chapel site in Holladay, Utah.

The location was more problematic, given competing requests from Georgia and New York. Brown argued that the mid-Atlantic location of Washington, D.C., would make the temple accessible for the entire East Coast. Brown also pointed out that hotelier J. Willard Marriott, a former president of the Washington D.C. Stake, was "very much enthusiastic over this site," to which Moyle replied, "I am in favor of it. I am not arguing against it.... We cannot go wrong by getting property if it is properly located." McKay was persuaded by their arguments: "If you Brethren think we should hold it, we had better do so." When Moyle asked about the probability of actually building a temple on the property at an unspecified time in the future, McKay replied, "I have no objection to having a temple in that area." He then instructed Brown to call Milan Smith. "Tell him to secure it, and to make no commitment, and not to call it a temple site." Moyle agreed with McKay saying that, for the time being, "this is just an investment." The meeting concluded with Moyle asking McKay if the purchase should go before the Expenditures Committee—composed of members of the Quorum of the Twelve—the same morning. "No, I think we had better not," replied McKay without giving a reason. And so the purchase was made without their knowledge.[45]

Six years after the purchase of the property, a delegation of church leaders from Washington, D.C., including Milan Smith and J. Willard Marriott, called on the First Presidency to propose the temple's construction. They presented charts and maps of the area east of the Mississippi River with an emphasis on the Atlantic seaboard, then focused on the site itself. Since its purchase, the Capital Beltway had been constructed, passing within one block of the property. The prominence of the site, elevated above the Beltway, would make it highly visible to hundreds of thousands of motorists daily, thus allowing the construction of a landmark. The site's central location would make it possible for 41,000 church members to drive to the temple and back again in one day. In addition to the other selling points, "Willard Marriott had indicated his full support and pledged a substantial sum of money to assist in the project... a half million dollars to start it out." The First Presidency expressed appreciation for the presentation but left "the matter...for further consideration and decision."[46]

Only one week later, however, the First Presidency discussed the proposal among themselves, and "President McKay then said that we should go forward with the project, announcing approval of it."[47] The following day, it was presented for the first time to the Quorum of the Twelve by N. Eldon Tanner and Alvin R. Dyer, with Tanner as spokesman. Neither McKay, who remained home upon his

physician's advice, nor Brown was present. McKay's diary entry, which was ex-
tracted from the minutes of the meeting, describes a frosty reception by some
members of the Twelve, particularly Harold B. Lee. Lee's vehement opposition to
changing the policy banning ordination of blacks (see chap. 4) likely served as the
basis for his objection:

> Elder Lee stated that there wasn't much that could be done about it,
> since it had been approved by the Presidency and this was like the
> Ogden and Provo Temples—the Quorum of the Twelve were merely
> informed that such were to be built. He stated that a Temple in Wash-
> ington D. C. was perhaps the poorest location in the East because of
> the tremendous amount of criminal disturbance in that area and the
> many Negroes that live in Washington and suggested that perhaps the
> Valley Forge area out of Philadelphia would be a more suitable place
> for the erection of a Temple. Elder Mark E. Petersen seemed to sus-
> tain the feelings of Elder Lee. Elder LeGrand Richards stated that he
> felt that a Temple at Washington was a proper location to serve the
> concentration of members in that area and other areas as well that
> would funnel into that point. The other members of the Quorum of
> the Twelve seemed non-committal and completely resolved [*sic*] to the
> fact that the President of the Church had made the decision for the
> erection of the Temple in Washington and therefore did not make
> any comments.[48]

Alvin R. Dyer, who had become an additional counselor in the First Presidency
in April 1968, was surprised at the harsh feelings of Lee and Petersen and suggested
to Tanner that they report the matter back to McKay, "that a re-confirmation be
asked for on the project in light of their opposition to it."[49] In a First Presidency
meeting the following morning, Dyer raised the issue. McKay responded, "After
listening to the comments by the brethren, I said that we should not hesitate to go
forward. President Brown asked me if it would be all right to ask Henry Smith [the
church's press liaison] to release the story and I said, 'Yes.'"[50]

David S. King, president of the Washington D.C. Temple during the early
1990s, commented on local views of the decision-making process: "The Washington Temple has reason to feel very kindly toward President McKay. He really
pushed that. I got my information from President Milan Smith and others that
President Lee was raising objections. He thought that the Blacks would be here
picketing and raising all kinds of trouble. He was opposed to the whole idea of a
temple here in Washington, but President McKay kept nudging it along. So, we
wouldn't have a temple here if it had not been for President McKay, as I understand it."[51]

McKay's resolve to move forward quickly with the project (he was ninety-five at the time) is clear in a First Presidency letter to church leaders in the nation's capital. Three days after deflecting Dyer's concerns, he announced: "Your recommendation has been approved and arrangements should go forward in the immediate future for the preparation of the plans and the breaking of the ground."[52] "Immediate future" was interpreted literally, and three days after sending the letter, McKay approved a groundbreaking ceremony for December 7, only two weeks away, even though not even a schematic drawing of the proposed building had been made.[53]

McKay's deteriorating health did not allow him to attend the groundbreaking ceremony, so he sent Hugh B. Brown to officiate, along with a message for the 4,500 people who attended the ceremony: "It is my great pleasure to be able to approve the erection of a House of the Lord to serve an area in which a Temple is so much needed." Apostle Ezra Taft Benson, who had served as the first president of the Washington D.C. Stake, echoed the satisfaction of many long-time local members when he recalled discussions "early in this century" in the home of Utah Senator Reed Smoot, where the prospect of a local temple was first raised.[54]

Four months after the groundbreaking ceremony, the First Presidency decided on the exterior design of the new temple, choosing a design created by architect Keith Wilcox, reminiscent of the Salt Lake Temple: "Several of the brethren expressed the thought that the temple with the six towers identifies itself with the Salt Lake Temple, which temple symbolizes the church throughout the world. The brethren present all favored the six tower structure and indicated that it could be seen from a long distance and particularly by people who would be traveling upon the freeways in that area."[55]

Indeed, as one drives on the outer loop of the Capital Beltway just beyond the Georgia Avenue exit and reaches the top of a slight incline, the white temple suddenly appears straight before the windshield, seemingly suspended in air. It has become one of the most famous landmarks in the nation's capital, so widely recognized that daily traffic reports, which used to identify Beltway traffic near "the Mormon Temple," now merely refer to "the Temple." McKay lived long enough to know what the temple would look like but died before it and two others in Utah were completed.

THE OGDEN AND PROVO TEMPLES

Ogden is within an hour's drive of the Salt Lake Temple, but for many years local residents had wished for a temple in their own city. By the time McKay became president, the growing population of northern Utah gave impetus to their desire.

Meeting in 1953 with stake presidents from Weber County, he noted their long-standing desire while moderating their enthusiasm:

> Several years ago a committee came from Ogden, giving figures show-ing the financial saving to the people of Ogden if we had a temple. They even went so far as to give a plan where the ordinances could be presented completely, saving time and all. It appealed to me at that time. To my surprise, the Building Committee and the Presidency already had a similar plan, and that plan will be used in Bern, Switzer-land, I hope, beginning this spring, and it will not cost more than $350,000. As far as Ogden is concerned, blessed are they who expect nothing, for they shall not be disappointed. If it should ever come to Ogden, however, wouldn't that up there be a wonderful place? Let us say nothing about this to the public.[56]

Six years later in another meeting, Thomas Smith, spokesman for the stake presidents of Weber County,

> said that they have heard indications that the Church is not ready to consider a temple in Ogden, but that they thought it would be wise to present the idea sometime to learn what President McKay's reac-tion might be. He said that the basis of the interest in a temple in Ogden is the convenience to the greatly increasing population, and the desire to encourage a larger number of people to participate in tem-ple work. He mentioned also the fact that the Logan and Salt Lake Temples are very busy, and are usually crowded. He said some of the people have been obliged to wait three hours for an opportunity to go through the Temple when they go to Logan or to Salt Lake.[57]

McKay's response this time was even less encouraging, perhaps because of the financial commitment the church had already made to temples recently completed or under construction in Switzerland, Los Angeles, England, New Zealand, and Oakland:

> President McKay said there are many places in greater need of a tem-ple than Ogden, and that no doubt the crowded conditions reported in the Logan and Salt Lake Temples can probably be overcome by introducing the new procedures. He explained that the new presen-tation is used in new temples in Switzerland, New Zealand, and Lon-don, and in part in the Los Angeles Temple.... He expressed the opinion that the crowded condition in the Salt Lake and Logan Tem-ples can be overcome in part by introducing the more efficient way of conducting the sessions.[58]

He concluded the meeting by saying what his audience had hoped not to hear: "I believe we will have to wait."

The issue lay dormant for another five years. Then, at the same time the Oakland Temple was completed, Lawrence Olpin, president of the Lorin Farr Stake, attempted to resuscitate the issue by offering to donate his own property as a temple site. Although no temples were then under construction, mismanagement of other building projects had placed the church in a financial bind. (See chap. 9.) The First Presidency "decided to express appreciation to President Olpin for his offer, and to tell him that we have no plans to build a Temple in Ogden."[59]

By 1967 the cash flow crisis had been resolved, and McKay began to consider not only a temple for Ogden, but also one for Provo. Mark Garff, chairman of the Building Department, suggested that "because of the students at the Brigham Young University and their travel to the Manti Temple in great numbers, he [McKay] might consider a small Temple in Provo and one in Ogden." Alvin R. Dyer, alarmed that Garff would preempt what he felt to be the prerogative of the president, "interjected the thought there should be no Temples built anywhere except those designated by revelation to the President of the Church." Garff held his ground, answering that "his suggestion was based on what his own personal observations and thinking are and he thought it well to mention this matter to the President."[60] McKay sided with Garff, and asked him to investigate further and make a report.

Three months later, Garff and his staff made their report to the First Presidency. Garff noted that "traffic in the Manti and Logan Temples is becoming so acute that it becomes necessary either to remodel those Temples or build new ones." He advised constructing new temples if for no other reason than economics, noting that remodeling the old temples would cost nearly twice as much as building the new ones. His assistant, Fred Baker, followed with an analysis of the workload of the Salt Lake Temple, noting that in 1966 it was 250 percent of what it had been in 1950. Church Architect Emil Fetzer concluded with a presentation on architectural options. The timing was right. McKay approved the concept and authorized Garff and his associates "to go forward and make provision for the location of the new Temples, prepare their plans, and so far as possible, have the same plan for both Temples."[61]

Unlike the other Utah temples, all four of which were architectural monuments representing the best of nineteenth-century Utah craftsmanship, the Ogden and Provo temples were to be strictly utilitarian. Emil Fetzer, who made virtually identical designs, recalled in detail in a later interview McKay's charge to him and how he fulfilled it:

He said to me, "Brother Fetzer, I'd like you to design an *economical* and *functional* temple for Ogden and for Provo." Those were my instructions. He didn't say they were going to be this big or this high—he said they were to be economical and functional temples. He said, "We can't continue to build huge monuments. We have to have temples that the membership can use to do efficient temple work."...

A week after this assignment had been given to me by President McKay, it was necessary for Brother [Fred] Baker and me to go to Europe on the meetinghouse program.... After we had settled in our seats and had a little meal at midnight, Brother Baker and I started to talk about this assignment that I had to design these temples.... All of a sudden it was in my mind as if I were walking through a building, and I started to describe to Brother Baker what I was seeing— the recommend desk, the inner foyer, the locker room, and then on the upper floor the sealing rooms. But the most important thing was on the floor above the sealing rooms. There was a central room surrounded by a cluster of six ordinance rooms.... I knew exactly how it was functioning, from the way I saw it. This was a very intriguing thing, a central Celestial Room surrounded by a cluster of six ordinance rooms. The idea was that the whole ceremony would be in one room, instead of going from room to room like in the Salt Lake Temple.... Well, when I was telling Brother Baker about this plan, the Celestial Room surrounded by a cluster of rooms, I looked out the window of the plane and it was daylight, and we were landing in Frankfurt. We had been discussing this temple all night long on the plane.

When I got home I sat down at my desk, took a clean piece of paper, and drew the first line that eventually became the Ogden and Provo Temples. It wasn't that hard to put this plan together, because I had walked through it in my mind. I'd seen it in my mind, and I knew exactly how this temple was organized and how it was going to function.[62]

Having addressed the mandate of functional temples, Fetzer made them economical by taking a minimalist approach on the exteriors. The result was not universally acclaimed, either in his initial presentation to the First Presidency or later:

I took the perspective of the building and put it up on the easel. You know how Ogden and Provo are, they are a little different than anything else. When I put it up, there was just a gasp! You could hear them suck in their breath. They were surprised and amazed at the design of the temple. After they took in their gasps, one of the counselors said to President McKay, "Does this design offend you?" I thought, "Oh boy, I could have said it a lot of ways, but that isn't the way I would have said it." Can you imagine that? It just about floored me. Well, as soon as he said that, there was a deathly silence in the room. Nobody said anything, and I think we all stopped breathing. In my mind I was turning it over, "How do I change this design to make it look like the Salt Lake Temple?" There was just this deathly silence, and it seemed like we all stopped breathing. "Does this design offend you?" Oh, I'll never forget that!

Then all of a sudden President McKay, in a strong and firm voice—before that you had to listen very carefully to hear what he was saying—said, "No, I like it very much." And all of a sudden I was on the side of the majority! It really didn't matter what anybody else said; the Prophet of the Lord had accepted it. That finished it! We went along those lines and built them like that.

Fetzer had succeeded in fulfilling McKay's charge to build temples that were both functional and economical. Addressing a group of General Authorities during the construction process, Fetzer confidently predicted that the two smaller temples would be able to accommodate as much ordinance work as the Salt Lake Temple, which at the time was accounting for one-third of temple ordinances in the entire church: "They all laughed! 'Those little temples will never do the amount of work that the Salt Lake Temple will do!' At that time the Salt Lake Temple was doing about 50,000 endowments a month, a great deal. A month after the Ogden Temple was dedicated [in January 1972], they did 75,000 endowments in one month! And they've done more than that since then. That was the first time that the Salt Lake Temple wasn't the top temple as far as endowments were concerned. It was #2. And then when Provo came on line and started going [in February 1972], Salt Lake became #3."

Fetzer's fundamental innovation of having multiple ordinance rooms—as few as two and as many as six—opening into a single celestial room has since become the central interior feature in new temples throughout the world. "Basically, everything that has been built since that time has a kernel of the Ogden and Provo Temples," he noted.

REBUILDING THE NAUVOO TEMPLE

While no other temples were initiated during McKay's lifetime, several were contemplated. While visiting Tonga in 1955, he told church members, "You know what I saw today in vision? A Temple on one of these islands where the members of the Church may go and receive the blessings of the Temple of God. You are entitled to it. We are not so far apart now."[63]

Four years later, in discussing South Africa with his counselors, he mused, "I think we should have a temple there some day. It is a long way for these people to go to a temple and the distances are great in that country and under present conditions they are obliged to live and die without having the blessings of the Temple and realize the significance of them."[64]

McKay also considered requests for temples in Germany, Sweden, Wyoming, Washington state, Texas,[65] and, notably, Nauvoo. The Nauvoo Temple was destroyed by fire shortly after the exodus of the Saints in 1846, and the entire city was ignored by the church for over a century. By the early 1960s, however, interest in historic Nauvoo had revived, due largely to the land acquisitions and reconstructions of LeRoy Kimball, a physician. Kimball was a descendant of Heber C. Kimball, a Nauvoo resident and member of the first Quorum of the Twelve Apostles in 1835. LeRoy Kimball purchased and restored the Heber C. Kimball home at his own expense. In a First Presidency meeting on May 15, 1962, McKay decided to organize Nauvoo Restoration, Inc., with LeRoy Kimball as president. Funded by the church, NRI's task was the purchase and preservation of historic Nauvoo properties. The incorporation documents were signed the following month.[66] The corporation then worked with experts from Colonial Williamsburg to plan the restoration and reconstruction of historic buildings in the city.

Although NRI had not completely restored any buildings by the time of McKay's death in 1970, interest in Nauvoo steadily increased following the organization's incorporation. By 1967, visitation by tourists stood at 110,000.[67] Church service missionaries staffed the historic sites, an effort paralleled by the Community of Christ on the sites it owned. The church had purchased the now-vacant temple site in December 1960,[68] maintained the lawn over it, built a fence around it, and in 1971 constructed a visitors center to interpret the site.

In January 1962 the First Presidency listened to a strategic plan that they had commissioned for the restoration of Nauvoo. After the presentation they met privately and "considered the advisability of this restoration." McKay recorded their deliberations:

> I said that the first decision to make before this project is undertaken
> is the location of a temple in the east, whether or not there should
> be a temple in Nauvoo and also one in Washington. President [Henry]
> Moyle stated that the only justification for spending the money
> necessary to restore any part of Nauvoo would be to restore the
> temple there. I said the restoration of the temple is the whole question before us, and transportation to the temple is another.... From

Mr. [Harold] Fabian's information at present, it does not seem to be an accessible and advisable center for a temple for our people.[69]

McKay elected to table the proposal of rebuilding the temple, while at the same time approving the restoration of other Nauvoo buildings. Nonetheless, he noted his vision of what the eventual restoration should be, saying, "I thought [the temple] should be restored as near to what it was as can be."[70] Forty years later under the church's fifteenth president, Gordon B. Hinckley, a Nauvoo Temple erected on the original temple's "footprint" and housing an abbreviated reproduction of its second-floor assembly room, was dedicated in June 2002.[71]

A TEMPLE TO SAIL ON THE WATERS

One proposal for a temple was unprecedented, both geographically and architecturally. Early in 1967, McKay asked Mark Garff, chairman of the Building Committee, "to look over the temples and to come back with a recommendation as to what our program should be in the matter of providing new temples and how we could accommodate our people who wish to go to the temples."[72] To study the matter, Garff traveled to Alaska, Hong Kong, the Philippines, New Zealand, and Australia—all areas with significant numbers of Latter-day Saints who were thousands of miles from the nearest temple. By his calculation, 30 percent (785,000) of church members had no access to temples. In response to their need, Garff made a novel proposal to McKay. According to his memo of the meeting, Garff

> asked the President to listen me out and see if I was foolish in what I was suggesting. He said he would be glad to listen and I told him I had just returned from the Far East; this is about the only time I have left my desk for the two and half years I have been working for President McKay and in my mind I tried to conceive a plan whereby we could bring Temple work to our people. I said cautiously to President McKay: "If you think I am out of bounds I want you to tell me, but I am proposing to you now, that the Church obtain or build a ship sufficient in size to run the oceans and we equip this ship as a temple ship; that we take the ship and outfit it as a temple, then take the ship into the ports and harbors where our people live. We could do this around the entire continent of South America, Europe, along the coast of China, Japan, Australia and even Africa if we wanted to." I was sure the cost would not amount to any more than what the cost of some of our temples has been. I suggested to the President that we do not have the money to build temples all over the world and it would be an impossibility because our funds are limited and if we

followed this procedure we could get at least those who want their
endowments done while they are still alive, we could move to the
ports where we would dock this ship; otherwise it would be impossible for them to have their own endowments and we might carry it even
further than their own endowments and move on to doing work for
the dead, making this a continuous tour of where there are people
needing the blessing of the temple and the holy endowment. After I
explained to the President my thinking he said to me: "That is not
foolish thinking and I want you to pursue this thought and pursue the
feasibility of it and make a report to me." He seemed to be greatly in-
trigued with the idea, he seemed to grasp it very quickly and thought
it would be a good idea, so I am going to pursue it a little further as
fast as my time will allow.[73]

Nothing more was said on the matter until Garff and his colleagues on the
Building Committee reported their proposal to the entire First Presidency almost
a year later on October 11, 1968. Repeating what he had earlier said to McKay, Garff
then estimated that a suitable ship could be purchased and remodeled for about two
million dollars, and operated for about a half-million dollars annually, "less money
than it costs us to build a temple anywhere in the United States or
elsewhere." Fred Baker, Garff's assistant, added that the ship they envisioned—a
thousand-ton vessel—would be able to sail both the high seas and the large rivers,
including the Mississippi and Missouri, and repeat its circuit every year or so.

Although McKay earlier had responded favorably to the idea, reaction from his
three counselors present (Tanner, Dyer, and Joseph Fielding Smith) was less than
enthusiastic. Smith "raised the question that Temples were to be constructed
according to revelation in Stakes of Zion," an argument that overlooked the fact
that he and his colleagues on the Twelve had approved temples for England,
Switzerland, and New Zealand where no stakes then existed.

Alvin R. Dyer "raised the question as to the cursing that has been placed upon
the waters in the last days, as to whether it would be proper in the light of that statement by the Prophet to construct a Temple to sail on the waters."[74] He also made
a curious point that was completely at odds with the notion of building *any* new
temples when he asked "why we should be so pressing and introducing such
urgency methods to get the Temple work done for people in remote places since
most of the Temple work will be accomplished in the Millennium." The meeting
concluded on a lukewarm note, with the First Presidency agreeing "that the matter was deserving of careful consideration," but stopping short of authorizing a
search for a ship.[75]

About two weeks later the First Presidency considered a query from Fred Baker about the idea's continuing viability. He reported that "a vessel is currently available in Europe at an extremely advantageous price which they would like to consider if there is a possibility that the brethren would approve such a project." McKay responded, without elaboration, that "as far as I was concerned we are not considering this proposition; that therefore they should not consider taking this vessel."[76] The subject was never discussed again.

Temple Marriage

In addition to building temples, McKay focused his attention on the ordinances carried out within them. One of the first items that landed on his desk when he became church president was the procedure for "cancellation of sealings" following a civil divorce. By tradition, only the church president could authorize such a cancellation. It was the bitter mirror image of a temple marriage and its promise of eternal union of husband and wife, and McKay referred to it as "the gloomiest duty I have in the Church."[77] Each case required extensive research and a recommendation. Joseph Anderson, secretary to the First Presidency, had previously written each report and recommendation for the church president's attention. However, McKay felt that the task was sufficiently important to merit the attention of a member of the Quorum of the Twelve and assigned it to Apostle Albert E. Bowen, formerly an attorney, in April 1951.[78]

In April 1954, McKay assigned Hugh B. Brown, also a former attorney, to the same task. Brown

> asked President McKay to advise me as to the grounds for divorce [i.e., cancellation of sealing], and as to what I was to look for in the investigation preparatory to making my recommendation to him. He explained that of course the initial fundamental reason for temple cancellation was immorality on the part of one of the parties concerned, but that was not the only cause. He explained that where a couple had learned that they could not live together, and where they had obtained a civil divorce and...there was no hope of reconciliation, and especially where no children were involved, "you should recommend that the cancellation be granted."[79]

Brown invested heavily in the assignment, and his performance was likely a factor in his subsequent calling to the First Presidency. Two years after beginning his work, Brown received a glowing note from McKay: "Having just completed [*sic*] most of this day on applications for cancellation of sealings, I feel impelled to send you this note of appreciation for your masterful attention to this arduous duty.

Your careful, intelligent consideration in each case merits the highest commendation and praise. Your assistance to me in this important phase of Church work is immeasurable. Please be assured of my deep gratitude. God bless you."[80]

Despite Brown's help, however, the task remained arduous for McKay, and he frequently spent Sundays at his office where, in the absence of distractions, he could devote uninterrupted attention to the cases. A diary notation from a Sunday in 1955 was typical: "Spent the hours between 10 A.M. and 7 P.M. at the office, with the exception of the dinner period, going over requests for cancellation of Temple sealings. Labored through more than 25 such requests with all the papers pertaining thereto—a very depressing experience."[81]

The problem never went away and, indeed, increased as the church grew and as the divorce rate rose. As McKay dealt with case after case, he grappled with the issue of how better to prepare church members for marriage, as well as the other ordinances that make up the overall temple experience: "More thought should be given on the part of bishops in letting the people understand what it means to go to the temple and enter into eternal covenants and then go out and violate them. It is a great thing to be sealed in the House of the Lord for time and all eternity— a wonderful blessing—and some of our men do not realize it."[82]

McKay's desire to enhance the temple marriage experience was manifest in the way he conducted the ceremony. Monroe McKay, a cousin, recalled President McKay's officiating at the wedding of Monroe's brother, Gunn, and Donna Biesinger:

> His performance of temple weddings was a thing of beauty. His commentaries were inspiring, but not flamboyant. They were beautiful. He made marriage really feel like a true sacrament, not just a ritual. My guess is that he introduced the exchanging of rings in the temple, as a side thing. He said at Gunn's wedding, "This is not a part of the temple ceremony, but we have recognized that people do exchange rings, and if you'll step over here, away from the altar, you may exchange rings." He probably even commented about what in society generally is the ritual meaning of the purity of the gold, and the perfect circle that represents your love, and so on. It would be my guess, although I don't know any way to document this, that he was probably the first to do that, because it is consistent with what he did in recognizing that there is more to the Church than just theology and marching down the line, that it's a whole thing, that we have to appeal to all that which is good.[83]

THE ENDOWMENT CEREMONY

Underlying temple marriage is the core of the temple experience, the endowment. A ritualized depiction of humankind's journey from the premortal existence through earth life and beyond, McKay referred to it as "one of the most beautiful things ever given to man," yet lamented that "there are very few people in the Church who comprehend it."[84] He was particularly concerned that the young people in the church, including those participating in the endowment just prior to being married in the temple, did so without comprehending its meaning or being jarred by the symbolism of the ritual. He lamented with his counselors "that many of our young people who go through the Temples gain a wrong impression, that they do not obtain a proper understanding of the Temple work and sometimes lose their faith by reason of the Temple ceremonies."[85]

His concern stemmed, in part, from his own first encounter with the endowment ceremony, which had not been favorable. With rare candor, he once spoke of the disappointment of that encounter:

> Do you remember when you first went through the House of the Lord? I do. And I went out disappointed. Just a young man, out of college, anticipating great things when I went to the Temple. I was disappointed and grieved, and I have met hundreds of young men and young women since who had that experience. I have now found out why. There are two things in every Temple: mechanics, to set forth certain ideals, and symbolism, what those mechanics symbolize. I saw only the mechanics when I first went through the Temple. I did not see the spiritual. I did not see the symbolism of spirituality. Speaking plainly, I saw men, physical state, which offended me. That is a mechanic of washing.... I was blind to the great lesson of purity behind the mechanics. I did not hear the message of the Lord, "Be ye clean who bear the vessels of the Lord." I did not hear that eternal truth, "Cleanliness is next to godliness." The symbolism was lost entirely.... And so with the anointing, following the washing. Do you see the symbolism?... How many of us young men saw that? We thought we were big enough and with intelligence sufficient to criticize the mechanics of it and we were blind to the symbolism, the message of the spirit. And then that great ordinance, the endowment. The whole thing simple in the mechanical part of it, but sublime and eternal in its significance.[86]

By the time McKay became church president, he had over a half-century of experience with the endowment ceremony, and thus was intimately familiar with its mechanics. But his concern with making the symbolic content of the ceremony more accessible to church members, particularly the young people, led him to review again and again the mechanics with the goal "of subordinating the mechanics to the important mission of the Temple, the impressing of each member with the fact that he is an important factor in God's Plan of Salvation for the human family."[87] Periodic diary entries indicate the intensity with which he approached this task: "My principal purpose in going through [participating in an endowment ceremony] that day was to observe the details of the ceremony and to study the mechanics of the presentation of the endowments." "Spent most of the day in the Salt Lake Temple considering and studying the Temple Ceremony. Will make recommendations covering several items in the presentation of the Temple Ceremony." "From 10 o'clock until 2 P.M. I was in the Salt Lake Temple, studying the ceremony for endowments." "I had planned to drive down to Salt Lake so that I could go to the Salt Lake Temple in order to study and make corrections on the master copy of the endowment ceremony."[88]

In 1959, after years of studying the formal procedures of the endowment, he finally introduced changes into the ceremony that would subordinate the physical aspects of the ceremony to the symbolic. Speaking to a group of stake presidents in Ogden, he commented on the alterations. According to the minutes of the meeting, "President McKay then briefly explained the new procedure as helping to overcome the consciousness of the people of the mechanics of the temple service, and in helping young people especially to understand the symbolism and the significance of the service. He briefly reviewed the purpose of the services to show the progress of men from the level of animal interests to spiritual forces which mold eternal life."[89]

12

CONFRONTATION WITH COMMUNISM

Throughout his long tenure as a General Authority, David O. McKay was consistently opposed to Communism. So, uniformly, were his fellow General Authorities. Ironically, once he had become president of the church, opposition to Communism became a seriously divisive issue among the Mormons. On the one hand, McKay gave his special blessing to Ezra Taft Benson as an opponent of Communism, enabling this strong-willed apostle to propagate his ultra-right-wing views among church members—views that included an endorsement of the John Birch Society, founded in Indianapolis, Indiana, on December 9, 1958, by Massachusetts candy maker Robert Welch. On the other hand, McKay also responded to General Authorities who, despite their own opposition to Communism, took exception to the extremism of Benson and the John Birch Society. These included Apostles Joseph Fielding Smith and Harold B. Lee, as well as Hugh B. Brown and N. Eldon Tanner, McKay's counselors in the First Presidency. Neither Benson nor his protesting colleagues among the apostles ever achieved a clear upper hand with the aging prophet. As a result, both Latter-day Saints who endorsed the extreme views of the John Birch Society and those who opposed them found reason to believe the prophet was on their side, and the divisive issue remained unresolved until McKay's death in 1970, when his successor, Joseph Fielding Smith, effectively silenced Benson on the subject.

THE INDIVIDUAL AND FREE AGENCY

McKay initially greeted the Russian revolution of 1917 with optimism, telling a general conference audience, "It looks as if Russia will have a government 'by the people, of the people, and for the people.'"[1] However, as Vladimir Lenin came to power later that year and imposed a Marxist rule on the nation, McKay saw that Communism was a threat to democracy and freedom. As he assumed his duties within the First Presidency in 1934 he was tutored on this threat by his ecclesiastical superior, First Counselor J. Reuben Clark Jr., whose many years of service in the State Department gave him a broad exposure to world politics. In 1936 the two counselors joined with President Heber J. Grant to issue the first LDS policy statement regarding Communism, a statement that would be cited repeatedly in coming decades:

> The Church does not interfere, and has no intention of trying to interfere, with the fullest and freest exercise of the political franchise of its members, under and within our Constitution....
>
> But Communism is not a political party nor a political plan under the Constitution; it is a system of government that is the opposite of our Constitutional government, and it would be necessary to destroy our government before communism could be set up in the United States.
>
> Since Communism, established, would destroy our American Constitutional government, to support communism is treasonable to our free institutions, and no patriotic American citizen may become either a communist or supporter of communism. . . .
>
> Communism being thus hostile to loyal American citizenship and incompatible with true Church membership, of necessity no loyal American citizen and no faithful Church member can be a Communist.[2]

Throughout the decade McKay remained convinced that Communism was a greater threat than the rising power of Germany. Writing to a correspondent as the 1940s dawned, he made it clear that he saw Communism as a clear and present danger, one that had already begun to infiltrate American society: "Communist rats are working here in the United States and are gnawing at the very vitals of our government, and I wish every one of them could be sent to Russia where he belongs."[3]

When the attack on Pearl Harbor brought World War II to America, Japan and Germany became an immediate threat and McKay's wartime rhetoric focused on them. In the first general conference after the attack, McKay decried war in principle but noted that there is one condition on which a righteous nation is justified in going to war: "To deprive an intelligent human being of his free agency is to commit the crime of the ages.... So fundamental in man's eternal progress is his inherent right to choose, that the Lord would defend it even at the price of war."[4] A common thread connecting wartime Germany and Japan with Soviet Communism was that all three systems deprived humankind of free agency, a gift from God that in McKay's view was second only to life itself. Time after time over the next three decades, McKay returned to the theme that the primary evil of Communism was its denial to the individual of free agency.

Following the war, McKay resumed his anti-Soviet rhetoric. Speaking on the "Church-of-the-Air" radio broadcast program in July 1947, he said, "Today America is reputedly the only nation in the world capable of sustaining western civilization. Opposed to her is Russia.... There can be no question about the outcome of the anticipated ominous clash, which we earnestly hope and pray will never come."[5] Addressing general conference the following spring, he said: "The choice today is between dictatorship with the atheistic teachings of communism, and the doctrine of the restored gospel of Jesus Christ, obedience to which alone can make us free."[6]

McKay's primary responsibility as second counselor in the First Presidency was supervising the church's forty-six missions worldwide; and as the 1940s came to a close, he watched anxiously as the Iron Curtain began to choke off church activity in Czechoslovakia, the only mission headquartered in a Communist bloc country.[7] In a move that forced the church's hand, Czech police arrested two LDS missionaries early in 1950, alleging that they had entered a restricted area.[8] The missionaries were held incommunicado for three weeks, and it gradually became apparent that their release was contingent upon the church's closing the mission.[9] This quid pro quo was a bitter pill for McKay to swallow; and a month after closing the mission, he remarked in his April 1950 conference address, "Every member of the Church should take a lesson from what has occurred in that communistically dominated land."[10]

The memory of Czechoslovakia was still fresh when McKay received news that carried even more ominous implications for his missionary portfolio: the invasion of South Korea by Communist North Korea on June 25, 1950. The drafting of young men greatly reduced the supply of missionaries, and the threat of an invasion of Hong Kong obliged McKay to instruct the mission president to abandon the Chinese Mission and move his remaining missionaries to Hawaii.[11] Furthermore, fear of an imminent Russian invasion of western Europe clouded McKay's plans for missionaries there.

Thus, in the year preceding his elevation to church president, McKay had to confront three assaults on his beliefs because of Communism: the forced abandonment of the Czechoslovak Mission, the preemptive abandonment of the Chinese Mission, and the reduction by over two-thirds of the missionary force. In his first interview after becoming president, he warned, "A third World War is inevitable unless Communism is soon subdued. Communism yields to nothing but force."[12]

In 1952, the first year of his presidency, McKay traveled to Europe to select sites for the first LDS temples outside of North America. Upon his return he reported that the trip "was a glorious one and that everything is promising and hopeful except for the threat of Communism."[13] Speaking to the First Presidency and Quorum of the Twelve, he used even stronger rhetoric. According to the minutes, "President McKay said we are facing Satan himself. They are anti-Christ. They want to destroy Christianity...[and] it looked to him as though there is only one way to meet them and that is by force, the only thing they understand."[14]

POLITICAL ASCENDANCY OF EZRA TAFT BENSON

The year 1952 had dual significance for McKay's confrontation with Communism. During that year, his trip to Europe made him an eyewitness to the ills of·Communism and Socialism and strengthened his resolve to battle both systems. Also during that year, the apostle destined to become McKay's staunchest ally in the battle, Ezra Taft Benson, began his political ascendancy.

Benson had entered the national spotlight in 1939 when he accepted a position in Washington, D.C., as executive secretary of the National Council of Farmer Cooperatives.[15] He rose in prominence over the next four years, at one point appearing on the cover of *Business Week*,[16] but his political career was temporarily curtailed by George Albert Smith's call in July 1943 to serve in the Quorum of the Twelve Apostles.

Benson's desire to combine political activities with his church calling was not unprecedented, for Apostle Reed Smoot had been elected to five terms in the U.S. Senate (1903–33) after being called to the Quorum of the Twelve. In August 1952, Benson approached the First Presidency for permission to serve as chair of the American Institute of Cooperation. His request was approved on condition that "he does not devote so much of his time to other interests that the Twelve would be deprived of his help."[17] It would not be long, however, before Benson accepted without a similar restriction an even more prestigious position as U.S. Secretary of Agriculture in the cabinet of the newly elected Dwight D. Eisenhower.

The latitude that McKay allowed Benson in this position is explained by his fervor for Eisenhower. That McKay was a Republican was not widely known. (See chap. 13.) Only a week prior to the 1952 presidential election, a church member called McKay's secretary, Clare Middlemiss, and said, "A group of us have had an argument regarding whether President McKay is a Republican or a Democrat, and we wonder if you will tell us." Middlemiss referred the caller to McKay's nonpartisan statement at the conclusion of the October general conference and added, "Therefore he is not proclaiming himself publicly" as a member of either party.[18]

Nonetheless, McKay was a Republican and privately rejoiced when Dwight Eisenhower won the election. The morning after the election he noted, "We were all thrilled with the News. In my opinion, it is the greatest thing that has happened in a hundred years for our country."[19] It was not surprising, then, that McKay responded favorably two weeks later when newly reelected Senator Arthur V. Watkins (R-Utah) "told me that Elder Ezra Taft Benson is being considered by General Eisenhower for the position of Secretary of Agriculture, and wondered if he would be permitted to accept the position should it be offered to him. I said yes that I thought he would be permitted to accept."[20]

The following morning McKay and Benson arrived in the parking lot of the Church Administration Building at the same time. According to Benson's son, Reed, "President McKay spotted my father and said to him, 'Elder Benson, I received a very important phone call last night, and my mind is clear on this matter. If this job is offered to you in the proper spirit, you are to take it.'"[21] Three days later, President-elect Eisenhower announced his selection of Benson, and in January 1953 Benson began an eight-year term as Secretary of Agriculture. Upon hearing the news, a reporter called McKay. "He desired to know if the report were true that Brother Benson would be given a leave of absence from his Church duties. I told him this was correct."[22]

At Benson's request, McKay bestowed on him a formal blessing that Benson thereafter considered a mandate to fight Communism by whatever means he chose: "We seal upon you the blessings of. . .sound judgment, clear vision, that you might see afar the needs of this country; vision that you might see, too, the enemies who would thwart the freedoms of the individual as vouchsafed by the Constitution,. . .and may you be fearless in the condemnation of these subversive influences, and strong in your defense of the rights and privileges of the Constitution."[23]

During the years Benson served in Eisenhower's cabinet, he avoided controversy regarding Communism, although he quickly became a lightning rod over agricultural policy. Often under fire from others,[24] he nonetheless had McKay's unwavering support and admiration. Indeed, McKay wrote in his diary, "I suppose it is not overstating the fact when I say that only the present responsibilities of the [U.S.] President himself exceed those which Brother Benson is carrying."[25]

MCCARTHY'S CRUSADE AGAINST COMMUNISM

McKay's focus on Communism remained sharp during the eight years that Benson worked in Washington. At a 1953 meeting of national executives of the Boy Scouts of America, he spoke of a death struggle between religion and Communism: "Today two mighty forces are battling for the supremacy for the world. The destiny of mankind is in the balance. It is a question of God and liberty, or atheism and slavery. The success of Communism means the destruction of Religion."[26]

The following year, at a time when the anti-Communist crusade reached a fever pitch, McKay gained national attention with a statement that ultimately proved prophetic. The *Los Angeles Times* reported: "People under Communist domination will some day rise against their rulers, the world leader of the Mormon church predicted today. White-haired Elder David O. McKay, Salt Lake City, said free will— the freedom to choose between right and wrong—is the people's most valuable possession. 'No power on earth,' he said, 'can take this freedom away.'"[27]

At about the same time that McKay made this statement, Senator Joseph McCarthy (R-Wisconsin) came under attack for employing extreme measures in his crusade against Communism. McKay's reaction was to support McCarthy. In June 1954, referring to "the farce that is going on now in Washington between McCarthy and the Army," he told his counselors and the Quorum of the Twelve that "the Communistic influence is being exerted there to lessen the influence of men who would ferret out the enemies in the high places of our government."[28] As the summer of 1954 wore on, however, and the extent of McCarthy's improprieties became evident, McKay switched sides on the issue.

Perhaps McKay's change of heart was facilitated by the fact that one of his Mormon friends, Senator Arthur V. Watkins (R-Utah), reluctantly accepted from Vice President Richard Nixon the assignment to chair the bipartisan committee investigating the censure charges against McCarthy. "In my more than 80 years with daily encounters and exchanges with people of diverse opinions," Watkins wrote in his memoirs, "I have never suffered such intense and continuing distress."[29] Nonetheless, Watkins's fairness in chairing the committee engendered respect from many quarters. None was more sincere than McKay, who shortly after the censure vote in early December, wrote to Watkins: "Now that your victory is won, permit me to extend to you many hearty congratulations and high commendation for your clarity, sound judgment, and true dignity manifested throughout the entire hearing and the final disposition of this most difficult case. You have won merited honor to yourself, retained the prestige of the Senate, and brought credit to your State and to the Nation."[30]

Watkins gratefully responded: "In all sincerity I want you to know that I appreciate that expression from you more than anyone in the country, not even excluding President Eisenhower."[31]

Even though McKay backed away from McCarthy's extremism, he remained fervent in his own opposition to Communism. When the Soviets forcefully put down the Hungarian revolt in November 1956, McKay sided with the Hungarians, who "should be called 'patriots' rather than 'rebels.'"[32]

In November 1957 McKay received a visit from Massachusetts Senator John F. Kennedy, who had already made known his intention to run for U.S. president in 1960. McKay asked Kennedy about the future of the Soviet Union. "Would the system break up first, or would it have to come to a clash of arms?" Kennedy replied that he expected to see continuing Soviet expansionism and that he did not expect to see Communism break up, since there was no alternative system to replace it. McKay responded that he could not see how the system could continue indefinitely. "They are fundamentally wrong. Free agency is inherent in every individual. Rule by force has been fought against by men throughout history." Kennedy was more realistic: "They have the power to continue. Their prospects for the immediate future are bright."[33]

McKay's philosophical objections to Communism were twofold: it was atheistic, and it robbed humankind of free agency, a principle that for McKay was of fundamental importance. He was willing to allow some curtailment of free agency, however, if limitations were necessary to fight Communism. Meeting with Stanley Tracy, a former assistant to FBI Director J. Edgar Hoover, McKay lamented Chief Justice Earl Warren's recent condemnation of Hoover for engaging in wiretapping: "I am in sympathy with Hoover in this regard, and think that sometimes it is necessary.... I look upon Communism as an enemy, whose sole purpose is destruction of Capitalism and our form of government, and the use of wiretapping is justifiable in the preservation of our government."[34]

But McKay's opposition to Communism became more complicated because of Ezra Taft Benson's activities. Benson returned to full-time activity as a member of the Quorum of the Twelve in January 1961, but he did not abandon his political activities. Ernest L. Wilkinson, president of Brigham Young University, noted in his diary after Benson spoke at the university in May 1961: "Presided at devotional, at which I introduced Elder Ezra Taft Benson. He gave a fine talk. It is apparent, however, it is very difficult for him to divorce himself from the active politics in which he has been engaged, and get into his work again as a member of the Quorum of the Twelve. While I agreed with every word that he said, I suspect there were some Democrats who did not, and he took one-third of his time talking on current political problems."[35]

Only a month later, McKay had to rein in Benson's political activities, recording in his diary: "Brother Benson has received an invitation from the senators and congressmen to go back to Washington as an adviser. I feel that if this matter comes up again that Brother Benson should remain here; that we need him at home."[36] Benson did remain "at home"; but before the year's end, he had entered an arena of political activity that required McKay's repeated attention for the remaining decade of his life and that caused acrimony and division among the church's highest leaders.

BENSON AND THE JOHN BIRCH SOCIETY

In December 1958, a Massachusetts candy maker, Robert Welch, founded a right-wing extremist organization that took up where Joseph McCarthy left off in attacking Communism but that went beyond McCarthyism to target civil rights and government in general, proclaiming that "the greatest enemy of man is, and always has been, government; and the larger, the more extensive that government, the greater the enemy."[37] Welch named the organization after an American soldier, John Birch, who was killed by Chinese Communists ten days after the end of World War II. Within a year, Ezra Taft Benson had a close association with one of the society's national leaders. During 1961 he became personally acquainted with Welch,[38] and the two men's political agendas quickly aligned. Benson's son recalled: "After his cabinet years, when he came back to Utah, he could see things happening in this country that put him on alert. He saw it with his eyes in Washington, but his focus was so much in the Department of Agriculture that he had enough problems there without him trying to take care of the problems in a lot of other areas."[39]

In August 1961, four days after the Soviets began constructing the Berlin Wall, Benson spoke up in a meeting of the First Presidency and Quorum of the Twelve: "Personally he thought the Communism threat is very real and very dangerous, and that there is need for some organized effort to meet this great threat." His colleagues, while acknowledging that Communism should be fought, cautioned against extreme measures, particularly against using the church as a platform. McKay tipped the emphasis the other way. He agreed that "our Sacrament meetings should be reserved for spiritual enrichment and spiritual instruction" but warned that "we must be careful about condemning any efforts that are anti-Communistic because Communism is a real danger in our country."[40] In taking this stand, McKay implicitly endorsed Benson's position, as he would do regularly in the future. Benson, in turn, never hesitated to remind people of McKay's support. "When the flak began to fly, my father, who didn't want to do anything to harm the church, would constantly be in touch with President McKay, and President McKay would *consistently* encourage him to keep speaking out," stressed Reed Benson.[41]

By September, Benson's outspokenness was causing enough turmoil that some church members began to complain to Hugh B. Brown of the First Presidency. Brown, a Democrat who had been politically active both before he became a General Authority and, to a limited extent, afterward, quickly became a sounding board for Latter-day Saints who felt that Benson's message and tactics were too extreme.

Benson, undaunted by the criticism, lashed out strongly in the October general conference, denouncing Communism, socialism, and socialist-style programs: "Communism is fundamentally socialism. We will never win our fight against communism by making concessions to socialism. Communism and socialism, closely related, must be defeated on principle.... No true Latter-day Saint and no true American can be a socialist or a communist or support programs leading in that direction."[42]

The conflict between Benson and moderate church leaders, particularly Hugh B. Brown, was tactical rather than strategic. "Certainly all of us are against Communism," Brown wrote to a personal correspondent in 1961. But that end did not justify certain means, and he was overtly critical of the means of the John Birch Society:

> The Church has not taken any stand officially relating to these various groups who nominate themselves as guardians of our freedom, except in the case of the John Birch Society, and we are definitely against their methods.... We do not think dividing our own people, casting reflections on our government officials, or calling everybody Communists who do not agree with the political views of certain individuals is the proper way to fight Communism. We think the Church should be a modifying, steadying institution and our leaders, or even members, should not become hysterical or take hasty action.[43]

The day after Brown wrote this letter, Ernest Wilkinson met sequentially with Benson and Brown. His diary entry captures the essence of the conflict between the two men: "I then had a conference with Brother Benson, who is very much concerned over the socialistic tendencies of Brother Brown. I then had a conference with President Brown, who is very much concerned over the super-patriotic tendencies of Brother Benson. It is apparent that I am caught in the center. I think Brother Benson, as a matter of principle, is right, but he has made some strategic mistakes."[44]

By early 1962 Benson's anti-Communist activities became the focus of an hour-long discussion within the First Presidency. McKay's two counselors, both of whom were Democrats, felt that Benson was too extreme in his tactics. Henry D. Moyle felt that it was not proper to discuss such controversial matters in church meetings, particularly when "the people were not well enough informed to discuss it" and when there had not yet been an official First Presidency statement on the subject to guide church members. Referring to Benson's talk in the October general conference, he noted that it had taken on the stature of an official church position without having been formally endorsed. McKay, who was consistently more concerned with the overall fight against Communism than with tactics, deflected this concern: he "knew nothing wrong with Elder Benson's talk, and thought it to be very good." Brown pointed out one consequence for church members of Benson's broad-brush attack: "All the people in Scandinavia and other European countries are under Socialistic governments and certainly are not Communists. Brother Benson's talk ties them together and makes them equally abominable. If this is true, our people in Europe who are living under a Socialist government are living out of harmony with the Church."[45]

The First Presidency decided to have Benson meet with them the following Monday to discuss the matter, with the possibility of reaching a consensus that would result in an official policy statement. That meeting ended inconclusively: "The First Presidency agreed that now was not the time for the Church to make a statement as to its stand against Communism, but that such a statement could be made at a later date."[46] In essence, this inaction left Benson's equation of socialism and communism unmodified.

As 1962 progressed, the tension within the hierarchy over the John Birch Society increased. McKay became more supportive of a hard-line approach toward Communism, while Brown continued to criticize extremism. Yet the public perception was that McKay agreed with Brown, as shown by the *Salt Lake Tribune's* report of an April conference address:

> The First Presidency of the Church of Jesus Christ of Latter-day Saints Saturday reaffirmed the Church's long standing opposition to the evils of communism in the world today, but denounced extreme anti-Communist movements as more of a hindrance than a help. Speaking for the presiding body of the church, Hugh B. Brown, second counselor in the First Presidency, told a packed Tabernacle crowd of priesthood bearers [that] "the leaders of the church now, as has always been the case, stand squarely against the ideals of communism. We'd like the world to know that. However," he added, "we urge you not to become extremists on either side. There is no place in the church or the priesthood of God for men to be fighting each other over a menace such as communism."[47]

Those who took offense at Benson received Brown's words gratefully. A UCLA graduate student wrote that the speeches and writings of Benson "have been the object of derision by competent scholars—not for being anti-Communistic, but rather because of apparent lack of scholarship in their analysis of current politics." Noting that he had occasionally been placed in the uncomfortable position of disagreeing with "what has appeared (until recently) to be the position of the Church," he complimented Brown for his general conference address, "which I interpreted to be a general censure of the 'Right Wing' trend in the Church." He acknowledged, however, that some of his fellow church members "refuse to see extremism in these movements,"[48] thus correctly characterizing a growing rift within the church.

Brown wrote in response, "It is encouraging to some of us who are on the firing line to find that our attempts to stem an undesirable tide of emotionalism are considered partially successful." However, he acknowledged the rift by noting that letters received since the general conference had come down on the other side of the issue. "The differences between some of the talks given in Priesthood Meeting and others in the General Conference leave some of the readers and listeners a bit confused. This I very much regret." Nonetheless, he did not apologize for his remarks, which clearly had been aimed at the John Birch Society. "While we do not think it wise to name names in our statements of Church policy, the cries which come from certain sources would indicate that somebody was hit by some of our statements and that was what we hoped would be the result."[49] However, while many complained to Brown, many others, perhaps indicative of the majority of Latter-day Saints, felt confirmed that Benson's hard-hitting approach was defending their freedoms. And knowing that he had McKay's explicit approval, Benson plunged forward fearlessly, occasionally requesting McKay's direct intervention to stem criticism. A month after Brown's general conference address, Benson phoned McKay to tell him that he would be traveling to Seattle for a church conference, where "there has been some reflection cast on him." McKay thereupon called the stake president in Seattle and said, "All I wish to say to you is that Brother Benson is not under any cloud whatever regarding his attitude towards communism."[50]

In October 1962 the world came to the brink of nuclear war over the issue of long-range missiles being deployed in Cuba. In the midst of this crisis, Ezra Taft Benson made his boldest move yet, attempting to solicit McKay's endorsement of the John Birch Society. In a telephone call, Benson explained that his son Reed, "after spending a year in studying the aims and purposes of the John Birch Society," wished to accept the position of state coordinator for Utah and wanted McKay to bless the move. McKay's response was not what Benson had hoped to hear. "I have heard about the John Birch Society, and everything so far has been negative, so it is up to you and Reed as to whether or not this position is accepted." Pressing the issue further, Benson said that he had read *The Blue Book,* Robert Welch's manifesto, and in meeting with Welch found him to be "a fine Christian gentleman." He referred to the John Birch Society as "the most effective organization we have in the country in fighting Communism and Socialism," and said his son "is convinced that he can best serve his country by working with this organization." McKay repeated his refusal to become involved. "I said, 'I have nothing whatever to do with it.' Brother Benson said that Reed would not go into this if I

told him not to, and I said that this is a matter that I shall leave entirely with him
and Reed."[51] The following day, Reed Benson announced his acceptance of the
position with the John Birch Society and his father's endorsement of the society thus
became public.[52] Newspapers across the country reported the story, and headlines
such as "Ezra Benson's Son Takes Birch Society Post," and "Benson Birch Tie Disturbs Utahans"[53] heightened the controversy.

Although Ezra Taft Benson never joined the John Birch Society, his position
as a senior apostle and his participation in both public and private activities of the
society lent the flavor of official church endorsement, a situation that infuriated
many Mormons. In a rare acknowledgement that public opinion can influence
church policy, Henry D. Moyle, second counselor in the First Presidency, wrote to
J. D. Williams, a professor in the Political Science Department at the University of
Utah: "When we pursue any course which results in numerous letters being written to the Presidency critical of our work, it should be some evidence we should
change our course."[54] As a result, on January 3, 1963, the First Presidency issued
its first policy statement dealing with the society:

> The following statement is made to correct the false statements and
> unwarranted assumptions regarding the position allegedly taken by
> the leaders of the Church on political questions in general and the
> John Birch Society in particular.... We deplore the presumption of
> some politicians, especially officers, co-ordinators and members of the
> John Birch Society, who undertake to align the Church or its leader-
> ship with their partisan views. We encourage our members to exercise
> the right of citizenship, to vote according to their own convictions,
> but no one should seek or pretend to have our approval of their
> adherence to any extremist ideologies. We denounce communism as
> being anti-Christian, anti-American, and the enemy of freedom, but
> we think they who pretend to fight it by casting aspersions on our
> elected officers or other fellow citizens do the anti-Communist cause
> a great disservice.[55]

Many church members welcomed the statement. J. D. Williams, then serving
as a bishop, wrote appreciatively to the First Presidency: "May this Bishop express
heartfelt gratitude for your forthright policy statement of January 3 on the Birch
Society. President Brown's declaration for the First Presidency at the Priesthood session of April Conference, 1962, decrying extremist groups of all sorts, seemed plain
enough. But apparently some of our number either refused to listen or could not
read."[56]

Apparently Benson had had no idea that the statement was coming. Blindsided, he called McKay the day after the statement was issued and asked for a meet-

ing. McKay, who was at his farm in Huntville, told him "to call my counselors [both of whom were Democrats] and tell them to hold a meeting with him this morning in the office of the First Presidency."[57] Two days after Benson's phone call, Brown visited McKay in Huntsville to discuss the matter, and at McKay's request wrote a memorandum describing the meeting:

> The first subject under discussion was the recent declaration made by the First Presidency and published in the newspapers regarding the John Birch Society and its officers, stating that the Church does not endorse them. You asked that I read a number of opinions from various sources, including the editor of the *Los Angeles Times,* the *New York Times,* the Attorney General of the State of California, the Ministerial Association of California, and others. After reading and discussing these, we agreed that we had done the right thing in letting the members of the Church and the world know that the Church does not in any way endorse or subscribe to the John Birch Society. You mentioned that we might have erred in that we did not call the Bensons in before making the announcement. I called your attention to the fact that we had called Brother Benson in and discussed Reed's activities during the campaign in disregarding our former statement regarding the use of our chapels and meeting places for political purposes. At that same meeting we discussed the John Birch Society, and Brother Benson denied having any association with them.[58]

Benson's denial of "any association" with the John Birch Society, if not overtly duplicitous, indicates that he was using the words in the narrowest possible manner such that, in his view, not being a card-carrying member of the society allowed him to deny having "any association." He used a similar tactic several years later when he nearly succeeded in getting McKay's photograph on the cover of *American Opinion,* the John Birch Society's monthly magazine.

In late January 1963, McKay finally met with Benson to discuss the First Presidency statement. It was one of the rare instances in which McKay came down hard on him—albeit in private—for his political activities: "Elder Benson said the statement seemed to be leveled against him and his son, Reed, and also Brother [W. Cleon] Skousen. I told Brother Benson that it was intended to apply to them. I said that the statement made by him (Elder Benson) in favor of the John Birch Society was made by him, one of the Twelve, who is an international character and received international publicity, and that that is one reason the Presidency had to make the announcement in the newspapers."[59]

A week later, Ernest Wilkinson met with McKay's secretary, Clare Middlemiss, and discussed the First Presidency statement. Wilkinson was sympathetic to the

John Birch Society and, at one point, traveled to Illinois for a multi-day Birch conference before deciding not to join. Middlemiss told Wilkinson that McKay had received "at least 25 letters vigorously protesting the statement of the First Presidency, many of them very intelligent letters." She then informed Wilkinson "that the President, himself, thinks that the First Presidency probably went a little too far."[60]

Four days later, Middlemiss showed McKay "hundreds of letters from all over the United States which have been received from members of the John Birch Society."[61] However, the letters were not spontaneous, but came in response to a notice in the *John Birch Society Bulletin* that urged Mormon members of the society to write McKay, thanking him for his stand against Communism and praising "the great service Ezra Taft Benson and his son Reed (our Utah Coordinator) are rendering to this battle, with the hope that they will be encouraged to continue."[62] At McKay's instruction, Middlemiss drafted a form letter to respond to any John Birch members who voiced concerns over their Church standing. The letter went out over her signature instead of his, although beneath her signature she always typed "Secretary to President David O. McKay." It read in part: "I have been directed to say that members of the Church are free to join anti-communist organizations if they desire and their membership in the Church is not jeopardized by so doing. The Church is not opposing The John Birch Society or any other organization of like nature; however, it is definitely opposed to anyone's using the Church for the purpose of increasing membership for private organizations sponsoring these various ideologies."[63]

The letter provided society members with an antidote to the First Presidency statement, and it was thereafter quoted frequently, although often in a truncated form that ended with the words "of like nature." Within a month of the statement, therefore, both sides had an authoritative source to quote in favor of their own position. Therefore, the sparring not only continued, but intensified.

Early in March 1963, Ernest Wilkinson met with W. Cleon Skousen, who though not a member of the society shared many of its views, and wrote: "I found out that despite the manner in which he [Benson] is being criticized by President Hugh B. Brown, President David O. McKay is squarely behind him and has told him to keep up his good work."[64] It was typical of McKay to allow his colleagues wide leeway in their public statements and not contradict them in public. In private, however, he made statements that were not always consistent, sometimes leading to major conflicts and misunderstandings.

The day after Wilkinson's meeting with Skousen, an article with the headline "Benson Not Speaking for Mormons on Birch" appeared in the *Los Angeles Times*.[65] It quoted Hugh Brown as saying that Benson was entitled to his own opinions but that, in expressing them, he spoke only for himself and not for the church. In a subsequent First Presidency meeting, McKay agreed with Brown and then criticized Benson, giving his own version of the meeting with Benson:

> Following the publication of the [First Presidency] statement, I was asked to apologize for what was said against Brother Benson and his son Reed because if we had called them "we would have done anything that you suggested." I said, "Yes, and nobody in the Church or in the world would have known that you were doing that, but everybody knew that you are a national character and everybody knew that you favor the Birch Society and that you approve your son representing it in Utah, and when the First Presidency gave that statement it received the same publicity which your statement received, and we offer no apology."[66]

Balanced against this strong, even testy, statement, however, were many other conversations and meetings in which McKay energetically encouraged Benson's anti-communist activities. The following week, on March 12, 1963, Lela Benson, wife of Ezra Taft Benson's other son, Mark, sent a handwritten request to Clare Middlemiss. The letter gives the appearance of having been engineered by other Bensons; it also gives the clearest known indication of Middlemiss's sympathy toward the John Birch Society: "Yesterday I talked to a Bishop who said he would like to see one of 'those' letters that President McKay has sent out regarding the John Birch Society. However he claims that it won't hold much weight unless it is signed by the President and not you. (I disagreed of course—but he stands firm!) Therefore, could you possibly send me one and have it signed by President McKay himself? I understand from Father Benson and his family that you are a dear, sweet, loyal, true blue soul."[67] There is no record of whether Middlemiss approached McKay with such a request.

The following day, in response to mounting pressure and after consulting with McKay, Ezra Taft Benson issued a statement published in the the *Church News*, a weekly tabloid-sized section inserted in the *Deseret News*. It affirmed that "only one man, President David O. McKay, speaks for the Church of Jesus Christ of Latter-day Saints on matters of policy." While on the surface the statement seemed to be conciliatory, in fact it was carefully crafted to have just the opposite effect. First, while disclaiming that he spoke for the church, Benson began the statement by reaffirming his own strong support for the John Birch Society: "I have stated, as my personal opinion only, that the John Birch Society is 'the most effective non-Church organization in our fight against creeping socialism and godless communism.'"[68] Second, by stating that only McKay could speak for the church authoritatively, Benson took a swipe at Brown's credibility as a spokesman for the First

Presidency. And third, Benson quoted only from the Middlemiss letter, which was sympathetic to the society and neglected to mention the January statement of the First Presidency, which was openly critical of the society.

Having issued his disclaimer, Benson continued to speak out publicly in support of the John Birch Society. The following week, the *Salt Lake Tribune* reported a "clarification" of his views: "Although he is not a member of the society, he 'strongly' believes in its principles.... 'I have stated, as my personal opinion only, that the John Birch Society is the most effective non-church organization in our fight against creeping socialism and godless communism.'...Elder Benson, whose son, Reed, is Utah coordinator for the John Birch Society, said he is completely impressed by the people who are pushing the work of the society and praised the 'honesty and integrity' of Robert Welch, the founder."[69]

Three weeks later, Ernest Wilkinson attended a social event that included two senior church officials: Henry D. Moyle of the First Presidency and senior apostle (and eventual church president) Harold B. Lee. Earlier in the day, Wilkinson had received a phone call from Benson, "who read me the riot act for having invited a Communist to speak to our students," a charge that proved to be untrue. As Wilkinson explained the unpleasant matter to Moyle and Lee, "Brother Lee commented that anyone who didn't agree with Brother Benson's mind was, indeed, a Communist. Brother Moyle said that he was happy that I was finding Brother Benson out, that when it came to this subject, he just didn't have any reason."[70] Lee was particularly distressed by Benson's actions and, according to an acquaintance, later said privately that "the brethren would never permit another member of the Twelve to serve in the Cabinet or in a high political position because, as he put it, 'Elder Benson had lost his spiritual tone and would no longer accept counsel.'"[71]

Moyle and Lee were not alone among the General Authorities in disapproving strongly of Benson's actions, yet Benson, as one General Authority later commented, continued to enjoy the support of "a majority of one":

> Early in my career I found that there was not a whole lot of support or appreciation for Benson constantly harping on the communist issue. Although, every time President McKay was present or in a meeting, he would be the endorser, or thanking President Benson for doing what he was doing. That kept the other elements sort of quiet. Hugh B. Brown really thought President Benson had gone overboard. And yet President Benson—I talked with him several times, not on this subject but just in conversation—would remind me that he was doing what the prophet had asked him to do.[72]

In August 1963, Robert Welch sent McKay a letter requesting that Ezra Taft Benson be permitted to join the National Council of the John Birch Society. While

McKay was broadly supportive of Benson's outspokenness, he drew a firm line in rejecting Welch's request, one that he never allowed Benson to cross in spite of repeated pleas: "I said that the letter will be answered that Brother Benson may not join that Board; that he cannot be a member of that Board and be a member of the Quorum of Twelve Apostles."[73] Deeply disappointed by the decision, Benson met with McKay later that month and said that he would "never say another word on the subject if that was President McKay's wish. [President McKay] said he wanted me to continue to speak out with the assurance I had his support as I have had in the past."[74]

Buoyed by the reaffirmed vote of confidence, Benson obtained McKay's consent to speak at a testimonial dinner for Robert Welch in Los Angeles the following month. On September 23, Benson delivered the speech. Although he called Welch "one of the greatest patriots in American history," the speech took a back seat to what Benson said to reporters afterwards. Welch had recently published a book, *The Politician,* in which he accused Dwight Eisenhower of being a tool of the Communists: "On January 20, 1953, Dwight Eisenhower was inaugurated as the thirty-fourth President of the United States. He thus became, automatically and immediately, captain and quarterback of the free-world team, in the fight against Communism. In our firm opinion he had been planted in that position, by Communists, for the purpose of <u>throwing the game</u>."[75] Asked if he agreed with Welch's statement, Benson sidestepped the question, refused to defend Eisenhower, and stated merely that Eisenhower "supported me in matters of agriculture. In other areas we had differences."[76]

The morning after the banquet, Reed Benson escorted Welch into McKay's office, where Welch "reviewed the success of the meeting of his organization in Los Angeles in which Elder Ezra Taft Benson was the featured speaker."[77] McKay's diary made no mention of the comment about Eisenhower, which had already ignited a firestorm in Washington, D.C., nor did it express a personal opinion about Welch.

ATTACK AGAINST BENSON IN CONGRESS

At the center of the protest in the nation's capital was Representative Ralph Harding. Harding and Ezra Taft Benson were both from Idaho. When Harding received a call to serve in the Central States Mission in 1949, he asked that Benson, his "favorite General Authority," set him apart. Benson complied with his request. After returning from his mission, Harding went into the U.S. Army and was at Fort Riley, Kansas, when Dwight Eisenhower was elected president in 1952. He recalled: "I remember the papers were full of President Eisenhower and his cabinet selections, and for Secretary of Agriculture it had been narrowed to Ezra Taft Benson of Utah and Clifford Hope, a Congressman from Kansas, whom all the Kansas papers were supporting. I can remember just as clearly as if it had happened yesterday kneeling down by my bunk when I was saying my prayers, and praying that Elder Benson would be appointed to that position. And he was."[78]

In 1960 Harding, a Democrat, won a Congressional seat from Idaho, arriving in Washington, D.C., just as Benson was completing his eight-year tenure as Secretary of Agriculture and returning to Utah. Harding was midway through his second term when Benson gave his speech in Los Angeles:

> I was on the House floor when that report came in over the wires, the Associated Press and UPI. I was upset, and I stayed up there all night, taking that report and the information I had, and I wrote a speech criticizing Brother Benson for using his Church position to promote the John Birch Society. Then I called Milan Smith, who was a staunch Republican and my stake president then. [Smith had been Benson's chief of staff during his eight years in the Department of Agriculture.] I told him I would appreciate it if he would come up to my office, that there was something that I needed to discuss with him. He did. I let him take the speech, and he went through it. He was crossing out things here and writing more there, and he toughened it up! He made it even tougher than I had. He, [former stake] President J. Willard Marriott and most of the leaders of the Church back here were very, very upset about Brother Benson's actions. Then I called President [Hugh B.] Brown. We didn't have faxes, so we sat right there in my office, with Milan Smith on an extension, and I read the speech to President Brown. After I finished he said, "Well, Brother Harding, can you stand the brickbats?" I said, "I think so, President Brown." But he said, "No, I mean can you *really* stand the brickbats?" I said, "I think so." He said, "You know this speech will probably defeat you." I said, "I realize there is a chance of that." He said, "Well, if you are willing to take that chance, and you are wide [*sic*] aware of the brickbats that are going to come your way, you can do the Church a real service by going ahead and delivering that speech." I said, "That's all I wanted to know, President Brown." So I gave it the next day. It broke loose, especially in Utah and Idaho![79]

In his speech to the House of Representatives, Harding recounted his personal relationship with Benson, saying that "it was just 14 years ago this month...that I was ordained by Ezra Taft Benson prior to my 2 years' service as a Mormon missionary." He described his pride while Benson served as Secretary of Agriculture but lamented that, when Benson "left his position as Secretary of Agriculture, if not before, he began to change.... It was only a short time later that he became a spokesman for the radical right of this Nation."[80]

Reaction to Harding's speech was both pointed and mixed. The majority of mail he received chastised him for criticizing Benson in public. As Brown had conjectured, he lost his campaign for reelection the following year. But other letters were highly complimentary of Harding's action. One was particularly noteworthy:

> I am grateful for your letter and for the speech that you made in Congress concerning the support and encouragement that the former Secretary of Agriculture, Ezra Benson, has allegedly been giving to a Mr. Welch, said to be the founder and leader of the John Birch Society. Your honest and unselfish effort to set the record straight is something that warms my heart.
>
> Frankly, because I rarely read such trash as I understand "The Politician" to be, I had never before read the specific accusations made against me by Robert Welch. But it is good to know that when they were brought to your attention you disregarded all partisan influences to express your honest convictions about the matter. It is indeed difficult to understand how a man, who professes himself to be an anti-Communist, can so brazenly accuse another— whose entire life's record has been one of refutation of Communist theory, practice and purposes—of Communist tendencies or leanings.
>
> With my best wishes and personal regard,
>
> Dwight D. Eisenhower[81]

A year later, when L. Ralph Mecham escorted Ernest L. Wilkinson, then running for the U.S. Senate, to meet with Eisenhower, the former president again brought up Benson's actions. Long afterward, Mecham recalled:

> When I took Ernest Wilkinson up to Gettysburg to visit with Eisenhower, I believe in the spring of 1964, to get Eisenhower's blessing for Wilkinson in his Senate campaign, Ike was almost wistful. We had a great conversation about many things. In the course of it he asked us quizzically, "Whatever happened to Ezra?" or something like that. The implication was clear. He could not understand, I believe, why a man to whom he had been so loyal had not reciprocated that loyalty but instead had adopted the extremist views of the John Birch Society.[82]

Benson's actions put McKay in a dilemma. On the one hand, McKay was uncomfortable with the rising tide of criticism directed at Benson, both from church members and from national media. On the other hand, McKay thought highly of Benson, prized his intense loyal support, and shared his deep, visceral disdain for Communism. While Benson's tactics occasionally caused embarrassment and distress for McKay, neither man ever questioned the goal.

BENSON CALLED TO THE EUROPEAN MISSION

Less than a month after the Robert Welch dinner McKay called Benson to preside over the European Mission, which meant that Benson would be out of the country (and out of the spotlight) for two years. McKay gave Benson the news privately, and the accounts that both men left of the meeting show that it was upbeat, with no hint that Benson was being "punished" or "exiled." McKay wrote that, after he announced the assignment, "Brother Benson expressed himself as being willing to go. He had a lovely spirit, and said he would do whatever I wanted him to do."[83] Benson's biographer described the meeting in similar terms: "'Brother Benson, I have a great surprise,' the prophet began. 'President McKay,' Ezra responded, 'this church is full of surprises.' Both men laughed and then President McKay announced that Elder Benson had been selected to preside over the European Mission with headquarters in Frankfurt, Germany."[84]

Regardless of McKay's intent, however, the move was widely seen as a rebuff to Benson's political activism, in spite of the fact that four other General Authorities—Mark E. Petersen, N. Eldon Tanner, Marion D. Hanks, and Alvin R. Dyer—had presided over missions in Europe within the previous three years. The same day that McKay met with Benson, one of McKay's sons expressed such a sentiment in a letter to Congressman Harding: "We shall all be relieved when Elder Benson ceases to resist counsel and returns to a concentration on those affairs befitting his office. It is my feeling that there will be an immediate and noticeable curtailment of his Birch Society activities."[85] Two weeks later, Harding received a letter from Joseph Fielding Smith, president of the Quorum of the Twelve, that conveyed a similar message: "I think it is time that Brother Benson forgot all about politics and settled down to his duties as a member of the Council of the Twelve.... It would be better for him and for the church and all concerned, if he would settle down to his present duties and let all political matters take their course. He is going to take a mission to Europe in the near future and by the time he returns I hope he will get all of the political notions out of his system."[86]

Reaction in the press was mixed. The church-owned *Deseret News* reported the story with a benign headline, "Elder Benson to Direct European Mission," while the story ran in the *Ogden Standard-Examiner* under the provocative headline:

"Apostle Benson Denies Being Sent into 'Exile' for Political Views."[87] The *National Observer* attempted a balanced perspective in a lengthy article, "Mormons Split over John Birch Society Campaign":

> The Benson connection with the John Birch Society has created somewhat of a "schism" in the Mormon Church. To a few Mormons, Birch philosophies appear to coincide with church doctrine.... But to others, especially those in the liberal Republican and Democratic ranks, the John Birch Society still meant political extremism, and they began asking for Ezra Taft's scalp.... When the elder Benson received his new assignment to Europe many of his critics said the Mormon Church was "shipping out Benson to get rid of him." But to this charge, the former Secretary of Agriculture declared: "Ridiculous—members of the Quorum of the Twelve Apostles are subject to call anywhere in the world anytime. That's our job, and I welcome the call with all my heart." President McKay, who called Mr. Benson on this mission, also termed the charge ridiculous. He, too, said the mission was a routine church assignment for a member of the Quorum of the Twelve Apostles.[88]

On the eve of his departure for Europe, Benson stirred up yet more controversy. On December 13, he delivered a farewell speech in Logan, a third of which was either a direct quotation or paraphrase from Robert Welch's manifesto, *The Blue Book*. Particularly inflammatory was a direct quotation from *The Blue Book* that was given wide publicity in a subsequent article by nationally syndicated columnist Drew Pearson.[89] Benson charged that the United States government was so infiltrated with Communists that the American people "can no longer resist the Communist conspiracy as free citizens, but can resist the Communist tyranny only by themselves becoming conspirators against established government."[90] When U.S. Senator Frank E. Moss (D-Utah) read an account of the speech, he wrote a candid letter to Hugh B. Brown:

> I read the account of Apostle Benson's speech in the Logan LDS Tabernacle in the December 15th issue of the *Herald Journal*. I won't comment on the contents of the speech except to say that it appears that he has not changed his position at all from that that he expressed in Los Angeles at the testimonial dinner for Robert Welch. On page 10 there is a picture of Reed Benson passing out copies of the speech of Ezra T. Benson, and on that same page the following paragraph in the article says: "Copies of Elder Benson's complete speech were available at the meeting or can be obtained by writing directly to him at the LDS Church Offices in Salt Lake City, the Apostle said." I

don't know how we could be tied in more closely as a Church with
the doctrines espoused by Ezra Taft Benson than by an announcement
of this sort. I continue to be bombarded daily by questions and criticisms back here.[91]

The same speech elicited a second, even franker, letter from Joseph Fielding
Smith to Congressman Harding: "I have the comments regarding Brother Benson's
speech in Logan, December 13, 1963. I am glad to report to you that it will be some
time before we hear anything from Brother Benson, who is now on his way to
Great Britain where I suppose he will be, at least for the next two years. When he
returns I hope his blood will be purified."[92]

In the midst of this controversy and on the same day that Smith wrote Harding the second time, McKay dictated a letter to Robert Welch responding to his
earlier request that Benson serve on the national board of the John Birch Society.
"I told Mr. Welch that Elder Benson's duties as European Mission President would
preclude his accepting his invitation."[93] The benignly worded letter, however, left
the door open for Welch and Benson to repeat their request after Benson returned
from Europe.

In late January 1964, McKay accepted an invitation from Lyndon B. Johnson
to meet with him at the White House, the first such invitation extended to any religious leader since Johnson assumed the Presidency after the death of John F.
Kennedy. Following lunch, Johnson invited the Mormon delegation in Congress,
including Congressman Harding, to join them. As Johnson led the group on a
tour of the White House, Harding seized the opportunity for a private word with
McKay: "I told President McKay, when we were walking out to the swimming
pool, 'President McKay, I want you to know that just because I've had my problems with Elder Benson over the John Birch Society, that I still have a strong testimony of the gospel.' He said, 'I know that, Brother Harding. Several of us have
had problems with Brother Benson over the Birch Society.'"[94]

DISSENSION AMONG THE BRETHREN

The controversy over Benson's departure to Europe had barely subsided when it
boiled up again. In late February, the *Idaho State Journal,* a daily paper printed in
Pocatello, published extracts from several of the letters Harding had received,
including Eisenhower's, Robert McKay's, and both letters from Joseph Fielding
Smith. The Associated Press promptly picked up the story and sent it out nation-
wide. The *Salt Lake Tribune,* in publishing extracts from the letters, rekindled the
debate over Benson's assignment. "There was speculation last December when

Mr. Benson was sent to Europe by the church that he was being exiled for his political views. The LDS Church officially denied the rumors."[95]

Although this issue was now public, McKay chose to handle it in private, a tactic he invariably opted for whenever controversy involved a General Authority. McKay was deeply upset by the publication of the letters, which included his son's, and told Middlemiss, "I shall have to take steps to have these accusations stopped." He authorized her to send an explanatory letter to inquirers stating that "Elder Ezra Taft Benson was not sent to Europe for any of the reasons given in your letter. Elder Benson was called by inspiration to preside over the European Mission."[96]

Then, in an unusually candid meeting of the First Presidency and Quorum of the Twelve (minus Benson, who was already in Europe), McKay broached the subjects of Benson, the John Birch Society, Congressman Harding, and the published letters. He began the "Very Important Meeting"[97] by saying, "Before partaking of the Sacrament this morning, I should like to refer to an unfortunate incident which has occurred since the Council last met in this capacity." McKay was particularly upset at letters he had received stating that "a lack of harmony among the leaders of the church" was "creating confusion among members and friends of the Church." He then put Joseph Fielding Smith on the spot: "I said that I should like to know today that there is no dissension among the members of this Council, and that we partake of the Sacrament in full fellowship and full support of one another. I mentioned that since President Smith's name is associated with Brother Benson, particularly in the matter of the John Birch Society, that I think it would be well for President Smith on this occasion to explain his association with the controversy."

Smith replied that "he was glad to do so." He acknowledged that "he did say that when Brother Benson comes home, he hoped he would not get into politics and would keep his blood pure." However, he did not intend his comments to be a personal attack on Benson, but rather as an acknowledgement "that in politics a lot of things are done that are somewhat shady. He said he was speaking of conditions that exist in the political world, and intended no reflection upon Brother Benson." Smith said that he had discussed the matter of his letters with Benson and asserted that the two were "on the best of terms and fellowship with each other." Refusing to capitulate on his main point, he repeated that he would not do anything to hurt Benson but "hoped Brother Benson would keep himself out of politics."

McKay accepted Smith's explanation, but defended Benson:

> I then said that Elder Benson had permission from the President of
> the Church to give the lecture that he gave in the auditorium in
> Hollywood. I mentioned that some people had said that that was one

activity wherein Brother Benson went contrary to the counsel of the
Presidency and General Authorities. I said that Elder Benson had full
permission to give that lecture and he gave a good talk.... I further
said that Brother Benson had said publicly that he was in favor of the
John Birch Society, and that I had told Brother Benson that he could
not, as one of the Twelve, join that Society. This was before Brother
Benson was called to be President of the European Mission, and his
call as President of that mission had nothing whatever to do with the
John Birch Society. I said that I had told him back in November last
that he could not join the Society as one of the Twelve.... Brother
Benson's call to preside over the European Mission had no relationship whatever to his desire to join that Society. I stated that so far as
this Council is concerned, we have no connection whatever with the
John Birch Society, no matter how good it may be and how noble its
purposes; that Brother Benson received his call to go to Europe without any thought of associating his call to the European Mission Presidency with his views regarding the John Birch Society, and that so far
as we are concerned this morning as the Council of the First Presidency and the Twelve, we have nothing whatever to do with it, and
Brother Benson's call over there had nothing to do with it. I then
said: "We shall partake of the sacrament this morning in the spirit of
the opening prayer; that we be one in all things pertaining to this
Church."

Although McKay's defense of Benson was impassioned and unequivocal, it sidestepped the issue that had catapulted Benson's talk into the national spotlight, namely,
Benson's implicit endorsement of Robert Welch's charges that Dwight Eisenhower, a
close friend of McKay, was a tool of the Communists. In fact, there is no record that
McKay ever took Benson to task on that issue, either publicly or privately.

With Benson in Europe, McKay tried, with little success, to put the whole matter of the John Birch Society to rest. In May 1964, Louis Midgley, a faculty member in Brigham Young University's Political Science Department, published a scald-
ing article in the student newspaper that again fanned the flames of controversy:

I have been asked by the Editor at the *Daily Universe* to make some
comments on the John Birch Society. It is difficult to believe that anyone at a university—anyone who reads books and thinks—would take
such a movement seriously.... The man who wrote *The Politician* did
so to inform his followers that former President Eisenhower was a
communist. Of course he provides no evidence but the usual collection of garbage. For absurdity, the charge against Ike would have to

be placed next to the belief, as far as I know, held by no one, that President McKay is secretly a Catholic. What Welch-Birch really wants is to return to a world without taxes, the U.N., labor unions, racial minorities demanding some kind of legal equality; Birchers want a world without fluoridation, the Soviet Union, large cities and emerging nations and all the rest that goes with our world.[98]

McKay reacted strongly to the article. He telephoned Earl C. Crockett, BYU's acting president, and directed him to meet with Midgley "and ask him why he should have written the editorial 'Birch Society Reviewed' for ten thousand students to read…. This matter of the John Birch Society should be dropped."[99] After Crockett reported holding the requested meeting and chastising Midgley, McKay repeated: "It would be well for faculty members to hold no discussions whatsoever on the John Birch Society, and to drop the matter entirely."[100]

Though continuing to distance himself from the society, McKay kept the heat up on Communism, in June authorizing the publication by the church-owned Deseret Book Company of a "Statements on Communism and the Constitution of the United States," a pamphlet that collected McKay's statements on the subject. For his part, Benson refused to stay out of politics, even from across the Atlantic. In August, Mark E. Petersen, Benson's colleague in the Quorum of the Twelve and president of the West European Mission (Benson was president of the European Mission), wrote in agitation to Hugh B. Brown "stating that he wished there was some way to keep Brother Benson out of politics." Europe, Petersen said, "hates" Barry Goldwater, the Republican presidential candidate, yet Benson had recently given an interview to Danish journalists that resulted in a story with the headline, "Mormon Apostle Says America Needs Goldwater." Petersen pointed out that this kind of publicity hurt the church in Europe, and asked if there was any way to stop it. Brown relayed the request to McKay, who sidestepped direct action: "I said that this ought not to be done, but asked that a communication be sent to Brother Benson calling attention to the report, and asking as to the accuracy of it."[101]

The following day, Benson wrote a note to Clare Middlemiss that confirmed his continuing political activities: "Hardly a week passes without someone writing, urging that I come home to help in the great fight to preserve our freedom."[102] A month later Arch Madsen, president of the church-owned KSL, relayed to the First Presidency an inquiry from a committee of broadcasters charged with selecting a new president of the National Association of Broadcasters. The committee wished to know if Benson, who was on their short list, would be available on a full-time basis to serve in that position. Meeting this request would involve, of course, terminating his assignment in Europe as well as giving him another leave of absence from his duties in the Quorum of the Twelve. "After hearing all the facts pertaining to the matter," McKay dictated in his diary: "I indicated that so far as the Church is concerned, Brother Benson would be available for such an appointment." Hugh B. Brown concurred with McKay's decision, but added a strong qualifier, saying "if Brother Benson severed his relationship with [the John Birch Society] and accepted this position as a non-partisan assignment for the benefit of the Church primarily, he could do a lot of good; otherwise, he could do us a lot of harm."[103] Benson was not offered the position, but McKay's strong support of such non-ecclesiastical activities was a clear message to other General Authorities.

In the meantime, Benson continued to act politically from afar, in October authorizing the John Birch Society to use his photograph on the cover of its monthly magazine.[104] Reed Benson, acting as a surrogate for his father, published full-page advertisements in Idaho newspapers quoting his father's endorsement of the society.[105]

Benson returned regularly to Salt Lake City for the church's semi-annual general conferences, using these occasions to press his political agenda. In April 1965, Ernest Wilkinson recorded his impressions of Benson's conference address: "Ezra Taft Benson gave a typical address against loss of our freedoms. He has great courage and I have great admiration for him. I'm sure some of his Brethren may have thought it was untactful, but it is apparent that Ezra is not going to give up in a cause in which he knows he is right. I know also that he has encouragement from President McKay."[106]

While Benson's general conference address pleased Wilkinson, it had the opposite effect on other church members. The *Washington Post* stated, "The Mormon Church revealed sharp and bitter differences among its leadership on civil rights during its recent conference here." Noting that Benson "spoke darkly but without specifics of 'traitors in the church,'" the *Post* quoted the most inflammatory portion of his speech: "Before I left for Europe I warned how the Communists were using the civil rights movement to promote revolution and eventual takeover of this country. When are we going to wake up? What do you know about the dangerous civil rights agitation in Mississippi?"[107]

According to the *Post* article, Hugh B. Brown "said tartly that Benson 'speaks strictly for himself.'"[108] Meeting later with his counselors, McKay raised the issue of Brown's outspoken critique of the John Birch Society, which had been the subject of many letters of protest that McKay had received: "I asked President Brown why he is so bitter against the organization. President Brown said that he did not consider it a good society, and he thought that they were doing more harm than good. He further stated that since I had told him about a year ago to be quiet on that subject, he had said and done nothing further regarding it. I said that it is wise not to mention the society."[109]

Brown seized the opportunity to bring up Benson's conference address, pointing out the negative publicity in the *Washington Post* and the many unfavorable reactions to Benson's remarks that he had heard. "Brother Benson," he concluded, "should be told to take care of his missionary work and leave such matters alone." McKay responded, "I had not noticed anything objectionable in what Brother Benson had said," and asked Brown to bring him a transcript of the talk. (Brown later did so; and upon reading it McKay agreed that the offensive paragraphs be deleted from the official published report of the conference.[110])

N. Eldon Tanner, McKay's second counselor, continuing the discussion in the first post-conference meeting, backed Brown up by citing other examples of negative feedback that he had received on Benson's talk. He concluded that it had "split the people down the center" in their church meetings. McKay, hoping to make the whole problem disappear, ended the meeting by saying, "I had told everyone not to mention the Birch Society but let the matter die out."[111]

THIRD-PARTY CANDIDATE

Benson concluded his European assignment and returned home in time for the October 1965 general conference. Soon afterward, he met with McKay to discuss some new political ambitions. As McKay recorded the meeting in his diary, "a very prominent man, representing a large group of Americans who are strongly in favor of freedom" had approached Benson about forming a third political party, because "even the Republicans are becoming soft toward socialism and Communism." McKay gave a mixed message, instructing Benson that "he must not have anything to do with a 'third party,'" but "should [still] look into what these men have in mind."[112]

Thorpe B. Isaacson, whom McKay had recently added as an extra counselor in the First Presidency, was present at the meeting and wrote a memo summarizing it in greater detail, which he sent to McKay. Benson and Senator Strom Thurmond (R-South Carolina) would take their crusade to the next Republican Convention during the summer of 1968; but if they could not get the party leadership to accept it, they would consider forming a third party. Benson, according to Isaacson, said that "the Republicans were becoming soft toward communism and drifting toward socialism and away from conservatism about as badly as the Democrats." When McKay cautioned him not to affiliate with a third party, Benson "stated that he did not care to get into politics, but he thought the Church should take a stand; that if somebody did not do something it would be too late. President McKay agreed with this."[113] In light of Benson's prior and subsequent political activities, his claim "that he did not care to get into politics" must be viewed skeptically.

In November, McKay again met privately with Benson, who "gave a report on the serious inroads the Communists have made in this country.... I am convinced that our country is already on the road to Socialism, and that the Communists are making gains here." Benson then suggested that McKay's new counselor, Thorpe Isaacson, be sent to a two-day John Birch Society seminar in December to learn about "Communism and conditions in our country." McKay agreed.[114]

It is easy to see how Hugh B. Brown became increasingly frustrated with Benson and the John Birch Society, as McKay repeatedly gave every indication of coming down hard on the society when he spoke in First Presidency and Quorum of the Twelve meetings, yet expressed support and encouragement on the same subject when he met privately with Benson. Although there is no record that Brown ever flared up at McKay, he at least once expressed his frustrations to Clare Middlemiss, whom he suspected of furthering her own political agenda with McKay. In November 1965, Middlemiss recorded a heated exchange: "President Brown said, 'Why cannot we have harmony?' Clare answered, 'Yes, why?' [Brown:] 'You got off the wrong track with me over the John Birch Society and Brother Benson.' [Middlemiss:] 'I have only wanted to fight Communism, and have answered letters on the John Birch Society the way President McKay has told me to.' President Brown said, 'I have wanted to fight Communism also, but not the way Benson or the John Birch Society are doing it—everybody is against them.'"[115]

THE AMERICAN OPINION MAGAZINE

As 1966 began, McKay noted that he had received complaints from church members who, understandably, were confused about the distinction between the church's stand on Communism on the one hand and the John Birch Society on the other: "I said that I think the time has come for the First Presidency to make a statement as to the Church's attitude regarding Communism; that this, however, should have nothing whatever to do with the Birch Society, and should be a message from the First Presidency of the Church. The Brethren agreed that there is a great need for such a message, and I was persuaded that I am the one who should prepare such a statement."[116]

McKay, however, was preempted by Benson, who five days later gave yet another public endorsement of the John Birch Society. Speaking in Boise, Idaho, Benson called the society "probably the most effective non-church group in the United States in the fight against galloping socialism and Godless communism." Still forbidden by McKay to join the society, Benson nonetheless suggested that he was everything but a formal member. "This is a fine group," he said. "I know their leaders, I have attended two of their all-day council meetings. I have read their literature. I feel I know their programs." He ended his remarks by emphasizing that McKay "has said he doesn't understand why the people do not become alerted and informed regarding the greatest evil in the world—the Communist conspiracy."[117] In the context of Benson's preceding remarks, it sounded as if McKay was endorsing the John Birch Society. Indeed, U.S. Senator Wallace F. Bennett (R-Utah) observed as much to McKay's son Lawrence: "I have just been reading the report in the *Tribune* of the 16th of the speech Brother Benson made in Boise in which he praised the John Birch Society and ended with a very clever statement about your father which would seem to give your father's endorsement."[118]

Benson's attempts to imply McKay's endorsement of the society did not end with speeches. Early the following month he met privately with McKay and presented his most audacious proposal yet. McKay described the meeting in his diary:

> Met by appointment Elder Ezra Taft Benson who said that the editors of the *American Opinion* magazine would like to have my portrait on the cover of their April issue. He said this magazine is published in Belmont, Massachusetts, and is a high-class publication. He showed me several past issues with pictures of Senator Barry Goldwater, the Honorable J. Edgar Hoover, Director of the FBI, and other prominent Americans. Brother Benson said that they needed a colored photograph and some biographical material, and I asked him to get these from my secretary, Clare. After discussing the matter, I could see no reason why I should not grant permission for the editors to use my picture.[119]

In presenting the matter to McKay, Benson had elected not to divulge one crucial detail: *American Opinion* was the monthly magazine of the John Birch Society.[120] At a subsequent First Presidency meeting, Apostle Mark E. Petersen dropped a bombshell by stating that the Church Information Service had received a bill for $25 for a color photograph of McKay for the cover of *American Opinion*, "which is the John Birch Society organ.... Elder Petersen said that if my picture is so published it will certainly look as though the Church is endorsing the John Birch Society." McKay reacted strongly, making it clear in the process that Benson had deceived him by failing to inform him that *American Opinion* was a John Birch publication:

> I said that my picture should not appear on this magazine; that the Church has nothing to do with the John Birch Society. I authorized Brother Petersen to tell Brother Benson that he had brought this matter to my attention, and had been told by me to stop the printing

of my picture on this magazine; that I do not want it used in that way. I said to Brother Petersen, "You are ordered in the presence of these men to stop it." I further said that I do not want to have anything to do with the John Birch Society; that the Church has had nothing to do with it in the past, and that so far as Brother Benson is concerned, I do not think we would hear anything more about it.[121]

The day after McKay's decision to withdraw his permission to print the picture, Benson met with him. According to McKay's diary entry, Benson avoided the issue of *American Opinion* being a John Birch Society publication, nor did McKay bring it up. Instead, he repeated that "the magazine is considered a high-type magazine" on whose cover the pictures of Senator Barry Goldwater, J. Edgar Hoover, and other prominent men had appeared. Furthermore, he reminded McKay that he had given his word on the matter. Although McKay had been adamant only two days before, he now decided "that they had better go ahead with it since I had given my permission for this to be done."[122] Unfortunately, McKay did not tell any of his other associates that he had reversed field on the issue.

Even with the benefit of over four decades of hindsight, it is not possible to conclude with certainty why McKay acted as he did on this issue, but the reason likely involved an interplay of factors. McKay was ninety-two, older than any previous church president. Although he was not intellectually impaired, his declining physical condition severely limited his direct contact with the outside world. According to the organizational chart, Hugh B. Brown and N. Eldon Tanner, his first and second counselors, should have been considered his closest confidants. However, a sharp exchange with Tanner a year earlier over the church's finances (see chap. 9) had led to a rift between McKay on the one side and Tanner and Brown on the other. Following that incident, McKay became increasingly dependent upon other voices within his inner circle. The most persuasive of those voices, when it came to the issue of Communism, were Ezra Taft Benson, Thorpe B. Isaacson, and Clare Middlemiss, all of whom were strong John Birch Society sympathizers. The *American Opinion* incident occurred less than a month after the massive stroke that permanently incapacitated Isaacson, with the result that Benson's and Middlemiss's voices became even more prominent. Furthermore, Middlemiss functioned as McKay's chief of staff, controlling access to him, giving Benson ready entrée but often blocking others from seeing the president.[123]

But perhaps most importantly, McKay, from the 1930s onward, was consistently and vehemently opposed to Communism. He was not speaking hyperbolically when he called it the greatest threat in the world to freedom and to the church, and he felt that way long before Benson embraced the same philosophy. If one can understand the depth of McKay's feelings against Communism, perhaps his continual waffling over Benson's involvement with the John Birch Society can better be appreciated.

Early in the morning of March 8, 1966, N. Eldon Tanner placed a phone call to McKay, who was resting in Huntsville. He said "it was very urgent" that he, Joseph Fielding Smith, Mark E. Petersen, and Lawrence McKay see him that morning. McKay agreed; and by 10:30 A.M. the four men, along with First Presidency secretary Joseph Anderson, who took minutes of the conversation, arrived in Huntsville.[124]

Tanner began by explaining that he had, the previous day, received a letter from Philip K. Langan, circulation manager of the *American Opinion*. The letter confirmed what McKay's colleagues had feared in the previous month's meeting on the subject—that the John Birch Society intended to use McKay's picture on the cover of the magazine to promote the society. The letter read in part:

> The cover of the April 1966 issue of *American Opinion* will feature the President of the Mormon Church, David O. McKay. We feel that our Standing Order Agents will want to increase their monthly shipment, as newsstand sales should improve with the well-respected President McKay on the cover. Our Subscription Agents now have a good selling point for any Mormon prospects they might be trying to "sign up." And for our regular Subscribers and John Birch Society Chapter leaders, you now have an opportunity to favorably impress your Mormon friends, who are not yet actively involved in the battle against Communism.

Upon reading the letter, Tanner had immediately called Petersen. The two men were baffled, because McKay's instructions to see that his photograph did not appear had been explicit. They called Lawrence McKay to see if he knew of any change in his father's wishes. He did not. At that point, Tanner moved quickly to arrange the meeting.

They then read to McKay the minutes of the First Presidency meeting of February 18, in which he had unambiguously ordered Petersen to stop the printing of his picture on the magazine. Without mentioning Benson by name, McKay replied, "They have resorted to everything they could to get me associated with that." Tanner said, "One reason we thought we should come this morning is if you thought it should be stopped we ought to get word to them immediately." McKay replied, "You get them by telephone. Tell them I do not want anything to do with it, that I do not want my name associated with John Birch." Tanner then showed McKay the issue of *American Opinion* with Benson's picture on the front cover and said, "That is the way they would want to put your picture, and even if they have it printed they could put a new cover on without any trouble." McKay replied, "I do not want my picture on it. Stop it!"

As Lawrence McKay attempted to reach John Birch headquarters in Massachusetts, Petersen raised the issue of Benson's role. As the discussion progressed, it was clear that, from McKay's point of view, Benson had not been forthcoming with him in their private discussions. It was also clear how deeply Benson had offended his closest associates by consistently overreaching the limits McKay placed on him.

At this point in the conversation, McKay asked Lawrence to get Benson on the phone. Joseph Anderson, recording the meeting in shorthand, naturally heard only McKay's part of the dialogue. Nonetheless, it is clear that, as as the president began to talk to Benson, his tone changed immediately. Like earlier occasions when he spoke privately with Benson, he simply could not come down hard on him. Unfortunately, the result was that he left the door open for Benson to continue his activities.

At McKay's direction, Lawrence then phoned the editorial office of *American Opinion* and required that they stop the publication of McKay's picture "no matter what the cost." At the conclusion of the phone call, Lawrence said to the other men in the room, "He says there is plenty of time to stop it." His father concluded the meeting by saying, "I am glad you came."

ROBERT WELCH VISITS SALT LAKE CITY

Having resolved one crisis, McKay was quickly brought into another. On the same day that he pulled the plug on his cover photograph for *American Opinion,* the chairman of a banquet in Salt Lake City honoring Robert Welch sent letters to bishops throughout the church. The timing of the event, April 7, was crucial, for the annual general conference, which would be attended by thousands of bishops throughout the church, was scheduled for April 6, 9, and 10; the $15-per-plate banquet would thus fill a gap in their schedule. The letter made strong reference to a Benson talk in the Assembly Hall the previous month, implying that McKay had sanctioned it (which he had not): "This talk was delivered to a turn-away crowd of over 2,000 persons. President David O. McKay had requested that he be allowed to view the proceedings over closed-circuit television." In order "to continue this education process respecting the things which threaten us today," Robert Welch would speak at the banquet. "Elder Ezra Taft Benson will be present and will introduce Mr. Welch." The letter concluded, "As you know, Conference will be held April 6th, 9th, and 10th this year. Thursday evening will be free for most people and we invite your attendance, along with your counselors and wives, at this dinner."[125]

The following day, the First Presidency published a "Notice to Church Members" to disclaim any church involvement in the banquet. It concluded: "In order to avoid any misunderstanding we wish to notify bishops, other church officers, and members of the Church in general, that the Church is not involved in this dinner in any way, and furthermore, that the Church has no connection with the John Birch Society whatever."[126]

The next day, Robert Hinckley, a friend and former neighbor of McKay, wrote an impassioned letter from New York City where he was working for the American Broadcasting Company, pleading with McKay to rein in Benson's extremist activities:

> The head of the Birch Society, Robert Welch, is due in Salt Lake City on April 6th or 7th, the time of General Conference. Efforts will be made to have him recognized in some way during Conference (Elder Benson may even propose to have him come to the stand to make some brief remarks). But this is the Robert Welch who slandered President Eisenhower by writing that "there is only one possible word to describe his purposes and actions. That word is 'treason.'" Welch bore the same kind of false witness against Eisenhower's Secretary of State, John Foster Dulles, calling him "a Communist agent." He also accused the late President John F. Kennedy, during his brief term in office, of being sympathetic to the Communist goals of world conquest.... President McKay, I beseech you to give heed on these matters to all of your dedicated Counselors in the First Presidency.... I fervently hope that Mr. Welch, the Birch head, will receive no recognition of any sort from you or the Church while he is in Salt Lake City. And I beseech you to require a decision from Elder Benson forthwith as to whether his life will be dedicated to Church or Birch. He is doing the Church a great, great disservice by mixing the two.[127]

A week later, McKay met privately with Benson to discuss the Birch Society banquet. McKay gave him a gentle message not to speak at the banquet or other society functions; but even according to his own diary notation, he couched the instructions in a way that left Benson plenty of maneuvering room if he chose to take it: "I told Brother Benson that I think it would be best for him not to speak at strictly John Birch Society meetings, but approved of his filling speaking appointments already accepted which were not associated with this group."[128]

On the following day, McKay and Benson attended the regular weekly meeting of the First Presidency and Quorum of the Twelve in the Salt Lake Temple. McKay's diary entry for the day gives no indication as to what was discussed in the meeting, merely stating, "Many problems and important Church decisions!"[129] However, a diary entry from the following week, immediately before April conference, described a portion of the meeting and an exchange between Tanner and

Benson about Benson's speaking at the Welch dinner: "Brother Benson inquired about the dinner, that in the letter that had been sent out it was announced that he would be in attendance and introduce the speaker. President Tanner said that he told Brother Benson that he could not give him any further answer than was given in the meeting on Thursday. Elder Benson asked President Tanner if he would clear this matter for him with President McKay, and President Tanner had said no, that he felt that it was just as clear as anything could be."[130]

The day after this meeting in the temple, the persistent Benson met privately with McKay to again discuss his speaking at the banquet. After he left, he wrote a memo summarizing their discussion that McKay "read and approved." Benson noted, "I desire to follow your counsel at all times," and then reaffirmed, without apology, his continuing and unqualified support of the John Birch Society, once again implying McKay's endorsement: "I am still convinced that the John Birch Society is a great patriotic, non-political, voluntary, educational organization which is doing great good in the fight against the Godless socialist-communist conspiracy which you have warned is the greatest evil in this world." He ended the memo by stating, "If you feel at any time I am getting off the right track please do as you promised and 'tap me on the shoulder.'"[131]

The combination of McKay's unwillingness to give Benson an ultimatum and Benson's willingness to assume *carte blanche* support from McKay, no matter what qualifications McKay had intended, ensured that Benson would continue to push his political agenda as long as McKay lived. It also ensured that Benson's fellow General Authorities who disagreed with his extremism would be continually frustrated in their attempts to rein him in, for he would always appeal directly to McKay.

Meanwhile, having been thwarted in his attempt to involve Benson in the banquet, Robert Welch shifted tactics and initiated a letter-writing campaign to lobby his cause directly with key church leaders. In the March issue of the *John Birch Society Bulletin*, he praised McKay's long-standing efforts to combat Communism, quoted part of McKay's general conference talk on the same subject, and then urged Birch members "to express their appreciation to this great religious leader, who is also—whether or not he would even recognize the word—a great Americanist."[132] Welch urged correspondents to keep their letters brief, "make it clear that you do not expect any answer," and mark both the letter and the envelope "Personal and Confidential," a move that would ensure that the letters would go directly to Clare Middlemiss, who pasted this issue of the *Bulletin* in her personal scrapbook.

The day after general conference began, Welch was honored at the announced banquet at the Hotel Utah. Benson attended but did not speak. In his speech, Welch described the church as "a very good recruiting ground."[133]

THE CHURCH'S STAND ON COMMUNISM

Two days later, in the priesthood session of general conference, McKay, who was in marginal physical health, asked his son Robert to read his statement regarding the church's stand on Communism. The statement said, in part:

> Church members are at perfect liberty to act according to their own consciences in the matter of safeguarding our way of life.... They are free to participate in non-Church meetings which are held to warn people of the threat of Communism or any other theory or principle which will deprive us of our free agency or individual liberties vouch-safed by the Constitution of the United States. The Church, out of respect for the rights of all its members to have their political views and loyalties, must maintain the strictest possible neutrality. We have no intention of trying to interfere with the fullest and freest exercise of the political franchise of our members under and within our Constitution... The position of this Church on the subject of Communism has never changed. We consider it the greatest Satanical threat to peace, prosperity, and the spread of God's work among men that exists on the face of the earth. In this connection, we are continually being asked to give our opinion concerning various patriotic groups or individuals who are fighting Communism and speaking up for Freedom. Our immediate concern, however, is not with parties, groups, or persons, but with principles. *We, therefore, commend and encourage every person and every group who are sincerely seeking to study Constitutional principles and awaken a sleeping and apathetic people to the alarming conditions that are rapidly advancing about us. We wish all of our citizens throughout the land were participating in some type of organized self-education in order that they could better appreciate what is happening and know what they can do about it. Supporting the FBI, the Police, the Congressional Committees investigating Communism, and various organizations that are attempting to awaken the people through educational means, is a policy we warmly endorse for all our people.*[134]

McKay's counselors saw the italicized passage as an implicit endorsement of the John Birch Society and promptly tried to control the potential use to which it would be put. Three days later, McKay summoned Henry A. Smith, editor of the

Church News, to his office. He had learned—he did not say from whom—that Smith did not plan to publish the statement on Communism in the forthcoming general conference issue of the *Church News.* Smith acknowledged the decision without explaining his rationale. McKay replied, "Well it should go in. I made that statement to 85,000 Priesthood members; the press has it, and many recordings have been made of it. I think it had better go in."[135] Accordingly, the statement was published in the *Church News* on April 16, but the controversial (here italicized) passage was deleted at McKay's request.[136]

When Clare Middlemiss discovered the deletion, she told McKay that "many recordings had been made of the statement and that many people are calling the office to find out why these paragraphs had been deleted." McKay replied that Lawrence McKay, at the instigation of Hugh B. Brown and N. Eldon Tanner, had urged that he leave them out, "pointing out that they would tie the Church in with the John Birch Society."[137] Three days later, Middlemiss again pressed the issue, expressing concern at the many letters she had received complaining about the deletion and also protesting a pre-conference editorial by Mark E. Petersen published in the *Church News* that had criticized the John Birch Society. It had said in part, "The Church has nothing to do with Communists, nothing to do with racists, nothing to do with Birchers, nothing to do with any slanted group."[138] Easily persuaded by these arguments, McKay reversed his previous position: "I told Clare that I did not wish these paragraphs deleted; that I gave them and the statement should stand as given; that many people have recordings of the full statement.... These things are very upsetting to me, and the deletion of what I said at Priesthood Meeting is causing a lot of people to question and to wonder what is going on."[139]

As a result, the deleted paragraphs were restored when McKay's statement appeared in the official *Conference Report* and in the church's monthly magazine, the *Improvement Era.* Middlemiss was not satisfied, however, and pushed for the statement's publication in full the following week in the *Church News.*[140] In doing so, however, she clashed directly with McKay's son Lawrence, who was firmly opposed to the society and who had taken the lead the first time in blocking publication of the disputed passage.

On April 21, the two met face-to-face in Middlemiss's office. Lawrence argued that the passage should not be published, "that it will do a lot of harm to the Church; that the John Birch Society will use it as meaning members of the Church should join their society." Middlemiss countered that she "did not see how they would take it that way; that they had already been called and said that the statement was not for them, and they are not to distribute it from their office."[141] The following day Middlemiss visited McKay in his apartment, again urged publication of the entire statement in the *Church News,* and reported her confrontation with

Lawrence. McKay, referring to his earlier discussion with his son, at which time it was agreed not to publish it in full, said, "I have never seen my son Lawrence so upset—he hates the John Birch Society."[142] The statement was not reprinted in the *Church News.*

BENSON'S BID FOR U.S. PRESIDENT

McKay's attention was deflected momentarily from the John Birch Society by another of Benson's political initiatives: his proposed candidacy for U.S. president. Months earlier, Benson had presented to McKay a rather nebulous plan whereby he and Senator Strom Thurmond would press the Republican Party for reforms, with the intent of forming a third party if they were not successful. That plan, however, had not included presidential aspirations. In mid-April 1966, Benson met with McKay and described "The 1976 Committee," to be composed of 100 prominent men from throughout the country, which proposed to nominate Benson for president and Thurmond for vice president. McKay repeated his resistance to forming a third party, to which Benson replied that he also was "opposed to this, but this Committee and movement might result in a realignment between the two political parties." McKay responded "that this nation is rapidly moving down the road of soul-destroying socialism, and that I hoped and prayed that the efforts of the 1976 Committee would be successful in stemming the tide." He told Benson "to let them go ahead and wait and see what develops." Benson presented him with proposed statements that he and McKay might make if the committee moved as planned to propose his nomination, to which McKay agreed. McKay's statement ended with the words "his doing so has my full approval."[143]

Three weeks later, when Benson was on a church assignment in Germany, the 1976 Committee announced its intention to draft Benson as a presidential candidate in 1968. Benson, speaking disingenuously in view of his prior conversation with McKay, told a reporter that he was in "shock" over the committee's proposal. "It's the first I've heard of it," he said. The same newspaper report indicated that "about half of the committee's 30 organizers are members of the Birch Society."[144]

Benson's bid for president of the United States ran out of momentum and was discontinued a year before the 1968 political conventions. Still, it placed McKay in the awkward position of trying to maintain political neutrality toward one Mormon presidential candidate who genuinely was a serious contender, Michigan's Governor George Romney, while at the same time endorsing the candidacy of Benson, who was never regarded as a serious candidate. A lengthy article in the *Wall Street Journal* noted the dilemma, pointing out that Benson "obtained from David McKay, the 92-year old prophet and president of the Mormon Church, an unpublished letter giving full approval to any campaign that Mr. Benson might make."

The article noted that political activity among American churches was on the rise; but while larger denominations such as Catholics, Methodists, Presbyterians and Lutherans had generally espoused liberal positions, the Mormons remained "deeply conservative." Summed the writer: "In great part this is due to certain doctrinal teachings unique to Mormonism. But it also is due to the energetic efforts of Mr. Benson, whose flirtation with the John Birch Society has produced deep divisions within the church. 'What Benson is doing could rend the church,' says a Western governor, 'and that would be bad for the church and bad for the West.'"[145]

In a nationally syndicated column, Drew Pearson also noted the shift in Mormon political philosophy, which he saw as atypical of McKay: "David O. McKay, president of the Church and now 93 years old, once championed the principle of free discussion, of letting Mormons have and listen to sharply divergent views. He still stands by that principle in theory. But the *Deseret News,* the Church-owned newspaper which circulates throughout Utah, shies away from publishing views not approved by the Church elders. Chief reason for the new Mormon trend toward political and philosophical isolation is probably the influx of outsiders into Utah, plus the steady drumbeat of John Birch Propaganda from Ezra Taft Benson."[146]

For his part, McKay disregarded the criticism and stood solidly behind Benson. Meeting with him in late October, McKay reread his letter of support, reaffirmed its content, and assured Benson that "I would support him in any effort which he might make in his efforts to help preserve the Constitution."[147]

In November, McKay's counselors met with him regarding a request Benson had made to duplicate and distribute widely his talk in the most recent general conference. The essence of Benson's talk, which was a thinly veiled criticism of his fellow General Authorities, whom he felt to be soft on Communism, is clear in the following paragraphs:

> In spite of the scriptural evidence and the counsel of modern-day prophets during the past more than 100 years, there are still some who seem to feel we have no responsibility to safeguard and strengthen our precious God-given freedom. There are some who apparently feel that the fight for freedom is separate from the gospel. They express it in several ways, but it generally boils down to this: Just live the gospel; there's no need to get involved in trying to save freedom and the Constitution or to stop Communism.
>
> Of course, this is dangerous reasoning, because in reality you cannot fully live the gospel without working to save freedom and the Constitution, and to stop Communism.

> In the war in heaven, what would have been your reaction if
> someone had told you just to do what is right—there's no need to get
> involved in the fight for freedom?[148]

Tanner, normally nonconfrontational, pointed out that "from this talk one would conclude that Brother Benson and President McKay stand alone among the General Authorities on the question of freedom." Brown strongly agreed: "I feel that this kind of talk is wholly objectionable because it does impugn the rest of us and our motives when we have advised the people to live their religions and stay away from extremist ideas and philosophies. Personally, I think we should not encourage the distribution of this kind of propaganda." McKay agreed that it went too far and "decided that the talk should not be mimeographed and distributed in pamphlet form."[149] Two weeks later, however, Benson met privately with McKay and asked him to reconsider his decision. After rereading Benson's talk, McKay made the opposite decision: "There is nothing wrong with the talk, so I told my secretary to tell Elder Benson he could have it mimeographed if he wished."[150]

While Ezra Taft Benson's bid for the presidency was still ongoing, he renewed his efforts yet again to obtain McKay's sanction for his formal affiliation with the John Birch Society. On February 24, 1967, McKay received a twelve-page letter from Robert Welch, "a cursory glance of which indicates or pleads for permission for Ezra Taft Benson to serve on the National Council of the Society."[151] In his conclusion, Welch indicated that Benson had already agreed to serve on the council, subject only to McKay's consent.[152] McKay postponed action until, a month later, Benson met with him privately to push for a decision. McKay told Benson, "I enjoyed reading Mr. Welch's letter and felt that he is sincerely dedicated, and that he displayed a very good spirit in his letter." For the second time he declined Welch's request. However, he worded his response in a way that left the door open: "It was agreed that Elder Benson would answer Mr. Welch and tell him that it would be impossible for him to serve on the Council at this time."[153]

It did not take long for Benson to raise the issue a third—and final—time. Only a month later he brought Robert Welch to meet McKay. Welch made an impassioned plea that included a letter to McKay. The letter began with the words, "This is probably the most important letter I have ever written." Welch pulled out all the stops in the letter, alleging that Communist infiltration of the United States government "has now reached so far that rampant treason is gradually but surely establishing Communist control over the United States." Standing between the Communists and complete takeover was but "one formidable, unshattered bulwark,...the one enemy which the Communists fear most anywhere in the world," the John Birch Society. Unhampered by modesty, Welch alleged that "but for the opposition of the John Birch Society our country would already have been carried

by Communist internal subversion beyond the point of 'no return.'" In concluding his letter, Welch called Benson "one of the world's truly great men," and said
that allowing Benson to join the John Birch national council would enable him "to
perform for his country an act of greatness equal to that of many another hero in
our history."[154]

Although McKay had for years hardened and then softened his stance on the
John Birch Society and, more particularly, Benson's interaction with it, he never
softened to the point of allowing Benson a formal affiliation. And on this occasion,
despite the intense pressure brought to bear by Benson and Welch, McKay held the
line. "I explained to him, as I have on two other occasions by letter, that it would
not be wise for Elder Benson to serve in this capacity."[155] This time the message
got through, and Benson did not ask the question a fourth time. Three days later,
McKay showed Welch's letter to Mark E. Petersen, who upon reading it said:
"President McKay, Elder Harold B. Lee has some hair-raising stories to tell about
the Birch Society which I am sure he will tell you, which I think would scare you
to death. We have the Church, and if we live up to its teachings, we do not need
to worry about what will happen to this country!"[156]

BENSON'S LOWERED PUBLIC PROFILE

Benson continued to pursue a conservative political agenda, though with a lower
profile once it became clear to him that McKay would never allow his formal affiliation with the John Birch Society. And Hugh B. Brown, for his part, continued to
be a sounding board for moderate and liberal Mormons who were upset at Benson's activities. Typical of the letters Brown received was one from a church member in Maryland: "I personally feel that Brother Benson is misusing his Priesthood
Authority.... I am finding it increasingly difficult to raise my right hand in Quarterly Conference and sustain Brother Benson as an Apostle. Isn't there something
that can be done to curb this type of political involvement of the Church in general?"[157]

While Brown's responses in the past had always been critical of the activities of
Benson and the society, he now responded even more strongly, suggesting that
McKay had finally realized that Benson's activities, if left unchecked, would do lasting damage to church members individually and to the church as an institution.
Three weeks after McKay's meeting with Benson and Welch, Brown wrote to a correspondent: "We did discuss your letter and numerous others like it on the same
subject with the First Presidency and are taking it to the Twelve as soon as Brother
Benson returns [from an assignment out of town]...and we prefer to have him
present when the matter is discussed. I think you can be assured that something
definite will be decided upon and activities in this connection will be curtailed."[158]

But Benson did not cut back on his political activities. Early in 1968, he asked McKay for permission to become the vice presidential candidate on the third-party ticket of Alabama Governor George C. Wallace. Unlike McKay's quasi-encouragement for Benson's earlier presidential aspirations with Strom Thurmond, this one met with McKay's immediate and unambiguous rejection. It is not clear how much of McKay's decision had to do with his already expressed aversion to a third political party, his personal feelings toward Wallace, his unwillingness to have an apostle square off against announced Mormon candidate George Romney, or merely growing weariness with Benson's political activities. In writing to Wallace, McKay couched his decision in ecclesiastical language: "Please be assured that my decision is not political in essence, but one that involves Mr. Benson's calling as a member of the Quorum of the Twelve Apostles of the Church."[159]

McKay's decision was not, however, an indication that he had softened his stance on Communism. Indeed, several months later when he learned of the Soviet invasion of Czechoslovakia he said: "The Communists will never surrender their main aim—that of world conquest—no matter what they say or do."[160]

Two months before the 1968 presidential election when George Romney had dropped out, Benson approached McKay one more time, again asking permission to run with George Wallace on a third-party ticket. McKay responded gently: "My decision is still the same;...I feel that Elder Benson should not launch out on this political campaign; that it could lead to confusion and misunderstanding in the Church."[161]

Shortly after the election, Hugh B. Brown summarized his feelings about Benson and the John Birch Society in an interview recorded by his grandson, expressing sentiments that proved to be accurate: "There are some [General Authorities]—I won't put it in the plural even—who sustain the John Birch Society. Others of us do not. I don't think that that should be an issue, should not be a question involving one's standing in the Church whether they approve of that or not. I do think that in this case all members of the General Authorities should keep out of that discussion. I think the John Birch Society will run its course and finally be rejected. That's my own opinion."[162]

In 1968, Benson made what proved to be his final attempt to recruit McKay's support of the John Birch Society. Telephoning Clare Middlemiss from New York City, he pleaded:

> Clare, President McKay has told me on various occasions that there are two things he regretted in his presidency: (1) the untimely decision, which was later changed, to move the college at Rexburg to Idaho Falls; and (2) the issuing of the statement in the public press against the John Birch Society. Now, in order to alleviate that feeling

about the John Birch Society, I wonder, since they are celebrating their 10th Anniversary tonight at a meeting and banquet in Indianapolis, Indiana, if President McKay would send a telegram similar to the following: "John Birch Society, c/o Mr. Robert Welch, Stauffer Inn, Indianapolis, Indiana—Congratulations upon reaching ten years of courageous and effective service in defense of our freedom and acquainting the American people with the insidious dangers of the atheistic communistic conspiracy. Best wishes for future success in the fight to preserve our God-given liberties."[163]

Middlemiss attempted to reach McKay with the request, but he was in a meeting and could not be interrupted. She then presented the matter to Alvin R. Dyer, a counselor in the First Presidency. Although Dyer was a Birch sympathizer, he vetoed the request before it could reach McKay.

McKay's Changing Attitude to Communism

In the final year of McKay's life, his relationship to Communism and to Benson changed slightly but significantly. While continuing to condemn Communism as forcefully as ever, he gradually acknowledged the difference between Communism as a system, and a Communist (and even more so, a Socialist) as a person. When N. Eldon Tanner inquired in May 1969 "if a man were an avowed communist, would our position be to excommunicate him or disqualify him for any position in the Church," McKay responded that he should not hold any church position, but allowed that he might remain a member of the church, a softening of his earlier stance.[164] It is likely that this change came with his belated realization that Socialist and even Communist parties in European countries carried far different baggage than in the United States. Indeed, one British member reminded even Benson of the difference: "Elder Benson was talking away to me and he said this and that. I said, 'Well, Elder Benson, I've got to be honest with you. I was very upset when I sat in the Tabernacle and heard you attack my politics.' 'What do you mean?' I said, 'Well, I'm a socialist. I've been a socialist all my life. My father was a great radical socialist. I don't think you know what socialists are when you come up and criticize them so harshly.' He explained to me the difference between the socialist he was attacking and the socialists I believed in at that time."[165]

McKay's friendship with Benson never waned, but his tolerance for the apostle's political extremism gradually eroded. In a First Presidency meeting eleven months before McKay's death, the subject of Benson's political remarks from the pulpit again came up. After McKay's counselors weighed in with assorted anecdotes highlighting the problem, McKay spoke:

I asked what conclusion the brethren had reached regarding the matter. President Tanner said the same conclusion that was arrived at about two years ago, that Elder Benson should discontinue this kind of thing, and particularly in stake conferences, and should limit himself to talking about the gospel and its applications. President Tanner said that he thought I made as clear a statement on the subject as he had heard made in the meeting of the Council of the First Presidency and the Twelve at that time. I said that there is no reason why we should not continue that understanding.[166]

When Benson gave an inflammatory speech at BYU three months later in which he criticized U.S. Government officials and the United Nations, McKay authorized Hugh B. Brown to go to BYU and give a strong rebuttal, stating, "I did not think that any government officials should be accused of these things."[167]

The Demise of Communism

Although McKay and Benson had both been willing to go to war to fight Communism, the war never came. Instead of going out with a bang, the Soviet Union went out with a whimper, collapsing in the late 1980s under its own weight. With its demise, Communism as a successful form of government quickly became discredited throughout the world. With the gradual opening of archives in the former Soviet Union and other Communist states, it has become apparent that some Communist infiltration of U.S. organizations and government institutions had occurred, yet the actual threat of the "Communist conspiracy" to the West never approached the cataclysmic dimensions of which Benson and Welch had warned.

Nor, despite Welch's claims, is there any convincing evidence that the John Birch Society was effective in combating Communism. It was *very* effective, however, in polarizing Americans, heightening political ill-will, and fostering an atmosphere of hate and intolerance. Welch's attacks on Dwight Eisenhower, John Foster Dulles, Martin Luther King, and other individuals and institutions gradually brought discredit and disdain to himself and his organization; and although the society still exists, it long ago ceased to have significant visibility within American society.

Benson's political activism diminished abruptly upon McKay's death, for he lost his patron and protector. McKay was succeeded by Joseph Fielding Smith and, subsequently, Harold B. Lee, both of whom had strongly objected to Benson's political activities during McKay's presidency. A comparison of Benson's general conference talks before and after McKay's death attests to their effectiveness in curtailing his political extremism.

Fifteen years after McKay died, Benson became church president; and to the surprise of many church members, whose memories of his earlier political activities were still vivid, he was a gentle, pastoral church president whose consistent message was a plea for Mormons to become reacquainted with the book that gave them their nickname, the *Book of Mormon*. The controversy that highlighted so many of his years as an apostle never returned.

Sadly, however, Mormonism's involvement in the 1960s with right-wing political extremism left a legacy that affects the church adversely to this day. As early as 1961, one Mormon Congressman, David S. King (D-Utah), warned McKay that the church seemed to be abandoning its position of neutrality in politics, to the extent that "Sunday School teachers are making broad hints and innuendoes in classes that those who follow the Democratic program are handmaidens of Communists, and cannot expect to consider themselves in full fellowship in the Church."[168] Mormonism's identification with right-wing politics did not go unnoticed in Communist countries, as indicated in a 1985 internal report by Stasi, the East German secret police: "In the May 18, 1985, political-operational report of Department XX...regarding the political-ideological orientation of the US-American Mormons, it was determined that they are to be classified as representatives of the right wing of American conservatism. There are close connections between their leadership and ruling circles within the government [at that time the Reagan administration]. Relationships also exist between persons and institutions of the church and the American secret service."[169]

Utah is now one of the most Republican states in the country, and Mormons have become so identified with the Republican Party that they have become almost invisible in Democratic presidential administrations. In recent years, this imbalance became of sufficient concern that the First Presidency, in 1998, assigned one of the few Democratic General Authorities, Marlin K. Jensen, to give an interview to the *Salt Lake Tribune* assuring readers that one may, indeed, simultaneously be a Democrat and a Mormon in good standing. He explained that church leaders "regret...that there would become a church party and a non-church party. That would be the last thing that we would want to have happen."[170]

Although McKay's fears of worldwide Communist conquest were overblown, his concerns that Communism was atheistic and that it robbed people of free agency remain well founded. One need only look at the countries formerly under Soviet domination to see the amount of damage inflicted on religion and individuals during seven decades of Communist oppression. And his prediction that Communist rulers would fall if they continued to rob people of their free choice between good and evil proved to be prophetic. His words spoken in 1954 are a potent reminder for all ages: "No power on earth can take this freedom away."[171]

13

POLITICS
AND THE CHURCH

The interface between politics and religion has always been an uncomfortable one within the United States, and the Founding Fathers took care to construct a wall to protect each from the excesses of the other. Within Mormonism, however, the wall has often been virtually, and sometimes actually, nonexistent. Joseph Smith envisioned a theocracy and came close to making it a reality in the brief period during which the city-state of Nauvoo flourished. Following the exodus to the Utah Territory, Brigham Young presided over both sides of the wall, simultaneously being church president and governor of Utah Territory.

Driven largely by a revulsion against plural marriage, the federal government eventually placed Utah Territory under non-Mormon (and generally antagonistic) political control.[1] Nonetheless, church leaders continue to exert significant influence over political affairs to this day. Of particular note during the twentieth century was the high-profile service within the federal government of two members of the Quorum of the Twelve Apostles. From 1903 to 1933 Reed Smoot served as U.S. senator from Utah, with the blessing of Church Presidents Joseph F. Smith and Heber J. Grant; and from 1953 to 1961 Ezra Taft Benson was Secretary of Agriculture in the administration of Dwight D. Eisenhower, with the blessing of David O. McKay.[2]

While no sitting church president since Brigham Young has held political office, the fact that each sat at the head of the largest voter constituency in Utah automatically conferred upon him political credibility and influence within Utah, and often nationally. However, experience taught that exercise of that influence was a two-edged sword and that even the best of intentions sometimes fell prey to the law of unintended consequences.[3]

David O. McKay's periodic forays into the world of politics met with mixed success, in large part because he did not see the world through the eyes of a politician. J. Bracken Lee, a non-Mormon who served two terms as Utah governor and whose terms overlapped McKay's presidency by five years, was particularly candid in assessing his political skills: "McKay as a politician would be the world's worst because his thinking didn't run along political lines."[4]

On issues that McKay defined as matters of faith and morals, he did not hesitate to take a strong, public stand; but in matters of partisan politics, he took pains to stay on the sidelines and show public neutrality, even though he was a lifelong Republican. Undoubtedly this discretion was a factor in his congenial relationships with several U.S. presidents of both political parties, most notably (and perhaps most surprisingly) with Democrat Lyndon B. Johnson.

MORAL ISSUES

McKay's first high-profile political stand came during his tenure on the Centennial Commission, which crafted the 1947 celebration of the Saints' arrival in the Salt Lake Valley a century earlier. Although he was already well aware of the moral turpitude in certain neighborhoods, McKay saw the centennial as a catalyst for cleaning up the city's image, for the celebration would bring the state into the national spotlight. Speaking at April general conference in 1946, he called first for a community face-lift, citing the "dilapidated structures marring the landscape.... Let us all join in the campaign to stimulate home owners to paint houses, fences, barns and other buildings and to maintain a general atmosphere of tidiness and neatness." Then he turned his focus inward: "What about our uniting for a moral cleanup? There is evidence of the presence of 'bunco' men in the city who are preying upon unsuspecting travelers.... Is it possible that Salt Lake is looked upon by these crooks as a 'fixed' city?...What about gambling, the slot machine racket, and race horse betting? What about beer and whiskey joints, and the flaunting of immorality on the public streets?"[5]

The statement, clearly an indictment of the local police force, brought a heated rebuttal from the police chief. He called McKay's statement a "slander of the entire Salt Lake City police department" and a "poor example of civic pride."[6] The following day, McKay shot back:

> The chief of police seems to be supersensitive regarding my suggestions about the desirability of having a moral as well as a landscape clean-up for the centennial.... Well, vastly more important than making pleasing our physical landscape is keeping our cities and towns clean morally.... If the chief of police whose inference may or may not be in harmony with my "implications," desires to know of some of the addresses of places in which gambling is being carried on, if he will call at my office I shall be pleased to give them to him as they have been reported to me.[7]

Heated exchanges continued for days, each publicized in the newspapers. Then, after a hiatus of three months, McKay again prodded civic government by charging that "the [Salt Lake City] commission in three months had failed to effect a moral cleanup of Salt Lake."8 The following day Mayor Earl J. Glade entered the fray and "pledged the support of the city administration in building a cleaner city."9 Three days later, the Salt Lake City police made their first arrest in the new clean-up campaign, thereby giving McKay a symbolic, albeit temporary, victory over vice.10

After becoming church president, McKay took on moral issues in a similarly public manner only twice. The first involved compulsory labor union membership, which he viewed as a violation of free agency and thus a moral issue, while others viewed it as strictly a political issue.

McKay's aversion to coercive activity on the part of labor unions dated to his early years in the First Presidency. Speaking to local church leaders in 1937, he stated: "You brethren and sisters should know the attitude of the church regarding the present efforts of some so called labor organizations in coercing members of our church into unions. I think we need not quibble. We have no apology to offer. It is un-American when 5 percent of this nation attempts to force the other 95 percent along a particular line of action."11

Over the next two decades, McKay periodically spoke out against compulsory union membership, most notably in a 1961 letter published by the U.S. Chamber of Commerce that linked the practice to the central religious doctrine of free agency: "We believe it is fundamental that the right to voluntary unionism should once again be reestablished in this nation and that state right to work laws should be maintained inviolate. At the very basis of all our doctrine stands the right to the free agency of man. We are in favor of maintaining this free agency to the greatest extent possible. We look upon any infringement thereof not essential to the proper exercise of police power of the state adversely."12

McKay's views drew broader attention four years later when right-to-work laws became a national issue. Acting on a campaign promise, U.S. President Lyndon B. Johnson sought legislation to repeal Section 14(b) of the Taft-Hartley Law. In a First Presidency meeting shortly after the announcement of the proposed legislation, McKay described it in moral terms: "We discussed the Right-to-Work Law which President Lyndon B. Johnson is proposing for federal legislation, which law would make it obligatory in all states that working people seeking employment join a union, which takes away the free agency of man." N. Eldon Tanner, McKay's second counselor, suggested that the First Presidency "write to our congressional delegation and tell them that we are definitely opposed to such legislation." Such action was unprecedented in McKay's presidency, and he responded, "I shall give the matter further thought before making a decision."13

The following day the First Presidency again considered the legislation and decided on the more moderate course of writing "a letter to be sent to President Johnson, stating that the Church is opposed to such legislation, this letter to be signed by the First Presidency."[14] They wrote and sent the letter the next day but five days thereafter returned to Tanner's earlier suggestion and sent a second letter to the eleven Latter-day Saint members of Congress (three Senators and eight Representatives). The concluding paragraph of the second letter sent a strong message: "We respectfully express the hope that no action will be taken by the Congress of the United States that would in any way interfere with the God-given rights of men to exercise free agency in seeking and maintaining work privileges."[15] The letter ignited a firestorm that swept through the national press.

Senator Frank E. Moss (D-Utah) was the first to respond and he did so publicly, issuing a statement to the church-owned *Deseret News* three days later. What McKay saw as a moral issue, Moss saw as purely political, and he minced no words in expressing his displeasure:

> I am rather surprised to learn that the First Presidency of the Church of Jesus Christ of Latter-day Saints has chosen to speak on a legislative and political matter, the repeal of Section 14(b) of the Taft-Hartley Act. It has been my position, and I thought it was the position of the Church, that the Church should stand aloof in matters of political controversy where members of the Church disagree by reason of honest difference of belief as to what political or governmental action is desirable.... As a Senator, I will form my judgment and I will vote my honest conviction in accordance with my conscience.[16]

Four days later Moss, along with four Latter-day Saint Congressmen (all Democrats), sent a second letter to the First Presidency. While slightly more measured in its tone, it nonetheless sent the same message: that the five men would not accept the First Presidency letter as binding upon them. Ironically, they turned the free agency argument on end to make their point:

> While we respect and revere the offices held by the members of the First Presidency of the Church, we cannot yield to others our responsibilities to our constituency, nor can we delegate our own free agency to any but ourselves. We know that each of you will agree that in this instance we act in conformity with the highest principles of our church in declining to be swayed by the view expressed in the communication of June 22nd under the signatures of the First Presidency. We hasten to assure you that we stand ready at any time to receive your views, that they will be considered and evaluated as the good faith

expression of men of high purpose, but we cannot accept them as binding upon us.[17]

Criticism also came from other quarters. On July 7, N. Eldon Tanner reported to the First Presidency that he had met with Utah Governor Calvin Rampton, a Democrat, at a charity breakfast. Tanner passed on Rampton's message that "when he and all other Democratic nominees accepted their nomination they made a commitment, including President Johnson himself, that they would work for the repeal of Section 14(b) of the Taft-Hartley Law, and that he had to carry out his commitment."[18] Four days later Tanner and Hugh B. Brown met with four union officials in Salt Lake City, all of them church members, at their request. They told McKay that the union representatives "were not militant but were positive in their opinion that Section 14(b) should be repealed."[19] The following day the *New York Times* publicized the issue nationally in an article that began, "The leaders of the Church of Jesus Christ of Latter-day Saints—the Mormon Church—have been rebuffed in an attempt to get Mormon members of Congress to cast votes as a matter of religious duty."[20]

Public opinion also generally went against the First Presidency's intervention. A particularly pointed editorial in an Idaho newspaper challenged McKay's assertion that the issue was moral:

> It could be pointed out there's a moral obligation to permit men to seek employment regardless of union membership. It also could be argued that there's a moral question involved and the church has every right to take an active interest in the well being of all its members. But basically the right-to-work issue involving the controversial section of the Taft-Hartley law, is a matter of politics. As such, it lies far outside the jurisdiction of any church leadership. It's just not a proper matter for expression of church views and certainly church pressure is improper, to say the least. Leaders of any church should speak up on clear-cut matters of theology or morals and all members of Congress should be happy to listen and try to profit from proper advice on such matters. But church influence should be limited to problems and issues that are clearly church problems and issues. Churches have no place in politics.[21]

On July 21, the controversy was on the First Presidency's agenda in the context of a set of questions from *Time* magazine. The news magazine was planning an article on the church's opposition to 14(b) and had sent in the written questions. One question went to the heart of the issue: "Is this statement considered by Church members to be a religious and moral declaration from the Prophet of God, being in effect an expression of the will of God that the law makers vote against the repeal of that section of the Taft-Hartley Law?" After "some discussion of the matter" with his counselors, McKay responded to this question:

> The answer is that the statement sets forth the attitude of the First Presidency of the Church; that, however, that part of the statement reading as follows is from the Lord: "It is our sincere desire and earnest prayer that no action will be taken by the President or the Congress of the United States that would tend to interfere with the God-given right of men to exercise free agency in seeking and maintaining work privileges."

Of the balance of the statement, McKay said, "It is only an opinion."[22]

Taking his lead from McKay's response, Hugh B. Brown took the initiative of making a statement to a reporter in New York City, where he was vacationing, that emphasized "opinion" while deemphasizing "from the Lord." It made national headlines: "A Mormon church leader eased the religious bind upon Mormon Congressmen today regarding repeal of the right-to-work section of the Taft-Hartley Act. Hugh B. Brown, right-hand man to David O. McKay, President of the Church of Jesus Christ of Latter-day Saints, softened Mr. McKay's recent stand on the law.... Mr. Brown, who is President McKay's first counselor, said the church leader's words had been intended as an expression of opinion and not a revelation from God."[23]

When McKay learned of Brown's statement, he "told Clare [Middlemiss] that I was amazed to read in the *[Salt Lake] Tribune* this morning the Right-to-Work statements made by President Brown in New York. I said that he had no authority nor any right whatever to make any additional statement to what was said on this subject by the First Presidency."[24] The following day, Apostle Delbert L. Stapley told McKay that Brown's statement had weakened the church's position. Without consulting his counselors, McKay promptly issued a statement designed to reverse the impact of Brown's remarks: "The First Presidency of the Church of Jesus Christ of Latter-day Saints Tuesday made clear it had not softened its opposition to repeal of Section 14-B of the Taft-Hartley Act despite contrary statements made recently in New York and Washington, D.C. 'This thinking and views as reported in the eastern press are unauthorized,' President David O. McKay and his two counselors, Hugh B. Brown and N. Eldon Tanner, said Tuesday. 'The statement as originally given and announced...remains unchanged.'"[25]

McKay's move was highly unusual and undoubtedly blindsided Brown, who was still out of town when the new statement, which was also attributed to him, was published. Two days later, at the next First Presidency meeting after Brown's return, no remark found its way into the minutes suggesting any further discussion of the matter.[26] However, the following day, July 30, Brown raised the issue in the First Presidency meeting, apparently to McKay's satisfaction:

> President Brown mentioned some rumor that is going around to the effect that he had softened the stand of the First Presidency as expressed in the statement regarding the proposed repeal of the Right-to-Work amendment. President Brown wanted me to understand what he did say. He stated that he said to the representative of Time Magazine who had called on him just what I had told him to say and no more, and that this man had come back yesterday and confirmed that and stated that he had reported exactly what President Brown had told him; that, however, when it went to New York, they changed it there and had given it headline value. President Brown then read to me the statement as contained in the minutes of the First Presidency's meeting which was agreed upon by the First Presidency at that time. He reiterated that he had done nothing that he was not authorized to do. I said that I am glad to hear that.[27]

Predictably, negative reactions continued to reverberate following the First Presidency's clarifying statement. *Newsweek* quoted Senator Moss as saying, "In my experience this is the most direct intervention in political matters I have ever seen the church attempt."[28] Drawing the obvious comparison to earlier anxiety over John F. Kennedy and possible Vatican influences, Congressman David S. King (D-Utah) stated, "If the Pope had sent such a letter to John F. Kennedy, or even the Catholic Congressmen, there would have been a major crisis," while Mormon Congressman Ken Dyal (D-California) wrote to a constituent: "I remember how the ward members and others used to stop me and say, 'How can you support [Kennedy]? Don't you know that the Pope will give him orders and we will be under the domination of Rome?'...What would you have said...if an encyclical had been issued by Pope Paul ordering, or requesting (as does the [First Presidency] letter of June 22) all of the Catholic members of the Congress to repeal Section 14(b)? What would the people of our nation have said?"[29]

The final aftershock occurred two weeks later, when a news article in the *Wall Street Journal* stated, "Many high-ranking Mormons feel the Church's attempt to influence Washington votes was an out-and-out tactical blunder. Even First Counselor [Hugh B.] Brown says he would just as soon forget the incident. 'They (the Congressmen) have the right to tell us to jump in the lake, and they did just that,' he comments."[30] McKay was understandably irritated when he read the article. Unlike the earlier incident, which Brown had brought up for discussion, McKay now confronted Brown "regarding the statement attributed to him in the article to the effect that 'Congressmen have the right to tell us we can jump in the lake.' President Brown said that he had made no such statement."[31]

The issue ended there. The article had been published while McKay was spending time at the seclusion of his Huntsville farm on doctor's order and was thus temporarily insulated from its impact. This meeting with Brown occurred ten days after its publication. McKay accepted Brown's explanation and returned the next day to Huntsville for another ten days. Perhaps because of his prolonged absence from the office, the story ran out of gas. It was not discussed in subsequent First Presidency meetings.

The irony of the whole affair was that none of it had any influence on the outcome of the repeal effort. Several months later in February 1966, having failed three times to break a Senate filibuster on the measure, the Johnson Administration gave up and the bill died.[32] The final vote was sixteen short of the two-thirds majority required, so the three Mormon votes would have had no effect regardless of how they were cast.[33] It was one of the few legislative defeats for Johnson since he took office in November 1963, following the assassination of John F. Kennedy.

The final moral issue that McKay tackled was liquor by the drink in Utah. In the aftermath of Prohibition's repeal in 1933, Utah became a "semi-dry" state, with distilled spirits available for purchase only in state-owned stores. The purchase of liquor by the drink in hotels and restaurants was prohibited, and the hospitality community in Utah periodically attempted to improve its bottom-line by rewriting the law.

McKay, while never wavering in his personal aversion to alcoholic beverages or a rigid requirement that church members adhere to the Word of Wisdom's prohibition against tea, coffee, alcohol, and tobacco,[34] was sympathetic to the plight of the restaurateurs and hoteliers when he met in April 1965 with first-term Governor Calvin L. Rampton. Citing his own opposition to liquor by the drink in spite of growing pressure to change the law in that direction, Rampton presented a compromise: a "proposal to place twelve small package agencies in hotels and large motels that cater to tourists.... He hoped that the package agency proposal would satisfy the situation." McKay agreed with Rampton's reasoning. "After listening to the Governor's presentation of the matter, I said this, too, is a matter of a governmental nature which I do not feel to oppose."[35] Later in the year, the State Liquor Commission moved quietly to establish small package stores in several hotels and motels.

During the same legislative session, however, as reported by the *Wall Street Journal,* an LDS state senator tried to broaden the package-store idea and, "with the backing of several prominent Church members and businessmen, introduced a bill to permit sale of miniature liquor bottles in bars and restaurants." When it looked as though public support was mobilizing behind the bill, the Church-owned *Deseret News* "opened fire editorially and the bill died a quick death."[36]

Three years later the debate reemerged, this time concerning a liquor-by-the-drink law that would go to the voters in the form of a referendum. McKay and his counselors agreed that this was a moral issue, and McKay decided that "we should pursue the matter of seeing to it that our people are informed on the policy of the Church concerning this important matter." Alvin R. Dyer, now a member of the First Presidency, suggested that the church not try to go it alone, recalling its earlier failure to prevent Utah from becoming the final state to ratify the Constitutional amendment repealing Prohibition. He recommended "that Weston E. Hamilton would be a good man to help with non-members of influence to work for the defeat of the referendum." McKay agreed, saying, "We should seek all the outside help we can get to help in defeating the measure."[37]

Two days later, Tanner told a joint meeting of the First Presidency and the Quorum of the Twelve: "The only way we can defeat it is to organize throughout the Church and throw this weight against it." McKay agreed. "I said that we must be prepared to prevent liquor by the drink; that if we were to get liquor by the drink, we would have trouble." Delbert L. Stapley proposed spending church funds—estimated by Gordon B. Hinckley to be as much as $100,000—in an organized campaign to fight the referendum, and the group of church leaders unanimously approved the proposal and appointed Marion G. Romney to head an action committee. McKay had the last word in the meeting: "I firmly stated: 'Let them know we mean something.'"[38]

On May 10, 1968, McKay met in his apartment with Alvin R. Dyer of the First Presidency, Marion G. Romney, Gordon B. Hinckley, Wilford Kirton (the church's attorney), and Joseph Anderson (secretary to the First Presidency). Hugh B. Brown, who was ill, and N. Eldon Tanner, who was out of town, did not attend. Romney reported that his committee had written for that evening's edition of the *Deseret News* an editorial opposing a petition to place the issue of liquor by the drink on the November ballot. However, he and his committee, concerned that the editorial might not be sufficient to stop proponents from gathering enough signatures, asked McKay for a First Presidency statement for publication the following day, in a further bid to thwart their efforts. At Dyer's prior prompting, Romney and Hinckley had drafted a statement and brought it to the meeting. Hinckley read the statement to McKay, who "energetically approved of the article and said most positively that we must do everything in our power to defeat the bill.... He authorized that his signature be attached to the statement and placed in the *Deseret News* on the front page in the May 11 issue in all editions."[39] McKay's statement concluded with an unambiguous call to action: "I call upon members of the Church throughout the State, and all citizens interested in safeguarding youth and avoiding the train of evils associated with alcohol, to take a stand against the proposal for 'liquor by the drink.'"[40]

Despite their efforts, church leaders were unable to keep the measure off the ballot, and so they mobilized outside support. On May 25 a coalition that included local Latter-day Saint leaders (but no General Authorities), Protestant clergy, and other individuals announced formation of "Citizens for a Better Utah Through Opposing Liquor-By-The-Drink."[41] Two weeks later the anti-liquor campaign received a boost from the Rev. Louis B. Gerhardt, president of the Salt Lake Ministerial Association and a member of the central committee of Citizens for a Better Utah, who concluded a lengthy statement by questioning the wisdom of having private citizens, rather than elected officials, decide the issue: "Revision of our liquor laws is certainly necessary. This is obvious and important, but even more important is that we see the entire issue in proper perspective. Surely circumventing our elected representatives with its deteriorating effect on the representative system is far more serious than the additional passage of time that may be required to make significant changes in the membership of our representative body who could, in turn, respond affirmatively to the voters who elected them."[42]

Public debate continued over the course of the summer, with numerous letters to the editor of the Utah newspapers on both sides of the issue, but no more public statements on the part of the church. In September, with the election only a few weeks away, the First Presidency renewed the call to battle in a circular letter to all Utah stake presidents and bishops. It stated in part: "We desire that all family heads become familiar with the facts on Liquor Initiative Petition #A to be voted on in the November election."[43] Two weeks later, McKay's address in October general conference drew national attention. The *New York Times* reported: "The 'evils of liquor' were assailed yesterday by David O. McKay...as the Mormons opened their 138th semi-annual world conference.... The church has always stood firm against the use of alcoholic beverages, and Mr. McKay hit the drinking issue hard. He expressed his concern for 'the moral breakdown caused by drinking,' and cited a number of experiences that have shown the damage drinking does to homes and families."[44]

Voters defeated the measure by a margin of 270,132 to 143,371, surprisingly large even with the church leading out on an issue that was clearly framed in moral terms.[45] Although a proposal allowing mini-bottles in private clubs easily passed the legislature the following year, the defeat had long-term effects, and even today unrestricted liquor by the drink is not available in Utah.

Shortly after the successful campaign to defeat liquor by the drink, the First Presidency issued an unprecedented circular letter defining the kinds of moral issues upon which the church might properly exert its influence. While no context was included, the letter seems to reflect both the church's recent success as well as its earlier embarrassment over right-to-work: "We recognize the urgent need of encouraging legislators and civic groups to use their good offices to combat the evils of drinking, gambling, immorality and other vices. While strictly political matters should properly be left in the field of politics where they rightfully belong, on moral issues the church and its members should take a positive stand. We urge all members of the church to wield their influence in the matter of encouraging the introduction of proper legislation that will, when enacted into law, combat evil of the kind mentioned, and safeguard the morals of members and nonmembers alike."[46]

NON-PARTISAN POLITICS

David O. McKay was sensitive both to the needs of the community in which church headquarters was located and also to how church resources might be used to meet some of those needs. During his service on the Centennial Commission in 1946–47 he worked closely with John F. Fitzpatrick, publisher of the *Salt Lake Tribune* and a prominent lay Roman Catholic, and Gus Backman, director of the Salt Lake City Chamber of Commerce. After the Centennial celebration was completed, the three men continued to meet informally in a relationship that was driven mostly by friendship, but occasionally by community activism. John Gallivan, who succeeded Fitzpatrick at the helm of the *Tribune* upon the latter's death in 1960, described a relationship that was not well understood publicly:

> John Fitzpatrick and Gus Backman who was also a very close friend of President McKay's started meeting with President McKay for breakfast every Wednesday morning in the old coffee shop at the Hotel Utah. They continued there for a couple or three years faithfully every Wednesday when they were all in town and then they moved to President McKay's office and that went on from 1947 until Fitzpatrick died in 1960. Then it was my great fortune to take his seat each Wednesday of those meetings.... They were wonderful. There was all kinds of speculation about what really went on there—but what went on there was just an exchange of stories and good fellowship.... This isn't to say that important things didn't happen at those meetings, and certainly they did lay the background for the telephone call that was often made to bring about a decision that was good for the business community and the Church's relationship to the business community.[47]

Perhaps the most important such decision had to do with the construction of Salt Lake City's first convention center. In the early 1960s, the average tourist stay in Salt Lake City was less than one day, while in nearby Denver it was nearly five days. Construction of the Salt Palace, a project completed in 1969, not only provided a magnet for businessmen and tourists, but also revitalized the downtown area by razing run-down buildings. According to Gallivan, "It turned skid row of Salt Lake into a hotel row. At the time we had 700 hotel rooms between the Newhouse Hotel and the Hotel Utah at Temple Square, and the ones at the Newhouse were pretty well run down. Now [1995] we've got about 14,000 within walking distance. That all came about on account of a favor—it might have happened anyway, but it would have taken much longer—a favor granted by President McKay."[48]

The favor came in the form of a dollar-a-year lease to Salt Lake County of prime church-owned land kitty-corner from Temple Square, with an option to purchase outright. Gallivan concluded his story: "[McKay] was really wonderful, and the rest is history. We have been so successful in the convention business that in 25 years we outgrew those facilities.... I would have to struggle to remember any time he ever asked me for anything. He was constantly anxious to help out in the business community, helping to build, to create the employment that we had to have."[49]

PARTISAN POLITICS

David O. McKay was a lifelong Republican, reportedly because the church, as part of the process of accommodating statehood by balancing political affiliations, asked some families to leave the Democratic Party in 1893 when it dismantled its own People's Party. Monroe McKay, interviewed in 1999, passed on a great second-hand story from Stewart Grow, head of BYU's Political Science Department. The popular folklore, still told today, is that Church President Wilford Woodruff (or sometimes Apostle John Henry Smith, a fervent Republican), instructed ward bishops to assign ward members evenly to the two national political parties and that, according to the folklore, many bishops simply stood at the pulpit, used the central aisle as the division point, and assigned half the house to one party and the other half to the other. Grow, trying to document this tale, "interviewed President McKay. President McKay told him that when his father was the bishop of the Huntsville Ward, he came home one Sunday and around the table he said, 'Now children, I have something to tell you. I have become a Republican.' President McKay said to Dr. Grow, 'I remember how ashamed we children were, because Father and Whiskey Olson were the only two Republicans in Huntsville.'"[50]

Once he became church president, McKay took great care to avoid the appearance of partisanship, generally with success. Even when Apostle Ezra Taft Benson became Secretary of Agriculture in Republican President Dwight D. Eisenhower's administration with McKay's explicit blessing, McKay tried to steer a public course of political neutrality.

The first test of that neutrality came the year following his assumption of the church presidency. Early in August 1952, Marriner Eccles, a prominent Utah banker who was the Republican candidate for the U.S. Senate, met with him and asked "if the Church would be against him in the campaign. I answered that the Church takes no stand whatever in politics, that there are members of the Church who are Democrats, and members who are Republicans, and that I personally am going to treat each group fairly."[51]

Two weeks later McKay was approached by Heber Bennion, the Democratic Secretary of State, who "had heard that the Church favors Mayor Earl Glade for Governor, and favored the Republicans." Again, McKay repeated what he had told Eccles: "I told him that the Church takes no stand whatever in politics—there are Democrats in the Church, there are Republicans in the Church, and I am President of the Church, and so far as I am personally concerned, I am going to treat each group in fairness."[52]

In spite of his even-handedness in private, rumors circulated widely that the church favored one party. Speaking in the October conference in 1952, one month before the general election in which Eisenhower and Adlai Stevenson were competing for the U.S. presidency, McKay tackled the issue head-on:

> Recently we heard that in one meeting, for example, it was stated authoritatively by somebody that two members of the General Authorities of the Church had held a meeting and had decided to favor one of the leading political parties over the other, here in this state, particularly.... This report is not true, and I take this opportunity here, publicly, to denounce such a report as without foundation in fact.... The President is President of the Church, not favoring in this election either political party. The welfare of all members of the Church is equally considered by the President, his Counselors, and the General Authorities. Both political parties will be treated impartially. *The Deseret News* is the organ of the Church. It will be equally fair and impartial in the treatment of both political parties.[53]

Upon seeing the newspaper headline, "General Dwight D. Eisenhower Wins by Landslide," he wrote in his diary, "We were all thrilled with the news. In my opinion, it is the greatest thing that has happened in a hundred years for our country."[54] He made a similar statement for attribution, enthusiastically telling a *Deseret News* reporter that Eisenhower's election in 1952 "is the turning point in United States, if not world history."[55] It was the last time, however, that he made such a statement in public; and the Kennedy–Nixon campaign of 1960 showed that he had good reason for such prudence.

McKay's neutrality did not mean that he discouraged Latter-day Saints from becoming involved in partisan politics. In 1956 Salt Lake attorney Oscar W. McConkie Jr., then a member of a stake presidency, met with McKay to discuss running for the U.S. Congress on the Democratic ticket. McKay summarized the meeting in his diary: "In view of the fact that Brother McConkie holds an important position in the Stake, he wondered if the church would have any objection to his accepting the nomination. I told Brother McConkie that he has my permission and my blessing if he cares to accept this nomination."[56] McConkie had McKay's personal blessing, tantamount to wishing him well, but neither asked for nor received his endorsement.

In the October 1956 general conference, McKay once again affirmed the church's neutrality in partisan politics, while encouraging individual church members to participate in the political process by voting. "We ask, we plead that every member of the Church go to the polls in November and cast your vote for the men and women whom you wish to occupy the offices named. Now you choose, and choose wisely and prayerfully, but cast your vote."[57]

In spite of his attempt to keep the church neutral, McKay had to deal with the fact that Ezra Taft Benson was a high-profile cabinet officer in a Republican administration. On at least one occasion, McKay encouraged a Democratic General Authority to counteract the perception that Republicans were being favored. Hugh B. Brown, who had been called as an apostle in April 1958, was invited in July to give the keynote address at the Utah Democratic state nominating convention. He met with McKay and "asked if it would be in keeping with the policy of the Church and his office as an Apostle to accept the invitation."[58] McKay responded: "Since some think we are one-sided in politics (having a member of the Twelve as Secretary of Agriculture during a Republican administration) it might be a good thing for him to accept this assignment and let the members of the Church know that both political sides are represented in the Church."[59]

The 1960 presidential campaign matched Senator John F. Kennedy against Vice President Richard M. Nixon in a very tight race. Although Utah had only four electoral votes, both candidates made campaign stops in Salt Lake City, spoke in the Tabernacle, and invited McKay to sit on the stand. He accepted both invitations, a demonstration of his policy of even-handedness. Kennedy's visit came first, in late September. When McKay received the senator in his office, he wished him well.

Two weeks later, Nixon spoke in the Tabernacle but in visiting McKay received a different message. The church-owned *Deseret News* reported the incident benignly: "During the interview, President McKay, speaking as a Republican, said to Vice President Nixon: 'I sat by your competitor in this office a few weeks ago and told him that if he were successful we would support him. In your case I'll say we hope you are successful.'"[60] The story immediately drew national attention. The news story in the *Chicago Tribune* called it "an Endorsement" and noted, "Local inhabitants were startled. It was the first time in history, they said, that the church, wielding great influence in the state, had laid a hand in blessing upon a Presidential candidate."[61]

What most startled many people was that religion had already become a campaign issue, but it was the Roman Catholic, not the Mormon, Church that was the focus. The *Washington Star* noted: "In a year when 'religion in politics' has been a burning issue, the first candidate to receive the formal endorsement of the head of a major church is not Senator Kennedy, the Catholic, but Mr. Nixon, the Quaker, who yesterday won the endorsement of the No. 1 Mormon in the land.... Local political reporters said they could recall no such positive endorsement of a presidential nominee by the head of the Mormon Church. Mr. McKay made no comparable declaration to President Eisenhower in 1952 or 1956, they said. His action was seen as having significance even beyond the borders of Utah."[62]

Embarrassed by the *faux pas* and its fallout, McKay enlisted his secretary, Clare Middlemiss, to act as his impromptu press secretary. When the Mormon *Intermountain News* telephoned for a clarification, she told the reporter: "The statement in the press is correct but it isn't the way President McKay meant it.... He wants it clarified that he was speaking 'as a personal voter and as a Republican' to the Republican candidate of his party."[63]

Although the incident quickly blew over and Utah's electoral votes went to Nixon, some questioned whether the church had, in fact, abandoned its official neutrality. A year later Congressman David S. King (D-Utah) visited McKay to discuss, according to McKay's summary of the meeting, "what he thought were actions that indicated that perhaps there was an abandonment by the Church of its neutrality in politics." King told of several instances where, in local church meetings, the Democratic Party was disparaged and asked that McKay rectify any misunderstanding. McKay's response suggests that he was still smarting from the Nixon endorsement:

> He [King] urged that the First Presidency say something in print as to where the Church stands on politics. He said he understood the Church had spoken officially sometime in the past, but he thinks that the average Democrat does not know where to find it. He then discussed the general direction of the Democratic administration which he thinks is in complete harmony with Gospel principles. He also set

forth his political philosophy. I remarked to him that the action of the President of the Church in choosing two Democrats for counselors [Henry D. Moyle and Hugh B. Brown] should be sufficient indication that the Democrats have a definite place in the Church. I said that all we need to do is to republish what we have heretofore said on the political stand of the Church.[64]

In 1962 the question of church neutrality again arose, this time in the context of California state politics where Nixon, the defeated presidential candidate in 1960, was competing against Democrat Edmund G. ("Pat") Brown for the gubernatorial chair. John M. Russon, president of the Los Angeles Stake, had given permission for Nixon to speak in the stake center and, as a result, other church members asked that Pat Brown be given equal time in the same venue. It turned out that Russon had not acted independently; rather, when the question of Nixon's speaking in the building came up, Russon had consulted the General Authority visiting at quarterly stake conference—Ezra Taft Benson. The apostle had approved it. Caught in a bind, McKay gave a qualified "yes" to the Democratic request: "I said that it is the rule of the Church that we do not open our houses for political purposes; that under the circumstances in this case, however, we should give Governor Brown the same privilege that was given to Nixon, and then tell them that this has to stop. I said that in fairness, both parties should be given the same privilege."[65]

Several months later the church officially closed the door to subsequent use of church buildings for partisan political meetings. In a circular letter to all U.S. stake presidents, the First Presidency instructed:

> The General Authorities of the Church as such do not favor one political party over another; the Church has no candidate or candidates for political office; we do not undertake to tell people how to vote.... It is contrary to our counsel and advice that ward, branch or stake premises, chapels or other Church facilities be used in any way for political campaign purposes, whether it be for speech-making, distribution of literature, or class discussions. Needless to say, we are unalterably opposed to the use of our Sacrament or other Church meetings for any such purposes, and those who attempt to use the Church facilities to further their political ambitions are injuring their cause and doing the Church a disservice.[66]

Only in one instance did McKay intentionally abandon his self-imposed public neutrality and that was during the presidential campaign of George Romney. Romney was a renowned and highly regarded Michigan Republican, who served simultaneously and effectively as president of American Motors and president of the

Detroit Stake. Although Michigan was a highly unionized and predominantly Democratic state, Romney had gained high marks from both parties for his efforts to improve relations between management and labor unions through an organization called Citizens for Michigan. Romney paid a courtesy call to the First Presidency early in 1960 and, in the course of that meeting, told them that he had been urged by some to seek election as governor and by others to run for the Senate. He had declined both suggestions.[67] Two years later, as the 1962 election season began, he again visited the First Presidency. Again he had been urged to run for governor, and this time he had not declined. He came to the First Presidency, not for either permission or endorsement, but for clarification of the church's ban on priesthood ordination of blacks, which would certainly become an issue in the election, given Michigan's large black population.

Though Romney did not press McKay to change the policy, his language suggested, according to McKay's diary, that he would welcome a change as helping his electability: "He said he has no race bias; that he has worked with the negroes in these programs as much as he has worked with others.... But he feels that there is no question but that this particular point will receive a great deal of publicity and public discussion, not only in Michigan, but more broadly."[68] McKay acknowledged that "there is no question but that the negro question will come up" but declined to do anything more than restate the current policy. He offered no hint of change and questioned, without giving a reason, whether it might not be preferable for Romney to delay his campaign for two years, although he stopped short of telling him what to do. Henry D. Moyle, McKay's first counselor, went a bit further by suggesting that Romney's position as stake president was more important than running for governor. "Are you not stepping down from a high pedestal to a lower one?" he asked. Romney, noncommittal, said "he would keep everything which had been said in mind in undertaking to arrive at a decision."[69]

One month later the First Presidency received a letter from Romney in which he all but announced his candidacy for governor, citing a wide array of support that included "the state's leading negro Democrats" and "conservative Republicans." According to McKay's summary of the letter, rather than pressing for a change on the ordination policy, Romney "expressed the desire that his candidacy would not be hurtful to the Church by reason of the negro question." McKay concluded the discussion by leaving the matter entirely in Romney's hands: "After careful consideration, I said that we do not want to take the responsibility of telling him not to run, and it is not right for him to give us that responsibility."[70]

McKay took no public stand on Romney's candidacy, but in private he made one decision, only two weeks before the election, that reflected full awareness of it. At issue was a request from thousands of Nigerians to be baptized, albeit with the knowledge that priesthood ordination was not possible. McKay's decision was a good-faith effort not to allow such a move to influence the election: "We felt that it was best that nothing be done about the matter until after the November election for the reason that if we were to baptize a considerable number of negro people at this time, certain politicians might take the view that it was done to influence the negro vote in favor of George Romney in his candidacy for Governor of Michigan."[71]

Romney won election and reelection; amid rising national popularity, he decided late in 1966 to seek the Republican nomination for U.S. president in the 1968 election. At this point, McKay, delighted with the possibility of seeing a Mormon in the White House, temporarily abandoned his public neutrality.

In November 1966, Dan L. Thrapp, a *Los Angeles Times* reporter, sent a written request for an interview with McKay, during which he asked McKay about Romney's candidacy. His story quoted McKay's unqualified endorsement: "If Michigan Gov. George Romney, a Mormon, wins the Republican nomination for President, he will have the full backing of his church but will be his own man, David O. McKay, President of the Church of Jesus Christ of Latter-day Saints, told The Times. 'I hope he gets it!' boomed Dr. McKay, 93. 'He would make a good President. Very good! He is an independent thinker. He will go his own way—and that usually is a very good way.'"[72]

Given the anxiety over the Vatican's possible influence over John F. Kennedy (which never materialized), the statement might easily have caused an uproar had it been made concerning Romney-as-nominee. But Romney was still only a candidate for the Republican nomination and never came close to winning it, and so McKay's statement was soon forgotten.

On one occasion early in his presidency, McKay became involved in a political matter that, while not overtly partisan, carried strong partisan implications and thus deserves mention within this section. At issue was a proposed amendment to the Utah State Constitution that would restructure the State Senate by allocating one senator to each of the state's twenty-nine counties. Other states had similar laws, but the difference in Utah was that such a restructuring would virtually have assured perpetual Latter-day Saint control of the legislature, for the rural counties were strongly Mormon—and, not coincidentally, strongly Republican, which made it a de facto partisan issue even though it was not initially presented as such.[73]

Both houses of the legislature easily passed the law in 1953; but since it was a constitutional amendment, it required voter ratification in the 1954 election. Nearly a year before that election, Milton Weilenmann, a University of Utah law student, chair of the State Democratic Committee, and a Mormon, saw clearly the partisan implications and requested a meeting with McKay. "Brother Weilenmann is of the opinion that this gives to one section of the Senate too great an advantage.... I told him I would take the matter under consideration and have another discussion with him next Wednesday morning."[74]

Weilenmann's words weighed on McKay, particularly because they raised the essential issue of fairness. After all, the proposed reapportionment would have given the rural counties, which had less than 27 percent of the population, 83 percent of the Senate seats. The following morning he discussed the matter with the First Presidency: "It is reported that Brother [Harold B.] Lee and Brother [Henry D.] Moyle have advocated that principle saying that the Church is back of it, and there seems to be a division of opinion among the legislators. The Brethren were agreed that the Church should not take a position on the question, that it is the responsibility of the legislature to make the decision, and if there are any who feel we have taken a position they should be corrected."[75]

Indeed, according to Weilenmann, "Moyle's speeches left Church members with the impression that the Church and President McKay were all for the one senator per county plan."[76] Moyle was particularly candid in explaining his support of the measure. Speaking to "several persons" who were not further identified, he said, "Brethren, don't you realize that if this proposal is passed the Church will control twenty-six of twenty-nine senators?"[77]

The follow-up meeting with Weilenmann took place in McKay's office, not on Wednesday but one day later, Thanksgiving Day. Weilenmann invited a fellow Democrat, J. D. Williams, a political science professor from the University of Utah, to accompany him. According to Williams, Weilenmann related that, when he had raised the fairness issue, McKay had given an interesting response: "We would have disapproved of a majority church in Missouri doing this to us and I don't see that the principle has changed because we are in the majority out here. Furthermore, fourteen of the General Authorities may have agreed to Church-backing of the rural apportionment amendment, but not fifteen—I was out of town when it was decided upon."[78]

Two Republican legislators also attended the meeting at McKay's invitation. In the course of the discussion, Williams asked whether it was even appropriate for the church to become involved in what was clearly a political issue. "President McKay," he said, "as an Elder's [Quorum] President and a faithful member of the Church, I find myself in a quandary when General Authorities of the Church commit the Church on political issues, in apparent violation of the 9th verse of Section 134 of the Doctrine and Covenants (which forbids intermingling of the Church and the State)." McKay's reply was unambiguous: "'Well let me make this clear. The Church has not and will not take an official position in this issue. Many of the General Authorities will express vigorous opinions on this apportionment issue, but as a Church we remain neutral.' Milt said, 'This means we can go out and campaign in the regular fashion?' President McKay replied, chuckling, 'That is correct and I promise you that you will not be excommunicated for your stand.'"[79]

While McKay gave Weilenmann and others free license to campaign against the amendment, he also allowed Lee and Moyle to carry on their campaign in favor of it. This "evenhanded" permission gave the reapportionment proponents a two-fold advantage. Because they were apostles, their words had extra weight for many Latter-day Saints, even though the issue was obviously political rather than religious. Furthermore, they had at their disposal considerable logistical assets if they chose to use them. They did so choose, without McKay's knowledge or approval. In May, six months after the Thanksgiving meeting, Weilenmann publicized McKay's statement at that meeting, quoting him as saying, "This is not a matter on which the Church will take a stand. Church officials may express their ideas. But those ideas will be the ideas of the individual and will not represent the official views of the Church."[80] Nevertheless, the apparent advantage of Lee and Moyle continued to be daunting.

In mid-October, with the election only three weeks away, Williams learned that stake presidents throughout the Salt Lake Valley, clearly acting on instructions from General Authorities, were using local church officials and church trucks to distribute tens of thousands of copies of pamphlets urging a vote in favor of reapportionment.[81] After quick investigation, Williams played a trump card—a First Presidency letter written a month earlier to political science professor Frank Jonas: "We acknowledge receipt of your letter under date of September 1 soliciting an expression of our attitude with reference to the so-called Reapportionment question. We advise you that we have consistently made the statement in response to inquiries on this subject that the Church takes no position with reference to it. It is regarded by us as a matter for the determination of the voters of the state, and no one is authorized to align us with either side of the controversy."[82]

Williams obtained both Jonas's and McKay's permission, and the letter appeared in the *Deseret News* the afternoon before the election and in the *Salt Lake Tribune* the morning of the election. Its effect on the election is not known, but the proposed amendment was soundly defeated (142,972 to 89,094), with the strongest negative vote, not surprisingly, coming from the urban counties.

Both Lee and Moyle were bitterly disappointed with the outcome. Weilenmann later stated, "Elders Lee and Moyle felt that President McKay didn't back them up. First he was for the resolution and then later against the plan and it seemed to them that he got out from under his commitments."[83] From McKay's perspective, he took a neutral position because Weilenmann had made a convincing argument that the amendment was both unfair and partisan. However, it is highly unlikely that Lee and Moyle would have staked out their initial positions without at least implied consent from McKay, so it is not surprising that they felt confused, if not abandoned, when he switched his own position and declared that both he and the church would remain neutral.

Heated though the battle for reapportionment was, the issue turned out to be moot. In the landmark case *Reynolds v. Sims* in 1961, the U.S. Supreme Court ruled that the federal Senate, with representation of two senators per state regardless of population, was the only exception to the "one man, one vote" rule. Thus, even if the amendment had passed, "rural rule" in Utah would have lasted only seven years.

THE DOUGLAS STRINGFELLOW HOAX

During the election campaign of 1954, a charismatic freshman Congressman from Utah, Douglas Stringfellow, was the subject of the popular television program, *This Is Your Life*. Stringfellow's administrative assistant, Keith Jacques, had arranged for him to be showcased, unbeknownst to Stringfellow.[84] Millions of viewers across America thus came to know the amazing saga of the self-proclaimed war hero that *Time* magazine later summarized: "A paraplegic veteran of World War II, he got a job as an Ogden, Utah, radio announcer. In his spare time he made scores of speeches to Mormon church gatherings and civic groups. The story, as it evolved after hundreds of repetitions, was that he had been assigned to the OSS, parachuted behind German lines with 29 other men and kidnapped a German atomic scientist named Otto Hahn. Every other member of the mission, Stringfellow said, was later killed. He said that he was captured and tortured, then escaped to France, where he was crippled by a land mine."[85]

Arthur V. Watkins, Utah's senior U.S. Senator, later added an even more impressive part of the story: "That achievement was small compared to Stringfellow's claim that Hitler's time table for world conquest was completely upset and with it the course of the war. As a consequence, the direction of history was changed by him and his brave companions under his leadership."[86]

The story was convincing, in large part because Stringfellow was a gifted orator. In 1954 he was named one of the ten most outstanding young men in America by the Junior Chamber of Commerce, and he was an overwhelming favorite to win a second term in Congress.

However, among the viewers of *This Is Your Life* were several retired Army officers in San Francisco's Presidio, one of whom had actually been in the group that had captured Otto Hahn. As he listened to the Stringfellow story, he remarked that he had no recollection of the Congressman having been in his unit.[87]

Rumors of a Stringfellow hoax had actually begun prior to the television show and did not subside afterward. Late in the summer Les Honeycutt, managing editor of *Army Times,* a privately owned weekly for servicemen and veterans, got a tip from a veteran and, with his senior editor's permission, began investigating Stringfellow's story.

In the meantime, Democrats and Republicans in Utah also got wind of a possible scandal and moved independently to exploit or control the damage. McKay first heard of it from Lynn Richards, son of his Democratic counselor Stephen L Richards, but took no action.[88] Lynn Richards also told Milton Weilenmann his suspicions.[89] Weilenmann, then a student at the University of Utah law school, consulted the dean of the law school, Spencer L. Kimball, the son of then-Apostle Spencer W. Kimball, who became church president in 1973. Weilenmann later recalled:

> Spence said, "I think we had better go down and see President McKay, because this young man (the Congressman) has instilled faith in a lot of people based on his exploits, and if the exploits aren't true, there will be a loss of faith on the part of a lot of young people." "But," I said, "I'm trying to elect a Democratic Congressman, and this is much too early to go down and see President McKay, because President McKay will have the authority to get this story released, and if it's released too early, they'll name a replacement, and the replacement will not be under the stigma that Stringfellow is under, and the whole plan will fail." Kimball said, in effect, "Well, we're after the truth. Truth doesn't wait until a week before an election."[90]

Weilenmann and Kimball met with McKay on Sunday morning, October 10, 1954. Kimball later recalled the essence of the meeting: "When we arrived at the President's office, Milt showed him the elaborate documentation of the case against Stringfellow. The case was a strong presumptive one, though there were certain gaps that needed filling before it would become airtight. After President McKay had seen the material, he was quite visibly disturbed about it, and asked that he be permitted to keep the dossier to use in an interview with Stringfellow. With this permission, the appointment terminated."[91]

McKay's direct intervention in partisan politics was a departure from his customary neutrality. While he held his thoughts on the matter closely, not involving his counselors in the meetings, it appears that his unusual actions were driven by four considerations: first, deep concern for church members whose faith had been buoyed by Stringfellow's many inspirational, if untrue, speeches to church groups; second, concern about a backlash of public opinion against the state and Stringfellow's constituency; third, a personal revulsion for dishonesty in any form, which was consistent with McKay's sense of integrity, and particularly for this sullying of the genuine heroism of America's soldiers, which was consistent with McKay's patriotism; and fourth, concern for Stringfellow's soul if he did not repent of this sin.

Senator Arthur V. Watkins, head of Utah's Congressional delegation, saw concern about the church's good name as a chief motivation for involving McKay:

> To many readers who are not members of the Mormon Church, it may seem strange or unusual for Senator [Wallace] Bennett (R-Utah) and me to call on President McKay about the Stringfellow matter. To these readers, I offer my personal explanation.
>
> Throughout the comparatively short history of the Mormon Church it became the custom of its critics and its enemies to blame the Church for the alleged misconduct of its members. Bad conduct of members and especially those holding high positions in the Church, or state, or both, might be very damaging to the Church before the peoples of the world, and would bring deep sorrow to its faithful members.
>
> Congressman Stringfellow held a position of trust and honor, and the charges against him were of grave concern, not only to Republican members of the Church but to Democratic members as well. Some of the leaders brought evidence of these charges to President McKay, I believe, because they didn't want the Church to get hurt if it could be avoided. I think they were acting in good faith. When President McKay was advised of the situation he brought the matter to the attention of Secretary Benson, a member of President Eisenhower's cabinet.[92]

The matter quickly dominated McKay's agenda. On Wednesday he held three meetings on the topic, the first with Stringfellow himself and Ezra Taft Benson, then Secretary of Agriculture and a political liaison to Eisenhower, who later weighed in on the matter. No others were present at this meeting, and McKay's diary records only that they discussed "a serious accusation."[93] He then met again with Weilenmann alone but recorded nothing of the meeting's substance. Finally, in the evening, he met with Stringfellow, Weilenmann, and Kimball. Kimball later described the third meeting: "At first Stringfellow insisted the whole thing was a frame-up, an attempt to smear an innocent man.... Once we had succeeded in getting down to a discussion of the details of his military record, it quickly became apparent to Milt and to me that this was one of the most elaborate fabrications imaginable.... Despite the strong case against him, Stringfellow conceded nothing in the interview; to the end he maintained his integrity and innocence. My impression was that President McKay was fully convinced of the fraud, though he said little."[94] Weilenmann related the substance of the meeting to his friend, J. D. Williams, who recorded in his diary: "As Stringfellow left the room, President McKay said to the other two something to the effect, 'We have certainly heard a lot less than the full truth.'"[95]

The following morning McKay phoned Benson, who had returned to Washington, D.C., and reported that the previous evening's meeting "had not brought forth any more facts than the conference we had with him yesterday morning. Representative Stringfellow stated that if the news was made public, he would answer it. I told Brother Benson that the news had already been released in an Army paper [*Army Times*] in Washington."[96]

Later that day McKay received a phone call from Preston Robinson, editor of the *Deseret News:*

> Dr. Robinson stated that they had had information on this matter
> since April and that they were running a story in the paper to-night.
> Dr. Robinson also stated that they had a letter from Representative
> Stringfellow which he had written to them last May. They had per-
> mission from the Representative to run this letter in the paper tomor-
> row evening. I said that I would withhold comment for the present.
> Dr. Robinson asked if he had approval to go ahead and dig out what
> information they could. I indicated that it would be all right for them
> to go ahead and obtain information in their capacity as a newspaper.[97]

Saturday, October 16, was a whirlwind of activity. Watkins had earlier worked through a contact at the Central Intelligence Agency in the hope of verifying Stringfellow's claims about Hahn's capture, but a thorough search found nothing that even mentioned the special army unit of which Stringfellow had spoken. Watkins asked his contact not to release the information to the media until he had a chance to confront Stringfellow directly. Early Saturday morning Watkins called his colleague, Senator Wallace F. Bennett (R-Utah), and briefed him on the CIA report. They also "discussed the rumors each of us had heard that the Democratic State Committee was preparing a broadside exposé of the Congressman to take place at an early date."[98] There was substance to the rumors. Walter Granger, a for- mer Democratic Congressman, was Stringfellow's opponent and told Weilenmann wistfully, "You know, if we could just prove that he was not an honest Congress- man, that this story was false, and we released that just a few days before the elec- tion, before the Republicans had a chance to name a replacement, we would be able to elect a Democratic Congressman."[99]

Next came a tense political huddle that involved Watkins, Bennett, Congress- man William Dawson (R-Utah), Governor J. Bracken Lee (a Republican), and the

State Republican Chairman and Chairwoman. Governor Lee later described the meeting:

> Immediately Watkins said, "We've got to keep him on. He has been a good representative. We've got to keep him on the ticket because the election is only a couple of weeks away. After all, he hasn't done anything too wrong except mislead the people with his war record." I said, "That doesn't make any difference. The man has shown that he won't tell the truth all the time. If we're going to have a party and work to the end of making it better instead of worse, we've got to insist that people who are in positions of power in the party try to live up to a moral standard." . . . While we were arguing, a phone rang in the other room. A woman in there called Senator Bennett to the phone. He was gone quite a while. In the meantime this argument between Watkins and [me] kept going on and getting worse all the time. Finally Bennett came back and said, "Arthur, you're wanted on the phone." So Watkins got up and went to the phone. Then Bennett told us, "That is Ezra Taft Benson. . . . He told us that Eisenhower said, 'You call Senator Bennett and Senator Watkins and the Central Committee out there and tell them that they've got to get Stringfellow off the ticket because this is a lie that he is telling. I know that it is a lie and I'm assured of it because no such thing ever existed that he is talking about.'" A little while later Watkins came back and he said, "Well, he has got to go. He has got to go."[100]

Watkins and Bennett then drove to Ogden to meet with Stringfellow, who was expecting them. Watkins confronted him with the CIA report, which documented several inaccuracies in Stringfellow's public statements. Watkins then gave Stringfellow an ultimatum:

> "You are the one person who knows for a certainty whether your story is true or false. You have been a missionary for the Mormon church and you have preached repentance with all that doctrine implies to peoples [*sic*] you met in your missionary service. If your story is false, you know what your duty is. If you do not confess your sin in this mortal life and make whatever restitution is within your power, you know you will have to face it in the life to come. Now, on the other hand, if you still insist, after all I have told you, that you have been telling the truth, that your story is true, I will stand by you." (Even some Army people were reluctant to say Stringfellow's story was false. If it were a deep secret operation there might be a good reason for the CIA to deny the story for reasons peculiar to the Agency's

future operations under similar circumstances.) "But we do want the truth and we want it now." There was a painful pause—the Congressman turned his back to us for a few moments, put his head in his hands and burst into tears. Sobs shook his body. Facing us he said, "I never was behind the German lines. I never did help kidnap Otto Hahn. The whole story is false."[101]

At this point the matter returned to McKay's office. Watkins and Bennett phoned McKay requesting an urgent meeting, then drove back to Salt Lake City and met with him early in the afternoon. The senators told McKay of Stringfellow's confession, then "the three of us considered how best Congressman Stringfellow could make his confession to the public. We concluded that he should do this before the CIA in Washington made public the fact that there is nothing in the record of the CIA to substantiate his claim that he ever flew across the sea on a secret mission. We further considered that arrangements be made to have Congressman Stringfellow appear on the Radio and Television to-night if possible."[102]

J. D. Williams, writing in his diary the following morning, described the sequence of events: "The President of the Church then called KSL and demanded television time and after he obtained it then called Stringfellow and actually ordered him to get down to the station to begin to make his repentance with the people. Consequently there was nothing voluntary about the confession. Stringfellow was absolutely up against the wall when his last hope disappeared (the CIA files)."[103]

At 7:00 P.M. Stringfellow made his confession. There was no time to publicize the event in advance nor to arrange air time on other television stations, but the confession was rebroadcast the following day and quickly made national headlines. Four days later, McKay received a telegram from the chair of the Utah Republican Party stating that the committee had accepted Stringfellow's resignation and that H. Aldous Dixon, president of Utah Agricultural College (now Utah State University), had agreed to accept the nomination.[104] Although only fifteen days remained between Dixon's decision and the election, he won in a victory that a *Deseret News* reporter termed "one of the astonishing performances in American political history."[105]

Although Weilenmann's hope of electing a Democratic Congressman failed, he viewed the whole affair philosophically: "The wonderful thing about President McKay was that he was willing to listen. He was willing to bring out the truth. He was not willing to cover up anything, and he wanted it done on his terms, as soon as he knew that it [Stringfellow's story] was false. He didn't want me or anyone else to have any advantage. . . . I've always had increased admiration for one who didn't need to do what he did. He knew the chance he was taking, as far as this young man was concerned, but he demanded that the truth be told, let the consequences fall where they may."[106]

President Harry S. Truman

David O. McKay did not like the New Deal as a political movement nor Harry S. Truman as the successor to its founder, Franklin D. Roosevelt. While traveling to Washington, D.C., in January 1953 to attend Eisenhower's inauguration, he pointed out the morning fog through which the train passed as it approached Union Station and told his wife, "This fog is typical of the fog that has been hanging over Washington politically for twenty years."[107]

Truman opted not to run for reelection in 1952; and as Adlai Stevenson and Dwight Eisenhower squared off in the campaign, Truman made a farewell trip across the country by train. Although he was not campaigning directly for Stevenson, the trip came right in the middle of the campaign and thus had political overtones. In September, the First Presidency learned that Truman's train would stop first in Salt Lake City, then go on to Provo, where Truman would give an address at BYU. Eisenhower and Stevenson were already scheduled to give speeches in the Tabernacle on Temple Square, and McKay and his counselors worried that Truman's trip might make it appear that they favored the Democrats. In a First Presidency meeting, they discussed their options. McKay's diary contains the minutes of that meeting: "It has been suggested that President McKay have breakfast with President Truman and travel with him to Provo for the political meeting. The brethren felt that I must have breakfast with the President if *he* requests it, that otherwise he [*sic*] need only to call on the President at his car and pay his respects."[108]

Local Democrats apparently got wind of the meeting, for two days later Weilenmann, the Utah State Democratic Chairman, phoned the White House. Kenneth Hechler, a White House aide, wrote a memo to Matthew J. Connolley, Truman's personal secretary, explaining that Weilenmann had asked "that David O. McKay, President of the Mormon Church[,] be allowed to board the train at Salt Lake City and ride to Provo. Mr. Weilenman [*sic*] stressed the importance of allowing Mr. McKay, whom the President has met, to be on the train."[109]

The following day, McKay received a telegram from Connolley that began, "The President hopes it will be possible for you to visit with him on the train between Salt Lake City, and Provo, Utah, October Sixth." McKay telegrammed his acceptance the same day.[110]

McKay met Truman's train at the Denver and Rio Grande Station on October 6, 1952, and was escorted onto the train:

President Truman then came in and said: "Oh, President McKay, you honor me in coming down!" I thanked him for his invitation: The President then introduced me to his daughter Margaret. The President then invited me to come out to the platform with him to have pictures taken, stating that if having the picture taken would embarrass me for me not to do it. I, however, accepted his invitation.... [On the ride to Provo], I had a very pleasant thirty minutes or so with the President, during which time, I saw the better Truman, and got a glimpse of his better nature—the cockiness was gone. He referred to the fact that this is his last official tour before retiring, saying, "When I get through with this, it is my last." He then told me what he wanted to do; viz. to spend his time instructing the youth of America in loyalty and American ideals. He mentioned some other men whom he would like to have join him in this project. I commended him for this desire, and told him that I think that is just what we need. I then gave him a few of my ideas on the subject, emphasizing the freedom of the individual; that that must be maintained at all cost.... I had a higher opinion of him today.[111]

Although McKay had hoped to avoid political fallout from the meeting, some Republicans were upset. Two weeks later, Arthur Watkins wrote the First Presidency "reporting that many people feel that my presence at the B.Y.U. with Pres. Truman was an indication that I favored the Democratic party. The Brethren could think of nothing that might be done under the circumstances to let the people know that Truman being the President of the United States and having invited me to accompany him, there was nothing else to do."[112]

Eisenhower's victory smoothed the ruffled Republican feathers, and shortly after the election Watkins wrote McKay a letter with apologetic overtones:

Now that the contest is over and the results are known, I can appreciate more than ever how well you handled the difficult situation you were placed in by the visit of President Truman. There were many of our people who were quite disturbed at the time, but I am sure they will agree with me that you faced a very embarrassing situation and that the way you handled it was the only possible way under the circumstances. My letter sometime before the election was prompted by so many requests from the Church members who were very much concerned over the effect of your appearance with President Truman. I calmed them the best I could, but, at their urging, I wrote the letter to which you so generously responded. May I thank you for your answering letter.[113]

President Dwight D. Eisenhower

McKay met Dwight Eisenhower prior to his election, and so it is not clear whether his post-election letter to the president-elect was based more on McKay's personal feelings or his Republican sentiments. Nonetheless, his words were of unrestrained praise: "Your being placed at the head of the United Sates Government at the time of the present crises in our history is more than just an expression of millions of honest hearts yearning for the preservation of liberties vouchsafed by the Constitution of the United States—it is a manifestation of Providential watchfulness over the destiny of this land of America."[114]

Two weeks after McKay sent this letter, he received a phone call from Watkins, relaying Eisenhower's request that Ezra Taft Benson serve as Secretary of Agriculture. "I said yes that I thought he would be permitted to accept."[115] Four days later, the White House announced Benson's appointment.

McKay and Eisenhower exchanged occasional notes over the years, but on one occasion they had significant personal contact. Eisenhower occasionally had "stag" (all-male) dinners in the White House and asked cabinet members for suggestions of invitees. Benson recommended McKay, who attended one of the dinners in 1955. Benson later told Clare Middlemiss about the evening's success:

> Although he often invited members of the Cabinet to attend some of these dinners, I did not attend the one at which President McKay was present. The Friday morning following the Thursday night dinner, President Eisenhower referred to the dinner. As I recall, it was the only time he ever singled out one individual. He said to the Cabinet, Friday morning, "Among the group was President David O. McKay, head of the Mormon Church." Then he added, "He was the life of the party." On another occasion President Eisenhower said to me he considered David O. McKay the greatest spiritual leader in the world."[116]

President John F. Kennedy

John F. Kennedy began his campaign for the U.S. presidency several years prior to the 1960 election. In late November 1957, he visited Salt Lake City and made a courtesy call on McKay. The conversation was substantive, revolving around the threat of Soviet Communism and the recent propaganda triumph of the successful launch of the world's first artificial satellite, Sputnik. Nonetheless, McKay's reaction, recorded in his diary entry, was only lukewarm: "Mr. Kennedy is a member of the Catholic Church. I enjoyed my visit with him, although not too much impressed with him as a leader."[117]

In 1959 Kennedy paid a second visit to McKay, this time bringing his wife Jacqueline. Although Kennedy's nomination was more than a year in the future, the issue of whether he, a Roman Catholic, would be subject to Vatican direction, had already become a high-profile issue. He had addressed the issue head-on in public, which had impressed McKay. "Mr. Kennedy seems to be a very fine young man," he dictated in his diary this time around. "His recent remarks regarding his belief in separation of Church and state are contrary to what the Catholics want."[118]

A third visit came in January 1960. This time Kennedy was accompanied by a large contingent of local Democrats, one of whom, Oscar W. McConkie Jr., later recounted:

> I took Senator Kennedy in to see President McKay. They had a really significant conversation, a lot more so than most political people, where you just bring them in and they kind of pass pleasantries, and this sort of thing. They had a serious talk about how it was going to be possible to bring democratic governments throughout the world. They discussed, for instance, such things as the fact that the difficulty the President would have in doing this was that there isn't any middle class in the rest of the world. The third world has extremely few very wealthy people, and then there is huge poverty. But President Kennedy was saying that it takes a middle class in order to make a democratic system work. It was a significant talk. As we walked out of President McKay's office, Senator Kennedy turned to me and said, "I have never met a man as ideally suited and qualified to be the spiritual leader of his people."[119]

The two men had little contact during Kennedy's brief presidency, although Kennedy stopped in Salt Lake City and had breakfast with McKay in late September 1963. Eight weeks later, he was assassinated in Dallas. McKay wrote in his diary: "All at our house are shocked and stunned at the news, as it is only a few weeks ago that it was our privilege to entertain the President in our apartment, and now to think that he has gone is unbelievable!"[120]

PRESIDENT LYNDON B. JOHNSON

David O. McKay and Lyndon B. Johnson had little in common politically. Not only were the two men in different political parties, but they were also at opposite extremes on civil rights, the issue which largely defined Johnson's domestic policy. Yet ironically, McKay came to have a closer personal relationship with Johnson than with any other U.S. president.

McKay met Johnson twice before Kennedy's death. The first time was during the 1960 campaign, and it left a different impression than McKay's first meeting with Kennedy: "I thoroughly enjoyed my conference with Senator Johnson and the others, and felt that Senator Johnson is a very fine person."[121] The second visit occurred in 1962, when Johnson was Kennedy's vice president. McKay recorded: "As I greeted Vice President Johnson, I said to him, 'I am glad you accepted the Vice Presidency.'...Vice President Johnson recalled his visit to Salt Lake City in 1960 and expressed appreciation for the opportunity to come again. He said he is always warmed and inspired by an opportunity to meet the First Presidency. He recalled that he had a roommate, Truman Young, who was a Mormon and who helped him very much at the time Senator [Reed] Smoot was leader in the Senate."[122]

Two months after Kennedy's assassination McKay received a phone call, the transcript of which read:

> "Mr. President, this is Lyndon Johnson.... I am an old friend of yours. I don't know whether you remember me or not, but you've been receiving me every time I come out there."
>
> "I remember you very well. I'm glad to hear your voice too."
>
> "I wonder if you feel like coming down to Washington and see me sometime in the next week or two?... I don't have anything emergency, but I just need a little strength and I think that would come from visiting with you an hour or so."[123]

The following week, the ninety-year-old McKay, accompanied by his son Lawrence and N. Eldon Tanner, flew to Washington, D.C., for lunch with Johnson. "President Johnson explained to President McKay that he had called him on an impulse, that he wanted his advice. He stated that President McKay had received him twice in Salt Lake City and each time he had come away inspired."[124] McKay was the first religious leader to be invited to the White House since Johnson became president. Senator Frank Moss (D-Utah) saw more than impulse behind the invitation:

> He just thought [McKay] was a very powerful man, and Lyndon Johnson was like that. Wherever there was a power structure, he wanted to have a little grab in there, a little hold, and he was convinced that McKay was the greatest single source of power in Utah. So, he had him come to the White House, you know.... That was just pure Lyndon Johnson. He looked out for elements of power wherever he could see them, and his conclusion was that the power in Utah really resided in McKay. It was a pretty low point for the Democrats to claim they had much power at that point, so that's Johnson.[125]

Edwin B. Firmage, who worked in the White House during the Johnson Administration, had a similar, though more benign assessment of Johnson's motives: "The administration didn't really think they would carry Utah, although Johnson and Humphrey did in 1964. They just wanted decent relations with the Mormon people."[126] Indeed, Utah was not much of a political plum for Johnson, with only four electoral votes, all of which had gone to Richard Nixon in 1960. Fifty-five percent of the state had voted Republican in that election, one of the largest Republican majorities in the country.

While Johnson's motivation may have been purely political, the primary result of the meeting was a genuine friendship between two men—even though they differed on key political issues such as the Civil Rights Act (1964) and the attempted repeal of Section 14(b) of the Taft-Hartley Act. After lunch, Johnson "told President McKay that events were crowding in on him: Cyprus, Viet Nam, the shooting of Americans over Berlin, Panama. He felt he needed help. When he was a boy he could rest his head on his mother's shoulder; now he needed another shoulder to rest on."[127]

After the visit, the two presidents frequently exchanged notes, telegrams, and telephone calls. One of McKay's secretaries recalled:

> President Johnson got so he called President McKay all the time. Jack Valenti was his executive secretary, and he called on the telephone. . . . I remember one time he called, and President McKay was over in the temple meeting. I said, "He's over in the temple in a meeting." He said, "How long would it take you to get him?" I said, "Let me see. Do you want me to call back, or do you want to call back?" He said, "I'll give you the number."... President Johnson would just want to talk. He would have ideas, and would just talk them out. . . . He really liked President McKay. He thought a lot of him. He respected President McKay.[128]

Late in October 1964, only five days before the election, Johnson and his wife visited the McKays in their Hotel Utah apartment, opting to breakfast with them and bypass a $500-a-plate fund-raising breakfast in another part of the hotel.[129] Five days later Johnson was reelected in a landslide victory over Republican Barry Goldwater. Utah voters, perhaps in part because of Johnson's open affection for McKay, shifted their voting pattern. In 1960, 55 percent of them had voted for Nixon, but now 57 percent voted for Johnson. The Democrats also won the governorship and other statewide offices, and majorities in both houses of the legislature. The evening after the election, Johnson called McKay from his ranch in Texas.[130]

Late in December, McKay received a phone call from Senator Frank E. Moss (D-Utah), relaying the information that Johnson had invited the choir to sing at his inauguration three weeks later. McKay "said that I considered the invitation an honor and that the Choir would be pleased to sing at the Inaugural at the President's invitation."[131]

Johnson's idea about the choir came late in the planning. To accommodate the entire choir, who sat in seats directly across from Johnson on the east side of the Capitol, it was necessary to reassign 300 seats originally reserved for the press. With relish, the *Deseret News* reported that the disgruntled correspondents appealed the decision, recommending "that the Choir be trimmed to about 100 voices. The President is reported to have told the standing committee, in salty language, that he had invited the Tabernacle Choir and he wasn't going to have half a choir, he wanted all three hundred, no matter how many seats it cost."[132]

McKay, because of poor health, was not able to attend the inauguration but watched the ceremonies on television. He noted in his diary:

> At 4:00 P.M. I was surprised to receive a telephone call from the President of the United States (Lyndon B. Johnson) who had been inaugurated in services between 10:00 A.M. and 12:00 noon today. President Johnson said: "Dr. McKay, I want you to know that I was thinking of you during the time I was delivering my address, and I think you will be pleased to know that the singing of the Tabernacle Choir was the best thing connected with the Inaugural Ceremonies— they did wonderfully well. They had a very difficult time in getting here and they were worn out, but their physical discomforts were not reflected in their voices. You can be mighty proud of your work with them, and the whole world heard them by Telstar, television, and radio. I think you will be getting some very fine reports about them."... It was indeed gratifying that he would call during this unusually busy time, right in the midst of his inaugural activities, to tell me that I was in his thoughts during his Inaugural Address, and to express appreciation for the singing of the Tabernacle Choir.[133]

Three U.S. flags flew over the Capitol during the inauguration. One went to Johnson, another to Vice President Hubert Humphrey, and the third to David O. McKay.[134]

A month after the inauguration, McKay asked for Johnson's assistance with a nagging problem. Several years earlier, the Armed Forces had changed the requirements for chaplains to include three years of formal theological training. This policy excluded new LDS applicants, as there was (and still is) no LDS theological seminary. Efforts spanning six years, either to change the policy or gain a special exception for LDS servicemen, had failed, so McKay wrote directly to Johnson on February 26, 1965: "There is a matter causing us considerable concern as a Church relating to the chaplaincy in the Armed Forces of the United States. This matter has been discussed with Senators Frank E. Moss of Utah and Howard Cannon of Nevada, who have suggested that it be presented to you personally. It would be greatly appreciated if a representative of our Servicemen's Committee, together with the two mentioned Senators, could meet with you to discuss this problem."[135]

Three days later Johnson replied, in words that underscore the depth of friendship between the two men: "It is always a source of comfort to me to hear from you either by letter or in person. I would be glad to meet with Senators Moss and Cannon and a representative of your Servicemen's Committee at any time that is mutually convenient. Please be assured that whatever problems or requests that you have will always be given warm and sincere consideration here."[136]

On March 3, only five days after McKay's letter, Moss, Cannon, Boyd K. Packer, then an Assistant to the Twelve and a member of the LDS Servicemen's Committee, and Joseph Anderson, secretary to the First Presidency, met with Johnson in the White House. Packer later reported the meeting to McKay:

> For the past six years we have not had a chaplain commissioned in the military forces of the United States. There has been a long and consistent effort to effect a change in Defense Department regulations which were discriminatory against the Church.... Thursday, March 3, at 12:30 P.M. I went to the White House with Senators Moss and Cannon and met with President Johnson. He indicated that he had already phoned Cyrus Vance, Deputy Secretary of Defense, concerning this matter, that he had taken that action immediately upon receipt of the letter from President McKay. He listened to a statement of the situation and then read to us from a memo from Cyrus Vance which proposed no solution to the problem and actually would have been negative in its effect.
>
> President Johnson immediately had Cyrus Vance on the telephone and instructed him to "give us what we wanted." He told Mr. Vance over the telephone something about the training our boys receive and that it was his wish that they get an exception or a waiver or a change in regulation that would clear this problem for us. He indicated to Mr. Vance that he did not want Dr. McKay to feel that he was not doing everything he could to solve this problem. There was some discussion on the matter and President Johnson made a final statement to Mr. Vance that he was to solve this problem. . . .

When I expressed appreciation for the action he had taken, and expressed appreciation from President McKay, he said, as nearly as I can quote, "I don't know just what it is about President McKay. I talk to Billy Graham and all of the others but somehow it seems as though President McKay is something like a father to me. It seems as though every little while I have to write him a letter or something."[137]

Within a month the final details were worked out, which required only that LDS chaplains have a college baccalaureate degree and the church's permission to serve. By that time, eleven new LDS chaplains had already been authorized. In a meeting of the First Presidency and Quorum of the Twelve on April 1, Apostle Harold B. Lee noted, "There is no question that the feeling of friendship and the power of President McKay have opened the door for us in this chaplain situation, that when we tried to handle the matter from every other avenue the door was shut."[138]

A final glimpse comes from the minutes that Joseph Anderson made of the meeting with Johnson. When Vance continued to protest against this policy change,

President Johnson said, "Listen here, these Mormons, from the minute they are out of their mothers' womb, have been praying and teaching and leading one another, and then they go out on missions." He said, "I would rather have one of their boys than one of the preachers you get out of the seminary, so you fix it up so that they can get their chaplains." Then he said, "I cannot have Dr. McKay out in Salt Lake City sitting there thinking I am not doing the thing he has asked me to do, so you do it." . . . Brother Packer said that the thing that solved this problem in spite of all that has been done is President Johnson's relationship with President McKay.[139]

14

AN
INTERNATIONAL
CHURCH

Many crucial issues confronted the church during David O. McKay's Presidency; and although historians may debate which one was the most significant, there was no question in McKay's mind. About a year before his death, he was interviewed by Alden Whitman of the *New York Times.* In response to the question, "What do you regard as the most outstanding accomplishment of your ministry as President of the Church?" he replied, "The making of the Church a world-wide organization."[1]

McKay, in comparison with all of his predecessors, was uniquely qualified to transform the church into a permanent international institution. While others had served foreign missions, in 1920–21 he became the first General Authority to circumnavigate the globe. The idea of such a journey was not new, having originated with Apostle Heber J. Grant in the early days of his apostleship. While serving a mission to Japan in 1906, Grant wrote to Church President Joseph F. Smith and requested that he be allowed to take such a trip upon leaving Japan. Instead, he was recalled to serve a mission to Great Britain. Fourteen years later, Grant as church president resuscitated the idea in a statement to the *Deseret News:*

> Now Elder McKay is to take the trip which I then advocated. He will make a general survey of the missions, study conditions there, gather data concerning them, and in short, obtain general information in order that there may be some one in the deliberations of the First Presidency and the Council of the Twelve thoroughly familiar with actual conditions. He will be gone several months; and if he finds it advisable, when he has completed his tour of the Pacific missions, to go on to South Africa and even to the European missions, entirely encircling the globe, he will be authorized to do so.[2]

A week later the term "actual conditions" was further explained to include "a study of the customs and needs of the people in general at each place visited."[3] Awareness of such customs and needs, which McKay first gained while on the journey, was a major first step toward comprehending that a worldwide church would consist of more than a series of copies of the Great Basin church. One General Authority who served during the McKay years later commented on the difficulty of such a transition: "It's been a Wasatch Front church and then it's been an American church. It's only been very recently, really, that this has been an international church the way it should have been right from the beginning."[4]

CIRCUMNAVIGATING THE GLOBE

Early in December 1920, McKay and his traveling companion, Hugh J. Cannon, left Salt Lake City and headed west. Almost immediately upon embarking upon the ocean journey to Japan, McKay was abruptly reminded of his propensity to develop seasickness. His extended diary account, written shortly after his recovery, managed to inject humor retroactively into a decidedly uncomfortable situation:

> Wednesday, December 8, 1920. Twenty-one years ago last August, I awoke in a berth in the "City of Rome" starting across the Atlantic from Glasgow to Montreal, with just the same feeling that I had this morning. It presaged ill. I had gloomy forebodings.... Knowing that it was the wise thing to get up on deck, I dressed and promenaded in the cold, stiff sea breeze. But a longing desire to be alone seized me, and I hurriedly sought the solitude of my stateroom, where the Jonathan apple and I parted company most unceremoniously. I lay down on my berth, wondering if a Jonathan apple and Jonah had any peculiar quality in common. At any rate my sympathy went to the whale rather than to Jonah.
>
> Feeling a little better, I started again for the deck, and was not a little comforted to pass a poor Chinaman with perspiration running down his jaundiced-looking face, and sitting holding his knees and looking, and I'm sure felt, the most forsaken, limpy lump of humanity I have ever seen. At any rate I had company in furnishing gratuitous amusement for the favored ones.
>
> This time I reached only the top of the stairs when the longing for solitude again overpowered me, and I returned to my room.
>
> As last evening's dinner followed my Jonathan, I was surprised at the slight effect my gastric juices had made upon it. The shrimps I had eaten seemed whole enough to start swimming as soon as they would strike the ocean. . . .

I remained in my berth all day, could eat nothing, and by night had given up everything as far back as my Rotary luncheon the day before. . . .

When I awoke the next morning the sea was still heaving, and as I tried to dress so was I. Hugh J. went to breakfast and brought back word that only a very few passengers took their morning meal. I know it was a selfish-dog-in-the-manger feeling, but I'll confess his information gave me a good deal of comfort.

Friday, December 10, 1920. Feeling somewhat better, but still shaky, and as gaunt as a starving coyote. It's no wonder, though, for I have eaten nothing except half a cup of beef tea and a little chicken broth for sixty-four hours, and have parted with everything I have eaten since mother weaned me.[5]

Not to be outdone, Cannon, a better sailor, added his account of the spectacle, invoking in the process the unique Latter-day Saint doctrine of baptism for the dead:

Brother McKay does nothing by halves. He treats every subject exhaustively, going to the very bottom of it, and this occasion was no exception. Seasickness is undertaken with the same vigorous energy which is displayed when he leaves a meeting in the Church office building with only two minutes to catch a Bamberger train. In neither case is it safe to get in his way.

He says he would like to change places right now with some of those who envied him this trip. The wish even entered his mind that the Japs and the Chinese, whom we are to visit, had all died. It would have been easier to have been baptized for them.[6]

Landfall brought relief from seasickness, but at times one hardship replaced another. Particularly troublesome were fleas, as Cannon noted of a short-term stay in a Calcutta hotel: "Within a short time we discovered that vermin had no more respect for our lives than we had for theirs. Sitting stripped under electric fans, each with a basin of water at his side, we began to defend ourselves. It seemed to be a survival of the fittest, and after a stinging conflict we finally won. Your correspondent caught 157 fleas while Brother McKay feels sure his victims numbered twice that many."[7]

McKay, writing to his son Llewelyn from Cairo, echoed Cannon's sentiment when he noted, "I accept as absolute facts every plague of Egypt named in the Bible, and add to them the plague of fleas, which Moses forgot to mention."[8]

Yet of far greater impact than the physical discomforts McKay endured were the lessons he learned about cultures far removed from Huntsville, Utah. Writing to fellow Apostle and U.S. Senator Reed Smoot, he noted: "Our visit here [China], as in Japan, has been one constant round of interest and surprises, and the best means of education in the world. The only right way to learn a people is to visit them in their own land and in their own homes."⁹ A particularly strong imprint came in Japan:

> In Japan everything is done backwards. Literally you have to stand on your head in Japan to understand things. Here you take off your hats, but there they take off their shoes. Wedding receptions are at the home of the man and not the bride. The bridegroom receives the wedding presents. (That is the place for us men.) The Japanese carpenter saws up and planes back. If you want to criticize, first find out the other's point of view. . . .
>
> Seeing their dinner we felt hungry. Brother Stimpson said, "Here is some lunch that we brought along with us." I reached across and took a sandwich in my hand. The first thing I noticed was a little girl on my right look over and try to keep back a "snicker." She did too. Then I noticed that bride looking over at me. I began to wonder what was interesting her. I then began to think, and try to look at myself as others did, and this is what I saw. Her chopsticks were sanitary. She didn't touch one morsel with her hands. That was in her mind. Then, I reached over, took the sandwich in my hands, and held it in them until I had eaten it. As I passed her, I thought I could hear her say, although I could not understand it, "Now that he has eaten his dinner he has washed his hands." To me eating food this way was all right, but to her it was not. Right from that moment on I said, I am going to try to see things here in Japan from the Japanese standpoint, and it is wonderful how things changed.¹⁰

Such experiences undoubtedly came to mind several decades later when, as church president, McKay made several extended trips to the Pacific Islands, Australia, Africa, South America, and Europe, and saw first-hand the challenges in adapting one church to many cultures. In a second letter to Smoot, written from Australia in August 1921, he sounded a theme that recurred frequently in later years: "Every new condition we meet as we continue our most interesting tour emphasizes the wisdom and inspiration of President Grant in having these missions visited. Whether they realize much immediate benefit or not from our visit, the fact remains that the authorities will be in closer touch than ever before with conditions in these somewhat neglected missions."¹¹

Although McKay did not challenge the church policy of "gathering" that had been in effect for nearly a century, whereby converts outside the United States were generally encouraged to emigrate to the Great Basin, he noted with compassion the difficulties encountered by those who remained in their native countries and suggested that a time would come when they would lack for nothing that the American Saints had. Particularly poignant was a speech he gave in New Zealand to a congregation that included the relatives of soldiers who had recently died at the hands of the German Army in World War I:

> Now what about your boys? Their bodies sleep in the dust, back to dust they go, but your boys, God bless them, live in the spirit world. They live! No German shell could touch that spirit, no bomb could maim that spirit.... You should be baptized for them by proxy. That is why you have a Temple at Laie [Hawaii].... Somebody said that he hoped there would be soon a temple in New Zealand. I want to tell you that when you are ready for it, when you can keep it busy, I have no doubt in my heart, but what you will get a Temple.[12]

Nearly forty years later he kept his promise, and returned to New Zealand to dedicate the temple.

Upon returning from his lengthy journey in 1921, McKay gave a report to the First Presidency that included strong recommendations on administering the church in foreign countries, recommendations that he, himself, took to heart upon becoming church president:

> In conclusion, Brethren, I desire to suggest that these missions be permitted to go at longest no more than two years without another visit from a member or members of the General Authorities of the Church. Also that the strongest available men who can possibly be found be chosen to preside over these missions. He who is chosen to carry the responsibility of conducting one of these missions is required to meet greater obstacles, to analyze more difficult situations, to meet more opposition, and to deal with more intricate problems than the average President of a Stake, and yet when we appoint the latter we give him two counselors, associate with these three High priests, twelve or eighteen other High Priests constituting a High Council, visit the stake from two to four times every year and give the officers the opportunity to meet with the General Authorities at least twice a year. While the Mission President is required to meet his difficulties, to carry his great responsibilities and to solve his problems practically alone. It doesn't seem quite right. Therefore, even though some of the stakes might be visited less frequently, I plead that more frequent visits be given to these missions, that the Presidents thereof may be benefited and strengthened by personal contact with members of the

General Authorities. The good thus to be accomplished cannot be overestimated.[13]

Reversing the Policy of Gathering

From its earliest days, Mormonism's message of a restoration of Primitive Christianity went hand-in-glove with a policy of gathering its converts to central locations: initially Ohio, then Missouri, then Illinois, and finally the Great Basin. For the first seven years of its existence, the church's converts came from the United States and Canada, then in 1837 its proselytizing activities extended to the British Isles, and subsequently to other European countries. At a time of economic depression in England, the excitement of the new religion combined with the lure of prosperity in the United States proved to be a potent attractant, and thousands of converts crossed the Atlantic Ocean to gather in Zion. Had it not been for the constant, heavy influx of European converts both before and after Joseph Smith's death in 1844, it is doubtful that the exodus to the Great Basin would have been as successful, if successful at all. In the latter decades of the nineteenth century, the flow of converts from the British Isles was nearly matched by that from Scandinavia. During thirty-five years of operation, the Perpetual Emigrating Fund subsidized the emigration of some 87,000 converts to America.[14]

In 1887, however, the dynamics of gathering changed irreversibly. Determined to blot out plural marriage, the U.S. Congress passed the Edmunds-Tucker Act, part of which dissolved the Perpetual Emigrating Fund. Almost simultaneously the frontier era was ending. By the end of the nineteenth century virtually all habitable locations within the Mormon domain that were suitable for agriculture had been occupied.[15] As the century drew to a close, the unrestrained encouragement—even requirement—to converts to immigrate, began to change. In a meeting of the First Presidency and Quorum of the Twelve in 1897, Apostle George Teasdale requested clarification of church policy on the subject. George Q. Cannon, a counselor in the First Presidency, "stated that the Presidents of Missions had been instructed not to encourage people to emigrate to Utah until they had become well grounded in the faith and not then until times in Utah became better, unless they have friends or means to provide a home on their arrival."[16]

Several months later, the same group discussed the issue at greater length. The discussion was precipitated by a letter from Ben E. Rich, president of the Southern States Mission, asking that the General Authorities stress emigration, since converts in the South "were not growing spiritually, their children were not receiving proper education, and in some instances they were marrying non-Mormons." Church President Lorenzo Snow and his counselor, George Q. Cannon, were sympathetic to Rich's request, but both acknowledged that non-selective immigration was no longer desirable, for "those who fail to secure employment soon become discouraged and want to return to their former homes. They either apostatize, or to a great extent neutralize the efforts of our missionaries laboring in those regions." Cannon further observed "that the spirit of the gathering rested upon the people after receiving the Gospel, but there were times when it was wise and proper to restrain that feeling, and this was the part of presiding men."[17] Apostle Anthon H. Lund suggested a middle ground: "We better not say much publicly to the Saints about restraining emigration because that would have a bad effect, but our missionaries could be instructed to not preach it publicly."[18]

Lund's compromise position reflected the de facto church policy on the issue for years to come: immigration was neither encouraged nor overtly discouraged. For example, a First Presidency message in 1907 noted, "The policy of the Church is not to entice or encourage people to leave their native lands."[19] Fourteen years later, after the close of World War I, an editorial in the *Millennial Star,* the Church's magazine in England, echoed the same sentiment: "Nowhere is it said that the gathering shall be incessant; of necessity there are periods of action in any great enterprise, which, like the avalanche, gathers additional force from a temporary delay. The counsel of the General Authorities to the yet ungathered saints is not to flock Zionward under existing conditions...but remain where you are until further instructions."[20]

A month later the First Presidency sent the same message to European mission presidents: "Many of the saints who immigrate here (the United States), could make themselves much more useful if they would built [*sic*] up and strengthen the church in their own lands.... For years now it has been evident that the emigration of the Saints to Utah and the surrounding area is not advantageous."[21]

The onset of the Great Depression worsened the economic climate in Utah; and in 1931 the First Presidency, noting that in earlier times "there was land and water for irrigation purposes in abundance for all of our members who gathered to Zion," pointed out that "conditions have changed since then." While not overtly reversing the policy of gathering, they sent a strong message by concluding, "Many of the saints who come here could be far more useful in assisting to strengthen and build up the Church in their native lands, than by making sacrifices to come to Zion where their expectations may not be realized."[22]

Economic prosperity returned with the onset of World War II, yet the message did not change. A First Presidency letter written the same month the war ended and published in the *Millennial Star* counseled:

> The missionaries should not hold out inducements to the Saints to gather to Zion on the score of bettering their material interest,...neither should they unduly influence the people to emigrate with a view

of hastening their deliverance from Babylon.... We have no desire to unnecessarily delay the gathering of Israel, or in the least to discourage the Saints from using every means in their power to economize with a view to saving means with which to emigrate. On the contrary we constantly pray for the gathering of Israel, and rejoice to see the Saints come to Zion.... But we wish to impress upon you and the missionary Elders generally, that in the gathering especially, as in all things else connected with the work of the Lord on earth great wisdom must be exercised in order that the best interests of gathered as well as ungathered Israel might be best conserved.[23]

While economics dictated the deemphasis of immigration, an ethical issue likely stood behind the consistent refusal to overtly and permanently *discourage* it, and that was the church's inability to deliver to members in foreign countries all of the spiritual advantages enjoyed by those in the Great Basin. Chief among those advantages were the blessings of the temple, but others such as patriarchal blessings also lay beyond the reach of foreign members, for until McKay's presidency there were no stakes outside of North America (including Hawaii) where such blessings could be obtained.[24]

Because of his earlier trip around the world, McKay had a keen understanding of the deprivation experienced by Saints in other lands, as he had noted in his 1921 speech in New Zealand. Two years later he had repeated the consoling message to British Saints, as president of the European Mission: "Some day we shall have temples built for them which will be accessible to all, so that the desired temple work can be done without uprooting families from their homeland."[25] In 1951 when Stayner Richards, president of the British Mission, requested a temple on British soil, he catalyzed the implementation of McKay's decades-old dream.[26]

Having delivered on the promise of temple blessings and full stake organizations, McKay was now in a position to end the church policy of gathering. Without fanfare, he began to send the message that the time for emigrating to the United States had now permanently passed. In April 1952 he pointed out to the Quorum of the Twelve: "For years it has been recommended that the branches in Great Britain and Europe be strengthened, but...members of the Church in those lands when they get the spirit of the Gospel realize the importance of temple work and notwithstanding some of them held good positions, they have given those positions up and have come here in order to go through the temple."[27]

Two months later he made his first public comment—fittingly, on a trip to Europe to select sites for temples in England and Switzerland. Speaking to a reporter, he said, "We aim to keep our adherents here instead of encouraging them to immigrate to Utah and other places in the United States."[28] In 1953 Senator

Arthur V. Watkins (R-Utah) informed McKay that he "was going to Europe in the interest of the new immigration program and he wondered if he could do anything to help immigrate our people from there." McKay refused the invitation, stating, "We should like our people to remain in Europe and build up strong branches, particularly now that we are taking temples to them. Many of them have good positions there. They can now remain there, build up the branches, receive their endowments and have their temple work taken care of there, both for themselves and their dead."[29] At the same time, the First Presidency directed foreign mission presidents to discourage emigration to America: "It is the present intention of the Church to . . . provide temples throughout the world that the members may remain in the areas and yet have opportunity to receive the blessings of the temple ordinance."[30] Monroe McKay, a cousin of David O. then serving a mission in South Africa, recalled the letter: "During my mission, the official announcement to end the gathering came out. We were told to quit singing, 'Think Not When Ye Gather to Zion.'"[31]

Coincident with the decision to urge people to stay in their native lands was a redefinition of the concept of "Zion." While it had earlier referred to a geographical location, now it was recast as a state of being. McKay's son Lawrence commented on the change: "[Father] preached that Zion was not so much a matter of geography as it was a matter of principle and feeling, that the Spirit of God is within you. He preached that people should stay where they are. The gathering place was no longer Missouri or Utah."[32]

In addition to building a permanent church presence in foreign countries, McKay hoped that Latter-day Saints in those countries would eventually become influential in the affairs of their countries. After a trip to Australia and New Zealand in 1955, he reported to his counselors: "Our men are holding leading positions in Government and other places; . . . We can have an influence in those countries far beyond anything we have had before." During the trip a member of the New Zealand Parliament had told McKay, "You have done more for our Maori people here than all the other churches put together."[33]

Supplementing First Presidency statements were instructions to new mission presidents. T. Bowring Woodbury, set apart to preside over the British Mission in 1958, heard the message clearly:

> After President McKay had set me apart and President [J. Reuben] Clark had set apart Sister Woodbury, President McKay took me by the hand and said: "With the building of the Temple in London, the proposed building of the New Chapel in Exhibition Road and the acquisition of a new Mission Home, this marks the beginning of a NEW ERA in the British Mission; and you, President Woodbury, are the first

to preside in this NEW ERA." We left the Administration Building
with the words "NEW ERA" ringing loud in our ears. The NEW
ERA became the watchword, the slogan, yes, the promise of a
Prophet to the British Saints. That this was a prophetic utterance is
attested to by the fact that out of one mission, the British Mission,
came eight missions and the organization of five stakes of Zion....
The Saints were advised to stay in the land in which they had been
placed by the Lord. Now that we had a new Temple, there was no
need to come to America, but to build the Kingdom and "lift where
they stood."[34]

The change in policy had a gradual effect. Clifton Kerr, who had preceded
Woodbury as president of the British Mission, commented:

In the beginning immigration was encouraged and was taught, but
even after it was no longer emphasized and the encouragement was
given to remaining in England, it was very hard to hold people there.
I made a little survey of the immigration from England of the people
who came into the Church during the first two years I was there. I
found that about a third of them emigrated.... It was usually the
people who were aggressive and good leaders who emigrated,
because they wanted to make a better life for themselves. There were
two factors. One was being near the center of the Church and the
temple, and then the other was economic. Some of our good people
would come over, and pretty soon they'd write home that they'd
bought a car and a refrigerator, something few had in England, and
they'd tell what money they were making, and that was pretty hard
to beat. . . .

I remember time and time again people would say, "There isn't
one chance in a thousand if we stay here of my children marrying in
the Church." I think probably that motivated them as much as any
other single thing, because all their schooling and their associations
were with non-members, and in that situation it was natural that they
would marry out of the Church.[35]

Following a slow start, the retention of church members in their native countries gradually grew. In 1950, the year before McKay became church president, 7.7
percent of the membership resided outside North America; a decade later that had
changed to 10.4 percent, even as total church membership increased by 50 percent
in the same period.[36] However, numbers alone did not result in a strong, permanent church presence overseas. Other elements of the transition included improving the public image of the church abroad and training local leaders.

REVERSING THE CHURCH'S NEGATIVE IMAGE

The image of the church in foreign countries, particularly Western Europe, had been poor for a full century prior to McKay's presidency, ever since the public acknowledgment of the practice of plural marriage in 1852. McKay had abundant personal contact with this poor image, first as a missionary in Scotland from 1897 to 1899, then as a global voyager from 1920 to 1921, and finally as president of the European Mission from 1923 to 1924. He made improving the church's image a personal priority by including abundant public appearances in his travel itineraries. Meetings with church members were interspersed with press conferences, public addresses, and meetings with business and government leaders including three heads of state: Queen Elizabeth II of England, Queen Juliana of the Netherlands, and President Juan Perón of Argentina.

The effect of his personal persona was dramatic, as one traveling companion reported: "[The purpose of the trips] was to let as many people see the President of the Church as was possible. And oh, the meetings and the government people! In Australia, the Governor General and the newspaper people and the people who interviewed him! The reports in the papers and the write-ups and the pictures that they took! He broke down so much prejudice. He looked the part of a prophet. Many people when he and Sister McKay would walk across the platform at an airport or getting onto a train or a ship, they'd all turn around. 'Who's that?' He looked the part of a prophet."[37]

A second public relations tool almost as influential as McKay's persona was the Mormon Tabernacle Choir. Although the choir was well known and respected within the United States, both from its weekly broadcast programs and occasional national tours, it had never ventured overseas. In 1953, following the public announcement of the temple in Switzerland, Warren J. ("Jack") Thomas, a retired Union Pacific Railroad executive, approached McKay with the proposal to send the choir to Europe at the time of the temple's dedication. According to the minutes of that meeting, Thomas had told McKay:

> He had never been on a mission but there is one thing he would like to do which he felt would be a great missionary factor and that he would have to have a year and a half to work it out. He said he would like to take the Tabernacle Choir to Switzerland when the temple there is dedicated and hold concerts in London and Paris and other centers. He said it would cost $250,000 and that he would raise every cent of it and not call on the Church for one dollar.... The President said that the more he thought about it the more favorably he was impressed.[38]

The choir gave concerts in London and Paris prior to the dedication of the Swiss Temple in 1955, and the result was dramatic. Speaking later to the choir, McKay noted the effect of the tour:

> I mentioned the great missionary work the Choir had done on their tour in Europe and reported to them the following statement given by Brother Harold W. Lee, recently released President of the French Mission, to the First Presidency a few days ago when he was making a report of his Mission—he said:
>
> "Before the choir came to Europe, the newspaper articles in France were very often, but not always, unfavorable to the Church. However, as soon as the Choir had sung the first concert in Europe, the articles were more or less neutral, just quoting what others had said.
>
> "After the choir had sung in Paris, the newspaper articles became most favorable. There were 125 newspaper write-ups on the concert itself, and these articles have been sent to the Historian's Office in the Church Office Building. Since that time nearly all the articles have been favorable, and none have been slanderous. We think the Choir is one of the greatest things that ever 'hit' Europe."[39]

TRAINING LOCAL LEADERS

Overseas converts to Mormonism generally came from lower socioeconomic strata with limited leadership skills. While prosperity and leadership skills often increased in the years following conversion, these qualities also predisposed their possessors toward emigration. As a result, the lack of local leadership internationally was a perennial problem for the church. A. Theodore Tuttle, a General Authority who presided over the South American Mission beginning in 1961, nearly a decade after the decision to discourage gathering, described the leadership vacuum he encountered: "The leadership training was, I suppose, in a sense non-existent on an organized basis.... In nearly every mission I guess more than 50 percent of all the branches were presided over by elders [American missionaries], and district presidents were likewise elders. We took a rather strong stand on that, particularly with mission presidents and just agreed on goals that in X amount of time, generally in the next six months, we would eliminate every elder from presiding in a branch, except in branches that were just opened."[40]

A similar situation existed in Europe, where the lack of local leaders became a source of public embarrassment. In a press conference in England in 1958, McKay was put on the defensive by a British journalist who asked: "Mr. McKay, the London President is an American. Is there no Englishman or man in Great Britain who could become the London President? Is there no English person who could become President in London of the Church? Most executives in the Mormon Church are American. Are there no Englishmen who could hold the post?" McKay's response acknowledged the reporter's observation but only described the policy, rather than its cause: "It is the custom of the Church to send Mission Presidents usually from the headquarters of the Church, but they might be natives of the country to which they are sent."[41] His private reaction showed that the question had stung. He urged the new mission president, T. Bowring Woodbury, to make the development of local leadership a priority. Woodbury later described his approach to the problem:

> Missionaries were eased out of the positions as branch presidents and district presidents. We asked every missionary branch president to recommend two counselors. We asked each missionary district president to do the same. Then, we began schools for the local brethren by having them come to London and also meeting with them in district conferences. In a matter of six months, we had reduced every district presidency to local brethren and the only missionary branch presidents were in the new small branches where we did not have the priesthood.... In Wales, where we could find few worthy brethren, we sent an older couple and his job was to challenge the individual priesthood bearers to make themselves worthy for a special calling that was to come to them. Within weeks, these brethren gave up their habits, started paying tithes and responded magnificently to the call. The surge of local leadership and their development was the forerunner of the stakes that have been formed.[42]

In addition to these local initiatives, McKay greatly increased central supervision of the international church. In 1955 he noted, "It is marvelous how close these missions are to us under the present means of transportation; that the Lord has opened up the way for His interests in all the world to be looked after by those who are called to look after them."[43] Only weeks later in general conference he announced a sweeping change in central supervision: "It is only recently that some of these missions have been visited by a General Authority. With modern means of transportation available, it is now possible and very practical to have these far off missions visited as the missions here in the United States have been visited. Accordingly, and this you will be pleased to hear, at a meeting of the First Presidency and Council of the Twelve held March 17, 1955, it was unanimously decided that these distant missions should be included with other missions in the annual appointments of members of the Council of the Twelve."[44]

Four years later, McKay extended headquarters influence by reopening the European Mission, which had been closed since the outbreak of World War II. This mission, which served as regional church headquarters for Europe, supervised the individual missions throughout Europe. McKay explained the model to the Twelve: "Instead of sending the Brethren of the General Authorities to visit the various missions over there," a General Authority would "preside as President of the European Mission, to work with the various missions just as the European Mission President formerly did.[45]

Called to fill this revitalized role was Alvin R. Dyer, an Assistant to the Twelve. The experiment was so successful that, two years later, McKay announced the assignment of all church missions units to one of nine geographical groupings, each presided over by a General Authority. For the European Mission, West European Mission, and South American Mission, the presiding General Authority lived on-site in Frankfurt, London, and Montevideo, respectively, while the other six regional president/General Authorities continued to reside in Salt Lake City. The new program, called a "precedent setting decision,"[46] was expanded four years later, this time with two General Authorities (one an apostle, the other either a member of the First Council of Seventy or an Assistant to the Twelve) over each area. Paul H. Dunn, a member of the First Council of Seventy, explained his duties and the benefits of the program:

> Before, it was everybody doing everything that the First Presidency would assign you to do. There was no coordination, no responsibility geographically for any area or Stake or Ward or Mission, or anything like that. It was just the Church, and everybody was available to do whatever the First Presidency wanted you to do, whether it was a Stake Conference, or mission tours, or whatever. . . .
>
> I had the assignment, under Tom [Monson] in my area, the South Pacific, to tour each mission (as I recall, we had twelve at that time) once a year and interview each missionary. Then a year or two later, a directive came for us to then, after each interview, write a note to the parents. That became a concern of the First Presidency that we were keeping close to our people throughout the world. . . . I was the first General Authority the Cook Islands and New Caledonia had seen since Matthew Cowley. You would have thought I was Quetzalcoatl when I got off the plane! That really commenced the international church. . . .
>
> It got to where you could call hundreds of people by their names, where that had never happened before. Before, you were working with Stake Presidencies and Bishops, and after you went over there for

one Stake assignment and came right home, nobody knew anybody. This way, you were with them constantly, and you were working with them on a daily basis. That had a very wholesome effect, in letting them know that the Church cared, that we got to know the brethren, and that we had an entree to ask questions that we hadn't been able to ask before.... To have a General Authority mingle with them and be a part of their lives was a very motivating and lifting thing.[47]

Thus, a combination of factors—abandoning the doctrine of gathering, the construction of temples and chapels, reversing the church's negative public image, and training local leaders—all worked together to effect a maturation of the international church. One hundred twenty-eight years after the founding of the church, the first stake outside North America was formed in New Zealand; a year later, England saw the formation of the first stake in Europe; and in 1966 the first South American stake was organized in Brazil. Between 1958 and McKay's death in 1970, thirty-four LDS stakes began operations outside North America.[48]

THE CHALLENGES OF INTERNATIONALIZATION

Growth and maturation brought a realization that international Mormonism could not be merely a duplication of Great Basin Mormonism. The process of internationalization continues to the present as one of Mormonism's most important and daunting challenges.

Early in his tenure as church president, McKay became acutely aware of differences between the church in which he had grown up and the church abroad. In 1953 his second counselor, J. Reuben Clark, drafted an anti-welfare letter to the president of the Western Canadian Mission that condemned "the acceptance by the people in Canada of gratuities of one sort and another granted by the Canadian government." McKay referred the draft to his first counselor, Stephen L Richards, like Clark an attorney, who replied:

It is very difficult for me to harmonize my feelings [with Clark's stand].... I just feel that we do not have to do things like that when we can leave the people to act for themselves, and while we cannot individually approve of everything governments do, I think the policy as outlined in the letter would lead us to take objection to what governments all over the world are doing. We, the Church, are worldwide, and it makes so many people feel that they are not in good standing because they are not fully following the counsel of our brethren.... We cannot regulate the affairs of all governments, and I wonder if the time has not come when we can say that we express no

official view; that we leave it to the people for determination themselves.... There is nothing in the law (Canadian) that prevents us
from teaching family solidarity, and from advocating those high principles in our Gospel, but when it comes to interfering with the policies of the government, I doubt that it is our function.

McKay agreed with Richards, and vetoed Clark's letter.[49]

The following year McKay took an extended trip to two areas of the world he
had not yet visited, South Africa and South America. The experience opened his
eyes. Writing from South Africa, he noted, "One must take this long journey to
realize what a vast continent Africa is and to sense the distances that the branches
in the Union are from Salt Lake City, or to put it in the words of the South African,
how far Salt Lake City is from Capetown!"[50]

In Uruguay, he found that conducting church business sometimes called for
unconventional measures. Lyman S. Shreeve, the mission president who greeted
him there, later described the scene:

> He said to me, "President Shreeve, we have noticed that you have a
> little more success than some of the other mission presidents in South
> America in getting things from the States into Uruguay. Would you
> like to tell me how you do that?" I thought, "Well, he's got me now.
> I've got to tell him how I do that, and I don't know if he's going to
> like it or not."
>
> So I said, "Sure, I'll be glad to show you how." We got in the mis-
> sion car and drove down to the port and went over to a bar where I
> called out a fellow by the name of António, who I introduced to Pres-
> ident McKay. António had a flat-bottomed green truck with a foot-
> high border around it, and I asked him to show President McKay the
> customs house and how he got our merchandise in. So we went
> through the gate into the port and around the customs house. . . .
>
> I said, "Now, here's the way it works, President McKay. António
> knows everybody who works here. He knows the fellow that works
> in the customs, he knows the guy out at the gate, and everybody.
> When this equipment comes in, it comes off the ships and is placed
> on the dock, and then should go into the customs house in their stor-
> age places, where it could be kept for months or even years. Some-
> times it gets in there and we never get it out. But António has got it
> fixed so that when it hits the dock he picks it up and puts it on this
> green flat-bottom truck and he gives a few pesos tip to this guy and
> a few pesos to that guy, and then he loads this all up—things like
> heaters for the chapel and all kinds of material that we bring in—and

then he drives the car around to the gate—it's all fenced in—and as he goes through he's inspected again, and there he has other friends and he pays them a few pesos and then he comes to the mission home."

Then I got to the real crucial question and I said, "What do you think about us doing it that way, President McKay?" He thought for a minute, and these are his exact words, "Oh, I don't know. They do things differently in Latin America, don't they?" That was the end of it, and was I glad.[51]

Upon returning to Salt Lake City, McKay told a joint meeting of the First Presidency and Twelve: "The concepts we get from reality are entirely different than the concepts we have from reports received."[52]

Accommodation to foreign cultures occurred slowly and on several fronts. Prior to 1962 few texts other than the *Book of Mormon* had been translated into languages other than English. For instance, when J. Thomas Fyans was called to preside over the Uruguayan Mission in 1960, accompanied by his wife, Helen, they found a startling shortage of church materials:

When we went to Uruguay, there was absolutely nothing in Spanish [except the Book of Mormon]. They'd send a manual down in English, and we'd have to translate it. When we first got there, they divided up the work of translation. The mission in Lima, Peru, did the Relief Society lessons. In Argentina, they did the Primary. In Chile they did the Sunday School. And we had the Mutual. And we went through that magazine, and we'd translate every lesson. Then, when we'd hold a mission presidents' seminar, we'd take all of our materials and share them with the other missions. That's the way we got started. I remember the Primary lessons mentioning Old Jack Frost in January, and George Washington in February, and spring in March. Well, [March] wasn't spring down there. So we had to look around and try and find something that meant something to them.[53]

Translation facilities in Salt Lake City slowly centralized and professionalized but lacked a comprehensive plan. In 1962 Henry D. Moyle, then McKay's first counselor, assigned Apostle Gordon B. Hinckley to head a task force to recommend a more systematic approach to the problem.[54] Three years later their efforts resulted in the formation of a new Translation Department, headed by Thomas Fyans, who also suggested standardizing the church magazines:

It was in Switzerland where I said, "Now, you have all these different magazines." Every mission had its own magazine in its own language.

The Church magazines were under us at that time. I said, "We do all the art work for the covers of the *Improvement Era,* and we'd be happy to print your art work for you, so we could have a standard cover throughout the world. This would save you a lot of wear and tear." I remember Elder [Howard W.] Hunter say[ing], "Why are you talking about just the cover? Why don't you do the whole thing for them?" So Elder Hunter brought this idea back, and said, "I think this organization ought to create this magazine for us." So what we created was the international magazine.... When we came back, we presented this to President McKay. We then had the magazine world-wide.[55]

General awareness of international issues gradually permeated church head-quarters. When reviewing proposed lessons for the 1967 Melchizedek Priesthood manual, the Correlation Committee acknowledged that some of the material was provincial. "Much of the information in the alternate study course that had been suggested pertains specifically to the United States and would not be appropriate for world-wide membership."[56]

As broadcasts of general conference reached the membership outside the United States, sensitivity to the needs and feelings of non-American Saints became an issue. Ironically, in one telling incident, McKay was the bottleneck: Apostle Richard L. Evans, who delivered the short sermon that accompanied each Sunday morning broadcast of the Mormon Tabernacle Choir, was keenly attuned to both the public relations advantages and the pitfalls of these broadcasts. When he saw that the Tabernacle Choir, joined by the congregation, was scheduled to sing "America" during one session of the April 1968 general conference, he pointed out that "criticism is received when we sing at the Broadcast sessions of Conference the patriotic songs of America." He urged McKay to have another song sub-stituted. McKay, bristling, telephoned the choir director, Richard P. Condie, who "could not see any objection to singing 'America' at this session. I stated that 'I don't care whether they like it or not, I want them to sing 'America' as listed.'" For unknown reasons—perhaps Evans's continued efforts—he learned within a few days that "'America' would be deleted from the Broadcast going overseas" and "gave permission to delete it from the [conference session] program."[57]

As already noted, Ezra Taft Benson's unwavering anti-Communism positioned socialism as its forerunner, bringing statements of stern denunciation. (See chap. 12.) In his October 1968 conference address, he lashed out at all forms of social-ism throughout the world, thus bringing to a head a problem that had been sim-mering for several years. A First Presidency meeting discussed the issue within the month:

Reference was made to questions that have been raised by presidents of stakes and mission presidents in Germany, the British Isles, etc., and also by the *[Improvement] Era*, regarding talks that have been given in conference by the brethren of the Authorities such as the one given by Brother Benson at the recent General Conference regarding the responsibilities we have to oppose socialism, etc. A letter had been received from the President of the Manchester Stake stating that certain talks at the conference could create a problem, and he asks for some clarification before the conference pamphlet is published. He mentioned an address by one of the brethren reminding the people that we are under obligation to heed the counsel of the General Authorities as being from the Lord, and that on Friday morning an address was given denouncing all forms of socialism in governments, and specifically mentioning England. He explains that over half of the members of his stake in England vote socialist and that members of the stake presidency, high council and bishoprics support that cause, that there is therefore some confusion in regard to how they should accept these statements.

Although this policy did little in terms of curbing Benson, "The brethren were agreed that in General Conference the Authorities should talk about principles and leave politics or pointed attacks on politics out of their talks."[58]

Later the same day N. Eldon Tanner, McKay's second counselor, brought the issue before the Council of the Twelve Apostles:

President Tanner mentioned that during the past three years we have had questions and complaints about talks given in General Conference that seem to be offensive to the German people or the British people, or whoever it may be, by just building up the United States of America and referring to things that are going on here. . . .

Elder [Harold B.] Lee mentioned that the overall problem we have constantly had in mind is to make our hearers conscious of the fact that we are a universal church, and that those things that go into our lessons must be applicable to the world; that when we set forth gospel principles this is very simple, but when we begin to relate it to governmental programs of this country and other countries we become involved in controversy. . . .

Elder [Spencer W.] Kimball felt that in the General Authorities meeting, which is held in the temple two weeks before conference, the brethren might be reminded that their talks should be geared to the world.

President Tanner said that he did not know that we could do any more this morning, but we should have in mind that it is a world church, and that when speaking in General Conference he thought we should be careful to tell people what we are trying to tell them regarding the gospel in a way that will not be offensive to other parts of the world.[59]

Other cultural differences needed to be addressed, but progress was often painfully slow. Not until 1969, less than a year before McKay's death, was there a serious discussion about architecture in the context of an international church: "Some of the brethren do not think that we should try to build the same kind of chapel in South America that we build in North America, that the conditions are different and the people are not housed the same as they are here. They are not as affluent as we are. President Tanner said that at a meeting of the Council the other day it was suggested that a committee be set up to study this matter and come in with recommendations as to what modifications we should make. I gave my approval."[60]

The committee delivered its report later that year,[61] but full implementation of a program to build chapels throughout the world that consistently reflected local conditions and cultures lay decades in the future.

The cumulative progress that David O. McKay made toward building a truly international church remains one of the most enduring parts of his legacy. Peter D. Olson, a businessman interviewed as one of Woodbury's former missionaries, recalled an unrelated but telling incident that captured the depth of McKay's concerns over reaching his worldwide constituency:

One of my former missionary companions lived in the basement of the Lawrence McKay home when he was attending the University of Utah. I went up there to see him one night and he had a book called *The Shoes of the Fisherman*. It's a fictional book about a Pope who had been chosen from Russia. He'd been in prison for many, many years, and finally he was let out of prison. He became the new Pope, and it goes through how this happened, and then the problems he struggled with as the Catholic Church dealt with their worldwide problems. They made a movie of it. Anthony Quinn was in it. Anyway, this former companion said, "Peter, here's a book that I've been reading. President McKay has just finished reading this book. It sure is interesting to see what he underlined." There were some pencil underlinings in that book, and I looked at that with great interest. I could see that some of the things he had underlined in that book were pertaining to the worldwide problems that the Catholic Church had. I know that he looked at that, as from the underlinings I could see this is a worldwide church that we're involved with and we have the same problems.[62]

MCKAY'S CROWNING ACHIEVEMENT

Shortly after David O. McKay's death, Sterling M. McMurrin, a prominent Mormon intellectual who had had a significant relationship with McKay (see chap. 3), wrote a tribute echoing McKay's earlier feeling that the transformation of the church into a worldwide organization was his crowning achievement:

> It is not difficult to identify the large difference that President McKay has made in the character and historical movement of the Church. I refer to the obvious fact that especially during the period of his presidency the Church has broken some of its parochial bonds and hopefully has begun to move toward universality. . . .
>
> The recent stirring of the Church toward universalism is represented not so much by its missionary expansion as by its building "foreign" temples, not by any change in doctrine, but by a change in disposition. The Church has always had quite extensive missions, but with the exception of the Polynesians served by the Hawaiian Temple, the converts came to America to become full-fledged Mormons. The doctrines taught and believed in foreign climes have been the same as those taught and believed in Utah, but a part of one's conversion to the gospel, if he were a native of Europe, South America, or the Orient, was to learn to sing the songs of Zion, to join the "gathering" to Israel, and all too often to abandon precious values in his native culture to become a "Utah" Mormon. . . .
>
> But that in this period the Church began to enlarge its perspectives on its place in the world, magnifying its vision, and moving, though slowly, toward an identification of itself with all men, was surely due in large part to President McKay's own moral disposition and ideals, ideals which were inclusive rather than exclusive, which included rather than excluded his fellowmen. That from an early date he possessed a quality of world-mindedness not commonly found in the Church is known to all who have followed his ministry. It was a world-mindedness made possible not so much through his acquaintance with the world, which was extensive, as through his insight into the condition of the human soul. . . .

Universality as a religious ideal is possible only where there is an authentic conception of the reality of the individual, a genuine concern for his dignity and worth, and a full measure of human sympathy.... I believe that the universalism of President McKay, his identification with humanity, was grounded in his respect and concern for the individual, his reverence for the freedom and autonomy of the moral will, his sympathy and compassion for every person.... We may hope that future historians will find that his ideal was in fact the beginning of a new era for the Church.[63]

15

FINAL YEARS

When Joseph Smith, Mormonism's founder, was assassinated in 1844 at age thirty-eight, it was not immediately clear who would succeed him, or what the pattern of succession would eventually become. Indeed, at various times Smith had suggested as many as eight means of succession.[1] Initially, power was assumed by the Quorum of the Twelve Apostles, acting as a group but with the senior apostle, Brigham Young, assuming a leadership role. Group leadership continued for over three years before Young sought and obtained from his fellow apostles a consensus that a new First Presidency should be formed, with him as church president. Similar periods of apostolic rule followed the deaths of Young in 1877 and his successor, John Taylor, in 1887. By the turn of the twentieth century, however, a firm precedent had been established by which the longest-tenured apostle, regardless of age, became the new president. While guaranteeing continuity of "institutional memory," the policy also ensured that all presidents would assume office at an advanced age.

David O. McKay was in his seventy-eighth year when he became president, an age when most of his peers in secular life had already been retired for over a decade, yet he was surprisingly fit. A hardworking farmboy, he further developed an athletic build as a member of the University of Utah football team, preserved it through periodic activity on the family farm well into his ninth decade, and entered the presidency with robust health and vitality. In celebrating his seventy-fifth birthday three years earlier, he had expressed pleasant surprise at his good fortune: "Old Age at seventy-five is not nearly so decrepit as years ago I had anticipated he would be. I used to think that at three score and fifteen a man is pretty close to the evening of life; but this birthday has convinced me that life at seventy-five is just as bright and joyous as ever when surrounded by Loved Ones and loyal friends."[2]

Five years later he upstaged two of his sons with a remarkable display of stamina. After attending a funeral one morning, he responded to a plea from Robert and Lawrence, who were trying futilely to load thoroughbred horses onto a trailer, and drove to Robert's farm to take control. In reading his account of the matter, one can imagine the octogenarian shaking his head at the limitations of the younger generation: "One of the horses stubbornly refused to go up the plank and into the trailer, and it took me until 6:30 P.M. to finally convince her that I did not give up easily. I was out in the hot sun all this time. Lawrence who was watching became very ill because of the heat and had to find a place in the shade. Robert had to leave to keep an appointment. Finally, after much struggling, I succeeded in getting the horse into the trailer and Lawrence and Mildred then drove her to Huntsville and I returned home."[3]

About three months later as he celebrated a milestone, he reflected on his good fortune: "It is a beautiful autumn day! It is hard for me to realize that today is my 80th birthday. In childhood and even throughout the gay realm of youth the '70's' and '80's' seemed far in the future, and weary and feeble those who had reached such an advanced old age. Today, however, I know that what seemed in youth to be a long journey is very short indeed; and what in anticipation was considered to be a joyless existence is one of the most wholesome contributive periods of life."[4]

Although McKay underwent several hospitalizations for a variety of causes, including several surgical procedures, he was free from systemic disease. In 1956 his physician, Dr. Louis Viko, remarked to him, "It is amazing—for your age and for a man who works as hard as you do, you are in wonderful condition—your heart, your blood pressure are good."[5] Dr. Viko, nonetheless, cautioned McKay to cut back on his strenuous schedule, advice that the patient—who survived his younger physician by a decade—summarily ignored.

As he moved through his ninth decade, however, McKay was well aware that age was taking its toll, although he admitted it more readily to himself than to his associates. After one Saturday at his Huntsville farm, he noted in his diary: "Had quite a time all afternoon working on the farm—ran the mowing machine, cutting the grass which had grown very high during the rains of the past few days. One thing, I found that I am not as young as I used to be—work on the farm is more tiring to me than it formerly was, so I suppose I shall have to admit that 'old age' is taking over."[6]

The following year, now eighty-five years old, he wrote even more candidly in his diary: "This morning I rested, trying to regain my physical health. The two operations for cataract this year, the dedication of two temples in foreign lands, the presiding at and conducting two General conferences of the Church, in addition to the myriads of Church problems which have arisen during this year, have taken a toll of my health, and I am having a difficult time regaining my strength."[7]

Respites at his Huntsville farm or at the church-owned home at Emerald Bay, California, became increasingly important; but even then his idea of relaxation would have been strenuous by anyone else's standards. Mrs. McKay noted ironically that once, when he was "in great need of a rest," he made arrangements to dedicate a meetinghouse in Oregon. On the first day of this "rest," the two left Salt Lake City at 7:30 A.M. and "drove 500 miles over [the Nevada] desert" before they stopped for the night.⁸ Even at Emerald Bay, he entertained a stream of visitors. Over time the therapeutic effect of days out of the office diminished because of the increasing workload that met him on his return. In a sense, he was a victim of his own success as church membership nearly tripled under his leadership. In late 1958 he noted: "Although I felt fine when I returned from California last Tuesday, three or four days of pressing problems and meetings have put me back where I was before leaving for California. The Church is growing, and duties are becoming heavier and more pressing!"⁹

Church members had long been accustomed to aged presidents, and even to long periods of failing health. McKay's two immediate predecessors, Heber J. Grant and George Albert Smith, had lengthy periods at the end of their lives when their deteriorating health effectively ceded day-to-day administration of the church to J. Reuben Clark Jr., who served as first counselor to both men. But Grant and Smith held office prior to the age of television; and without visual images as a cue, most church members were unaware of the degree of their infirmities. In contrast, McKay was a televised church president from the start; and as broadcast coverage of general conferences gradually increased, his visual image and the sound of his voice, combined with a steady stream of photographs in church publications, conveyed to church members his gradual physical decline.

To those in his inner circle, the change was even more obvious, and it accelerated in the aftermath of the sudden death of his closest friend and associate, First Counselor Stephen L Richards. Richards had had a long history of heart problems, but his fatal heart attack on May 19, 1959, at age seventy-nine, came as a great shock to the eighty-five-year-old McKay. Minutes after receiving the news, McKay wept openly as he told two associates, "He was as dear to me as a brother—a true and loyal friend, a wise counselor, with one of the greatest minds in the Church. Oh! how I shall miss him!"¹⁰

Two weeks later, BYU President Ernest L. Wilkinson met with J. Reuben Clark, who had been elevated to first counselor at Richards's death, and the two discussed McKay's condition. The sixty-year-old Wilkinson reported that Clark, who was eighty-seven, said, "The president is failing fast," and added, "I suppose I am also, but don't know it." Wilkinson, never strong on tact, wrote ruefully in his diary: "All I could do was to assure him that he was not failing as fast as President McKay. This was a quick response, and of course carried the admission he was failing, which I think he noted, and after I left the room I wondered if my statement was entirely accurate, because they are both failing very fast."¹¹ Wilkinson's diagnosis proved to be flawed, however, for Clark died two years later while McKay rallied, as he would repeatedly, and lived another decade.

Two years after this diary entry, Wilkinson noted that McKay's health again appeared precarious, and he confided to the diary his prediction that McKay would not survive another two years (McKay lived another eight years), although this time he added a disclaimer: "In saying this, I don't pretend to be a prophet. I had thought a few years ago that Stephen L Richards would survive all members of the Presidency, and he went first."[12]

A month later, on the occasion of his eighty-eighth birthday, McKay mused philosophically about his accommodation to the realities of old age:

> For the past several years I have been prone to consider Old Age as a disagreeable unwelcome trespasser, skulking along to claim any faculty that might show the strain and usage of the passing years; this year at eighty-eight I look upon him with a degree of compassion akin to appreciation. Indeed, if it were not for 'Old Age' I should not have seen seventy-five, or eighty, or eighty-five, and most assuredly not Eighty-eight. Now I am content to let him walk by my side, but shall continue as long as possible to deny the demands of Old Age to take from me the good health Kind Providence still gives me![13]

The following year he gave in to one of those demands and, for the first time since becoming president eleven years earlier, asked one of his counselors, Hugh B. Brown, to conduct the priesthood session of general conference.[14] Yet even as he made some concessions to age, he continued to relish whatever remaining years he might have, often exuding humor in the process. After being assisted to the podium by two university officials at a dedicatory service at Utah State University, "he said he was 'fit as a fiddle' but had experienced some difficulty getting on the platform because he had to drag two others up with him."[15] He made a similar quip to David M. Kennedy, later Nixon's U.S. Secretary of the Treasury, at a gathering in Chicago: "We had luncheon at John Kaye's home, and John was on one side of him and I was on the other, and we were walking up kind of an incline from the curb on his grass slope there. President McKay stopped and smiled at us and looked at John and then he looked at me and he said, "You know, I can pull one of you up here, but I can't pull both of you up this hill."[16]

During a general conference session in 1963, Hugh B. Brown was particularly impressed with the dynamism being displayed by fellow General Authorities as they addressed the congregation. Leaning over to McKay, he whispered, "With men like that, we do not have to worry about what will happen to the Church after we are gone." McKay quickly riposted, "I do not know about you, President Brown, but I am not going anywhere."[17]

Feeling chipper as he approached his ninetieth birthday, McKay decided on the spur of the moment one Tuesday to spend the day at his Huntsville farm. He called his son Llewelyn, who accommodated him on short notice and drove him to the farm, where he handily ignored his age:

> After taking care of some chores, decided to take a ride on "Sonny Boy." He has been out in the fields all winter and has fattened up. He looks wonderful, however, is very nervous. My son Llewelyn was putting the saddle on him, and I was holding the rope which was around his neck, when the saddle blanket slid off his back. This scared "Sonny Boy," and as he bolted from fright, I was knocked down and pulled along on the ground for about a block. However, he stopped and I was not hurt. We finally saddled him, and he was his usual self, and I had a very good ride on him, which I enjoyed thoroughly. When I returned home in the later afternoon, I said nothing about this incident to Sister McKay as she would have worried a great deal about it.[18]

Love and concern about his wife, Emma Ray, was the focal point of his personal life during this period as it had been ever since their marriage in 1901. A man who assisted the McKays for a short time asked daughter-in-law Lottie McKay for pointers on how best to act around them. "'What do I do? How do you treat him?' Lottie responded, 'You just be sure that Mama Ray is okay, and he'll be just fine.'"[19] One General Authority noted the effect on others of McKay's relationship with his wife:

> His love for Emma Ray was something that was always at the forefront. He demonstrated it very beautifully. I remember that we were out at a cemetery, and it was a blustery, wintry day. His white hair was blowing in the wind. As he approached the car, one of his attendants, Brother Acomb, had Sister McKay around the other side of the car to help her in. He said, "Brother Acomb, just a minute, just a minute. Hold on there." And he walked all the way around the car with this cold wind blowing, and he opened the door for Emma Ray, and he said, "This is my responsibility," and he helped her in. Here he was, ninety years old. It was a great lesson, and it showed that you endure to the end, even in the little things.[20]

McKay's tender affection for his wife also had its moments of puckish good-humor. One associate recalled a time when both, living in their Hotel Utah apartment, were using wheelchairs for mobility. On their way to a general conference session, their attendants wheeled them "down the hall towards the elevators." McKay "put his hands on the wheels and said, 'Emma Ray, I'll race you to the elevators!'"[21]

Shortly after turning ninety, McKay reported to his fellow General Authorities on his health: "I have been under the weather somewhat this past week, but the doctors can find nothing wrong with me but age. I said that I do not mind being ninety years of age; that I am looking forward to more years. I said that I supposed I would have to be here until the Lord says that I am ready to go, and that I would work as long as I can."[22]

While McKay's work was periodically compromised by bodily limitations, his mind continued to function well, unclouded by dementia, lack of reasoning ability, or memory loss. Arch Madsen, whom McKay had recruited to run the church's broadcasting interests, recalled, "He was the youngest man I ever worked with, and he was ninety years old then."[23] Along with a crisp intellect, he maintained an impressively optimistic vision of the future. At the time when the Apollo Program aimed to land astronauts on the moon, McKay discussed its implications with an associate:

> He said, "Brother Jacobsen, the United States is trying to put a man on the moon. How would you like to be the first one to fly to the moon?" I had never thought about that question. I said, just quickly, "President McKay, I think maybe I'd rather be the second man to fly to the moon, so the first one would have some experience." He spoke right up and he said, "You know, I'd love to be the first man to fly to the moon. How do you suppose we are going to travel from one planet to another in the hereafter unless we learn how to do some of it on this earth?" Then he quoted the old song in the hymnbook called "If You Could Hie to Kolob." He quoted every word from memory, all verses of that song to me. And he said, "Now this is just not a figment of imagination. There's a lot of truth in what this man has put in this song."... He [McKay] was a kind of forward-looking man, and he was not one who didn't think that it was possible for us to go to the moon. He wanted to be there also.[24]

In November 1963, McKay suffered a stroke and spent several weeks convalescing. Upon returning to the office and attending a council meeting in the Salt Lake Temple for the first time in over two months, he told his colleagues, "I think this condition is only temporary; that the doctors say I am getting along fine .... I am inclined to accept their word, but do not believe all that they say." The stroke had affected his right side, and thus his ability to write, but he had managed to regain the ability to sign his name. "It does not look like the same old signature," he told them, "but it passes on checks all right."[25]

Two weeks later, reacting to obvious concern from his secretary, he soothed her, "Don't fret, I'll be here another five years!"[26] (He lived another six.) At about

the same time, his youngest grandchild was born. When McKay's son Bob brought
the baby over for a visit and said, "I thought you'd like to see your newest grandson," McKay replied, "You mean before I go? You needn't worry, because I'm not
going anywhere for the next six years. That's how long it will take me to complete
my work, and the Lord won't take me before then."[27] In fact, McKay lived just a
few weeks longer than six years.

As 1964 proceeded, McKay became discouraged at the slow pace of his recovery from the stroke. In February he wrote, "I am not gaining very much in
health;…it makes me angry that I have to drag my feet; that they will not perform
as I should like them to."[28] His son noted the extent of the impairment: "At dinner before the stroke, he always carried the conversation. After the stroke he could
hardly speak. When he asked the blessing on the food, we couldn't understand
him. We had to ask him to repeat when he said something, and he was embarrassed
to have to repeat what he'd said."[29]

In August, he suffered another setback. Early in the morning he felt weak and
began to perspire profusely. He was taken to the LDS Hospital, where it was determined that he had had a minor heart attack. The doctor reassuringly told Lawrence
McKay: "It is small and is on the side of his heart which will not do too much damage."[30] A medical student from the University of Utah at the time was assigned to
draw blood from McKay:

> He appeared moderately ill and in some distress. Yet, when I ex-
> plained my task, he smiled patiently, asked my name and graciously
> submitted to my search for the right vein, the scrubbing and prepa-
> ration of the venipuncture site, the needle stick and the pressure and
> staunching once the blood had been drawn. He must have sensed my
> apprehension, as he was reassuring and kind. When I placed the
> tourniquet and probed his arm with my fingers, I was struck by how
> muscular and well preserved was this 90 year-old man. Once com-
> pleted, I was grateful and indelibly touched by his patience and kind-
> ness toward me despite his own pain and obvious discomfort.[31]

Two days after being hospitalized, McKay had difficulty in breathing and was
placed in an oxygen tent, where he remained for several days. A week later, well
aware of the seriousness of his condition, he made a special request of his fellow
General Authorities:

> Now this is very important: I feel the need of the united prayers and
> faith of the Brethren. I should like to ask my counselors and the
> Twelve to have a special meeting next Monday morning. I was going
> to have this blessing following one of my sacred visits to the Holy of

Holies in the Temple, but I cannot leave this hospital room. It is going to be a problem to arrange this so that the greatest good can come out of the blessing.... I think I shall ask President Brown to represent the First Presidency in anointing me, and then have Brother Joseph Fielding Smith seal the anointing as President of the Council of the Twelve. Members of the First Presidency and Brother Joseph can come here to my room in the hospital and the Twelve, the Assistants to the Twelve, the Seventies, and the Presiding Bishopric can hold a special prayer meeting in the First Presidency's room at the same hour that the Presidency are giving the blessing.[32]

Two days later, as McKay had requested, his colleagues gathered for a special meeting of fasting and prayer: "They gathered around President McKay's bedside and he asked President Tanner to anoint him and President Smith to seal the anointing. At the same time, Elder Harold B. Lee was voice in representing the other General Authorities gathered in the First Presidency's room in the Church Administration Building in offering a prayer in President McKay's behalf. President Smith has never been so inspired—his blessing was indeed an inspiration!"[33]

No miraculous restoration of health followed this special blessing. A few weeks later, he was obliged to watch October 1964 general conference on television from his apartment—the first time he had missed a conference due to illness since becoming an apostle in 1906 and the first time that his address was read by one of his sons. Characteristically, he found the silver lining in this situation, reporting, "It was the first time that I had enjoyed the privilege of watching the Brethren's faces as they spoke."[34] However, he lamented to a correspondent the following week: "For the first time in all my years of church experience excepting when I was on my World Tour and when I was President of the European Mission, I was unable to attend Conference. At the last moment I gave in to the pleas of the doctors and members of the family not to put the added strain on my heart. I am trying to obey the orders of the doctors, but it has been very difficult."[35]

For weeks after the conference McKay was confined to his apartment on doctor's orders. In the meantime, a signal event in church history approached as the Oakland Temple was completed and readied for dedication on November 17—the first temple dedicated since the London Temple in September 1958. Given McKay's state of health, his colleagues assumed that he would still be unable to travel and that they would have to act in his stead to dedicate the building. However, as the event drew nearer, McKay made no assignments, leaving both family and colleagues in a state of anxious uncertainty. Because he had asked his sons, Robert and Lawrence, to read his prepared addresses at the October general conference, Lawrence began to "worry" that he or Robert might be tapped for this responsibility. In late October, he brought the subject up with his brother: "'Has he asked you, Bob?'... 'No,' my brother answered. 'Has he asked you?' 'No.' There seemed to be no more to say. President Hugh B. Brown, then Father's first counselor, asked a week or so later, 'Lawrence, has your father said anything about who is going to dedicate the Oakland Temple?' 'No,' I reported."[36]

Early in November, McKay surprised everyone by announcing in a First Presidency meeting, "In all probability I shall go to the dedication of the Oakland Temple." He acknowledged, however, that "my doctors are advising against my going."[37] A week later, he indicated in another First Presidency meeting that his role in the ceremony would be limited. (At earlier temple dedications, he had delivered a major address and the dedicatory prayer at each of several daily sessions.) "I said that it is my intention at the opening session to give a few words of greeting, and later in the session to make brief remarks, and then to read the dedicatory prayer."[38] Two days later, in a meeting of the First Presidency and Twelve in the Salt Lake Temple, he reported: "The doctors were really surprised yesterday morning at my improved condition, and gave me hope that I would overcome the impediment in my speech and that I would not have to stutter so much." Nonetheless, he reiterated that his role would be limited, "that the responsibility for the sermons would rest upon the Brethren of the Council." He concluded by referring to the special fasting and prayers of his colleagues in August, to which he attributed the recent improvement in his health: "I told the Brethren that I feel better, and thanked them again for their prayers on the occasion when Presidents Brown, Tanner and Joseph Fielding Smith came to the hospital and administered to me, and the other Brethren of the General Authorities met together fasting and praying for me."[39]

McKay's entourage included his daughter, Emma Rae Ashton, and his sons, Lawrence, Robert, and Edward. Edward, who was a physician, brought "a portable oxygen tank and a suitcase full of medicines."[40] The party flew from Salt Lake City to San Francisco on Monday, November 16. After arriving at the hotel in Oakland, McKay held a press conference, at which "it was still hard for [Father] to speak. We realized more than ever the necessity of his getting someone to read his speeches and prayer." Yet McKay still gave no indication that he would designate a stand-in. The following morning, with the opening session of the dedication only moments away, Hugh B. Brown knocked on the door of McKay's room and asked, "President McKay, have you any instructions for me?" It was clear what he thought those instructions should be, but McKay simply replied, "No, President Brown."[41]

As they entered the temple, McKay was the first to realize that something extraordinary was about to happen:

As I entered the Celestial Room, tears welled up in my eyes as I looked around at those gathered there in the rooms on either side of the pulpit, and at the Choir members dressed in white. I knew then that our prayers had been answered, and I felt grateful that the Lord had granted me the privilege of being in attendance at the dedication of this beautiful Temple.... I then delivered the Dedicatory Address and Prayer. I stood at the pulpit for over an hour at this time, and I knew that the Lord had blessed me as I stood there without any support of any kind.[42]

For over a year, since suffering a stroke, McKay had been unable to stand unassisted. In fact, he had required assistance to stand and move to the pulpit, which, though solid, was temporary, not fastened to the floor. As he stood alone, his hands resting on the sides of the pulpit, the effect on the congregation was electrifying. Lawrence recalled with emotion:

He...began to speak. His diction became just as clear as it had been ten years before that. Mildred turned to me with tears in her eyes and running down her cheeks. She said, "Lawrence, we're witnessing a miracle!" I nodded and looked over at the members of the Council of the Twelve, who were also crying. [Father] finished his speech and offered the dedicatory prayer. After the services I asked Dr. Louis Schricker, who was there for President Brown, "Can he do this this afternoon again?" He said, "Lawrence, this is beyond us. It's out of our hands entirely." He did it again that afternoon and the next morning and the following afternoon.[43]

Shortly after returning to Salt Lake City, McKay commented on the temple dedication to Clare Middlemiss: "I am still thinking about the dedicatory services of the Oakland Temple. Just before rising to the pulpit there in the Temple, I wondered if I would be able to go through with standing there for over an hour to give the address and prayer, and then there came to my soul the assurance that I could go through with it; I had no doubt, and I was able to give an address at each session and to read the dedicatory prayer so that everyone could hear them!"[44]

Early in 1965, McKay suffered another setback and was hospitalized. After Middlemiss telephoned BYU President Ernest Wilkinson to cancel their appointment that day, Wilkinson wrote, "She was greatly concerned over his condition, and was regretting very much that she had not been able to see him before he left. Her attitude was such that it was apparent she feared this might be the last."[45] The effects of the illness lingered, and six weeks later McKay confided, "I was very tired and discouraged because I do not feel that I am getting better."[46] Later in the same week, just before April general conference, Wilkinson spoke with McKay over the phone: "Apparently from what I heard they had to pretty much sit President McKay up in bed to talk to me. While I am no doctor, I could tell he was having heart failure as I talked to him. He was having evident difficulty in breathing, and only said a few words to me. I immediately suggested that I wait until after the General Conference, because I could tell he was not in any position to hold a conference now. It is apparent to me that he could be taken at any time, even before this conference is through."[47]

While Wilkinson's prognosis was, once again, premature, it was clear to McKay's colleagues that his physical health was gradually, inevitably declining. In August 1965 he suffered another setback, which kept him away from the weekly meetings of the First Presidency and Quorum of the Twelve for two months. Upon his return, he minimized his condition: "I have been under the weather," he reported, "I suppose because of a slight stroke. I have been blessed in that I have not had any pain."[48]

At this time he was visited by Dr. Norman Vincent Peale, one of the leading religious figures of the time, who was deeply impressed by the experience:

> President McKay, at the age of ninety-two, is spiritual leader of over two million people. His mind is alert and keen, and there is about him an indefinable sweetness—almost, I would say a saintliness. As I took leave of him, after a half-hour of gay repartee and delightful conversation, I asked him if he would offer a prayer. He came to his feet slowly, due to the infirmity of his years, put his arm through mine, and talked to the Lord in a way most lovely and unforgettable. He talked about the sweetness, as he put it, of friendship in Christ. I shall always remember that prayer.[49]

As the October 1965 general conference approached, McKay made contingency plans for the possibility that poor health would not allow him to attend the conference. The day before the opening session, he had technicians from the church-owned television station, KSL, come to his apartment and tape him giving his address. The following morning, however, he rallied in a manner reminiscent of what had happened at the Oakland Temple dedication: "Following the opening exercises, I arose and walked over to the pulpit. Someone had thoughtfully placed a high stool at the pulpit, but I moved it aside. I was remarkably blessed of the Lord in giving the opening address, for I stood the entire forty minutes which it took to complete my talk. My voice was strong, and the people seemed to have no trouble in hearing me."[50]

Six months later, at the next general conference, he chose to use the stool as he addressed the audience. His secretary commented, "This was the first time President McKay had ever relented and given in to the appeals of the doctors and others not to try to stand, and to conserve his energy while talking."[51]

In short, from about 1959 on when Wilkinson made his first "failing fast" observation, McKay repeatedly suffered health crises that seemed serious, but would then surprise his colleagues by the extent to which he rallied. Utah Governor Calvin L. Rampton recalled vividly one such incident:

> Over his last five or six years, he had sort of a cyclical situation. He'd get very weak, and you'd think he was going to die, and then he'd get better. In about 1968, he was having one of these times when he was just sort of fading. Clare Middlemiss called me, and said, "The President can't meet with you any more, but he wants you to keep meeting with people," and he named a committee which consisted of Hugh Brown, Eldon Tanner and Alvin Dyer. So I did for several times. And then he got feeling better. The day that one of the buildings was dedicated...there was a little celebration in the lobby. He was down there in a wheelchair, with his son, Robert. He signaled for me to come over. He couldn't speak very loudly, so I leaned over, and he said, "I'm feeling a lot better. Forget what I told you about those other fellows, you come to see me."[52]

McKay's presence at the general conferences provided most church members with their only glimpses of his condition, and they watched with sadness as his attendance gradually became more sporadic. Even when he was present, he generally had one of his sons deliver his addresses. In April 1969 Dr. Alan MacFarlane, his personal physician, visited him shortly before the conference began and advised him not to attend any of the sessions. McKay reluctantly agreed with him, yet "said if he felt better he would change his mind." As MacFarlane left the apartment, he spoke briefly with Clare Middlemiss who admitted that "she had never seen the President so tired and weak."[53]

In July 1969, McKay made his last public appearance, speaking at the dedication of a new hospital in Ogden that bore his name. In his remarks he referred to an earlier promise that he now fulfilled: "Three years ago on April 22, 1966, when I attended the ground-breaking services for the hospital, I made a promise to the audience that I would be present at the dedicatory services to be held two or three years from that date."[54] At the conclusion of the ceremony, the architect, Keith Wilcox, and the general contractor, Jack Okland, helped McKay toward the car for the return to Salt Lake City.

He reached over and took my arm, and he took Jack's arm, and wouldn't let us go. I looked at Jack and he looked at me, and we didn't know what was going on here.... Then President McKay looked at me, and then he looked over at Jack, and he looked at me and he looked at Jack, and then he made this statement. "Brethren, this has been the happiest day of my life." We just sat there dumb-founded. Were we hearing right? He looked at us a couple of times again, and smiled and said, "Thank you, brethren." We closed the door and the big old car drove off, and Jack and I just stood there. What was behind that? How could President McKay, who had all these miles of things in his life, say this was the happiest day? Family, everything in the world, the prophet of the Church. Then it suddenly hit us why he said that. A prophet had been honored in his own coun-try. Even though the scriptures say a prophet is without honor in his own country, here the prophet, David O. McKay, had been honored right here in Weber County, in Ogden, Utah, his home country. That satisfied him.[55]

In spite of his physical decline, McKay remained intellectually active. "Mentally he was alert right up to his death," his son Lawrence recalled. "Physically it was hard for him to get around."[56] Joseph Anderson, secretary to the First Presidency, agreed with the assessment: "He was still quite keen. He had slowed up a little, but he certainly had his mental and spiritual faculties, I will say that. He was very keen, very sharp. Sometimes you might present a matter, and he would perhaps ask you to present it again so he could get it clearly in his mind, but when he did he had the right answer."[57]

Even during the final weeks of life, he had moments of startling resilience. His housekeeper recalled one such incident about a week before his death:

He wasn't coherent with us at times, but believe me, I swear to that, when the Lord wanted him to say something to help his Counselors, the Spirit was there. He knew what he was talking about. And then, the minute they left, the Spirit left him. He was sick like any normal being. But if the Lord needed him for something, this I swear to my deathbed, the Lord gave him consciousness and a bright spirit, and he knew what he was talking about. Like when those Counselors said, "We have been worried three months about that problem, and here in less than ten minutes you give us the answer." Now, don't tell me the Lord wasn't with him until the end. That was maybe three days before he died! So, to me, it is a testimony you cannot kill. The Lord

---

was with his servant until the last. He could barely talk to us, we wouldn't even ask him to say the prayer, because we couldn't hear his voice. But then, I know when the Lord needed him for something for the Church, he got clear-minded. To that I swear to my deathbed.[58]

Early on Sunday morning, January 18, 1970, David O. McKay died peacefully at age ninety-six. Later in the day, as his fellow General Authorities met to plan the funeral, they discussed four hymns that were his favorites. Three dealt directly with his relationship to Deity: "I Need Thee Every Hour," "O My Father" and "I Know That My Redeemer Lives." The fourth went in a different direction: "O Say, What Is Truth?" Written by John Jaques (1827–1900), an English convert who worked for the *Deseret News* and was an assistant church historian, it captured McKay's expansive view of the world that had enabled him to transform Mormonism from a colloquial Great Basin organization into a respected worldwide church:

> Yes, say, what is truth? 'Tis the brightest prize
>
> To which mortals or Gods can aspire.
>
> Go search in the depths where it glittering lies,
>
> Or ascend in pursuit to the loftiest skies:
>
> 'Tis an aim for the noblest desire.
>
> . . .
>
> Then say, what is truth? 'Tis the last and the first,
>
> For the limits of time it steps o'er.
>
> Tho the heavens depart and the earth's fountains burst,
>
> Truth, the sum of existence, will weather the worst,
>
> Eternal, unchanged evermore.[59]

McKay's body lay in state in the rotunda of the Church Administration Building for three days. Nearly 50,000 people paid their final respects, having stood silently for several hours in lines wrapping around the block as a light winter rain fell. At his funeral two men who succeeded him as church president paid tribute to his greatness. Joseph Fielding Smith, his immediate successor, said: "If ever a man of modern history left his world better for having lived in it, that man was David Oman McKay. Wherever he passed, men lifted their heads with more hope and courage. Wherever his voice was heard there followed greater tolerance, greater love. Wherever his influence was felt, man and God became closer in purpose and in action."

And Harold B. Lee, who succeeded Smith only two years later, gave voice to the sentiment of countless Latter-day Saints then and now when he said, "If I were an artist who had been retained to paint a picture of a prophet, I could think of no one better suited than David Oman McKay."[60]

The final entry in his diary, written by Clare Middlemiss, describes the funeral procession's journey from the Tabernacle to the Salt Lake City Cemetery. Ironically, it ends with a reference, not to the church over which he presided, but to the one with which he had made his peace, and which reciprocated in a gracious gesture of shared sorrow: "As the procession proceeded up South Temple, crowds lined the streets in reverent respect for their Prophet, Leader, and Friend, and bells tolled from the Cathedral of the Madeleine."[61]

16

EPILOGUE

The final years of the McKay administration, while conveying a legacy of benevolence, tolerance, and inclusiveness to church members in general, were nonetheless bittersweet at the highest levels of church administration. When Heber J. Grant and George Albert Smith suffered failing health that often removed them from day-to-day control of the church, J. Reuben Clark Jr., their capable and assertive first counselor, took a firm grip on the reins of leadership, effectively becoming acting church president. In contrast, there was no dominant counselor within the First Presidency during the late McKay years whose influence could replicate Clark's. Furthermore, sharp philosophical differences often divided his counselors and led to impasse. Ernest Wilkinson, who as BYU president was part of McKay's inner circle but viewed the scene from a distance, expressed his frustration in his diary several times during 1969, as he watched the effects of the power vacuum:

> [July 25] Problems are multiplying. We will have to face them some way or another. The difficulty is that President McKay does not have the physical energy to give directions, and others are going off in many directions. It's a time of lack of top leadership in the Church, which causes no end of problems.
>
> [September 8] The balance of the day I spent on miscellaneous matters having to do with the complete turmoil in Salt Lake City occasioned by President McKay's illness, and therefore lack of leadership. Everyone seems to be trying to fill in, with all kinds of cross-currents going.
>
> [September 9] I had a confidential visit with President McKay this morning, with respect to the future of the Church School System. . . . Because of turmoil in Salt Lake in the leadership at the present time, and everyone sparring for the ascendancy of his ideas, I haven't yet decided just yet what kind of an announcement will be made.[1]

THE OFFICE OF CHURCH PRESIDENT

Although the cross-currents within the First Presidency added to the turmoil, the root cause of the situation was the very nature of the office of church president. Unlike the U.S. government, where the vice president assists the president but, more importantly, automatically assumes the presidency upon his death or incapacitation, the First Presidency is dissolved immediately upon the death of the church president, at which time all authority reverts to the Quorum of the Twelve, acting as a group, until the new president is designated. Counselors in the First Presidency have authority limited by three facts: they are not "presidents-in-waiting," they are totally dependent upon the president whom they serve, and their role terminates automatically upon his death.

In the event that a president becomes incapacitated, however, the First Presidency is not dissolved. For such a situation, the authority of the counselors has never been sharply defined. During the first century of the church's existence, this issue was moot as no president went through a protracted period of incapacitation. This situation was due largely to the rudimentary state of medical care, which could seldom prolong life once a terminal illness began. However, ever since the early 1940s, all but one of seven church presidents experienced prolonged periods of physical impairment, ranging from months to as much as five years, that precluded their day-to-day leadership of the church. Clark's assumption of a de facto role as acting church president averted a leadership crisis when Heber J. Grant and George Albert Smith were ailing, but Clark died in 1961, his prior role was never institutionalized, and no one stepped forward to perform a similar function for McKay. Furthermore, the church had nearly tripled in membership during McKay's tenure and spread throughout the world, resulting in a far greater ongoing burden for a president and a greater potential crisis for his counselors in the event of his incapacitation.

McKay and his colleagues had long been aware of the problem and had begun to institute remedies in 1961 with the correlation movement. Until that time virtually all church organizations and programs reported directly to the First Presidency, with the Quorum of the Twelve acting almost exclusively in a staff function to the First Presidency. While the stated purpose of correlation was to place all organizations and programs "under the Priesthood" (clearly a euphemism since they had always functioned under the church president, the presiding priesthood leader), the real goal was to have them function under the Quorum of the Twelve, which would thus switch from staff to line authority. The switch, while not completed until after McKay's death, marked perhaps the most important administrative change in the church during the twentieth century.

Another part of the problem was more intractable, for it involved powers traditionally reserved for the president alone, not shared even with his counselors. Only weeks before McKay's death, these powers became the focal point of a crucial meeting of top church officials, a meeting McKay did not attend because of failing health.

Legal matters were first discussed, the issue being whether the proper instruments were in place to ensure that others could function legally, in McKay's absence, in his role as corporation of the president sole for the church. After some discussion that relied heavily on the expertise of Howard W. Hunter, who had practiced law for many years prior to being called to be an apostle, all were satisfied that the church's legal position was sound and that other men could act legally in McKay's behalf.[2]

A more vexing problem was ecclesiastical. Although no manual of church government existed until the twentieth century, a strong tradition that defined the ecclesiastical authority of the church president began with Joseph Smith and was well entrenched by the time of the McKay presidency. Any change in that authority, particularly one made in the absence of the president, would be a matter of enormous gravity. The possibility of such change became the focal point of the meeting.

One issue was the calling of full-time missionaries. Although a Missionary Committee did all the legwork preceding the calling of the 12,000 missionaries then serving missions, the actual call was issued by a letter signed by the church president, phrased to indicate his personal role in the process. In that November 1969 meeting, Gordon B. Hinckley said that "all missionary calls carry only one signature and that is the signature of the President of the Church. It is supposed that the President authorized that when he had his full competence, and we have acted under that authorization and instruction, but more and more people are beginning to ask questions."[3] Since McKay had not attended either April or October general conference, members of the church were widely aware of his failing health at this point.

N. Eldon Tanner, McKay's second counselor, suggested that such letters, already signed by autopen, continue to go out, as "it was felt that nobody could be hurt by this being done." The alternative was to delay indefinitely the calling of an average of 500 new missionaries each month, a prospect that would wreak havoc on the missionary system during a prolonged period of presidential incapacitation. (Full-time missionaries generally serve for two years, so requiring a personal signature a few years later, when President Spencer W. Kimball was completely incapacitated for nearly four years, would have resulted in involuntary termination of the entire program.) Harold B. Lee, acting president of the Quorum of the Twelve and second in line for the presidency, said "he did not suppose that there was any question on that matter," and the men voted unanimously to continue the use of the autopen.

With respect to certain ecclesiastical issues, however, the discussion moved in the opposite direction. The specific issue at hand was the "sealing" authority, conferred upon only a few men associated with each of the church's temples, by which they perform marriages that endure beyond death. Such marriages are one of the unique aspects of Mormonism, and authority to perform them is granted only by the church president. Could an exception be made if McKay was unable to act in this capacity? Lee cut to the heart of the matter by quoting his mentor, J. Reuben Clark Jr.:

> Brethren, the President is here by the Lord's appointment, not by our appointment. I do not understand that in his absence his first counselor or his second counselor, or both counselors acting in concert can assume the responsibility that belongs solely to the President of the Church. Until the Lord releases the President we cannot do anything about things he has never delegated to us, and one of the things he has never delegated is the conferring of the sealing power upon the president of a temple. Until he does, or the Lord acts to remove the President and has someone installed in his place, we will have to continue to carry on.[4]

To drive his point home even more forcefully, Lee then extended the principle beyond the sealing authority to include any new policy, stating that "none of us, not the first counselor or the second or both counselors, or any of us can determine a new policy or new changes without the President of the Church until the Lord releases him"[5]—that is, until the death of the president. Lee's primary concern in asserting this argument was not the sealing authority, but Hugh B. Brown's ongoing attempt to change the ban on ordaining black men to the priesthood.[6] Lee was then in the process of drafting an unprecedented First Presidency Circular Letter which McKay's two senior counselors, Brown and N. Eldon Tanner, signed, Brown only under heavy pressure from Lee. This letter reiterated the ban. By getting his colleagues in the meeting to agree that First Presidency counselors could not implement any "new policy or new changes," he succeeded in blocking Brown's attempt. The circular letter, which was signed a month later, merely formalized what occurred in the meeting.

Deferring action on policies did not cause the church undue inconvenience at this time, as McKay died only two months after this meeting. However, two subsequent church presidents, Spencer W. Kimball and Ezra Taft Benson, were each incapacitated for several years at the end of their lives, creating a situation where some decisions could not be delayed indefinitely. The current president, Gordon B. Hinckley, was a counselor to both men, and described the caution with which he exercised his office:

> I was counselor to President Kimball. Then he became sick, then President [N. Eldon] Tanner died, then President [Marion G.] Romney became indisposed, and I was alone. I was then second counselor. I tried to be very, very careful in those circumstances. And later, when I was a counselor to President Benson—I was first counselor and Brother [Thomas S.] Monson was second counselor—again, I tried to be very, very careful. The policies were well established. We didn't need a lot of new things. The church was getting along well, doing well. And I resisted efforts to move on some things where I was urged at times to do so. I did not want to get ahead of the president. I was his counselor, and as long as there was no need to do it, I felt not to do it. Now President McKay, when he appointed five counselors, was still mentally alert himself, so that that was all in his hands. My situation was different with President Kimball, because he failed—he began to fail—then President Tanner died and President Romney became indisposed, and I was here alone for quite a long time. But it was a different situation from what it was with President McKay.[7]

While Hinckley refrained from acting in the president's stead "as long as there was no need to do it," his action was required on some occasions. When Apostle LeGrand Richards died in January 1983, Kimball was already incapacitated and Hinckley declined to name a new apostle. A year later, Apostle Mark E. Petersen died, leaving a second vacancy. Faced with the prospect of yet a third vacancy, as Apostle Bruce R. McConkie had terminal cancer, Hinckley announced the two new appointments at the April 1984 general conference but did so with a preface that made it clear that he was in no way attempting to preempt Kimball's authority: "Though [President Kimball] is advancing in age, he is the prophet of the Lord, and he will be with us for so long as the Lord wills. And as the Lord's appointed servant, no major decision concerning this work will be made without his consideration and his direction. As we begin this conference, we shall take care of several items of business according to his expressed will and consent."[8]

Thus, while Lee had insisted that no policies be introduced or changed by counselors in the First Presidency in the event of an incapacitated president, Hinckley chose a more moderate approach that acknowledged a more complex reality: There were times when decisions had to be made; on such occasions, the counselors could step forward and make them, giving all consideration to the condition of the president and acting only on an ad hoc basis.

Hinckley also continued the process Lee had begun in the correlation movement, which shifted an increasing amount of responsibility and power from the First Presidency to the Twelve, thereby ensuring continuity regardless of the president's health. In an interview, Hinckley explained: "My feeling has been to use the Twelve more.... They're all in place.... They're a council, and my disposition is to call on them more, use them more. The Church is growing so tremendously, just leaping forward in a tremendous way. Rather than think of more counselors in the Presidency, I've simply felt to use the Twelve."9

SUCCESSION IN THE PRESIDENCY

The dilemma of an incapacitated president is closely linked to the fact that the succession policy of the church ensures that new presidents will assume office at an advanced age. Indeed, the six presidents who have succeeded McKay took office at the average age of eighty-three, six years older than McKay when he took office. The oldest of those six and McKay's immediate successor, Joseph Fielding Smith, was ninety-three. The succession policy had evolved gradually over a half-century; and since it never carried the imprimatur of revelation, it had been considered susceptible to change. Although nothing was said in a public setting, the possibility of bypassing Smith for Harold B. Lee, who was twenty-three years younger, was on the minds of some. One was BYU President Ernest Wilkinson, who wrote in his diary:

> Thursday, August 18, 1960: In the evening, we had baccalaureate services for the university, presided over by President Joseph Fielding Smith. While he still seems in good health physically, he certainly gave no dynamics to his presiding.
>
> Friday, August 19, 1960: In the evening, we had the commencement services, presided over by Elder Harold B. Lee. His dynamic presiding was a sharp contrast to that of the night before. This prompts me to make an unorthodox comment. I do not believe there is any scripture anywhere to justify the practice in the Church that the senior member of the Quorum of the Twelve must be the President, and I think that it would be much better for the Church if the selection were made on the basis of leadership, rather than seniority. At the time when Brigham Young was named President of the Quorum, there was a heavenly manifestation that he should be selected. Further, he was still a relatively young man. The present practice of selecting by seniority, when that senior person no longer has the vigor that is needed, does not lend itself for proper advancement of the Church. If this be treason, make the most of it.

Tuesday, September 6, 1960: My own unorthodox feeling is that, while there is no sense of any kind in people being required to retire at 65, as they do generally in this country, nevertheless there does come a time when, in the conduct of the affairs of the Church, younger men should take over. I should think the Quorum of the Twelve ought to find some way to accomplish this.[10]

Wilkinson was not the only one who wondered whether this was the time to make a change in the succession policy. Utah Governor Calvin L. Rampton observed during an interview:

In the early summer of 1969 Lucybeth and I had a dinner party at the residence to which we invited the leaders of the Mormon Church .... There was great speculation as to what would happen if, in fact, President McKay should die because President Joseph Fielding Smith was already at or approaching ninety, and Harold B. Lee, who was the second in line in seniority in the Council of the Twelve, was some twenty years younger than President Smith. There was great speculation that because of Joseph Fielding Smith's advanced age the Twelve Apostles might, as they could do if they chose to do so, not follow the tradition of appointing the senior Apostle as President of the Church and select the next man.

On this particular night I was at one end of the table and Lucybeth was at the other. On my right sat Jessie [Evans Smith, Joseph Fielding Smith's wife]; beyond her, on her right, sat Harold Lee, the second senior Apostle. We sort of had a triangle at the corner of the table. As we were eating dinner, suddenly out of the clear blue sky, with nothing to give rise to it that anybody else had said, Harold Lee—ostensibly talking to me—started to talk about the succession to the Presidency of the LDS Church. What he was saying to me in effect, although certainly I wasn't the logical person for him to be addressing on this subject, was that under no circumstances would the Mormon Church ever depart from the tradition of advancing to the Presidency the senior Apostle. He said this not once, but reiterated it, went back—even though I was kind of surprised at the turn of the conversation, and Jessie sat silent. Harold went back and recounted the tradition and how it had grown up and finally I realized that he really wasn't talking to me at all; he was talking at me, but he was really talking to Jessie. He was, in effect, assuring her that when President McKay died, if he did before Joseph Fielding Smith died, as appeared probable, in no way would Harold B. Lee insert himself and attempt to usurp the position that by tradition belonged to the senior Apostle, Joseph Fielding Smith.[11]

Several months later, two counselors in the First Presidency discussed the same issue. Alvin R. Dyer recorded in his journal that Hugh B. Brown broached the subject, asking "how I felt with regard to President Joseph Fielding Smith becoming the President of the Church in the event of President McKay's death." Brown said that Smith was "too old" for the job, and since the succession policy was "simply a tradition and need not be followed," he should be bypassed and Harold B. Lee chosen in his place. Dyer, a strong traditionalist, shot back with a lengthy defense of the status quo, ending his argument with: "Brother Lee's time will no doubt come, but...it is the right of President Smith to hold an office. If the Lord does not want President Smith to be the President, He would make it known to him or would remove him. I told President Brown that I could not in any way sustain his thinking regarding this fundamental matter."[12]

At McKay's death there was no challenge to the existing policy of succession. The First Presidency dissolved automatically; and Joseph Fielding Smith, by virtue of being the longest tenured apostle and thus president of the Quorum of the Twelve, became the presiding officer. The day after McKay's funeral, the Quorum of the Twelve met and ordained Smith, age ninety-three, to the office of church president. Smith chose seventy-year-old Harold B. Lee as his first counselor and N. Eldon Tanner as his second. Smith died after two and a half years in office, whereupon Lee became president. Lee died unexpectedly after only eighteen months in that capacity.

Two other initiatives relating to the McKay years brushed against the issue of presidential succession. In the mid-1960s McKay instructed the seven members of the First Council of Seventy—a group one level subordinate to the Quorum of the Twelve—to reevaluate the function of their council.[13] Among the issues discussed by the group as they studied the historical record concerning the council was the concept of emeritus status, by which council members would retire at the age of seventy rather than serve for life. Two of the seven men objected to the idea; and since McKay's instructions had been to produce a position paper that reflected the unanimous sentiment of the group, this proposal was omitted from their report.[14] A decade later, after the deaths of those two, it was inserted into a new position paper and approved by Church President Spencer W. Kimball.

Emeritus status for the First Council of Seventy had no bearing on succession to the office of church president, but Hugh B. Brown, McKay's first counselor at the time of his death, attempted to introduce it within the Quorum of the Twelve, a move that would certainly have altered succession. Brown's grandson described the initiative:

He concluded that there needed to be an emeritus system, that age would take its toll. Whether the person was a prophet or not, they were still humans, and age could take its toll. There should be a system of removing people from sort of lock-step advancement to the presidency. So, he proposed an emeritus system.... I don't remember the age, but whenever he proposed it, he was just over it. It might have been eighty, I don't remember the age, but he proposed it in such a way that he was the first and only victim at that time, or at least among the first.... The president wouldn't be asked to step down, but the people advancing to the presidency would at least enter the presidency, presumably, with their faculties about them.[15]

McKay's Legacy

Calvin L. Rampton, whose three terms as governor of Utah overlapped the final six years of David O. McKay's presidency, captured much of the essence of McKay and his administration: "I was asked on an interview on television here several years ago, out of the clear blue sky, 'Who would you say was the most valuable player in Utah life of this century?' And I said this [in]stinctively, 'President McKay.' I still believe that's true. He was genuinely loved. That's not true of all presidents of the church."[16]

The greatness of David O. McKay is not captured in facts and figures. Other church presidents have served longer, traveled farther, presided over greater growth, built more buildings, defined more doctrines, and instituted more sweeping changes in organization and policy. Yet to this day countless people who knew him or who never met him but were part of the church over which he presided, describe him in terms that emphasize his striking appearance and distinctive presence. But appearance alone did not account for his overall effect on the church.

A parallel might be found in two American presidents of the past half-century, John F. Kennedy and Ronald Reagan. By objective measures neither was a stellar administrator. Indeed, the legislative skills of Kennedy pale by comparison to those of Lyndon B. Johnson, as do those of Reagan compared to those of Bill Clinton. But Kennedy and Reagan both ignited a spirit of optimism and self-confidence that changed the mood and changed the direction of the entire country. Both took office at a time when America had seen better days and was looking for change. Kennedy faced a heated-up Cold War and a daunting Soviet military and space machine that caused many to question whether American democracy would be able to stand up against Soviet Communism. Reagan faced an economy shackled with high interest rates, high unemployment, a stagnant economy, and the admission by President Jimmy Carter that America's future no longer looked better than its past. Kennedy and Reagan both put themselves forward as symbols of change, and the symbols became the reality.

David O. McKay inherited a church that was provincial and backward looking. His immediate predecessors wore beards and came from polygamous families, two powerful symbols that were out of touch with modernism. "Zion" meant the Great Basin; and for over a century, the church policy of gathering had transplanted the best and brightest converts from abroad to the geographical Zion, leaving behind a struggling vestige that never moved beyond adolescence.

Clean-shaven, immaculately dressed, and movie-star handsome, McKay immediately caught the attention of member and nonmember alike, and held it. He democratized Mormonism, calling upon every member to be a missionary and thus participate in moving the church into a "New Era." He told converts to grow where they were planted, and built chapels and temples to allow them to do it without feeling like second-class citizens.

Perhaps most importantly, he adjusted the relationship between church and member. For a full century, since Brigham Young announced to the world that the rumored practice of plural marriage was more than rumor, church members had been asked to sacrifice themselves for the good of the institution. McKay reversed that, asserting that the church was made for the members, not the members for the church. He emphasized the paramount importance of free agency and individual expression, for he understood that improvement of the parts would inevitably improve the whole. "Let them conform" was replaced by "Let them grow." He willingly discarded institutional uniformity for the higher goal of individual excellence. He pitched a wide tent and then told members of all stripes that he welcomed them to join him and build the church within it.

Perhaps, as Walter Reuther said of McKay, "I doubt that another generation will produce a man like that." But we should try.

APPENDIX

THE CLARE MIDDLEMISS RECORDS

From 1925 to 1927, shortly before the country plunged into the Great Depression, an intrepid young secretary fresh out of business college penetrated the male-dominated world of the Mormon missionary program and served in the Western States Mission, with headquarters in Denver, Colorado. Following her mission at a time when the Depression was well entrenched, she landed a temporary secretarial job at church headquarters.[1] "Temporary" turned out to be four decades, the last thirty-five years of which involved but one boss, David O. McKay. During those years, Clare Middlemiss, the only woman ever to serve as the private secretary to a church president, became arguably the most powerful woman in the history of the LDS Church. Although her official title remained secretary, in fact she functioned as McKay's chief of staff, often to the chagrin of the otherwise exclusively male church hierarchy. Along the way she compiled probably the most extensive record of any church president.

Clare Middlemiss was one of the ten children (eight daughters and two sons) of William Middlemiss and Roselind Bridge Middlemiss. She was born in Salt Lake City on February 27, 1901, and, with the exception of her mission, lived there her entire life.

She attended West High School and LDS Business College, and took additional courses through the University of Utah Extension.

Never shy, once she began to work for McKay in 1935 she quickly took charge of his office and remained in charge throughout her career. She possessed superb organizational and writing skills that allowed her not only to manage the day-to-day affairs of the office, but also to compile along the way the extraordinary collection of records that made possible the current biography.

She was extremely loyal and devoted, first to David O. McKay as church president, and then to the church over which he presided. She was aware of her position and power—and adept at using them to promote or protect McKay and the church, even if it meant inserting herself between them and other church leaders. Generally of a pleasant and friendly disposition, she could become remote and intimidating at the first indication that the interests of her two charges were being threatened.

Clare Middlemiss was an attractive, stylish woman, as shown by the accompanying photograph taken in the mid-1930s. Though she never married, she did not consider herself an "old maid." Her extended family, which included nineteen nieces and nephews, became her posterity; and although her modest church salary never brought her close to financial independence, she was generous to them and to others throughout her life as benefactor, mentor, and confidant.

Middlemiss's ascent to power was inadvertent on her part:

> In the Spring of 1935 I was the only secretary in the general Financial and Missionary office of the Church, working as secretary for Arthur Winter, financial adviser to the First Presidency, and Harold Reynolds, the Mission Secretary and Transportation Agent for the Church. One morning Brother Winter told me that the First Presidency wanted me to serve in their office as secretary to President David O. McKay, who had been appointed second counselor to President Grant, just a few months previous to that time. I remember saying to Brother Winter, "Do I have to go?," as I was really frightened at the thought of working for these great men. His answer to me was: "Sister, when the First Presidency speaks, you go." So I commenced my work as the immediate secretary to President McKay.[2]

Shortly after beginning her work as McKay's secretary, Middlemiss turned her attention to the compilation of the record that became the nucleus of the current biography. As she explained in 1948, she discovered that "nothing has ever been compiled on President McKay's activities until 1934" and began to fill that gap by making "a complete record."[3]

A secretarial career for the church in those years required a special level of commitment, for church policy (since changed) required that all female secretaries be single. Early in her career, she reminisced, "I had plans to get married, such as every other young girl does, you know, and I was dating three or four boys at the time."[4] As matters turned out, she remained single, but her decision apparently was not driven by career aspirations. Her nephew Robert Wright, coauthor of this volume, remembers: "She had suitors who wanted to go out with her, and I think at least one or two of them really wanted to get married, but she didn't want to get married to them. She told me she just never found a person that she wanted to get married to . . . . After a few years went by, she wished that she had a family. I know that. And she would have been a good mother, but she just put all her energy into her job."[5]

Her fortunes changed dramatically in April 1951. As had been the case in 1935, it was inadvertent on her part. A fellow secretary related the story:

[Clare] told me one time when [President McKay] was called to be President of the Church that Joseph Anderson assumed he was going to be the President's secretary. Now, he had worked for Heber J. Grant and for George Albert Smith. He sort of treated Clare like her days were numbered. And President McKay had never said a word, one way or the other. So they were getting ready to move into the office where President McKay was going to sit, and she said to President McKay, "Well, I guess you'll be bringing in Brother Anderson. I suppose you'll want to bring him in here." And he said, "You're my secretary." She said, "Well, it's customary to have a man be the secretary to the President." He said, "I don't see why. You're my secretary, and you're going to stay my secretary." She said she just sat down and cried, because she was so worried that she'd lost her job. Brother Anderson was not happy about that, because he really, fully expected to be President McKay's secretary, too. That's when they started the First Presidency's office, and he was in the First Presidency's office.[6]

David O. McKay was seventy-seven years old when he became church president; and although he was a vigorous man, he had a history of health problems. As a result, Middlemiss was protective of him from the outset and became increasingly protective as advancing age gradually drained his strength. While others saw her efforts as less than benign, McKay trusted her implicitly and appreciated her protectiveness. McKay's housekeeper recalled, "Everybody knew that she was a little overpowering. When I made a remark to President McKay at one time, he said, 'Well, I know, Gaby, but she's a very good secretary.' He needed her, she was very good in her job.... He knew her weakness, but she was smart, and he appreciated her."[7]

McKay's eldest son agreed with the housekeeper's assessment, but spoke also of the downside. "She was devoted to Father and did everything she could to protect him, and in the process aroused the antagonism of nearly everybody else, including the members of the Twelve."[8] One such member was senior Apostle Harold B. Lee, who told a fellow General Authority, "It's interesting...that I have to go through a non-priesthood-bearer to get certain things done in my assignment."[9] Even members of the First Presidency were occasionally antagonized by her protectiveness. Charles M. Brown, son of McKay's counselor Hugh B. Brown, recalled: "She was probably the supreme example of a totally dedicated secretary, and men in that position need totally dedicated secretaries. But she might have overstepped her bounds.... Dad and Eldon Tanner couldn't get in to see him quite frequently, and they would work through his son, David Lawrence, to try to get to him, rather than through Clare."[10]

Yet others within the hierarchy saw Middlemiss as unqualifiedly positive. Apostle Ezra Taft Benson "had a high regard for her and her love for the Prophet, and her protectiveness of him, too."[11] And Marion D. Hanks, another General Authority, wrote to her, "I still think that of the factors that may have preserved the President's life beyond what might normally have been, your loyalty and wisdom and devotion rank high."[12]

Some women saw in Clare Middlemiss a unique role model. Elaine Anderson Cannon, who spent decades working in close approximation to the General Authorities, was particularly appreciative. "She had *power!* When women were just all saluting the Brethren, Clare was just manipulating and doing all of this stuff, and being charming and accepting the chocolates—and working the wonders."[13]

Still other people viewed Middlemiss with an ambivalence that was results driven. For example, in 1962 Ernest L. Wilkinson was highly critical of her when she was an obstruction to his own plans. "One of the most constant frustrations I have at the Church Office Building (I am not alone in this) is that of trying to get to see President McKay through his secretary."[14] Yet seven years later, when she enabled rather than obstructed, his attitude changed. "One of the difficulties of the present situation is that generally mail does not get through to the President, but through Clare Middlemiss we had arranged to get these letters through to him, and I think the conference we had will result in a decision in all three of these matters which had been pending for some time."[15]

The most balanced, and perhaps fairest, assessment of Clare Middlemiss came from Robert L. Simpson who, as a counselor in the Presiding Bishopric, worked with her and McKay for nearly a decade:

> She believed implicitly that she had a responsibility to protect President McKay, and to do everything she could to conserve his energy and strength, and give him peace of mind. And she did that to the very utmost of her ability. I never saw one occasion when she did anything but when she thought it was for the benefit of the Church, and President McKay personally. A lot of people were a little taken aback by her, because she held the line, but she had to, and in her mind she was doing what the Lord wanted her to do. Even other members of the [First] Presidency or the Twelve that would try and make an end run—she just didn't let that happen. And I think President McKay appreciated it.... He never wavered in his trust.... I think Clare Middlemiss was meant to be for just exactly what she did, and the role she played.[16]

As significant—and unprecedented—as her activities were in McKay's office, the most important legacy of Clare Middlemiss, and the longest lasting, was the record

she kept. An astounding 130,000 or so pages in length, it consists of three compo-
nents: diaries, discourses, and scrapbooks. Keeping the record became the focus of
her life away from the office. Her nephew recalled, "She would always bring something home to do. She got to the point where she had an office there.... She did
an awful lot of work at home, even after being at the office all day for a long
time."[17]

So consumed with the record was she that she took no holidays, spending
them in work at the office or home; took not even one week of vacation time in a
decade; and worked overtime nearly as many hours as regular time, without compensation.[18] Speaking at a national conference, Middlemiss stated, "I have not
been able to work on these journals during the regular working hours, they have
been written in the evenings, on holidays and week-ends."[19] She rarely deviated
from her daily commute of home-to-office-to-home, a round trip of some three
miles, and in twenty years drove her car an average of less than a thousand miles
annually.[20]

Of greatest historical significance are the diaries, some 40,000 pages of typescript
in length. Middlemiss began to write the diary a few months after beginning work
for McKay, and continued through his death:

> I noticed that President McKay kept a little black notebook in his
> pocket in which he kept a record of his appointments and activities for
> each day.... One day I picked up President McKay's notebook, and
> noted that he had stopped keeping a record along about March. I
> asked him if he had another book in which he was keeping his diary.
> He smiled and said, "Oh, I keep a diary until about March, and then
> I give up—I never seem to have the time to keep up with it."... From
> then on I became a little more conscientious about keeping a record
> of the more important items and activities, little realizing that one
> day President McKay would become the spiritual leader of over two
> and one-half million members of the Church. I have to smile now, as
> I go back to those early diaries, and see how meager they are com-
> pared to the diaries I have kept since.[21]

After McKay became church president in 1951, the size of the annual record
grew greatly, transformed from little more than a briefly annotated schedule into
a comprehensive daily record. Another secretary noted, "She would actually make
the draft of his day's work, and go over minutes of meetings he attended (Council,
etc.) and take excerpts from it where President McKay had made a decision, or said
something noteworthy."[22] Rounding out the McKay diaries are letters, memos,
newspaper clippings, and, from 1967 onward when her cousin Alvin R. Dyer
became a member of McKay's inner circle, copies of his detailed diary entries.

For his part, McKay fully understood the crucial role Middlemiss played in chronicling his life. "If it had not been for her," he said, "there would be no journals, no scrapbooks, and few if any records."[23] Even more to the point, he said, "So far as my life's work is concerned, there would be hardly one word written if it had not been for her; that she had really 'saved' my life in that regard."[24]

The second component of the McKay record consists of some 10,000 pages of discourses. Middlemiss gathered existing transcripts of McKay's discourses that predated her employment, then made a concerted effort to record as many of his ongoing discourses as possible. Her work of gathering was rendered much simpler when voice recording devices became portable shortly after he became church president. McKay's use of one such device, which accompanied his entourage on his first European tour in 1952, was duly noted in a company newsletter:

> One day late last fall, President David O. McKay of the Church of Jesus Christ of Latter Day Saints, which is commonly known as the Mormon Church, called for me at the Waldorf Astoria in New York City. I, complete with traveling case, had just arrived in New York from the Pembroke Stationery Co. in Salt Lake City.... President McKay and his wife told me their plans for a trip to Europe and the Scandinavian countries to visit branches of the Church.... Incidentally, I am a Master Model Audograph, and I'm proud that I'm still working for the McKay's [sic] in Salt Lake City. In fact, I'm a permanent part of the Church equipment and I attend all the dedication services at new temples and churches where President McKay presides. Members throughout the world can now hear the words of their beloved President almost as soon as I record them.[25]

The final component of the record consists of 215 legal-sized scrapbooks, comprising some 80,000 pages. It is a remarkably broad record of virtually every aspect of McKay's ministry and, by Middlemiss's own admissions, far more ambitious than originally envisioned: "I think one of the biggest projects I have undertaken is the keeping of scrapbooks covering all items and published materials concerning President McKay's life. I did not realize when I started this project what a task it was going to be, or how far-reaching it would become."[26]

Clare Middlemiss intended to use her record herself to write a biography of McKay. Her nephew noted:

> She was an historian, really. She wanted a history of President McKay, what he'd done in his life, and she thought it was really important to have that. But by the time she was able to do it after she retired, she really didn't have the health to do it. She was not well and she was

worn out. I talked to her about that. She said, "I don't have the energy to do it." Probably two years after President McKay's death, she told me she wanted me to have what she had up there at home, and she wanted it to be used.[27]

In addition to the three categories of records produced by Clare Middlemiss, this biography relies upon three additional categories: published works, including books, journals and newspapers; unpublished archival materials; and scores of interviews conducted by the authors. All six categories of records were essential for the writing of this biography, but the latter three would have been insignificant had they not stood on the foundation of the former three. It is for this reason that we have dedicated it to Clare Middlemiss, for compiling the record. It is our hope that her desire has finally been fulfilled.

When David O. McKay died in 1970, Middlemiss was one month short of her sixty-ninth birthday and in diminishing health. Prior to his death, she had had heart surgery that delayed but did not prevent further cardiovascular problems. She hoped to be able to continue working for the Church but was asked to stay on only long enough to finish the tasks of organizing McKay's records and completing the diaries. On April 4, 1983, after a long, debilitating battle with congestive heart disease, Clare Middlemiss died in Salt Lake City. She was buried in the Salt Lake City Cemetery.

NOTES

ABBREVIATIONS

The following abbreviations are used in the notes for frequently cited sources. Complete citations will be found in the bibliography.

DOMD—David O. McKay Diaries

DOMP—David O. McKay Papers

DOMS—David O. McKay Scrapbooks

ELWD—Ernest L. Wilkinson Diaries

Complete citations for interviews will be found in the bibliography. The notes cite the person interviewed and the date if more than one interview was conducted.

INTRODUCTION

1. Doctrine and Covenants 93:24.
2. Juanita Brooks's statement in Floyd A. O'Neil's presence. He related it to me October 3, 2003, and later reconfirmed its accuracy.

CHAPTER 1 – PROPHET AND MAN

1. DOMD, March 21, 1951.
2. Ibid., April 2, 1951.
3. Although the "senior" apostle had, in fact, assumed the church presidency ever since the death of Joseph Smith, several significant changes in interpreting "senior" had developed during the late nineteenth century.
4. DOMD, April 4, 1951.
5. Eldred G. Smith interview. Smith, a cousin and close friend of George Albert Smith, was present in the bedroom.
6. Stephen L Richards had no middle name, only the initial "L," and hence no period after the "L."
7. Clark's relationship to McKay and his reaction to the change in counselors are discussed in D. Michael Quinn, *Elder Statesman: A Biography of J. Reuben Clark.*
8. DOMD, April 17, 1951.
9. See Appendix.
10. Clare Middlemiss, address at the Ogden Twenty-First Ward, November 12, 1967, DOMP.
11. Valoy Eaton to Prince, June 16, 2000.
12. Keith Wilcox interview.
13. William Bates interview, October 5, 1999.
14. Robert L. Simpson interview.
15. Quinn McKay interview.
16. Edward R. McKay, Remarks at a special Devotional Assembly at Brigham Young University, at which time the "1968 Exemplary Manhood Award" was presented to David O. McKay by the Associated Men Students, DOMS #117.
17. David Lawrence McKay interview, January 5, 1984.

18. "Apostle David Oman McKay," *Juvenile Instructor* 41 (June 15, 1906): 354; "The New Leader of the LDS Church," *Salt Lake Tribune,* October 7, 1951, DOMS.

19. Edward R. McKay, Remarks, DOMS #117.

20. David O. McKay to an unnamed missionary who wanted to give up his mission and return home, March 2, 1949, DOMP.

21. Platte D. Lyman, Diary, July 20, 1899.

22. Hugh Nibley interview.

23. DOMD, June 6, 1958. More than six decades later, the stone on which the words were carved was salvaged by LDS missionaries when the building was being razed. It is on permanent display in the Museum of Church History and Art adjacent to Temple Square in Salt Lake City.

24. David O. McKay, remarks in General Priesthood Meeting, October 6, 1934, DOMS #120.

25. Joseph Anderson interview, 1970.

26. James E. Talmage diary, April 8, 1906.

27. Samuel E. Bringhurst to David O. McKay, April 18, 1951, DOMP.

28. *Salt Lake Tribune,* October 7, 1907, quoted in O. N. Malmquist, *The First 100 Years,* 309–10.

29. David Lawrence McKay interview, January 5, 1984.

30. Joseph Anderson, *Prophets I Have Known,* 129–31.

31. David O. McKay to President Francis M. Lyman and Members of the Council of the Twelve, April 2, 1916, DOMS #185.

32. Anderson, *Prophets I Have Known,* 129–31.

33. Lucy Grant Cannon to David O. McKay, September 1, 1963, DOMP.

34. David O. McKay, Diary, September 27, 1934 holograph, DOMP, Box 7, Fd. 12.

35. David O. McKay to Connie Cannon Wilson, May 8, 1951, DOMP.

36. "Answers to Questions Submitted President David O. McKay," DOMP.

37. Gunn McKay interview.

38. Monroe G. McKay interview.

39. David O. McKay, Emigration Stake Quarterly Conference, August 25, 1957, DOMP.

40. Anderson, *Prophets I Have Known,* 121–22.

41. Clare Middlemiss, interviewed on KSXX radio station, January 20, 1970, DOMS #110.

42. Quinn McKay interview.

43. Gunn McKay interview.

44. Richard McKay interview.

45. J. E. McCulloch, *Home: The Savior of Civilization.* I am indebted to Frederick Buchanan for providing me with the source of this quotation.

46. David O. McKay, Diary, holograph, DOMP, Box 7, Fd. 11.

47. Emma Ray Riggs McKay, *The Art of Rearing Children Peacefully,* 4–5. David Lawrence McKay, *My Father, David O. McKay,* 13, quotes the same account and confirms parenthetically that "Father and I actually did that once with the upstairs mattresses."

48. Midene M. Anderson, quoted by her husband, Howard B. Anderson, February 7, 1997.

49. David Lawrence McKay, *My Father, David O. McKay,* 100.

50. Paul W. Hodson interview.

51. Franklin J. Murdock interview.

52. DOMD, July 1, 1956.

53. John T. Bernhard interview.

54. Martha LaVern Watts Parmley interview.

55. Katherine McKay Iba interview.

56. Vivian McKay interview.

57. Edward H. Rich to David O. McKay, November 15, 1934, DOMS #120.

58. Angus H. Belliston to David O. McKay, September 6, 1960, DOMP.

59. Elaine Anderson Cannon interview.

NOTES TO PAGES 17–25

60. Peggy Card to David O. McKay, February 24, 1953, DOMS #22. One of McKay's popular illustrations of the effects of sin involved releasing a drop of ink from his fountain pen into a glass of water.

61. Vivian McKay interview.

62. Wilcox interview.

63. "Mr. McKay," *Salt Lake Tribune* (Magazine Section), October 4, 1953.

64. Douglas D. Alder interview.

65. Elaine Reiser Alder interview.

66. Robert Anderson interview.

67. Quinn McKay interview.

68. Cannon interview.

69. David O. McKay, "The Aaronic Priesthood," dedicatory address and prayer given at the dedication of the Aaronic Priesthood Monument, Salt Lake Tabernacle, October 10, 1958, DOMP.

70. Arnold Friberg interview.

71. David N. Fairbanks to Elly Srobel Card, January 24, 2002, photocopy in Prince's possession.

72. Paul H. Dunn interview, February 18, 1995.

73. Alan Macfarlane interview.

74. DOMD, May 17, 1962.

75. ELWD, July 31, 1960.

76. Don L. Christensen interview.

77. Bernard P. Brockbank interview.

78. Quinn McKay interview.

79. Midene Anderson interview, October 1, 1996.

80. No author identified, *Gospel Doctrine Class News,* a publication of the Eighteenth Ward Gospel Doctrine Class, March 19, 1939, DOMS #5.

81. Arch L. Madsen interview, January 14, 1996.

82. Murdock interview, March 28, 1973.

83. Simpson interview.

84. David O. McKay, "Courtship and Marriage," address given at a Youth Meeting of the East Millcreek Stake, October 23, 1945, DOMS #10.

85. Thomas S. Monson, "Eternal Principles from Prophets' Lives," BYU Devotional, October 10, 1989. In fairness to Widtsoe, his biographer emphasizes that it was Leah, rather than John Widtsoe, who had the most rigid views on nutrition and includes several stories from grandchildren recalling fondly how John, while driving, would pretend to be helpless as the automobile allegedly insisted on swerving into the parking lot of ice cream stores "almost weekly." Alan K. Parrish, *John A. Widtsoe,* 670–71.

86. Leonard J. Arrington, *Adventures of a Church Historian,* 41–42.

87. Edward Barner interview.

88. David O. McKay, address at Weber College, January 7, 1938, DOMP.

89. David O. McKay, address at Los Angeles Stake Aaronic Priesthood and LDS Girls, February 1, 1952, DOMP.

90. Lola Gygi Timmins interview, October 28, 1998.

91. David O. McKay, remarks at the German–Austrian Missionary Association Banquet, January 21, 1939, in *Contact,* the publication of the German Missionary Association, March 1939, DOMS #5.

92. Albert L. Bott, quoting McKay at the First Annual David O. McKay Honor Day, Ogden, Utah, February 25, 1965, DOMS #118.

93. Gabrielle Baruffol, *Through the Pantry Window,* 54.

94. Cathy McConnell interview.

95. David O. McKay, *Conference Report* (April 1951), 157.

96. Joseph Anderson interview, 1970.

97. Marion G. Romney, address at the Auckland (New Zealand) District Conference, July 1955, DOMS #31.

98. Charles M. Brown interview, June 3, 1995.

99. David Timmins interview.

100. Wm. Robert Wright interview.

101. Gabrielle Baruffol interview.

102. Barner interview.

103. Dunn interview, January 11, 1997.

104. Vivian McKay interview.

105. Ibid.

106. Clare Middlemiss note, April 13, 1955, DOMS #31.

107. Sterling M. McMurrin interview.

108. DOMD, July 26, 1956. Hanks related this story to Clare Middlemiss, who included it in McKay's diary entry for the day.

109. Marion Isabell "Belle" Spafford interview.

110. Donald H. Rasmussen interview.

Chapter 2 – Revelation and Prophecy

1. "The Greatest Need of the World Today—Faith in God," an address by President David O. McKay at the Berlin Conference, June 29, 1952, DOMP.

2. David O. McKay, "Witnesses to the Truth," *Improvement Era* 54 (1951): 542.

3. David O. McKay, "The Greatest Possession," *Instructor* 99 (1964): 130.

4. "David O. McKay, Mormon President, Was Ardent Advocate of Universal Expansion," *New York Times,* January 19, 1970.

5. David O. McKay, "The Power of Prayer," 190.

6. Address delivered at the Ninetieth Semi-Annual Conference of the Church, afternoon session, third overflow meeting, Barratt Hall, Sunday, October 5, 1919, presided over by Elder David O. McKay, DOMP. Published in *Conference Report,* October 1919, 181–82.

7. David O. McKay, "Great Power of Personal Influence in Missionary Work," address to the missionaries of the North British Mission, Manchester, England, March 1, 1961, DOMP.

8. Ibid.

9. David O. McKay, Address delivered at the Ninetieth Semi-Annual Conference.

10. A summary of the accounts is in Stan Larson and Patricia Larson, eds., *What E'er Thou Art Act Well Thy Part,* xxxiii–xl.

11. DOMD, May 29, 1899. Quoted in ibid., 239–41.

12. James L. McMurrin Diary, May 29, 1899, quoted in DOMS #190.

13. David O. McKay, Address delivered at the Ninetieth Semi-Annual Conference.

14. David O. McKay, Remarks at the General Priesthood Meeting, Saturday, October 6, 1934, his first General Conference address after being sustained as Second Counselor in the First Presidency, DOMP.

15. David O. McKay, Address delivered at the Ninetieth Semi-Annual Conference.

16. David O. McKay to Ira C. Fletcher, March 21, 1949, DOMS #185.

17. David O. McKay to Ramona Carlsen, March 23, 1956, DOMS #156.

18. David O. McKay to Catherine Farey, March 23, 1956, DOMS #156.

19. Selvoy J. Boyer interview.

20. Alistair James McWilliam Smith interview.

21. Robert L. Simpson interview.

22. Transcript of the movie footage. DOMS #185.

23. Ted L. Cannon, "Interview of President McKay by John Cook," DOMD, January 5, 1961.

24. DOMD, Sunday, May 19, 1957; Sunday, August 4, 1957; Sunday, February 1, 1959; Sunday, May 3, 1959.

25. "Testimony of President David O. McKay Regarding the Whispering of the Spirit," June 14, 1956, in "Testimonies" section, DOMP. Photocopy in authors' possession.

CHAPTER 3 – FREE AGENCY AND TOLERANCE

1. David O. McKay, "The Responsibility and Opportunities of Religious Teachers," address given ca. 1930, DOMS #3.

2. David O. McKay, "Religion and Life," commencement address at the Logan Institute of Religion, May 25, 1947, DOMS #12.

3. Doctrine and Covenants 93:36.

4. David O. McKay, "Whither Shall We Go, or Life's Supreme Decision," June 8, 1935, DOMP. The text of this hymn, which has been dated to 1805 and which was included in the church's first hymnal (1835) is No. 240 in the current edition *Hymns of the Church of Jesus Christ of Latter-day Saints* (Salt Lake City: Deseret Book, 1985).

5. DOMD, May 9, 1955.

6. David O. McKay, "Whither Shall We Go, or Life's Supreme Decision."

7. See chapter 12.

8. David O. McKay, "Freedom of Choice," 356. McKay's account of the war in heaven is a paraphrase of Moses 4:1–5, in the Pearl of Great Price, one of the LDS standard works of scripture.

9. David O. McKay, April 6, 1950, *Conference Report,* April 1950, 32, 36.

10. Drew Pearson, "Drew Pearson on the Washington Merry-Go-Round," Bell Syndicate, July 5, 1962, DOMS #202.

11. "David O. McKay Dies at 96; Head of Mormons Since 1951," *Evening Star* (Washington, DC), January 19, 1970.

12. David O. McKay, "Jesus, The Master Storyteller," *Instructor* 87 (November 1952): 322, 339. The parable of the wheat and the tares appears in Matthew 13:24–30.

13. Hugh B. Brown, speaking at the First Annual David O. McKay Honor Day, Ogden, Utah, February 25, 1965, DOMS #118.

14. Richard L. Evans, "Tribute to David O. McKay," remarks made at the Testimonial Dinner Party given in honor of David O. McKay's ninetieth birthday, September 5, 1963, DOMS #204.

15. Paul H. Dunn interview, October 6, 1995. George Boyd was an Institute of Religion Teacher at the University of Utah who, because of his liberal views, was transferred to the institute at the University of Southern California for the remainder of his career. Lowell L. Bennion was the director at the same institute. In the spring of 1962, he was fired from his position by decision of Ernest L. Wilkinson, then Church Commissioner of Education. After President McKay declined to meet with Bennion, he accepted a joint appointment as assistant dean of students at the University of Utah and as director of community services of the Utah Center for the Prevention and Control of Juvenile Delinquency. A center for student volunteer service at the University of Utah now bears his name. Mary Lythgoe Bradford, *Lowell L. Bennion,* chap. 8.

16. ELWD, June 15, 1954.

17. Richard Sherlock, "'We Can See No Advantage to a Continuation of the Discussion.'" After hearing the pro- and anti-evolution General Authorities state their cases, President Grant declared that neither view could claim to be doctrinal and ordered both groups to cease the debate.

18. DOMD, October 28, 1960.

19. David O. McKay, remarks at the funeral of May Anderson, June 14, 1946, in DOMS #11.

20. The meeting, described in more detail later in this chapter, occurred on March 14, 1954, in the Union Building of the University of Utah. Sterling W. McMurrin, "Account of Events of 1952–54."

21. Carlfred B. Broderick, "The Core of My Belief," 87–88.

22. DOMD, July 9, 1954.

23. DOMD, July 14, 1954.

24. DOMD, August 18, 1954.

25. ELWD, August 25 and 28, 1954.

26. DOMD, September 13, 1954.

27. George Boyd interview.

28. Sterlin M. McMurrin and L. Jackson Newell, *Matters of Conscience,* 184.

29. ELWD, June 10, 1955.

30. The speech was given to Seminary and Institute personnel on July 7, 1954, and published as "Church Leaders and the Scriptures," in J. Reuben Clark Jr., *Immortality and Eternal Life,* vol. 2 (Salt Lake City: Corporation of the President, 1969), the Melchizedek Priesthood Course of Study, 1969–70, 215–25.

31. Brown related this story to George Boyd, and Boyd quoted it in his interview.

32. Bertrand F. Harrison, "The Relatedness of Living Things," *The Instructor* 100 (July 1965): 272–76.

33. Stokes received this permission in writing from Joseph Anderson, secretary to the First Presidency, on October 18, 1968, but did not publish the letter for another decade. See Stokes, "An Official Position," 90.

34. Quoted in DOMD, January 7, 1960.

35. DOMD, February 6, 1959.

36. Lola Gygi Timmins interview, August 4, 2000.

37. DOMD, March 5, 1959.

38. DOMD, January 7, 1960.

39. DOMD, January 8, 1960.

40. DOMD, January 27, 1960.

41. DOMD, January 28, 1960.

42. DOMD, July 5, 1966.

43. Bruce R. McConkie to Clare Middlemiss, July 8, 1966, DOMD, July 5, 1966. After McKay's death, his successor, Harold B. Lee, called McConkie to the Quorum of the Twelve Apostles.

44. For a discussion of the theological influence of McConkie's and Joseph Fielding Smith's writings in Mormonism, see David John Buerger, "Speaking with Authority," and O. Kendall White Jr., *Mormon Neo-Orthodoxy.*

45. William Bates interview, October 3, 2000.

46. Levi S. Peterson, *Juanita Brooks,* 40–41.

47. R. J. Snow interview.

48. Peterson, *Juanita Brooks,* 273.

49. Snow interview. Juanita Brooks, *John Doyle Lee: Zealot—Pioneer Builder—Scapegoat* (Glendale, CA: Arthur H. Clark, 1961), was published in an edition of 209 copies without the notice of Lee's reinstatement. The notice of Lee's reinstatement was added to the first trade edition, which was published by Clark in 1962.

50. Delves, "'Leave Her Alone.'"

51. DOMD, March 14, 1954.

52. Sterling W. McMurrin, "Account of Events of 1952–54." McMurrin was the grandnephew of James McMurrin, who was David O. McKay's mission president in Scotland.

53. Sterling M. McMurrin to David O. McKay, March 24, 1954, DOMD, March 14, 1954.

54. M. Lynn Bennion to David O. McKay, April 8, 1954, DOMD, March 14, 1954.

55. DOMD, March 18, 1960.

56. Sterling M. McMurrin to David O. McKay, September 13, 1960, DOMP.

57. David O. McKay to Sterling M. McMurrin, November 1, 1960, DOMP.

58. DOMD, June 26, 1968.

59. DOMD, July 16, 1968.

60. DOMD, March 15, 1946.

61. Quoted in Newell G. Bringhurst, *Fawn McKay Brodie,* 113.

62. David Lawrence McKay interview.

63. DOMD, July 4, 1951.

64. A. Russell Mortensen interview.

65. Ann Hinckley interview.

66. Mortensen interview.

CHAPTER 4 — BLACKS, CIVIL RIGHTS, AND THE PRIESTHOOD

1. David Lawrence McKay interview.

2. DOMD, February 6, 1962.

3. DOMD, March 30, 1898. Quoted in Frederick S. Buchanan, "Missionary Roots of Change." This article is a review of Stan Larson and Patricia Larson, eds., *What E'er Thou Art, Act Well Thy Part.*

4. David O. McKay, "Persons and Principles," *Millennial Star* 86 (January 31, 1924): 72–74.

5. Thomas F. O'Dea, *The Mormons,* chap. 9.

6. Quoted in Paul W. Hodson to Prince, June 8, 1996. Hodson was a member of a study group to which Bennion also belonged.

7. DOMD, February 25, 1949.

8. J. Reuben Clark Jr. Office Diary, August 30, 1944. Quoted in D. Michael Quinn, *Elder Statesman,* 344.

9. George Albert Smith diary, June 16, 1945. Quoted in Quinn, *Elder Statesman,* 339–59.

10. J. Reuben Clark, Jr. Office Diary, December 2, 1957. Quoted in Quinn, *Elder Statesman,* 339–59.

11. DOMD, June 22, 1961. There is no further mention of this proposal in McKay's papers.

12. DOMD, June 19, 1963.

13. "Editor's Note," *Look,* October 22, 1963, 74–78.

14. ELWD, November 10, 1960.

15. Maureen Lee Wilkins, quoted in Ramona Bernhard interview.

16. *Deseret News,* December 14, 1963. In Lester E. Bush, "Compilation on the Negro in Mormonism," 280. Bush copied this clipping from Journal History of the Church of Jesus Christ of Latter-day Saints (chronology of typed entries and newspaper clippings, 1830–present), LDS Church Archives, where the clipping is filed under December 13.

17. DOMD, September 22, 1967.

18. Mark E. Petersen, "Race Problems—As They Affect the Church," 27 August 1954. In Bush, "Compilation on the Negro in Mormonism," 260–61.

19. ELWD, May 5, 1960.

20. Alvin R. Dyer, "For What Purpose?" March 18, 1961. Reprinted in Bush, "Compilation on the Negro in Mormonism," 267–68.

21. "Grandfather's release from the First Presidency was absolutely, directly related to the race issue." Edwin B. Firmage interview, June 6, 1995.

22. Quinn, *Elder Statesman,* 339–59.

23. Quoted in Bush, "Compilation on the Negro in Mormonism," 262.

24. Ibid., 261–62.

25. Ibid., 261.

26. "Extremism Is Never the Answer," *Deseret News,* April 3, 1956.

27. DOMD, April 2, 1956.

28. DOMD, September 19, 1958.

29. DOMD, June 13, 1961.

30. Stewart L. Udall to Henry D. Moyle and Hugh B. Brown, September 18, 1961. Quoted in F. Ross Peterson, "'Do Not Lecture the Brethren.'" There is no indication in McKay's papers that the First Presidency discussed Udall's letter.

31. DOMD, June 13, 1963.

32. DOMD, June 19, 1963.

33. DOMD, July 2, 1963.

34. Hugh B. Brown to Stewart L. Udall, July 22, 1963. Quoted in Peterson, "'Do Not Lecture the Brethren.'"

35. DOMD, October 4, 1963.

36. Sterling M. McMurrin and L. Jackson Newell, *Matters of Conscience,* 198–213.

37. Sterling M. McMurrin to Prince, October 30, 1994.

38. *Conference Report,* October 1963, 91.

39. McMurrin, "A Note on the 1963 Civil Rights Statement."

40. "A Clear Civil Rights Stand," editorial, *Deseret News,* March 8, 1965.

41. *Salt Lake Tribune,* October 7, 1963. In Bush, "Compilation on the Negro in Mormonism," 279.

42. Quoted in *Indianapolis Star,* November 6, 1963. In Journal History.

43. *Deseret News,* December 14, 1963. In Journal History, December 13, 1963.

44. David O. McKay, telegram to Lyndon B. Johnson, July 2, 1964, DOMD, July 2, 1964.

45. Ibid. There is no indication that McKay actually served on this committee, probably due to his failing health.

46. "NAACP Calls March for LDS Appeal," *Salt Lake Tribune,* March 7, 1965.

47. DOMD, March 8, 1965.

48. "Benson Ties Rights Issue to Reds in Mormon Rift," *Washington Post,* April 13, 1965. DOMS #78. This controversial passage was deleted from the text of the speech that was published in the official *Conference Report.*

49. Quoted in *Deseret News,* May 3, 1966. In Bush, "Compilation on the Negro in Mormonism," 289.

50. Hugh B. Brown Journal, August 6–12, 1967.

51. DOMD, August 6, 1967.

52. DOMD, September 1, 1967.

53. DOMD, September 22, 1967.

54. *Conference Report,* October 1967, 34–39.

55. *Conference Report,* April 1968, 3. Parentheses in original.

56. DOMD, April 5, 1968.

57. For an authoritative overview of the subject, see Lester E. Bush and Armand L. Mauss, eds., *Neither White nor Black.*

58. "Minutes of a Special Meeting by President David O. McKay, 17th January, 1954," in DOMD, January 19, 1954.

59. Heber Meeks to Lowry Nelson, June 1947. Quoted in Nelson, *In the Direction of His Dreams,* 335.

60. Lowry Nelson to Heber Meeks, June 26, 1947. Quoted in ibid., 335–37.

61. Lowry Nelson to George Albert Smith, June 26, 1947. Quoted in ibid., 337–38.

62. First Presidency (George Albert Smith, J. Reuben Clark Jr., and David O. McKay) to Lowry Nelson, July 17, 1947. Quoted in ibid., 339–40.

63. Ibid., 340–41.

64. Book of Abraham 1:21–27. According to this passage, Egypt was founded by the daughter of Ham and his wife Egyptus. Egyptus was descended from the Canaanites, presumed to be descendants of Cain, cursed, in Mormon belief, with a dark skin, for killing his brother Abel. Because of his marriage to Egyptus, Ham was cursed by Noah, his father. Since the Egyptians were descended from Ham and Egyptus, they were barred from holding the priesthood because of Noah's curse.

65. David O. McKay letter dated November 3, 1947. Quoted in Llewelyn R. McKay, *Home Memories of President David O. McKay,* 226–31.

66. DOMD, April 25, 1948.

67. Evan P. Wright, *A History of the South African Mission,* 419–20.

68. Evan P. Wright to First Presidency, November 23, 1949. Quoted in ibid., 87.

69. Evan P. Wright to First Presidency, April 14, 1952. Quoted in ibid., 225.

70. Evan P. Wright to First Presidency, June 17, 1952. Quoted in ibid., 438–48.

71. Ibid.

72. Ibid., 181.

73. Greetings to the Elders and Other Church Members in the South African Mission, December 1951, DOMS #18.

74. Monroe G. McKay interview.

75. A. Hamer Reiser interview, October 16, 1974.

76. "Minutes of a Special Meeting by President David O. McKay, 17th January, 1954," in DOMD, January 19, 1954. The secretary is not identified.

77. Ibid.

78. David O. McKay to Stephen L Richards and J. Reuben Clark Jr., January 19, 1954, DOMD.

79. Le Roy H. Duncan to David O. McKay, February 23, 1954, DOMS #137.

80. Lowell Bennion interview.

81. DOMD, June 13, 1957.

82. DOMD, August 21, 1959.

83. John H. Vandenberg interview, November 15, 1984.

84. Sterling M. McMurrin, affidavit, March 6, 1979. Italics Prince's.

85. Leonard J. Arrington, *Adventures of a Church Historian,* 183.

86. DOMD, February 17, 1955.

87. DOMD, October 11, 1956.

88. DOMD, May 13, 1958.

89. The first Fijians were ordained later in 1958 (day and month not specified). Armand L. Mauss, "The Fading of the Pharaoh's Curse," 36n13.

90. DOMD, September 4, 1958.

91. DOMD, February 24, 1961.

92. Council minutes, October 24, 1946, Adam S. Bennion Papers. Reprinted in Bush, "Compilation on the Negro in Mormonism," 360.

93. Council minutes, October 9, 1947, Adam S. Bennion Papers. Reprinted in Bush, "Compilation on the Negro in Mormonism," 360.

94. LaMar Stevenson Williams interview.

95. Glen Fisher, "Report [to the First Presidency]," September 16, 1960. Quoted in James B. Allen, "Would-Be Saints," 213.

96. DOMD, June 22, 1961.

97. DOMD, June 30, 1961.

98. DOMD, July 1, 1961.

99. DOMD, October 13, 1961.

100. Williams interview.

101. LaMar S. Williams to David O. McKay, undated, in DOMD, November 21, 1961.

102. DOMD, January 9, 1962.

103. Latter-day Saint priesthood organization consists of the lesser (or Aaronic) Priesthood, a preparatory priesthood composed primarily of boys ages twelve through eighteen, while the Melchizedek Priesthood is composed of male adults (who become eligible for ordination at eighteen) and includes all general church officers.

104. DOMD, March 1, 1962.

105. DOMD, March 3, 1962. McKay set Williams apart as a missionary to Nigeria on November 21, 1962 (DOMD). Williams, who was never set apart as mission president, referred to himself as "presiding elder" in Nigeria. McKay (DOMD, January 11, 1963) used the term "Supervising Elder," observing, "Nigeria would not be called a mission."

106. James B. Allen, "Would-Be Saints," 227.

107. David O. McKay to N. Eldon Tanner, September 4, 1962, in DOMD, August 30, 1962. Tanner's roles changed frequently during this period. He became an Assistant to the Quorum of the Twelve, October 8, 1960; served as president of the West German Mission April 9, 1961, to December 26, 1962, was called to the Quorum of the Twelve on October 6, 1962, and ordained five days later, and became second counselor in McKay's First Presidency on October 4, 1963.

108. DOMD, October 18, 1962.

109. DOMD, October 11, 1962.

110. Ibid.

111. Quoted in Allen, "Would-Be Saints," 227–28.

112. Quoted in DOMD, January 10, 1963.

113. DOMD, January 10, 1963.

114. "Church to Open Missionary Work in Nigeria," *Deseret News,* January 11, 1963.

115. *Nigerian Outlook,* March 5, 1963. In Bush, "Compilation on the Negro in Mormonism," 361–63.

116. Ibid., 363–64.

117. DOMD, March 8, 1963.

118. DOMD, March 12, 1963.

119. DOMD, March 20, 1963.

120. DOMD, May 13, 1963.

121. N. Eldon Tanner, memorandum dated June 3, 1963, DOMD, May 28, 1963.

122. Wallace Turner, "Mormons Weigh Stand on Negro," *New York Times,* June 7, 1963.

123. DOMD, June 5, 1963.

124. DOMD, June 7, 1963. Available biographical sources on Brown do not explain this episode with Turner.

125. DOMD, October 10, 1963.

126. "Clare Boothe Luce Says Romney '64 Deadlock Choice," *Arizona Republic* and other newspapers nationally, September 1, 1963.

127. Henry D. Moyle to Clare Boothe Luce, September 13, 1963, in DOMD, September 13, 1963. This letter was apparently never published. Clare Boothe Luce (1903–87) was a playwright, magazine editor, legislator, and diplomat. She served as a member of the House of Representatives from Connecticut. President Eisenhower appointed Luce as ambassador to Italy.

128. "Mormons: The Negro Question," *Time,* October 18, 1963, 83.

129. Thomas E. Cheney interview.

130. Ibid.

131. DOMD, January 14, 1964.

132. Allen, "Would-Be Saints," 233.

133. DOMD, April 22, 1965.

134. DOMD, June 3, 1965.

135. *Time,* June 18, 1965. In Bush, "Compilation on the Negro in Mormonism," 365.

136. DOMD, June 15, 1965.

137. DOMD, June 23, 1965.

138. DOMD, August 20, 1965.

139. DOMD, August 25, 1965.

140. DOMD, October 14, 1965.

141. Minutes of Council Meeting, November 4, 1965, DOMD, November 4, 1965.

142. DOMD, March 20, 1963.

143. Minutes of Council Meeting, November 4, 1965.

144. Ibid.

145. Williams interview.

146. DOMD, November 10, 1965.

147. Ibid.

148. Williams interview.

149. Quoted in Marjorie Newton, *Southern Cross Saints,* 209–10.

150. DOMD, February 24, 1961.

151. DOMD, July 5, 1966.

152. DOMD, August 15, 1966. Temple ordinances, the most notable being the "endowment," are held by Latter-day Saints to be essential for salvation. It is the responsibility of each Latter-day Saint to have such ordinances performed, by proxy, for all known progenitors.

153. DOMD, September 27, 1966. Latter-day Saints whose marriages are performed in an LDS temple are assured that they and their children will live together in eternity. "Sealing" is an ordinance performed in a temple that extends the same privilege to families whose initial weddings were not conducted in a temple, as well as for those adopting children.

154. DOMD, December 14, 1966. This decision was actually a restatement of a decision made in 1910 by Church President Joseph F. Smith. See Bush, "Compilation on the Negro in Mormonism," 215.

155. Stewart L. Udall, "Letter to the Editor."

156. Stewart L. Udall to David O. McKay, May 16, 1967, DOMD, May 24, 1967. McKay's papers contain no record of a reaction or response.

157. DOMD, May 24, 1967.

158. "U. Professor Rues LDS Negro Stand," *Salt Lake Tribune,* June 22, 1968. In DOMS #98.

159. DOMD, June 26, 1968.

160. DOMD, July 16, 1968.

161. Both men spent the majority of their professional careers at the university. At the time he wrote the letter, McMurrin was dean of the Graduate School and McKay, a French professor, was chair of the Languages Department.

162. Sterling M. McMurrin to Llewelyn McKay, August 26, 1968.

163. Sterling M. McMurrin, "Account of Events of 1952–54."

164. Ibid.

165. Edward R. McKay to Sterling M. McMurrin, September 19, 1968.

166. McMurrin, "Account of Events of 1952–54."

167. Stephen Taggart died of Hodgkin's disease before his manuscript was published. His wife, Pamela R. Taggart, completed it and published it as Stephen G. Taggart, *Mormonism's Negro Policy: Social and Historical Origins* (1970), which was also after the death of David O. McKay.

168. Alvin R. Dyer Diary, September 10, 1969, in DOMD, September 10, 1969. Stephen Taggart's father, Glen Taggart, had been selected as president of Utah State University from his position as dean of international education at Michigan State University.

169. Ibid.

170. Minutes of the First Presidency meeting of September 17, 1969, DOMD, September 17, 1969.

171. DOMD, September 24, 1969. George Albert Smith was McKay's immediate predecessor as church president.

172. Ibid. The note on McKay's condition was added to the diary entry by McKay's personal secretary, Clare Middlemiss.

173. Dyer Diary, October 8, 1969, in DOMD, October 8, 1969.

174. ELWD, October 27, 1969.

175. Lee's role was discussed in a meeting between Dyer, Mark E. Petersen, and McKay on December 26, 1969. Dyer's account, which is included in DOMD, December 26, 1969, does not record a response from either Petersen or McKay.

176. L. Brent Goates, *Harold B. Lee,* 380.

177. Edwin B. Firmage, *An Abundant Life,* 141–43.

178. Ibid., 142.

179. First Presidency Circular Letter, December 15, 1969.

180. "LDS Leader Says Curb On Priesthood to Ease," *San Francisco Chronicle,* December 25, 1969, D–4.

181. Sterling M. McMurrin to Prince, October 30, 1994.

182. DOMD, December 26, 1969.

183. Dyer Diary, December 26, 1969, DOMD.

184. The process by which this revelation occurred is recounted in Edward L. Kimball, *Lengthen Your Stride.* Our appreciation to Kimball for making this work available to us in manuscript.

185. Quoted by Midene McKay Anderson interview, September 2, 2004. Her mother was Mildred Calderwood McKay.

186. Marion D. Hanks interview.

187. Lola Gygi Timmins interview, January 17, 2003.

188. Richard Jackson interview.

CHAPTER 5 – ECUMENICAL OUTREACH

1. Pearl of Great Price, "Joseph Smith—History," 2:19.

2. McKay, "The Mission of the Church and Its Members," 781.

3. Sterling M. McMurrin to David O. McKay, September 6, 1963, DOMS #203.

4. *Time,* February 2, 1970, 50. Quoted in Richard N. Armstrong, *The Rhetoric of David O. McKay,* 7.

5. Hayes Gory, "The Ninth Prophet."

6. The Right Reverend Arthur Wheelock Moulton (1873–1962) served as the fifth Episcopal Bishop of Utah from 1920 until his retirement in 1946. Bishop Moulton promoted good relations with the Mormons.

7. DOMD, September 8, 1951. Note the artist's recreation of this event among the illustrations.

8. Warren Bainbridge to David O. McKay, December 13, 1962, DOMS #115. Rev. Bainbridge had been unable to attend the community tribute to McKay at Hotel Utah earlier that week.

9. C. Sumpter Logan to David O. McKay, June 13, 1961, DOMD, June 15, 1961.

10. Reverend A. Cadman Garretson, Master of Ceremonies, "A Report on the Proceedings of the 'David O. McKay Ceremonies' Held in Honor of President and Mrs. McKay in the Ballroom of the Ben Lomond Hotel, Ogden, Utah, July 16, 1954," DOMS #113.

11. For further information about Mormon views on lineage, race, and Israelite identity, see Armand L. Mauss, *All Abraham's Children.*

12. DOMD, January 12, 1951.

13. DOMD, October 14, 1952.

14. Israel Goldstein to David O. McKay, April 26, 1955, DOMS #31.

15. Rose L. Halprin to David O. McKay, April 11, 1955, DOMS #31.

16. Joseph Rosenblatt, "President David O. McKay Honored," 111.

17. Gory, "The Ninth Prophet," 37.

18. Book of Mormon, 1 Nephi 13:5, 8.

19. Ibid., 1 Nephi 13:34, 14:11.

20. William Miller, *Evidence from Scripture and History of the Second Coming of Christ, about the Year 1843* (1838), v, 141. Quoted in Whitney R. Cross, *The Burned-Over District,* 233.

21. U.S. Conference of Catholic Bishops, "A Statistical Profile of the Church in the United States 1789 to 2000," retrieved May 5, 2004, from http:www.nccbuscc.org/comm/profile.htm.

22. DOMD, June 17, 1923.

23. *Deseret News 2001–2002 Church Almanac,* 426–27.

24. Msgr. Jerome Stoffel, "The Hesitant Beginnings of the Catholic Church in Utah," 56.

25. Millard Everett, "Centenary of Mormonism Coincides with Successful Catholic Radio Work in Utah."

26. Duane G. Hunt to Most Rev. John A. Floersh, December 12, 1946. Duane G. Hunt Papers.

27. J. Reuben Clark Jr. Office Diary, February 25, 1948. Quoted in D. Michael Quinn, *Elder Statesman,* 121.

28. Ibid.

29. Typescripts of Hunt's radio addresses are in the Archives of the Catholic Diocese of Salt Lake City.

30. J. Reuben Clark Jr. Office Diary, March 2, 1948. Quoted in Quinn, *Elder Statesman,* 121.

31. J. Reuben Clark Jr., *On the Way to Immortality and Eternal Life.*

32. Msgr. Jerome Stoffel interview.

33. DOMD, February 19, 1949.

34. DOMD, March 2, 1949.

35. David O. McKay discourse at the dedication of the Darby Ward Chapel, Driggs, Idaho, July 31, 1949, DOMS #14.

36. Leo J. Steck, "A Foreign Mission Close to Home!" (n.p., 1949).

37. DOMD, August 28, 1949.

38. Duane G. Hunt to John F. Fitzpatrick, August 28, 1949. Hunt Papers.

39. David O. McKay to Duane G. Hunt, November 7, 1949. Hunt Papers.

40. Minutes of a meeting held in the Harvard Ward Chapel, September 22, 1949. Hunt Papers.

41. Minutes of a meeting held in the 10th Ward Chapel, October 13, 1949. Hunt Papers.

42. DOMD, October 7, 1949.

43. DOMD, October 12, 1949.

44. Duane G. Hunt to David O. McKay, October 21, 1949. Carbon copy in Hunt Papers.

45. David O. McKay to Duane G. Hunt, November 7, 1949. Hunt Papers.

46. The Italian Mission was reopened on August 2, 1966. *Deseret News 2001–2002 Church Almanac,* 434.

47. DOMD, December 16, 1951.

48. Duane G. Hunt, undated circular letter, "My dear People." Hunt Papers. A handwritten note at the top of the letter by Bernice Mooney, former archivist of the diocese, indicated that this was read in all parishes between September and November 1952.

49. DOMD, February 28, 1953.

50. Asael Sorensen interview.

51. David B. Haight interview. Several years after McKay's death, Haight was called to serve as an apostle.

52. Formally known as the Cistercian Order of the Strict Observance, the Abbey of the Holy Trinity in Huntsville was founded by monks from the Abbey of Gethsemani in Kentucky.

53. DOMD, June 3, 1954.

54. DOMD, April 29, 1957.

55. DOMD, May 20, 1957.

56. DOMD, October 2, 1957.

57. DOMD, October 10, 1957.

58. Smith was the senior member of the Quorum of the Twelve Apostles and succeeded McKay as church president in 1970. He remarked that he "did not know anything about it until it was published." DOMD, January 7, 1960. See chapter 3.

59. DOMD, February 6, 1959.

60. DOMD, January 7, 1960.

61. Bruce R. McConkie, *Mormon Doctrine,* 108, 129.

62. David S. King interview.

63. Robert L. Simpson interview.

64. David Lawrence McKay interview.

65. David O. McKay to Duane G. Hunt, June 1, 1959, DOMS #44.

66. DOMD, March 31, 1960.

67. DOMD, April 5, 1960.

68. The new First Presidency expressed its appreciation to Bishop Federal for this kind act in a letter dated January 28, 1970. Joseph Lennox Federal Papers.

CHAPTER 6 – RADIO AND TELEVISION BROADCASTING

1. Bruce L. Christensen, "Broadcasting," 232. KSL was an NBC affiliate from 1929 to 1933 when it switched to CBS.

2. DOMD, October 4, 1953.

3. DOMD, April 4, 1954.

4. "First Presidency Urges Greater Missionary Service," *Church News,* April 10, 1954.

5. Quoted in DOMD, June 3, 1958.

6. DOMD, January 22, 1959. Sharp's "retirement" was made retroactive to January 1, 1959.

7. Arch L. Madsen interview, January 14, 1996.

8. Ibid.

9. ELWD, May 31, 1960.

10. ELWD, June 11, 1960.

11. DOMD, November 23, 1960.

12. ELWD, December 16, 1960.

13. DOMD, January 12, 1961.

14. ELWD, January 22, 1961.

15. Madsen interview, June 11, 1981.

16. Madsen interview, February 19, 1995. In the same interview, Madsen gave an example of the kind of intervention about which McKay cautioned him. An unnamed General Authority went to McKay to complain about Madsen: "President McKay let him say just a few words, that I was the wrong person, incompetent, etc., and doing things wrong, and that the broadcasting should be turned over to him. President McKay said, 'Well, if you're going to talk about Brother Madsen, we'll get him to come.'... When I went in the room, there sat [the individual]. I sat down, and President McKay greeted me and thanked me for coming, then turned to him and said, 'Now, you were about to criticize Brother Madsen. Will you proceed?' Well, he did. He listed the things that I was doing wrong, which indicated my incompetence. President McKay turned to me and said, 'Did you do those things, Brother Madsen?' And I said, 'I certainly did, President McKay, and you approved every one of them.' Boy, the tension in that room! That guy couldn't get out of there fast enough. And that was only one of the episodes."

17. Madsen interview, February 19, 1995. Bonneville International is the holding company for the church's broadcasting properties.

18. Madsen interview, June 11, 1981.

19. Madsen interview, February 19, 1995.

20. ELWD, May 11, 1961. Moyle quoted McKay's comment to Wilkinson in a meeting on several issues that the two men subsequently had.

21. Kenneth L. Hatch interview.

22. Michael Grilikhes interview.

23. DOMD, April 26, 1962.

24. DOMD, May 8, 1962.

25. Joseph Kjar interview.

26. DOMD, May 8, 1962.

27. J. Reuben Clark Jr., "Memorandum: Radio Holding Corporation," October 20, 1937, J. Reuben Clark Papers, Box 358.

28. DOMD, April 13, 1962.

29. DOMD, May 8, 1962.

30. Ibid.

31. DOMD, May 18, 1962.

32. Ibid.

33. DOMD, September 6, 1962.

34. DOMD, October 10, 1962.

35. DOMD, December 9, 1962.

36. DOMD, February 26, 1963.

37. DOMD, March 13, 1963.

38. DOMD, November 5, 1963.

39. DOMD, April 16, 1964.

40. DOMD, July 15, 1964.

41. DOMD, December 15, 1964. Thorpe B. Isaacson, a businessman, had served as a counselor in the Presiding Bishopric (1946–61), but at this point was an Assistant to the Quorum of the Twelve. Even in 1964, McKay trusted Isaacson's judgment as an informal advisor and called him into the First Presidency as an additional counselor on October 28, 1965. His advice and participation in the First Presidency were short-lived, for only a few weeks later he suffered a severe stroke that disabled him for the remainder of his life. He was released at McKay's death in January 1970 and died that November.

42. DOMD, December 21, 1964.

43. DOMD, July 30, 1965.

44. DOMD, December 20, 1966.

45. DOMD, September 2, 1966.

46. DOMD, December 20, 1966.

47. DOMD, March 16, 1967.

48. Christensen, "Broadcasting," 232.

49. J. Alan Blodgett to Prince, July 31, 2003.

50. Madsen interview, June 11, 1981. The church sold KIRO TV in the mid-1990s for $160 million.

51. William F. Edwards interview.

52. J. Alan Blodgett to Prince, July 31, 2003.

53. Madsen, October 1, 1966, *Conference Report*, October 1966, 92.

54. DOMD, February 3, 1967.

55. DOMD, February 11, 1969.

56. Spencer W. Kimball, "Priesthood Missionary Work in the Church."

57. Madsen interview, January 14, 1996.

58. Blodgett to Prince, July 31, 2003.

59. Madsen interview, January 14, 1996.

60. Arch L. Madsen, Memorandum of meeting with DOM on January 7, 1964, DOMD.

61. Madsen interview, February 19, 1995.

62. Madsen interview, January 14, 1996.

63. Ibid.

64. Madsen interview, February 19, 1995.

CHAPTER 7 – CORRELATION AND CHURCH ADMINISTRATION

1. For a detailed account of such accommodations that occurred within the lifetime of Joseph Smith, see Prince, *Power from On High*.

2. For recent studies of the impact of the Smoot hearings on the church, see Kathleen Flake, *The Politics of American Religious Identity*.

3. Joseph F. Smith, *Conference Report*, April 1906, 3.

4. By the end of the nineteenth century, these included the women's Relief Society, Sunday School, Young Men's Mutual Improvement Association (YMMIA), Young Ladies' Mutual Improvement Association (YLMIA, later YWMIA), Primary Association, and Genealogical Society of Utah. Additional organizations continued to sprout and grow well into the twentieth century. For an overview of grassroots-initiated programs within the Church, see W. Keith Warner and Edward L. Kimball, "Creative Stewardship."

5. General Priesthood Committee, Minutes of Meetings, April 8, 1908. Quoted in Dale C. Mouritsen, "Efforts to Correlate Mormon Church Agencies in the Twentieth Century: A Review," 6.

6. Although some see 1961 as the beginning of "Correlation," neither the concept nor the name was new.

7. General Priesthood Committee, Minutes of Meetings, November 8, 1912. Quoted in Mouritsen, "Efforts to Correlate Mormon Church Agencies," 7.

8. First Presidency and Council of the Twelve, Temple Meeting Minutes, November 4, 1920, quoted in General Priesthood Committee Minutes. Quoted in Mouritsen, "Efforts to Correlate Mormon Church Agencies," 8. At the time the committee was formed, David O. McKay was circumnavigating the world, on assignment from Grant, to assess the state of all of the Church's foreign missions.

9. "Report of the Correlation–Social Advisory Committee [C-SAC] to the First presidency on the Definition and Assignment of Auxiliary Functions and Organizations, April 12, 1921." Quoted in Mouritsen, "Efforts to Correlate Mormon Church Agencies," 8.

10. Correlation Executive Committee, Meeting Minutes, I:4, June 7, 1922, LDS Church Archives. Quoted in Mouritsen, "Efforts to Correlate Mormon Church Agencies," 9.

11. David O. McKay to Stephen L Richards, June 6, 1923, DOMS #132.

12. McKay, "The Church Sunday School," 300.

13. John A. Widtsoe to J. Reuben Clark Jr., September 23, 1938. Quoted in Mouritsen, "Efforts to Correlate Mormon Church Agencies," 11.

14. Joseph T. Bentley interview, June 28, 1976. The Mutual Improvement Associations raised funds by advertising in the *Improvement Era*, while the Relief Society had a traditional annual fund-raising bazaar (handmade and cooked items) among other activities. The Sunday School, however, while soliciting funds at an annual "Dime Sunday," did not advertise in its magazine, *The Instructor*.

15. Lynn S. Richards interview.

16. A. Theodore Tuttle interview, October 11, 1977.

17. Loren C. Dunn interview.

18. John H. Vandenberg interviews, November 15 and December 6, 1984.

19. Theodore M. Burton interview. For an in-depth study of the Genealogical Society of Utah, see James B. Allen, Jessie L. Embry, and Kahlile B. Mehr, *Hearts Turned to the Fathers*.

20. Wilford W. Kirton Jr. interview.

21. Paul H. Dunn interview, May 21, 1996.

22. YMMIA General Superintendency and YWMIA General Presidency to First Presidency, August 13, 1952. Quoted in Antone K. Romney, "History of the Correlation of L.D.S. Church Auxiliaries." This typescript report, well over 100 pages in length, contains no pagination, table of contents, or index.

23. First Presidency Circular Letter, December 24, 1952.

24. First Presidency Circular Letter, March 25, 1953.

25. DOMD, September 10, 1953.

26. DOMD, March 6, 1956.

27. First Presidency to General Priesthood Committee, March 24, 1960. Quoted in Romney, "History of the Correlation of L.D.S. Church Auxiliaries."

28. L. Brent Goates interview.

29. Education Committee of the General Priesthood Committee, to Relief Society General Presidency, April 22, 1960. Quoted in Romney, "History of the Correlation of L.D.S. Church Auxiliaries."

30. ELWD, 18 May, 1960.

31. Romney, "History of the Correlation of L.D.S. Church Auxiliaries."

32. Report of Correlation Research Committee, March, 1961. Quoted in Romney, "History of the Correlation of L.D.S. Church Auxiliaries." This document contains all of the material referenced in the meetings in October 1960, January 24, 1961, and March 15, 1961.

33. Ibid.

34. Harold B. Lee Diaries, March 22, 1961. Quoted in L. Brent Goates, *Harold B. Lee*, 367.

35. Harold B. Lee, *Conference Report*, September 30, 1967, 100.

36. Romney, "History of the Correlation of L.D.S. Church Auxiliaries."

37. David O. McKay, September 30, 1961, *Conference Report*, October 1961, 76–77.

38. Harold B. Lee, September 30, 1961, *Conference Report*, October 1961, 81.

39. Rex D. Pinegar to Benson Young Parkinson, December 14, 1993. Quoted in Benson Young Parkinson, "S. Dilworth Young of the First Quorum of Seventy," 247.

40. Goates, *Harold B. Lee*, 367.

41. DOMD, September 30, 1961.

42. DOMD, June 21, 1962.

43. "Note by C.M.," DOMD, May 17, 1962.

44. DOMD, September 18, 1962.

45. DOMD, September 19, 1962; italics ours.

46. DOMD, September 28, 1962; italics ours.

47. Barbara Bradshaw Smith interview.

48. Harold B. Lee, October 6, 1962, *Conference Report*, October 1962, 79.

49. Marie Moyle Wangeman interview.

50. DOMD, April 3, 1963.

51. Ibid.

52. Ibid. According to McKay's diary, Lee "presented to us the Correlation Program.... After a discussion of these matters, Elder Harold B. Lee was authorized to present the program to the General Priesthood Meeting Saturday evening." McKay adds a "see" reference to Council of the Twelve minutes for details, but these minutes are not currently available to researchers.

53. DOMD, September 8, 1964.

54. Harold B. Lee, October 4, 1964, *Conference Report,* October 1964, 137–38.

55. Goates interview.

56. DOMD, May 30, 1967.

57. DOMD, June 1, 1967.

58. Quoted in Goates, *Harold B. Lee,* 368.

59. Gordon B. Hinckley interview.

60. Paul H. Dunn interview, October 6, 1995.

CHAPTER 8 – THE EDUCATION SYSTEM

1. DOMD, February 14, 1949.

2. "True Education," remarks made by President David O. McKay at the dedication of the Church College of New Zealand, Temple View, New Zealand, April 24, 1958. DOMP.

3. Hugh W. Nibley interview, June 5, 1995.

4. "Five Faiths That Deeply Concern Every Progressive-Minded Youth," address delivered by David O. McKay at Convention of Church School Teachers, Sunday School Board Room, Salt Lake City, January 18, 1941. DOMP.

5. David O. McKay, "True Education."

6. General Board of Education Minutes, March 23, 1926. Quoted in Ernest L. Wilkinson, *Brigham Young University,* 2:75.

7. David O. McKay, October 9, 1920. *Conference Report,* October 1920, 42.

8. Gary J. Bergera, "Ernest L. Wilkinson's Appointment as Seventh President of Brigham Young University." The search committee consisted of Joseph Fielding Smith (chair), Stephen L Richards, Joseph F. Merrill, John A. Widtsoe, and Albert E. Bowen. Wilkinson, *Brigham Young University,* 2:497.

9. Monroe G. McKay interview.

10. Alice Wilkinson Anderson to Prince, August 9, 1999.

11. DOMD, April 9, 1951.

12. DOMD, April 11, 1951.

13. John T. Bernhard interview, December 5, 1998.

14. John T. Bernhard interview, October 18, 1998.

15. Gabrielle Baruffol interview.

16. Paul H. Dunn interview, October 6, 1995.

17. Edward R. McKay interview.

18. Brigham D. Madsen, *Against the Grain,* 207.

19. Faye Fletcher interview.

20. Charles M. Brown interview, June 3, 1995.

21. Joseph T. Bentley interview, July 19, 1976.

22. Charles M. Brown interview, June 3, 1995. This compliment is third-hand. Clark told Hugh B. Brown, the other counselor in the First Presidency, and Brown related the information to his son, Charles.

23. Dale T. Tingey interview.

24. Bernhard interview, December 5, 1998.

25. Joseph Rosenblatt interview.

26. Richard D. Poll interview.

27. Dunn interview, October 6, 1995.

28. David O. McKay, "The Mission of Brigham Young University," speech given at BYU April 27, 1948. DOMP.

29. DOMD, March 28, 1953.

30. Quoted in Mary L. Bradford, *Lowell L. Bennion,* 127.

31. "Church Unites Schools Under One Director," *Deseret News and Telegram,* July 9, 1953.

32. "Address to Institute and Seminary Teachers at a Convention Held on the BYU Campus," August 20, 1953. Quoted in William E. Berrett and Alma P. Burton, *Readings in L.D.S. Church History,* 3:348.

33. Dunn interview, October 6, 1995.

34. ELWD, December 18, 1953.

35. ELWD, October 25, 1957.

36. DOMD, December 8, 1958.

37. ELWD, October 29, 1959.

38. ELWD, December 3, 1959.

39. ELWD, December 4, 1959.

40. Quoted in ELWD, February 24, 1960.

41. Report and McKay's comments in DOMD, October 3, 1966.

42. Wilkinson, memorandum, in DOMD, July 25, 1969.

43. Poll interview.

44. DOMD, October 8, 1951.

45. Wilkinson, address to Institute and Seminary Teachers, August 20, 1953, quoted in Berrett and Burton, *Readings in L.D.S. Church History,* 3:348.

46. Harold B. Lee, address to Institute and Seminary Teachers at a convention held on the BYU campus, August 21, 1953. Quoted in Berrett and Burton, *Readings in L.D.S. Church History,* 3:351.

47. DOMD, March 3, 1958.

48. ELWD, March 13, 1959.

49. ELWD, April 23, 1959.

50. ELWD, April 26, 1959.

51. ELWD, April 28, 1959.

52. ELWD, April 29, 1959.

53. ELWD, April 30, 1959.

54. Gary J. Bergera and Ronald Priddis, *Brigham Young University,* 70.

55. ELWD, June 15, 1954.

56. ELWD, entry under the date of December 29, 1958–January 16, 1959.

57. ELWD, April 23, 1959.

58. Ibid. Wilkinson's diary does not include the minutes.

59. ELWD, February 24, 1960.

60. ELWD, March 3, 1960.

61. In 1965 Wilkinson attended a three-day John Birch Society symposium in Illinois. He and two other attendees "agreed individually among ourselves that we would not join the society, even though in general we agree with its purposes and objectives." ELWD, August 19–22, 1965.

62. Wilkinson, memorandum, in DOMD, March 7, 1962.

63. DOMD, December 17, 1963.

64. Ray C. Hillam, *The BYU Spy Episode,* 28.

65. DOMD, November 10, 1964.

66. DOMD, December 2, 1964. The entry does not indicate whether the vote was unanimous.

67. DOMD, January 3, 1965.

68. DOMD, February 2, 1965.

69. ELWD, February 3, 1965.

70. ELWD, February 5, 1965; italics ours.

71. DOMD, April 19, 1965.

72. Hillam, *The BYU Spy Episode,* 1. The Forum series, held Thursday mornings at 10:00 A.M., featured speakers addressing national political, cultural, and/or educational issues. The Devotional series,

held at the same time Tuesday mornings, featured addresses by General Authorities. No classes were scheduled at these hours, and Wilkinson made it clear that all students were expected to attend.

73. DOMD, February 5, 1967.

74. DOMD, March 6, 1967.

75. Ibid.

76. Hillam, *The BYU Spy Episode*.

77. DOMD, March 6, 1967.

78. Quoted in Hillam, *The BYU Spy Episode,* 16.

79. Wilkinson, "Memorandum of Conference with President David O. McKay on Wednesday, March 15, 1967," DOMD.

80. Ibid. There is no record that Wilkinson subsequently hired anyone with FBI experience.

81. Hillam, *The BYU Spy Episode,* 13.

82. Ibid., 24. The two professors who accompanied Hillam were Ed Morrell and Richard Wirthlin.

83. DOMD, July 25, 1969.

84. Wilkinson, *Brigham Young University,* 3:745.

85. John T. Bernhard interview.

86. McKay quoted in Reuben D. Law, *The Founding and Early Development of the Church College of Hawaii,* 29.

87. Edward Lavaun Clissold interview.

88. Ibid.

89. Ibid.

90. Leon R. Hartshorn, "Mormon Education in the Bold Years," 202.

91. Clissold interview.

92. Michael Grilikhes interview. Mendenhall had involved Howard Anderson, then president of the California Mission, in the Polynesian Cultural Center's planning, and Anderson had introduced Grilikhes, a CBS executive, to Mendenhall. Anderson, Grilikhes, and Prince were all members of the Westwood Ward at the time.

93. Howard B. Anderson interview, February 7, 1997.

94. Grilikhes interview.

95. Ibid.

96. Howard B. Anderson interview, October 5, 1999.

97. Ibid.

98. Clissold interview.

99. Anderson interview, October 5, 1999.

100. Grilikhes interview.

101. Ernest L. Wilkinson, "Statement of sequence of events, information considered by, and reasons for the decision of the Board of Education of the Church of Jesus Christ of Latter-day Saints, to move Ricks College to Idaho Falls—Reasons for its change of mind," DOMD, December 21, 1958.

102. Executive Committee, General Board of Education of the Church of Jesus Christ of Latter-day Saints, Minutes, February 8, 1928. Quoted in William P. Miller, "Weber College, 1888 to 1933," 37.

103. Minutes, Church General Board of Education, February 20, 1929. Quoted in ibid., 32.

104. Executive Committee, General Board of Education of the Church of Jesus Christ of Latter-day Saints, Minutes, February 24, 1931. Quoted in Ibid., 42.

105. "Lee Advises Church [Will] Get 3 Schools," *Deseret News,* February 15, 1951.

106. DOMD, February 16, 1951.

107. DOMD, August 31, 1953.

108. ELWD, November 12, 1953.

109. Paraphrased in DOMD, December 10, 1953.

110. ELWD, December 14, 1953.

111. ELWD, December 21, 1953.

112. ELWD, December 27, 1953.

113. Stephen L Richards to David O. McKay, January 11, 1954, DOMS #138.

114. J. Bracken Lee to the First Presidency, May 14, 1954, DOMS #30.

115. "Church Stand on Colleges Told to Lee," *Deseret News,* May 28, 1954.

116. DOMD, August 18, 1954.

117. DOMD, August 30, 1954.

118. ELWD, November 12, 1954.

119. DOMD, September 28, 1954.

120. David O. McKay to Frank M. Browning, October 23, 1954, DOMD, October 23, 1954.

121. "McKay Denies LDS Drive for Colleges," *Salt Lake Tribune,* October 29, 1954.

122. "Utah Voters Defeat Three Ballot Issues," *Deseret News,* November 3, 1954.

123. ELWD, November 12, 1954.

124. ELWD, May 24, 1957.

125. J. Bracken Lee interview.

126. For a detailed account of the Ricks College issue see Val G. Hemming, "Ricks College."

127. Ibid., 60–61.

128. ELWD, March 25, 1954.

129. ELWD, July 7, 1954.

130. ELWD, April 16, 1957.

131. DOMD, April 25, 1957.

132. ELWD, April 26, 1957.

133. DOMD, May 21, 1957.

134. ELWD, July 11, 1957.

135. DOMD, July 11, 1957. Ten days later Wilkinson wrote in his diary, "I should here record that my indignation is not that President McKay decided to leave the school at Rexburg, but that the decision was made on the ground that notwithstanding every argument was in favor of moving it to Idaho Falls, he felt that he had promised a few years previously that it would be left at Rexburg." ELWD, July 21, 1957.

136. DOMD, July 11, 1957.

137. ELWD, June 30, 1958.

138. ELWD, October 13, 1958. Nearly all of Wilkinson's diaries are typed from his dictations. This entry, in contrast, is in his handwriting. He does not say who made the proposal about building a junior college in Idaho Falls.

139. DOMD, October 31, 1958. McKay's papers do not include this letter from the stake presidents nor the information about whether personnel in the stake presidency had changed since 1957.

140. ELWD, entry dated "October 29–November 3, 1958."

141. "Move 'Final' for Ricks, Church Leader Says," *Salt Lake Tribune,* November 16, 1958.

142. ELWD, entry dated "November 18–November 28, 1958."

143. DOMD, December 28, 1958.

144. DOMD, February 10, 1959.

145. DOMD, February 13, 1959.

146. ELWD, May 6, 1960.

147. DOMD, May 2, 1960.

148. ELWD, June 11, 1960.

149. DOMD, June 25, 1960.

150. DOMD, June 30, 1960.

151. ELWD, October 19, 1960.

152. DOMD, September 20, 1961.

153. ELWD, November 4, 1959.

154. ELWD, December 4, 1959.

155. DOMD, January 7, 1960.

156. ELWD, January 11, 1960.

157. ELWD, April 28, 1960.

158. ELWD, June 23, 1960.

159. ELWD, September 7, 1960.

160. ELWD, November 23, 1960.

161. ELWD, May 11, 1961.

162. ELWD, May 22, 1961.

163. ELWD, August 16, 1962.

164. ELWD, October 9, 1962.

165. DOMD, March 5, 1963. This is the first mention of Packer's letter in the McKay diary, so it is not clear when he received it, when he gave it to the executive committee, or what instructions he transmitted with it.

166. Dale Tingey interview. The executive committee consisted of Joseph Fielding Smith, chair, Harold B. Lee, Delbert L. Stapley, Marion G. Romney, LeGrand Richards, Howard W. Hunter, Gordon B. Hinckley, and Boyd K. Packer. All were apostles with the exception of Packer. Romney did not attend this meeting.

167. DOMD, March 5, 1963.

168. Ibid.

169. ELWD, March 5, 1963.

170. ELWD, March 13, 1963.

171. ELWD, May 28, 1963.

172. Wilkinson, *Brigham Young University,* 3:170.

173. J. Alan Blodgett to Prince, November 5, 1999.

174. *Deseret News 2004 Church Almanac,* 6.

CHAPTER 9 – THE BUILDING PROGRAM

1. DOMD, August 27 and 28, 1897. In Stan Larson and Patricia Larson, eds., *What E'er Thou Art Act Well Thy Part,* 11–12.

2. McKay, "A Dream Fulfilled."

3. "Record of Missionary Work in South Australian Conference, 1913–1923," August 21, 1921. Quoted in Marjorie Newton, *Southern Cross Saints,* 80.

4. Reed Smoot, Diary, July 19 and 20, 1923, in Harvard S. Heath, ed., *In the World,* 545–46.

5. David O. McKay to the First Presidency, November 7, 1923, DOMS #132.

6. David O. McKay to James E. Talmage, September 10, 1924, DOMS #132.

7. Edgar B. Brossard interview.

8. James B. Allen and Richard O. Cowan, *Mormonism in the Twentieth Century,* 116.

9. A. Hamer Reiser interview, September 10, 1974.

10. Clark's role in church government as well as his personal and administrative relationship to McKay are described in D. Michael Quinn, *Elder Statesman.*

11. J. Reuben Clark Jr., April 5, 1940, *Conference Report,* April 1940, 17.

12. DOMD, June 8, 1950.

13. Arch L. Madsen interview, June 11, 1981.

14. Howard B. Anderson interview, February 7, 1997.

15. "Mormons' Leader Visits Los Angeles," *Los Angeles Times,* April 29, 1951.

16. "Record Crowds Expected to Attend LDS Meeting," *Salt Lake Tribune,* October 1, 1951. The "indefinite date" proved to be a half-century later, when the fifteenth church president, Gordon B. Hinckley, constructed a slightly smaller Conference Center, seating 21,000, on the site McKay had chosen.

17. DOMD, April 17, 1952.

18. LeGrand Richards interview.

19. Ibid.

20. Clifton G. M. Kerr interview.

21. Bernard P. Brockbank interview. In 1962, Brockbank became as an Assistant to the Twelve, later a member of the First Quorum of the Seventy.

22. DOMD, June 23, 1952.

23. "Mormon Church to Expand: More Chapels for Union, Says U.S. Leader," *Cape Times,* January 13, 1954.

24. David O. McKay, October 3, 1952, *Conference Report,* October 1952, 8.

25. "Howard McKean, Church Building Chairman, Dies," *Deseret News & Salt Lake Telegram,* April 18, 1955.

26. DOMD, May 4, 1955.

27. Edward Lavaun Clissold interview.

28. DOMD, February 3, 1954.

29. David W. Cummings, *Mighty Missionary of the Pacific,* 38.

30. DOMD, March 16, 1955.

31. "Church Appoints Head of Building Committee," *Deseret News & Salt Lake Telegram,* July 19, 1955. Mendenhall appointed an all-new committee consisting of John H. Vandenberg, businessman; Harry E. McClure, contractor; Harold W. Burton, architect; and Raymond H. Bradfield, contractor.

32. Michael Grilikhes interview.

33. John H. Vandenberg interview, November 15, 1984.

34. J. Alan Blodgett to Prince, October 19, 1999.

35. Ibid.

36. Richard D. Poll, *Working the Divine Miracle,* 194.

37. DOMD, October 6, 1958; "Labor-Missionary Program Adopted for European Chapels," *Church News,* July 9, 1960.

38. DOMD, September 7, 1960.

39. Robert L. Simpson interview.

40. J. Howard Dunn interview. Dunn was a member of the Church Building Committee under Mendenhall and was released with him.

41. Owen Cook interview.

42. Robert Sears interview.

43. Paul H. Dunn interview, June 5, 1995. In the church at that time, oversight for ecclesiastical functions (missions, stakes, and wards) was separate from physical facilities (building construction/mainte-nance, real estate, etc.). Both functions are now coordinated through area presidents.

44. William S. Erekson interview.

45. Stanford Bird interview.

46. Levi Berg Thorup interview.

47. A. Hamer Reiser interview, September 24, 1974.

48. "800 Chapels to be Built by Church in '60," *Church News,* July 23, 1960.

49. DOMD, September 22, 1961.

50. McKay, "I Feel Your Welcome."

51. "Tributes to President David O. McKay," *Improvement Era* 66 (September 1963): 747.

52. Henry D. Moyle Jr. interview.

53. William Bates interview, October 3, 2000. Kingdom Hall is the name Jehovah's Witnesses give to their unadorned, often rented meeting places.

54. Blodgett to Prince, October 15, 1999. For details about the BYU expansion, see chapter 8.

55. Howard B. Anderson interview, October 5, 1999.

56. Richard Moyle interview.

57. ELWD, October 22, 1959.

58. ELWD, December 4, 1959.

59. ELWD, October 13, 1960.

60. ELWD, October 19, 1960.

61. DOMD, October 25, 1960.

62. DOMD, December 27, 1960.

63. ELWD, September 21, 1961.

64. ELWD, September 25, 1961.

65. DOMD, November 1, 1961; ELWD, December 29, 1961.

66. ELWD, November 9, 1961.

67. DOMD, December 1, 1961.

68. Blodgett to Prince, November 2, 1999.

69. Goates, *Harold B. Lee,* 381–82.

70. DOMD, May 25, 1962.

71. DOMD, July 14, 1962.

72. DOMD, July 19, 1962.

73. DOMD, July 20, 1962.

74. David M. Kennedy interview.

75. Blodgett to Prince, November 2, 1999.

76. DOMD, January 18, 1963. He recorded only the percentage, not the dollar amount.

77. DOMD, May 1, 1963.

78. DOMD, March 27, 1963.

79. DOMD, July 23, 1963.

80. Poll, *Working the Divine Miracle,* 216. Joseph Fielding Smith, president of the Quorum of the Twelve, replaced him.

81. Bird interview.

82. DOMD, April 25, 1963.

83. Ibid.

84. DOMD April 25, 1963.

85. B. Z. "Bud" Kastler interview.

86. DOMD, January 24, 1964.

87. DOMD, March 5, 1964.

88. DOMD, March 20, 1964.

89. DOMD, July 15, 1964.

90. DOMD, September 29, 1964.

91. DOMD, October 13, 1964.

92. Richard W. Jackson, *Places of Worship,* 312; DOMD, October 23, 1964.

93. Quoted in DOMD, October 23, 1964.

94. DOMD, December 10, 1964.

95. Blodgett to Prince, November 3, 1999.

96. DOMD, October 21, 1964.

97. Ibid.

98. DOMD, November 13, 1964

99. DOMD, December 15, 1964.

100. DOMD, December 21, 1964.

101. DOMD, December 31, 1964.

102. DOMD, January 5, 1965.

103. "First Presidency Administrative Problems," January 5, 1965, DOMD.

104. Ibid.

105. G. Homer Durham, *N. Eldon Tanner,* 215.

106. Clare Middlemiss, "Notes," March 19, 1965.

107. Paul H. Dunn interview, January 11, 1997.

108. Memo to David O. McKay, January 21, 1965, signed by Delbert L. Stapley (Chairman), LeGrand Richards, Howard W. Hunter, Franklin D. Richards, and Thorpe B. Isaacson, DOMD.

109. DOMD, March 31, 1965.

110. DOMD, April 8, 1965.

111. DOMD, April 15, 1965. The minutes of the Quorum of the Twelve and First Presidency are not currently open to researchers.

112. DOMD, April 16, 1965.

113. DOMD, April 22, 1965.

114. "Building Chief Resigns Job with LDS Church," *Salt Lake Tribune,* April 28, 1965.

115. DOMD, May 19, 1965.

116. DOMD, June 10, 1965.

117. DOMD, July 15, 1965.

118. Grilikhes interview.

119. Blodgett to Prince, November 2, 1999.

120. Ibid.

121. DOMD, April 27, 1965.

122. DOMD, May 6, 1965.

123. DOMD, May 19, 1965.

124. DOMD, May 20, 1965.

125. DOMD, June 1, 1965.

126. DOMD, June 9, 1965. Garff's committee consisted of Fred Baker, Julian S. Cannon, Emil Fetzer, Victor Laughlin, and Horace A. Christiansen.

127. Horace A. Christiansen interview.

128. DOMD, September 23, 1965. One striking example of over-building was given by Paul H. Dunn, interview, June 2, 1995: "I was on a kind of fact-finding trip with Harold B. Lee in the Pacific, on the Building Committee.... In Tahiti—I don't mean just the main island, I'm talking about some atolls—there'd be a stake center the size of downtown Salt Lake, and there might be a membership of 35."

129. DOMD, September 24, 1965.

130. One year following this report, Prince arrived in Brazil to serve a two-year mission, which included five months in the city of Uruguaiana. The recently completed chapel in that city, as large as the average LDS chapel in the United States, was home to a congregation whose average weekly attendance was fewer than thirty.

131. DOMD, March 30, 1966.

132. DOMD, December 20, 1966.

133. Blodgett to Prince, November 9, 1999.

134. DOMD, April 25, 1967.

135. DOMD, September 17, 1969.

136. Blodgett to Prince, October 19, 1999.

137. Paul H. Dunn interview, June 5, 1995.

138. Garff reported to McKay that during his first three years on the job, he was so preoccupied with church matters that he neglected his own company, whose failure cost him $1 million. DOMD, July 5, 1968.

139. Blodgett to Prince, November 3, 1999.

CHAPTER 10 – THE MISSIONARY PROGRAM

1. Doctrine and Covenants 16:6, 17:6.

2. Doctrine and Covenants 18:14–15.

3. Quoted in Richard D. Poll, *Working the Divine Miracle,* 199.

4. Alice Moyle Yeates interview.

5. "Special Missionary Conference—127th Annual General Conference," *Church News,* April 13, 1957, DOMS #37.

6. Thomas Bowring Woodbury II interview.

7. DOMD, July 30, 1958.

8. Woodbury interview.

9. Henry D. Moyle Jr. interview. The Reiser family disputes the accuracy of the statement attributed to A. Hamer Reiser.

10. Richard Mavin, "The Woodbury Years," 56–57.

11. DOMD, December 7, 1951.

12. "Church Progress in Europe," Editorial, *Deseret News,* November 27, 1959.

13. DOMD, February 3, 1960.

14. DOMD, March 15, 1960.

15. "New Program to Intensify Supervision of World-wide Church Missions," *Church News,* July 1, 1961.

16. "Good-bye Nineteen Twenty-three," Editorial, *Millennial Star* 85 (December 27, 1923): 824.

17. DOMD, September 6, 1953.

18. T. Bowring Woodbury diary, November 27, 1959.

19. Asael Sorensen interview.

20. Edgar B. Brossard interview.

21. First Presidency circular letter, February 3, 1960, DOMS #47.

22. Moyle interview.

23. Howard B. Anderson interview, February 7, 1997.

24. Moyle interview.

25. Joel Izatt interview.

26. Woodbury diary, January 23, 1959. The Dyer lesson outlines should not be confused with the six-lesson Anderson plan developed in the Northwestern States Mission in the 1950s, which later became standard worldwide.

27. Levi B. Thorup interview.

28. Howard B. Anderson interview, February 7, 1997.

29. Moyle interview.

30. Brent Rushforth interview.

31. Gary L. Browning interview.

32. Yeates interview.

33. Kahlile B. Mehr, "The Trial of the French Mission."

34. Woodbury diary, May 23, 1959.

35. William Bates interview, October 3, 2000.

36. Woodbury diary, August 3, 1959.

37. Ibid., March 27, 1960.

38. Ibid., June 25, 1960.

39. T. Bowring Woodbury to David O. McKay, June 29, 1960, DOMS #199.

40. David O. McKay to T. Bowring Woodbury, July 19, 1960, DOMS #199. Emphasis McKay's.

41. Bernard P. Brockbank to David O. McKay, September 3, 1960, DOMS #199.

42. "British Missions Pass Goal of 1,000 Converts," *Church News,* September 17, 1960.

43. Woodbury diary, November 27, 1960.

44. "Missionary Activity Boosts Baptisms to New High in 1960," *Church News,* December 31, 1960.

45. "8,000 Missionaries, Serving Full-time, Carry Gospel Message," *Church News,* December 31, 1960.

46. T. Bowring and Beulah Woodbury to David O. McKay, September 8, 1961, DOMS #200.

47. Several such letters are in the DOMS #200.

48. *Conference Report,* April 1961, 27–28; ibid., April 1962, 22–23.

49. "Spirit of Conversion Places 75,700 on Mission Records," *Church News,* December 20, 1961.

50. Undated [1965] memo from Theodore L. Cannon, Church Information Service, to Clare Middlemiss, DOMS #150.

51. Woodbury diary, May 23, 1959.

52. T. Bowring Woodbury, "To All Supervising Elders," Bulletin M-13 3/59.

53. T. Bowring Woodbury, "To Traveling and Supervising Elders," Bulletin M-26 4/59.

54. Irene Bates interview.

55. Woodbury diary, January 1, 1961.

56. Ibid., October 29, 1960.

57. Ibid., November 27, 1960.

58. Ibid., January 1, 1961.

59. Izatt interview.

60. Franklin J. Murdock interview, March 29, 1973.

61. Clifton G. M. Kerr interview.

62. Browning interview.

63. Thorup interview.

64. Paul H. Dunn interview, June 5, 1995.

65. William Clayton ("Tony") Kimball interview.

66. Gary Stevens interview.

67. Kerr interview.

68. Hyrum Smith interview.

69. Mavin, "The Woodbury Years," 57.

70. Ronald Watt interview.

71. Albert Roy interview.

72. Mavin, "The Woodbury Years," 57.

73. Ibid., 58.

74. Arch J. Turvey interview.

75. Peter L. Morley interview.

76. Wilfrid Clark interview.

77. ELWD, September 6, 1960.

78. Joseph Fielding Smith to Lowell L. Bennion, March 13, 1961. Quoted in Mary L. Bradford, *Lowell L. Bennion,* 142. Two years later, when Moyle was relieved of his duties on the Missionary Committee and Smith became chairman of the committee, Smith wrote a stinging letter to a mission president who was still engaging in questionable baptisms: "I hold in my hand a long list of reported baptisms from your mission of children who never should have been baptized and evidently without the consent of their parents.... It appears to me that what we are working for is a record and making such sacred ordinances of the church a farce. Missionaries are not sent into the field to compete in baptisms and no person should be baptized without conforming with the covenant of baptism and no child without the full consent of parents. This action is causing a condition that could bring serious trouble and someone might eventually lose his life." Joseph Fielding Smith to Delmont H. White, Central Atlantic States Mission, October 25, 1963. Photocopy in Prince's possession.

79. ELWD, May 25, 1961.

80. Copy of presentation in Richard D. Poll Papers, Box 68, Fd. 11.

81. Hugh B. Brown, "Don't Lose the Shepherds," *Improvement Era* 64 (October 1961): 724–36.

82. A. Hamer Reiser interview, August 30, 1974.

83. DOMD, February 16, 1961.

84. DOMD, February 28, 1961.

85. Ibid.

86. David O. McKay, "What It Means to Be a Missionary," address to the missionaries of the Scotch-Irish Mission, Glasgow, Scotland, February 28, 1961, DOMP.

87. "Mormons and Young Converts," *Glasgow Herald,* March 1, 1961, DOMS #148.

88. "Challenge to the Kirk—From Mormon Leader," *Scottish Daily Express,* March 1, 1961, DOMS #148.

89. Woodbury diary, March 3, 1961.

90. Marion D. Hanks interview.

91. First Presidency to T. Bowring Woodbury, October 11, 1961. In Woodbury diary, November 12, 1961.

92. DOMD, December 5, 1962. J. Alan Blodgett, who was a financial officer for the church at this time, confirmed that Woodbury remained in good standing with McKay: "After his mission, By Woodbury

took a job with Zions First National Bank in a customer relations role. I became rather well acquainted with By, and recall no evidence whatsoever that he had fallen in disrepute. There was talk about the 'baseball baptisms,' but that was merely regarded as an overly exuberant program with no real harm done. It would be very difficult not to like By. He was a genuine, warm and interesting person who displayed a great respect for church leaders and love of the gospel. His appearance was striking, he was proper, a dapper dresser, trim and erect, always cheerful and friendly. Roy Simmons, CEO of Zion's First National Bank, was acutely tuned in to the attitudes of the brethren. If he had detected that By had a cloud over him, I doubt he would have assigned By to interface with the church." J. Alan Blodgett to Prince, November 4, 1999.

93. Marion D. Hanks to Clare Middlemiss, December 15, 1965, DOMS #83.

94. First Presidency circular letter, "To All Mission Presidents," November 30, 1962.

95. Thorup interview.

96. Peggy Petersen Barton, *Mark E. Petersen*, 122.

97. DOMD, January 31, 1963.

98. DOMD, June 28, 1963.

99. Dunn interview.

100. Quoted in Poll, *Working the Divine Miracle*, 216.

101. DOMD, July 25, 1963.

102. DOMD, August 26, 1963.

103. DOMD, October 9, 1963.

104. DOMD, February 19, 1964. At that time, the only mechanism for removing a name from membership records was excommunication, done by convening a formal "bishop's court." In 1989, the procedure was modified so that an individual can request name removal by letter. In such cases, the term "excommunication" is no longer used.

105. Stevens interview.

106. James Foulger interview.

107. Smith interview.

108. David Timmins, undated letter [1999] to Prince. For another missionary's experience during the "clean-up" phase see D. Michael Quinn, "I–Thou vs. I–It Conversions: The Mormon 'Baseball Baptism' Era."

109. DOMD, October 17, 1968.

110. *Conference Report*, April 1960 and April 1963.

111. A. Theodore Tuttle interview, November 22, 1977.

112. Moyle interview.

113. J. Alan Blodgett to Prince, November 2, 1999.

114. *Deseret News 1983 Church Almanac*, 135–38.

115. Kerr interview.

116. Spencer W. Kimball, "Priesthood Missionary Work in the Church."

117. *Conference Report*, April 1975 and April 1982.

118. J. Alan Blodgett to Prince, November 4, 1999.

CHAPTER 11 – TEMPLE BUILDING

1. Luke 24:48.

2. For a detailed account of the development of endowment and temple theology, see Prince, *Power from On High*.

3. Title to the Kirtland "House of the Lord" eventually went to the Reorganized Church of Jesus Christ of Latter Day Saints (now Community of Christ), while the Nauvoo Temple was destroyed by fire shortly after the main body of church members emigrated to the Salt Lake Valley.

4. Chad M. Orton, *More Faith than Fear*, 119–21.

5. J. Reuben Clark to David O. McKay, June 14, 1937, J. Reuben Clark Papers, Box 358.

6. Report of Preston Richards and Edward Anderson to David O. McKay, DOMD, September 14, 1951.

7. Ibid.

8. DOMD, September 22, 1951.

9. DOMD, February 3 and 18, 1952.

10. DOMD, October 27, 1953.

11. DOMD, February 1, 1953.

12. DOMD, August 11, 1952.

13. Ibid.

14. John M. Russon interview.

15. DOMD, September 11 and 15, 1953.

16. DOMD, October 13, 1953.

17. DOMD, July 11, 1954.

18. Arnold Friberg interview.

19. DOMD, August 5, 1954.

20. Friberg interview.

21. DOMD, March 10, 1956.

22. DOMD, April 14, 1956.

23. Eugene Hilton, "Temple Hill (Oakland)," DOMD, January 23, 1961.

24. DOMD, April 6, 1943.

25. DOMD, May 21, 1957.

26. DOMD, June 12, 1957.

27. DOMD, November 22, 1960.

28. DOMD, January 23, 1961. McKay did not give the source of the quoted prophecy.

29. DOMD, November 30, 1951.

30. DOMD, January 3, 1952.

31. DOMD, April 17, 1952.

32. DOMD, July 26, 1952; McKay, quoted in Doyle L. Green and Albert L. Zobell, Jr., "A New Era in Church History," 634.

33. David O. McKay to Samuel E. Bringhurst, October 24, 1952, DOMS #134.

34. David O. McKay to Samuel E. Bringhurst, November 24, 1952, DOMS #151.

35. David O. McKay, Minutes of Report on European Trip, Given to the First Presidency and Quorum of the Twelve, August 27, 1953, DOMS #136.

36. David O. McKay to Cecil Bryant Kenner, March 24, 1959, DOMD, March 23, 1959.

37. DOMD, February 20, 1953.

38. DOMD, December 24, 1953.

39. David O. McKay, remarks in General Priesthood Meeting of the 125th Annual General Conference, April 2, 1955, DOMS #37. In his remarks, McKay indicated that Mendenhall had made this trip in December 1954.

40. DOMD, February 17, 1955.

41. Edward R. McKay, remarks at the David O. McKay Symposium.

42. DOMD, November 1, 1961.

43. DOMD, April 18, 1962.

44. In autumn 1999, the temple names, usually identified by country or state, were standardized to include the city name. For example, the Swiss Temple became the Bern Switzerland Temple. Contemporary stake and mission names likewise omit punctuation on this model. The London Temple had been finished three years earlier in September 1958.

45. DOMD, September 18, 1962.

46. DOMD, November 6, 1968.

47. Alvin R. Dyer diary, November 13, 1968, DOMD.

48. DOMD, November 14, 1968. According to the minutes, no one mentioned McKay's by-passing the Committee on Expenditures. Lee was church president while the temple was still under construction, and two concessions to his fears were incorporated into the building: the complete absence of exterior windows (sunlight enters the building through translucent marble), and the presence of riot gates that could quickly be dropped to block unauthorized entrance to the building.

49. DOMD, November 14, 1968.

50. DOMD, November 15, 1968.

51. David S. King interview.

52. First Presidency to Milan D. Smith, Julian C. Lowe, Robert W. Barker, J. Willard Marriott, Wilford M. Burton, and Edgar B. Brossard, November 18, 1968, DOMD.

53. DOMD, November 21, 1968.

54. DOMD, December 7, 1968.

55. DOMD, April 7, 1969.

56. Minutes of a meeting held in the Ogden Third Ward Chapel, February 28, 1953, DOMD.

57. Minutes of a meeting held in the Ogden Stake Tabernacle, March 2, 1959, DOMD.

58. Ibid.

59. DOMD, October 22, 1964.

60. DOMD, April 25, 1967.

61. DOMD, August 8, 1967.

62. Emil B. Fetzer interview. Emphasis his. The Fetzer quotations that follow are from the same interview.

63. David O. McKay, discourse given in the Ha'alaufuli, Vava'u Branch Chapel, Tongan Mission, January 13, 1955, DOMP.

64. DOMD, June 18, 1959.

65. DOMD, March 12, 1954; October 27, 1955; December 28, 1955; May 7, 1964; June 18, 1968.

66. DOMD, May 15, 1962; June 28, 1962.

67. DOMD, April 17, 1968.

68. DOMD, December 1, 1960.

69. DOMD, January 4, 1962.

70. Ibid.

71. The new Nauvoo Temple is a working temple, meaning that most of the interior space is taken up by ordinance rooms. The original Nauvoo Temple accommodated only one endowment ordinance at a time, conducted in the attic story.

72. DOMD, October 11, 1968. McKay's papers do not include a record of the first meeting with Garff in which he gave him the exploratory assignment.

73. Mark Garff, Minutes of a Meeting between Mark Garff and David O. McKay, November 30, 1967, DOMD.

74. Dyer was alluding to Doctrine and Covenants 61:14–19, a revelation given through Joseph Smith on August 12, 1831, which reads in part: "Behold, I, the Lord, . . . in the last days . . . cursed the waters. Wherefore, the days will come that no flesh shall be safe upon the waters."

75. DOMD, October 11, 1968.

76. DOMD, October 24, 1968.

77. DOMD, March 8, 1959.

78. DOMD, April 17, 1951.

79. Hugh B. Brown interview.

80. Quoted in Eugene E. Campbell and Richard D. Poll, *Hugh B. Brown*, 225.

81. DOMD, May 15, 1955.

82. DOMD, March 8, 1959.

83. Monroe G. McKay interview.

84. DOMD, November 8, 1961.

85. DOMD, June 21, 1966.

86. Address delivered by David O. McKay at the dedicatory services of the additions to the Arizona Temple, Mesa, Arizona, December 30, 1956, DOMS #162.

87. DOMD, December 27, 1957. Because the details of the endowment are considered so sacred that they are covered by a covenant of secrecy made by all participants, we provide no description.

88. DOMD, March 28, 1951; August 15, 1954; February 2, 1958; July 20, 1958.

89. Minutes of a meeting with Presidents of Stakes of Weber County, held in the Ogden Stake Tabernacle, March 2, 1959, DOMD.

Chapter 12 – Confrontation with Communism

1. David O. McKay, *Conference Report,* April 1917, 49.

2. First Presidency, "Warning to Church Members," July 3, 1936. *Improvement Era* 39, no. 8 (August 1936): 488.

3. David O. McKay to Jeremiah Stokes, April 19, 1940. Quoted in D. Michael Quinn, *J. Reuben Clark,* 190.

4. McKay, *Conference Report,* April 1942, 71–73.

5. "Faith Triumphant," Church-of-the-Air Broadcast, July 20, 1947. DOMS #12.

6. McKay, *Conference Report,* April 1948, 70.

7. A mission was also operating at this time in the Soviet sector of Germany.

8. Senator Elbert D. Thomas to David O. McKay, February 14, 1950, DOMD. Unless otherwise noted, all correspondence is filed under the date of writing in the McKay diary.

9. Elbert D. Thomas to David O. McKay, February 23, 1950, DOMD.

10. McKay, *Conference Report,* April 1950, 175.

11. DOMD, January 13, 1951.

12. "LDS President Concerned over Red Attitude toward Christianity," *Salt Lake Telegram,* April 26, 1951.

13. "Church Leader Tells Rotary Club of Trip to European Missions," *Deseret News,* August 6, 1952.

14. Minutes of a meeting of the First Presidency and Quorum of the Twelve, August 28, 1952, DOMD.

15. Sheri Dew, *Ezra Taft Benson,* 124. Although 565 pages long, the biography skirts the issue of Benson and Communism to the point where the terms "Communism," "John Birch Society," and "Robert Welch" do not appear in its index.

16. *Business Week,* October 30, 1943.

17. DOMD, August 1 and 5, 1952.

18. DOMD, October 27, 1952.

19. DOMD, November 5, 1952.

20. DOMD, November 20, 1952.

21. Reed Benson interview.

22. Telephone conversation between David O. McKay and Ned Redding, publisher of the *California Intermountain News,* notes in DOMD, November 25, 1952.

23. Transcription of blessing quoted in Dew, *Ezra Taft Benson,* 259.

24. Benson's autobiographical account of his cabinet years was entitled *Cross Fire: The Eight Years with Eisenhower.*

25. DOMD, August 19, 1954.

26. "Forward In Spiritual Ideas," an address delivered by President David O. McKay at a meeting of the Executives of the National Council of the Boy Scouts of America, held in the Statler Hotel, Los Angeles, California, July 17, 1953, DOMP.

27. "Head of Mormons Predicts Revolt in Red Countries," *Los Angeles Times,* April 26, 1954.

28. DOMD, June 3, 1954.

29. Arthur V. Watkins, *Enough Rope,* ix.

30. David O. McKay to Arthur V. Watkins, December 11, 1954. Quoted in Watkins, *Enough Rope,* 195.

31. Arthur V. Watkins to David O. McKay, December 31, 1954. DOMD, December 13, 1954.

32. DOMD, November 15, 1956.

33. DOMD, November 12, 1957.

34. DOMD, June 6, 1958.

35. ELWD, May 24, 1961.

36. DOMD, June 29, 1961.

37. Robert Welch, *The Blue Book,* 108. For an overview of the John Birch Society, see Seymour Martin Lipset and Earl Raab, *The Politics of Unreason.*

38. D. Michael Quinn, "Ezra Taft Benson and Mormon Political Conflicts," 7–8.

39. Reed Benson interview.

40. DOMD, August 17, 1961.

41. Reed Benson interview. Emphasis his.

42. Ezra Taft Benson, *Conference Report,* October 1961, 73–74.

43. Hugh B. Brown to Alicia Bingham, December 28, 1961, Box 48, fd. 21, Firmage Papers.

44. ELWD, December 29, 1961.

45. DOMD, February 15, 1962.

46. DOMD, February 19, 1962.

47. "LDS Hits Extremes in Anti-Red Battle," *Salt Lake Tribune,* April 7, 1962.

48. Harley R. Hammond to Hugh B. Brown, April 24, 1962.

49. Hugh B. Brown to Harley R. Hammond, April 25, 1962.

50. DOMD, May 18, 1962.

51. DOMD, October 26, 1962.

52. "Reed A. Benson Takes Post in Birch Society," *Deseret News,* October 27, 1962.

53. "Ezra Benson's Son Takes Birch Society Post," *Sacramento Bee,* October 27, 1962; "Benson Birch Tie Disturbs Utahans," *New York Times,* November 4, 1962.

54. Henry D. Moyle to J. D. Williams, January 9, 1963. Photocopy in authors' possession.

55. "Church Sets Policy on Birch Society," *Deseret News,* January 3, 1963.

56. J. D. Williams to the First Presidency, January 4, 1963. Photocopy on authors' possession.

57. DOMD, January 4, 1963.

58. DOMD, January 6, 1963. McKay's diaries make no earlier reference to Reed Benson's use of LDS chapels.

59. DOMD, January 23, 1963.

60. ELWD, January 31, 1963.

61. DOMD, February 4, 1963.

62. *John Birch Society Bulletin,* February 1963, 28–29. McKay eventually received more than two thousand such letters. See DOMD, February 26, 1963.

63. DOMD, February 4, 1963.

64. ELWD, March 3, 1963.

65. "Benson Not Speaking for Mormons on Birch," *Los Angeles Times,* March 4, 1963.

66. DOMD, March 6, 1963.

67. Lela (Mrs. Mark A.) Benson to Clare Middlemiss, March 12, 1963. There is no other correspondence from Lela Benson in Middlemiss's papers.

68. "Elder Benson Makes Statement," *Church News,* March 16, 1963.

69. "Benson Clarifies Views on Birch Society Stand," *Salt Lake Tribune,* March 21, 1963.

70. ELWD, May 13, 1963.

71. Quoted in L. Ralph Mecham to Prince, March 21, 2001.

72. Paul H. Dunn interview, May 21, 1996.

73. DOMD, August 9, 1963.

74. Quoted in Dew, *Ezra Taft Benson,* 371–72.

75. Robert Welch, *The Politician,* 133. Emphasis in original.

76. "Benson Speaker at Testimonial Dinner," Associated Press Wire Service, Los Angeles, September 24, 1963.

77. DOMD, September 24, 1963.

78. Ralph R. Harding interview, October 24, 2000.

79. Ibid.

80. Harding, *Congressional Record, House of Representatives,* 109 (September 25, 1963): 18125–28. The original was not titled; however, Harding had the speech reprinted at his expense by the Government Printing Office. That version is titled: "Ezra Taft Benson's Support of John Birch Society Is Criticized."

81. Dwight D. Eisenhower to Ralph R. Harding, October 7, 1963. Photocopy in authors' possession.

82. L. Ralph Mecham to Prince, March 21, 2001.

83. DOMD, October 18, 1963.

84. Dew, *Ezra Taft Benson,* 371–72.

85. Robert R. McKay to Ralph R. Harding, October 18, 1963. Photocopy in authors' possession.

86. Joseph Fielding Smith to Ralph R. Harding, October 30, 1963.

87. "Elder Benson to Direct European Mission," *Deseret News,* October 24, 1963; "Apostle Benson Denies Being Sent into 'Exile' for Political Views," *Ogden Standard-Examiner,* October 29, 1963.

88. Nelson Wadsworth, "Mormons Split over John Birch Society Campaign," *National Observer,* November 4, 1963. The *National Observer,* published in Washington, D.C., was a Dow-Jones Company newspaper published 1962–77.

89. Drew Pearson (1897–1969) was an influential columnist and radio broadcaster. His column "Merry-Go-Round" was published in newspapers throughout the United States. A strong supporter of the New Deal and the United Nations, he openly opposed Joseph McCarthy and helped bring about his downfall.

90. Ezra Taft Benson, "We Must Become Alerted and Informed." Attached to the typescript is the analysis tying it to the *Blue Book,* which was prepared by B. Delworth Gardner, N. Keith Roberts, and E. Boyd Wennergren. Pearson's column, "Benson's Cure for Communism," appeared in the *Washington Post* on January 4, 1964.

91. Frank E. Moss to Hugh B. Brown, December 20, 1963, Moss Papers.

92. Joseph Fielding Smith to Ralph R. Harding, December 23, 1963. Photocopy in authors' possession.

93. DOMD, December 23, 1963. McKay's delay in answering this request, which he had received four months earlier, was no doubt because he had suffered a stroke several weeks earlier and had been convalescing.

94. Ralph R. Harding interview.

95. "Ike Praises Idaho Solon for Benson Criticism," *Salt Lake Tribune,* February 21, 1964.

96. DOMD, February 20, 1964.

97. A lengthy account of the meeting, from which the succeeding quotations are taken, is in DOMD, March 5, 1964.

98. Louis Midgley, "Birch Society Reviewed by Prof. Louis Midgley," *(BYU) Daily Universe,* May 22, 1964.

99. DOMD, May 26, 1964.

100. David O. McKay to Earl C. Crockett, June 4, 1964, DOMD, May 26, 1964. Crockett was acting BYU president while Ernest Wilkinson ran unsuccessfully for the U.S. Senate. Wilkinson returned to BYU in 1965 and, after McKay's death, lamented to Benson that McKay's instructions had blocked any attempts to establish a chapter of the John Birch Society at BYU: "I would personally like to have one at BYU, and I am seeing what I can do, but my lieutenants insist I would be violating the letter that President McKay sent us sometime ago if I did." Ernest L. Wilkinson to Ezra Taft Benson, May 4, 1971. Photocopy in authors' possession.

101. DOMD, August 18, 1964.

102. Ezra Taft Benson to Clare Middlemiss, August 19, 1964. Photocopy in authors' possession.

103. DOMD, September 17, 1964.

104. *American Opinion,* October 1964.

105. Jack Anderson, "Reed Benson Spreads Birch Gospel," *Washington Post,* January 15, 1965. In response to Anderson's column, the *John Birch Society Bulletin* in its March 1965 issue, referred to Anderson as Drew Pearson's "right-hand stooge,...viciously attacking what Anderson referred to as 'the Benson father-and-son team.'" Jack Anderson (1922–) began his career as a journalist when he was hired by Drew Pearson to work at the *Washington Post*. Following Pearson's death, he took over the "Merry-Go-Round" column. Like his mentor, Anderson openly opposed Joseph McCarthy and helped bring about his downfall.

106. ELWD, April 6, 1965.

107. "Benson Ties Rights Issue to Reds in Mormon Rift," *Washington Post,* April 13, 1965.

108. Ibid.

109. DOMD, April 23, 1965. There is no documentation in the McKay papers on the instructions to which Brown refers.

110. DOMD, May 3, 1965.

111. DOMD, April 23, 1965.

112. DOMD, October 21, 1965.

113. Thorpe B. Isaacson to David O. McKay, October 21, 1965, DOMD.

114. DOMD, November 19, 1965. Isaacson later elected not to go to the seminar. In January 1966, Isaacson suffered a massive stroke which immobilized him until his death in November 1970.

115. Clare Middlemiss, "Notes," November 24, 1965.

116. DOMD, January 11, 1966.

117. "LDS Apostle Backs up Birch Group," *Salt Lake Tribune,* January 16, 1966.

118. Wallace F. Bennett to David Lawrence McKay, January 21, 1966. Bennett Papers.

119. DOMD, February 9, 1966.

120. Three years earlier, Benson had described the John Birch Society's activities to McKay, including the fact that "they have a magazine called *American Opinion.*" DOMD October 26, 1962. However, 1966 events make it clear that the ninety-two-year-old McKay had no recollection of this previous conversation.

121. DOMD, February 18, 1966.

122. DOMD, February 19, 1966.

123. There was concern on the part of some correspondents that Middlemiss might intercept mail addressed to McKay. For example, Robert H. Hinckley, who worked for the American Broadcasting Company in New York, wrote a letter to McKay on March 17, 1966 (photocopy in authors' possession), to which he added the following postscript: "Forgive me for sending this letter via your son, but I am concerned that some letters may not be getting beyond the desk of Miss Middlemiss."

124. DOMD, March 8, 1966. Subsequent quotations from the meeting come from this source, all of which were included under the same date in McKay's diary.

125. J. Reese Hunter, Dinner Chairman, to "Dear Brethren," March 8, 1966. In DOMD, March 15, 1966.

126. "Notice to Church Members," *Deseret News,* March 16, 1966.

127. Hinckley to McKay, March 17, 1966.

128. DOMD, March 23, 1966.

129. DOMD, March 24, 1966.

130. DOMD, March 29, 1966.

131. Ezra Taft Benson to David O. McKay, March 25, 1966, DOMD.

132. *John Birch Society Bulletin,* March 1966, 22–24.

133. Robert Gottlieb and Peter Wiley, *America's Saints,* 78.

134. McKay, *Conference Report,* April 1966, 109. Italics ours.

135. DOMD, April 12, 1966.

136. "Statement Concerning the Position of the Church on Communism," *Church News,* April 16, 1966.

137. DOMD, April 15, 1966.

138. [Mark E. Petersen], "Politics and Religion," editorial, *Church News,* March 26, 1966.

139. DOMD, April 18, 1966.

140. DOMD, April 16, 1966.

141. Middlemiss, "Notes," April 21, 1966.

142. Middlemiss, "Notes," April 22, 1966.

143. DOMD, April 16, 1966.

144. "Presidential Draft for Elder Benson," *Deseret News,* May 3, 1966.

145. "Mormons & Politics—Benson's Influence Helps Keep Growing Church on Conservative Track," *Wall Street Journal,* August 8, 1966.

146. Drew Pearson, "Mormons Reverse Clock," *Washington Post,* October 16, 1966.

147. DOMD, October 31, 1966.

148. Benson, *Conference Report,* October 1966, 122.

149. Hugh B. Brown to David O. McKay, November 9, 1966. In Hugh B. Brown file on the John Birch Society, Edwin B. Firmage Papers, Box 48, fd. 21; Notes from First Presidency meeting, November 16, 1966, DOMD.

150. DOMD, December 2, 1966.

151. DOMD, February 24, 1967.

152. Robert Welch to David O. McKay, February 21, 1967, DOMD, March 22, 1967.

153. DOMD, March 22, 1967.

154. Robert Welch to David O. McKay, April 18, 1967, DOMD.

155. DOMD, April 18, 1967.

156. DOMD, April 21, 1967.

157. Dorothy L. Skinner to Hugh B. Brown, March 24, 1967. Photocopy in authors' possession.

158. Hugh B. Brown to Burns S. Hanson, May 11, 1967. Firmage Papers, Box 48, fd. 21.

159. DOMD, February 13, 1968.

160. DOMD, August 26, 1968.

161. DOMD, September 9, 1968.

162. Hugh B. Brown interview.

163. "Note by C.M.," December 7, 1968, DOMD.

164. DOMD, May 29, 1969.

165. Arthur Forbes Herbertson interview.

166. DOMD, February 12, 1969.

167. DOMD, May 12, 1969.

168. Notes on a meeting between McKay, Brown, and King in McKay's office, DOMD, November 16, 1961.

169. Karlheinz Leonhardt, *Die Ersten Hundert Jahre,* 358.

170. Dan Harrie, "LDS Official Calls for More Political Diversity, *Salt Lake Tribune,* May 3, 1998.

171. "President McKay Predicts Fall of Red Leaders," *Deseret News,* April 26, 1954.

CHAPTER 13 – POLITICS AND THE CHURCH

1. Two recent works that can be read sequentially with profit on the Mormon-federal contest immediately preceding McKay's apostleship are Sarah Barringer Gordon, *The Mormon Question,* which analyzes the Constitutional questions involved in the federal crushing of Mormon theocracy, with polygamy as a focus, and Kathleen Flake, *The Politics of American Religious Identity,* which provides an insightful analysis of the Reed Smoot hearings, a direct result of which was the calling of monogamist David O. McKay to the apostleship.

2. Analyses of Reed Smoot's political career, including the tension-fraught years of hearings, include Thomas G. Alexander, *Mormonism in Transition;* Harvard S. Heath, ed., *In the World: The Diaries of Reed Smoot,* although, unfortunately, no diary exists for the period of the hearings; and Milton R. Merrill, *Reed Smoot: Apostle in Politics.*

3. D. Michael Quinn, *The Mormon Hierarchy: Extensions of Power,* chap. 9, is a historical overview of the "partisan politics" engaged in by the church from the Kirtland period onward. He identifies as "the low point of the hierarchy's influence" (358) the 1930s when the church president was Heber J. Grant and David O. McKay was a senior apostle. The church suffered three checks in its attempt to exercise political influence. First, Republican Apostle-Senator Reed Smoot lost to a Democrat in 1932. Second, in the election of 1936, J. Reuben Clark campaigned openly for Alf Landon, Church President Heber J. Grant, who was opposed to Franklin D. Roosevelt and alarmed by his proposal to pack the U.S. Supreme Court, publicly endorsed Landon, though "speaking for himself," and the *Deseret News* ran a front-page editorial endorsing Landon. However, Utahns, like the nation, voted overwhelmingly (70 percent) for Roosevelt. And third, to the church's "chagrin," Utah became the decisive thirty-sixth state to ratify Prohibition's repeal. James B. Allen and Glen M. Leonard, *The Story of the Latter-day Saints,* 2d ed., 526–27. McKay, in the 1950s, had no desire to repeat the embarrassments of his predecessor in the 1930s.

4. J. Bracken Lee interview.

5. David O. McKay, *Conference Report,* April 1946, 139–40.

6. Police Chief L. C. Crowther, quoted in "Police Chief Raps Talk at LDS Meet," *Salt Lake Tribune,* April 10, 1946.

7. McKay, quoted in "LDS Leader Replies to Police Blast," *Salt Lake Tribune,* April 11, 1946.

8. Bruce McConkie, "City Officers Fail in Duty, Says Pres. McKay," *Deseret News,* August 6, 1946.

9. Earl J. Glade, quoted in "Mayor to Back Fight for Cleanup," *Deseret News,* August 7, 1946.

10. "Police Make First Arrest as Cleanup Begins," *Deseret News,* August 10, 1946.

11. McKay, quoted in "Unionism 'Coercion' Assailed Vigorously by L.D.S. Church," *Salt Lake Telegram,* July 2, 1937.

12. McKay, quoted in "LDS Leader Supports 'Work' Law," *Salt Lake Tribune,* September 17, 1961.

13. DOMD, June 15, 1965.

14. DOMD, June 16, 1965.

15. First Presidency to "Dear Senators and Representatives," June 22, 1965, DOMD, June 25, 1965. The Latter-day Saints in Congress included three U.S. Senators: Wallace F. Bennett (R-Utah), Frank E. Moss (D-Utah), and Howard Cannon (D-Nevada); and eight U.S. Representatives: Laurence J. Burton (R-Utah), David S. King (D-Utah), John E. Moss (D-California), Morris K. Udall (D-Arizona), Ken W. Dyal (D-California), Richard T. Hanna (D-California), Delwin M. Clawson (R-California), and George V. Hansen (R-Idaho).

16. "Statement of Senator Frank E. Moss (D-Utah) with Regard to Repeal of Section 14(b)." Moss sent a copy of the statement, dated June 25, with a cover letter, dated June 28, to the First Presidency. Both are in DOMD, June 25, 1965.

17. Letter to the First Presidency, June 29, 1965, signed by Senator Frank E. Moss and Congressmen Ken W. Dyal, Richard T. Hanna, John E. Moss and Morris K. Udall. In H. George Frederickson and Alden J. Stevens, "The Mormon Congressman and the Line between Church and State," 125–26.

18. DOMD, July 7, 1965.

19. DOMD, July 13, 1965.

20. Wallace Turner, "'Right-to-Work' Bid by Mormons Fails," *New York Times,* July 14, 1965.

21. "Wrong Field," editorial, *Twin Falls Times-News,* July 19, 1965.

22. DOMD, July 21, 1965.

23. "Mormons Soften Opposition to 'Right-to-Work' Section," *New York Times,* July 26, 1965.

24. DOMD, July 26, 1965. "Amazed" may be a euphemism. The following week, Ernest L. Wilkinson spoke with Thorpe B. Isaacson, who became an additional counselor in the First Presidency in October 1965, and made this entry in his diary: "I also learned from Thorpe Isaacson that President McKay was furious over the statement given to the press in New York City by President Brown, that the Church was softening its stand on right-to-work." ELWD, August 4, 1965.

25. The statement and the account of Stapley's visit are in DOMD, July 27, 1965. It was published as "Rap Unauthorized Thinking. LDS View on Work Law Unchanged," *Salt Lake Tribune,* July 28, 1965.

26. DOMD, July 29, 1965.

27. DOMD, July 30, 1965

28. Moss, quoted in "The Right to Vote," *Newsweek,* July 26, 1965.

29. King and Dyal are quoted in Frederickson and Stevens, "The Mormon Congressman and the Line between Church and State," 125–26.

30. Glynn Mapes, "Utah & the Mormons: As State Bids for Business It Comes Into Conflict with Church," *Wall Street Journal,* August 10, 1965.

31. DOMD, August 20, 1965.

32. Marjorie Hunter, "Labor Backers Give Up, Can't Repeal 14–B Now," *Salt Lake Tribune,* February 11, 1966.

33. The three Mormon senators were Wallace F. Bennett (R-Utah), Frank E. Moss (D-Utah), and Howard Cannon (D-Nevada).

34. The Word of Wisdom, a revelation dating to 1833, outlawed not alcoholic beverages per se but rather "strong drink," then interpreted as distilled spirits. Church President Heber J. Grant changed the application of the revelation nearly a century later to prohibit any alcoholic beverage.

35. DOMD, April 23, 1965.

36. Mapes, "Utah & the Mormons." McKay's diary does not mention this episode.

37. DOMD, April 16, 1968.

38. DOMD, April 18, 1968.

39. Alvin R. Dyer diary, May 10, 1968. Photocopy in DOMD.

40. "Statement by President David O. McKay of the Church of Jesus Christ of Latter-day Saints," *Deseret News,* May 11, 1968; "Statement by President David O. McKay of the Church of Jesus Christ of Latter-day Saints," *Salt Lake Tribune,* May 12, 1968.

41. "Group Opposes Liquor Vote, Asks New Law," *Salt Lake Tribune,* May 26, 1968.

42. "Ministerial President Opposes 'By-Drink' Petition," *Deseret News,* June 8, 1968.

43. First Presidency Circular Letter, "To Presidents of Stakes and Bishops of Wards in Utah," September 23, 1968, DOMS #100.

44. "Liquor Assailed by Mormon Head," *New York Times,* October 6, 1968.

45. Q. Michael Croft, "Influence of the L.D.S. Church on Utah Politics," 89–91.

46. First Presidency Circular Letter, "To Presidents of Stakes and Bishops of Wards in the United States and Canada," January 27, 1969, DOMD.

47. John W. Gallivan interview.

48. Ibid.

49. Ibid.

50. Monroe G. McKay interview. Quinn, *The Mormon Hierarchy,* 322, identifies McKay as an "ardent Republican" in a table giving the political affiliations of church presidents and apostles.

51. DOMD, August 7, 1952.

52. DOMD, August 22, 1952.

53. Closing address by President David O. McKay at the 123rd Semi-Annual Conference of the Church of Jesus Christ of Latter-day Saints, Sunday, October 5, 1952, DOMP; *Conference Report,* October 1952, 129–30.

54. DOMD, November 5, 1952.

55. Quoted in Quinn, *The Mormon Hierarchy,* 360.

56. DOMD, June 18, 1956.

57. General Conference Address, October 7, 1956, DOMD, October 7, 1956; *Conference Report,* October 1956, 124.

58. By "policy of the Church," Brown was evidently referring to the effects of the "political manifesto" instituted a half-century earlier. Well before McKay's presidency, the church had negotiated an internal arrangement contrasting with its frankly theocratic period in which Joseph Smith served as mayor of Nauvoo and head of the Nauvoo Legion and when Brigham Young was governor of the Territory of Utah and George Q. Cannon, a counselor to three church presidents, was a territorial delegate. The abrasive election of 1895—which elected the first senator who would serve when Utah became a state in 1896—pitted the political ambitions of Apostle Moses Thatcher, a Democrat, against those of the Republi-

can First Presidency, under Joseph F. Smith. Thatcher lost but the First Presidency proposed a "political manifesto" before April conference in 1896 that disclaimed any intention of interfering in politics and requiring any "leading" Mormon officer to get clearance for a political office. When Thatcher refused to sign it, he was dropped from the quorum and would have been excommunicated except that he reversed field after several months and signed. During this same election, B. H. Roberts, senior president of the First Council of the Seventy, also accepted nomination on the Democratic ticket, and was likewise punished when he refused to recant by being dropped from his position before April conference, 1896. The First Presidency gave him three weeks to make up his mind, and at the last moment he wrote a letter of apology that enabled him to keep his position. This divisive incident set the church's public policy of not interfering in politics and also established the tradition that political service by a General Authority required First Presidency clearance. The best general work on the social and political accommodations made by the church during this transitional period is Thomas G. Alexander, *Mormonism in Transition*. For specific treatments of these elections, the Political Manifesto, and its aftermath, see also Kenneth W. Godfrey, "Moses Thatcher in the Dock," Quinn, *The Mormon Hierarchy: Extensions of Power*, 350–52, and Jean Bickmore White, "Utah State Elections, 1895–1899."

59. DOMD, July 8, 1958. McKay's papers make no further mention of this incident nor does Brown's biography, Eugene E. Campbell and Richard D. Poll, *Hugh B. Brown*.

60. Dexter Ellis, "Nixon Calls on Pres. McKay for Chat," *Deseret News*, October 11, 1960. "President McKay 'Interviews' Nixon," *Salt Lake Tribune*, October 11, 1960, gave a sidebar account of McKay's quotation: "I sat next to your competition recently.... I told him that if he is successful we would all support him. And I say to you, I hope you are."

61. Willard Edwards, "Head Mormon Gives Nixon an Endorsement," *Chicago Tribune*, October 11, 1960.

62. David S. Broder, "Mormon Church Leader Strongly Backs Nixon," *Washington Star*, October 11, 1960.

63. "President McKay Clarifies Nixon 'Endorsement,'" *California Intermountain News*, October 13, 1960. This clarification apparently did not receive attention in the national press, as the heated campaign moved on to other issues. Furthermore, since the national Democratic Party probably assumed (correctly) that Utah's electoral votes would go to the Republican candidate, neither the statement nor its clarification would have influenced the election's outcome.

64. DOMD, November 16, 1961.

65. DOMD, May 3, 1962.

66. First Presidency Circular Letter, August 22, 1962, DOMD, August 22, 1962.

67. DOMD, March 23, 1960.

68. DOMD, December 5, 1961.

69. Ibid.

70. DOMD, January 3, 1962. McKay's diary does not indicate who drafted the response to Romney nor include a copy of it.

71. DOMD, October 18, 1962.

72. Dan L. Thrapp, "Mormons See Romney in Race on His Own, But Full Church Backing Is Assured," *Los Angeles Times*, November 15, 1966. McKay records receiving Thrapp's request on November 15, 1966.

73. Quinn, *The Mormon Hierarchy*, 361–62, analyzes the reapportionment battle, Sunday closing, released-time legislation for seminary classes, and other political efforts by the church during the 1950s and 1960s. F. Ross Peterson, "Utah Politics since 1945," has a brief but cogent discussion of "The Role of the Mormon Church" (516–18) in which he discusses the involvement of high-ranking officials in party politics, Sunday-closing laws (twice passed by the legislature but vetoed by two governors), the liquor-by-the-drink referendum, and right-to-work bill (both discussed in this chapter), and other issues outside the McKay period.

74. DOMD, November 23, 1953.

75. DOMD, November 24, 1953.

76. Weilenmann, interviewed by Kenneth L. Mitchell, January 6, 1956. Quoted in Mitchell, "The Struggle for Reapportionment in Utah," 104.

77. Henry D. Moyle, interviewed by Kenneth H. Mitchell, April 4, 1956. Quoted in ibid., 96–97.

78. Weilenmann quoted in J. D. Williams Diary, November 26, 1953.

79. Ibid.

80. "Demo Chief Quotes Lee, LDS President to Clear Reapportionment Confusion," *Salt Lake Tribune,* May 4, 1954.

81. Williams Diary, October 17, 1954.

82. First Presidency (David O. McKay, Stephen L Richards, J. Reuben Clark Jr.) to Frank H. Jonas, September 16, 1954. Quoted in Mitchell, "The Struggle for Reapportionment in Utah," 164.

83. Weilenmann, interviewed by Kenneth H. Mitchell, January 6, 1956. Quoted in ibid., 125.

84. Weilenmann, interviewed by Frank H. Jonas, September 6, 1957.

85. "The Hoax," *Time,* October 25, 1954.

86. Arthur V. Watkins, *Enough Rope,* 159.

87. Weilenmann interview, September 6, 1957.

88. DOMD, October 21, 1954.

89. Weilenmann interview, September 6, 1957.

90. Weilenmann, interviewed by Prince, February 20, 1995.

91. Spencer L. Kimball to Prince, September 24, 1996.

92. Watkins, *Enough Rope,* 161.

93. DOMD, October 13, 1954.

94. Kimball to Prince, September 24, 1996.

95. Williams Diary, October 17, 1954.

96. DOMD, October 14, 1954.

97. Ibid.

98. Watkins, *Enough Rope,* 160.

99. Quoted in Weilenmann interview, February 20, 1995.

100. J. Bracken Lee interview.

101. Watkins, *Enough Rope,* 162.

102. DOMD, October 16, 1954.

103. Williams Diary, October 17, 1954.

104. DOMD, October 20, 1954.

105. LaVor K. Chaffin, "The 'Dixon Story'—A 15-Day Political Wonder," *Deseret News,* November 3, 1954.

106. Weilenmann interview, February 20, 1995.

107. DOMD, January 19, 1953.

108. DOMD, September 23, 1952. Emphasis his.

109. Kenneth W. Hechler, White House memo to Matthew J. Connolley, September 25, 1952. Harry S. Truman Library, Independence, MO.

110. DOMD, September 26, 1952.

111. DOMD, October 6, 1952.

112. DOMD, October 21, 1952.

113. Arthur V. Watkins to David O. McKay, November 22, 1952, DOMS #21.

114. David O. McKay to Dwight D. Eisenhower, November 6, 1952, DOMS #22.

115. DOMD, November 20, 1952.

116. Ezra Taft Benson to Clare Middlemiss, May 28, 1966, DOMS #169.

117. DOMD, November 12, 1957.

118. DOMD, March 6, 1959.

119. Oscar W. McConkie Jr. interview.

120. DOMD, November 22, 1963.

121. DOMD, October 27, 1960.

122. DOMD, October 19, 1962.

123. Transcript of telephone conversation between President Lyndon B. Johnson and David O. McKay, January 25, 1964. White House Recordings and Telephone Notes, Box 1, Lyndon B. Johnson Library and Museum.

124. David Lawrence McKay, "Memorandum of Visit of President David O. McKay with Lyndon B. Johnson, President of the United States, at the White House, Friday, January 31, 1964, at 1:00 P.M.," DOMD.

125. Frank E. Moss interview.

126. Edwin B. Firmage interview, October 10, 1996.

127. David Lawrence McKay, "Memorandum of Visit."

128. Lola Gygi Timmins interview, August 3, 2000.

129. DOMD, October 29, 1964.

130. DOMD, November 4, 1964.

131. DOMD, December 31, 1964.

132. "Choir Takes Press Seats," *Deseret News,* January 9, 1965.

133. DOMD, January 20, 1965.

134. DOMD, May 3, 1965.

135. David O. McKay to Lyndon B. Johnson, February 26, 1965, DOMD.

136. Ibid.

137. Boyd K. Packer, "Report on the Interview with President Lyndon B. Johnson," March 10, 1965, DOMD.

138. Minutes of the First Presidency and Quorum of the Twelve, April 1, 1965. Photocopy in Prince's possession.

139. Joseph Anderson, Minutes, March 10, 1965, DOMD.

Chapter 14 – An International Church

1. Alden Whitman, "David McKay, Mormon President, Was Ardent Advocate of Universal Expansion," *New York Times,* January 19, 1970. The interview took place on October 23, 1968, DOMS #110.

2. "Two Church Workers Will Tour Missions of Pacific Islands," *Deseret News,* October 15, 1920.

3. "Plan Visit to Island Missions," *Deseret News,* October 23, 1920.

4. Theodore M. Burton interview.

5. David O. McKay, Diary of his world tour, December 8–10, 1920, DOMS #127.

6. Hugh J. Cannon, letter of December 18, 1920, DOMS #126.

7. Hugh J. Cannon, letter of January 21, 1922, DOMS #126.

8. David O. McKay to Llewelyn McKay, October 27, 1921, DOMS #127.

9. David O. McKay to Reed Smoot, January 17, 1921, DOMS #127.

10. David O. McKay, remarks in a missionary meeting at Huntly, New Zealand, April 26, 1921, DOMS #126.

11. David O. McKay to Reed Smoot, August 30, 1921, DOMS #127.

12. David O. McKay, remarks at the Puke Tapu Branch, Waikato District, Huntly, New Zealand, April 24, 1921, DOMS #126.

13. "The Missions, Summary and Report, Tour of Inspection of Missions and Schools," 1921, DOMS #127.

14. Mormon emigration has been the subject of a large number of scholarly studies, beginning with William Clayton's *The Latter-day Saints' Emigrants' Guide* (1848). Book-length studies over the past few decades include William Mulder, *Homeward to Zion;* Wallace Stegner, *The Gathering of Zion;* P. A. M. Taylor, *Expectations Westward;* James B. Allen and Thomas G. Alexander (eds.), *Manchester Mormons;* two works by Conway B. Sonne, *Saints on the Seas* and *Ships, Saints, and Mariners;* Ronald D. Dennis, *The Call of Zion;* Frederick S. Buchanan (ed.), *A Good Time Coming: Mormon Letters to Scotland;* and Maurine J. and Scot F. Proctor, *The Gathering.*

15. Norman C. Hill, "The Changing Concept of Gathering," 8.

16. Minutes of the First Presidency and Quorum of the Twelve, September 16, 1897, Journal History.

17. Minutes of the First Presidency and Quorum of the Twelve, January 19, 1899, Journal History.

18. Anthon H. Lund Diary, January 19, 1899.

19. First Presidency "To The Saints in the Netherlands Mission," December 14, 1907. In James R. Clark, *Messages of the First Presidency,* 165.

20. Editorial, "Stand Where You Are!", *Millennial Star* 83 (September 15, 1921): 585.

21. First Presidency letter, October 18, 1921. Quoted in James B. Allen and Richard O. Cowan, *Mormonism in the Twentieth Century,* 52.

22. First Presidency Circular Letter, ca. November 1931, LDS Archives, CR 1/1.

23. "Editorial," *Millennial Star* 107 (October 1945): 304–5.

24. A patriarchal blessing, so-called after the blessings given by the Old Testament patriarch Jacob ("Israel") to his sons, is an individualized blessing given to church members that serves as a spiritual guide throughout their lives. The blessings are given by patriarchs chosen in each stake throughout the world. The absence of overseas stakes prior to 1959 meant that church members residing outside the United States could not receive such blessings unless they could obtain them from the church's presiding patriarch, either as he traveled (which he did rarely) or, more commonly, by coming to Salt Lake City.

25. "London Temple Progress," *Millennial Star* 118 (August 1956): 248.

26. DOMD, November 30, 1951. See chap. 11.

27. Minutes, April 17, 1952, DOMD. Unless otherwise noted, correspondence, minutes, and reports are filed in McKay's diary under the date of writing.

28. DOMD, June 23, 1952.

29. DOMD, August 26, 1953.

30. Keith C. Warner, "History of the Netherlands Mission of the Church of Jesus Christ of Latter-day Saints 1861–1966" (M.A. thesis, Brigham Young University, 1967), 146. Quoted in Bruce Van Orden, *Building Zion: The Latter-day Saints in Europe,* 162.

31. Monroe G. McKay interview.

32. David Lawrence McKay interview.

33. "Report and Recommendations by President David O. McKay on Matters in the South Pacific Missions," February 17, 1955, DOMD.

34. Thomas Bowring Woodbury, report to the First Presidency, December 5, 1962, DOMD.

35. Clifton G. M. Kerr interview.

36. James B. Allen and Glen Leonard, *The Story of the Latter-day Saints,* 564.

37. Franklin J. Murdock interview.

38. First Presidency meeting minutes, September 1, 1953, DOMD.

39. DOMD, January 30, 1958.

40. A. Theodore Tuttle interview, August 23, 1977.

41. Transcript of press conference in Grosvenor House, London, September 4, 1958, DOMD, September 10, 1958.

42. Woodbury, report to the First Presidency.

43. Report to the First Presidency and Council of the Twelve on a tour of the South Pacific Missions, February 24, 1958, DOMD.

44. David O. McKay, General Conference Address, April 3, 1955, *Conference Report,* April 1955, 25.

45. DOMD, November 19, 1959.

46. "New Program to Intensify Supervision of World-Wide Church Missions," *Church News,* July 1, 1961.

47. Paul H. Dunn interviews, January 15, 1996 and March 21, 1997.

48. *Deseret News 1983 Church Almanac,* 135–43.

49. DOMD, March 2, 1953.

50. David O. McKay to Stephen L Richards and J. Reuben Clark Jr., January 19, 1954, DOMD.

51. Lyman S. Shreeve interview.

52. McKay, Report given to the First Presidency and Quorum of the Twelve, February 25, 1954, DOMD.

53. Helen Cook Fyans interview.

54. DOMD, April 17, 1962.

55. J. Thomas Fyans interview. Fyans was appointed to head the Translation Department on June 18, 1965.

56. Report of the Executive Committee of the Correlation Committee, n.d., DOMD, December 21, 1965.

57. DOMD, March 15, 1968.

58. Minutes of a Meeting of the First Presidency and Quorum of the Twelve, October 24, 1968. Summarized in DOMP; verbatim report in Clare Middlemiss, "Notes."

59. Ibid.

60. DOMD, May 26, 1969.

61. DOMD, August 27, 1969.

62. Peter D. Olson interview. The novel is Morris West, *The Shoes of the Fisherman* (New York: William Morrow, 1963).

63. Sterling M. McMurrin, "President David O. McKay—1873–1970."

CHAPTER 15 – FINAL YEARS

1. D. Michael Quinn, "The Mormon Succession Crisis of 1844."

2. DOMD, September 8, 1948.

3. DOMD, June 15, 1953.

4. DOMD, September 8, 1953.

5. DOMD, July 6, 1956.

6. DOMD, May 18, 1957.

7. DOMD, November 23, 1958.

8. Emma Ray McKay Diary, quoted in David Lawrence McKay, *My Father, David O. McKay,* 213.

9. DOMD, December 5, 1958.

10. DOMD, May 19, 1959.

11. ELWD, June 3, 1959.

12. ELWD, August 9, 1961.

13. DOMD, September 8, 1961.

14. DOMD, April 7, 1962.

15. Quoted in Leonard J. Arrington, *Adventures of a Church Historian,* 46.

16. David M. Kennedy interview.

17. DOMD, April 7, 1963.

18. DOMD, May 7, 1963.

19. Edward Barner interview.

20. Robert L. Simpson interview.

21. Ibid.

22. DOMD, September 19, 1963.

23. Arch Madsen interview, January 14, 1996.

24. Ted Jacobsen interview. W. W. Phelps (1792–1872) authored the hymn text in 1856 and it was first included in the LDS hymnal in 1950.

25. DOMD, January 9, 1964.

26. DOMD, January 22, 1964.

27. Robert R. McKay interview.

28. DOMD, February 20, 1964.

29. David Lawrence McKay interview.

30. David Lawrence McKay, quoted in DOMD, August 20, 1964.

31. Val G. Hemming to Prince, February 15, 2003.

32. DOMD, August 29, 1964.

33. "A report of President David O. McKay's activities from June to October, 1964," DOMS #76.

34. DOMD, October 4, 1964.

35. David O. McKay to Dr. C. Lowell Lees, October 13, 1964, DOMS #74.

36. David Lawrence McKay, *My Father, David O. McKay,* 262–64.

37. DOMD, November 6, 1964.

38. DOMD, November 10, 1964.

39. DOMD, November 12, 1964.

40. David Lawrence McKay interview.

41. McKay, *My Father, David O. McKay,* 262–64.

42. DOMD, November 17, 1964.

43. David Lawrence McKay interview.

44. DOMD, December 1, 1964.

45. ELWD, February 14, 1965.

46. DOMD, March 24, 1965.

47. ELWD, March 28, 1965.

48. DOMD, August 19, 1965.

49. Norman Vincent Peale, quoted by Clare Middlemiss, meeting sponsored by the Weber County Commissioners, held in the Ogden Second Ward, December 6, 1965, at which time President McKay was presented with the Hall of Fame Award, DOMS #83.

50. DOMD, October 1, 1965.

51. Clare Middlemiss, "Note," in DOMD, April 9, 1966.

52. Calvin L. Rampton interview.

53. Clare Middlemiss, "Note," in DOMD, April 2, 1969.

54. Remarks at the dedication of the David O. McKay Hospital, July 9, 1969, DOMS #118. During a remodeling, it was renamed the McKay-Dee Hospital.

55. Keith Wilcox interview.

56. David Lawrence McKay interview.

57. Joseph Anderson interview, January 12, 1963.

58. Gabrielle Baruffol interview.

59. John Jacques, "Oh Say, What Is Truth?" *Hymns of the Church of Jesus Christ of Latter-day Saints* (Salt Lake City: Deseret Book, 1985), No. 272.

60. Transcription of the funeral service by Clare Middlemiss, DOMD, January 22, 1970.

61. Ibid.

CHAPTER 16 – EPILOGUE

1. ELWD for the indicated dates.

2. Alvin R. Dyer Journal, November 13, 1969, DOMD. Unless otherwise noted, correspondence, minutes, and reports are filed in McKay's diary under the date of writing.

3. Ibid.

4. Ibid.

5. Ibid.

6. See chapter 4.

7. Gordon B. Hinckley interview.

8. Gordon B. Hinckley, April 7, 1984, *Conference Report,* April 1984, 3.

9. Hinckley interview.

10. ELWD for the indicated dates.

11. Calvin L. Rampton oral history.

12. Alvin R. Dyer Journal, October 8, 1969, DOMD.

13. Benson Y. Parkinson, "S. Dilworth Young of the First Quorum of Seventy."

14. Paul H. Dunn interview, June 5, 1995.

15. Edwin B. Firmage interview, October 10, 1996.

16. Calvin L. Rampton interview.

APPENDIX

1. Clare Middlemiss, interviewed on KSXX Radio, Salt Lake City, broadcast January 20, 1970, DOMS #110.

2. Clare Middlemiss, "President Heber J. Grant" (remarks describing her feelings when asked to work for President McKay), n.d., DOMP.

3. Clare Middlemiss to Mrs. Joseph Morrell, October 8, 1948, DOMP. Mrs. Joseph Morrell was David O. McKay's younger sister, Jeanette.

4. Middlemiss, interviewed on KSXX radio.

5. Wm. Robert Wright interview.

6. Lola Gygi Timmins interview, October 28, 1998. Up to this point, there had not been a secretary to the First Presidency. Joseph Anderson fulfilled that responsibility, including taking minutes at the meetings of the First Presidency and the joint meetings of the First Presidency and Quorum of the Twelve.

7. Gabrielle Baruffol interview.

8. David Lawrence McKay interview.

9. Paul H. Dunn interview, October 6, 1995.

10. Charles M. Brown interview, June 3, 1995.

11. Mark Benson interview.

12. Marion D. Hanks to Clare Middlemiss, October 26, 1962, DOMP.

13. Elaine Anderson Cannon interview. Emphasis hers.

14. ELWD, September 14, 1960.

15. ELWD, December 28, 1967.

16. Robert L. Simpson interview.

17. Wright interview.

18. DOMD, April 26, 1966; Clare Middlemiss, "Notes," July 13, 1969, photocopy in authors' possession.

19. Clare Middlemiss, Remarks at the United States Civil Service Conference held at the Hotel Utah, February 26, 1965, DOMS #77.

20. Wright interview.

21. Middlemiss, Remarks.

22. Lola Gygi Timmins to Prince, April 20, 1998.

23. DOMD, June 29, 1965. McKay made this comment to Middlemiss, which she included in this date's diary entry, after discussing with her the ultimate disposition of the diaries, the original of which he intended to go to his family. He also intended that the minutes of First Presidency meetings, to be placed in the LDS Church Archives, be the official record of his activities.

24. DOMD, December 20, 1966.

25. "Audograph Delivers Messages During Goodwill Tour Abroad," *Gray Audograph News,* Gray Manufacturing Company, March 1953, DOMS #22.

26. Middlemiss, Remarks.

27. Wright interview.

BIBLIOGRAPHY

The bibliography is divided into two sections: published sources and manuscript sources. Manuscript items by individuals in archival collections cataloged under that individual's name are not listed separately.

PUBLISHED SOURCES

Alexander, Thomas G. *Mormonism in Transition: A History of the Latter-day Saints, 1890–1930*. Urbana: University of Illinois Press, 1986.

Allen, James B. "Would-Be Saints: West Africa before the 1978 Priesthood Revelation." *Journal of Mormon History* 17 (1991): 207–47.

Allen, James B., and Thomas G. Alexander, eds. *Manchester Mormons: The Journal of William Clayton, 1840 to 1842*. Santa Barbara, Calif.: Peregrine Smith, 1974.

Allen, James B., and Richard O. Cowan. *Mormonism in the Twentieth Century*. Provo, UT: Brigham Young University Press, 1969.

Allen, James B., and Glen M. Leonard. *The Story of the Latter-day Saints*. Salt Lake City: Deseret Book, 1976.

Allen, James B., and Glen M. Leonard. *The Story of the Latter-day Saints,* 2d ed. Salt Lake City: Deseret Book, 1992.

Allen, James B., Jessie L. Embry, and Kahlile B. Mehr. *Hearts Turned to the Fathers: A History of the Genealogical Society of Utah, 1894–1994*. Provo, UT: Brigham Young University Press, 1995.

Anderson, Jack. "Reed Benson Spreads Birch Gospel." *Washington Post,* January 15, 1965.

Anderson, Joseph. *Prophets I Have Known*. Salt Lake City: Deseret Book, 1973.

"Apostle Benson Denies Being Sent into 'Exile' for Political Views." *Ogden Standard–Examiner,* October 29, 1963.

Armstrong, Richard N. *The Rhetoric of David O. McKay*. New York: Peter Lang, 1993.

Arrington, Leonard J. *Adventures of a Church Historian*. Urbana: University of Illinois Press, 1998.

Barton, Peggy Petersen. *Mark E. Petersen: A Biography*. Salt Lake City: Deseret Book, 1985.

Baruffol, Gabrielle Antoinette Chappuis. *Through the Pantry Window*. N.p., 1979.

Benson, Ezra Taft. *Cross Fire: The Eight Years with Eisenhower*. New York: Doubleday, 1962.

"Benson Birch Tie Disturbs Utahans." *New York Times,* November 4, 1962.

"Benson Clarifies Views on Birch Society Stand." *Salt Lake Tribune,* March 21, 1963.

"Benson Not Speaking for Mormons on Birch." *Los Angeles Times,* March 4, 1963.

"Benson Speaker at Testimonial Dinner." Associated Press Wire Service. Los Angeles, September 24, 1963.

"Benson Ties Rights Issue to Reds in Mormon Rift." *Washington Post,* April 13, 1965.

Bergera, Gary James. "Ernest L. Wilkinson's Appointment as Seventh President of Brigham Young University." *Journal of Mormon History* 23, no. 2 (Fall 1997): 128–54.

Bergera, Gary James, and Ronald Priddis. *Brigham Young University: A House of Faith*. Salt Lake City: Signature Books, 1985.

Berrett, William E., and Alma P. Burton. *Readings in L.D.S. Church History from Original Manuscripts*. Salt Lake City: Deseret Book, 1958.

Bradford, Mary Lythgoe *Lowell L. Bennion: Teacher, Counselor, Humanitarian*. Salt Lake City: Dialogue Foundation, 1995.

Bringhurst, Newell G. *Fawn McKay Brodie: A Biographer's Life*. Norman: University of Oklahoma Press, 1999.

"British Missions Pass Goal of 1,000 Converts." *Church News*, September 17, 1960.

Broder, David S. "Mormon Church Leader Strongly Backs Nixon." *Washington Star*, October 11, 1960.

Broderick, Carlfred B. "The Core of My Belief." In *A Thoughtful Faith: Essays on Belief by Mormon Scholars*, edited by Philip L. Barlow, 85–101. Centerville, UT: Canon Press, 1986.

Brown, Hugh B. "Don't Lose the Shepherds." *Improvement Era* 64 (October 1961): 724–36.

Buchanan, Frederick S., ed. *A Good Time Coming: Mormon Letters to Scotland*. Salt Lake City: University of Utah Press, 1988.

———. "Missionary Roots of Change." *Dialogue: A Journal of Mormon Thought* 33, no. 2 (Summer 2000): 193–96.

Buerger, David John. "Speaking with Authority: The Theological Influence of Elder Bruce R. McConkie." *Sunstone* 10, no. [2] (March 1985): 8–13.

"Building Chief Resigns Job with LDS Church." *Salt Lake Tribune*, April 28, 1965.

Bush, Lester E., Jr., and Armand L. Mauss, eds. *Neither White nor Black: Mormon Scholars Confront the Race Issue in a Universal Church*. Midvale, UT: Signature Books, 1984.

Campbell, Eugene E., and Richard D. Poll. *Hugh B. Brown: His Life and Thought*. Salt Lake City: Bookcraft, 1975.

Chaffin, LaVor K. "The 'Dixon Story'—A 15-Day Political Wonder." *Deseret News*, November 3, 1954.

"Choir Takes Press Seats." *Deseret News*, January 9, 1965.

Christensen, Bruce L. "Broadcasting." In *Encyclopedia of Mormonism*, 4 vols. Edited by Daniel H. Ludlow, 1:232–34. New York: Macmillan Publishing, 1992.

"Church Appoints Head of Building Committee." *Deseret News & Salt Lake Telegram*, July 19, 1955.

"Church Leader Tells Rotary Club of Trip to European Missions." *Deseret News*, August 6, 1952.

"Church Progress in Europe." Editorial. *Deseret News*, November 27, 1959.

"Church Sets Policy on Birch Society." *Deseret News*, January 3, 1963.

"Church Stand on Colleges Told to Lee." *Deseret News*, May 28, 1954.

"Church to Open Missionary Work in Nigeria." *Deseret News*, January 11, 1963.

"Church Unites Schools Under One Director." *Deseret News and Telegram*, July 9, 1953.

"Clare Boothe Luce Says Romney '64 Deadlock Choice." Syndicated column. *Arizona Republic*, September 1, 1963.

Clark, James R., ed. *Messages of the First Presidency of the Church of Jesus Christ of Latter-day Saints, 1833–1964*, 6 vols. Salt Lake City: Bookcraft, 1965–75.

Clark, J. Reuben, Jr. *Immortality and Eternal Life*, vol. 2. Salt Lake City: Corporation of the President, 1969.

———. *On the Way to Immortality and Eternal Life: A Series of Radio Talks by President J. Reuben Clark Jr. of the First Presidency of the Church of Jesus Christ of Latter-day Saints*. Salt Lake City: Deseret Book, 1949.

Clayton, William. *The Latter-day Saints' Emigrants' Guide: Being a Table of Distances, Showing All the Springs, Creeks, Rivers, Hills, Mountains, Camping Places, and All Other Notable Places, from Council Bluffs, to the Valley of the Great Salt Lake*. 1848; rpt., edited by Stanley B. Kimball. Gerald, MO: Patrice Press, 1983.

"A Clear Civil Rights Stand." Editorial. *Deseret News,* March 8, 1965.

Conference Reports. Report of the Semi-Annual Conference of the Church of Jesus Christ of Latter-day Saints. Salt Lake City: Church of Jesus Christ of Latter-day Saints, semi-annual.

Cross, Whitney R. *The Burned-Over District: The Social and Intellectual History of Enthusiastic Religion in Western New York, 1800–1850.* New York: Harper & Row, 1965.

Cummings, David W. *Mighty Missionary of the Pacific.* Salt Lake City: Bookcraft, 1961.

"Demo Chief Quotes Lee, LDS President to Clear Reapportionment Confusion." *Salt Lake Tribune,* May 4, 1954.

Dennis, Ronald D. *The Call of Zion: The Story of the First Welsh Emigration.* Provo, UT: Religious Studies Center, Brigham Young University, 1987.

Deseret News 1983 Church Almanac. Salt Lake City: Deseret News, 1982.

Deseret News 2001–2002 Church Almanac. Salt Lake City: Deseret News, 2000.

Deseret News 2004 Church Almanac. Salt Lake City: Deseret News, 2003.

Dew, Sheri L. *Ezra Taft Benson: A Biography.* Salt Lake City: Deseret Book, 1987.

Durham, G. Homer. *N. Eldon Tanner: His Life and Service.* Salt Lake City: Deseret Book, 1982.

"Editorial." *Millennial Star* 107 (October 1945): 304–5.

"Editor's Note." *Look,* October 22, 1963, 74–78.

Edwards, Willard. "Head Mormon Gives Nixon an Endorsement." *Chicago Tribune,* October 11, 1960.

"800 Chapels to be Built by Church in '60." *Church News,* July 23, 1960.

"8,000 Missionaries, Serving Full-time, Carry Gospel Message." *Church News,* December 31, 1960.

"Elder Benson Makes Statement." *Church News,* March 16, 1963.

"Elder Benson to Direct European Mission." *Deseret News,* October 24, 1963.

Ellis, Dexter. "Nixon Calls on Pres. McKay for Chat." *Deseret News,* October 11, 1960.

Everett, Millard F. "Centenary of Mormonism Coincides with Successful Catholic Radio Work in Utah." *Intermountain Catholic Register,* August 31, 1930.

"Extremism Is Never the Answer." *Deseret News,* April 3, 1956.

"Ezra Benson's Son Takes Birch Society Post." *Sacramento Bee,* October 27, 1962.

Firmage, Edwin B., ed. *An Abundant Life: The Memoirs of Hugh B. Brown.* Salt Lake City: Signature Books, 1999.

Flake, Kathleen. *The Politics of American Religious Identity: The Seating of Senator Reed Smoot, Mormon Apostle.* Chapel Hill: University of North Carolina Press, 2004.

Frederickson, H. George, and Alden J. Stevens. "The Mormon Congressman and the Line Between Church and State." *Dialogue: A Journal of Mormon Thought* 3, no. 2 (Summer 1968): 121–29.

Goates, L. Brent. *Harold B. Lee: Prophet and Seer.* Salt Lake City: Bookcraft, 1985.

Godfrey, Kenneth W. "Moses Thatcher in the Dock: His Trials, the Aftermath, and His Last Days." *Journal of Mormon History* 24 (Spring 1998): 55–58.

"Good-bye Nineteen Twenty-three." Editorial. *Millennial Star* 85 (December 27, 1923): 824.

Gordon, Sarah Barringer. *The Mormon Question: Polygamy and Constitutional Conflict in Nineteenth-Century America.* Chapel Hill: University of North Carolina Press, 2002.

Gory, Hayes. "The Ninth Prophet." *Time,* December 21, 1962, 37.

Gottlieb, Robert, and Peter Wiley. *America's Saints: The Rise of Mormon Power.* New York: G. P. Putnam's Sons, 1984.

Green, Doyle L., and Albert L. Zobell Jr. "A New Era in Church History Begins as President David O. McKay Visits Europe." *Improvement Era*, September 1952, 632–34, 658–64.

"Group Opposes Liquor Vote. Asks New Law." *Salt Lake Tribune*, May 26, 1968.

Harrie, Dan. "LDS Official Calls for More Political Diversity." *Salt Lake Tribune*, May 3, 1998.

Harrison, Bertrand F. "The Relatedness of Living Things." *The Instructor* 100 (July 1965): 272–76.

"Head of Mormons Predicts Revolt in Red Countries." *Los Angeles Times*, April 26, 1954.

Heath, Harvard S., ed. *In the World: The Diaries of Reed Smoot*. Salt Lake City: Signature Books, 1997.

Hemming, Val G. "Ricks College: The Struggle for Permanency and Place, 1954–1960." *Journal of Mormon History* 26, no. 2 (Fall 2000): 51–109.

Hill, Norman C. "The Changing Concept of Gathering." In *Conference on the Language of the Mormons*, 6–10. Provo, UT: Language Research Center, Brigham Young University, 1974.

Hillam, Ray C. *The BYU Spy Episode, 1966–68*. N.p, 2001.

"The Hoax." *Time*, October 25, 1954.

"Howard McKean, Church Building Chairman, Dies." *Deseret News & Salt Lake Telegram*, April 18, 1955.

Hunter, Marjorie. "Labor Backers Give Up, Can't Repeal 14–B Now." *Salt Lake Tribune*, February 11, 1966.

"Ike Praises Idaho Solon for Benson Criticism." *Salt Lake Tribune*, February 21, 1964.

Jackson, Richard W. *Places of Worship: 150 Years of Latter-day Saint Architecture*. Provo, UT: Religious Studies Center, Brigham Young University, 2003.

Jacques, John. "Oh Say, What Is Truth?" *Hymns of the Church of Jesus Christ of Latter-day Saints*. Salt Lake City: Deseret Book, 1985. No. 272.

Kimball, Edward L. *Lengthen Your Stride: The Presidency of Spencer W. Kimball, 1973–1985*. Provo, UT: BYU Press, 2004.

"Labor-Missionary Program Adopted for European Chapels." *Church News*, July 9, 1960.

Larson, Stan, and Patricia Larson, eds. *What E'er Thou Art Act Well Thy Part: The Missionary Diaries of David O. McKay*. Salt Lake City: Blue Ribbon Books, 1999.

Law, Reuben D. *The Founding and Early Development of the Church College of Hawaii*. St. George, UT: Dixie College Press, 1972.

"LDS Apostle Backs up Birch Group." *Salt Lake Tribune*, January 16, 1966.

"LDS Hits Extremes in Anti-Red Battle." *Salt Lake Tribune*, April 7, 1962.

"LDS Leader Replies to Police Blast." *Salt Lake Tribune*, April 11, 1946.

"LDS Leader Says Curb on Priesthood to Ease" *San Francisco Chronicle*, December 25, 1969, D–4.

"LDS Leader Supports 'Work' Law." *Salt Lake Tribune*, September 17, 1961.

"LDS President Concerned over Red Attitude toward Christianity." *Salt Lake Telegram*, April 26, 1951.

"Lee Advises Church [Will] Get 3 Schools." *Deseret News*, February 15, 1951.

Lipset, Seymour Martin, and Earl Raab. *The Politics of Unreason: Right-Wing Extremism in America, 1790–1970*. New York: Harper & Row, 1970.

"Liquor Assailed by Mormon Head." *New York Times*, October 6, 1968.

"London Temple Progress." *Millennial Star* 118 (August 1956): 248.

Madsen, Brigham D. *Against the Grain: Memoirs of a Western Historian*. Salt Lake City: Signature Books, 1998.

Malmquist, O. N. *The First 100 Years: A History of the Salt Lake Tribune, 1871–1971*. Salt Lake City: Utah State Historical Society, 1971.

Mapes, Glynn. "Utah & the Mormons: As State Bids for Business It Comes into Conflict with Church." *Wall Street Journal,* August 10, 1965.

Mauss, Armand L. *All Abraham's Children: Changing Mormon Conceptions of Race and Lineage.* Urbana: University of Illinois Press, 2003.

Mauss, Armand L. "The Fading of the Pharaoh's Curse: The Decline and Fall of the Priesthood Ban against Blacks in the Mormon Church." *Dialogue: A Journal of Mormon Thought* 14, no. 3 (Autumn 1981): 10–45.

Mavin, Richard. "The Woodbury Years: An Insider's Look at Baseball Baptisms in Britain." *Sunstone* 19, no. 1 (March 1996): 56–60.

"Mayor to Back Fight for Cleanup." *Deseret News,* August 7, 1946.

McConkie, Bruce. "City Officers Fail in Duty, Says Pres. McKay." *Deseret News,* August 6, 1946.

McConkie, Bruce R. *Mormon Doctrine.* Salt Lake City: Bookcraft, 1958.

McCulloch, J. E. *Home: The Savior of Civilization.* Washington, D.C.: The Southern Cooperative League, 1924.

McKay, Emma Ray Riggs. *The Art of Rearing Children Peacefully.* Provo, UT: Extension Publications, Brigham Young University, 1966.

McKay, David Lawrence. "Memorandum of Visit," DOMD, January 3, 1964.

———. *My Father, David O. McKay.* Salt Lake City: Deseret Book, 1989.

McKay, David O. "The Church Sunday School: Its Growth and Comprehensiveness." *Juvenile Instructor* 63, no. 6 (1928): 299–303.

———. "A Dream Fulfilled: Remarks of President David O. McKay at the Dedication of the Hyde Park Chapel, morning session, February 26, 1961." *Millennial Star* 123 (April 1961): 172–79.

———. "Freedom of Choice." *Relief Society Magazine* 31 (July 1944): 355–59.

———. "The Greatest Possession." *Instructor* 99 (April 1964): 129–30.

———. "'I Feel Your Welcome,' President Tells Merthyr." *Millennial Star* 125 (1963): 265–66, 296.

———. "Jesus, The Master Storyteller," *Instructor* 87 (November 1952): 321-22, 339.

———. "The Mission of the Church and Its Members." *Improvement Era* 59 (November 1956): 781–82.

———. "Persons and Principles." *Millennial Star* 86 (January 31, 1924): 72–74.

———. "The Power of Prayer." *Millennial Star* 125, no. 8 (August 1963): 190.

———. "Witnesses to the Truth." *Improvement Era* 54 (1951): 493–94, 542.

"McKay Denies LDS Drive for Colleges." *Salt Lake Tribune,* October 29, 1954.

McKay, Llewelyn R. *Home Memories of President David O. McKay.* Salt Lake City: Deseret Book, 1956.

McMurrin, Sterling M. "A Note on the 1963 Civil Rights Statement." *Dialogue: A Journal of Mormon Thought* 12, no. 2 (Summer 1978): 60–63.

———. "President David O. McKay—1873–1970." *Dialogue: A Journal of Mormon Thought* 4, no. 4 (Winter 1969): 54–55.

McMurrin, Sterling M., and L. Jackson Newell. *Matters of Conscience: Conversations with Sterling M. McMurrin on Philosophy, Education, and Religion.* Salt Lake City: Signature Books, 1996.

Mehr, Kahlile. "The Trial of the French Mission." *Dialogue: A Journal of Mormon Thought* 21, no. 3 (Autumn 1988): 27–45.

Merrill, Milton R. *Reed Smoot: Apostle in Politics.* Logan: Utah State University Press, 1990.

Midgley, Louis. "Birch Society Reviewed by Prof. Louis Midgley." *(BYU) Daily Universe,* May 22, 1964.

"Ministerial President Opposes 'By-Drink' Petition." *Deseret News,* June 8, 1968.

"Missionary Activity Boosts Baptisms to New High in 1960." *Church News*, December 31, 1960.

"Mormon Church to Expand: More Chapels for Union, Says U.S. Leader." *Cape Times,* January 13, 1954.

"Mormons & Politics—Benson's Influence Helps Keep Growing Church on Conservative Track." *Wall Street Journal*, August 8, 1966.

"Mormons' Leader Visits Los Angeles." *Los Angeles Times,* April 29, 1951.

"Mormons: The Negro Question." *Time,* October 18, 1963, 83.

"Mormons Soften Opposition to 'Right-to-Work' Section." *New York Times,* July 26, 1965.

"Move 'Final' for Ricks, Church Leader Says." *Salt Lake Tribune,* November 16, 1958.

"Mr. McKay." *Salt Lake Tribune* (Magazine Section), October 4, 1953.

Mulder, William. *Homeward to Zion: The Mormon Migration from Scandinavia*. Minneapolis: University of Minnesota Press, 1957.

"NAACP Calls March for LDS Appeal." *Salt Lake Tribune,* March 7, 1965.

Nelson, Lowry. *In the Direction of His Dreams: Memoirs*. New York: Philosophical Library, 1985.

"New Program to Intensify Supervision of World-wide Church Missions." *Church News,* July 1, 1961.

Newton, Marjorie. *Southern Cross Saints: The Mormons in Australia*. Laie, HI: The Institute for Polynesian Studies, 1991.

"Notice to Church Members." *Deseret News,* March 16, 1966.

O'Dea, Thomas F. *The Mormons*. Chicago: University of Chicago Press, 1957.

Orton, Chad M. *More Faith than Fear: The Los Angeles Stake Story*. Salt Lake City: Bookcraft, 1987.

Parkinson, Benson Young. "S. Dilworth Young of the First Quorum of Seventy." *Journal of Mormon History* 27, no. 1 (Spring 2001): 215–51.

Parrish, Alan K. *John A. Widtsoe: A Biography*. Salt Lake City: Deseret Book, 2003.

Pearson, Drew. "Mormons Reverse Clock." Column. *Washington Post,* October 16, 1966.

[Petersen, Mark E.] "Politics and Religion." Editorial. *Church News,* March 26, 1966.

Peterson, F. Ross. "'Do Not Lecture the Brethren': Stewart L. Udall's Pro-Civil Rights Stance, 1967." *Journal of Mormon History* 25, no. 1 (Spring 1999): 272–87.

———. "Utah Politics since 1945." In *Utah's History,* edited by Richard D. Poll, Thomas G. Alexander, Eugene E. Campbell, and David E. Miller, 514–44. Provo, Utah: Brigham Young University Press, 1978.

Peterson, Levi S. *Juanita Brooks: Mormon Woman Historian*. Salt Lake City: University of Utah Press, 1988.

"Plan Visit to Island Missions." *Deseret News,* October 23, 1920.

"Police Chief Raps Talk at LDS Meet." *Salt Lake Tribune,* April 10, 1946.

"Police Make First Arrest as Cleanup Begins." *Deseret News,* August 10, 1946.

Poll, Richard D. *Working the Divine Miracle: The Life of Apostle Henry D. Moyle*. Salt Lake City: Signature Books, 1999.

"President McKay Clarifies Nixon 'Endorsement.'" *California Intermountain News,* October 13, 1960.

"President McKay 'Interviews' Nixon." *Salt Lake Tribune,* October 11, 1960.

"President McKay Predicts Fall of Red Leaders." *Deseret News,* April 26, 1954.

"Presidential Draft for Elder Benson." *Deseret News,* May 3, 1966.

Prince, Gregory A. *Power from On High: The Development of Mormon Priesthood*. Salt Lake City: Signature Books, 1995.

Proctor, Maurine J., and Scot F. Proctor. *The Gathering: Mormon Pioneers on the Trail to Zion*. Salt Lake City: Deseret Book, 1996.

Quinn, D. Michael. *Elder Statesman: A Biography of J. Reuben Clark*. Salt Lake City: Signature Books, 2002.

———. "Ezra Taft Benson and Mormon Political Conflicts." *Dialogue: A Journal of Mormon Thought* 26, no. 2 (Summer 1993): 1–87.

———. "I–Thou vs. I–It Conversions: The Mormon 'Baseball Baptism' Era." *Sunstone* 16 (December 1993): 30–44.

———. *J. Reuben Clark: The Church Years*. Provo, UT: Brigham Young University Press, 1983.

———. *The Mormon Hierarchy: Extensions of Power*. Salt Lake City: Signature Books, 1997.

———. "The Mormon Succession Crisis of 1844." *BYU Studies* 16, no. 2 (Winter 1976): 187–233.

"Rap Unauthorized Thinking. LDS View on Work Law Unchanged." *Salt Lake Tribune*, July 28, 1965.

"Record Crowds Expected to Attend LDS Meeting." *Salt Lake Tribune*, October 1, 1951.

"Reed A. Benson Takes Post in Birch Society." *Deseret News*, October 27, 1962.

"The Right to Vote." *Newsweek*, July 26, 1965.

Rosenblatt, Joseph. "President David O. McKay Honored." *Improvement Era* 66 (February 1963): 85, 111–12.

Sherlock, Richard. "'We Can See No Advantage to a Continuation of the Discussion': The Roberts/Smith/Talmage Affair." *Dialogue: A Journal of Mormon Thought* 13, no. 3 (Fall 1980): 63–78.

Sonne, Conway B. *Saints on the Seas: A Maritime History of Mormon Migration, 1830–1890*. Salt Lake City: University of Utah Press, 1983.

———. *Ships, Saints, and Mariners: A Maritime Encyclopedia of Mormon Migration, 1830–1890*. Salt Lake City: University of Utah Press, 1987.

"Spirit of Conversion Places 75,700 on Mission Records." *Church News*, December 20, 1961.

"Stand Where You Are!" Editorial. *Millennial Star* 83 (September 15, 1921): 585.

"Statement by President David O. McKay of the Church of Jesus Christ of Latter-day Saints." *Deseret News*, May 11, 1968.

"Statement by President David O. McKay of the Church of Jesus Christ of Latter-day Saints." *Salt Lake Tribune*, May 12, 1968.

"Statement Concerning the Position of the Church on Communism." *Church News*, April 16, 1966.

Steck, Leo J. *A Foreign Mission Close to Home!* N.p., 1949.

Stegner, Wallace. *The Gathering of Zion: The Story of the Mormon Trail*. 1964; rpt., Lincoln: University of Nebraska Press, 1992.

Stewart, John J. *Mormonism and the Negro*. Orem, UT: Bookmark Division of Community Press Publishing Company, 1960.

Stoffel, Monsignor Jerome. "The Hesitant Beginnings of the Catholic Church in Utah." *Utah Historical Quarterly* 36, no. 1 (Winter 1968): 41–62.

Stokes, William Lee. "An Official Position." *Dialogue: A Journal of Mormon Thought* 12, no. 4 (Winter 1979): 90–92.

Taggart, Stephen G. *Mormonism's Negro Policy: Social and Historical Origins*. Salt Lake City: University of Utah Press, 1970.

Taylor, P. A. M. *Expectations Westward: The Mormons and the Emigration of Their British Converts in the Nineteenth Century*. 1965; Ithaca, NY: Cornell University Press, 1966.

Thrapp, Dan L. "Mormons See Romney in Race on His Own, But Full Church Backing Is Assured." *Los Angeles Times,* November 15, 1966.

"Tributes to President David O. McKay." *Improvement Era* 66 (September 1963): 747.

"Two Church Workers Will Tour Missions of Pacific Islands." *Deseret News,* October 15, 1920.

Turner, Wallace. "Mormons Weigh Stand on Negro." *New York Times,* June 7, 1963.

———. "'Right-to-Work' Bid by Mormons Fails." *New York Times,* July 14, 1965.

Udall, Stewart L. "Letter to the Editor." *Dialogue: A Journal of Mormon Thought* 2, no. 2 (Spring 1967): 5–7.

"Unionism 'Coercion' Assailed Vigorously by L.D.S. Church." *Salt Lake Telegram,* July 2, 1937.

"Utah Voters Defeat Three Ballot Issues." *Deseret News,* November 3, 1954.

Van Orden, Bruce A. *Building Zion: The Latter-day Saints in Europe.* Salt Lake City: Deseret Book, 1996.

Warner, W. Keith, and Edward L. Kimball. "Creative Stewardship." *The Carpenter* 1, no. 4 (Spring 1971): 17–26.

Watkins, Arthur V. *Enough Rope: The Inside Story of the Censure of Senator Joe McCarthy by His Colleagues—the Controversial Hearings That Signaled the End of a Turbulent Career and a Fearsome Era in American Public Life.* Englewood Cliffs, NJ: Prentice-Hall, 1969.

Welch, Robert. *The Blue Book of the John Birch Society.* Belmont, MA: Robert Welch, Inc., 1961.

———. *The Politician.* Belmont, MA: privately printed, 1963.

White, O. Kendall Jr. *Mormon Neo-Orthodoxy: A Crisis Theology.* Salt Lake City: Signature Books, 1987.

Whitman, Alden. "David O. McKay, Mormon President, Was Ardent Advocate of Universal Expansion." *New York Times,* January 19, 1970.

Wilkinson, Ernest L. *Brigham Young University: The First One Hundred Years.* Provo, UT: Brigham Young University Press, 1975.

Wright, Evan P. *A History of the South African Mission, Period III, 1944–1970.* N.p.: 1987.

"Wrong Field." Editorial. *Twin Falls Times-News,* July 19, 1965.

MANUSCRIPT SOURCES

Alder, Douglas D. Interviewed by Prince, June 3, 1995. Historian; president, Dixie College.

Alder, Elaine Reiser. Interviewed by Prince, June 3, 1995. Secretary, office of David O. McKay.

Anderson, Alice Wilkinson, to Prince, August 9, 1999. Daughter of Ernest L. Wilkinson.

Anderson, Howard B. Interviewed by Gregory A. Prince, December 8, 1996; October 5, 1999. Interviewed by Stephen L. Prince, February 7, 1997. Transcript in authors' possession. Businessman; grandson-in-law of David O. McKay.

Anderson, Joseph. Interviewed by Jay Todd, 1970 (no month or day indicated). MS 443, LDS Church Archives. Interviewed by Davis Bitton, January 12, 1963. MS 200 29, LDS Church Archives. Secretary to the First Presidency; First Quorum of the Seventy, 1976–78.

Anderson, Midene McKay. Interviewed by Prince, October 1, 1996, September 2, 2004. Daughter of David Lawrence McKay.

Anderson, Robert. Interviewed by Wright, June 14, 1996. David O. McKay's barber.

Arrington, Leonard J. Interviewed by Prince, June 6, 1995. LDS Church Historian.

Barner, Edward. Interviewed by Prince, October 1, 1996. Businessman.

Baruffol, Gabrielle. Interviewed by Prince, May 28, 1994. David O. McKay's housekeeper.

Bates, Irene M. Interviewed by Prince, October 3, 2000. Historian; British member.

Bates, William. Interviewed by Prince, October 5, 1999; October 3, 2000. Engineer; counselor in the first stake presidency in Europe (Manchester, England), and later Manchester Stake president.

Bennett, Wallace F., to David Lawrence McKay, January 21, 1966. Wallace F. Bennett Papers. MS 290, Box 24, Fd. 3, Manuscripts Division, J. Willard Marriott Library, University of Utah. Businessman; U.S. Senator, 1951–75.

Bennion, Lowell L. Interviewed by Maureen Ursenbach Beecher, March 9, 1985. MS 200 730, LDS Church Archives. Instructor, Church Educational System; professor, University of Utah.

Benson, Ezra Taft, to Clare Middlemiss, August 19, 1964. Photocopy in authors' possession. Quorum of the Twelve Apostles, 1943–85; church president, 1985–94.

———. "We Must Become Alerted [*sic*] and Informed." December 13, 1963. Utah State Historical Society, Salt Lake City.

Benson, Lela, to Clare Middlemiss, March 12, 1963. Photocopy in authors' possession. Daughter-in-law of Ezra Taft Benson.

Benson, Mark. Interviewed by Prince, May 21, 1999. Businessman; son of Ezra Taft Benson.

Benson, Reed A. Interviewed by Prince, September 15, 1999. National officer, John Birch Society; son of Ezra Taft Benson.

Bentley, Joseph T. Interviewed by Gordon Irving, June 28, July 19, 1976. MS 200 205, LDS Church Archives. Vice-president, Brigham Young University; general superintendent of Young Men's Mutual Improvement Association, 1952–62.

Bernhard, John T. Interviewed by Prince, October 18, December 5, 1998. Dean, College of Humanities and Social Sciences, Brigham Young University.

Bernhard, Ramona. Interviewed by Prince, December 5, 1998. Friend of Maurine Lee Wilkins, a daughter of Harold B. Lee.

Bird, Stanford. Interviewed by Richard D. Poll, January 17, 1981, Richard Douglas Poll Papers. MS 674, Box 66, Fd. 33, Manuscripts Division, J. Willard Marriott Library, University of Utah. Taped interview transcribed by Prince. Photocopy in the Gregory A. Prince Papers. J. Willard Marriott Library. Employee, Church Building Department.

Blodgett, J. Alan, to Prince, October 15, 19, November 2, 3, 4, 5, 9, 1999; July 31, 2003. Chief Financial Officer, LDS Church.

Boyd, George. Interviewed by Robert Miller, November 15, 1985. Everett L. Cooley Oral History Project, Accn 814, Interview 104, Manuscripts Division, J. Willard Marriott Library, University of Utah. Instructor, Church Educational System.

Boyer, Selvoy J. Interviewed by Gordon Irving, December 12, 1978. MS 200 467, LDS Church Archives. President of the British Mission.

Brockbank, Bernard P. Interviewed by Prince, May 20, 1996. President of North British Mission, Assistant to the Quorum of the Twelve Apostles, 1962–76; First Quorum of the Seventy, 1976–80.

Brossard, Edgar B. Interviewed by Davis Bitton, February 21, 1973. MS 200 51, LDS Church Archives. President of French Mission.

Brown, Charles M. Interviewed by Prince, June 3, 1995. Interviewed by Richard D. Poll, June 7, 1973, Richard Douglas Poll Papers. MS 674, Box 51, Fd. 25. Taped interview transcribed by Prince. Photocopy in the Gregory A. Prince Papers. J. Willard Marriott Library. Professor, University of Southern California; son of Hugh B. Brown.

Brown, Hugh B. Interviewed by Edwin B. Firmage, November 9, 30, 1968, Edwin Brown Firmage Papers. MS 674, Box 51, Fds. 26, 28, Manuscripts Division, J. Willard Marriott Library, University of Utah. Assistant to the Quorum of the Twelve, 1953–58; Quorum of the Twelve Apostles, 1958–61; counselor in the First Presidency, 1961–70; Quorum of the Twelve Apostles, 1970–75.

———. Journal. In Edwin Brown Firmage Papers. MS 674, Box 52, Fd. 14, Manuscripts Division, J. Willard Marriott Library, University of Utah.

———. Letter to Alicia Bingham, December 28, 1961. Edwin Brown Firmage Papers, Box 48, Fd. 21, Manuscripts Division, J. Willard Marriott Library, University of Utah.

———. Letter to Harley R. Hammond, April 25, 1962. Photocopy in authors' possession. Second counselor, First Presidency.

———. Letter to Burns S. Hanson, May 11, 1967. Edwin Brown Firmage Papers, Manuscripts Division, J. Willard Marriott Library, University of Utah.

———. Letter to David O. McKay, November 9, 1966. Edwin Brown Firmage Papers, Manuscripts Division, J. Willard Marriott Library, University of Utah.

Browning, Gary L. Interviewed by Christen L. Schmutz, July 14, 1978. MS 200 377, LDS Church Archives. Served mission in Finland.

Burton, Theodore M. Interviewed by Bruce Blumell, February 4, 18, 1976. MS 200 219, LDS Church Archives. Assistant to the Quorum of the Twelve, 1960–76; First Quorum of the Seventy, 1976–89.

Bush, Lester E. "Compilation on the Negro in Mormonism." 1973. Unpublished typescript. Photocopy in author's possession.

Cannon, Elaine Anderson. Interviewed by authors, June 5, 1995. Young Women general president, 1978–84.

Cheney, Thomas E. Interviewed by J. Roman Andrus, October 10, 1979, UA OH 46, L. Tom Perry Special Collections, Harold B. Lee Library, Brigham Young University. Professor of English, Brigham Young University.

Christensen, Don L. Interviewed by Prince, October 25, 1995. President of Danish Mission.

Christiansen, Horace A. Interviewed by Bruce Blumell, October 29, 1973. MS 200 81, LDS Church Archives. Employee, Church Building Department.

Clark, J. Reuben, Jr. Papers. MSS 303, L. Tom Perry Special Collections, Harold B. Lee Library, Brigham Young University.

Clark, Wilfrid. Interviewed by Prince, October 20, 1999. British member.

Clissold, Edward Lavaun. Interviewed by R. Lanier Britsch, June 11, 1976. MS 200 394, LDS Church Archives. President of Hawaii Stake (Honolulu).

Cook, Owen. Interviewed by Prince, October 28, 1999. Member, Pacific Board of Education.

Croft, Q. Michael. "Influence of the L.D.S. Church on Utah Politics, 1945–1985." Ph.D. diss., University of Utah, 1985.

Delves, William H. "Leave Her Alone: The Dynamic Triangle—David O. McKay, Delbert L. Stapley and Juanita Brooks." Unpublished manuscript in authors' possession.

Dunn, J. Howard. Interviewed by Richard D. Poll, undated interview conducted between 1980 and 1982. Richard Douglas Poll Papers. MS 674, Box 66, Fd. 36, Manuscripts Division, J. Willard Marriott Library, University of Utah. Taped interview transcribed by Prince. Photocopy in the Gregory A. Prince Papers. J. Willard Marriott Library. Employee, Church Building Department.

Dunn, Loren C. Interviewed by Matthew K. Heiss, March 6, 1991. MS 200 1086, LDS Church Archives. First Council of the Seventy, 1968–76; First Quorum of the Seventy, 1976–2000.

Dunn, Paul H. Interviewed by the authors, February 18, June 5, 1995; and by Prince October 6, 1995; January 15, May 21, 1996; January 11, March 21, 1997. First Council of the Seventy, 1964–76; First Quorum of the Seventy, 1976–89.

Eaton, Valoy, to Prince, June 16, 2000. Artist.

Edwards, William F. Interviewed by Oliver Smith, October 21, 1983, UA OH 122, L. Tom Perry Special Collections, Harold B. Lee Library, University of Utah. Vice-president, Brigham Young University.

Eisenhower, Dwight D., to Ralph R. Harding, October 7, 1963. Photocopy in authors' possession.

Erekson, William S. Interviewed by Christen L. Schmutz, June 26, 1979. MS 200 403, LDS Church Archives. President of Swiss Mission.

Fairbanks, David N., to Elly Srobel Card, January 24, 2002. Photocopy in authors' possession. Physician.

Federal, Joseph Lennox. Papers. Archives of the Catholic Diocese of Salt Lake City.

Fetzer, Emil B. Interviewed by authors, September 20, 2002. LDS Church architect.

Firmage, Edwin Brown. Interviewed by Prince, June 6, 1995, October 10, 1996. Professor of law, University of Utah; grandson of Hugh B. Brown.

Firmage, Edwin Brown. Papers. Accn 1074, Manuscripts Division, J. Willard Marriott Library, University of Utah.

First Presidency and Quorum of the Twelve Apostles. Minutes, April 1, 1965. Photocopy in authors' possession.

First Presidency Circular Letters. CR 1, LDS Church Archives.

Fletcher, Faye. Interviewed by Prince, August 20, 2000. Wife of James C. Fletcher, who was president of the University of Utah.

Foulger, James. Interviewed by Prince, September 3, 2002. Served in British Mission.

Friberg, Arnold. Interviewed by Prince, August 4, November 16, 2000. Artist.

Fyans, Helen Cook. Interviewed by Prince, June 3, 1995. Wife of J. Thomas Fyans.

Fyans, J. Thomas. Interviewed by Prince, June 3, 1995. President, Uruguayan Mission; chairman of the Translation Department; Assistant to the Quorum of the Twelve Apostles, 1974–76; First Quorum of the Seventy, 1976–89.

Gallivan, John W. Interviewed by Wright, March 7, 1995. Publisher, *Salt Lake Tribune*.

Goates, L. Brent. Interviewed by Prince, May 20, 1996. Son-in-law and biographer of Harold B. Lee.

Grilikhes, Michael. Interviewed by Prince, October 1, 2000. CBS executive.

Haight, David B. Interviewed by Prince, May 21, 1996. Assistant to the Quorum of the Twelve Apostles, 1970–76; Quorum of the Twelve Apostles, 1976–2004.

Hammond, Harley R., to Hugh B. Brown, April 24, 1962. Photocopy in authors' possession. Graduate student.

Hanks, Marion D. Interviewed by Prince, May 27, 1994. First Council of the Seventy, 1953–68; Assistant to the Quorum of the Twelve Apostles, 1968–76; First Quorum of the Seventy, 1976–92.

Harding, Ralph R. Interviewed by Prince, September 19, October 24, 2000. Congressman (D-Idaho), 1961–65.

Hartshorn, Leon R. "Mormon Education in the Bold Years." Ph.D. diss, Stanford University, 1965.

Hatch, Kenneth L. Interviewed by Tim Larson, May 20, 1988. Everett L. Cooley Oral History Project, Accn 814, Interview 186, Manuscripts Division, J. Willard Marriott Library, University of Utah. KSL employee.

Hechler, Kenneth W. White House memo to Matthew J. Connolley, September 25, 1952. Harry S. Truman Library, Independence, MO.

Hemming, Val G., to Prince, February 15, 2003. Physician.

Herbertson, Arthur Forbes. Interviewed by Gordon Irving, April 2, 1986. MS 200 752, LDS Church Archives. British member.

Hinckley, Ann. Interviewed by Newell Bringhurst, November 28, 1988. Transcript in authors' possession. Friend of Fawn McKay Brodie.

Hinckley, Gordon B. Interviewed by Wright, December 10, 1996. Assistant to the Quorum of the Twelve Apostles, 1958–61; Quorum of the Twelve Apostles, 1961–81; counselor in First Presidency, 1981–95; church president, 1995–present.

Hinckley, Robert H., to David O. McKay, March 17, 1966. Photocopy in authors' possession. Executive, American Broadcasting Company.

Hodson, Paul W. Interviewed by Prince, May 23, 1996. Vice-president, University of Utah.

———. Letter to Prince, June 8, 1996.

Hunt, Duane G. Papers. Archives of the Catholic Diocese of Salt Lake City.

Iba, Katherine McKay. Interviewed by Prince, October 2, 2000. Granddaughter of David O. McKay.

Izatt, Joel. Interviewed by Prince, October 22, 1994. Served in British Mission.

Jacobsen, Theodore Christian ("Ted"). Interviewed by Prince, September 24, 1997. President of New York Mission.

Jackson, Richard W. Interviewed by Prince, October 19, 1999. Architect, Church Building Department.

Johnson, Lyndon B. Papers. Lyndon B. Johnson Library and Museum, Austin, Texas.

Jonas, Frank Herman. Research Files. MS 641, Manuscripts Division, J. Willard Marriott Library, University of Utah.

Journal History of the Church of Jesus Christ of Latter-day Saints. Chronology of typed entries and newspaper clippings, 1830–present. LDS Church Archives.

Kastler, B. Z. ("Bud"). Interviewed by Prince, June 3, 1997. President, Mountain Fuel Supply.

Kennedy, David M. Interviewed by Gordon Irving, December 13, 1982. MS 200 968, LDS Church Archives. President, First Continental Bank; U.S. Secretary of the Treasury, 1969–71.

Kerr, Clifton George Mercer. Interviewed by Gordon Irving, October 23, 1980. MS 200 541, LDS Church Archives. British Mission president.

Kimball, Spencer L. to Prince, September 24, 1996.

Kimball, Spencer W. "Priesthood Missionary Work in the Church." Seminar for Regional Representatives of the Twelve, September 27, 1967. Photocopy in authors' possession.

Kimball, William Clayton ("Tony"). Interviewed by Prince, August 22, 1999. Served in German Mission.

King, David S. Interviewed by Prince, February 1, 1995. General Superintendency, Young Men's Mutual Improvement Association; Congressman (D-Utah), 1959–61, 1963–67; U.S. Ambassador to Madagascar.

Kirton, Wilford W., Jr. Interviewed by Gordon Irving, March 31, 1981. MS 200 525, LDS Church Archives. Church General Counsel.

Kjar, Joseph. Interviewed by Tim Larson, August 5, 1988. Everett L. Cooley Oral History Project, Accn 814, Interview 221, Manuscripts Division, J. Willard Marriott Library, University of Utah. KSL employee.

Lee, J. Bracken. Interviewed by J. Keith Melville, November 28, 1979. MSS OH 431, L. Tom Perry Special Collections, Harold B. Lee Library, Brigham Young University. Utah governor, 1948–56.

Leonhardt, Karlheinz. *Die Erste Hundert Jahr: Eine Geschichte der Gemeinde Friberg.* Freiberg, Germany: privately published by Karlheinz Leonhardt, 2000. English translation by Raymond Kuehne in Prince's possession.

Lund, Anthon H. Diary. MS 288, LDS Church Archives.

Lyman, Platt D. Diary. Library of Congress Collection of Mormon Diaries. Microfilm copy at Bancroft Library, University of California, Berkeley, Photographic Service No. 2804. The Lyman diary is on Roll 3.

Macfarlane, Alan. Interviewed by Prince, February 19, 1995. David O. McKay's physician.

Madsen, Arch L. Interviewed by Prince, February 19, 1995; and by authors, January 14, 1996. Interviewed by Richard D. Poll, June 11, 1981, Richard Douglas Poll Papers. MS 674, Box 67, Fd. 3, Manuscripts Division, J. Willard Marriott Library, University of Utah. Taped interview transcribed by Prince. Photocopy in the Gregory A. Prince Papers. J. Willard Marriott Library. President, KSL radio and television; founding president of Bonneville International Corporation.

McConkie, Oscar W., Jr. Interviewed by Prince, August 24, 1998. Attorney.

McConnell, Cathy. Interviewed by Prince, November 18, 2000. Registered nurse.

McKay, David Lawrence. Interviewed by Gordon Irving, January 5, March 30, 1984. MS 300 734, LDS Church Archives. Attorney, son of David O. McKay.

McKay, David Oman. Diaries, 1897–99; 1920–23; 1932; 1936–70. Cited as DOMD. In the David Oman McKay Papers (DOMP). MS 668, Manuscripts Division, J. Willard Marriott Library, University of Utah.

———. Scrapbooks, 215 volumes with assorted contents and no pagination. MS 4640, LDS Church Archives. Cited as DOMS.

McKay, Edward R. Interviewed by Prince, February 16, 1995. Physician; son of David O. McKay.

———. Remarks at David O. McKay Symposium, Brigham Young University, October 1996. Typescript in the authors' possession.

———. Letter to Sterling M. McMurrin, September 19, 1968, photocopy in authors' possession.

McKay, K. Gunn. Interviewed by Wright, January 14, 1995. Congressman (D-Utah); cousin of David O. McKay.

McKay, Monroe G. Interviewed by Prince, March 5, 1999. Federal judge, U.S. Court of Appeals for the Tenth Circuit; cousin of David O. McKay.

McKay, Quinn G. Interviewed by Prince, May 21, 1999. Professor of business administration, Brigham Young University; cousin of David O. McKay.

McKay, Richard. Interviewed by Prince, May 21, 1996. Dentist; grandson of David O. McKay.

McKay, Robert R. Interviewed by authors, March 21, 1995. Businessman; son of David O. McKay.

———. Letter to Ralph R. Harding, October 18, 1963. Photocopy in authors' possession.

McKay, Vivian. Interviewed by Prince, May 21, 1996. Granddaughter-in-law of David O. McKay.

McMurrin, Sterling M. "Account of Events of 1952–54." Tape recorded approximately 1980. Transcribed by and in the possession of the authors. Vice-president, University of Utah; U.S. Commissioner of Education, 1961–62.

———. Affidavit, March 6, 1979. Photocopy in authors' possession.

———. Interviewed by Prince, June 6, 1995.

———. Letter to Llewelyn R. McKay, August 26, 1968. Photocopy in authors' possession.

———. Letter to Prince, October 30, 1994.

Mecham, L. Ralph, to Prince, March 21, 2001. Director, Administrative Office of the U.S. Courts.

Middlemiss, Clare. "Notes." Photocopy in authors' possession.

Miller, William P. "Weber College, 1888 to 1933: Historical Information Obtained from Original Sources in the Archives of the Church of Jesus Christ of Latter-day Saints in Salt Lake City." Stewart Library, Weber State University, Ogden, Utah.

Mitchell, Kenneth H. "The Struggle for Reapportionment in Utah." M.S. thesis, University of Utah, 1960.

Monson, Thomas S. "Eternal Principles from Prophets' Lives." Brigham Young University Devotional, October 10, 1989. Typescript in authors' possession.

Morley, Peter L. Interviewed by Douglas F. Tobler, October 10, 1974. MS 200 744, LDS Church Archives. British member.

Mortensen, A. Russell. Interviewed by Newell Bringhurst, October 9, 1987. Everett L. Cooley Oral History Project, Accn 814, Interview 367, Manuscripts Division, J. Willard Marriott Library, University of Utah. Professor, University of Utah. Historian; Director, Utah State Historical Society.

Moss, Frank E. Interviewed by Prince, October 10, 1996. U.S. Senator (D-Utah), 1959–77.

———. Letter to Hugh B. Brown, December 20, 1963. Frank E. Moss Papers. Box 122, Fd. 3, Manuscripts Division, J. Willard Marriott Library, University of Utah.

Mouritsen, Dale C. "Efforts to Correlate Mormon Church Agencies in the Twentieth Century: A Review." August 1974. Photocopy in authors' possession.

Moyle, Henry D., Jr. Interviewed by Prince, June 2, 1997. President of the French Mission; son of Henry D. Moyle.

Moyle, Henry D., [Sr.], to J. D. Williams, January 9, 1963. Photocopy in authors' possession. Counselor in the First Presidency, 1959–63.

Moyle, Richard. Interviewed by Richard D. Poll, June 20, 1980. Richard Douglas Poll Papers. MS 674, Box 67, Fd. 10, Manuscripts Division, J. Willard Marriott Library, University of Utah. Taped interview transcribed by Prince. Photocopy in the Gregory A. Prince Papers. J. Willard Marriott Library. Son of Henry D. Moyle.

Murdock, Franklin J. Interviewed by Gordon Irving, March 28 and 30, 1973. MS 200 89, LDS Church Archives. Secretary, LDS Church Missionary Committee.

Nibley, Hugh. Interviewed by Prince, June 5, 1995. Professor of ancient scriptures, Brigham Young University.

Olson, Peter D. Interviewed by Prince, September 29, 1996. Served in British Mission.

Parmley, Martha LaVern Watts. Interviewed by Jill Mulvay, November 19, 1974. MS 200 296, LDS Church Archives. Primary Association general president, 1951–74.

Poll, Richard D. Interviewed by Maureen Ursenbach Beecher, May 28, 1985. Richard Douglas Poll Papers. MS 674, Box 66, Fd. 29, Manuscripts Division, J. Willard Marriott Library, University of Utah. Professor of history, Brigham Young University.

Poll, Richard Douglas. Papers. MS 674, Manuscripts Division, J. Willard Marriott Library, University of Utah.

Prince, Gregory A. Papers. Accn 1334, Manuscripts Division, J. Willard Marriott Library, University of Utah.

Rampton, Calvin L. Interviewed by authors, February 21, 1995. Utah governor, 1964–76.

———. Oral History, Accn 814, Manuscripts Division, J. Willard Marriott Library, University of Utah.

Rasmussen, Donald H. Interviewed by Prince, June 6, 1995. Businessman.

Reiser, A. Hamer. Interviewed by William G. Hartley, August 30, September 10, 24, October 16, 1974. MS 200 334 3 LDS Church Archives. President of the British Mission; assistant secretary to the First Presidency.

Richards, LeGrand. Interviewed by William G. Hartley, March 15, 1974. MS 200 77, LDS Church Archives. Presiding Bishop, 1938–52; Quorum of the Twelve Apostles, 1952–83.

Richards, Lynn S. Interviewed by Prince, January 15, 1996. Counselor in general superintendency, Deseret Sunday School Union.

Romney, Antone K. "History of the Correlation of L.D.S. Church Auxiliaries." Prepared for the Research Committee of the Melchizedek Priesthood Education Committee, August 1961, part B, CR 2/21, LDS Church Archives.

Rosenblatt, Joseph. Interviewed by Wright, March 1995. Businessman.

Roy, Albert. Interviewed by Ronald K. Esplin, April 1, 1987. MS 200 763, LDS Church Archives. Served in British Mission.

Rushforth, Brent. Interviewed by Prince, January 9, 2002. Served in Berlin Mission.

Russon, John M. Interviewed by Chad M. Orton, June 11, 1986. MS 200 729, LDS Church Archives. President of Los Angeles Stake.

Sears, Robert. Interviewed by Richard D. Poll, January 15, 1981. Richard Douglas Poll Papers. MS 674, Box 67, Fd. 18, Manuscripts Division, J. Willard Marriott Library, University of Utah. Taped interview transcribed by Prince. Photocopy in the Gregory A. Prince Papers. J. Willard Marriott Library. Businessman.

Shreeve, Lyman S. Interviewed by Gordon Irving, October 18, 1974. MS 200 110, LDS Church Archives. President of Uruguayan Mission.

Simpson, Robert L. Interviewed by Prince, June 2, 1995. Counselor in Presiding Bishopric, 1961–72; Assistant to the Quorum of the Twelve Apostles, 1972–76; First Quorum of the Seventy, 1976–89.

Skinner, Dorothy L., to Hugh B. Brown, March 24, 1967. Photocopy in authors' possession. LDS Church member, Maryland.

Smith, Alistair James McWilliam. Interviewed by Ronald K. Esplin, July 14, 1987. MS 200 917, LDS Church Archives. Local Church leader, British Isles.

Smith, Barbara Bradshaw. Interviewed by Prince, July 31, 2000. Relief Society general president, 1974–84.

Smith, Eldred G. Interviewed by Prince, October 5, 1995. Presiding Patriarch.

Smith, Hyrum. Interviewed by Prince, January 19, 2004. Served in British Mission.

Smith, Joseph Fielding, to Delmont H. White, October 25, 1963. Photocopy in authors' possession. President of the Quorum of the Twelve Apostles.

———. Letters to Ralph R. Harding, October 30, 1963, and December 23, 1963. Photocopy in authors' possession.

Snow, R. J. Interviewed by Everett L. Cooley, October 23, 1984. Everett L. Cooley Oral History Project, Accn 814, interview 8, Manuscripts Division, J. Willard Marriott Library, University of Utah. Vice-president, Brigham Young University.

Sorensen, Asael. Interviewed by Prince, November 18, 2000. President Brazilian Mission.

Spafford, Marion Isabell ("Belle"). Interviewed by Jill Mulvay Derr, January 12, 1976. MS 200 344, LDS Church Archives. Relief Society general president, 1945–74.

Stevens, Gary. Interviewed by Prince, October 20, 2000. Served in British Mission.

Stoffel, Jerome. Interviewed by Prince, October 6, 1995. Monsignor, Catholic Diocese of Salt Lake City.

Talmage, James E. Diaries. MSS 229, L. Tom Perry Special Collections, Harold B. Lee Library, Brigham Young University.

Thorup, Levi Berg. Interviewed by Richard L. Jensen, June 5, 1975. MS 200 474, LDS Church Archives. President of Danish Mission.

Timmins, David. Interviewed by Prince, March 18, 2000. Foreign Service officer.

———. Letter to Prince, undated 1999.

Timmins, Lola Gygi, to Prince, April 20, 1998. Foreign Service officer; secretary, office of David O. McKay.

———. Interviewed by Prince, October 28, 1998; August 4, 2000; January 17, 2003.

Tingey, Dale T. Interviewed by Prince, September 23, 1997. Assistant Administrator, LDS Institutes of Religion.

Transcript of telephone conversation between President Lyndon B. Johnson and David O. McKay, January 25, 1964. White House Recordings and Telephone Notes, Box 1, Lyndon B. Johnson Library and Museum, Austin, TX.

Truman, Harry S. Papers. Harry S. Truman Library, Independence, Missouri.

Turvey, Arch J. Interviewed by Gordon Irving, April 3, 1986. MS 200 753, LDS Church Archives. British member.

Tuttle, A. Theodore. Interviewed by Gordon Irving, August 23, October 11, November 22, 1977. MS 200 354, LDS Church Archives. First Council of the Seventy, 1958–76; First Quorum of the Seventy, 1976–86.

Vandenberg, John H. Interviewed by Gordon Irving, November 15, December 6, 1984. MS 200 727, LDS Church Archives. Presiding Bishop, 1961–72; Assistant to the Quorum of the Twelve Apostles, 1972–76; First Quorum of the Seventy, 1976–78.

Wangeman, Marie Moyle. Interviewed by Richard D. Poll, June 14, 1981. Richard Douglas Poll Papers. MS 674, Box 67, Fd. 21, Manuscripts Division, J. Willard Marriott Library, University of Utah. Taped interview transcribed by Prince. Photocopy in the Gregory A. Prince Papers. J. Willard Marriott Library. Daughter of Henry D. Moyle.

Watt, Ronald G. Interviewed by Prince, November 15, 2000. Served in British Mission.

Weilenmann, Milton L. Interviewed by Prince, February 20, 1995. Interviewed by Frank H. Jonas, September 6, 1957. Frank Herman Jonas Papers. MS 641, Box 97, Fd. 20, Manuscripts Division, J. Willard Marriott Library, University of Utah. Chairman, Utah Democratic Party.

White, Jean Bickmore. "Utah State Elections, 1895–1899." Ph.D. diss., University of Utah, 1968.

Wilcox, Keith W. Interviewed by Prince, October 7, 1996. Architect, designed the McKay-Dee Hospital in Ogden, Utah, and several Church buildings; First and Second Quorums of the Seventy, 1984–89.

Wilkinson, Ernest L., to Ezra Taft Benson, May 4, 1971. Photocopy in authors' possession. President, Brigham Young University.

———. Diaries. In Ernest L. Wilkinson Personal Papers. UA 1000, L. Tom Perry Special Collections, Harold B. Lee Library, Brigham Young University. Cited as ELWD.

Williams, J. D. Diary. Photocopy in authors' possession. Professor, University of Utah.

———. Letter to First Presidency, January 4, 1963. Photocopy in authors' possession.

Williams, LaMar S. Interviewed by Gordon Irving, May 6, 1981. MS 200 692, LDS Church Archives. Church Missionary Department; intended to be but not set apart as president of the Nigerian Mission.

Woodbury, T. Bowring. "Bulletins and Ideas, 1958–61." Photocopy in authors' possession.

———. Diary. MS 8000, LDS Church Archives.

Woodbury, Thomas Bowring, II. Interviewed by Prince, March 25, 2000. Son of T. Bowring Woodbury.

Wright, Wm. Robert. Interviewed by Prince, August 23, 1997. Attorney; nephew of Clare Middlemiss.

Yeates, Alice Moyle. Interviewed by Prince, February 19, 2001. Daughter of Henry D. Moyle.

INDEX

Australian aborigines, excluded from ban on priesthood ordination, 94

Backman, Gus, alliance with DOM over local nonpartisan issues, 333

Benson, Ezra Taft, charged that civil rights movement was "fomented almost entirely by the Communists," 64; civil rights movement "part of the pattern for the communist take-over of America," 70; Communists using civil rights movement to take over the country, 71; obtained permission from DOM to speak on civil rights in general conference, 72; Communists plan "to destroy America by spilling Negro blood," 72; accused Martin Luther King Jr. of being a Communist agent, 93; accused NAACP of being a Communist front organization, 93; recommended recall of LaMar Williams and closure of Nigerian Mission, 93; urged by DOM not to visit pope while on official visit to Italy, 121; highlights of pre-church career, 282; call to Quorum of the Twelve, 282; given leave-of-absence to be Eisenhower's Secretary of Agriculture, 283; DOM denied request to return to job in Washington following Eisenhower years, 285; met Robert Welch in 1961, 286; DOM consistently supportive of his anti-Communist rhetoric, 286; "No true Latter-day Saint...can be a socialist or a communist," 287; DOM reaffirmed support for his attitude towards Communism, 289; sought DOM's endorsement of Reed Benson's

becoming John Birch Society officer, 289; called John Birch Society "most effective organization we have in the country in fighting Communism and Socialism," 289; DOM acknowledged that First Presidency statement denouncing John Birch Society was also directed at Benson, 291; other General Authorities critical of Benson's extremism, 294; in spite of criticism from others, enjoyed continued support from DOM, 294; wanted to join National Council of John Birch Society, 294; DOM declined request, 295; spoke at testimonial dinner for Robert Welch, 295; refused to counter Robert Welch allegation that Dwight Eisenhower was a tool of the Communists, 295; called to preside over European Mission, 298; mission call widely seen as rebuff to his political activities, 298; gave inflammatory speech in Logan prior to departing for Europe, 299; Joseph Fielding Smith: "When he returns I hope his blood will be purified," 300; DOM: "Several of us have had problems with Brother Benson over the Birch Society," 300; DOM denied allegation, 301; DOM met with Twelve to set record straight, 301; continued political activities while in Europe, 303; continued support from DOM, 304; openly endorsed John Birch Society, allowing his picture on the cover of their magazine, 304; spoke in general conference of "traitors in the church," 304; wanted to form national third political party with Strom Thurmond, 305;

implied DOM endorsement of John Birch
Society, 307; obtained approval for DOM
picture on cover of John Birch Society magazine, 307; slated to introduce Robert Welch
at tribute banquet, 310; DOM vetoed Benson's participation at Welch banquet, 311;
obtained permission from DOM to run for
president of the United States, 315; public
endorsement by DOM for presidential candidacy, 315; renewed attempt to join National
Council of John Birch Society, 317; DOM
declined request, 317; complaints from
church members over his political activism,
318; sought permission to run as vice presidential candidate with George Wallace, 319;
final attempt to obtain DOM's endorsement
of John Birch Society, 319; inflammatory
speech at BYU counteracted by Hugh B.
Brown, 321; political activism greatly diminished following death of DOM, 321; discussed with DOM allegations against Douglas Stringfellow, 346; conveyed Eisenhower's
demand that Stringfellow be removed from
ticket, 347

Benson, Reed, accepted position as Utah coordinator for John Birch Society, 290

blacks, exclusion from priesthood, policy pre-
dating Civil War, 60; origins of policy, 74;
DOM did not encounter policy until 1921,
74; First Presidency vaguely tied policy to
pre-existence, 74; DOM cited Book of Abraham, pre-existence in support of policy, 75;
DOM declined to invoke "curse of Cain"
rationale, 75; DOM characterized it as muta-
ble "policy," not immutable "doctrine," 75;
en route to South African Mission, ponders
what to do about practice, 77; policy to
remain "until the Lord gives us another revelation," 77; DOM changed policy regarding
genealogical research, 78; when in doubt,
DOM acted on the side of mercy, 78; South
Africa trip caused DOM to reexamine policy,
79; "a practice, not a doctrine, and the practice will some day be changed," 79; special
committee of the Twelve to reexamine the
policy, 80; though a policy, change would
require a revelation, 80; authorizes ordination of Fijians, 81, 94; DOM abandoned pre-
existence rationale for policy, 81; Hugh B.
Brown suggested ordination to Lesser Priesthood, 83; DOM declined to ordain Nigerians
to Lesser Priesthood, 83; DOM declined to
present matter to the Twelve, 84; only the
Lord can change it, 85; Hugh B. Brown
announced reconsideration of policy, 87;
DOM reaffirmed that change could only
come through a revelation, 88; Australian
aborigines excluded from ban, 94; Egyptians
without evidence of Negro blood excluded
from ban, 94; allowed to hold leadership
roles in auxiliary organizations, 95; questions
relating to temple ordinances, 95; DOM
declined to publish official position, 95;
DOM "much more liberal on this subject
than many of the brethren, 97; First Presidency discussion of policy in light of
McMurrin letter, 99; Hugh B. Brown pushed
to reverse policy in light of McMurrin letter,
99; Hugh B. Brown "tried twice of late" to
get DOM to reverse policy, 100; Harold B.
Lee wrote First Presidency statement reaffirming policy, 101; First Presidency statement signed by Hugh B. Brown under pressure from Harold B. Lee, 101; text of First
Presidency statement, 101; statement omitted
mention of "divine curse," 102; after initial
delay, First Presidency statement published,
102; 1978 revelation reversed policy, 103;
DOM petitioned the Lord for change on
several occasions, 103

Blodgett, J. Alan, overheated building program
led to financial overextension, 209; challenge
was to implement new accounting system
that could keep up with building program,
212; made retrospective analysis of problems
with building program, 222

Bonneville International Corporation, formed in
1964 as holding company for church broadcasting interests, 135; rapid acquisition of
broadcasting properties, 135

Brigham Young University, DOM felt it had the
greatest responsibility of any university in the
world, 165; unprecedented building program
initiated by Wilkinson, 166; development
office created in 1955, 166; operating budget
doubled between 1951 and 1956, 166; budget
crisis of 1959 affected BYU, 166; enrollment
quadrupled between 1951 and 1966, 167;
eighty buildings constructed between 1951
and 1966, 167; by 1969, largest private university in the United States, 167; Gospel "is the
proper subject to teach in all classes," 169;

DOM required high standard of orthodoxy for BYU professors, 171; 1961 budget money shifted to Building Committee, 211

broadcasting, church broadcasting experience began in 1925, 124; first televised broadcast of general conference, 124; expanding television coverage of general conference, 124; DOM's vision of the role of broadcasting in the church, 127; request from CBS for programming beyond Tabernacle Choir, 128; *Let Freedom Ring* won Peabody and Freedom Foundation awards, 129; acquisition of KIRO, Seattle, 134; plans to broadcast to the entire world, 136; factors causing abandonment of plans to broadcast to the entire world, 136; shift in focus from ownership to content, 137; drop in popularity of Tabernacle Choir broadcasts, 137; origin of "Homefront" series, 138

Brockbank, Bernard P., purchased over 28 building sites in Scotland, 204

Brodie, Fawn McKay, niece of DOM, 58; published *No Man Knows My History*, 58; DOM privately condemned "viciousness and inaccuracy," 58; excommunicated by local Church leaders, 58; no evidence DOM involved in excommunication; mutual acrimony between her and DOM, 58; DOM refused to recognize and accept her, 58; DOM became reconciled to her, 59; "Fawn, you're one of my favorite nieces," 59

Brooks, Juanita, genesis of *Mountain Meadows Massacre,* 53; ostracized by local church for publishing *Mountain Meadows Massacre,* 53; research led to reinstatement of John D. Lee's church membership, 54; published account of John D. Lee reinstatement despite threats to her, 54; Delbert Stapley urged her excommunication, 54; DOM to Stapley: "Leave her alone," 54; tears upon learning of DOM's instructions, 55

Brossard, Edgar, deplored poor condition of rented meeting halls in France, 200

Brown, Hugh B., sent by DOM to BYU to moderate conservative theology, 49; sole voice of moderation on civil rights, 65; activism over civil rights caused release from First Presidency following DOM's death, 66; brought into First Presidency as extra counselor, 68; met with NAACP leaders to prevent picketing of general conference, 69; through body language, gave civil rights statement the impact of an official statement, 70; eulogized Martin Luther King Jr. in general conference despite DOM's refusal to do so, 73; announced reconsideration of policy on ordination of blacks, 87; incurred displeasure of DOM for stand on blacks and priesthood, 88; debated with Alvin R. Dyer that policy should be reversed, 99; "tried twice of late" to get DOM to reverse policy, 100; signed First Presidency statement reaffirming policy, under pressure from Harold B. Lee, 101; dropped from First Presidency following death of DOM, 103; warned mission presidents against pushing too hard for baptismal goals, 245; complimented by DOM for research work relating to cancellation of sealings, 275; became sounding board for those opposed to Ezra Taft Benson's anti-Communist extremism, 286; criticism of John Birch Society and political extremism, 287; denounced Benson support of Society in *Los Angele Times* article, 292; flare-up with Clare Middlemiss over John Birch Society, 306; assigned by DOM to counteract inflammatory speech given by Ezra Taft Benson at BYU, 321; public conflict with DOM over Taft-Hartley law, 328; attempted to distance church from Taft-Hartley controversy, 329; allowed to address Utah Democratic convention to counteract impression that church favored Republicans, 336

building program, DOM dismayed by poor meeting halls in Europe, 199; church-constructed buildings necessary to build strong, permanent presence in foreign countries, 200; "a good building is worth twenty full-time missionaries," 200; total church expenditures on buildings fell to $320,000 in 1935, 201; WWII put church construction projects on hold, 201; J. Reuben Clark imposed building moratorium in 1950, 201; surplus of cash accumulated during war years was springboard for new building program, 202; "focus of the Mormon Church today is upon building," 202; plans for 30,000-seat conference center announced, 202; building of temples in foreign countries necessary to reverse policy of gathering, 202; building program placed directly under First Presidency, 203;

approval of construction of Relief Society Building, 203; purpose of buildings was to allow church members to stay in their native countries, 204; "took off like a shot" under Wendell Mendenhall, 205; labor missionaries contributed greatly to its success, 206; accelerated with calling of Henry D. Moyle to First Presidency, 206; unprecedented acquisition of building sites in Europe, 207; unprecedented level of spending approved by DOM, 208; over half of all chapels in church built between 1951 and 1963, 208; chapel construction succeeded in lifting church image abroad, 209; integral to proselytizing successes, 209; overheated program led to financial overextension, 209; Twelve passed 1959 resolution to keep annual spending within income, 210; deficit for 1960 projected to be $17,000,000, 210; deficit for 1961 projected to be $20–25,000,000, 211; deficit for 1962 projected to be $60,000,000, 211; renewed emphasis on tithing to decrease deficits, 212; overheated building program outpaced accounting system, 212; church leaders sought financial assistance from First National City Bank of New York, 212; consideration of sale of church assets to finance deficit, 213; eastern bankers knew church was in "serious financial difficulties," 213; more construction costs shifted to local congregations, 213; DOM rejected recommendation from N. Eldon Tanner to have committee of General Authorities oversee program, 215; all of 1964 building budget spent in first half of year, 216; despite budget problem, Mendenhall told to proceed without change, 216; Tanner identified cost overruns, 216; building program needed to be cut in half to meet budget, 216; recommendation to deal with problems without changing personnel, 216; DOM commissioned separate committee to look into building program, 217; committee, independent of Tanner, recommended releasing Building Committee, 218, 220; list of grievances against Building Committee, 220; Twelve voted unanimously for Mendenhall's release, 221; audit showed mismanagement, but no financial impropriety, 221; retrospective analysis of problems with

building program, 222; success of program in building overseas church, 222; DOM initially approved Quorum of Twelve oversight of building program, then changed mind, 223; under Mark Garff, conditions improved dramatically, 225
Bunche, Ralph, refused accommodation at Hotel Utah, 66
BYU Hawaii. *See* Church College of Hawaii

Cannon, Hugh, predicted in 1921 that DOM would become church president, 11
Catholic Church, DOM's attitude contrasted with that toward other churches, 112; anti-Catholic sentiment in America at time of founding of church, 112; DOM did not explicitly link Book of Mormon and Catholicism, 112; DOM's anti-Catholic feelings in 1923, 113; DOM suspected organized Catholic campaign to proselytize Mormons, 115; DOM warned against attempted inroads, 115; pamphlet misconstrued by LDS leaders, 115; anti-Catholic meetings initiated by Mark E. Petersen, 116; Duane Hunt letter to DOM sought to clarify role of Catholic Church in Utah, 118; DOM accepted Hunt's explanation, 119; opening of LDS mission to Italy, 119; DOM complimented spirituality of Brazilian Catholics, 120; DOM told colleague, "Catholic Church is an anti-Christ," 120; DOM suspected it was undermining LDS Church, 121; DOM urged Agriculture Secretary Ezra Taft Benson to avoid audience with pope while on official trip, 121; called "Church of the Devil" by Bruce R. McConkie, 122; following publication of *Mormon Doctrine,* DOM abandoned public criticism of Catholic Church, 122; bells of Cathedral of the Madeleine tolled in respect to DOM funeral procession, 123
Celestial Kingdom, "That is what the Celestial Kingdom looks like," 27
character, the most important purpose of life, 11; without development of character, technology will lead to calamity, 160; aim of true education, 160
Cheney, Thomas, predicted that policy on ordination of blacks would change, 89; denied BYU promotion because of prediction, 89

children, "President McKay spoke to us children, and we could understand what he meant," 17; DOM thrilled with visits from children, 17

Chinese Mission, threat of Communist invasion of Hong Kong forced closure, 281

Chukwuo, Ambrose, published inflammatory article causing delay in opening Nigerian Mission, 86

Church College of Hawaii, DOM recommended formation following 1921 trip to Hawaii, 179; decision to locate college in Laie, 179; opened in 1955, 179; succeeded in increasing college attendance by Polynesians, 180

civil rights, DOM had lifelong distrust of civil rights, 60; disturbed at racist remarks made by fellow missionaries in 1897, 61; "I do not care much for a negro," 61; DOM refused to intervene when black soldiers were excluded from Deseret Gymnasium, 62; DOM defended rights of businessmen to discriminate, 62; discrimination in Utah "almost as severe as in the South," 66; civil rights legislation consistently blocked in Utah Legislature, 66; *Deseret News* editorial called for gradual desegregation, 67; DOM blocked *Deseret News* from advocating school desegregation, 67; DOM objected to JFK's civil rights initiatives, 67; DOM declined JFK invitation to White House conference on civil rights, 68; DOM defended businessmen's right to discriminate, 68; NAACP threatened to picket general conference, 69; DOM refused to make civil rights statement an official First Presidency statement, 69; *Deseret News* later referred to statement as "official," 70; Utah has "potentially the worst race problem in the United States," 70; DOM accepted LBJ invitation to serve on national civil rights committee despite personal reservations, 71; Church declined to advocate equal opportunity in housing and employment, 71; DOM initially opposed republication of civil rights statement, 71; rumor of attempts to bomb Temple Square, 72; hysteria over civil rights led to unprecedented security measures for General Authorities, 72; linkage between policy on priesthood and aversion to civil rights, 73

Clark, J. Reuben, Jr., role reversal upon death of George Albert Smith, 2; "demoted" to Second Counselor, 2; sent by DOM to BYU to affirm unique position of church president to define doctrine, 49; authorized local church leaders to "restrict and control negro settlement" in Salt Lake City, 63; urged General Relief Society President to oppose "negro equality," 63; began anti-Catholic campaign, 114; wrote anti-Catholic treatise, 114; advised Wilkinson to "get rid of" some BYU faculty, 172; opposed construction of new junior colleges, 194; opposed construction of elaborate church buildings, placed moratorium on new construction, 201

Clissold, Edward Lavaun, transmitted vision of Polynesian Cultural Center to DOM, 180

Communism, DOM approved Wilkinson request to hire a former FBI agent to monitor alleged Communist activities at BYU, 177; 1936 First Presidency statement opposing, 280; DOM's opposition grounded in belief in free agency, 280; it is an anti-Christ, 282; success of Communism means destruction of religion, 284; DOM supported limited incursions into civil liberties in fight against Communism, 285; DOM published anti-Communism pamphlet, 303; clarification of church stand on Communism read in general conference, 313; DOM softened stance forbidding church membership by Communists, 320

Conkling, James, appointed director of International Educational Broadcasting Corporation, 130; tendered resignation amid mounting losses, 133

correlation, 1906 prophecy foreshadowing shift to overall supervision by priesthood councils, 140; auxiliary organizations began as grassroots initiatives, 141; autonomous functioning of auxiliary organizations, 141; 1908 formation of General Priesthood Committee on Outlines, 141; 1912 formation of Correlation Committee, 141; 1920 formation of Correlation–Social Advisory Committee, 141; 1923 suggestion by DOM to place Presiding Bishopric under the Twelve, 142; organizational and financial autonomy of auxiliary organizations, 142; ambiguous job description of Presiding

Bishopric, 143; what ought to be taught was not being taught, 144; opposition from auxiliaries to come under closer supervision, 144; recommendation for new committee to correlate courses of study, 145; Harold B. Lee chosen to head correlation initiative, 146; went beyond original mandate restricted to coordination of curriculum, 147; recommendation to abolish existing auxiliary organizations, 148; recommendation rejected, 148; ward teaching overhauled, 148; revised recommendation that created age-group coordinating committees, but left auxiliaries intact, 149; formation of All-Church Coordinating Council, 149; Lee foreshadowed reforms extending beyond curriculum, 149; DOM: "We cannot run the Church as we would run a business," 150; First Presidency alarmed at incursion into its prerogatives, 151; DOM wanted correlation limited to curriculum coordination, 151; DOM: "There will be no change in Church Government," 152; home teaching program first noncurriculum aspect of correlation, 153; Henry D. Moyle objected to home teaching as overextension of correlation mandate, 153; by inaction, DOM validated correlation's incursion into other arenas, 154; First Presidency concern that it will "get out of hand," 154; shift in power from First Presidency to Quorum of the Twelve, 155; resistance from auxiliary organizations, 155; DOM declined to reverse flow from First Presidency to Twelve, 156; report card of correlation achievements, 157; shift from merely correlating to interpreting, 158

Cowley, Matthew, originally envisioned Polynesian Cultural Center, 180

Czechoslovakian Mission, closure followed arrest of two LDS missionaries, 281; DOM: "Every member of the Church should take a lesson," 281

death, like going from this room to that room, 27

deity, "The finite cannot conceive of the infinite," 19

DeMille, Cecil B., introduced to DOM by Arnold Friberg, 259; escorted by DOM through Los Angeles Temple, 259

Dempsey, Jack, told by DOM of stone in Scotland, 7

divorce, "the most depressing duty there is," 15

Dixon, Henry Aldous, nominated to replace Douglas Stringfellow 15 days before election and won, 348

Dyal, Kenneth, condemned First Presidency attempt to influence vote on Taft-Hartley law, 329

Dyer, Alvin R., added to First Presidency as an extra counselor, 65; blacks rejected priesthood in pre-existence, 65; pushed unsuccessfully for First Presidency statement on policy banning blacks from priesthood, 96; moved to block reconsideration of policy, 99; moved to block effort by Hugh B. Brown to reverse policy, 99; enlisted aid of Harold B. Lee to block Brown initiative to reverse policy, 100; presided over Central States Mission, 228; radically different approach to conversion, 228; called as president of European Mission, 228; explanation of "manner of conversion," 234; "If you're not baptizing, there is something wrong with *you*," 241; released as president of European Mission, 249

ecumenism, DOM affirmed distinctive claim of LDS Church to divine authority, 106; *Time* tribute to DOM ecumenism, 107; DOM exposed to other churches via international travel, 108; DOM received from and gave blessing to Episcopalian bishop, 108; Methodist minister paid tribute to DOM's ecumenism, 109; Presbyterian minister paid tribute, 109; president of American Jewish Congress paid tribute, 111; Jewish businessman paid tribute, 111; DOM complimented spirituality of Brazilian Catholics, 120

education, paramount interest of DOM for his entire professional life, 159; education not to be confined by narrow limits of dogma or creed, 159; development of character is aim of true education, 160; expense of church schools justified by secularization of world, 161

Eisenhower, Dwight D., DOM favored his election to presidency, 283; requested Ezra Taft Benson as Secretary of Agriculture, 283; reaction to Benson's failure to defend him against allegation of Robert Welch, 297;

"Whatever happened to Ezra?" 297; DOM privately expressed satisfaction with Eisenhower's election, 335; DOM congratulatory message upon election in 1952, 351; invited DOM to attend White House dinner, 351; called DOM "greatest spiritual leader in the world," 351

evolution, debate curtailed by Heber J. Grant, 45; DOM used as an argument in favor of resurrection, 46; "I believe in evolution," 46; "the Lord has not revealed the details," 46; anti-evolution views pushed by Joseph Fielding Smith, 47; DOM authorized BYU professor to write pro-evolution article for church magazine, 49

family, "No success in life can compensate for failure in the home," 14

Faust, James E., instructed by DOM to attend White House conference on civil rights to "find out what President Kennedy is trying to do," 68

Fetzer, Emil, designed new interior architecture for temples, 269

Fijians, excluded from ban on priesthood ordination, 94

Fitzpatrick, John, alliance with DOM over local, nonpartisan issues, 333

free agency, most important principle driving life, 41; fundamental next to life itself, 41; God can't make men like himself without making them free, 41; men without free agency are only puppets, 41; DOM opposition to Communism driven by concerns for free agency, 41; Christ died to give us freedom of choice, 42; any organization can be judged by its attitude toward free agency, 42; church must champion free forum of ideas, 43; obituary: brought to presidency a strong sense of individual freedom, 43; the people's most valuable possession, 284

Gallivan, John, alliance with DOM over local, nonpartisan issues, 333

Garff, Mark E., appointed to replace Wendell Mendenhall as chairman of Building Committee, 221; called for independent audit of building program, 221; presented plan to DOM to contain building program costs, 224; by 1967, reported cumulative savings of $32,000,000, 225

gathering, policy quietly de-emphasized at turn of twentieth century, 199; building of temples in foreign countries necessary to reverse policy of gathering, 202; initiation of policy in 1830s, 363; passive de-emphasis coinciding with Edmunds-Tucker Act, end of frontier, 363; announcement of foreign temples allowed active de-emphasis of policy, 365; redefinition of concept of "Zion," 366

Grant, Heber J., pronounced blessing of healing on DOM, 10; took special notice of DOM as a young man, 10; called DOM to First Presidency, 11

Grilikhes, Michael, commissioned by DOM to direct cultural and entertainment aspects of Polynesian Cultural Center, 180

Hafen, Orval, worked with Ernest Wilkinson to draft legislation returning junior colleges to church, 184

Hall, Mosiah, DOM's role model as an educator, 159

Hanks, Marion D., related incident of DOM petitioning the Lord for change in policy banning ordination of blacks, 103; called to preside over British Mission in wake of allegations of baptismal irregularities, 248; later told by DOM he was unaware of extent of irregularities, 248; authorized removal of bogus memberships without formal church court action, 252

Harding, Ralph, set apart for mission by Ezra Taft Benson, 295; elected to Congress in 1960, 296; denounced Benson's extremism on the floor of the Congress, 296; mixed reaction to speech, 297; commended by Dwight Eisenhower for speech, 297

home teaching, first noncurriculum aspect of correlation, 153; Henry D. Moyle objected to it as over-extension of correlation mandate, 153

Hunt, Duane, 1930 radio addresses on Roman Catholicism, 113; astonishment at J. Reuben Clark's anti-Catholic rhetoric, 114; contacted DOM to clarify possible misunderstanding, 115; despair at LDS misunderstanding of Catholic pamphlet, 116; contacted DOM to resolve misunderstanding, 117; sought to clarify role of Catholic Church in Utah, 118; DOM accepted Hunt's explanation, 119; encouraged Utah

Catholics to be good neighbors to Mormons, 119; DOM paid high compliment to Hunt, 120; complained to Congressman David King about *Mormon Doctrine* attacks on Catholicism, 122; complained to DOM about *Mormon Doctrine,* 122; attended funeral of Stephen L Richards, 122; DOM expressed grief at sudden death of Hunt, 123; DOM attended funeral mass, 123

Institutes of Religion, given additional resources following demise of junior college program, 196; now enroll over 600,000 students annually, 198

intellectuality, DOM strongly defended, 40; "intellectual fire" of the Savior, 40; appeal to seek the higher intellectual life, 40; "Let us seek to live intellectually," 161

international church, DOM's "most outstanding accomplishment" was making church a worldwide organization, 358; DOM assigned by Heber J. Grant to circumnavigate globe to visit foreign missions, 358; "The only right way to learn a people is to visit them in their own land," 361; insight gained through global trip, 361; recommendation for regular visits to foreign missions by General Authorities, 362; change of policy of "gathering" had gradual effect, 367; DOM's personal influence in reversing negative image of church abroad, 368; effect of Mormon Tabernacle Choir tour in reversing negative image, 369; importance of training local leadership, 369; increased central supervision of international church, 370; formation of first stakes outside North America, 372; difficulty in fighting tendency to transplant American culture to church in other countries, 372; "how far Salt Lake City is from Capetown," 373; DOM tolerance for practices unacceptable in America, 374; more than language needed to be translated in adapting curriculum to other countries, 374; formation of Translation Department, 374; creation of unified church magazine, 375; de-emphasis of Americanism in general conferences, 375; tolerance of socialism as part of internationalization process, 376; difficulty in adapting building program to international needs, 377; DOM's sensitivity to international needs,

377; tribute to DOM's success in internationalizing church, 378

International Educational Broadcasting Corporation. *See* shortwave radio

Isaacson, Thorpe B., asked by DOM to look into problems with building program, 216; part of committee commissioned by DOM to investigate building program, 217; met with DOM and recommended releasing Building Committee, 218

Jackson, Richard, related incident of DOM petitioning the Lord for change in policy banning ordination of blacks, 104

Jews, DOM viewed in special light, 110; church purchased Israel bonds, 111

John Birch Society, founded by Robert Welch in 1958, 286; despite pleas from Ezra Taft Benson, DOM refused to endorse society, 289; First Presidency statement denouncing society, 290; BYU censured by DOM for campus newspaper article, 302; published Ezra Taft Benson's picture on cover of monthly magazine, 304; DOM told associates "not to mention the Birch Society," 305; DOM's picture to appear on cover of monthly magazine, 307; DOM vetoed proposal when he found *American Opinion* was Birch Society magazine, 307; DOM general conference statement thought to imply support of Society, 313; *Church News* editorial distanced church from Society, 314; final, unsuccessful attempt by Ezra Taft Benson to obtain DOM endorsement of Society, 319; summary of effects of Society, 321

Johnson, Lyndon B., DOM was first religious leader he invited to White House, 70; invited DOM to serve on national civil rights committee, 71; phone call inviting DOM to White House, 353; Senator Moss: White House invitation purely political, 353; visit led to close friendship, 354; frequent notes, phone calls from LBJ to DOM, 354; invited Mormon Tabernacle Choir to sing at his inauguration, 355; phoned DOM during inaugural events, 355; gave inaugural flag to DOM, 355; intervened, at request of DOM, to reverse armed forces policy on LDS chaplains, 356; "President McKay is something like a father to me," 357

Jonas, Frank, letter from First Presidency affirming non-commitment in Utah State Senate reapportionment amendment was a factor in its defeat, 342

junior colleges, financial strains caused church to seek divestiture, 183; DOM voted against First Presidency proposal to divest, 183; Dixie, Gila, Snow, and Weber junior colleges transferred to state ownership in 1930s, 183; Gov. Bracken Lee recommended returning Dixie, Snow, and Weber to church ownership, 183; DOM in favor of return, 184; immediate opposition from Ogden community to returning Weber to church, 184; opposition resulted in ballot referendum, 185; ambivalent First Presidency response to questions on referendum, 185; DOM declined to urge church members how to vote, 185; mixed signals to church leaders on referendum position, 186; DOM publicly stated church neutrality on referendum, 186; referendum blocking transfer passed by 3–2 margin, 186; church purchased college sites in several states, 193; church financial crisis put junior college program on hold, 193; fifteen-year master plan proposed by Wilkinson, 194; discontinuation of program, 196; resources shifted to Institutes of Religion, 196

Kennedy, David M., consulted over church's financial difficulties, 213

Kennedy, John F., invited DOM to White House conference on civil rights, 68; visited DOM in 1957, 285; DOM unimpressed after first visit, 351; DOM impressed after second visit, 352; said of DOM, "I have never met a man as ideally suited and qualified to be the spiritual leader of his people," 352; breakfast with DOM two months prior to assassination, 352

Kerr, Clifton, instructed by DOM to find chapel site in center of London, 203

Kimball, Spencer L., met with DOM to challenge Douglas Stringfellow claims, 344

Kimball, Spencer W., energized missionaries in Germany, 235; pleaded for corrections in abuses of missionary program without killing the program, 255

King, David S., confronted by Duane Hunt over anti-Catholic rhetoric in Mormon Doctrine, 122; criticized First Presidency attempt to influence vote on Taft-Hartley law, 329

King, Martin Luther, Jr., DOM refused to acknowledge his death in general conference, 73; eulogized by Hugh B. Brown in general conference, 73; accused by Ezra Taft Benson of being Communist agent, 93

KIRO. See broadcasting

KSL, financial turmoil, 124; recommendation for reorganization, 125; poor condition when Madsen assumed leadership, 128; strategic plan for rebuilding, 128; conversion to color broadcasting, 129; turnaround of KSL operations, 129; profitability of KSL led to acquisition of other broadcasting properties, 134

labor missionary program, began in 1950 with labor shortage in Tonga, 206; promoted by Wendell Mendenhall, 206; provided job skills to hundreds of young men, 206

Lee, Harold B., "The world produces few David McKay's, and it's those few who change the world," 29; favored banning blacks from BYU, 64; vowed to exclude blacks from priesthood as long as he lived, 64; moved to delay opening of Nigerian Mission, 92; would not consent to any change in policy banning ordination of blacks, 100; wrote First Presidency statement reaffirming policy, 101; chosen to head correlation initiative, 146; desire to reorganize church dated to early 1940s, 146; foreshadowed reforms extending beyond curriculum, 149; opposition to Polynesian Cultural Center, 181; apologized for opposition to Polynesian Cultural Center, 182; opposed to construction of new junior colleges, 195; led attempt to gain perpetual church control over Utah State Senate, 341

Lee, J. Bracken, recommended return of junior colleges to church, 183; asked church clarification on junior college referendum, 185; expressed dismay at church refusal to take public stand supporting return of junior colleges, 186

Lee, John D., membership restored by DOM following Juanita Brooks's research, 54; attempt by church leaders to suppress news of reinstatement, 54

liquor-by-the-drink, church successfully campaigned against initiative, 330
literature, DOM cited it more frequently than
scripture, 40

Madsen, Arch L., early broadcasting career, 125;
interviewed by DOM, 126; offered presidency of KSL, 127; told to report directly to
DOM, 127; outlined strategic plan for
rebuilding KSL, 128; enlisted talent outside
of KSL to broaden focus of broadcasting,
129
marriage, "Always admire her new hat," 15;
DOM condemns spousal abuse, 16
Marriott, J. Willard, Sr., urged DOM not to
attend White House conference on civil
rights, 68; spearheaded initiative to build
Washington D.C. Temple, 265
McCarthy, Joseph, DOM initially favored his
extremism against Communism, 284; DOM
changed positions and favored his censure,
284
McConkie, Bruce R., published *Mormon Doctrine* without approval of Reading Committee, 49; DOM avoided public embarrassment over *Mormon Doctrine*, 51; instructed
not to publish second edition of *Mormon
Doctrine*, 51; spared public censure over
publication of *Mormon Doctrine*, 52; misconstrued DOM's caution over second edition of *Mormon Doctrine*, 52; referred to
Catholic Church as "Church of the Devil,"
122
McCulloch, J. E., author of "No success in life
can compensate for failure in the home," 14
McKay, David, teaches DOM to avoid fault finding, 12
McKay, David Lawrence, suggested to DOM
that ban on ordination of blacks might be
changed, 98; confronted Clare Middlemiss
over attempt to publish DOM statement
implying support of John Birch Society, 314
McKay, David O., shocked upon realizing immi-
nence of George Albert Smith's death, 1;
sustained as ninth church president, 2; told
secretary, "I know my course," 3; projected
aura to onlookers, 3, 4, 5; rowdiness and
tenacity as a child, 5; patriarchal blessing
promised leadership positions, 5; studied literature while carrying mail, 6; class president, valedictorian at the University of
Utah, 6; accepted mission call reluctantly, 6;

dealt with doubts while on mission, 6;
related skepticism to new missionaries, 7;
"Whate'er thou art, act well thy part," 7;
prophecy concerning future church role
while in Scotland, 8; married to Emma Ray
Riggs, 8; fourth principal of Weber Academy, 8; called to Quorum of the Twelve, 9;
nearly died in accident after ignoring pre-
monition, 9; healed miraculously, 10; called
to First Presidency, 11; self-discipline as a
youth, 12; how he controlled anger, 12;
stubbornness, 13; "When you stop, you
die," 14; discipline of children, 15; always
rose when a woman entered the room, 16;
"I'm not that unapproachable," 17; "kindliest, fairest and most understanding man,"
18; style of dress, 18; intentionally left hair
long, 18; projected an uplifted image for the
entire church, 19; failure as a young man,
19; taught reverence for Sacrament, 20; "I
don't know. The Lord hasn't told us yet,"
20; church cannot be run as a business, 21;
great spiritual leader, but poor executive,
21; delegation of authority, 21; administrative power of his aura, 22; preached a cheerful religion, 22; sense of humor, 22; tolerance of imperfections, 23; "as long as there
is a Coke in the cup," 23; Scottish humor,
24; "I believe in having good times," 24;
"You've got too much of me!" 25; deep
spirituality, 25; "He was directed by the
Lord," 25; "When was the last time you
talked to God?," 26; used early morning
hours to meditate, 26; retreats in Huntsville, 27; "The most god-like man I have
ever met," 28; doubtful another generation
will produce a like character, 28; "The
world produces few David McKays, and it's
those few who change the world," 29;
refused to censure General Authorities publicly, 52; insisted that church members had a
right to believe as they pleased, 56; symbol
of a religion that includes rather than
excludes, 56; commended for defending
man's right to freedom to think, 56; complimented for "unfailing humaneness and
sincere compassion," 57; eventual reconcili-
ation with Fawn Brodie, 58; despite aversion to civil rights, was progressive on
changing policy banning blacks from priesthood, 73; gained understanding of other
churches through international travel, 108;

received from and gave blessing to Rev. Arthur Moulton, 108; gave correlation portfolio to Harold B. Lee, 145; began career in education in eighth grade, 159; liberal philosophy of education, 159; shocked by condition of commoners in Scotland in 1897, 199; foreign missionary experience spanned three missions, 227; "Every member a missionary," 230; prophesied concerning a "new era" of missionary work, 231; made temple marriage ceremony "a true sacrament," 276; concerned that young people were not comprehending endowment, 277; disappointed in own first temple experience, 277; worked to make temple ceremony more meaningful, 278; consistent opposition to Communism, 279; initially greeted Russian Revolution with optimism, 279; Republican affiliation, 334; propensity to develop seasickness, 359; remarkable stamina in later years, 380; health report in 1956, 381; beginning of physical decline, 381; delegated conducting of general conference for first time, 383; optimism despite physical decline, 383; constant deference to Emma Ray, 384; suffered stroke in 1963, 385; missed general conference for first time because of health, 387; miraculous recovery at dedication of Oakland Temple, 389; pattern of health setbacks and rallies, 391; last public appearance, "a prophet in his own land," 391; death at age 96, 393; funeral, 393; tribute from Catholic Church during funeral procession, 394

McKay, Emma Ray Riggs, met DOM while student at the University of Utah, 6; married DOM, 8; patient with DOM, 14

McKay, Jennette Evans, spent entire inheritance on children's education, 6

McKay, Llewelyn, received letter from Sterling McMurrin recounting 1954 meeting with DOM on policy banning ordination of blacks, 96; verified McMurrin account with DOM, 97

McKay, Monroe G., urged DOM to visit South African Mission: "I've already decided to go," 77

McMurrin, James, miraculous testimony meeting in Scotland, 8, 34

McMurrin, Sterling M., vice president of the University of Utah, United States Commissioner of Education, 55; threatened with excommunication for unorthodox beliefs, 55; met with DOM over excommunication threat, 55; DOM offered to be witness in his behalf, 55; treated by DOM with affection, 56; DOM displeased with his statements on civil rights, 56; DOM affirmed friendship, 57; excommunication recommended by Joseph Fielding Smith, 58; DOM ignored recommendation to excommunicate him, 58; intervened with NAACP to prevent picketing of general conference, 69; drafted First Presidency statement on civil rights, 69; criticized continuation of ban on ordination of blacks at NAACP meeting, 96; wrote letter to Llewelyn McKay describing 1954 meeting with DOM on priesthood policy, 96; letter verified by DOM, 97; informed by Hugh B. Brown that he signed First Presidency statement under great pressure, 102; paid tribute to ecumenical spirit of DOM, 107

meditation, hours spent in meditation and prayer, 39

Mendenhall, Wendell B., appointed chairman of Building Committee in 1955, 205; reported directly to DOM, 205; Henry D. Moyle became his ally upon entry into First Presidency, 206; direct reporting to DOM insulated him from other General Authorities, 211; became vulnerable after death of Moyle, 214; commended by DOM for his "fine work" even as budget crisis worsened, 216; Twelve voted unanimously for his release, 221; request for one-year extension denied, 221; tribute to his successes, 226; critique of his shortcomings, 226

Middlemiss, Clare, only woman to serve as secretary to church president, 2; signed letter, authorized by DOM, stating church did not oppose John Birch Society, 292; pushed for publication of DOM statement implying support of John Birch Society, 314

missionary program, 1829 revelations established priority of proselytizing, 227; reorganization of Missionary Committee in 1954, 230; all missions placed under direct General Authority supervision, 230; "Every member a missionary," 230; DOM prophesied that a "new era" of missionary work was to break forth, 231; at London Temple dedication DOM spoke of "new era" of missionary work, 231; First Presidency letter: "There is no limit to our conversions," 232; effect of upgraded mission homes on proselytizing success, 232; calling of younger mission presidents, 233; bold new ideas for proselytizing, 233; new proselytizing plan lessened time to baptism, 235; first European stake organized in 1960, 237; superiority of member referrals to tracting, 237; worldwide baptisms increased 70 percent in 1960, 238; missions set increasingly higher baptismal goals, 238; worldwide baptisms increased 83 percent in 1961, 238; worldwide baptisms increased only 30 percent in 1962, 238; worldwide baptisms decreased by 10 percent in 1963, 238; baptismal quotas, begun in British Mission, spread to other missions, 240; competition between missions, 241; psychological problems of missionaries subjected to too much stress, 241; bribery and other excesses used to meet baptismal goals, 241; the "baseball baptism" program, 241; authentic success in early stages, 242; baseball baptism program abused under pressure to meet baptismal goals, 243; baptism of children without parental permission, 243; opposition from some General Authorities to accelerated missionary program, 244; DOM initially disbelieved reports of baptism of children without parental permission, 246; First Presidency letter cautioning against unauthorized baptisms, 249; strategic changes to address baptismal irregularities, 249; cleanup in aftermath of bogus baptisms, 250; First Presidency letter outlining procedure for removing names from church records, 251; drop in convert baptisms, 251; analysis of missionary program, 253; Korean War forced drastic reductions in missionary force, 281

Mormon Doctrine, published without approval of Reading Committee, 49; resulted in policy requiring First Presidency approval of books written by General Authorities, 50, 51; Mark E. Petersen noted 1,067 errors, 50; second edition not approved, 51; discussed in meeting of First Presidency and Quorum of the Twelve, 51; DOM approved second edition with reservations, 52; one of the all-time best sellers among LDS books, 53; referred to Catholic Church as "Church of

the Devil," 122; following publication of anti-Catholic statements, DOM abandoned public criticism of Roman Catholicism, 122

Mormon Tabernacle Choir, 1955 European tour helped dispel Church's negative image, 232

Moss, Frank E., public criticism of First Presidency attempt to influence Taft-Hartley vote, 326; "the most direct intervention in political matters I have ever seen the church attempt," 329

Moulton, Arthur, gave to and received blessing from DOM, 108

Mountain Meadows Massacre, published by Stanford University Press in 1950 despite efforts to block it, 53

Moyle, Henry D., attempted to dissuade army from deploying black soldiers to Utah, 63; strongly opposed civil rights, 63; alarmed at incursion of correlation into First Presidency prerogatives, 151; friendship with Harold B. Lee deteriorated when he was called into the First Presidency, 153; opposed construction of new junior colleges, 194; accelerated building program upon entry into First Presidency, 206; possessed risk-taking character of an oil wildcatter, 207; had vision of improving church image internationally by upgrading mission homes, 207; accelerated acquisition of chapel sites, 207; church image abroad improved as result of building program, 209; viewed construction expenses as excellent investment, not deficit spending, 210; began service on Missionary Committee in 1954, 228; missionary work "the greatest work I have ever been engaged in," 228; given missionary portfolio upon entering First Presidency, 228; effect on Germany, 228; reorganized missionary system, 230; DOM said, "You are going to have a revelation," 231; prophesied while touring Brazilian Mission, 231; upgraded mission homes, 232; urged calling of younger mission presidents, 233; energized missionaries in France, 235; removed from Missionary Committee, 249; "I have been relieved of every responsibility except my title," 250; philosophy of conversion process challenged, 254; led attempt to gain perpetual church control over Utah State Senate, 341

NAACP, threatened to picket general conference over civil rights, 69; called off picketing in return for First Presidency statement on civil rights, 69; praises 1963 statement on civil rights, 70; despite statement, says Utah "has potentially the worst race problem in the United States," 70; pressed church to advocate equal opportunity in housing and employment, 71; organized protest marches in front of Church Administration Building, 71; disbanded marches when church republished statement on civil rights, 71; criticizes church for failure to support anti-discriminatory practices, 71; DOM declined to yield to pressure, 88; accused by Ezra Taft Benson of being Communist front organization, 93

Nelson, Lowry, stunned to learn of policy excluding blacks from priesthood, 74; wrote to First Presidency requesting clarification of policy, 74; First Presidency response vaguely tied policy to pre-existence, 74

Nibley, Hugh, recalled DOM's rehearsal of doubts, 6

Nigeria, 1946 letter requested missionaries, 81; 1947 decision to delay proselytizing pending reexamination of policy, 81; second request, for missionaries and literature, 82; self-organization, pending formal proselytizing, 82; "we cannot escape the obligation of permitting these people to be baptized," 82; a problem greater than the ancient church faced when taking the Gospel to the gentiles, 82; fact-finding mission to assess logistics of establishing church in Nigeria, 82; Nigerians willing to have Gospel without priesthood, 83; 5,000 Nigerians wished baptism, 83; DOM proposed opening mission in Nigeria, 84; mission placed on hold in deference to George Romney's gubernatorial candidacy, 84; DOM decides to proceed with mission, without ordaining blacks, 84; dedicated for missionary work by N. Eldon Tanner, 85; public announcement of mission, 85; opening of mission delayed by publication of inflammatory article, 86; over 4,000 awaiting baptism, 87; approval to open mission denied by Nigerian government, 90; 7,000 people awaiting baptism, 90; Harold B. Lee moved to delay opening of mission, 92; Mark E. Petersen moved to block opening of mission, 92; Ezra Taft

Benson recommended recall of LaMar Williams and closure of mission, 93; unanimous vote by Quorum of Twelve to recall Williams and close mission, 93; Williams estimated 20,000 people were awaiting baptism, 94; First Presidency postponed opening of mission indefinitely, 94; outbreak of Biafran civil war in Nigeria, 94

Nixon, Richard M., DOM inadvertently gave public endorsement to candidacy, 337

Packer, Boyd K., wrote position paper that ended Ernest Wilkinson's junior college program, 196

Petersen, Mark E., noted 1,067 errors in *Mormon Doctrine,* 50; "The Lord segregated the Negro," 65; moved to terminate Nigerian Mission initiative, 92; initiated anti-Catholic meetings with LDS leaders in Salt Lake Valley, 116; complained of lavish furnishings of mission homes, 214; called to preside over West European Mission, told by DOM to discontinue youth baptisms, 249; wrote *Church News* editorial distancing church from John Birch Society, 314

politics, church viewed by East Germany as "representatives of the right wing of American conservatism," 322; political influence of church within Utah, 323; assessment of DOM's political skills, 324; DOM's 1946 calls for cleanup of Salt Lake City politics, 324; First Presidency letter to Mormon congressional delegation urged vote against repeal of Taft-Hartley law, 326; backlash from Mormon congressmen over First Presidency letter, 326; Taft-Hartley letter "the most direct intervention in political matters I have ever seen the church attempt," 329; successful campaign against Utah liquor-by-the-drink initiative, 330; First Presidency letter defining moral issues in which church would become politically involved, 332; DOM involvement in local, nonpartisan politics, 333; DOM participation in Salt Lake City urban renewal, 334; DOM's expressed nonpartisanship, 334; general conference statement by DOM reaffirming church nonpartisanship, 335; Hugh B. Brown allowed to address Utah Democratic convention to counteract impression that church favored Republicans, 336; DOM's inadvertent public

endorsement of Richard M. Nixon caused
controversy, 337; decision to discontinue
use of church buildings for political purposes, 338; DOM gave public endorsement
to George Romney's presidential candidacy,
338; 1953 attempt to have one state senator
per county, 340; local leaders used church
apparatus to campaign for Utah State Senate reapportionment, 342; defeat of reapportionment amendment, 342
Poll, Richard D., political science professor at
BYU targeted by Wilkinson for liberal
views, 174
Polynesian Cultural Center, originally envisioned
by Matthew Cowley, 180; built by church
members and nonmembers, 180; initially
opposed by some church leaders, 180; initial
plan disapproved by Quorum of the
Twelve, 181; became largest tourist attraction in Hawaiian Islands, 181; provided millions of dollars of scholarship money, 181

Rampton, Calvin L., opposition to church
attempt to influence attempted repeal of
Taft-Hartley law, 327
Redding, Lady, "I have never met a greater
man," 29
Reiser, A. Hamer, recommended closure of
British Mission, 229; received call from
Scottish journalist concerning baptism of
children without parental consent, 245
resurrection, springtime is its metaphor, 27
Reuther, Walter, "I doubt that another generation will produce a character like that," 28
revelation, bedrock principle of LDS theology,
30; importance of personal revelation, 30;
use of the phrase, "Thus saith the Lord,"
31; answer to DOM's prayer as a child, 32;
manifestation of God's power and presence
of his angels, 32; manifestation of angels in
1899, 34; private nature of manifestations,
35; selecting workers for London Temple,
36; discerning an adulterer, 36; whisperings
come when we are relaxed, 39
Richards, Stayner, recommended construction of
first overseas temple, 202
Richards, Stephen L, sustained as First Counselor, 2; supported transfer of Ricks College
to Idaho Falls, 190
Ricks College, vote to transfer ownership to state
of Idaho narrowly defeated, 183; Wilkinson

tried in 1954 to transfer it to Idaho Falls,
188; DOM told Rexburg residents, "There
will be no change in Ricks College," 188;
second proposal, in 1957, to move college
approved by Board of Education, 189; 1954
assurance to Rexburg citizens caused DOM
to veto recommendation of Board, 189;
proposal for state junior college in Idaho
Falls caused Wilkinson to renew his campaign for transfer of Ricks, 190; in 1958,
First Presidency reversed itself and
approved move to Idaho Falls, 190; in face
of Rexburg opposition, DOM reversed
approval and left Ricks in Rexburg, 192
Roman Catholic Church. See Catholic Church
Romney, Antone K., chaired committee
researching history of correlation efforts,
147; committee recommended abolition of
existing auxiliary organizations, 148; revised
recommendation created age-group coordinating committees but left auxiliaries intact,
149
Romney, George, gubernatorial candidacy placed
Nigerian Mission initiative on hold, 84;
DOM gave public endorsement to presidential candidacy, 338; during gubernatorial
candidacy, asked First Presidency for clarification of policy on blacks and priesthood,
339; DOM declined to interfere with gubernatorial candidacy, 339; sought 1968 Republican presidential nomination, 340
Rosenblatt, Joseph, paid tribute to DOM's ecumenism, 111; organized banquet honoring
DOM's community achievements, 112

Salt Lake Tribune, called DOM one of only two
"acceptable" General Authorities, 9
Scopes Trial, DOM invited William Jennings
Bryan to speak, 46
shortwave radio, DOM instructed Arch Madsen
to obtain station, 130; "the first great step
to reach the world," 130; James Conkling
appointed managing director, 130; to be
self-supporting through advertising, 131;
"a bound into space in this space age," 131;
decision to purchase WRUL rather than
build new station, 131; purchase of WRUL
for $1,750,000, 131; "We have hoped for
short-wave for 25 years," 131; station operated at a financial loss, 132; escalating losses
remove hope of station ever being self-

sustaining, 132; concern over poor quality of broadcast signal, 132; N. Eldon Tanner expressed serious reservations over purchase of WRUL, 133; losses continued to escalate, 133; divestiture of shortwave properties, 134; analysis of failure of shortwave venture, 134

Simpson, Robert L., interview hadn't consisted of a single question, 37

Smith, George Albert, retained Clark and DOM as counselors, 1; death, 2

Smith, Joseph F., nothing by way of DOM's name that suggested importance in the Church, 9

Smith, Joseph Fielding, published anti-evolution book in 1954, 45; attempted to insert anti-evolution views into church curriculum, 47; promoted anti-evolution views to Institute teachers, 47; book not authoritative nor authorized, 47; free to write and speak but not to enunciate church doctrine, 48; rumors of rift with DOM, 48; recommended excommunication of Sterling McMurrin, 58; "Darkies" have a place in the church, 64; critical of accelerated baptism program, 244

Smoot, Reed, senatorial hearings resulted in restructuring of church, 140; lamented poor meetinghouse conditions in 1920s Europe, 200

South African Mission, catalyst for DOM to rethink policy excluding blacks from priesthood, 75; no man to be ordained until all genealogy traced out of Africa, 75; church in South Africa paralyzed for lack of priesthood, due to requirement to trace genealogy out of Africa, 76; until 1954, only mission never visited by General Authority, 77; "To observe conditions as they are" was reason for DOM's trip, 77; DOM changed policy regarding genealogical research, 78; effect of changed policy on mission, 78

spy scandal, BYU, began in 1966 with Wilkinson effort to covertly monitor liberal professors, 175; disclosure by student spy led to national publicity, 175; justified by Wilkinson to DOM, 175; resolved favorably to Wilkinson by direct appeal to DOM, 176; DOM approved Wilkinson request to hire a former FBI agent to monitor alleged Communist activities at BYU, 177

Stake Academies, predecessors to church junior colleges, 182

Stapley, Delbert L., threatened Juanita Brooks with adverse action, 54; urged DOM to excommunicate Juanita Brooks, 54; told by DOM to "Leave her alone," 54

Steck, Leo J., authored pamphlet that incited strong LDS anti-Catholic reaction, 115

Stringfellow, Douglas, elected to Congress in 1952, 343; appeared on *This is Your Life* in 1954, 343; claimed he led secret operation to kidnap German atomic scientist Otto Hahn, 343; alleged that his exploits altered Hitler's timetable for world conquest, 343; named one of ten most outstanding men in America in 1954, 343; rumors that his stories were a hoax, 344; DOM met with political and church leaders to determine his credibility, 345; DOM: "We have certainly heard a lot less than the full truth," 346; damage control meeting involving Senators Watkins and Bennett, Congressman Dawson, Governor Lee, 346; Eisenhower demanded Stringfellow's removal from ticket, 347; confronted by Arthur Watkins, who demanded confession, 347; Senators Watkins and Bennett reported Stringfellow's confession to DOM, 348; DOM demanded a public confession on KSL-TV, 348; confession and withdrawal from ticket, 348

succession to the presidency, evolution to current policy of senior member of Twelve, 380; policy ensures Presidents will take office at an advanced age, 380; power vacuum within First Presidency during final years, 395; transfer of power from First Presidency to Quorum of Twelve, 396; suggestions for change in succession policy, 400

Taft-Hartley law, repeal part of Lyndon B. Johnson's platform, 325; First Presidency letter to Mormon congressional delegation urged vote against repeal, 326; backlash from Mormon congressmen over First Presidency letter, 326; public opposition to church attempt to influence vote, 327; dispute within First Presidency over statement regarding law, 328; Hugh B. Brown attempted damage control, 329; measure defeated by Senate filibuster, 330

Taggart, Stephen, wrote dissertation on policy excluding ordination of blacks, 97; dissertation brought 1954 meeting between DOM and Sterling McMurrin to attention of other General Authorities, 97

Tanner, N. Eldon, dedicated Nigeria for missionary work, 85; called to First Presidency, 89; expressed serious reservations over purchase of WRUL, 133; changed position on Polynesian Cultural Center, 181; replaced Henry D. Moyle in First Presidency, 215; unique skills for "managing tough situations," 215; given financial portfolio of church, 215; recommended to DOM that building program be supervised by committee of General Authorities, 215; identified cost overruns, 216; recommended dealing with budget crisis without changing personnel, 216; objected to Thorpe B. Isaacson's intervention in building program, 217; "expressed himself freely" in First Presidency meeting regarding building program, 218; "felt he might possibly be released because of the strong position he had taken," 219; defended Mendenhall in face of call for his release, 220

temples, building of temples in foreign countries necessary to reverse policy of gathering, 202; first-time temples built without existing stakes, 202; number of temples, either completed or under construction, doubled under DOM's leadership, 256; history of Los Angeles Temple, 256; DOM escorted Cecil B. DeMille through Los Angeles Temple, 259; purpose is "to take man from physical man to spiritual man," 259; history of Oakland Temple, 260; proposal to construct first European temples, 261; new, reduced architectural style for overseas temples, 261; overseas temples to allow church members to stay in native countries, 262; revelation authorizing overseas temples, 263; plans for New Zealand Temple, 263; unusual events at dedication of Swiss Temple, 263; history of Washington D.C. Temple, 264; opposition to Washington D.C. Temple, 266; history of Ogden Temple, 267; proposal to build temples in Ogden and Provo, 269; new internal architectural plan, 269; initial reaction to design of Ogden and Provo temples, 270; new internal plan far more efficient, 271; other temples contemplated, 271; consideration of rebuilding of Nauvoo Temple, 272; proposal for floating temple, 273; cancellation

of sealings, 275; DOM made temple marriage "really feel like a true sacrament," 276; DOM concerned that young people were not comprehending endowment, 277; DOM disappointed in own first temple experience, 277; difference between mechanics and symbolism, 277; DOM worked to make temple ceremony more meaningful, 278

testimony, distinction between manifestations and testimony, 33; "not so loud as I had anticipated," 33; "I know because I have heard His voice," 38; evidences stronger even than sight, 38

Timmins, Lola Gygi, related incident of DOM petitioning the Lord for change in policy banning ordination of blacks, 103

tolerance, DOM set a tone of tolerance not since equaled, 43; don't rush to remove the "tares," 43; God does not judge us until the end, 44; solve the problem without hurting a tender heart, 44; if you take action on him, "you'd better take action on me," 45; teachers at BYU held to a different standard of expression, 45

Truman, Harry S., DOM privately critical of Truman Administration, 349; made 1952 farewell trip by train, 349; First Presidency decision not to have DOM appear with Truman, unless directly requested to do so by him, 349; direct request from Truman 349; DOM unexpectedly impressed by Truman, 350

Udall, Stewart, as Secretary of Interior, urged First Presidency to modify resistance to civil rights, 68; second attempt to persuade First Presidency to modify stand on civil rights, 69; published article critical of exclusion of blacks from priesthood, 95

unions, DOM aversion to compulsory union membership, 325; proposed repeal of right-to-work law opposed by DOM, 325

Watkins, Arthur V., assigned by Richard Nixon to chair Senate committee investigating Joseph McCarthy, 284; commended by DOM for outstanding work on the committee, 284; attempted to verify Douglas Stringfellow's claims through CIA contact, 346; confronted Stringfellow, demanded confession, 347; reported confession to

DOM, 348; upset at DOM appearance with Harry Truman, 350

Weilenmann, Milton, elicited pledge from DOM to remain uncommitted on Utah reapportionment amendment, 341; attempted to exploit Douglas Stringfellow hoax, 344; met with DOM to challenge Stringfellow claims, 344; applauded DOM's integrity in handling of Stringfellow case, 348; learned of DOM's aversion to appearing with Truman, arranged direct request by Truman, 349

Welch, Robert, founded John Birch Society in 1958, 286; met Ezra Taft Benson in 1961, 286; asked DOM to allow Benson to join National Council of John Birch Society, 294; Benson spoke at testimonial dinner in his honor, 295; accused Dwight Eisenhower of being a tool of the Communists, 295; met with DOM, 295; letter sent to LDS bishops inviting them to a banquet honoring Welch, in connection with general conference, 310; Ezra Taft Benson slated to introduce Welch, 310; urged Birch Society members to write letters of support to DOM, 312; called LDS Church "a very good recruiting ground" for Society, 313; sent DOM twelve-page letter requesting Benson's membership on National Council of John Birch Society, 317; DOM declined request, 317; met with DOM to make final plea for Benson to join National Council, 317; DOM declined request, 318

Wilkinson, Ernest L., we are obliged to discriminate against blacks, 65; alliance with DOM transformed BYU into largest church-owned university in the United States, 159; representation of Ute Indians in U.S. lawsuit brought him financial independence, 161; began tenure as BYU president in 1951, 161; nature of relationship with DOM, 162; used frequent, personal contact with DOM to accomplish agenda, 162; cultivated relationship with Clare Middlemiss to facilitate access to DOM, 162; often bypassed Twelve and appealed directly to DOM, 163; prodigious energy key to success at BYU, 163; covertly tape recorded board meetings, 164; ongoing conflict with Harold B. Lee over BYU issues, 165; became Administrator of Church Unified School System in 1953, 165; established policy encouraging all LDS college students to attend church schools, 165; initiated unprecedented building program at BYU, 166; doubled operating budget between 1951 and 1956, 166; summary of his achievements at BYU, 168; attempted to enforce tithing compliance by BYU professors, 169; attempted to rid BYU of liberal professors, 171; admired John Birch Society but did not join, 172; accused Kennedy Administration of being socialistic, 172; secured DOM's permission to dismiss BYU faculty member who was sympathetic to welfare state, 173; given leave-of-absence in 1963 to run for U.S. Senate, 173; defeat in senatorial election left him embittered, 173; despite objections from DOM, not reinstated as Chancellor of Unified Church School System, 173; in aftermath of senatorial defeat, targeted politically liberal professors, 174; obtained permission from DOM to purge liberal professors from BYU, 174; recruited students to covertly monitor liberal BYU professors, 175; justified spy scandal to DOM as being consistent with DOM's mandate to him, 175; achieved favorable outcome on spy scandal by appealing directly to DOM, 176; DOM approved Wilkinson request to hire a former FBI agent to monitor alleged Communist activities at BYU, 177; reassured of DOM's support in 1969, 178; resigned months after death of DOM, 178; positive and negative aspects of his legacy at BYU, 178; grand plan of church-owned junior colleges to feed students into BYU, 184; worked with Orval Hafen to draft legislation returning junior colleges to church, 184; dismayed over DOM's public statement of neutrality on junior college transfer referendum, 186; first attempted in 1954 to transfer Ricks College from Rexburg to Idaho Falls, 188; proposal for state junior college in Idaho Falls caused him to renew his campaign for transfer of Ricks, 190; abandoned junior college initiative when he ran for U.S. Senate, 197; complained about "reckless expenditures" of Building Committee, 211; attended John Birch Society meeting but did not join, 291; visited Eisenhower during senatorial campaign, 297

Williams, J. D., predicted in *Time* that policy on ordination of blacks would change within

his lifetime, 89; succeeded in having First
Presidency letter to Frank Jonas published,
to counteract Utah State Senate reapportionment amendment, 342

Williams, LaMar S., sent church literature to
Nigeria, 82; sent to Nigeria on fact-finding
mission, 82; reported that 5,000 Nigerians
wanted baptism, 83; designated mission
president for Nigeria, 84; set apart as mission president, 85; received temporary visa
to Nigeria, 90; failed to obtain government
approval to open Nigerian Mission, 90;
return trip to Nigeria, with instructions to
report directly to First Presidency, 91;
attempted to obtain permanent visa, 91;
recalled from Nigeria, 93; pleaded unsuccessfully with First Presidency to return to
Nigeria, 94

Woodbury, T. Bowring, successful businessman,
228; served as counselor to Alvin R. Dyer in
Central States Mission, 229; called to preside over British Mission, 229; flamboyant
persona, 229; "one of the most charismatic
and powerful personalities I had yet
encountered," 229; public relations initiatives in British Mission, 233; implemented
streamlined proselytizing plan, 234; dramatic effect of Mutual Improvement Association youth conference, 236; emphasized
development of local leadership in addition
to proselytizing, 237; emphasized member
referrals over tracting, 237; pledged 1,000
baptisms as birthday present for DOM, 237;
set increasingly higher baptismal goals, 238;
began rewards program for missionaries,
239; changed goals from number of work
hours to number of baptisms, 239; punished
missionaries who did not meet goals, 240;
reported to DOM that youth baptisms
were decreasing, 248; extended honorable
release as mission president, 248

Wright, Evan P., as new president of South
African Mission, told by First Presidency
not to ordain any men with *any* proportion
of black ancestry, 75; assigned six missionaries full time to trace genealogy, 76; church
in South Africa paralyzed for lack of priesthood, due to requirement to trace genealogy out of Africa, 76; pleads with First Presidency to change genealogy requirement,
76; tells First Presidency of thousands of
blacks wanting baptism in South Africa, 76;
urged First Presidency to visit South African
Mission, 77

WRUL. *See* shortwave radio